An Introduction to Contact Linguistics

Language in Society

1 Language and Social Psychology
edited by Howard Giles and Robert N. St Clair

2 Language and Social Networks (second edition)
Lesley Milroy

3 The Ethnography of Communication (third edition)
Muriel Saville-Troike

4 Discourse Analysis
Michael Stubbs

5 The Sociolinguistics of Society: Introduction to Sociolinguistics, Volume I
Ralph Fasold

6 The Sociolinguistics of Language: Introduction to Sociolinguistics, Volume II
Ralph Fasold

7 The Language of Children and Adolescents: The Acquisition of Communicative Competence
Suzanne Romaine

8 Language, the Sexes and Society
Philip M. Smith

9 The Language of Advertising
Torben Vestergaard and Kim Schrøder

10 Dialects in Contact
Peter Trudgill

11 Pidgin and Creole Linguistics
Peter Mühlhäusler

12 Observing and Analysing Natural Language: A Critical Account of Sociolinguistic Method
Lesley Milroy

13 Bilingualism (second edition)
Suzanne Romaine

14 Sociolinguistics and Second Language Acquisition
Dennis R. Preston

15 Pronouns and People: The Linguistic Construction of Social and Personal Identity
Peter Mühlhäusler and Rom Harré

16 Politically Speaking
John Wilson

17 The Language of the News Media
Allan Bell

18 Language, Society and the Elderly: Discourse, Identity and Ageing
Nikolas Coupland, Justine Coupland, and Howard Giles

19 Linguistic Variation and Change
James Milroy

20 Principles of Linguistic Change, Volume I: Internal Factors
William Labov

21 Intercultural Communication: A Discourse Approach (second edition)
Ron Scollon and Suzanne Wong Scollon

22 Sociolinguistic Theory: Language Variation and Its Social Significance (second edition)
J. K. Chambers

23 Text and Corpus Analysis: Computer-assisted Studies of Language and Culture
Michael Stubbs

24 Anthropological Linguistics
William Foley

25 American English: Dialects and Variation
Walt Wolfram and Natalie Schilling-Estes

26 African American Vernacular English: Features, Evolution, Educational Implications
John R. Rickford

27 Linguistic Variation as Social Practice: The Linguistic Construction of Identity in Belten High
Penelope Eckert

28 The English History of African American English
edited by Shana Poplack

29 Principles of Linguistic Change, Volume II: Social Factors
William Labov

30 African American English in the Diaspora
Shana Poplack and Sali Tagliamonte

31 The Development of African American English
Walt Wolfram and Erik R. Thomas

32 Forensic Linguistics: An Introduction to Language in the Justice System
John Gibbons

33 An Introduction to Contact Linguistics
Donald Winford

34 Sociolinguistics: Method and Interpretation
Lesley Milroy and Matthew Gordon

An Introduction to Contact Linguistics

Donald Winford

BLACKWELL PUBLISHING
350 Main Street, Malden, MA 02148-5020, USA
108 Cowley Road, Oxford OX4 1JF, UK
550 Swanston Street, Carlton, Victoria 3053, Australia

First published 2003 by Blackwell Publishing Ltd
Reprinted 2005

Library of Congress Cataloging-in-Publication Data

Winford, Donald.
An introduction to contact linguistics / Donald Winford.
p. cm. — (Language in society ; v. 33)
Includes bibliographical references and index.
ISBN 0–631–21250–7 (alk. paper) — ISBN 0–631–21251–5 (pbk. : alk. paper)
1. Languages in contact. I. Title. II. Language in society (Oxford, England) ; v. 33.
P130.5 .W56 2003
306.44—dc21
2002026252

A catalogue record for this title is available from the British Library.

Set in 10/12.5 pt Ehrhardt
by Graphicraft Ltd, Hong Kong
Printed and bound in India
by Gopsons Papers Ltd, Noida

The publisher's policy is to use permanent paper from mills that operate a sustainable forestry policy, and which has been manufactured from pulp processed using acid-free and elementary chlorine-free practices. Furthermore, the publisher ensures that the text paper and cover board used have met acceptable environmental accreditation standards.

For further information on
Blackwell Publishing, visit our website:
www.blackwellpublishing.com

For my students, past, present, and to come

Contents

Series Editor's Preface xv
Acknowledgments xvi

1 Introduction: The Field of Contact Linguistics 1

1.1 The Subject Matter of Contact Linguistics 1
1.2 History of Research on Language Contact 6
1.3 The Field of Contact Linguistics 9
1.4 Types of Contact Situation 11
1.4.1 Language maintenance 11
1.4.2 Language shift 15
1.4.3 Language creation: new contact languages 18
1.5 Overview of Contact Situations and their Outcomes 22
1.6 The Social Contexts of Language Contact 24
1.6.1 Language contact in its social settings 25

2 Language Maintenance and Lexical Borrowing 29

2.1 Introduction 29
2.2 "Casual" Contact and Lexical Borrowing 30
2.2.1 English influence on the Japanese lexicon 31
2.3 Contact in Settings Involving "Unequal" Bilingualism 33
2.3.1 French influence on the lexicon of Middle English 34
2.3.2 Chinese influence on the Japanese lexicon 36
2.4 Lexical Borrowing in Equal Bilingual Situations 37
2.5 Social Motivations for Lexical Borrowing 37
2.6 The Processes and Products of Lexical Borrowing 42
2.7 The Integration of Loanwords 46
2.7.1 Phonological integration of loanwords 46
2.7.2 Morphological integration of loanwords 48

2.8 Linguistic Constraints on Lexical Borrowing 51
2.9 Structural Consequences of Lexical Borrowing 53
2.9.1 Impact of lexical borrowing on phonology 54
2.9.2 Impact of lexical borrowing on morphology 56
2.9.3 Impact of lexical borrowing on the lexicon 58
2.10 Summary 59

3 Structural Diffusion in Situations of Language Maintenance 61

3.1 Introduction 61
3.2 Is there Direct Borrowing of Structural Features? 63
3.3 Factors Affecting Structural Convergence 64
3.4 Structural Convergence in Stable Bilingual Situations 65
3.4.1 Spanish in LA 66
3.4.2 A situation of unstable bilingualism: French/English contact on Prince Edward Island 68
3.5 Sprachbünde: Contact Across Contiguous Speech Communities 70
3.5.1 The Balkan Sprachbund 71
3.6 A Case of Intimate Inter-Community Contact: Arnhem Land 74
3.6.1 Ritharngu and Ngandi 76
3.6.2 Nunggubuyu and Warndarang 78
3.6.3 Factors regulating convergence in Arnhem Land 78
3.7 Heavy to Extreme Structural Diffusion: Borrowing or Substratum Influence? 79
3.7.1 Old Norse influence on Old English 80
3.7.2 Situations in level 5 of Thomason and Kaufman's borrowing scale 83
3.7.3 Convergence in Kupwar 84
3.7.4 Convergence in Northwest New Britain 86
3.8 The Social Contexts of Structural Convergence 90
3.9 Linguistic Constraints on Structural Diffusion into a Maintained Language 91
3.9.1 Constraints on borrowing of morphology 91
3.9.2 Constraints based on congruence 93
3.9.3 Constraints based on transparency/markedness 94
3.9.4 Functionally based constraints 96
3.10 Constraints on Syntactic Diffusion 97
3.11 Summary 99

4 Code Switching: Social Contexts 101

4.1 Introduction 101
4.2 Defining Code Switching 102
4.2.1 Code switching versus borrowing 107
4.2.2 Code switching versus "interference" 108
4.3 Social Motivations for Code Switching 110
4.3.1 Code switching and sociolinguistic domains 110
4.3.2 Micro-level analysis: code switching and conversation 114
4.3.3 Toward a theory of the social meaning of conversational code switching 117
4.3.4 Code switching and Communication Accommodation Theory 119
4.4 Summary 124

5 Code Switching: Linguistic Aspects 126

5.1 Introduction 126
5.2 Structural Constraints on Code Switching 126
5.2.1 Equivalence-based constraints 127
5.2.2 Government-based approaches to code switching 134
5.3 A Production-Based Model of Code Switching 137
5.3.1 Hypotheses of the MLF model 139
5.3.2 Establishing the matrix language 141
5.4 Constraints on Code Switching Within the MLF model 146
5.4.1 Constraints on switching of system morphemes 146
5.4.2 Constraints on switching of content morphemes 152
5.5 Constraints on Multi-Word Switches (EL Islands) 154
5.5.1 The EL Island Trigger Hypothesis 155
5.5.2 EL islands and the notion of congruence 158
5.6 Further Issues 163
5.7 Summary 165

6 Bilingual Mixed Languages 168

6.1 Introduction 168
6.2 Definition and Classification 170
6.3 Media Lengua 175
6.3.1 Structural characteristics 176
6.3.2 Adaptation of Spanish items to Quechua structure 177
6.3.3 Processes of change: the Relexification Hypothesis 181

6.4 Michif 183
6.4.1 Sociohistorical background 183
6.4.2 Sources of Michif structure 184
6.4.3 Phonology 185
6.4.4 NP structure 186
6.4.5 VP structure 187
6.4.6 Syntax of Michif 188
6.4.7 Convergence and innovation in Michif 189
6.4.8 Mechanisms and processes in the genesis of Michif 190
6.5 Creations Associated with Language Shift 193
6.6 The Case of Ma'a 193
6.6.1 Historical backgound 194
6.6.2 Structural features 194
6.6.3 The genesis of Ma'a 196
6.7 The Strange Case of Copper Island Aleut 198
6.7.1 Sociohistorical background 199
6.7.2 Structural characteristics of Copper Island Aleut 199
6.7.3 Processes and constraints in Copper Island Aleut origins 203
6.8 Summary 205
6.8.1 Sociohistorical background and social motivations 205
6.8.2 Processes and origins 206

7 Second Language Acquisition and Language Shift 208

I An Overview of Individual Second Language Acquisition 208
7.1 Introduction 208
7.2 L1 Influence in SLA 209
7.2.1 L1 influence on the TL lexicon 211
7.2.2 L1 influence on L2 phonology 212
7.2.3 L1 influence on L2 morphology 213
7.2.4 L1 influence on TL syntax 214
7.3 Simplification in SLA 217
7.4 Internal Developments in L2 Systems 219
7.5 Developmental Stages in SLA 220
7.5.1 General characteristics of early interlanguage 222

7.6 Strategies and Processes in SLA 223
7.7 Principles and Constraints on SLA 225
7.7.1 The early stages of SLA: processing and learning principles 225
7.7.2 Constraints in the elaboration of L2 grammar 227
7.7.3 Typological universals and SLA 230
7.7.4 Markedness constraints and L1 influence in SLA 231
7.7.5 Constraints on transfer 233
7.7.6 Cognitive principles and IL development 234
II Group Second Language Acquisition or Language Shift 235
7.8 Introduction 235
7.9 Irish English 237
7.9.1 Substratum influence on Irish English 239
7.10 "Indigenized" Englishes and Similar Contact Varieties 241
7.11 Issues in the Study of Language Shift 243
7.11.1 Processes of formation 243
7.11.2 Degrees of "fossilization" or approximation in group SLA 245
7.11.3 Colloquial Singapore English: a case of early IL "fossilization"? 245
7.12 Linguistic Constraints in Language Shift 247
7.12.1 Constraints on L1 influence 247
7.12.2 The concept of "transfer" in group SLA 248
7.12.3 Transfer as psycholinguistic process 251
7.13 Non-Structural Factors in Language Shift 252
7.14 Questions of Classification 254
III First Language Attrition and Death 256
7.15 Introduction 256
7.16 External (Social) Factors in Language Death 257
7.16.1 Macro-level social factors 257
7.16.2 Stages of language attrition and death 258
7.16.3 Sociolinguistic factors within the shifting community 259
7.17 The Linguistic Consequences of L1 Attrition 259
7.17.1 Language decay 261
7.18 Language Attrition in Relation to Other Contact Phenomena 263
7.19 Summary 264

8 Pidgins and Pidginization 268

8.1 Introduction: Definitions 268
8.2 Social Contexts of Pidgin Formation 270
8.3 Russenorsk: A Brief Sketch 273
8.4 Structural Characteristics of Pidgins 275
8.4.1 Pidgin morphology and syntax 275
8.4.2 Pidgin lexicon 276
8.4.3 Pidgin phonology 277
8.5 Pidgin Formation in Relation to Early SLA 278
8.5.1 Processes of pidgin formation 280
8.5.2 Principles and constraints in pidgin formation 286
8.6 Elaborated or Extended Pidgins 288
8.6.1 The origins and development of extended pidgins 289
8.6.2 Social contexts of early Pacific Pidgin English 289
8.6.3 The emergence of early Melanesian Pidgin 291
8.6.4 Further elaboration of MP grammar 293
8.7 Simplified Languages 297
8.8 Issues of Classification Revisited 299
8.9 Summary 301

9 Creole Formation 304

9.1 Introduction 304
9.2 Defining Creoles 305
9.3 The Sociohistorical Background to Creole Formation 309
9.3.1 Portuguese colonization 309
9.3.2 The social contexts of creole formation 310
9.3.3 Community settings and codes of interaction 312
9.4 The Emergence of "Intermediate" Creoles: Bajan 314
9.4.1 The social context 314
9.4.2 Linguistic inputs and outcomes in Barbados 315
9.5 The Emergence of Radical Creoles: Suriname 316
9.5.1 The sociohistorical background 317
9.6 Some Aspects of Creole Grammar 319
9.6.1 Creole phonology 319
9.6.2 Creole lexicon 321
9.6.3 Creole morphology and morphosyntax 322
9.6.4 Creole TMA systems 324
9.6.5 Creole syntax 326
9.7 Theories of Creole Formation 329
9.7.1 Reconstructing creole formation: a caveat 330

9.8 Radical Creole Formation as SLA 331
9.8.1 The target of acquisition 331
9.8.2 Restructuring in creole grammar 333
9.9 Mechanisms, Constraints, and Principles in Creole Formation 340
9.9.1 Constraints on the linguistic inputs 341
9.9.2 Substrate influence: mechanisms and constraints 341
9.9.3 Leveling in creole formation 345
9.10 Universal Principles and Creole Formation 346
9.10.1 Universals and L1 influence 347
9.10.2 Universals and internal developments 348
9.10.3 Grammaticalization in creoles 350
9.11 Externally Motivated Change in Later Creole Development 352
9.12 Summary 355

References 359
Index 387

Series Editor's Preface

Contact between human beings from different ethnic and other groups is obviously a social phenomenon; but it nearly always involves a linguistic dimension as well. A number of books in our Language in Society series have dealt with particular aspects of contact between speakers from different language backgrounds, such as intercultural communication. Others have been concerned with some of the outcomes of this type of contact, such as (undeniably) new-dialect formation, bilingualism, and pidgin and creole languages, as well as (more controversially) African American Vernacular English. This book, however, is the first we have published which deals with the phenomenon as a whole. We are therefore very fortunate that the author is one of the world's leading authorities in this area – not only someone who comes, personally, from a background of very interesting linguistic complexity, but also a scholar who has been at the forefront of descriptive and theoretical language contact research for the last three decades. *An Introduction to Contact Linguistics* represents the very latest scholarship on issues which will be of profound concern to all linguists working on language contact, including not only the topics I have just mentioned, but also very many others, including language shift, language death, language mixing, and second language acquisition. The book is exciting because of its innovative thinking, but it is also enormously erudite, and comprehensive in its coverage of all the major theories and issues in the field.

Peter Trudgill

Acknowledgments

The writing of this book has been a highly rewarding experience that added much to my knowledge of contact phenomena in general and of the creoles that are the main focus of my research. Contributing to this personal enrichment was the generous and enthusiastic support provided to me by many colleagues, friends, and students. Several of them shared their extensive knowledge in their own areas of specialization and made me rethink many of the entrenched ideas and assumptions I had not previously questioned.

I owe a special debt of gratitude to Jeff Siegel, whose engaging (and lengthy) e-mail exchanges with me were always enlightening. Jeff commented extensively on chapters 7, 8, and 9 of the book, which are greatly improved as a result. Brian Joseph also found time to comment on several chapters despite his busy schedule, while Panos Pappas went through the manuscript with a fine-tooth comb, pointing out many errors and infelicities of expression. Others who devoted their time to commenting on various chapters were Jacques Arends, Bettina Migge, and Terence Odlin. Among the colleagues who provided helpful information are Mary Beckman, Carol Myers-Scotton, David Odden, Carmen Silva-Corvalán, and Jeanine Treffers-Daller.

I also received valuable feedback from many students, including Robin Dautricourt, Hope Dawson, Shelome Gooden, Craig Hilts, Hannah Lin, Andrea Sims, Shravan Vashishth, Jinyi Wang, and others.

I am very grateful for the comments made by reviewers of the first drafts of chapters 1 to 4, who pointed out serious flaws and offered very useful suggestions for improvement. Among them were Michel DeGraff and Salikoko Mufwene, both of whom have been most generous with their advice over the years. My friends and house-mates Taiwan and Jermaine put up with my grumpiness especially in the last stages of writing, and provided moral support throughout. Many other friends and colleagues contributed in various ways to the completion of this book, and I apologize for not mentioning them all. Special thanks also to Beth Remmes for her encouragement, and to Fiona Sewell for keeping the editing on track.

Above all, I wish to express my appreciation to my students who motivated me to develop the lectures that were the basis of this book, and provided much-needed feedback. I owe them a great deal for helping me to develop my understanding of contact linguistics over the years. By dedicating this book to them, I hope I can repay a small part of that debt.

1

Introduction: The Field of Contact Linguistics

1.1 The Subject Matter of Contact Linguistics

In offering his account of Caló, the mixture of Spanish and Romani used as an in-group language by Roma (Gypsies) in Spain, Rosensweig (1973) referred to it, in the very title of his book, as "Gutter Spanish." A flyer from a West Sussex bookseller advertising publications on "dialect and folk speech, pidgins and creoles," describes these forms of language, in boldface capitals, as "vulgar and debased English." Language mixture has always prompted strong emotional reaction, often in the form of ridicule, passionate condemnation, or outright rejection. Language purists have proscribed it as an aberration of the "correct" language, and their attitude is reflected in a lay perception of mixed languages as deviant, corrupt, and even without status as true languages. Thus Ambrose Gonzales, self-proclaimed student of the Gullah language, a "creole" language of mixed English and African ancestry spoken on islands off the South Carolina coast, explained its origins in this way:

> Slovenly and careless of speech, these Gullahs seized upon the peasant English used by some of the early settlers and by the white servants of the wealthier colonists, wrapped their clumsy tongues about it as well as they could, and, enriched with certain expressive African words, it issued through their flat noses and thick lips as so workable a form of speech that it was gradually adopted by the other slaves and became in time the accepted Negro speech of the lower districts of South Carolina and Georgia. (Gonzales 1922: 17–18)

While linguists and others might cringe at the sheer idiocy of this racist statement, many members of the public would probably accept the notion that languages like Gullah are the result of clumsy and ineffective learning. The truth, of course, is that these languages are testaments to the creativity of humans faced with the need to break down language barriers and create a common medium of communication. Far from being deviant, language mixture is a creative, rule-governed process that affects all languages in one way or another, though to varying degrees. The kinds of mixture that characterize languages like Caló and Gullah may be extreme, but they are by no means unusual, and have played a role in the development of just about every human language, including some that are regarded as models of correctness or purity. Whenever people speaking different languages come into contact, there is a natural tendency for them to seek ways of bypassing the communicative barriers facing them by seeking compromise between their forms of speech.

Such contact can have a wide variety of linguistic outcomes. In some cases, it may result in only slight borrowing of vocabulary, while other contact situations may lead to the creation of entirely new languages. Between these two extremes lies a wide range of possible outcomes involving varying degrees of influence by one language on the other. More accurately, of course, it is the people speaking the respective languages who have contact with each other and who resort to varying forms of mixture of elements from the languages involved. The possible results of such contact differ according to two broad categories of factors – internal (linguistic) and external (social and psychological). Among the relevant linguistic factors is the nature of the relationship between the languages in contact, specifically the degree of typological similarity between them. There is also a variety of other linguistic constraints which operate in such situations, some of them specific to particular areas of linguistic structure (e.g., the lexicon, phonology, morphology, etc.), others of a more general, perhaps universal nature. These are discussed more fully in later chapters. Relevant social factors include the length and intensity of contact between the groups, their respective sizes, the power or prestige relationships and patterns of interaction between them, and the functions which are served by intergroup communication. Sociopolitical factors which operate at both individual and group level, such as attitudes toward the languages, motivations to use one or the other, and so on, are also important.

Most, if not all, languages have been influenced at one time or another by contact with others. In some cases, externally induced changes do not even require speakers of the different languages to have actual social contact. For instance, lexical borrowing can be accomplished through book learning by teachers, writers, lexicographers, and the like who pass on the new vocabulary to others via literature, religious texts, dictionaries, and so on. In other cases, prolonged social interaction between members of different speech communities may result in varying degrees of mixture and structural change in one or the other of the languages involved. In extreme cases, pervasive contact may result in new creations distinct from their original source languages. The following examples illustrate some of the contact-induced changes that have affected English in various contact settings, leading to very different outcomes in each case. We might well ask whether these varieties are indeed forms of English, and if so, in what sense we can say they belong to the family of English dialects.

Sample (1) is an example of the form of pidgin English used as a lingua franca among ethnic groups of different linguistic background (English, Hawaiian, Japanese, Chinese, and Portuguese, among others) on the plantations of Hawaii during the nineteenth century. This particular extract is from a recording of an older male Japanese immigrant. Like all pidgins, this one shows evidence of loss of inflectional morphology, absence of grammatical categories such as tense and aspect, and overall simplification or reduction of grammatical apparatus as well as vocabulary:

(1) samtaim gud rod get, samtaim, olsem ben get, enguru get, no? enikain seim.
Sometimes good road get, sometimes like bend get, no? everything same.
Olsem hyuman laif, olsem. Gud rodu get, enguru get, mauntin get, no? awl, enikain,
Like human life, all-same. Good road get, angle get, mountain get, no? all, any kind
Stawmu get, nais dey get – olsem. Enibadi, mi olsem, smawl taim.
Storm get, nice day get – all-same. Anybody, me too, small time.

"Sometimes there's a good road, sometimes there's, like, bends, corners, right? Everything's like that. Human life's just like that. There's good roads, there's sharp corners, there's mountains, right? All sorts of things, there's storms, nice days – it's like that for everybody, it was for me too, when I was young." (Bickerton 1981: 13)

Sample (2) is taken from Sranan Tongo ("Suriname Tongue"), a creole language spoken in Suriname, which emerged as a medium of interethnic communication among African slaves brought in thousands to the coastal plantations of this country in the seventeenth to eighteenth centuries. Like other creoles, its lexicon is drawn mostly from the language of the colonizers, while its grammar bears the mark of substantial influence from the native languages of the subjected peoples who created it. This of course is a simplistic way to describe the complex process of creole formation, but it will suffice for now. In this extract, an older woman talks about the good old days, when children had respect for their elders:

(2) Ma di mi ben e gro kon, mi no ben mag taigi wan bigi
but when I PAST IMP grow come, I NEG PAST may tell one big
suma wan wortu. Uh? Efu mi seni a pikin a no go, en mama
person one word. Uh? If I send the child s/he NEG go, his mother
yere, a e fon en. Taki sanede meki te owma seni yu,
hear, she IMP beat him. Say why make when granny send you,
yu no go?
you NEG go?
Direct a e priti en skin gi en.
Immediately she IMP split 3p skin for 3p.

"But when I was growing up, I wasn't allowed to say a word to an adult. Uh? If I sent a child [on an errand], and s/he didn't go, and his/her mother heard this, she would spank the child. [She'd] say why didn't you go when granny sent you? Right then she'd cut his/her skin for him/her." (Winford 2000a: 429)

Sample (3) comes from Singapore colloquial English, one of the so-called New Englishes which arose in former British colonies, in many cases becoming the everyday vernacular of the community. These "indigenized" varieties are the result of "imperfect" (creative) second language learning, and are characterized by varying degrees of influence from the first languages of the groups who created them. For instance, features such as the use of sentence-final discourse marker *lah* and existential *get* parallel similar features in Cantonese, one of the native languages involved in the contact. Here a taxi driver talks about his job:

(3) Passenger(s) depen(d) lah – good one(s) also go(t), bad one(s) also go(t). Some ah taxi driver(s) they wan(t) to go to this tourist area(s) like hotel(s) ah. They par(k) there, y'know. Then if the touris(ts) want to go an buy things, buy anything ah, they brough(t) the passengers go and buy thing(s) already. Then the shop(s) ah give commission to the taxi driver(s) lah.

"With passengers, it depends, you know. There are good ones and bad ones. Some taxi drivers like to go to tourist areas such as hotels, yeah. They park there, you know. Then if the tourists want to go and buy things, they take them to the shops and straightaway they are buying things. Then the shops give a commission to the taxi drivers, yeah." (Platt et al. 1983: 35)

Finally, extract (4) is from Anglo-Romani, a well-known example of a bilingual mixed or "intertwined" language. Its grammar is English, but much of its lexicon derives from the Romani dialects brought by Roma (Gypsies) to England. Romani items are italicized in the extract:

(4) Once *apré* a *chairus* a *Rommany chal* *chor*ed a *rāni chillico*
'Once upon a time a Gypsy stole a turkey (lit. lady bird)
and then *jāll*ed *atut* a *prastraméngro* *'pré* the *drum*
and then met (went on) a policeman on the road
Where did *tute chore adovo rāni*? *putcher*ed the *prastraméngro*.
Where did you steal that turkey? asked the policeman.
It's *kek rāni*; it's a *pauno rāni* that I *kinn*ed *'drée* the
It's no turkey; it's a goose (lit. white lady) that I bought in the
gav to *del tute*. – *Tácho*, *penn*ed the *prastraméngro*, it's the *kusht*iest
village to give you. – Really, said the policeman, it's the finest
pauno rāni mandy ever *dick*dus. *Ki* did *tute kin* it?
goose I ever saw. Where did you buy it?
(Leland 1879: 208)

Exercise 1
Discuss the ways in which each one of samples (1)–(4) differs from Standard English, and list the features that characterize each. In what sense would you say these are varieties or dialects of English?

Examples such as these can be multiplied. Indeed, there are in principle no limits (except those imposed by Universal Grammar) to what speakers of different languages will adopt and adapt from one another, given the right opportunity. How can we explain such phenomena? What combinations of social and linguistic influences conspire to produce them? What kinds of situation promote one type of outcome rather than another? Questions like these are all part of the subject matter of contact linguistics. Its objective is to study the varied situations of contact between languages, the phenomena that result, and the interaction of linguistic and external ecological factors in shaping these outcomes. The diverse kinds of mixture, change, adaptation, and restructuring that result from interaction between (the users of) different languages have long been of interest to linguists. At the same time, scholars in the social sciences have devoted much attention to the social aspects of contact between different linguistic groups. For instance, they have investigated the nature of group relationships and group loyalty and how they are reflected in processes of accommodation in some circumstances, and by divergence and conflict in others. These two broad lines of research have converged significantly over the last few decades, resulting in a new cross-disciplinary approach to language contact that attempts to integrate the social and the linguistic in a unified framework. To understand how this approach evolved, it is useful to survey briefly the history of research on language contact.

1.2 History of Research on Language Contact

The study of the effects of language contact has been a focal point of interest to linguists ever since the earliest period of scientific study of language in the nineteenth century. In fact, interest in the topic among students of language dates back much earlier than this. For instance, Schuchardt (1884: 30) (cited by Michael Clyne 1987: 452) mentions G. Lucio's discussion in 1666 of the mixture of Croatian and Romance dialects in Dalmatia based on Dalmatian records of the fourteenth century. During the heyday of historical linguistic scholarship in the nineteenth century, research on language contact became an integral part of the field and played a vital role in debate over the nature of language change. As Michael Clyne (1987: 453) reminds us, it was a topic to which such great linguists as Müller (1875), Paul (1886), Johannes Schmidt (1872), and Schuchardt (1884), among others, devoted a great deal of their attention. It continued to be a central topic well into the twentieth century, and was addressed by Sapir (1921), Bloomfield (1933), and other early pioneers of structuralism. In the heyday of structuralism during the 1940s to the 1960s, it became rather less central, though not completely marginalized.

The major impetus for the concern with language contact among historical linguists arose from disagreement about the part played by contact-induced change in the history of languages. There was intense debate among nineteenth-century scholars as to whether the conventional Stammbaum or "family tree" model of genetic relationships among languages was compromised in any way by the growing evidence that many languages contained a mixture of elements from different source languages. The field split into two camps, though many scholars occupied a middle ground between the two. On the one hand there were those who maintained that language mixture – especially mixture in grammar – was rare if not non-existent and that each language evolved from a single parent as a result of purely internal developments over time. For instance, Müller (1875) claimed that languages with mixed grammar did not exist, and this belief in the impenetrability of grammatical systems was echoed later by scholars like Meillet (1921: 82) and more recently by Oksaar (1972: 492) (cited by Thomason and Kaufman 1988: 2). On the other hand there were many scholars who were equally convinced that language mixture was not only possible, but clearly evidenced by actual cases of contact. For instance, Whitney (1881), responding to Müller, argued that both lexical and grammatical transfer occurred in cases of contact. In his (1884) paper, Schuchardt, the first great creolist and pioneer in the study of contact languages, provided numerous examples of structural mixture and contact-induced change from a variety of situations, including Slavic/German, Slavic/Italian, and Balkan contact, as well as pidgin and creole situations.

The evidence of mixture provided by these and other scholars posed a serious challenge to orthodox Stammbaum theory (with its insistence on a single-parent source for every language and its belief that practically all language change resulted from internal causes.) From another angle, the work of scholars like Johannes Schmidt (1872) also provided evidence that changes could enter languages as the result of diffusion from external sources – a process which his "wave" model of change attempted to capture. The issue of how contact affects "genetic" affiliation is still a highly controversial one today. On the one hand, "traditional" historical linguists argue that a distinction should be made between "normal" and "abnormal" transmission (Thomason and Kaufman 1988: 11). The former would apply to languages whose components can for the most part be traced back to a single source language, even if they might have been subject to some external influence in the past. Such languages lend themselves to reconstruction via the traditional comparative historical model of single-parent genetic affiliation and gradual internal change. The label "abnormal transmission" would then apply to mixed languages whose various subsystems cannot all be traced back to a single parent language. They result from "broken transmission" and therefore have no genetic links to other languages in the standard sense of the term (1988: 11). Such cases include pidgins, creoles, and bilingual mixed languages, the three major types of contact language referred to earlier. However, many scholars have challenged this approach. They point, for instance, to the fact that all languages are mixed to some extent, and that the processes of change found in highly mixed languages such as creoles can be found in varying degrees in the cases of so-called "normal" transmission (Mufwene 1998; Thurston 1994; DeGraff to appear). From this standpoint, it is perhaps unfortunate that contact-induced change and its outcomes are still viewed by many as secondary, even marginal, to the central pursuits of historical-comparative linguistics.

Despite (or perhaps because of) the disagreement in the field, there developed during the nineteenth to mid twentieth centuries a strong tradition of research in contact-induced change, both within the ambit of Historical Linguistics, and in other disciplines. In addition to the theoretical issues referred to above, research within the former field focused on specific geographic areas of contact; linguistic processes and types of contact-induced change; specific instances of mixture such as bilingual code switching or processes of pidgin and creole formation; and the possible constraints on contact-induced change. Most of the current topics in the field were already the object of serious enquiry as early as the nineteenth century. For instance, the language situation in the Balkans has attracted the attention of scholars since Kopitar (1829) and Schuchardt (1884), and there is a considerable body of research on this linguistic area. Troubetzkoy (1928) (cited in Weinreich 1953: 112, n. 4) provided the first definition of a Sprachbund ("union of languages" or "linguistic area"), and since then there have been numerous studies of linguistic areas around the world. Other topics such as lexical borrowing and the role of substratum influence (discussed later) in language change were investigated. And of course much attention was paid to pidgins and creoles, as classic examples of "new" mixed languages. Schuchardt's pioneering work in this field was complemented by that of Hesseling (1899, 1905), Olaf Broch (1927), and others. Early in the twentieth century, the phenomenon of code switching was studied by Braun (1937), who observed switches between Russian and German in the speech of a bilingual.

This line of more linguistically oriented research was complemented by other approaches concerned more with the social context of language contact. For instance, some scholars devoted their attention to the problems of long-established ethnic minorities faced with the strong influence of a majority national language. Systematic study of language maintenance began with Kloss (1927, 1929). Other scholars became interested in the fate of immigrant languages in North America and elsewhere (Herzog 1941; Reed 1948; Pap 1949; etc.). Studies like these established the foundation for the discipline known as the sociology of language, focusing on language maintenance and shift (see Fishman 1964; Fishman et al. 1966). It provided important insights into the social and psychological factors that determine the outcomes of language contact. Closely associated with this tradition is the growing body of research on the social psychology of language choice as exemplified, for instance, by the approach known as Speech Accommodation Theory, developed by Howard Giles and his associates (Street and Giles 1982). Within the historical linguistics tradition too, many scholars stressed the importance of social factors in language contact. They included Whitney (1881) and Schuchardt (1884), who was in many ways far ahead of his time. Much of Schuchardt's discussion of the linguistic aspects of language contact is accompanied by details of the social context, the groups in contact, and other relevant sociocultural data.

New vigor was injected into the field by the important work of Weinreich (1953) and Haugen (1950a, 1950b, 1953). Working within the structural paradigm, they both emphasized the importance of studying language contact from both a linguistic and a sociocultural perspective. Michael Clyne (1987: 453) suggests that their work can be considered the beginning of American sociolinguistics. If so, it is also true that their work established the ground for the re-emergence of language contact as a topic of central importance and as a subdiscipline of linguistics in its own right.

All of these various lines of approach, some primarily linguistic, others primarily sociological or anthropological, contributed to the emergence of the new field of contact linguistics. According to Nelde (1997: 287), the term was introduced at the First World Congress on Language Contact and Conflict, held in Brussels in June 1979. As noted earlier, the major turning point in the discipline was the work of Haugen and Weinreich, particularly the latter. As Michael Clyne (1987: 456) notes, despite all the previous research, "there was, before Weinreich (1953), no systematized theory of language contact." Both Weinreich and Haugen attempted to integrate linguistic analysis with social and psychological explanations to account for language contact and its consequences. Their major contribution to this enterprise was undoubtedly their formulation of a comprehensive framework for the study of language contact in its social setting. Perhaps the strongest recent impetus to research in this area came from Thomason and Kaufman's (1988) book-length study of a wide variety of contact phenomena, and their attempt to lay the foundations for both a typology of contact outcomes and an empirical/theoretical framework for analyzing such outcomes. Their work constitutes a major contribution to historical linguistic scholarship, in attempting to resolve the old controversy over the role of external linguistic influence as distinct from internal motivations and mechanisms in language development. Like earlier researchers, they emphasized the need for an interdisciplinary approach and refined several aspects of the terminology and descriptive framework employed in previous studies. The emerging field of contact linguistics owes its existence primarily to the work of all these pioneers.

1.3 The Field of Contact Linguistics

Despite Appel and Muysken's (1987: 7) assertion that "Bilingualism or language contact in itself is not a scientific discipline," the study of language contact is in fact a fairly well-defined field of study, with its own subject matter and objectives. It employs an eclectic methodology that draws on various approaches, including the comparative-historical method, and various areas of sociolinguistics. It is this very interdisciplinary approach that defines it and gives it its strength. One of the clearest statements of the goals of this subdiscipline is the following, from Weinreich (1953: 86): "To predict typical forms of interference from the socio-linguistic description of a bilingual community and a structural description of its languages is the ultimate goal of interference studies."

Though Weinreich focuses specifically on the phenomenon of bilingualism, his statement can, *mutatis mutandis*, apply equally well to the study of all contact situations. Moreover, the field of contact linguistics is not limited to just the study of "interference," but covers all the linguistic consequences of contact, including phenomena such as simplification and various other kinds of restructuring that characterize the outcomes of contact. Weinreich's goal of "prediction" is perhaps ambitious, but he himself is well aware of the complexity of the problem. In particular, he emphasizes that the components of an explanatory framework must include "purely structural considerations . . . psychological reasons. . . . and socio-cultural factors" (1953: 44). The need to explore the latter two types of factor arises from the fact that, first, contact situations which appear quite similar in terms of the linguistic inputs present can and do result in quite different linguistic outcomes. Moreover, for any given contact situation, predictions of contact-induced changes based solely on structural factors fail miserably. This point will be discussed in later chapters, when we consider the various linguistic constraints on such changes. Weinreich's outline of the main concerns of "interference" studies is worth quoting in full. He notes:

> In linguistic interference, the problem of major interest is the interplay of structural and non-structural factors that promote or impede such interference. The structural factors are those which stem from the organization of linguistic forms into a definite system, different for every language and to a considerable degree independent of non-linguistic experience and behavior. The non-structural factors are derived from the contact of the system with the outer world, from given individuals' familiarity with the system, and from the symbolic value which the system as a whole is capable of acquiring and the emotions it can evoke. (1953: 5)

It follows, first, that we need to distinguish among the various social contexts of language contact if we are to understand the nature and direction of contact-induced change. Second, it is necessary to examine, where possible, the actual speech behavior of persons in each contact situation in order to uncover the factors that motivate them to change their language in one way or another.

Scholars have long been aware that differences in the social setting lead to differences in the outcomes of contact. For instance, Wackernagel (1904) distinguished three kinds of contact situation – when a conquered group adopts the language of its conquerors, when the reverse occurs, and when there is mutual influence leading to a "mixed language." Every outcome of language contact has associated with it a particular kind of social setting and circumstances that shape its unique character. The goal of contact linguistics is to uncover the various factors, both linguistic and sociocultural, that contribute to the linguistic consequences of contact between speakers of different language varieties. Toward that end, we need a framework of analysis that includes a variety of components. In the rest of this chapter, we provide a broad overview of types of contact situation, their outcomes, and the social settings in which they emerge. We will consider each of these situations in more detail in subsequent chapters. There too we will explore the mechanisms and types of change involved as well as the factors, both linguistic and non-linguistic, which influence the patterns of cross-linguistic influence.

1.4 Types of Contact Situation

We can in general distinguish three broad kinds of contact situation: those involving language maintenance, those involving language shift, and those that lead to the creation of new contact languages. Most cases of language contact can be assigned clearly to one or another of these categories. However, as we will see, there are many situations that cannot be classified so readily. Some are characterized by interplay between maintenance and shift, like the "fuzzy" cases found in Sprachbünde or linguistic areas such as the Balkans, discussed in chapter 3. Others involve types of interaction and mutual accommodation which make it difficult to place them in a single category, for instance the kinds of extreme structural convergence found in Northwest New Britain, where languages of the Austronesian and non-Austronesian families have become structurally isomorphic (see chapter 3). Similar difficulties arise in the case of the so-called "new" contact languages, pidgins (chapter 8), creoles (chapter 9), and bilingual mixed languages (chapter 6). These are cases neither of maintenance nor of shift in the strict sense, though they share characteristics with the latter situations. Each of them presents its own problems of definition and classification.

1.4.1 Language maintenance

1.4.1.1 Borrowing situations

Language maintenance refers simply to the preservation by a speech community of its native language from generation to generation. Preservation implies that the language changes only by small degrees in the short run owing to internal developments and/or (limited) contact with other languages. Hence the various subsystems of the language – the phonology, morphology, syntax, semantics, and core lexicon – remain relatively intact.

Cases of maintenance may involve varying degrees of influence on the lexicon and structure of a group's native language from the external language with which it is in contact. This kind of influence is referred to as "borrowing." Since this term has been used in a variety of senses, it is necessary to emphasize that it is used here, following Thomason and Kaufman (1988: 37), to refer to "the incorporation of foreign features into a group's native language by speakers of that language." This makes it clear, first, that the borrowing language is maintained, though changed in various ways by the borrowed features, and that the agents of change are its native speakers. As van Coetsem (1988: 3) points out, borrowing involves recipient language agentivity, and this crucially distinguishes it from the other major type of cross-linguistic influence that involves source language agentivity in cases of second language learning (see section 1.4.2 below). The borrowing language may be referred to as the recipient language, and the foreign language as the source language. Both of these terms may also be used in a wider sense, to refer respectively to (a) any language that incorporates features from another and (b) any language that provides the relevant input.

Borrowing is also sometimes referred to as "borrowing interference" (as opposed to "interference via shift"), reflecting a tendency within the field to use the term "interference" as a cover term for all kinds of contact-induced change (Thomason and Kaufman 1988). Since the term "interference" has been used in a variety of conflicting senses, some general, some rather narrow (for instance, Weinreich 1953: 1 defines it as "deviations from the norm of either language which occur in the speech of bilinguals as a result of their familiarity with more than one language"), the term will be avoided as far as possible here. Instead, we will use terms like "contact-induced changes" and "cross-linguistic influence" as general labels to cover all kinds of influence by one language on another.

Borrowing may vary in degree and kind from casual to heavy lexical borrowing, and from slight to more or less significant incorporation of structural features as well. As already noted, situations involving primarily lexical borrowing, that is, borrowing of content morphemes like nouns, verbs, etc., are extremely common, and most, if not all, languages have been subject to this kind of influence at some time or another. Sometimes, as we shall see later, significant lexical borrowing may have effects on the lexical semantics as well as other aspects of a language's structure. Situations involving structural borrowing, that is, borrowing of features in phonology, morphology, syntax, and semantics, are somewhat rarer, though examples can be found. Borrowing situations will be discussed in chapter 2.

1.4.1.2 Situations of structural convergence

Structural diffusion often occurs where languages are spoken in close geographical proximity, for example in border areas, or in communities characterized by a high degree of multilingualism. Examples of the former type of situation are Sprachbünde or linguistic areas. Perhaps the best-known of these is the Balkan Sprachbund, where long-standing contact between languages like Albanian, Bulgarian, Greek, Macedonian, and others led to significant diffusion of structural features. In cases involving bi- or multi-lingualism within the same speech community, the results of language contact are often manifested in increasing structural convergence between the languages involved. A well-known case in point is the village of Kupwar in India. Here, a long history of interaction between speakers of Marathi, Kannada, and Hindi-Urdu led to a surprising degree of isomorphism in structure, to the point where it has been claimed that simple replacement of lexical items from each language within the same structural frame is often possible. Long-term pressure on the language of a minority group surrounded by a larger dominant group can sometimes lead to significant structural and lexical diffusion from the latter to the former. This can in some cases lead to a radically altered version of the recipient language. Cases in point include Asia Minor Greek, which incorporated many features from Turkish, and Wutun, a Chinese language heavily influenced by Tibetan.

Sometimes, diffusion of features across languages may be so widespread that the boundaries between the languages become blurred, even for the speakers themselves. Thurston (1987, 1994) describes situations like this in Northwest New Britain, an island that forms part of Papua New Guinea. Here, as in Kupwar, convergence has led to structural isomorphism among the languages involved, with lexicon serving as the primary means of distinguishing one from the other. Thus, though they belong to quite distinct language families (Austronesian versus non-Austronesian), or to different subgroups within these families, all languages use practically the same syntactic strategies. For example, requests for items follow the same pattern: first the requested item is named, followed by a third person form of the verb come; then there is a first person verb expressing what the speaker will do with the desired item. The following examples illustrate. Anêm is non-Austronesian. Mouk and Lusi belong to the Bibling and Bariai subgroups of Austronesian respectively. Amara is an Austronesian isolate:

(5)	Anêm:	uas	gox	o-mên	da-t
	Mouk:	uas	silaŋ	max	ŋa-ŋan
	Lusi:	uasi	eta	i-nama	ŋa-ani

Amara:	aguas	kapso	i-me	e-kenen
	tobacco	some	3s-come	1s-eat

"Hand me some tobacco to smoke" (Thurston 1987: 69)

In cases like these, it is often difficult to identify the agents of change, whether they may be native speakers of language A who maintain it while borrowing, or speakers of language B who shift to A and introduce features of B which native speakers of A eventually adopt. These situations will be discussed more fully in chapter 3.

1.4.1.3 Code-switching situations

Language maintenance situations also include more or less stable bilingual speech communities in which bilingual mixture of various types is usual, leading to the phenomena known collectively as code switching. This involves the alternate use of two languages (or dialects) within the same stretch of speech, often within the same sentence. For example, Puerto Ricans in New York city switch between Spanish and English with great facility, as illustrated in the following example from Blanca, a 9-year-old girl living in Spanish Harlem, New York city. Spanish items are italicized:

(6) Hey Lolita, but the Skylab, the Skylab *no se cayó pa(-ra) que se acabe el mundo*. It falls in pieces. *Si se cae completo*, yeah. The Skylab *es una cosa que (e-)stá rodeando el* moon taking pictures of it. *Tiene tubos en el medio. Tiene tubos en el medio*. It's like a rocket. It's like a rocket.

(Hey Lolita, but the Skylab, the Skylab ("didn't fall for the world to end"). It falls in pieces. ("If it falls whole"), yeah. The Skylab ("is something that's going around the") moon taking pictures of it. ("It has tubes in the middle") [repeated]. It's like a rocket [repeated]. (Zentella 1997: 117)

Notice how Blanca switches languages from clause to clause, but also mixes items from the two languages within the same clause. These are examples of inter- and intra-sentential switching, which reflect somewhat different kinds of bilingual competence, as we shall see.

In many bi- or multi-lingual communities, the choice of one code or another is dependent on the situation or domain of use, so that the codes tend to be used in mutually exclusive functions. Such situations are referred to as cases of diglossia, or (where more than two languages are involved) polyglossia. An example of the former is Spanish/Guaraní bilingualism in Paraguay, while the latter is exemplified by the situations in Singapore and Malaysia, where speakers alternate between English, Malay, and other ethnic languages like Mandarin depending on the interlocutor and the situation (Platt 1977). Situations like these, of course, also allow for a certain degree of code alternation and code mixture within a single interaction. The social and linguistic aspects of code switching will be discussed in chapters 4 and 5 respectively.

1.4.2 Language shift

In other situations, contact between different linguistic groups can lead to language shift, the partial or total abandonment of a group's native language in favor of another. In some cases, the shift results in successful acquisition of the target language (TL), with little or no influence from the native language (L1) of the shifting group. For instance, by the third generation, most immigrant groups in the United States succeed in achieving native proficiency in American English. In many cases, however, shift is accompanied by varying degrees of influence from the group's L1 on the TL. Such situations fall into two broad categories. First, there are cases involving immigrant or other minority groups that shift either partially or completely to the language of the dominant majority, but carry over features of their L1 into their version of the TL. Sometimes, the shifting group is eventually absorbed into the TL community and the innovations that they introduced are imitated by the TL community as a whole, thus becoming permanently established in the language. This happened, for instance, when speakers of Norman French shifted to English in the late Middle English period, leading to significant lexical and some structural (especially phonological) influence from French on English. In other cases, a minority group may preserve its L1 for certain functions, while acquiring the dominant language for other uses. Such situations typically result in significant L1 influence on the TL, as for example in the second language varieties of German used by "guestworkers" in Germany from the late 1950s on. Such influence tends to be confined to the minority group and does not usually spread into the language of the host community as a whole.

The second category of situation where shift leads to L1 influence on a recipient language involves languages that become targets of shift after being introduced into new communities by invaders or colonizers. The indigenous community then adopts the foreign language either as a replacement for its original native language(s), or as a second language to be used in addition to the latter. Such "indigenized" varieties of a foreign language are especially common in areas that were formerly colonized by external powers. Indian English and Irish (Hiberno-) English are two examples. Second language versions of target languages such as these, which result from untutored learning in "natural" community settings, are clearly similar in certain ways to the varieties of second or foreign languages acquired in formal settings such as the classroom. "Interlanguage" phenomena in classroom second language acquisition (SLA) often arise from the same kinds of L1 influence that characterize "untutored" SLA, that is, targeted language shift. Moreover, both types of learning may be subject to other principles and constraints, such as the universal tendency toward simplification of target structures, at least in the early stages of learning. There is therefore much to be gained from a close comparison of all these types of language acquisition.

Language shift obviously implies the gradual or complete abandonment of a previous native language in favor of the TL. Such situations provide interesting insight into the phenomenon of *language death*, the slow attrition and decay of the language previously used by the shifting group.

As noted above, many of the changes in a TL which accompany shift are the result of influence from the shifting group's L1. Such changes have been referred to by various names, including "interference through shift," "transfer," "substratum influence," and "imposition." Some of these labels are problematic in one way or another. We've already seen that "interference" is used in several conflicting senses. The same is true of "transfer," which is used by some as a cover term for all kinds of contact-induced change (hence "borrowing transfer" versus "substratum transfer"), and by others to refer only to L1 influence on an L2. Most SLA researchers use the term "transfer" to refer only to L1 influence on (learner versions of) a target language. Van Coetsem (1988: 3) introduced the term "imposition" to refer to this kind of contact-induced change. Though this term has failed to gain currency, his description of the change itself is quite insightful. As he notes, it involves the agentivity of source language speakers who "impose" their L1 habits on the recipient or target language.

The term "substratum influence" is popular among creolists, who use it to refer to much the same phenomena that SLA researchers describe as (L1) transfer – hence the growing rapport between these fields, as we shall see in chapter 9. Creolists use the term in a somewhat different sense from historical linguists. The latter generally use it to refer to influence from the language of a subordinate group, distinguishing it from "superstratum" and "adstratum" influence from the languages of dominant and equal groups respectively. Creolists on the other hand use it to refer specifically to influence from a subordinate group's language on pidgin and creole formation. Henceforth, we will use the term "L1 influence" or "substratum influence" to refer to the influence from a speaker or group's L1 on an outcome of language contact. It is immaterial whether the outcome is a second language variety of a TL or a new creation such as a creole, or what the relative statuses of the languages (groups) in contact may be.

Thomason and Kaufman seem to have this sense in mind when they define substratum influence as the result of "imperfect group learning during a process of language shift" in the course of which the learning group commits "errors" that may spread to the TL as a whole. This definition may not be precise enough. In the first place, the results of "imperfect learning" may include strategies ("errors") other than substratum influence, such as simplification of TL structures. Second, not all cases of substratum influence result in spread of such influence to the TL as a whole. There are indeed such cases, usually when the shifting group is absorbed by the TL community. However, there are also cases where the shifting group constitutes a separate community in its own right, and the changes they introduce remain restricted to their version of the TL (e.g., Hiberno-English and other "indigenized" Englishes). In addition, we may want to distinguish between individual and group shifts. Thomason and Kaufman are right to note that group shifts promote substratum influence in a TL. But we can gain much insight into this type of cross-linguistic influence by investigating the strategies employed by individual learners in both "natural" and "tutored" contexts. As Mufwene (1990: 2) notes, "interference" from an L1 at the individual level is the first stage in the establishment of substrate influence in the language of the group. When the same types of change are replicated by various individuals and are adopted by many others, they become conventionalized as part of the community's linguistic system and at this point they can be described as substratum features.

Substratum or L1 influence, like borrowing, may be found at all levels of linguistic structure. But, in general, borrowing begins with vocabulary, and the incorporation of structural features into a maintained language comes only after substantial importation of loanwords. By contrast, substratum influence begins with sounds and syntactic patterns and sometimes also morphology, and is therefore characterized by more structural than lexical influence from the L1 on the TL. Thomason and Kaufman offer a sketch of the difference between borrowing and shift as illustrated by Rayfield's (1970: 85) description of mutual influence between English and Yiddish as spoken by a group of bilinguals in the United States (see table 1.1).

As table 1.1 shows, the process of borrowing from English into the Yiddish of these immigrants involves the lexicon much more than either phonology or morphosyntax. On the other hand, structural influence from Yiddish on the English of this group is much more pronounced than lexical influence.

These differences in the patterns of contact-induced change in borrowing as opposed to shift situations appear to be quite common, perhaps even predictable, and the distinction is therefore crucial to our understanding of what goes

Table 1.1 Degrees of "interference" in bilinguals' languages

	English → Yiddish (borrowing)	Yiddish → English (substratum influence)
Lexicon	Very strong	Moderate
Phonology	Weak	Strong
Morphosyntax	Moderate	Strong

Source: Thomason and Kaufman 1988: 40, table 2

on in different contact situations. It has important implications for both our methodology and our theories of contact-induced change. Methodologically, it means that we must understand the precise nature of the contact situation to determine the directionality of change and its agents. As far as theory is concerned, it means that explanations or predictions of the results of contact will vary depending on which of the two major vehicles of change is involved.

Exercise 2

Rayfield (1970) predicts that in situations of second language learning, lexical borrowing from the L2 will be much more frequent than structural borrowing in the L1 of the learners, while structural changes due to L1 influence will be more frequent in the learner's version of the L2. Investigate the use of English or any other language as a second language by international students at your university. Does Rayfield's prediction hold true as far as their usage is concerned?

1.4.3 Language creation: new contact languages

In addition to maintenance and shift situations, there are other kinds of contact setting which have yielded rather special outcomes: the contact languages referred to as pidgins, creoles, and bilingual mixed languages. These outcomes involve such extreme restructuring and/or such pervasive mixture of elements from more than one language that they cannot be considered cases of either maintenance or shift in the strict senses of those terms. It is also difficult at times to decide which outcomes of contact should be included in each of the above categories of contact language. The labels "pidgin" and "creole," for instance, have each been applied to a very heterogeneous group of languages, which differ both in the circumstances of their creation and in their structural characteristics. For this reason, it is necessary to refer to "prototypical" examples of each category, and attempt as far as possible to relate other potential members of the class to the prototype (Thomason 1997c).

1.4.3.1 Bilingual mixed languages

Bilingual mixed or intertwined languages arose in settings involving long-term contact between two ethnic groups leading to bilingualism and increasing mixture of the languages. In these cases, that mixture became conventionalized as a community norm, resulting in the creation of hybrid languages whose components could clearly be traced to one or the other source language. We saw one example of a bilingual mixed language, Anglo-Romani, earlier in this chapter. Another example is the Media Lengua of Ecuador, a language which incorporates Spanish lexicon into a virtually unchanged Quechua grammatical framework. The latter preserves intact not just the syntactic rules of Quechua, but also its highly complex morphology. Here is a brief example, in which a Media Lengua speaker explains how the language is made up. Items derived from Spanish are in italics:

(7) *Media Lengua*-ga *así* Ingichu-munda *Castallanu*-da *abla*-na
Media Lengua-TOP thus Quechua-from Spanish-ACC talk-NOM
kiri-xu-sha, *no* *abla*-naku-ndu-mi *asi*, chaupi-ga *Castellanu* laya,
want-PROG-SUB not talk-pl-SUB-AFF thus, half-TOP Spanish like,
i chaupi-ga Ingichi laya *abla*-ri-na ga-n.
and half-TOP Quechua like talk-REFL-NOM-be-3.

"Media Lengua is thus if you want to talk Spanish from Quechua, but you can't, then you talk half like Spanish, and half like Quechua." (Muysken 1997a: 377)

Other somewhat similar examples are Michif, a language in which Cree VP structure is wedded to French NP structure, and Mednyj Aleut, in which Russian finite verb morphology and other structural features have been fused with Aleut grammatical systems. In general, it is fair to say that these vernaculars fuse the grammar of one source with the lexicon (at least the phonological representations of the lexical items) of another. However, this picture is simplistic, since it ignores many respects in which a bilingual mixed language may differ from either of its source languages. Moreover, no single formula can be applied to describe or predict the mixture, even though there are many similarities in design among them. These and other aspects of the genesis and structure of bilingual mixed languages will be discussed further in chapter 6.

1.4.3.2 Pidgins

Trading contacts between groups speaking different languages have often led to various types of linguistic compromise to facilitate communication. Such compromises often result in pidgins, highly reduced languages with minimal vocabulary and grammar whose functions are restricted primarily to barter and exchange. An example of the pidgin English used for trading between English speakers and Pacific islanders in the nineteenth century was provided earlier in this chapter. Pidgins are a rather mixed bag of languages. Some involve more lexical mixture than others. For instance, Russenorsk, used in trade between Russians and Norwegians up to the nineteenth century, employed vocabulary from both groups' languages. Other pidgins, like Eskimo Trade Pidgin and Chinese Pidgin English, derive their vocabulary primarily from one source, Eskimo in the former, English in the latter. The primary source language in these cases tends to be the language of the group that has control of the trade or its location. Pidgins have also arisen in contexts other than trade, for instance in cases of military occupation (Pidgin English in Japan during the post-war period) or in domestic settings for communication between employers and servants of different language backgrounds (Indian Butler English) or on plantations (Hawai'i Pidgin English).

The cases mentioned so far are all examples of prototypical pidgins. The label is necessary because there is in fact a great deal of controversy over the scope of reference of the term "pidgin." The reason is that the degree of reduction in structure as well as range of functions may differ significantly from one case to another. Prototypical pidgins are severely restricted in terms of their social functions, and clearly reduced in form and structure, containing a minimal lexicon and a rudimentary grammar. Bickerton (1981) describes them as lacking inflectional morphology, tense/mood/aspect sytems, movement rules, embedding strategies, and other structural characteristics associated with fully developed natural languages. The sociohistorical and structural criteria by which such pidgins are defined will be outlined further in chapter 8.

By contrast, other languages to which the term "pidgin" has been applied, for example, Tok Pisin, Nigerian Pidgin, etc., are far more elaborate in terms of social function and structure, and hardly meet the criteria for inclusion in this class. These more elaborate contact languages may be placed in two broad categories: extended pidgins and simplified languages, though once more, the boundaries between these two are not always clear.

So-called extended pidgins apparently began as highly reduced (prototypical) pidgins which then underwent varying degrees of elaboration in both vocabulary and grammar when their range of functions extended beyond the confines of their original contexts of use. In such cases, there is usually incorporation of features from both the lexifier (superstrate) language and the native (substrate) languages of indigenous groups. Contact vernaculars like these can achieve such a degree of elaboration in this way that they become indistinguishable from other fully developed natural languages. Examples include Tok Pisin and Bislama, official languages of Papua New Guinea and Vanuatu respectively, both descended from an earlier plantation pidgin, in turn rooted in early Pacific Trade Pidgin. Other examples include varietes of West African Pidgin English, such as Nigerian Pidgin English, that are used as lingua francas in various parts of West Africa. These contact languages have much more in common, both functionally and structurally, with creoles than with prototypical pidgins.

There are other contact vernaculars to which the label "pidgin" has been applied which do not appear to involve the degree of structural reduction characteristic of prototypical pidgins. For instance, languages like Trade Motu or Pidgin Yimas appear to be somewhat simplified forms of Motu and Yimas respectively, only partially reduced so as to facilitate their use by non-native speakers in trading and other contacts with native speakers. Their degree of reduction is not nearly as extensive as that found in, say, Russenorsk. Hence they should arguably be referred to as simplified languages, rather than pidgins. All of these cases and others like them will be discussed more fully in chapter 8.

1.4.3.3 Creoles

European colonial expansion during the fifteenth to nineteenth centuries led in many cases to the creation of new communities peopled primarily by groups transplanted from distant regions of the world. In the plantations of the New World, where huge numbers of slaves were transplanted from West Africa, contact between the latter and European settlers led to the emergence of creole languages, so called because they were used by the creole or locally born descendants of slaves (as well as Europeans and other freemen) in the colonies. A typical example is Sranan Tongo, a brief sample of which was provided earlier in this chapter. Other well-known Caribbean creoles include Jamaican and Guyanese creole (English lexicon); Haitian creole (French lexicon); Papiamentu, a creole used in the former Dutch islands of Aruba, Bonaire, and Curacao (Spanish/Portuguese lexicon) and Berbice Dutch, once spoken in the interior of modern Guyana (Dutch lexicon).

Similar languages emerged in the Indian Ocean and other areas where European colonies were established. For instance, there is Isle de France creole, a French-lexicon creole with varieties spoken in Mauritius and the Seychelles. In South East Asia, we find creoles such as Daman Creole Portuguese, spoken in India, and Papia Kristang, spoken in Malaysia and Singapore. There are also several other creole languages spoken in West Africa, including Krio (English-lexicon), spoken in Sierra Leone, and Guinea Kriyol (Portuguese-lexicon), spoken in Guinea-Bissau. Some of the earliest creoles known arose on plantation settings on islands off the West African coast. Well-known examples include Cape Verde Crioulo and other Portuguese-lexicon creoles spoken on São Tomé, Principe, and other islands in the Gulf of Guinea.

The formation of these languages involved varying degrees of input from the superstrate languages of the colonizers and the native languages of the subjected peoples. Creoles, like other contact vernaculars, differ significantly in the nature and extent of the respective inputs. Just about every aspect of these languages, their origins and sources, their typological characteristics, their classification, etc., remains a matter of controversy. These issues will be discussed more fully in chapter 9.

As with "pidgins," there are substantial differences among so-called "creoles" in terms of both their processes of formation and their structural make-up. Essentially, such differences have to do with the nature and extent of the substratum contribution to the creole's formation. On the one hand, there are radical creoles like Sranan and its Surinamese relative Saramaccan, and varieties of the Eastern Maroon Creole, a substantial part of whose grammar can be traced to West African (especially Gbe) sources. For this reason, it is difficult to accept Thomason and Kaufman's characterization of them as cases of shift "whose structure can be accounted for under a hypothesis of extreme unsuccessful acquisition of a TL" (1988: 48). One might just as well argue that they are akin to cases of maintenance, though, as usual, the truth lies somewhere between these two extremes.

By sharp contrast, the so-called intermediate creoles of the Caribbean, such as Bajan, urban Guyanese, or Trinidadian creole, are arguably cases of shift and far more akin to products of "unsuccessful" acquisition of a TL such as Hiberno-English, Singapore English, Taiwanese Mandarin, etc. than they are to radical creoles. Once more, between these poles lie many other points on a continuum that includes contact vernaculars in the Caribbean, Pacific, Indian Ocean, and elsewhere to which the label "creole" has traditionally been applied.

1.5 Overview of Contact Situations and their Outcomes

At this point, it may be useful to provide a brief taxonomy of contact situations and the types of cross-linguistic influence they involve. Table 1.2, based partly on Thomason and Kaufman (1988: 50), illustrates the major outcomes of language contact. The table distinguishes three general categories of outcome, those

Table 1.2 Major outcomes of language contact

(A) Language maintenance

I Borrowing situations

Degree of contact	Linguistic results	Examples
Casual	Lexical borrowing only	Modern, English borrowings from French, e.g., *ballet*
Moderate	Lexical and slight structural borrowing	Latin influence on Early Modern English; Sanskrit influence on Dravidian languages
Intense	Moderate structural borrowing	German influence on Romansh

II Convergence situations

Type of contact	Linguistic results	Examples
Contiguous geographical location	Moderate structural diffusion	Sprachbünde, e.g., the Balkans
Intra-community multilingualism	Heavy structural diffusion	Marathi/Kannada influence on Kupwar Urdu
Intense pressure on a minority goup	Heavy structural diffusion	Tibetan influence on Wutun; Turkish influence on Asia Minor Greek
Intense inter-community contact (trade, exogamy)	Heavy lexical and/or structural diffusion	The languages of Northwest New Britain; the languages of Arnhem Land, Australia

(B) Language shift

Type of shift	Linguistic results (substratum)	Examples
Rapid and complete (by minority group)	Little or no substratum interference in TL	Urban immigrant groups shifting to English in the US
Rapid shift by larger or prestigious minority	Slight to moderate substratum interference in TL	Norman French shift to English in England

Table 1.2 (*cont'd*)

Type of shift	Linguistic results (substratum)	Examples
Shift by indigenous community to imported language	Moderate to heavy substratum interference	Shift to English by Irish speakers in Ireland (Hiberno-English); shift to English dialects in seventeenth-century Barbados (intermediate "creole")

(C) Language creation (new contact languages)

Type	Characteristics
Bilingual mixed languages	Akin to cases of maintenance, involving incorporation of large portions of an external vocabulary into a maintained grammatical frame
Pidgins	Highly reduced lingua francas that involve mutual accomodation and simplification; employed in restricted functions such as trade
Creoles	Akin to cases of both maintenance and shift, with grammars shaped by varying degrees of superstrate and substrate influence, and vocabulary drawn mostly from the superstrate source

pertaining to language maintenance situations (here subdivided into borrowing and convergence situations), those relating to language shift, and those involving the creation of new contact vernaculars, viz., pidgins, creoles and bilingual mixed languages.

1.6 The Social Contexts of Language Contact

Precisely what factors determine the varied outcomes of the contact situations we have just surveyed? We have already emphasized the complementary roles of external and internal factors in shaping such outcomes. Early scholars such as Müller (1875) and Jakobson (1938) argued that structural (linguistic) constraints were the primary determinants of contact-induced change. But the wide body of evidence available to us now shows that practically any linguistic feature can be transferred from one language to another, if the circumstances are right. The reason is that extralinguistic factors – the social ecology of the contact situation itself – can override any purely structural resistance to change. Moreover, it is such factors that explain one of the key problems of language contact studies – why all potential forms of contact-induced change may not actually materialize in a given situation. This does not mean, of course, that explanations in terms of purely linguistic constraints are not possible or relevant. It is of prime importance for us to seek explanations as far as possible in linguistic structure, But ultimately, as Weinreich (1953: 3) so aptly stated: "A full account of interference in a language contact situation, including the diffusion, persistence and evanescence of a particular interference phenomenon, is possible only if the extra-linguistic factors are considered."

We will consider the various linguistic constraints on contact-induced change in some detail in our discussions of specific contact situations and their outcomes in later chapters. For the present, let us survey briefly the sociocultural factors that play so important a role in regulating these outcomes.

1.6.1 Language contact in its social settings

It bears repeating that the broad distinctions we have made between situations involving language maintenance, language shift, and the creation of new contact languages are crucial to explaining the linguistic outcomes of contact. Without a clear understanding of the history and social dynamics of the contact situation, we are in no position to explain anything. Not just the mechanisms of change but also its directionality and agentivity vary according to the type of situation involved. It follows that the constraints on the changes that can occur will vary from one case to another as well. In general, however, the same set of sociocultural factors is present in every contact situation, though the particular mix varies from case to case, with consequent variation in the results. These sociocultural factors include the types of community settings, the demographics of the populations in contact, the codes and patterns of social interaction among them, and the ideologies and attitudes that govern their linguistic choices. Other factors that play a role include the degree of bilingualism among the individuals and groups in contact, the history and length of contact, the power relationships between the groups, and so on. Obviously, it is no easy task to integrate all the relevant factors into a comprehensive and coherent picture of the social ecology of a given contact situation. In the following chapters, we will try to examine the social setting of each type of contact in more detail, and show, as far as possible, how it contributes to the particular outcome in question. For the moment, let us just attempt a broad outline of some types of setting.

1.6.1.1 Speech communities and language contact

The unit of analysis for investigating the social ecology of language contact is the speech community. The concept has sometimes been difficult to pin down but it has proven useful and revealing in the study of language in its social and cultural setting. Speech communities can be defined at different levels of generalization, from communities of practice to the local neighborhood to the nation state. They can also be identified in terms of social criteria such as ethnicity, social class, gender, and so on. What unites each of these social constructs is the fact that its members share certain linguistic repertoires and rules for the conduct and interpretation of speech. Essentially, it is social interaction within and across speech communities that leads to diffusion of linguistic and other cultural practices. So, in order to understand the products of language contact, we have to understand the speech economies of the communities in contact, and the dynamics of their patterns of interaction.

It would be very useful to design a comprehensive classification of all the community settings within which language contact takes place. But this would be a daunting and immensely complex task, one that is well beyond the reach of the present chapter. By way of illustration, however, we can at least attempt a broad overview of some types of community setting. For instance, Loveday (1996: 16) has suggested that communities might be categorized according to the degree of bi- or multi-lingualism within them. He suggests that there are six "archetypal contact settings," each characterized by different arrays of contact phenomena. I here follow the broad outlines of Loveday's typology, but amend his labels and descriptions where it seems appropriate to do so.

At one end of the spectrum we find relatively homogeneous communities of monolinguals most of whom have little or no direct contact with speakers of other languages. Still, foreign influence may be introduced into the language by individuals who travel, or by the mass media, or through language teaching in schools, churches, etc. Such "distant" contact typically results in lexical borrowing alone. Examples include Japanese, Russian, and other languages that have borrowed words from English. Further discussion can be found in chapter 2.

In the middle of the spectrum we find a variety of situations involving varying degrees of bi- or multi-lingualism within the community. One such setting involves contact between linguistic minorities and a dominant host group. In some cases, the minority group may be relatively isolated or socially distant from the majority group. Some examples include Gaelic speakers in Scotland, Basques in southern France, and the Pennsylvania "Dutch" of the midwestern US. Such groups may preserve their language(s) for a long time, though shift to the dominant language may eventually take place. Other bilingual situations are characterized by higher levels of individual bilingualism. There are cases where minority groups become bilingual in the host community's language, for example, Hispanics in the US. There are also cases where different ethnic groups vie for equal status in the same territory, each preserving its own language, but also learning the other. Examples include French and English in Montréal, and Flemish and French in Brussels. We can also find communities that typically employ two or more languages in everyday interaction, and treat them as relatively equal or at least appropriate in their respective domains of use. These communities are characterized by "diglossia," a situation in which two languages, one High (H) and the other Low (L), fulfill complementary functions in the community. Examples include the use of Spanish and Guaraní in Paraguay, and Standard German and Schwyzertüütsch in Switzerland.

When stable bilingualism collapses, through either the erosion of ethnolinguistic boundaries or the resolution of diglossia or some other cause, the result is language shift. This is a common outcome of situations involving bilingualism among minority groups subject to strong cultural pressure from a dominant group. A classic example is the community of Oberwart in Austria, which has undergone shift from Hungarian to German (Gal 1979). Many immigrant groups in the United States have lost their ancestral languages and shifted to English.

Some situations involve bilingualism in an ancestral language as well as a superposed (usually colonial) official language. This can lead to the emergence of new vernaculars which draw on the resources of both the H and L languages, as witness the "New Englishes" in India, Singapore, and various African countries.

Finally, at the other extreme of the continuum, we find highly heterogeneous communities characterized by high degrees of individual multilingualism, such as the village of Kupwar in India, described by Gumperz and Wilson (1971). There are also situations where different speech communities engage in constant interaction, and the fluidity of their social boundaries is matched by the fluidity of their linguistic practices. The Aboriginal groups of Arnem Land, Australia (Heath 1978), and the villages of Northwest New Britain in Papua New Guinea (Thurston 1987, 1994) are examples of this type. They are discussed further in chapter 3.

All of these multilingual communities offer a rich range of possibilities for contact-induced changes of one type or another. There may be borrowing across languages, code-switching behaviors, substratum influence on varieties acquired as second languages, various types of convergence, and so on. The particular outcomes, as usual, have to do with a range of social factors, some favoring the preservation of language boundaries, others favoring different degrees of language mixture, switching, and convergence, yet others promoting language shift. It is simply impossible to list here all the factors that may be relevant to the nature and outcome of the contact.

It should also be obvious that there is no clear or consistent correspondence between the type of community and the pattern of contact-induced change within it. Bilingual communities, for instance, may be characterized by stable maintenance in some cases, by language shift in others, or by both. Long-term stability can translate into rapid shift, given the right circumstances.

Finally, it bears repeating that this overview of contact settings is far from complete. For instance, it does not include the social contexts that lead to the formation of pidgins, creoles, or bilingual mixed languages. These contact outcomes and their social settings will be discussed more fully in the relevant chapters.

Exercise 3

The following are some questions you might want to ask of a particular contact situation, in order to understand the outcomes of the contact:

1 What is the nature of the community setting in which the contact takes place?
2 What are the demographics of the groups in contact?
3 Is the situation one of language maintenance or shift?
4 What languages are spoken by the groups in contact?
5 What is the direction of influence?

Suggest other questions you might want to ask about the social setting of the contact, the linguistic inputs, and the processes of change that may occur.

2

Language Maintenance and Lexical Borrowing

2.1 Introduction

Most English speakers would be surprised to learn that 75 percent of the words in their language were "borrowed" from other languages during the course of its history. Few speakers are aware that many commonplace words derive from foreign sources, for instance *people*, *nation*, and *clergy* from French, *cheese* and *table* from Latin, *zero* from Arabic, and so on. Some words originally borrowed from a language may be re-borrowed by it in such altered form that they appear totally foreign. For instance, English speakers think of *pokémon* as a Japanese word, when in fact it originally derives from *pocket monster*. Lexical borrowing is an extremely common form of cross-linguistic influence, and few, if any, languages are impervious to it. Such borrowing can occur under a variety of conditions, ranging from casual familiarity with the source language (even without real contact with its speakers) to close interaction between recipient and source language speakers in bilingual communities.

It has been claimed that there is a continuum ranging from relatively slight lexical borrowing under casual contact to extreme structural borrowing under very intense contact. An example of this is Thomason and Kaufman's borrowing scale, a modified version of which is presented in table 2.1. The scale consists of five stages or levels representing increasing intensity of contact, and increasing typological distance. (Readers should consult the original scale for full details of the lexical and structural features included under each stage.) Features at the top of the scale are borrowed first. The presence of borrowed features lower on the scale implies the presence of features placed higher.

Two broad issues arise here. First, we need to clarify notions such as "intensity of contact" and "cultural pressure" if we are to understand the social influences on various types and degrees of borrowing. Is it true that there is a clear correspondence between degrees of contact and cultural pressure on the one hand, and degrees of structural borrowing on the other? Answers to this can be found only in a thorough examination of the social contexts of borrowing.

Table 2.1 Borrowing scale

Stage	Features
1 Casual contact	Lexical borrowing only
2 Slightly more intense contact	Slight structural borrowing; conjunctions and adverbial particles
3 More intense contact	Slightly more structural borrowing; adpositions, derivational affixes
4 Strong cultural pressure	Moderate structural borrowing (major structural features that cause relatively little typological change)
5 Very strong cultural pressure	Heavy structural borrowing (major structural features that cause significant typological disruption)

Source: summarized from Thomason and Kaufman (1988: 74–6)

Second, we might question whether the kind of extreme structural changes claimed for stages 4 and especially 5 of Thomason and Kaufman's borrowing scale are really cases of borrowing at all, in the strict sense of that term, that is, as changes initiated by recipient language speakers.

It seems uncontroversial that (heavy) lexical borrowing can result in the transfer of structural features as well. This kind of indirect structural borrowing is well attested, as we will see. However, it seems somewhat unusual for structural features to be directly borrowed. Why would native speakers of a language ever adopt purely structural features from an external language, if equivalent features in their own language are already quite adequate to their needs? Still, there are many contact situations in which there is a significant degree of structural diffusion from one system to another. We will examine such situations in more detail in the following chapter, and ask whether borrowing is the only mechanism of change involved in these cases of structural convergence. For the moment, let us restrict our attention to the clear cases of lexical borrowing and its structural consequences.

2.2 "Casual" Contact and Lexical Borrowing

A great deal, perhaps the majority, of lexical borrowing results from only marginal contact with other languages. Such contact may be due to travel, exploration, or conquest, or it may be due to exposure to the donor language in the mass media, foreign language instruction, and the like. Loveday (1996) refers to these as settings involving "distant" contact with the external language. Typically, in these situations, the recipient language community does not achieve bilingualism in the donor language, though some of its members may.

Situations in which contact is initiated by exploration and/or conquest were extremely common in the period of European colonial expansion from the fifteenth to the twentieth centuries. This led to varying degrees of lexical borrowing into European languages from the languages of the indigenous peoples whom they conquered. For instance, English colonization of North America introduced borrowings such as *skunk, moccasin, teepee, wigwam*, and others from Algonquian languages into American English. The names of states like Illinois, Ohio, Michigan, Wisconsin, etc. are derived from Native American languages. This kind of borrowing is typical of colonial Englishes generally. For instance, Australian English adopted words like *kangaroo, billabong*, etc. from Aboriginal languages.

Lexical borrowing in the other direction, from the languages of the colonizers to those of the colonized, is even more common. Spanish, for example, has been the source of numerous lexical borrowings and innovations in the Amerindian languages of Central and South America. Similarly, English has supplied numerous loans to languages like Navajo and others in the United States.

Exercise 1
Find out at least ten words that have been borrowed into English or Spanish from Native American languages, and ten that have been borrowed in the opposite direction. Compare your findings with those of your classmates, and try to determine what semantic fields are represented in the borrowings.

Another type of "distant" contact leading to lexical borrowing can be found in the spread of global avenues of communication such as radio, television, and the internet. These have facilitated the spread of vocabulary from (American) English in particular to many other languages. In some cases, that influence has been strong and pervasive, even though the contact is supposedly "distant." A case in point is Japanese.

2.2.1 *English influence on the Japanese lexicon*

Japanese contact with English dates back to the opening up of Japan to Western influence from the mid-nineteenth century on. The defeat of China in the

Opium Wars with Britain (1839–42 and 1850–60) impressed on the Japanese the need to learn about Western concepts, and particularly Western scientific and military know-how. There was a significant influx of English loans, especially in the late nineteenth to early twentieth centuries. As Ishiwata (1986: 457) notes, these borrowings were motivated by the need for modernization in areas such as science, technology, and higher learning.

But the greatest impetus to borrowing from English came from growing exposure to it via radio, cinema, newspapers, and other forms of mass media, which spread popular American culture among the Japanese, especially the more well-to-do youth. The first phase of this influence occurred from the 1910s to about 1930, ending with the growth of strong anti-Western feeling which culminated in the war of 1941–5. The post-war occupation of Japan set the stage for even greater exposure to English, which became an avenue to social advancement and education. In this period, many English-derived words spread quickly into Japanese. The result is that such words now make up some 7.29 percent of the modern Japanese lexicon, second only to Chinese, from which as much as 48 percent of the Japanese lexicon is derived (Loveday 1996: 41). In addition to domains such as science and technology, English loans abound in areas that reflect the influence of Western fashion, cosmetics, sport, music, and the like. Table 2.2 illustrates this.

Exercise 2
The examples in table 2.2 show that English loanwords have been adapted in various ways to Japanese phonology. Describe informally the kinds of change that are involved in this process of adaptation.

Table 2.2 Some English loans in Japanese, by domain

Food:	Sport:
sarada < salad	*batto < bat*
keeki < cake	*geemu setto < game and set*
sofuto (aisu) kariimu < soft ice cream	*bodiibiru(dingu) < bodybuilding*
Dress/Fashion:	Music/Leisure:
supaiku shuuzu < spiked shoes	*songu < song*
ooba (cooto) < overcoat	*paati < party*
sangurasu < sun glasses	*terebi(jon) < television*

Source: examples from Ishiwata (1986)

Not all cases of borrowing from English into Japanese are as straightforward as these. In many cases, forms from English have been subjected to a variety of other processes, including "truncated compounding" (*wa-pro* < *word processor*); innovative compounding (*goo sutoppu* "traffic light" < *go* + *stop*); blending or hybridization (*dai-sutoraiku* < Japanese "big" + *strike*), and so on. Many loans have also undergone semantic restriction, extension, or shift. For instance, *ranchi* (< *lunch*) is used to refer to "restaurant cooking," while *handoru* (< *handle*) refers only to the driving wheel of a car or the handlebar of a bicycle, and *namba* (< *number*) refers only to the "licensed number plate of a car" (Loveday 1996; Ishiwata 1986). On the whole, English items "borrowed" into Japanese have been thoroughly "japanized" and integrated into the phonology and morphology of the language.

2.3 Contact in Settings Involving "Unequal" Bilingualism

So far we have been concerned with cases of relatively limited contact in which quite distinct speech communities borrow lexical items from each other. In cases where speakers of different languages come together within the same general community and bilingualism develops, lexical and other forms of borrowing may be even more common. Some of these situations correspond to what Loveday (1996: 20) refers to as settings of "bounded" or "subordinate" bilingualism, where there is more or less restricted contact between a dominant group and a linguistic minority.

This kind of contact may be the result of sociohistorical forces such as immigration, invasion, or military conquest, the realignment of national boundaries, or the establishment of inter-group contact for purposes of trade, marriage, and so on. According to Lewis (1978), some of the factors associated with settings of this type include the following:

- geographical isolation (e.g., Gaelic speakers in the Scottish Highlands);
- urban segregation (e.g., Hispanics in the United States);
- the persistence of ethnic minority enclaves (e.g., Basques in southern France)
- a tradition of limited cultural contact (e.g., the Pennsylvania Dutch in the US).

The languages of immigrant groups and ethnic minorities absorbed into a larger host community are particularly susceptible to lexical borrowing from the dominant language. Eventually, such minority groups tend to become bilingual, or to shift entirely to the host language. The greater intensity of contact during the phase of bilingualism and shift, as well as the asymmetry in power and prestige of the languages involved, promote borrowing, primarily into the subordinate language. A classic example of such a situation is the contact between Norwegian immigrants and English speakers in the US, as described by Haugen (1953).

Of course, borrowing in the opposite direction, from subordinate to dominant language, also occurs, though not usually to the same degree. American English in particular is replete with borrowings from the languages of immigrant groups who have settled in the United States over the last couple of centuries. Examples of the former type include loanwords such as *kosher* from Hebrew via Yiddish, *taco* and *margarita* from Spanish, *sauerkraut* from German, *sushi* from Japanese, and so on.

There are also numerous cases of unequal contact brought about by invasion, colonization, and the like. The contact between the European languages that serve official functions and indigenous languages in African, Asia, South America, etc. provides examples of this kind of setting. Two of the most interesting cases, however, involve earlier English and Japanese, both of which were once subject to massive influence from more prestigious external languages – French and Chinese respectively.

2.3.1 *French influence on the lexicon of Middle English*

The history of English offers two excellent examples of contact through invasion – the major incursions into the Danelaw by Norse Vikings and Danes in the ninth and tenth centuries, and the invasion by the Norman French in the eleventh century. The resulting contacts had a major influence on the vocabulary and indeed the general character of English. We will consider the Norse influence on Old English in the next chapter. For the present, let us examine the influence of Norman French on Middle English (ME).

The impact of French on ME was so great that scholars like Bailey and Maroldt (1977) have suggested that ME was in fact a creole or mixed language. However, Thomason and Kaufman (1988: 306f) argue that the degree and type of mixture was not similar to that found in creoles, but rather represented a case of category 3 borrowing on their scale.

After French-speaking Normans conquered England between 1066 and 1070, French became established as the language of the court and nobility, the church officials and clergy, and the feudal lords who owned the best agricultural land. For much of the period until the thirteenth century, English lost its status as a literary and official language, being relegated to that of a less prestigious vernacular. But it remained the native language of the majority of the population, and within three generations after the conquest, all classes except for the very highest levels of the nobility used English as their mother tongue. French (and Latin) were restricted to the nobility and intellectuals, among whom they enjoyed great prestige. Hence French influence on English was not due to widespread bilingualism. The sociolinguistic situation in England in the eleventh to twelfth centuries was more like one of diglossia (see chapter 4, section 4.3.1), in which the High language was fast losing ground to the Low language (Dalton-Puffer 1996: 6–8).

It is interesting to note that borrowing from French into ME was relatively moderate during the period 1066–1250 while French was spoken as the first and primary language of the Norman elite and clergy. French speakers made up a small minority of the population, though of course their ratios were higher in some urban centers in the south. During the thirteenth century, the Normans increasingly shifted to English, and French words began to flow into their newly adopted language. It would appear that, in this early ME period, speakers who were bilingual in French and English (a majority of whom were Norman) were primarily responsible for the introduction of French lexicon into English, whose native speakers imitated their use. The character of the early loans probably reflects this scenario. They tend to be simplex words borrowed from Old Northern French, e.g., *carpenter, canon, kennel*, etc. (the initial /k/ is a clue to their source – Dalton-Puffer 1996: 9). Moreover, the number of loans was not huge.

The situation in the later ME period from 1300 on was rather different. When the Norman lords severed their ties with Normandy and opted for allegiance to England, they increasingly abandoned French in favor of English. This process of shift set the stage for the massive influx of French loans into English over the next century or two. The period 1350–1450 witnessed the greatest influx, so great that it had repercussions on English morphology, as we shall see. A major cause of the borrowing was the fact that English started regaining various functions it had not had for some two centuries. During this transition, French was still used for official purposes (along with Latin), and also remained the medium of instruction at universities until the mid-fifteenth century. While it is impossible to determine the relative impact of spoken as opposed to written language contact in promoting borrowing, it seems likely that the latter was more influential during this period. This is supported by the nature of the loans – more complex, learned words like *acquaintance, adversity, temptation*, and the like, many with sources in Old Central French.

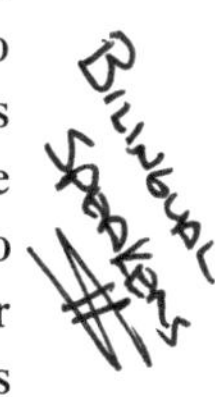

A great deal of native English vocabulary was also replaced by French borrowings, but the proportion only reached about 7 percent in the basic vocabulary. The preservation of native lexicon is one way in which English reveals itself as a Germanic language, despite the fact that some 65–75 percent of its present vocabulary is of non-Germanic origin. Borrowings from French included many words that are now commonly used, such as *atom, engine, finance, machine*, and *nation*. Many of these were motivated by need, since the concepts they expressed were new to English culture. Other borrowings seem to have been motivated more by prestige, since English already had native equivalents. Among such loans are dining terms like *beef, pork*, and *veal*, as well as terms related to areas of administration and the law, e.g., *arms, court, justice, legal, royal*, etc.

French writing continued to exert influence on Early Modern English, acting as a conduit for the importation of many Latin-derived words in the mid-fifteenth to mid-sixteenth centuries. Extensive borrowing of this sort through the medium of writing has parallels in other situations as well, for instance the introduction of thousands of Chinese borrowings into Japanese during the Middle Ages.

2.3.2 Chinese influence on the Japanese lexicon

The influence of French on Middle English is far surpassed by the massive influence of Chinese on Japanese between the seventh and twelfth centuries AD. During this period, Chinese became the main source of the technological and cultural innovations that promoted this earlier phase of Japanese modernization. There had been limited and distant contact between the two languages over the fourth to sixth centuries. This introduced a number of loans in areas such as silk and rice cultivation, metalwork, weaving, etc. Borrowings such as *uma* "horse," *shio* "salt," and *ine* "rice" date from this period (Loveday 1996: 30).

But contact was greatly increased after 594, when Japan adopted Chinese Buddhism and launched a program of sinicization. The contact setting evolved into a case of diglossia with restricted bilingualism within Japan in the eighth century. Chinese functioned as a High language, acquired via exclusive schooling and employed in domains of administration, law, literature, religion, science and technology, and the like. The most significant impetus to this development was the wholesale adoption of the Chinese writing system by the Japanese, who had none of their own. As Loveday (1996: 31) notes, this meant that Japan was forced to adopt the Chinese language along with its writing system. As a result, there was a proliferation of borrowings from Chinese, at first primarily in "higher" spheres. The parallel with French influence on Middle English is strong. In time, Chinese loanwords filtered down from those higher domains into the "lower" spheres of spoken and written Japanese. The result of this long process of influence was that Chinese contributed no less than 48 percent of the lexicon of modern Japanese. These borrowings include first person pronouns such as *boku* "I" (for males) and the imperial "I," *chin*, reserved for the emperor. Such "intimate" borrowings testify further to the strength of the Chinese influence.

2.4 Lexical Borrowing in Equal Bilingual Situations

In the cases of bilingual contact examined so far, the power and prestige differences between the (speakers of the) languages involved played an important role in promoting lexical borrowing from the High to the Low language. We would expect, then, that in cases of more or less equal bilingualism, this effect would be mitigated, and borrowing would be both more limited and more bi-directional. To some extent, this turns out to be true. For instance, Treffers-Daller (1999) reports on the low rate of lexical borrowing in two situations – Flemish–French contact in Brussels, and French–Alsatian contact in Strasbourg (Gardner-Chloros 1991). Based on a count of all tokens, she finds that in both cases the proportion of French borrowings into the other language is only around 2.0–2.5 percent, while borrowings in the other direction make up only about 0.29 percent of all words in her corpus. The differences reflect the higher status of French in both situations, but the low rate of borrowing indicates a high degree of language loyalty to the minority language. Interesting questions arise here as to why borrowing is so extensive in cases of "distant" contact or in diglossic situations, while it is so limited in cases of "equal" bilingualism. To understand this, we need to examine the social motivations for lexical borrowing.

2.5 Social Motivations for Lexical Borrowing

The motivations for and extent of lexical borrowing depend on a range of social factors that vary from one contact situation to another. Two factors that have been frequently mentioned are "need" and "prestige." Most of the borrowing associated with "distant" contact seems to be motivated by "the need to designate new things, persons, places and concepts" (Weinreich 1953: 56). This is especially true in cases where a community is exposed to new areas of cultural knowledge and experience through contact with others.

For instance, all speech communities have experienced the need to modernize and keep abreast of developments in science, technology, etc. This is what motivated much of the borrowing from Chinese into Japanese in the Middle Ages, and from French, Latin, and Greek into English in the Early Modern

English period. Similarly, the instrumentalization of modern vernaculars as official and national languages has prompted elaboration of their lexicons to meet the new demands placed on them. Through borrowing, they can fill gaps in the lexicon, or introduce finer distinctions of meaning not available in native words. For example, Indonesian did not clearly differentiate related nouns and adjectives by morphological means, as English does. Hence it created noun–adjective pairs based on English words such as *doktor* versus *doktoral* and *norma* versus *normal* (Moeliono 1994: 383).

Exercise 3

Weinreich (1953) suggests a number of factors that seem to promote borrowing by monolinguals and bilinguals alike. All of these are related to the concept of "need" as a factor promoting lexical borrowing. They include:

- the existence of homonyms in the recipient language, creating the need to resolve potential ambiguity (p. 57);
- the ever-present need for synonyms in certain semantic fields (p. 58);
- a perception that certain semantic fields are insufficiently differentiated in one of the languages (p. 59).

Examine in detail any case of substantial lexical borrowing involving a newly standardized vernacular (such as Indonesian) and try to determine which loans are motivated by each of Weinreich's factors. Suggest other motivations of your own.

Other kinds of borrowings under distant contact seem to be motivated more by considerations of fashion or prestige. The spread of English loanwords into many languages across the globe since the mid-twentieth century may be attributed partly to these factors. As we have seen in the case of Japanese, the growth of global avenues of communication such as television and the internet has had enormous influence on the spread of American English in particular.

In situations of bilingualism, the reasons for lexical borrowing are more complex. The motivations in these situations depend on a range of macro- as well as micro-sociolinguistic factors that vary from one community to another. The macro-level factors include those relating to notions like "intensity of contact," "cultural pressure," and language attitudes. As we've seen, intensity of contact is a function of factors such as demographic ratios, the sociopolitical relationships between the groups, the length of the contact, and the degree of bilingualism across groups. Cultural pressure is a function of the social motivations that promote the adoption of foreign features into a group's L1. These include the social and economic advantages that follow from such borrowing, among them social advancement, employment, educational opportunity, etc. Finally, degree of borrowing is dependent on the social values attached to each language, that is, their relative prestige, the degree of loyalty to each, and other ideologies regarding the tolerance of foreign interference or language mixture of any type.

As Bloomfield (1933) noted, borrowing is usually from a more prestigious into a socially subordinate language. Speakers may find it more sophisticated to borrow from the higher language. The French–Dutch contact described earlier for Brussels is a good example. Treffers-Daller (1994) finds that there are ten times as many (tokens of) French borrowings in her Dutch data (2.55 percent) as there are in her French data (0.29 percent). This can be attributed to the relatively high status of French, reflecting the historical dominance of French-speaking Walloons over Dutch-speaking Flemings, as well as the numerical preponderance of French speakers in Brussels itself. Another often-cited example is the borrowing of items like *beef, pork, veal*, etc. from French into Middle English. English, of course, already had equivalent words, *cow, pig*, etc., but apparently the French items had a more sophisticated air to them. A similar motive appears to lie behind the use of English loanwords in Japanese advertising. The borrowings place the products or services offered in a superior or more appealing light (Loveday 1996). Borrowing may also provide speakers with stylistic choices, allowing them to display their learning by using both foreign and native words with the same meaning. Thus educated Indonesians may use *kontrol* and *pengendalian*, *spesial* and *khusus*, and so on (Moeliono 1994: 383).

In general, then, notions like "need" and "prestige" must be understood in relation to the social aspects of the contact situation, particularly the kinds of culture contact and social interaction that characterize the relationships between the groups involved. For example, the pattern of borrowing from English into American Norwegian, as described by Haugen (1953), is directly related to the new domains in which Norwegian immigrants had to interact with speakers of English. Thus, "the chief foci of influence were the store, the government and the American neighbor" (1953: 93). Hence there was a preponderance of lexical borrowings in the economic and official spheres of activity. One the other hand, very little borrowing affected the vocabulary used at home or in religion, where interaction remained within the group.

Other factors that may come into play in bilingual situations relate to degrees of social solidarity and accommodation (Giles et al. 1991). Much research has been done on these kinds of motivation for code switching (chapter 4). But there have been few studies of how they influence patterns of lexical or other borrowing.

Poplack et al. (1988) were the first to attempt a detailed examination of the macro- and micro-level factors that influence the degree and type of lexical borrowing in a given community. They examined the frequency of English loanwords in the French of monolingual and bilingual speakers in the Canadian urban area of Ottawa/Hull – a community on the border of Ontario, where English is the majority language, and Quebec, where the majority speak French. They found that the rates of borrowing correlated with differences in social class (upper-class speakers use fewer loans than members of other classes) and neighborhood (with higher rates of loanwords in Ottawa). Other factors such as sex, age, and language proficiency had relatively little effect on rates of borrowing.

Overall, their subjects displayed few differences in the rates of "established" loans (that is, loans that are frequent throughout the community and permanently established as part of French vocabulary). However, bilingual speakers used more "nonce" (that is, not widely used) borrowings, particularly in Ottawa neighborhoods where English is dominant. This higher frequency of nonce borrowings was also typical of speakers who were more proficient in English. The general conclusion that Poplack et al. draw from these findings is that rate of borrowing (especially of nonce loans) is dependent on the norms of community behavior, rather than on lexical need. In that sense, nonce borrowing is similar to code switching, which varies according to convention as well. To put it differently, borrowing here seems to be motivated by accommodation to the conventions of use in the social networks of the speakers.

Support for Poplack et al.'s findings comes from a comparison of borrowing and code-mixing patterns in Anderlecht and Brussels, two municipalities that are part of the greater Brussels metropolitan area in Belgium. Treffers-Daller (1994) shows that French borrowings and code switches in (municipal) Brussels Dutch are significantly more frequent than in Anderlecht. These differences are related to the fact that Anderlecht residents have attended Dutch-speaking schools more than French-medium ones, have had more exposure to Dutch in the mass media, and are generally more proficient in Standard (Belgian) Dutch, which they use in many situations. Thus, their need for borrowings is satisfied by Standard Dutch rather than by French, and they may resist code mixing because of the puristic norms of the standard language. By contrast, Brusselers tend to have more contact with French (speakers), and therefore incorporate more of it into their Dutch. A social networks analysis reveals that the occurrence of French borrowings is significantly higher among subjects whose networks include more French speakers (1994: 80). Once more, it seems that degree of borrowing and mixture is determined by the behavioral norms and network structures of each community.

Another important factor affecting degree of borrowing is language ideology. Loyalty to one's native language and pride in its autonomy may encourage resistance to any foreign incursions. Indeed, some nations have enacted language policies, even legislation, to prevent or eliminate foreign borrowings into their languages. A well-known example of this is the continuing effort by the French to rid their language of foreign, especially English, loans. On the other hand, there are situations where borrowing from external sources may be favored because it avoids taboo associated with some native words. For instance, Herbert (1995: 59) suggests that the borrowing of click consonants and new words from Khoesan into Southern Bantu languages (particularly the Nguni subgroup) was motivated by the practice of *hlonipha*. The term conveys the sense of "respect through avoidance," and refers to a range of social avoidance customs practised by Nguni speakers. For instance, it is taboo for women to pronounce the names of senior male relatives such as their fathers-in-law. In some cases, even the syllables contained in such names must be avoided. According to Herbert (1995), Nguni speakers accomplished this either by substituting other native sounds or foreign sounds such as Khoesan clicks for the sounds that had to be avoided. In some cases, inherited words were replaced with a foreign *hlonipha* alternative.

Differences in borrowing or code-mixing patterns across bilingual communities have also been explained in terms of differences in perceptions of group identity. For instance, mixing of Alsatian and French in Strasbourg is common and well tolerated by members of the community, who regard the mixed vernacular as a symbol of their ethnic identity (Gardner-Chloros 1985: 166). By contrast, the relative rarity of language mixture in Brussels, especially among younger speakers, reflects the fact that such mixture is no longer seen as a marker of Brussels identity. The growing social distance between French and Dutch speakers encourages each group to identify more exclusively with its own language (Treffers-Daller 1994: 85). Despite the differences in patterns of code mixing, however, both Strasbourg and Brussels display a relatively low incidence of actual lexical borrowing between the languages in contact. Moreover, there is practically no structural borrowing across any of the languages. Despite what appears to be a situation of close contact, each language seems to preserve its autonomy quite well. Precisely what social factors are responsible for this is difficult to say. At any rate, it is clear that borrowing in the strict sense and code mixing in bilingual situations must be viewed as potentially quite different phenomena, governed by separate dynamics. The process by which foreign vocabulary becomes established as an integral part of a group's native language must be distinguished from the processes of accommodation that lead bilinguals to adopt "nonce" borrowings from an external source language when they engage in code mixing or code switching. The line between the two, however, is often hard to draw. More comparative studies are clearly needed to determine more clearly how sociolinguistic factors influence patterns of lexical borrowing, and determine which items become permanently installed in the recipient language, as distinct from being employed as nonce switches in bilingual code switching. Further discussion of the similarities and differences in code-switching patterns in bilingual contact situations will be found in chapter 4.

2.6 The Processes and Products of Lexical Borrowing

What exactly is a lexical borrowing? We've proceeded so far as though the answer to this question was clear. However, the phenomena that have been referred to by this label are quite varied. Some are close imitations of foreign items (e.g., *rendezvous* borrowed from French into English). Others are items that have been thoroughly transformed in shape (e.g., Costan Rican Spanish *chinchibí* from English *gingerbeer*), while still others are inventions that employ only recipient language materials in imitation of some foreign pattern (e.g., Spanish *rascacielos* modeled on English *skyscraper*). In fact, many so-called "borrowings" are not the result of a direct or complete adoption of a foreign item with both its form and meaning intact. The process of borrowing can be very selective, adopting a foreign form but assigning it a new meaning (e.g., Japanese *sumato* "slim, slender" < Eng. *smart*), or adopting a foreign meaning or concept and assigning it to a native form (e.g., Japanese *sara*, extended to include Western-style "plate"). Also, many of the outcomes of lexical borrowing involve innovations or creations that have no counterpart in the donor language. Some of these innovations may be created out of donor materials (e.g., Japanese *wan-man-ka* "bus without a conductor" < English *one+man+car*). Others may be created out of native materials, for example Zapotec *éxxuwí* "fig" < *exxu* "avocado" + *wí* "guava" and (older) coinages in the Pima language such as "wrinkled buttocks" for "elephant" and "dog person" for "monkey" (Herzog 1941: 68). Still other creations are blends of native and foreign items (e.g., Yaqui *líos-nóoka* "pray" < Span. *Dios* "God" + Yaqui *nóoka* "speak"). It would appear that the composition of lexical entries can be manipulated and rearranged in a variety of ways to produce these outcomes of contact. [1]

Attempts to establish a coherent framework for dealing with contact-induced changes in the lexicon began as early as the nineteenth century with Paul (1886) and others, and continued in the first decades of the twentieth century with scholars like Seiler (1907–13) and later Eugen Kaufman (1939). Perhaps the most comprehensive of the early frameworks was that of Betz (1949), whose basic distinction between *Lehnwort* (loanword) and *Lehnprägung* (loancoinage) still forms the basis for current descriptions.

Haugen (1950a, 1950b, 1953) added a new dimension to existing classifications with his distinction between importation and substitution – a dichotomy based on the presence or absence of foreignness markers (1950b). Importation refers to the adoption of a foreign form and/or its meaning, and may involve complete or only partial imitation. Substitution refers to the process by which native sounds or morphemes are substituted for those in the donor model. For example, in producing *rendezvous*, English speakers generally fail to reproduce the uvular [R] of French, using their own continuant [ɹ] instead. This is a case of phonemic substitution. Cases where a meaning or concept is borrowed but expressed by a native form are instances of morphemic substitution. An example is Spanish *rascacielos*, discussed above. In short, for Haugen, "every loan [is] part importation and part substitution" (1953: 388).

Following Haugen (1953), we can classify lexical contact phenomena into two broad categories – *lexical borrowings*, which involve imitation of some aspect of the donor model, and *creations*, which are entirely native and have no counterpart in the donor language. Lexical borrowings can be further subdivided into two categories. First, there are *loanwords* in which all or part of the morphemic composition of the loan derives from the external source language. Second, there are *loanshifts*, in which the morphemic composition of the item is entirely native, though its meaning derives at least in part from the donor language. Each of these categories can be further subdivided, according to the types of importation and substitution involved.

Loanwords may be divided into two categories; "pure loanwords" and "loanblends." Pure loanwords may consist either of single words like *rendezvous* or compounds like *chincibiri*. Sometimes these undergo semantic modification of some sort. For instance, the English word *corner* is borrowed into Dutch only in its football (soccer) sense, to refer to a corner kick. As usual, borrowed compounds or phrases may also be adjusted both phonologically and syntactically, like the phrase *objetores conscientes* borrowed into Florida Spanish from English *conscientious objectors* (Ortoz 1949, cited in Weinreich 1953: 50).

"Loan blends" involve the transfer of part of the foreign model and the reproduction of the rest (importation of a foreign morpheme combined with substitution of a native one). Examples of such "hybrids" include Pennsylvania German (PG) *esix-jug* "vinegar jug" and *home-plato* in Tampa Spanish (Weinreich 1953).

Loanshifts or loan meanings fall into the following subtypes. In some cases, a native word may undergo extension of its meaning on the model of a foreign counterpart. These are cases of "extensions" or "semantic loans." For example, Yakut *tahym*, originally "water level," was extended to mean all kinds of level, both concrete and abstract (e.g., of water, of skill, of development, etc.) on the model of Russian *uroven*" (Mordinov and Sanžejev 1951: 41, cited by Weinreich

1953: 48). In other cases, native morphemes are employed to express new meanings imported from foreign sources. For instance, American Portuguese (Am. Port.) *humoroso*, originally "capricious," acquired the meaning "humorous" on the model of its English counterpart.

Loanshifts or coinages involving compounds allow for a wider variety of results combining direct transfer with "substitutions" of various types. For example, loanshifts may take the form of "pure loan translations" or calques in which the foreign model is replicated exactly by native words, for example American Portuguese *estar direito* "to be right" modeled on English. Sometimes the model is adjusted somewhat to fit native patterns of order, like Spanish *rascacielos* modeled on English *skyscraper*. Similar to this are "loan renditions" in which the model compound provides a general hint for the native imitation, like German *Wolkenkratzer*, lit. "cloud scraper," also based on English *skyscraper*. We also find "loan creations," (that is, new coinages based on a foreign model,) for example Yiddish *mitkind*, lit. "fellow-child," modeled on English *sibling*, German *Geschwister*, and the like (Weinreich 1953: 51). For the sake of simplicity, we will refer to all of these compound loan formations as "loan translations."

Table 2.3 presents a brief summary of types of lexical contact phenomena, based on Haugen's (1953) classification. I have modified his terminology and description somewhat. I have also expanded his category of "native creations" to include a third subcategory ("creations using only foreign morphemes," e.g., Japanese *wan-man-ka*), which was not included in Haugen's classification.

Many of the lexical phenomena included in table 2.3 are not direct results of the process of borrowing itself, but rather due to additional processes applied to borrowed items. Most "loanblends," for instance, arise when native (recipient language – RL) derivational processes are applied to previously imported words, for example, PG *bassig*. Others may result from applying a foreign derivational process to a native item, such as Japanese *ichigo-edo* "strawberry" + *-ade*. Loanblends of the first type are really due to the more general process of integrating loan items into the morphology of the recipient language.[2]

In the process of morphological adaptation, loanwords can be subjected to various other processes, such as clipping. This can affect single words, for example, Japanese *baito* "part-time job" < German *Arbeit*, as well as imported compounds, such as Japanese *wa-pro* < *wo[rd] pro[cessor]*. As Loveday (1996: 79) notes, these processes help to simplify the pronunciation of the loans and facilitate their integration.

Creative word formation involving imported items is another interesting by-product of lexical borrowing, which Haugen includes in his category of "native creations." New compounds may be built entirely out of native materials to express new concepts, for example Pima "wrinkled buttocks." As we saw earlier, some of these "native creations" may also be blends of foreign and native

Table 2.3 A classification of lexical contact phenomena

Types	Processes involved	Examples
I Borrowings (modeled on the donor language)		
A Loanwords:		
1 "Pure" loanwords	Total morphemic importation of single or compound words	*rendezvous*
	Varying degrees of phonemic substitution[a]	*chinchibiri*
	Possible semantic change	Dutch *corner*
2 Loanblends[b]	Combination of native and imported morphemes	
2a Derivational blend	Imported stem + native affix	PG *bassig* Eng. *boss* + Germ. *-ig*
	Native stem + imported affix	Jap. *ichigo-edo* "strawberry" + *-ade*
2b Compound blend	Imported stem + native stem	PG *blaumepie* "plum" + *pie*
B Loanshifts (loan meanings):		
1 "Extensions" (semantic loans)	Shifts in the semantics of a native word under influence from a foreign word	
	a Phonological resemblance	Am. Port. *humoroso* "humorous"
	b Partial semantic resemblance	Am. Port. *frio* "cold infection"
2 Loan translations (calques)	Combination of native morphemes in imitation of foreign pattern	Germ. *Wolkenkratzer* cf. Eng. *skyscraper*
II Native creations		
1 Purely native creations	Innovative use of native words to express foreign concepts	Pima "wrinkled buttocks" for "elephant"
2 Hybrid creations	Blends of native and foreign morphemes to express foreign concepts	Yaqui *líos-nóoka* "pray"
3 Creations using only foreign morphemes	Combinations of foreign morphemes for new concepts	Jap. *wan-man-ka*

Notes:

a Some cases that appear to belong in this category involve the phonological adjustment of a native word on the model of a foreign one, without change in content. Weinreich (1953: 50) cites the example of Tampa Spanish *europa* becoming *uropa* on the model of English *Europe*, and American Yiddish *vakátsje* becoming *vekejʃn* on the model of American English *vacation*. It's difficult to say whether these are really cases of phonological adjustment of the native word as distinct from importation (imitation) of the foreign counterpart.

b Haugen (1953: 399) includes what he calls "blended stems" under the category of "loanblends." He gives the example of American Norwegian *kårna*, which appears to be a blend of English *corner* and Norwegian *hyrna*. Such cases seem to be rare, and might well be treated as cases of morphemic importation with phonemic substitution. Hence I omit them from the present classification.

words, like Yaqui *líos-nóoka* "pray." But we also find new compounds being created entirely out of foreign materials. Examples include Japanese *wan-man-ka*, *gaadoman* "guard" < *guard* + *man*, and, most interestingly, *sukinshippu* "intimate, physical closeness" < Eng. *skin* + *-ship*. All of these are innovations based on native patterns, or creative extensions of a foreign pattern, which have no counterparts in the source language. We therefore need to distinguish the process of lexical borrowing from other processes that may apply to imported items. Moreover, we should distinguish all such processes (borrowing, adaptation, integration) from the products they create.

Exercise 4

The following are a number of Japanese lexical items that are products of lexical borrowing and attendant processes of integration. First, try to assign each item to one of the categories in Haugen's classification (table 2.3). What difficulties do you have with this, and what changes in classification would you suggest to resolve them? Second, describe the processes of adaptation and change that the borrowings have undergone. The examples are from Loveday (1996) and Ishiwata (1986):

apaato "apartment" < English *apartment*
dai-sutoraiku < Jap. *dai* "big" + Eng. *strike*
dansu paati "dance" < Eng. *dance* + *party*
dorai "unsentimental" < Eng. *dry*
goo-sutoppu "traffic signal" < Eng. *go* + *stop*
han-suto "hunger strike" < Eng. *hunger strike*
kaa "car, bus or truck" < Eng. *car*
ofisu redi "office girl" < Eng. *office* + *lady*
poteto furai "fried potatoes" < Eng. *potato* + *fry*
raisu "rice served on a plate with a Western-style dish" < Eng. *rice* (Compare *gohan* "cooked rice served in a bowl and eaten with chopsticks" and *kome* "uncooked rice.")

2.7 The Integration of Loanwords

2.7.1 Phonological integration of loanwords

In cases of relatively light to moderate contact, lexical borrowings tend to be adapted in terms of the phonology and morphology of the recipient language, and become essentially indistinguishable from native items. It is quite easy to find examples of this kind of integration (or, in Haugen's words, importation with phonological and morphological "substitution"). For instance, English loanwords in Japanese tend to be adapted to Japanese pronunciation as well as its preferred CV syllable structure. Japanese accomplishes this adaptation by various means, including epenthesis (e.g., *baseball* > *besuboru*), cluster simplification (*sweater* > *seta*), and syllabification of glides (*quizz* > *kuizu*). Another excellent illustration of the processes of integration is provided by the integration of borrowings from English and other languages into Hindi (and other Indic languages). Part of this involves a complex pattern of substitution of foreign stops and fricatives by perceived equivalents in Hindi. Hock (1991: 393) calls this an example of a system-based pattern of substitution. The pattern is summarized as follows:

Foreign	/p^h, t^h, k^h/	→	Indic	/p, t̪ , ʈ, k/
	/f, θ, x/	→		/p^h, t^h, k^h/

English →	*Hindi*	*Example*
p^h	p	proof → prup^h
t^h	ʈ	tin → ʈin
k^h	k	concrete → kaŋkrit
f	p^h	phone → p^{h}o:n
θ	t̪^{h}	thermos → t̪^{h}armas
x (Arabic)	k^h	xatam → k^{h}atam

To find reasons for these substitutions, we need first to compare the very different structures of the Hindi and English obstruent systems, as in the following chart:

English				*Hindi*				
p	t	č	k	p	t̪	ʈ	č	k
				p^h	t̪^{h}	ʈ^h	č^h	k^h
f	θ	s	š	s			š	

Hock (1991: 394) suggests that foreign non-sibilant fricatives (f, θ, x) are "nativized as the corresponding Hindi voiceless aspirated stops because the friction noise of these aspirates approximates the acoustic impression of the foreign fricatives." Hence: English /θ/, a genuine dental, is rendered as Hindi dental /t̪^{h}/.

English /t/ is really alveolar, post-dental, and it is this "post-dentality" that is captured by the post-dental retroflex /ʈ/ of Hindi. Also, English aspirated stops like [p^h, t^h, k^h] may not be perceived as turbulent enough to be considered instances of "true" aspiration by Hindi speakers, where aspiration has a much higher level of turbulence.

Hock's explanation of the substitutions recalls Weinreich's notion of "interlingual identifications" at the phonetic and other levels.

Exercise 5
Revisit exercise 4 in this chapter. Find out about Japanese phonemes and phonotactics and try to explain how Japanese rules of phonology might have influenced these changes.

2.7.2 Morphological integration of loanwords

In general, loanwords pose little problem for syntactic adaptation, simply behaving like their counterparts of different syntactic categories in the recipient language. However, morphological adaptation can prove more difficult, especially if the recipient language has complex rules involving case, number, gender, and the like. In many cases, borrowed words are treated like native stems of equivalent categorial status, and take the bound morphology and other properties appropriate to the class they are assigned to. But class assignment itself may be problematic. In (standard) Swahili, for example, nouns fall into 15 morphologically defined subclasses, each with its own pair of singular and plural suffixes, some of which are covert (Mkude 1986: 519). Differences in class membership are signaled by agreement markers appearing on demonstratives and other word classes which have to agree with the noun in question. Some examples are sufficient to illustrate:[3]

Class	*Sing. prefix*	*Plur. prefix*	*Examples*
Class 1–2	m(u)-	wa-	*mtu*, *watu* "person(s)"
Class 3–4	m(u)-	mi-	*mkia*, *mikia* "tail(s)"
Class 5–6	ø	ma-	*harage*, *maharage* "bean(s)"
Class 7–8	ki-	vi-	*kiti*, *viti* "chair(s)"
Class 9–10[4]	ø	ø	*nyama* "meat"
Class 11	u	n/a	*uhuru* "freedom"

In some cases, foreign loans are assigned to a noun class simply on the basis of a formal similarity to native stems. Thus, Arabic *kitab* "book" has been reanalyzed as *ki-tabu* and assigned to class 7–8, with the plural *vi-tabu*. A similar example is *ki-biriti* "match" (< Arabic *kibrit*), with the plural *vi-biriti*. Whiteley (1967) reported on some interesting cases of adaptation among the speakers he observed. For example, some speakers assigned English loans like *madigadi* (< *mudguard*) and *machingoda* (< *marching-order*) to the *ø-/ma-* (5–6) class on the basis of their initial CV sequence. Even more interestingly, they created singular forms like *digadi* and *chingoda* from these loans (via "back formation") by analogy with native singular items. These kinds of adaptation are not found in today's Swahili. It may be that they are a function of the degree of bilingualism and proficiency in the foreign language among borrowing speakers. The more usual strategy is to place foreign loans into classes 5–6 and especially 9–10, which lack overt class prefixes. Some estimates suggest that loanwords now make up more than 50 percent of the total words in these classes (Mkude 1986: 520).

Another interesting aspect of morphological adaptation involves the treatment of borrowed nouns and adjectives in languages like Dutch, French, German, etc., which assign grammatical gender to such items. The conventional wisdom is that the rules of the recipient language determine the assignment. But this may depend on various factors, including formal criteria (similarity in phonological shape), meaning, and analogy. For instance, English loanword *stress* is assigned masculine gender in German by analogy with nouns like *kampf* "struggle" which are semantically similar.

Poplack et al. (1988) investigated the role of five factors in gender assignment to English nouns borrowed into Montréal French: sex of (animate) referent; phonological shape; (semantic) analogy; homophony; and shape of suffix. They found that only the first of these was significant, though other factors played some role as well. This seems to be the case as well with French borrowings into Dutch. French nouns which refer to males (*agent* "agent," *facteur* "postman," etc.) receive masculine gender, while nouns referring to females (*danseuse* "female dancer," *madame* "madam") are assigned feminine gender (Treffers-Daller 1994: 130). As in Montréal, analogy plays a small role, but only in the case of disyllabic nouns with stress on the second syllable (*canon* "cannon," *palais* "palace," *prison* "prison"). These tend to be assigned neuter gender in Dutch by analogy with native deverbal nouns, whether or not they are masculine or feminine in French. In many cases too, Dutch assigns gender to foreign nouns on the basis of formal criteria. For instance, French nouns ending in *-ment* (*gouvernment* "government," *appartement* "apartment," etc.) generally receive neuter gender, while loans ending in *-iteit* (e.g., *variabiliteit* "variability") are assigned feminine gender on the basis of the suffix (Treffers-Daller 1994: 124).

There is also evidence that social factors such as degree of bilingualism and proficiency in the foreign language may influence the gender assignment of borrowed nouns. This seems to be the case with French nouns borrowed into Brussels Dutch, which tend to keep their original gender (either masculine or feminine). This might be explained by the fact that the Brussels Dutch speakers are mostly bilingual in French, and familiar with gender assignment in the latter language. Moreover, the gender systems of the two languages match to a large extent, since Brussels Dutch distinguishes masculine, feminine, and neuter genders. Treffers-Daller (1994) finds that approximately 80 percent of the borrowed French nouns keep their gender in Brussels Dutch. This contrasts with French nouns borrowed into Standard Dutch, many of which are assigned neuter gender despite being either masculine (e.g., *bureau* "office," *numero* "number") or feminine (e.g., *station* "station," *terasse* "terrace") in French. Part of the explanation for this is that the gender systems of the two languages do not match, French nouns being classified as either masculine or feminine, while Standard Dutch nouns are either neuter or non-neuter. The fact that many French-origin nouns are assigned neuter gender in Standard Dutch may be due in part to borrowing speakers' unfamiliarity with French gender assignment (Treffers-Daller 1994: 125).

On the whole, it is clear that no single general rule applies to the way gender is assigned to borrowed nouns from one contact situation to another. The interplay of linguistic and social factors may vary significantly from one case to another, yielding different results.

The integration of loan items into the morphological structure of the recipient language can also involve creative processes of adaptation that yield additional lexical entries. In Japanese, for example, English loans are treated as uninflected nouns or stems which can be converted to other classes by the addition of suffixes or a helping verb (Loveday 1996: 118). For example, borrowed nouns may be converted into adjectives (or adjectival nouns) by attaching the suffix *-na* (e.g., *romanchikku-na* "romantic") or into adverbs via affixation of *-ni* (e.g., *romanchikku-ni* "romantically"). Borrowed nouns may also be converted for use as verbs by adding the dummy verb *suru* "do, make," for example *sain suru* "sign," *enjoi suru* "enjoy," etc. These strategies conform fully to Japanese patterns of derivation. Even the "clipping" of loan items common in Japanese (e.g., *han-suto* < *hanga-sutoraiki* < *hunger strike*) is a way of making such importations conform more closely to native Japanese morpho-phonology (Loveday 1996: 118).

The various types of integration we have examined here demonstrate that so-called "borrowing" involves complex patterns of lexical change that create new lexical entries or modify existing ones in response to culture contact. In all cases, borrowed items are manipulated so that they conform to the structural and semantic rules of the recipient language. This is what distinguishes the mechanisms of change associated with borrowing from those that characterize other vehicles of cross-linguistic influence, such as substratum influence. The kinds of adaptation and integration found in borrowing are also quite common in code switching and other outcomes of bilingual contact such as bilingual mixed languages, as we will see in chapters 5 and 6.

2.8 Linguistic Constraints on Lexical Borrowing

In addition to social factors, there are structural (linguistic) constraints which condition the degree and type of lexical borrowing. The most general constraint involves the well-known "hierarchy of borrowability," according to which open-class content items like nouns and adjectives lend themselves most easily to borrowing, while closed-class function items like pronouns and conjunctions are least likely to be adopted. Hierarchies of borrowing were proposed as early as the nineteenth century by Whitney (1881), and later by Haugen (1950b) and Muysken (1981b). The most comprehensive of these is the following, from Muysken:

> nouns > adjectives > verbs > prepositions > co-ordinating conjunctions > quantifiers > determiners > free pronouns > clitic pronouns > subordinating conjunctions

Part of the reason for the greater accessibility of nouns and adjectives lies in the fact that they form less tightly knit subsystems of the grammar than functional morphemes do. Moreover, they occur frequently in contexts where they can be isolated and extracted as loans. At the same time, the open-ended nature of these categories in the recipient language makes them more receptive to new additions. By contrast, the structuredness of classes such as pronouns, prepositions, etc. makes them highly resistant to borrowing. This reflects the more general hierarchical constraints on lexical versus structural borrowing to be discussed in chapter 3. Muysken supports his hierarchy with evidence from Spanish borrowings in Quechua. But the borrowing hierarchy in this case may not be fully representative of all situations. Appel and Muysken (1987: 171) emphasize the need to distinguish counts of tokens as distinct from types to ensure a more accurate picture of the hierarchy of borrowing. Still, the general outlines of the borrowing hierarchy are supported by other research, such as Poplack et al.'s study of English loans in Ottawa/Hull French, and Treffers-Daller's study of French loans in Brussels Dutch.

Syntagmatic constraints relating to the morphological and syntactic properties of lexical classes may also operate to favor or inhibit borrowing. This may explain why categories like verbs or prepositions, which govern other categories and assign case, tend not to be as heavily borrowed as nouns and

adjectives. Moreover, the greater the degree of morphological complexity in the paradigms of a lexical class, the more resistant it is to borrowing. Again, this may be why verbs, which tend to be morphologically complex as well as central to the syntax of the sentence, tend to be borrowed less than other open-class categories. The borrowing of verbs tends to be facilitated in cases where there is close typological similarity in verbal structure between the languages in contact, or where the borrowed item can be fitted easily into the morphology of the recipient language. Thus, most French verbs borrowed into Brussels Dutch tend to be from the *-er* class, since these lend themselves most readily to incorporation into the class of regular Dutch verbs whose infinitival suffix is *-en*. So we find *blesseren* "hurt" (< Fr. *blesser*); *rappeleren* "remember" (< Fr. *rappeler*), and so on (Treffers-Daller 1994: 110). In fact, so many of these French verbs have been borrowed that the French suffix *-er* has become somewhat productive in Brussels Dutch as a means of incorporating French verbs which do not even belong to the *-er* class. Thus we get BD *ofreren* "offer" (< Fr. *offrir*) and *finisseren* "finish" (< Fr. *finir*). Indeed, *-er* is often combined with French- or Latin-derived nouns to form verbs that aren't found in French, such as *fantaseren* "to fantasize" (ibid.: 111). We will see other examples of typologically favored borrowing of verbs in the discussion of convergence in Arnhem Land, Australia, in the following chapter.

Constraints having to do with degree of structural complexity may also explain the preference for morphologically simple lexical items over more complex ones in bilingual borrowing (Poplack et al. 1988: 60). In some cases, borrowing speakers may resort to strategies of simplification to facilitate the borrowing of verbs. A well-known example is provided by languages like Mayan, whose speakers borrow Spanish infinitives and use a Mayan verb meaning "do" as an auxiliary to which Mayan inflections can be added to convey tense/aspect meanings. A similar strategy is also found in Persian borrowings from Arabic, Japanese borrowings from English, and many other cases throughout the world. The same strategy is used in code switching (see chapter 5). Other languages follow the Brussels Dutch strategy of borrowing an infinitive and attaching a verb-forming suffix to it, for example, German borrowings from French and Russian borrowings from various languages (Thomason and Kaufman 1988: 349). Cases like these led Weinreich to suggest that the reasons why nouns tend to be borrowed more frequently than verbs has less to do with structural constraints than with "lexical-semantic" motivation. Still, structure does seem to have much to do with it.

Weinreich (1953: 61) also notes that typological differences in word structure may inhibit direct borrowing and promote the use of strategies like loanshifts or loan translations instead, when contact is sufficiently intense. He cites as an example the different types of borrowing from Sanskrit and Chinese into

Tibetan. Tibetan has borrowed directly from Chinese because of the similarity in word structure between the two languages, but has resorted to loan translations in borrowing from Sanskrit because of the mismatch between their word structures. Loan translations are particularly common when compounds are involved. Thus we find new formations in Brussels Dutch such as *ijzerweg* "railway" modeled on French *chemin de fer*, and *schoonbroer* "brother-in-law" (modeled on French *beau-frere* (Treffers-Daller 1994: 98). Some scholars, such as Heath (1984: 367), prefer to view such cases of "pattern transfer" or "calquing" as instances of structural convergence rather than lexical borrowing per se.

While there is much evidence for structural constraints on lexical borrowing, there are nevertheless many exceptions that do not follow the predicted patterns. Weinreich (1953: 62) provides several examples of the borrowing of words whose structure is typologically different from that of words in the recipient language. As always, structural constraints may not apply when the right social conditions prevail. As Weinreich (ibid.) puts it: "The unequal degrees of resistance to transfers and the preference for loan translations over transfers are a result of complex sociocultural factors which are not describable in linguistic terms alone."

We might note, finally, that there are strong constraints on the borrowing of basic or core as opposed to peripheral vocabulary. Indeed, the assumption that basic vocabulary is almost immune to replacement via borrowing is vital to assessments of language relatedness via the comparative-historical method. Some scholars use this criterion to establish whether contact-induced change is due to borrowing under language maintenance or to changes induced by shift. Thomason and Kaufman (1988), for example, argue that Ma'a, a bilingual mixed language, is a result of massive grammatical borrowing from Bantu languages into a previous Cushitic language, since most of the core vocabulary of Ma'a is of Cushitic origin. It's not clear that this conclusion rests on solid ground. In the following chapter, we will see cases in which a great deal of core vocabulary diffuses across language boundaries, suggesting that the constraints on such diffusion may not be as absolute as the traditional wisdom holds. However, it is difficult to say precisely what factors – structural or sociocultural – facilitate or impede changes in core vocabulary.

2.9 Structural Consequences of Lexical Borrowing

In cases of relatively intense contact, heavy lexical borrowing can be accompanied by the introduction of new sounds as well as morphemes which can affect the phonology and morphology of the recipient language. In fact, it has been claimed that heavy lexical borrowing is a prerequisite for phonological and morphological borrowing, an implicational constraint that might be stated as follows:

Implicational constraint 1:
No structural borrowing without lexical borrowing.

2.9.1 *Impact of lexical borrowing on phonology*

The borrowing of phonological features has been attested in many cases of relatively intense contact. One of the conditions under which this tends to occur is the substantial importation of foreign lexical items along with foreign phones or phonemic distinctions. Weinreich (1953: 27) provides examples such as the introduction of new phonotactic sequences with initial /v/ and /z/ into English because of importation of words with these initial sounds from French. We might add to this the emergence of a phonemic distinction between /ʃ/ and /ʒ/ as a result of the same influence. (See Thomason and Kaufman 1988: 78–9 for further examples.) Of course, it is also possible that native speakers of a language A will eventually adopt foreign features that have been introduced into second language varieties of A used by speakers of another language. In such cases, which are not rare, the resulting changes are due first to substratum influence, and second to a kind of borrowing. Weinreich (1953: 25) provides examples such as the merger of /l/ and /l'/ in Czech under German influence.

The massive lexical borrowing from French into Middle English described above had some influence on English phonology as well as morphology. For instance, the introduction of French loans with initial [v ð z] led to the phonemicizing of Old English (OE) allophonic variants such as [f] and [v], [θ] and [ð], and [s] and [z]. In OE, these fricatives were voiced in intervocalic position, but voiceless elsewhere; thus, [wi:f] "woman" versus [wi:vas] "women." Borrowings from French such as *veal, zeal*, etc. led to the development of contrasts, for example between *feel* and *veal*, *seal* and *zeal*, leading to a phonemic opposition between the voiced and voiceless fricatives. This was further reinforced by numerous French borrowings with initial [v], such as *village, vine, very*, etc. On the whole, however, phonological changes were few, confined to the pairs above, as well as the phonemicizing of [j] versus [dʒ] and [ʃ] versus [ʒ]. No new sounds were introduced into English. Moreover, the tendency toward phonemicization of certain allophonic pairs may have existed even before French influence intervened. For example, the loss of geminate consonants in words like [pyfan] (< pyffan) may have created a contrast between intervocalic [f] and the [v] in words like [dri:van] "drive" (Kurath 1956). In addition, some English dialects apparently had a contrast between [f] and [v] in initial position, as in

Table 2.4 Types of "borrowing" of phonology

Features borrowed	Example	Mechanism
Introduction of new phones or phonemic distinctions	Emergence of opposition between /v/ and /f/ in ME	Indirect borrowing via loanwords
Loss of phonemic distinctions	Merger of /l/ and /l'/ in Czech under German influence	Substratum plus borrowing

fox versus *vixen* (Brian Joseph, p.c., Feb. 2002). At any rate, English phonology changed rather little under direct French influence. The effects of the massive borrowing of Latin-derived vocabulary via French writing in the mid-fourteenth to mid-fifteenth centuries were more pronounced. This, along with the earlier borrowings from French, led to a significant altering of the English lexicon. One structural consequence was the emergence of the so-called "romance" phonological rules that apply to the Latinate elements of English vocabulary. Table 2.4 sums up the types of phonological borrowing.

2.9.1.1 Constraints on phonological borrowing

On the whole, phonological borrowing, even under heavy lexical borrowing, appears to be quite rare and subject to strong constraints. In his discussion of phonological "interference," Weinreich pays attention mostly to constraints on substratum influence (1953: 22). But one of his structural constraints – the existence of suitable "holes in the pattern" or "empty cases" – may apply equally well to borrowing situations. The constraint may be formulated as follows for borrowing:

> *Phonological constraint 1 (borrowing):*
> The existence of gaps in the phonemic inventory of the recipient language facilitates the importation of new phonemes or phonemic oppositions that fill such gaps.

The phonemicization of voiced fricatives and affricates in opposition to their respective voiceless counterparts in Middle English, as described above, fits this scenario. The change was further facilitated by the fact that these phones already existed in Middle English, as non-distinctive allophones.

Cases involving the borrowing of phonological rules under conditions of close typological fit can also be found. Thomason and Kaufman (1988: 97) provide examples such as the borrowing of a neutralization rule and allophonic rules among Mayan languages (Campbell 1976: 184–5). All such innovations are facilitated by the fact that they fit well with the phonological structure of the recipient language.

We might propose the following constraint for such cases:

Phonological constraint 2 (borrowing):

Borrowing of phonological rules is facilitated when such changes do not affect the basic phonemic inventory, and are restricted to patterns of allophonic distribution.

It should be noted once more that new phonological features are sometimes introduced into a TL by shifting speakers and then imitated by native speakers. It's difficult to say how typological constraints like the above affect the extent to which native speakers are willing to incorporate such innovations in these cases. Recall also that, in cases involving intense contact and a high degree of bilingualism, the transfer of phonological features and rules may not be subject to such typological constraints. An example is the diffusion of several Turkish phonological features, including vowel harmony, into Asia Minor Greek (Thomason and Kaufman 1988: 94, citing Dawkins 1916). It isn't clear whether these types of diffusion can be described as "borrowings" in the strict sense of that term. On the whole, there is need for much more research on the constraints that govern the diffusion of phonological features, whether due to "borrowing" or to substratum transfer.

2.9.2 *Impact of lexical borrowing on morphology*

In cases where words are borrowed along with affixes, new morphological patterns may also be introduced, and may or may not become productive. Examples include the borrowing of singular and plural pairs like *focus/foci* and *formula/formulae* from Latin into English. It is clear from examples like these that lexical change due to contact can involve varying degrees of structural change as well. We saw earlier that heavy lexical interference can introduce new phones or phonemic distinctions into the recipient language. It can also introduce new morphemes or morphological processes.

The borrowings from French discussed earlier also had some impact on English morphology, particularly on derivational processes. Several derivational affixes were imported along with French words, and several of these were extended to use with native stems. Thus, borrowings such as *dis-connect, de-flee, en-rich, em-bolden*, etc. yielded new prefixes. Similarly, items like *conspir-acie,*

Table 2.5 Examples of Romance suffixes entering ME through French loanwords

Abstract noun suffixes:		Agentive noun suffixes.	
-acioun	*creacioun, temptacioun*, etc.	*-ant*	*servant, ascendent*, etc.
-age	*mariage, pilgrimage*, etc.	*-ard*	*dotard, Spaignard*, etc.
-aunce	*acquaintance, obedience*, etc.	*-esse*	*countesse, goddess*, etc.
-erie	*flatterie, villainie*, etc.	*-our*	*confessour, prechour*, etc.
-ment	*ornement, instrument*, etc.		
-ite	*adversite, chastete*, etc.		
Adjectival suffixes:		Verbal suffixes:	
-able	*charitable, credible*, etc.	*-ate*	*translate*, etc.
-al	*natural, spiritual*, etc.	*-ify*	*magnify, glorify*, etc.
-ive	*defective, subjectif*, etc.	*-ize*	*baptise, chastise*, etc.
-ous	*amorous, corageous*, etc.		

Source: Dalton-Puffer 1996

cert-ify, charit-able, declar-acioun, statu-ette, etc. yielded a variety of suffixes, some of which became relatively productive as early as the Middle English period itself. For instance, the adjective-forming suffix *-able*, introduced along with loans like *equatable, legible, potable*, etc., was soon extended to native stems to yield words like *spekable, knowable*, etc., and has become very productive. Abstract noun-forming suffix *-erie*, introduced in loans like *flatterie, robberie, chivalry*, etc., was also attached to native stems to yield words like *aldermanrie, husbondrie*, etc. Table 2.5 gives some idea of the variety of suffixes that entered ME via French loanwords.

Despite the apparent wealth of new affixes, the overall influence of French on Middle English morphology was not that great. French loans were overwhelmingly adapted to native morphological processes, so that formations involving a French stem and a Germanic affix far outnumbered those involving native stems with French suffixes.

Sometimes, lexical borrowing can also lead to borrowing of inflectional morphemes. An example is the introduction of the plural inflection *-im* into Yiddish with pairs from Hebrew such as *mín/mínim* "sort," *gíber/gibójrim* "strong man," etc. This ending was later generalized to other nouns (Thomason and Kaufman 1988: 21). The borrowing of many Latin and Greek words into Early Modern English also introduced a number of foreign inflectional morphemes, some of which, though not productive, have survived. Thus from Greek we have *criterion/criteria, phenomenon/phenomena*; and from Latin *focus/foci, formula/formulae*, etc. Some of these plural endings are being lost as the borrowings are adapted to English rules, thus *criteria* (sing. and plur.), *formulas*, etc.

2.9.2.1 Constraints on the productivity of imported morphemes

It is not easy to predict which of the morphemes imported via lexical borrowing are likely to become part of the recipient language's morphemic inventory. However, Dalton-Puffer (1996) does provide some insight into this question. Working within the framework of Dressler's (1985) "natural morphology," she attempts to explain why certain derivational morphemes imported as part of French loanwords became productive in Middle English. In this approach, morphological processes can be evaluated along two complementary dimensions: semantic and morphotactic transparency. Morpheme combinations are ranked in terms of how clearly they can be decomposed semantically as well as in terms of how well the phonological shapes of their parts coincide with their respective meanings. Rankings are assigned on two scales. For example, a compound like *freedom (free+dom)* is both semantically and morphotactically transparent, and is ranked high on both scales. On the other hand, *conclusion (conclude+ion)* is ranked high for semantic transparency but lower for morphotactic transparency, while cases like *length (long+th)* are ranked low on both scales. The two scales complement each other and provide a combined assessment of the degree of transparency of the combination.

Using this approach, Dalton-Puffer found that those borrowed French suffixes which were most transparent in both senses were the ones which tended to become most productive in later Middle English. They included suffixes like *-erie, -able, -age*, and others which began to combine productively with native (Germanic) stems, for example, *husbondrie, aldermanrie; spekable, knowable; bondage*, etc. She concludes that "Processes with higher constructional iconicity are more natural so that suffixes with good MTT [morphotactic and semantic transparency] scores are acquired and suffixes with low MTT scores are lost from the language (or, if encountered in a contact situation, not borrowed)" (1996: 224).

2.9.3 Impact of lexical borrowing on the lexicon

Lexical borrowings can also have consequences for the wider semantic fields of which the imported items become part. Indeed, entirely new lexical fields may be created in a recipient language, for instance, in science and technology, agriculture, or other areas of new cultural knowledge. A modern example is the spread of "computerese" across the world's languages. Another effect of heavy lexical borrowing may be the creation of distinct choices of vocabulary reflecting different levels of style, when both native and imported words are retained. An example is the distinction between the more formal vocabulary borrowed into English from French, Latin, and Greek, and the more informal native Germanic lexicon.

A final issue raised by heavy lexical borrowing is how far it may affect the genetic affiliation of the recipient language. It's been estimated that some 65 percent or more of English vocabulary is of foreign (non-Germanic) origin. Yet English is still classified as Germanic, mainly because most of its structure as well as its basic vocabulary can be traced to Germanic roots. The same is true of Swedish, which has over 65 percent foreign (mostly Low German) vocabulary. Similarly, Albanian is said to have 90 percent of its vocabulary drawn from foreign sources, especially Greek, Latin, and Slavic, which belong to different branches of the Indo-European family. The extent of borrowing in these cases, by contrast with others such as Icelandic where foreign loans are minimal, only highlights the difficulty of predicting which factors promote or inhibit the borrowing of vocabulary.

2.10 Summary

We've seen that lexical changes due to contact involve not just direct importation of words, but a variety of other processes leading to innovations in the lexicon of the recipient language. Lexical borrowings are integrated in varying degrees into the phonology, morphology, and syntax of the borrowing language. They are also subject to different kinds of semantic change, as they vie for a place in the lexicon with native items that may already occupy similar semantic space. Once incorporated, they become fair game for both derivational and inflectional processes internal to the recipient language. Many of the products of these processes – loanblends, loan creations, and the like – are not strictly speaking borrowings, but innovations that have no counterparts in the source language.

Lexical borrowing must therefore be seen as just one aspect of a creative process of lexical change under contact, which builds on both native and foreign resources. This process not only adds to the lexicon, but also enriches its potential for further expansion. Foreign additions to the lexicon may also trigger phonological and morphological innovations. These structural changes appear to be subject to strict constraints, not least of which is the extent of the lexical borrowing involved. The higher the latter, the more likely it is that some structural features will be transferred. But since these structural innovations have to fit into the existing phonology and morphology of the recipient language, they are subject to typologically based constraints as well. Hence they tend to be rare even in cases of substantial lexical borrowing. The conditions under which structural features diffuse to more significant degrees across language boundaries will be the subject of the next chapter.

Notes

1 See Hilts (2001) for an interesting attempt to show how various components of form and meaning can be rearranged to produce various lexical contact phenomena in Atepec Zapotec, under Spanish influence.
2 Moeliono (1994: 382) provides an interesting example of the coining of new items by way of extending a native derivational pattern to imported words. In the domain of sports, Indonesian had native terms like *petinju* "boxer" and *pegulat* "wrestler," which correlate with *bertinju* "box" (v) and *bergulat* "wrestle" respectively. By analogy, a new paradigm of sport terms has arisen, each consisting of the prefix *pe-* and a (borrowed) stem. Hence we find *petenis* "tennis player," *pehoki* "hockey player," *pejudo* "judo player," etc.
3 I am very grateful to David Odden for providing examples as well as most helpful comments on the integration of loanwords into various noun classes.
4 David Odden (p.c. Jan. 2001) points out that some stems in this class begin with *n-*, which appears historically to have been a prefix, but most stems in the class don't appear with *n-*, so synchronically it seems that there is no overt prefix, even for words beginning in *n-*.

3

Structural Diffusion in Situations of Language Maintenance

3.1 Introduction

We saw in the last chapter that languages can import large numbers of foreign lexical items while still retaining their basic grammar, and indeed their genetic affiliation to earlier forms of the language. But do languages also import structure from external sources, and if so, under what conditions? What kinds of agency are involved in the diffusion of structural features? And what limits are there on it?

We have already seen that significant lexical borrowing can introduce new derivational morphemes and processes, as well as new phonemic distinctions (though not necessarily new phones) to a language. Does this mean that all structural borrowing is mediated by lexical borrowing? Or can structure be borrowed separately, in its own right?

Some scholars, for example, Thomason and Kaufman (1988), distinguish between "lexical" and "structural" borrowing as though the two could in fact proceed independently of each other. Indeed, Thomason and Kaufman give many examples of what they call "structural borrowing" and even go so far as to claim that, under conditions of intense contact, massive structural borrowing can result in entire grammatical systems being replaced. But despite the many claims concerning the "borrowing" of phonology, morphology, and even syntax, there has been no convincing demonstration that such structural change occurs without mediation by some other medium or process.

In fact, when we examine cases of language maintenance in which the maintained language is subject to extensive lexical borrowing from an external language, we find that in many if not most cases, little structural innovation occurs. Moreover, such structural change is practically always mediated by lexical transfer. This tends to support the traditional wisdom that (maintained) languages put up stiff resistance to importation of foreign structural elements. This constraint appears quite valid for structural borrowing in the strict sense of that term. It would be very strange indeed for speakers of a maintained language to single out structural features from a foreign source and install them as part of their native grammar. In the first place, why would they? Second, how could they identify and access such features for importation? Speakers do not have access to a list or a complete inventory of structural features from which they can select at will the ones they wish to import. For instance, when Middle English speakers "borrowed" derivational morphemes like *-tion*, *-able*, etc. from French, it certainly wasn't because they isolated them in the relevant French words and imported them independently of the stems to which they were attached. The process of borrowing – which, recall, involves the agency of recipient language speakers – would therefore appear to be subject to very strong constraints indeed, when it applies to structure. Such constraints may be weaker in the case of derivational morphology (which is more lexical in nature anyhow), but are more robust in the case of phonology, inflectional morphology, and syntactic structure.

This is not to say that such structural features can never be diffused from one language into another. Indeed, it was suggested in chapter 1 that there is in principle no limit to what can be transferred across languages, given the right circumstances. But when structural features are transferred, it is rarely the result of direct borrowing. Rather, such transfer is either mediated by lexical borrowing (as noted) or introduced under the agency of speakers of the external source language, whose innovations are then adopted by other speakers of the recipient language. In most if not all cases, as we shall see, the speakers who initiate such structural change are bilinguals.

The distinction being made here between direct borrowing and structural diffusion that is mediated by source language (SL) agentivity is similar to the distinction that Heath (1984: 367) makes between "direct transfer of forms from the other language" and "structural convergence (using native morphological material)." For Heath, "direct transfer" includes borrowing and code switching, while "structural convergence, also called pattern transfer or calque, is the rearrangement of inherited material because of diffusional interference" (ibid.).[1] As Heath notes, such "interference" can cause recipient language (RL) morphemes, words, or phrases to undergo rearrangements that make the RL structures more similar to those of the source language. This would suggest that abstract structural patterns may be transferred at the morphological and syntactic levels. It isn't clear, however, what mechanisms underlie this type of convergence. It will be argued later that these mechanisms involve L1 or substratum influence under the agency of bilinguals who impose SL features on the RL.

To summarize briefly at this point, we can distinguish several types of contact-induced structural changes in cases of language maintenance. They include direct borrowing of structural elements (quite rare), indirect structural diffusion via lexical borrowing (fairly common), and indirect structural transfer via SL agentivity in situations of bilingualism and mutual accomodation between the linguistic groups. Strictly speaking, all of these types of transfer are vehicles of convergence, since they all lead to greater structural similarity between the languages involved. In general, then, two languages can be said to have converged structurally when previous differences in grammar between them are reduced or eliminated either because one adopts structural features from the other as a replacement for its own, or because both adopt an identical compromise between their conflicting structures. The vehicles of convergence may include direct borrowing, substratum influence, and other mechanisms of leveling such as simplification. As we shall see, it is not always easy to determine which of these applies in a given instance. In the following sections, we will explore various instances of structural convergence and examine the sociolinguistic as well as structural factors which brought about the diffusion of linguistic features.

Let us first examine cases where it has been claimed that structural features have been directly borrowed.

3.2 Is there Direct Borrowing of Structural Features?

As we saw in chapter 2, there is good evidence that certain function words such as conjunctions, prepositions, and even complementizers can be borrowed directly. For example, various Amerindian languages in Latin America have borrowed Spanish conjunctions like *pero* "but," *como* "as, like," and so on. However, such borrowings have had little or no impact on the grammar of the recipient languages.[2]

It has been claimed that direct borrowing of inflectional morphology can occur in cases of close typological fit between the languages in contact. Thus Weinreich (1953: 32) informs us that Meglenite Rumanian speakers have replaced the native verb inflections *-u* (first person indicative) and *-i* with Bulgarian inflections *-um* and *-iš* respectively. Such importation of inflections appears to be generally rare in situations of language maintenance, though it does occur if there is sufficient congruence between the inflections involved. Another type of structural borrowing that has been claimed to occur involves changes in the semantics and/or grammatical function of native morphemes under foreign influence. An example is the extension of the function of American Yiddish *ver* from interrogative pronoun to both interrogative and relative pronoun on the model of English *who* (Weinreich 1953: 30). Cases like these are the morphosyntactic equivalent of lexical calquing, or "loanshifts."

The so-called "borrowing" of morphology may take various other forms, such as the introduction of new morphological categories or the loss of existing categories. An example of a newly introduced morphological category is the development in Balkan languages of a distinction between two complementizers, one used in factives after verbs like *say, think*, etc. (e.g., Rumanian *că*), the other after desideratives like *want, demand*, etc. (e.g., Rumanian *să* – (Weinreich 1953: 40). This distinction corresponds to the Middle Greek distinction between *óti* and *ná* (ibid.). Examples of the loss of morphological categories include the demise of the usual Dravidian distinction between exclusive and inclusive "we" and the old Dravidian gender system in Brahui under Balochi influence (Thomason and Kaufman 1988: 93, citing Emeneau 1962: 56). Many other examples of these kinds of contact-induced change can be found in Weinreich (1953: 39–42) and Thomason and Kaufman (1988: 78–97).

The problem is that all of these cases are cited without any explanation of the processes by which the changes occurred, or of the agentivity involved. Many of the situations in which these changes took place involved bilingualism and/or ongoing language shift. Hence the mechanisms involved might have included heavy lexical borrowing or code mixing on the part of recipient language speakers, as well as substratum influence by bilingual SL speakers whose innovations were imitated by RL speakers. In short, the case for direct borrowing of structure in any of these situations has yet to be convincingly made.

In order to find explanations for contact-induced changes in structure, we need to consider specific cases of contact and examine their social settings and the dynamics of language use by the groups involved.

3.3 Factors Affecting Structural Convergence

The extent and nature of structural convergence depend, as usual, on a range of social, historical, and linguistic factors. In the first place, there are differences in the sociohistorical circumstances that gave rise to each situation. In many cases, it is difficult to reconstruct the earlier history of the contact, and one must rely more on speculation (aided by linguistic evidence) to establish the sources and directionality of change. Second, the social contexts of the contact vary significantly from one situation to another. Some situations involve shift from a minority language to a dominant one with one-way bilingualism within the minority group, while others involve a high degree of bi- or multi-lingualism across groups. To complicate matters, there may be differences in degrees of bilingualism between different groups in the same community. Some situations involve diffusion of features across geographical and linguistic boundaries, while others involve relatively close contact within the same community. Finally, there are cases where diffusion has taken place gradually over long periods without extensive multilingualism, as opposed to those where diffusion has been swift as a result of intense contact and pervasive communal multilingualism. It is clear also that many of these convergence situations overlap considerably with those in which we find contact phenomena such as code switching. As usual, the task is to determine what combination of historical, demographic, sociocultural, and other factors is responsible for these different outcomes. In some cases, this may prove impossible.

We also need to account for convergence in terms of linguistic processes and constraints. The first problem is how to distinguish internally motivated changes from those due to diffusion from external sources. Second, we must identify the precise external source, as well as the agents of change – a task made all the more difficult by the absence of relevant sociohistorical data for many contact situations in the distant past. Finally, in cases where we have the necessary data, we must explain the mechanisms of change – whether borrowing, substratum influence, or other causes – as well as the constraints that affect their spread.

3.4 Structural Convergence in Stable Bilingual Situations

Let us first examine those situations involving more or less stable bilingualism within the community. These settings correspond to some of those examined in the previous chapter. We saw that, in general, such situations tend to promote varying degrees of lexical borrowing with only marginal diffusion of structural features. Indeed, even minority languages that are under heavy cultural pressure from a dominant host language resist importation of structure, with the exception of derivational morphology and some function words, as already noted. For instance, Pennsylvania German (PG) appears to have undergone very little structural change as a direct result of contact with English (Louden 1997). Fuller (1996) claims that PG is converging toward English in structure. But the changes she documents are relatively few in number, and most of them involve no new (morpho)syntactic patterns in PG. In fact, several of the changes involve minor adjustments in the subcategorization properties of verbs, similar to those discussed in the following section for Los Angeles Spanish. Finally, Fuller (1996: 511) notes that "few overt English system morphemes are being brought into PG."

Similarly, the French spoken in the Ottawa/Hull region of Ontario, Canada, shows very little evidence of structural influence from English. Concerning this contact situation, Poplack (1996: 286) informs us that, despite extensive code switching and lexical borrowing among bilingual speakers, there is no evidence that French grammatical structure has been replaced by more "English-like mechanisms." Similar conclusions apply to many other minority languages in bilingual situations, for example Alsatian and Flemish, both in contact with French, or Spanish in many Hispanic communities in the United States. Let's look briefly at the last of these situations.

3.4.1 Spanish in LA

Silva-Corvalán (1994) presents many examples of apparent structural changes in Los Angeles Spanish that have been attributed to English influence. Such changes are particularly characteristic of the varieties of Spanish spoken by persons bilingual in Spanish and English. But Silva-Corvalán argues that such changes do not in fact represent anything new to Spanish syntax. For instance, an apparent change in the "affected dative" construction yields structures like (1a) in LA, whereas Spanish normally has (1b):

(1)	a.	LA Span.:	y quebraron mi, mi jaw
			and they-broke my, my jaw
	b.	Gen. Span.:	y me quebraron la mandibula
			and to-me they-broke the jaw
			"And they broke my jaw"

Yet Spanish does allow structures like (1a) under different pragmatic conditions, for example when the affected object is not an inalienable possession, as in (2):

(2) Tiraron una piedra y quebraron mi portalápices
"They threw a stone and broke my pencilholder" (Silva-Corvalán 1994: 139)

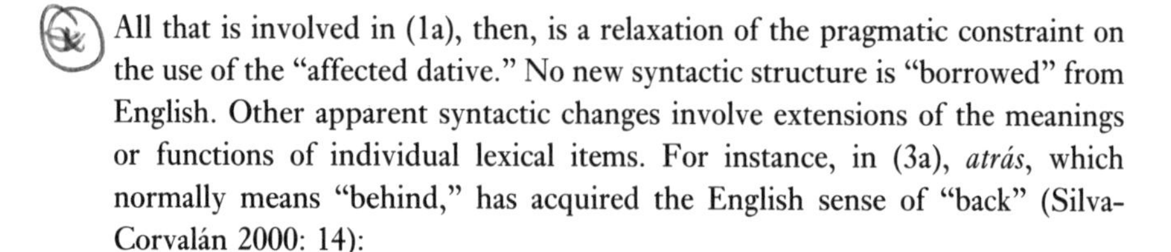

All that is involved in (1a), then, is a relaxation of the pragmatic constraint on the use of the "affected dative." No new syntactic structure is "borrowed" from English. Other apparent syntactic changes involve extensions of the meanings or functions of individual lexical items. For instance, in (3a), *atrás*, which normally means "behind," has acquired the English sense of "back" (Silva-Corvalán 2000: 14):

(3) a. LA Span.: Se lo dió p'atrás (< para atrás)
to-him it she-gave back
b. Gen. Span.: Se lo volvió
to-him it she returned
"She gave it back to him"

By way of final example, in (4a) *jugar* "to play" (games) has had its meaning extended to include the playing of musical instruments, a sense normally conveyed in General Spanish by *tocar*. The change also involves modification of the subcategorization frame of *jugar*, as in the following example from Otheguy (1995: ex. 2):

(4) a. LA Span.: Cuando no tengo nada que hacer, juego música
b. Gen. Span.: Cuando no tengo nada que hacer, toco música
when NEG I-have nothing what to-do I-play music
"When I have nothing to do, I play music"

Exercise 1

The following are some more examples of changes in LA Spanish under English influence, provided by Silva-Corvalán. What exactly has changed in these cases, and to what extent do they support the view that no new syntactic structure has been "borrowed" from English?

1 LA Span.: Mi padre es seis pies [de altura]
English: My father is six feet [tall]
Gen. Span.: Mi padre mide seis pies
My father measures six feet (2000: 13)

2 LA Span.: Y tu carro que compraste, ¿cómo te gusta?
And your car that you-bought, how to-you it-pleases
English: And the car that you bought, how do you like it?
Gen. Span.: Y el carro que compraste, te gusta? (1998: 232)

Compare:

3 Gen. Span.: ¿Cómo te gusta el café?
"How do you like coffee?"
Me gusta cargado.
"I like it strong."

Silva-Corvalán (1998) discusses several other examples like these, and argues that the changes involved are not the outcome of direct borrowing of syntactic structures or rules from one language into another (1998: 225). Rather, what is involved is a kind of "lexico-syntactic calquing" (ibid.) triggered by partial congruence between Spanish and English words. This results in Spanish words assuming the semantic and/or subcategorization properties of the apparent English equivalents (*faux amis*). Her findings lead her to the conclusion that "what is borrowed across languages is not syntax, but lexicon and pragmatics" (1998: 226). This claim certainly seems to hold for cases of language maintenance with bilingualism such as that in LA. Clearly, intense contact and heavy cultural pressure are insufficient to bring about significant structural change in many minority languages. Under what conditions, then, do such changes occur? To answer this, let us examine certain bilingual situations in which structural diffusion has taken place.

3.4.2 A situation of unstable bilingualism: French/English contact on Prince Edward Island

One such situation involves contact between English and Acadian French on Prince Edward Island, one of the three Maritime provinces of Atlantic Canada. The Acadian variety spoken here has been subjected to heavy lexical borrowing from English, as have all varieties of French in Canada. But, unlike other varieties, Prince Edward Island (henceforth PEI) French has also borrowed a number of function items, including prepositions, *wh*-words and the adverbial particle *back*. Each of these has led to certain structural changes in PEI French. Space permits only a brief look at the borrowing of prepositions and its structural consequences.

King (2000: 142) informs us that borrowed verb + preposition combinations like *ender up, finder out, hanger around*, etc. make up no fewer than 17.6 percent of all English-origin verbs in her corpus of PEI French. In addition, a variety of English-origin prepositions occur with verbs of French origin, for example, *parler about* "talk about," *aller on* "go on," *faire up* "make up," etc. Similarly, French prepositions occur with verbs of English origin, for example, *crasher dans* "crash into," *picker su* "pick on," *lander su* "land on," etc. (2000: 143). The result of this mixture in the prepositional system is that a property peculiar to English prepositions, viz. preposition stranding, has been transferred to PEI French prepositions. Thus, *wh*-interrogative strategies like that in (5) are quite acceptable in this and some other Acadian French varieties, though they are ungrammatical in other varieties of French, both in Canada and elsewhere:

(5) a. Quoi ce-qu'ils parlont about?
what that they are-talking about
"What are they talking about?"
b. Où ce-qu'elle vient de?
"Where does she come from?"

In addition, preposition stranding is allowed in relatives and passives, as in the following examples:

(6) a. Je cherche une fille à avoir confiance en
I am-looking-for a girl to to-have confidence in
"I'm looking for a girl to trust"
b. Ce lit-là-a été couché dedans
"This bed has been slept in"

By contrast, other varieties of Canadian French have borrowed few, if any, prepositions, and do not permit preposition stranding.[3] King concludes, justifiably, that "there is a close relationship between borrowing prepositions and having preposition stranding" (2000: 145). Crucially, though, she argues that the structural change is not the result of direct syntactic borrowing, however much it may seem that way. Rather, "lexical borrowing has triggered reanalysis of the PEI French prepositional system" (ibid.: 136). Once more we have evidence that an apparent case of structural "borrowing" is actually mediated by lexical borrowing, this time of function words.

It would appear that the agents of this change were fluent bilinguals who practiced frequent code mixing. Their practice of freely mixing French verbs with English prepositions and vice versa appears to have promoted a gradual change in which French prepositions assumed the syntactic properties of their English counterparts. This kind of agentivity seems to be one of the factors that promote structural change in an ancestral language. Another important factor appears to be ongoing shift in the community. It turns out that, while all varieties of Acadian French are under intense pressure from English, PEI French is particularly at risk, and some communities there are undergoing more rapid language attrition. Mougeon and Beniak (1991: 180) suggest that situations of unstable bilingualism promote structural influence from the dominant language on the minority language. This is certainly borne out by the PEI French situation. It turns out that other cases of contact conform to this pattern.

Exercise 2
Examine and compare at least two contact situations, one involving stable bilingualism (e.g., French–Flemish contact in Brussels) and the other unstable bilingualism (e.g., French–English contact in Prince Edward Island). What differences do you find in the social settings and patterns of use? To what extent are these reflected in differences between the types of contact-induced changes in the minority language?

3.5 Sprachbünde: Contact Across Contiguous Speech Communities

Another kind of setting which can lead to structural diffusion is prolonged contact across geographically contiguous language communities. The groups involved may develop close links and patterns of interaction for purposes of trade, or because of cultural practices such as exogamy, or because they are subsumed through conquest within a larger political conglomerate. A situation of this type, involving the diffusion of linguistic features across geographically adjacent languages, is referred to as a Sprachbund or linguistic area. The term "Sprachbund" was coined by Troubetzkoy (1928), who apparently saw it as a counterpart to the notion of "language family." It has been translated roughly as "language association," "language league," and "union of languages." Other terms that have been used include "convergence area," "diffusion area," and "affinité linguistique." But the term "Sprachbund" is now the generally accepted choice.

Sprachbünde or linguistic areas have been proposed for various parts of the world, on the basis of a variety of criteria, ranging from sharing of a few structural features to substantial similarities in several subsystems of the grammar. For instance, South East Asian languages like Chinese, Thai, Vietnamese, etc. have been treated as a Sprachbund since they share the feature of phonemic tone as well as certain morphological characteristics (Henderson 1965). Similarly, the diffusion of a series of click consonants from Bush-Hottentot languages into neighboring Bantu languages is the basis for treating this area as a Sprachbund (Guthrie 1967–71).

There are other more complex linguistic areas characterized by far greater degrees of convergence at more than one level of structure. Among the best-known are the Balkan Sprachbund, Meso-America (Campbell et al. 1986), South Asia (Emeneau 1980; Masica 1976), and the Pacific Northwest (Sherzer 1976).

3.5.1 The Balkan Sprachbund

The Balkan Sprachbund is perhaps the best-known and most widely researched convergence situation in the field of areal linguistics, its study dating back to the nineteenth century. The primary languages of the Sprachbund include Albanian (whose dialects include Geg in the north and Tosk in the south), Greek, Romanian (a Romance language), and the Slavic languages Bulgarian, Macedonian, and Serbo-Croatian (especially the Torlak dialects of the south-east). Other languages more marginally involved include Judezmo (also known as Ladino or Judeo-Espagnol), Romany, and Turkish. In keeping with practice in the field, the languages of the Balkan Sprachbund will be referred to as the Balkan languages (as distinct from the geographically based term "languages of the Balkans" in general).

The sociohistorical background to this situation involved prolonged contact among the above language groups during the period roughly from AD 800 to 1700. Contact was due to a variety of causes, including war and conquest, trade, animal herding, etc. Invasions by different groups (Southern Slavs, Bulgars, etc.) led to a long period of migration across language boundaries, leading to the emergence of multilingual communities. One important factor in the areal diffusion of linguistic features appears to have been the widespread use of Greek as a High language across these communities. This was related to the spread of Byzantine civilization and in particular the unifying role played by the Greek Orthodox church. Hence Greek seems to have been the source of, or the vehicle for, many of the diffused features. However, Greek was also the recipient in some cases, so the picture is not that clear.

The full details of this contact situation are still unknown. However, the linguistic consequences can be seen in various types of convergence at all linguistic levels (Sandfeld 1930; Schaller 1975). In phonology, the Balkan languages share the absence of suprasegmental features such as length and nasalization in vowel articulation, as well as the presence of a mid-to-high central vowel /ɨ/ or /ə/ (not present in Greek or Standard Macedonian, though it occurs in some Macedonian dialects). Schaller also pointed out that the vowels systems of the languages had merged to some extent, all having at least the vowels *i*, *e*, *a*, *o*, *u* (Joseph 1986: 106).

In morphology, we find the following convergence features (among others):

1 A post-posed enclitic definite article (all languages except Greek and Turkish) as in the following examples:

	Noun	*Noun + article*	*Meaning*
Bulgarian:	voda	voda-ta	"water"
Romanian:	lup	lup-ul	"wolf"
Albanian:	shok	shok-u	"comrade"

2 A periphrastic future marker derived from a verb meaning "want":

Greek:	θa ɣrafo (cf. *θa* < *θeli na* "he wants that")
Romanian:	o să scriu (cf. *va* "he wants")
Albanian:	do të shkruaj (cf. *do* "s/he wants")
Serbo-Croatian:	pisa-ću (cf. *hoću* "I want")
	"I will write"

3 A periphrastic perfect formed with an auxiliary verb corresponding to "have" (except for Bulgarian).
4 The merger of dative and genitive cases in Albanian, Bulgarian, Greek, and Romanian.
5 The merger of locative and directional expressions in Bulgarian, Greek, and Romanian. Thus Greek *stin eláða* "in Greece" or "into Greece."

In syntax, we find the following shared features:

1 Loss of infinitival structures in favor of finite complements. This is found in all of the Balkan languages. Joseph (1983) provides a thorough account of this development:

Greek:	θelo na ɣrafo
Serbian:	hoću da pišam
	I-want that I-write
	"I want to write"

2 The use of pleonastic personal pronouns to cross-index direct or indirect animate objects:

Romanian:	I-am scris lui Ion
	to-him I wrote him John
	"I wrote to John"

In addition, there has been a great deal of diffusion of lexical items across the Balkan languages. Some examples include:

1 The borrowing of single lexical items such as Greek *ðromos* > Alb. *dhrom*, Bulg. *drum*, S.Cr. *drum*, Rom. *drum* "drum." Also, Turkish *boya* "paint, color" > Alb. *bojë*, Bulg. *boja*, Greek *boyá*, Rum. *boia*, S.Cr. *boja*.

2 Numerals 11–19 are expressed by combinations whose literal meanings are "one on ten," "two on ten," etc. (not found in Modern Greek, though occurring in Medieval Greek):[4]

Albanian:	një -mbë- dhjetë [nyəmbəðyet]
Bulgarian:	edi(n)-na-deset
Rumanian:	un-spre-zece (< *unu-supre-dece)
	one on ten "eleven"

3 Various calques on idiomatic expressions. For example:

(a) "without a doubt" is expressed by "without other":

Albanian:	pa tjetër
Bulgarian:	bez drugo
Greek:	xorís álo

(b) The expression "whether one VERBS or not" is conveyed by the structure "VERB-not-VERB. Joseph (2000: 147) suggests that Greek may have been the source of this pattern:

Bulgarian:	pie ne pie	"whether one drinks or not"
Greek:	fíji ðe fiji	"whether one leaves or not"
Romanian:	vrea nu vrea	"whether one wants or not"
Turkish:	ister istemez	"willingly or not"

It has been suggested that both borrowing and substratum influence were involved in the creation of the Balkan Sprachbund. However, it is difficult to determine which type of change applies in a given instance. Sandfeld (1930) proposed that the diffusion was due to borrowing from a single language (Greek) into the others. But some of the evidence points to asymmetrical patterns of diffusion. For instance, it has been claimed that Bulgarian is genarally the recipient language in grammar, but the source of phonological innovations, especially in Romanian. But this claim remains controversial. As for the role of substratum influence, this has been interpreted to mean the influence of a pre-existing speech community on the linguistic groups that came to settle in the Balkans. But as Joseph (1983) suggests, it is equally likely that mutual accommodation and shift among the immigrant groups themselves promoted the spread of features. On the whole, the Balkan Sprachbund remains problematic for any attempt to explain the directions, agency, and mechanisms of convergence in a principled way. Moreover, as Joseph (1986: 111) points out, "there is an entire sociolinguistic dimension to the Balkan Sprachbund which must be confronted" before we can fully understand how it came into being. A better understanding of both the mechanisms of change and the factors that constrained them can be gained by examining situations for which more sociohistorical and linguistic information is available.

Despite all the scholarly attention that the Balkan Sprachbund has attracted, the fact is that the degree of lexical and structural diffusion found in most of the languages involved is not that extensive. Heath (1984: 378) in fact claims that "ongoing mixture involving European languages and native vernaculars in former colonies is at least as extensive as in the Balkans." This is perhaps what we might expect in situations of language maintenance, particularly when the groups involved belong to quite distinct communities. Resistance to extreme structural change remains strong in such cases. Even when there is intimate inter-community contact leading to massive lexical diffusion, structure seems to resist externally motivated change.

3.6 A Case of Intimate Inter-Community Contact: Arnhem Land

A case in point is the situation in Arnhem Land, Australia, where several Aboriginal languages belonging to quite distinct language families have converged remarkably over the centuries (Heath 1978). The major language families involved are the Yuulgnu languages, including Ritharngnu, Dhayʔyi, and others, and the "Prefixing" languages, divided into a northern subgroup containing Ngandi, Nunggubuyu, and others, and a southern subgroup containing Warndarang, Alawa, and others. These languages came together in the distant past in Arnhem Land as a result of migration. The clans affiliated to each language group congregated during the dry season to hold major ceremonies, to which clans from other language groups were invited. All groups practiced strict exogamy, so that marriage across language boundaries has long been common. For instance, a typical group consisting of four clans and 200 persons would typically have about 50 percent inter-group marriages (Heath 1981: 359). The wife joined her husband's group, and children would acquire both their father's language (as their primary vernacular) and their mother's language, which was used in ceremonies and other rituals. The groups that were closest became most similar culturally and linguistically, and those with the longest history of close association now exhibit the highest degree of convergence. It's important to note that groups in Arnhem Land spent long periods without close contact; hence individuals might not use their second language for several months during the wet season. This may have helped preserve language boundaries despite the widespread diffusion.

There is clear evidence of convergence among the Arnhem Land languages in the following areas (Heath 1978):

1 *Morphosyntax:*
  (a) Pronominal systems.
  (b) Demonstrative determiners and adverbs.
2 *Syntax:*
  (a) Free word order in all languages.
  (b) Juxtaposition as the primary strategy of clause linking, with occasional formal subordination.
  (c) Lack of agentive or passive participial formation.
  (d) Similar uses of potential verb forms (e.g., in counterfactual conditions).
  (e) Similar structure for causal sentences, etc.

In addition, there has been massive lexical diffusion across the languages, often involving significant portions of basic vocabulary. Many of these instances of convergence developed in the distant past, and are difficult to demonstrate now. However, using a combination of historical reconstruction and comparison of synchronic structures, Heath was able to document several instances of more recent structural and lexical diffusion across several of the Arnhem Land languages. Two pairs of language groups in particular have had close recent contact – Ritharngu (Yuulnu family) and Ngandi (North Prefixing) on the one hand, and Nunggubuyu (North Prefixing) and Warndarang (South Prefixing) on the other. Both pairs have developed very strong connections through intermarriage and joint ceremonies. The Ritharngu (Ri), Nunggubuyu (Nu), and Warndarang (Wa) groups appear to have been of fairly large size prior to contact, numbering approximately 200–300. The Ngandi (Ng) group was fairly small, numbering perhaps 60–70 persons. The disparity in size between the Ri and Ng groups has some implications for the kinds of convergence that occurred, as we shall see. The Ng group is gradually shifting to Ri, and the Ng language is becoming extinct, being now restricted to a few fluent speakers (Heath 1981: 358). The close association between the Nu and Wa groups has led to a gradual absorption of the latter by the former, and in fact the Wa language has recently become extinct. This too is a clue to the types of convergence that took place between Nu and Wa.

3.6.1 Ritharngu and Ngandi

Convergence between Ri and Ng involved heavy lexical as well as structural diffusion. There has been massive exchange of lexicon across the two languages, including significant portions of core vocabulary. In lexicon, Ng has borrowed more from Ri than vice versa, probably because of the larger size of the latter group. According to Heath (1981), the borrowing extends over a variety of lexical fields such as trees and shrubs, insects, physical feature nouns, body part nouns, kinship terms, and so on. Some idea of the extent of diffusion is given by the fact that Ri and Ng share some 65 percent of a set of 106 tree/shrub terms, 35 percent of 40 insect names, and 28 percent of 69 body part nouns (Heath 1981: 355). Borrowed items include nouns and verbs, as well as other categories such as directional terms ("north, south, up, down") and numerals. On the whole Ri and Ng share about 50 percent of all the noun and verb stems (about 1300) examined by Heath (1978: 29). The borrowing of so-called "thematic" verbs, especially from Ri into Ng, was accomplished in spite of significant differences in verb morphology between the two languages. Thematic verbs have isolatable root forms to which a thematizing suffix *-d̪u-* can be attached, with inflectional endings placed last, for example:

(Ng) *ḍak* = root for "cut" *ḍak-d̪u-ŋi* = past continuous "was cutting"

To facilitate the transfer of such verbs, Ng also borrowed the thematizing suffix *-d̪u-* from Ri, along with the root forms themselves. This meant that roots in this class could be borrowed back and forth, and indeed this class of verbs is the largest and most productive in both languages now (Heath 1981: 350).

Another interesting aspect of the diffusion between the two languages is the (mediated?) borrowing of grammatical morphemes, especially from Ri into Ng. These included the following:

- Ergative/instrumental suffix -t̪u- (< Ri *-d̪u-*), attached to nouns to express ergative or instrumental case, for example, Ri *ŋaya-t̪u* (I-ergative).
- Inchoative verbalizer *-t̪i-* (a derivational suffix attached to nouns to form intransitive verbs), for example, Ri *ḍaːl* "strong, firm" > *ḍaːl-t̪i* "to become strong, firm."
- Genitive/dative/purposive suffix *-ku-* (< Ri *-gu-*).

Ri for its part acquired negative suffix *-ʔmayʔ* and the kin-term dual suffix *-kaʔ* from Ng (Heath 1978: 143). In addition, there are several other shared affixes and postpositions for which the directionality of diffusion is unclear. It seems reasonable to assume that the spread of these structural features was facilitated, at least in part, by heavy lexical exchange, as in other situations we have examined.

There is also clear evidence of structural diffusion from Ng into Ri involving "pattern transfer" of the type associated with substratum influence. Interestingly, there appears to be no such influence in the opposite direction. In phonology, Ri has become more similar to Ng in the distribution of glottal stops. Other than this, there has been very little phonological diffusion between the two, perhaps because their phonological systems were already quite similar, though not entirely so in the case of vowels. Heath suggests that the present congruence in the consonant systems was probably due to a long history of convergence whose details cannot now be uncovered. In morphosyntax, several innovations in Ri can be traced to Ng influence. For instance, Ri developed a series of enclitic pronouns marking subjects and objects on the pattern of Ng, which, like the other Prefixing languages, has obligatory pronominals indexed to subjects and objects in all clauses. This feature is not found in the other Yuulngu languages to which Ri is closely related genetically. An example of this use of pronominal clitics follows (Heath 1978: 126):

(7) Ri: n̺a:-wala d̺ali-ña ŋay d̺inʔ-wač-n̺a ḍaramu-y
saw them he the women (acc.) man (erg.)
"The man saw the women"

Note that Ri did not imitate the word order of Ng clauses, only the pattern of a nuclear clause consisting of verb + pronominals, fleshed out by NPs identifying the subject and object, as in the example above.

Under Ng influence, Ri has also developed a strategy for creating relative clauses and gerunds by attaching a subordinating suffix *-ŋu* to a clause, as in the following (Heath 1978: 128):

(8) wa:ni-na—ŋu ra baŋguḷʔ
having gone I return
"Having gone, I returned" OR "I, who had gone, returned"

This pattern is quite different from that in other Yuulgnu languages, where infinitives are used in relative clauses. It seems clear that the new Ri pattern has its source in Ng, which uses a subordinating prefix *ga-* in the same function as Ri suffix *-ŋu*.

Finally, Ri has made changes in certain verbal (TMA) categories under Ng influence. These include the following:

- Merger of imperative and future in the same verb form, for example, *bu-ŋu* "Kill!" or "will kill."
- A distinction between present (*bu-ma*) and future (*bu-ŋu*).
- The emergence of a new potential category (bu-w-a "would kill") for use in counterfactual conditionals.

None of these features is found in Dhuwal, a close relative of Ri, yet they have clear equivalents in Ng. The effect of all these changes was to make the Ri verbal inflectional system more similar to that of Ng than that of Dhuwal. Again, it seems reasonable to assume that these innovations were introduced to Ri by Ng speakers learning the former language, and are therefore instances of substratum influence.

3.6.2 Nunggubuyu and Warndarang

The patterns of diffusion just described for Ri and Ng are quite similar to those for Nu and Wa. Briefly, they involve significant direct borrowing of lexicon and (indirectly) structural features from Nu into Wa, and some degree of substratum influence from Wa on Nu. Morphemes adopted from Nu into Wa include instrumental suffix *-miri*, elements of the noun class prefix system, and possibly ablative case marking suffix *-wala* (Heath 1978: 144). There is evidence of significant substratum influence from Wa on the phonology of Nu. Innovations in the latter include the loss of a fortis/lenis opposition in stops, loss of glottal stops, and the restructuring of the vowel system into three basic sounds (/i, a, u/) with length distinctions, by contrast with Nu's close relative Ng which has five vowel qualities. Heath (1978: 64) suggests that these changes in Nu were brought about by Wa speakers who pronounced Nu sounds with their own substituted native phones. This is reminiscent of Weinreich's "phone substitution" by learners shifting to a target language, a classic example of substratum influence.

3.6.3 Factors regulating convergence in Arnhem Land

The situation in Arnhem Land is highly instructive with regard to the conditions under which significant structural diffusion takes place. The assymetrical patterns of diffusion we have found in these two language pairs are in keeping with the kinds of dominance relationship that seem to hold between their members. In both cases we have a numerically superior group (Ri and Nu) exerting influence on a smaller group (Ng and Wa respectively) which is increasingly adopting the language and culture of its larger neighbor. In both cases, language shift has occurred, with the smaller group gradually giving up its language in favor of that spoken by the larger group. Indeed, as noted earlier, Wa is now extinct, and Ng is fast becoming so. Yet both of these languages have maintained their distinctiveness and their full complexity to the end. This would provide an explanation for the patterns of diffusion – heavy borrowing from the dominant into the subordinate languages, and substratum influence in the other direction, consistent with the pattern of shift and language death. From this perspective, the situation in Arnhem Land has much in common with other known cases of language attrition and death.

However, our focus here is on language maintenance, and on the innovations that take place in maintained languages as a result of contact. In most of the cases considered in this chapter, the communities concerned have continued to maintain their languages, despite varying degrees of external influence. In the cases involving extreme diffusion of both lexical and structural features, the vehicles of change include both borrowing and substratum influence, and in some cases it is difficult to separate the two. For this reason, it is not practical to equate language maintenance only with borrowing situations. For instance, no one would deny that both Ritharngu and Ngandi continued to be maintained for generations, yet the former changed primarily under substratum influence, while the latter changed primarily as a result of structural borrowing. The agents of change in a maintained language can include native speakers of that language, speakers of some other language, or speakers bilingual in both. If that is the case, then it calls into question the conventional wisdom concerning several other cases of convergence that have been attributed to borrowing alone.

3.7 Heavy to Extreme Structural Diffusion: Borrowing or Substratum Influence?

Thomason and Kaufman (1988: 66) argue that "the traditional prerequisite for structural borrowing . . . is the existence of a bilingual group within the borrowing language speaker population." This seems to be supported by all the cases examined so far. However, their definition of structural borrowing as "structural interference initiated by native speakers of the recipient language" (ibid.) is rather vague as to the actual mechanisms of change involved in these cases. It seems to imply, at first glance, that structural features can be incorporated and integrated into an RL in the same way as "direct" borrowings, for example, of lexicon, are. But this is clearly not the case. The "native speakers" who initiate the structural changes are in fact also proficient, to varying degrees, in the SL. This familiarity with the SL allows them to change the RL via imposition or transfer from the former. This would mean that the actual mechanisms or processes by which such structural diffusion occurs are similar to those found in cases of shift or second language acquisition. The only distinction would be that shifting speakers are less familiar with the RL (their target language) than bilinguals, at least in the earlier stages of shift. If that is the case, then the boundaries between "structural borrowing" and "interference through shift" are at best fuzzy. In this instance, as in all cases of contact-induced change, we need to distinguish the mechanisms of change (e.g., importation versus imposition) from their results (the "borrowings").

In addition to the cases we have considered, there are many other maintained languages that have experienced significant structural change under pressure from an external source. Thomason and Kaufman (1988) explain several cases of this type as instances of heavy to extreme structural borrowing, placing them in category 4 or 5 of their "borrowing scale" (see table 2.1 in chapter 2 above). In light of what we have discussed so far, there is good reason to ask whether these kinds of convergence may involve not (just) borrowing under RL agentivity, but rather change under SL agentivity, via mechanisms of transfer or imposition. Among the situations that raise such questions is the contact between Old Norse and Old English, which has been traditionally regarded as a case of "structural borrowing."

3.7.1 Old Norse influence on Old English

The invasion and settlement of northern and midland areas of England by Norse-speaking Norwegians and Danes lasted from roughly 865 to 955. The size and duration of the settlement led to a situation of relatively intense contact between Norse and English speakers, resulting in considerable lexical and some structural influence from Norse on the English spoken in the Danelaw. Norse speakers gradually shifted to English over the next hundred years or so, but their language left its mark on Northern and Midland varieties of English. Thomason and Kaufman (1988: 292–8) demonstrate that these dialects, and especially Northern ME, adopted a large number of Norse function words, derivational and inflectional affixes, as well as several hundred lexical items. Among the grammatical traits adopted were:

- Pronouns: *they, them, their*, replacing Old English equivalents *hie/he:o, him/hira, heom/heora* respectively.
- Quantifiers: *minne* "less," *seer* "various," (replacing OE *læ:ssa, syndrig/sundrij* respectively.
- A variety of strong forms of verbs, for example, *give(n), gaf, geeven* "to give," versus OE *jefa(n)/jifan, jæf/je:fon, jefen/jifen.*

Table 3.1 A comparison of grammatical features in Old English, Viking Norse, and Northern Middle English

Feature	OE	Viking Norse	Northern ME
Pronouns	*hi:e, he:o* "they"	*θei-r*	*they*
	him "them"	*θei-m*	*theim*
	hira "their"	*θei-ra*	*theire*
Quantifiers	*twejen, twa* "two"	*twinr-r* "twofold"	*twinne*
	lae:ssa "less"	*minne*	*minne*
	syndrij/sundrij "various"	*se:r* (dat. and pl. of refl./recip. pro.)	*seer*
Prepositions	*to:* "to"	*til*	*til*
	fram/from	*fra:*	*fraa/froa*

Source: Thomason and Kaufman (1988: 293, table 6)

- Locatives such as *whedhen* "whence" and *hedhen* "hence."
- Prepositions such as *til* "to," *fraa/froa* "from," etc.

Table 3.1 compares a few grammatical features in (Northumbrian) Old English, Viking Norse, and Northern Middle English. It shows the close correspondence between the latter two languages, by contrast with OE.

Thomason and Kaufman (1988: 292) list a total of 57 grammatical traits of Norse origin in northern varieties of ME, which make up 20 percent of all comparable traits (a total of 269) in these dialects. Most of these grammatical features were close phonological variants of their counterparts in OE. The diffusion was facilitated by the close typological similarity between OE and Viking Norse, reinforced by the close contact between Norse and English speakers, leading to extensive bilingualism. The intimate association of the two languages is reflected in the fact that many items of basic vocabulary were adopted from Norse to replace native English equivalents. English speakers may have been motivated to use Norse features by the prestige of the latter group, and the economic advantages that followed from knowledge of the language. At the same time, it appears likely that Norse speakers simply retained many features of their language when they "switched" to English. Though Norse influence was and still is most pronounced in the (rural) dialects of the North and Midlands, it spread somewhat into Southern varieties and eventually into London English, via Leicester (East Midlands). This influence can be seen in contemporary Standard English, where we still find Norse survivals such as *give, run, thrive, get*, etc., pronominal forms *they, them, their*, and function words like *though, till*, and *again(st)*.

Thomason and Kaufman appear somewhat indecisive about the causes of the Norse impact on Northern ME, ascribing it either to level 3 borrowing or to "influence through shift [i.e., substratum influence] or (more likely) both" (1988: 281). Elsewhere they refer to it as an instance of typologically favored borrowing (ibid.: 97). If we extrapolate from the other situations examined in this chapter, it would appear that substratum influence played a significant role in the structural changes that occurred in Northern ME. In other words, Norse features were introduced by Norse speakers into the variety of Northern English that was the outcome of the contact. In addition, the high degrees of morphological simplification found in this dialect might be attributed to the effects of language learning, as well as leveling across the typologically similar varieties. As is well known, such leveling is quite common in cases of contact between dialects or closely related languages (Siegel 1985; Trudgill 1986).

Hope Dawson (2001) suggests that the variety of Northern English that emerged from the contact between Viking Norse and Northern Old English was in fact a koiné – a blend of elements from the two languages. The formation of this compromise variety involved selections from both varieties, with gradual elimination of competition between variants through leveling (selection of one option). This suggestion is attractive, since it explains the retention of Norse grammatical features more satisfactorily than a borrowing scenario does. We saw in the previous chapter, as well as earlier in this one, that the direct borrowing of structural features (under RL agentivity) is rather rare. The massive diffusion of Norse grammatical features into Northern Old English is therefore not what we would expect if the agents of change were speakers of Old English importing Norse features into their speech. A more feasible explanation is that both Norse and English speakers continued to use their own varieties to each other, and that later generations of bilingual or bidialectal

Exercise 3

Compare any two case studies of koiné formation – for example, Siegel's (1987) study of Fiji Hindi; the studies of convergence among European dialects in Hinskens and Mattheier (1996); or Kerswill and Williams's (2000) study of Milton Keynes English. What processes of change are involved in these kinds of dialect convergence? What part do structural and social factors play in facilitating or impeding koiné formation? Discuss the relative importance of children and adults in this process.

speakers (especially children) forged a compromise language, as tends to happen in so many situations of contact. This explanation would be in keeping with other scenarios in which koinés have emerged (Siegel 1985; Hinskens 1998; Kerswill and Williams 2000).

3.7.2 Situations in level 5 of Thomason and Kaufman's borrowing scale

The situations that Thomason and Kaufman (1988) assign to level 5 of their borrowing scale include Wutun, a Chinese dialect that has undergone extensive structural change under Tibetan influence, and Asia Minor Greek, which changed significantly under Turkish influence. These situations are characterized by significant changes in syntax as well as morphology, phonology, and lexicon. Wutun, for instance, experienced the loss of phonemic tones, the development of several new cases, and changes in word order, to mention just a few.

Asia Minor Greek underwent similar changes at all levels of structure, including a variety of changes of a sort typically associated with substratum influence. The Cappadocian variety of Greek in particular was subjected to far more Turkish influence than those in other areas such as Silli and Phárasa (also in Central Asia Minor), while Greek varieties in Pontus on the western coast showed much less influence. Dawkins's (1916) study showed that Cappadocian Greek had converged considerably toward Turkish – in his famous words, "the body has remained Greek, but the soul has become Turkish." Just a few examples will suffice here to illustrate this. In phonology, vowel harmony is found on Greek suffixes attached to Turkish-derived words, and various morphophonemic rules from Turkish were introduced into the Greek dialect (Thomason and Kaufman 1988: 218). In morphology, we find such developments as an agglutinative pattern of inflection on nouns and verbs – a feature of Turkish, not at all typical of Greek. For example, the Greek genitive suffix *-yu* (as in *spityu* "of the house") was reinterpreted as an agglutinative suffix and extended to all nouns. The model for this was the genitive suffix *-in* (as in *ev-in* "of the house"), which was used with all nouns in Turkish (Sasse 1992b: 66). Finally, in syntax we find a frequent use of SOV order on the Turkish model (where Greek has SVO) and other kinds of structural diffusion.

Once more, treating the changes in languages like Wutun and Asia Minor Greek as instances of structural borrowing in the strict sense is problematic. With respect to the latter language, Thomason and Kaufman (1988: 216) argue that "if Turks did not shift to Greek, all the interference must be due to borrowing." But this overlooks the possibility that bilinguals, especially those that were Turkish-dominant, played a key role. In other words, the dramatic changes seem rather to be the result of substratum influence under the agency of SL-dominant bilinguals who reinterpreted RL grammar on the model of the SL. This would bring Asia Minor Greek (and Wutun) in line with other cases of massive structural change in an ancestral language, due to continuing shift toward an external language. In chapter 7, we will consider other cases of language obsolescence due to ongoing shift.

Interestingly, Thomason and Kaufman offer this very explanation for similar kinds of structural change in (other) situations that involve language shift. For example, they discuss "changes in Ethiopic Semitic from VSO, Aux-Verb, Noun-Adjective (probably) and Head Noun-Relative Clause word orders with prepositions to SOV, Verb-Aux, Adjective-Noun and Relative Clause-Head Noun word orders with postpositions to match the patterns of the substrate Cushitic languages" (1988: 131). Though these changes have been installed in Ethiopic Semitic as a maintained language, Thomason and Kaufman attribute them to substratum influence on the Semitic learnt by Cushitic speakers. Such developments make one wonder whether many such changes that have been ascribed to "borrowing" may not have involved an intermediate stage of substratum influence. Even in cases where native speakers of the recipient language were the agents of change, it is arguable that they must have had a substantial degree of bilingualism in the source language. Hence the cause of change in these cases must have been substratum influence, via processes of transfer or imposition, as is typical in shift. Once more, the distinction between borrowing and substratum influence becomes blurred in these cases.

3.7.3 *Convergence in Kupwar*

If extensive linguistic diffusion can take place across geographically contiguous communities, it is not surprising that convergence also occurs in single speech communities made up of different linguistic groups. A well-known example is the village of Kupwar situated in southern India to the north of the Mysore border (Gumperz and Wilson 1971). Here, three distinct languages – Urdu and Marathi of the Indo-European family, and Kannada of the Dravidian family – have converged extensively as a result of diffusion over a long period of intimate contact.

As a result, the languages have developed virtually identical constituent structures and grammatical categories, leading to an extraordinary ease of translation among them. Even their phonologies have become quite similar. Hence a structure in one can be converted to any of the others by simply substituting the corresponding morphs, one for one. Gumperz and Wilson found it possible to postulate a single syntax for all three languages, though they are kept distinct by different lexical items and grammatical morphs.

According to Gumperz and Wilson, the changes in the Kupwar languages become apparent when they are compared with the respective (standard) varieties spoken outside the village. The most striking changes are found in Kupwar Urdu (KU), which we can use for purposes of illustration. In the first place, we find changes in the KU system of gender agreement, to conform to patterns in Kannada. For instance, the KU system of grammatical gender is changed to one of semantically determined gender. Hence words with non-human referents which are assigned feminine gender in Standard Hindi/Urdu (HU) are reassigned to the masculine category, as example (9) illustrates:

(9) HU: wəhã nədii a-ii
KU: hwa nədi ay-a
there river came
"There was a flood"

Gumperz and Wilson also describe other changes in the gender system, such as the loss of gender distinctions in the verb "be" and in future tense constructions. Another morphological change is the introduction of an inclusive/exclusive "we" distinction in KU, on the model of both Kupwar Kannada (KK) and Kupwar Marathi (KM).

There are also several changes in word order, for instance in complex sentences with purpose clauses on the model of Kannada, as in example (10):

(10) HU: wo [bhæs cərane-ke liye] gəy-a th-a
KU: o gəe t-a [bhæs carn-e-ko]
KM: tew gel hot-a [mhæs car-ay-la]
KK: aũ hog ida [y'mmi mes ka]
he go Past-Agr [buffalo graze-Obl-to]
"He went to graze the buffalo"

Other examples of (morpho-)syntactic change in KU include the use of compound verbs and the use of *wh*-questions with "should" on the model of Marathi and Kannada. Finally, there are some examples of what appears to be direct borrowing of morphemes from Marathi. For example, the dative suffix *-na* replaces the native Urdu suffix *-ko*, as in (11):

(11) KU: hwa-si həm-na bula ne-ko pəwne ae
there-from us-to calling-for cousins came
"Our cousins came from there to call for us"

Various questions have been raised concerning the validity of Gumperz and Wilson's findings. For instance, the study is based on a corpus of only 10,000 words, and very scant illustration (one supporting example) is provided for each of the 16 convergent changes described. Moreover, Gumperz and Wilson fail to locate convergence in Kupwar within the larger context of widespread convergence in the surrounding region. As a reviewer of this book pointed out, "regional varieties of Urdu, Kannada and Marathi would have provided more appropriate reference points than the standard varieties, possibly revealing that convergent change in Kupwar itself is less impressive than assumed." Various other criticisms have been leveled against the study.

Despite this, the situation remains of some interest as an example of extreme structural diffusion (whether in Kupwar itself, or in the region as a whole). The precise motivations – social and linguistic – for these developments are difficult to pin down. One factor seems to be the extensive code switching that has been practiced in the village for generations. As we shall see in chapter 5, code switching is a powerful vehicle for diffusion of structural and other features across languages. Other motivations may lie in economy, in that speakers need only learn a single grammar for inter-group communication. But we still do not know the details of the convergence process, that is, the agency and precise mechanisms of the changes. As Gumperz and Wilson acknowledge:

> To what extent the adaptation in each language has been initiated by its home-group speakers under the influence of their knowledge of the languages of others, and to what extent adaptation has been initiated by others using a language to its home-group speakers, or in the case of Marathi, to others, we are not able to say. (1971: 269)

The preservation of separate vocabularies might be explained by the need to preserve distinct group identities and a separate code for in-group and familiar use. Such cultural pressures to keep some semblance of autonomy for languages that are converging can be found in other situations as well, including that in Northwest New Britain, the subject of the next section.

3.7.4 Convergence in Northwest New Britain

The Northwestern area of New Britain in Papua New Guinea (NWNB) has a long history of contact between the earlier established Papuan or Non-Austronesian (NAN) languages and the Austronesian (AN) languages introduced in the distant past by seafaring groups from other parts of the Pacific. At present, only one of the original NAN languages, the isolate Anêm, continues to survive in the area. It is in contact with eight AN languages, including the

Table 3.2 Languages in contact in Northwest New Britain

Non-Austronesian	Austronesian		
	Bibling family	Bariai family	Whiteman family
Anêm (isolate)	Aria Lamogai Mouk Tourai	Kabana Kove Lusi	Amara (isolate)

isolate Amara, four languages of the Bibling subgroup (Aria, Mouk, Lamogai, and Tourai), three belonging to the Bariai subgroup (Kabana, Kove, and Lusi) and Tok Pisin, the general lingua franca of Papua New Guinea. Table 3.2 is a sketch of the main languages involved.

Anêm appears to be the sole survivor of a larger group of NAN languages that were once spoken throughout the area, and which have gradually lost ground to the AN languages. Today, it is spoken by only about 350 people in small mountain villages where it is in contact with AN languages like Lusi, Mouk, and others. Contact among languages is the norm, so that everyone in NWNB is multilingual in three or more languages, including Tok Pisin.

Demographically and geographically, the contact situation in the pre-colonial past was somewhat different from that in Kupwar, in that contact was spread across contiguous languages spoken by different speech communities in a broad geographical area, a situation akin to a Sprachbund. In other respects, however, the situation is similar to that in Kupwar in that each village has long been characterized by intimate contact among groups who interact on a daily basis. For instance, the Anêm and Mouk speak each other's language since they have a long tradition of cultural relationships and are very much alike in social structure. The Anêm speak Mouk or Lusi as their secondary vernaculars, while speakers of the other isolate, Amara, speak either Kabana or Mouk, and in some cases Anêm, as their secondary language. The general pattern is that the Anêm and Amara (the two minority groups) typically use a Bariai language such as Lusi or Kabana for out-group communication, since these languages act as lingua francas across the area.

Just as in Kupwar, switching between languages in NWNB involves mostly changing vocabulary while using a common grammatical and semantic structure. The following examples from Thurston (1994: 687) illustrate:

(12)

NAN isolate	Anêm:	doxa	led	u-tl-î	aba	kan	abul
AN isolate	Amara:	o-togou	ane	i-se	esŋei	ne	e-ila
BIBLING	Mouk:	gute	ka	mtex	abax	tan	uala
BARIAI	Kabana:	eaba	ne	i-gal	gaea	ŋan	ido
BARIAI	Lusi:	tanta	ne	i-gali	gaea	ŋani	izo
		man	this	3sg-spear	pig	with	spear

"This man speared the pig with a spear"

(13)

Anêm:	nê-b-î	kaoa	êbêl
Amara:	pun	o-goune	kate
Mouk:	om-mluk	oulei	sakam
Kabana:	rau	kaua	mina
Lusi:	u-rau	kaua	mina
	2sg-hit	dog	don't

"Stop hitting the dog" OR "Don't hit the dog"

The major structural characteristics that are shared among the languages of NWNB include the following (Thurston 1994: 587–8):

- Fairly rigid SVO order, and similar constituent structure.
- Absence of tense as a grammatical category. Time reference is indicated optionally by temporal words.
- No verbal inflection for distinctions of voice or focus.
- Use of clause-final words to indicate aspect and negation.
- Absence of articles (though there are nominal prefixes in Amara).

There are various other similarities among the languages in causative, reciprocal, possessive and adverbial constructions, as well as in lexicon.

Most of these similarities seem to have developed as a result of changes in the AN languages under influence from Anêm or very similar NAN languages in their prehistory. A comparison of the AN languages of NWNB with their relatives outside the area makes this clear. As Thurston (1994: 585–6) points out, most AN languages outside Melanesia share the following characteristics:

- The verb phrase occurs initially in neutral statements.
- TMA categories (tense, aspect, negation, etc.) are expressed within the VP either by pre-verbal particles or by verbal inflections.
- Noun phrases are marked by particles which have the properties of both articles and prepositions.

The AN languages of NWNB show significant departures from the above typology, and marked similarity to NAN languages like Anêm. What processes of contact-induced change could have brought about this high degree of structural convergence? The major factor seems to have been continuing shift over the centuries from NAN to AN languages. As the influx of AN speakers grew, they merged with the indigenous NAN groups, who gradually adopted more and more of the former's culture, including their languages. It was this that led to the gradual expansion of the groups speaking the AN languages and the areas they occupy. It would appear then that the primary vehicle of convergence among the AN languages was (common) substratum influence from the NAN languages, bolstered by widespread borrowing under conditions of extensive multilingualism. The shift scenario is supported by the fact that the AN languages appear to have undergone extensive simplification and regularization of structure, in areas such as their pronominal and tense-aspect systems. Such simplification is commonplace in cases of untutored second language acquisition leading to the creation of new contact vernaculars, particularly when the new creations serve as lingua francas for groups speaking mutually unintelligible languages, as is the case in NWNB. This is particularly true of the Bariai languages, Kabana, Kove, and Lusi. The isolates, Amara and Anêm, present a clear contrast to these languages, in that they seem to have largely preserved their original grammars.

In addition to the kinds of structural convergence outlined above, there has also been a great deal of diffusion of lexical items across the languages of NWNB. They differ from one another primarily in basic vocabulary, but much of their non-basic vocabulary is shared. The interior languages (especially Anêm and Amara) have borrowed extensively from the Bariai languages in domains such as fishing, canoe building, and other maritime activities, while the Bariai languages have borrowed vocabulary from Anêm in areas pertaining to sound and motion, and the rainforest. The combinations of lexical and structural diffusion that have led to convergence among all these languages make it difficult to classify the outcomes strictly in terms of maintenance versus shift, since both seem to apply. Moreover, the mechanisms of convergence include both substratum influence under the agency of learners acquiring new means of communication, and borrowing under the agency of speakers maintaining their native languages. The situation in NWNB does not fall neatly into any one category, and poses a problem for Thomason and Kaufman's view that shift and borrowing situations can be clearly distinguished by the degree of structural versus lexical diffusion that takes place.

It remains for us to relate the cases of structural convergence discussed here to a typology of the social and linguistic factors that regulate these kinds of contact-induced change in maintained languages.

3.8 The Social Contexts of Structural Convergence

As Thomason and Kaufman (1988: 67) note, the classic situation that promotes structural borrowing involves heavy cultural pressure exerted on a subordinate population by a politically and numerically superior group. The various situations discussed here seem to bear this out, though not all cases of heavy pressure have resulted in the same degrees of structural change. The extent of structural diffusion is dependent on a broad range of social and linguistic factors, many of which are specific to each situation.

A full account of the social contexts of these contact situations is beyond the scope of this chapter. Suffice it to say that they vary according to the parameters outlined in chapter 1, which are the basis for establishing typologies of contact settings. They include:

- The demographics of the groups involved, including numerical ratios, power and prestige relationships, etc.
- The community settings in which the contact occurred.
- The frequency and type of social interaction among the groups.
- The ideologies concerning language and its relation to social identity in each group, and, hence, attitudes toward language mixture.
- The directionality of change, and the degree of stability or shift in the contact setting.

All of the cases of extensive structural convergence we have considered here involve stable multilingualism as an integral part of the social relations among the groups in contact. But each situation has led to different kinds of outcome. In Kupwar, convergence has resulted in near isomorphism of grammars, though lexical differences are preserved. Language boundaries here have proven weak and permeable. The major reason seems to be the extensive use of code switching and mixture in everyday interaction, and the fact that Marathi is used by everyone as a lingua franca. In NWNB, both structural and lexical convergence has occurred, leading to considerable isomorphism of structure. This seems to be due primarily to shift-induced changes resulting in common substratum influence from NAN on AN languages, though regular borrowing seems to have played some role as well. Moreover, the conservative interior languages preserve their distinctive complexity of grammar, while the AN languages which serve as lingua francas show evidence of simplificatory change. Finally, in Arnhem land, multilingual contact has resulted in a pattern of diffusion very different from that of either Kupwar or NWNB. Convergence here is to a large extent due to borrowing, both structural and lexical, with shift-induced changes playing a secondary role. There is no evidence of the kind of structural isomorphism found in Kupwar, or the simplification and regularization found in NWNB. The languages preserve distinct and rather complex morphological systems and areas of lexicon.

Clearly, then, convergence in multilingual situations can take different forms, and lead to quite different outcomes. One explanation for this may lie in the kinds of multilingual interaction practiced in each community, as described earlier. The full details of the different contact settings and patterns of social interaction that contributed to these different outcomes are yet to be fully understood. Some of these social factors will be discussed more closely in the following chapter, with particular reference to the kinds of bilingual language mixture known as code switching.

3.9 Linguistic Constraints on Structural Diffusion into a Maintained Language

The traditional view held by historical linguists such as Meillet, Sapir, and others was that grammatical subsystems and morphology in particular were highly resistant to cross-linguistic influence. This belief has proven untenable in the face of evidence from many contact situations. But it appears that structural diffusion is for the most part the result of substratum influence under SL agentivity, rather than direct borrowing. Hence Meillet and others may well have been right as far as the latter is concerned. In seeking constraints on structural diffusion, then, we need to be clear as to which vehicle of change is involved, since constraints that apply to one may not apply to the other. For the present, let us confine our attention to constraints on direct structural borrowing, in the strict sense. The constraints that apply to substratum influence (in cases of language shift) will be discussed in chapter 7.

3.9.1 Constraints on borrowing of morphology

There is still much disagreement on the extent and type of structural borrowing possible under contact. With regard to morphology, there seems to be consensus that derivational morphemes are more likely to be borrowed than inflectional ones. Moreover, it would appear that derivational morphology tends to be introduced via lexical borrowing, as we have seen.

There is rather less agreement as to whether inflectional morphology can be borrowed, either directly or indirectly. The cases we have examined here suggest that both are possible, under the right circumstances. Weinreich (1953) attempted to identify various structural constraints on such diffusion. According to him, the borrowing of morphemes follows these tendencies:

- Highly congruent structures allow for substitution of one morpheme by another.
- Zero morphemes tend to be replaced by overt ones, and bound morphemes by free forms.
- Allomorphic variants are likely to be leveled into a single form.
- Morphemes with opaque and complex grammatical functions are less likely to be borrowed than those with a single transparent function.
- Morphological borrowing is favored by functional factors such as gaps in the recipient language's system.

While these observations are supported by many examples in Weinreich's own data, they do not predict what will happen in all contact situations. Heath (1978: 73), for instance, discusses several instances of morphosyntactic borrowing in Arnhem land which run counter to some of Weinreich's claims. Heath therefore suggests alternative characteristics of morphemes which seem to favor their "diffusability", as follows (1978: 105):

- Syllabicity (morphemes that are independently pronounceable).
- Sharpness of boundaries (morphemes which are in opposition to zero).
- Unifunctionality (morphemes with a single function, as opposed to portmanteau morphs).
- Categorial clarity (morphemes whose function is clear without having to examine the broader environment in which they occur).
- Analogical freedom (morphemes that are not dependent on other morphemic systems in the same language).

The factors or constraints proposed by Weinreich and Heath are not mutually exclusive, and indeed complement one another. They fall into three general categories:

- Constraints based on congruence of morphological structures.
- Constraints based on transparency.
- Constraints based on functional considerations.

As will become apparent, these constraints involve considerations of typological distance and markedness.

3.9.2 Constraints based on congruence

The typological constraint most frequently proposed for morphological borrowing is some version of Weinreich's suggestion that "the transfer of morphemes is facilitated between highly congruent structures." This may be formulated as follows:

> *Morphological constraint 1 (borrowing):*
> The greater the congruence between morphological structures across languages in contact, the greater the ease of borrowing.

When there is both functional and structural congruence between morphological elements, even highly bound morphemes can be transferred. In addition to the example given earlier (Meglenite Rumanian borrowing of Bulgarian verb inflections), Thomason and Kaufman (1988: 57) cite the example of case and number suffixes from Standard Serbo-Croatian replacing older suffixes in Chakavian dialects of that language. Changes like these, involving the importation of morphemes to express functional categories already present in the recipient language, seem to be among the most common types of morphological borrowing (Thomason and Kaufman 1988: 54), and are especially frequent in dialect contact situations. The Viking Norse influence on Northern ME may be a case in point. As noted earlier, Thomason and Kaufman treat this as a case of "typologically favored borrowing" (1988: 97), a claim which may have validity to the extent that native speakers of OE imitated Norse speakers. It is certainly reasonable to argue that the diffusion of Norse features into Northern ME was facilitated by the close typological fit between the languages.

In cases involving contact between less closely related languages, typological similarities or congruence in certain subsystems of the grammar can also favor structural borrowing. The changes in Kupwar Urdu under Kannada influence (discussed earlier) seem to fall into this category, though it isn't clear that they were borrowings in the strict sense. The various changes in gender marking and agreement patterns were facilitated by the close similarity in morphosyntactic structure between the languages. The same is true of the diffusion of some morphemes from Marathi into Kupwar Urdu, a pattern which may be compared with the spread of certain Marathi morphemes into Standard Hindi (Thomason and Kaufman 1988: 98).

Most of the borrowings from Ritharngu into Ngandi in Arnhem Land also fit the pattern described here. The morphological structures of the two languages are quite similar, particularly in the case of verbal derivation and inflection. For instance, the borrowing of thematizing suffix *ḑu* by Ngandi was facilitated by the fact that the two languages shared a verb-inflectional pattern of the form: *Vroot + thematizing suffix + inflection* – as well as the fact that the favored shape of a thematizing suffix in Ngandi is CV (Heath 1978: 110). Similarly, the sharing of a verb-forming pattern of the form: *Noun stem + Verb-forming suffix + inflection* made it easier for Ngandi to borrow the derivational suffix which converts nouns to verbs. Other instances of borrowing in Arnhem Land seem to involve the replacement of a native morpheme by one from the external language – a process once more facilitated by a close typological fit between the languages. Examples include the borrowing of inchoative verbalizer *ṯi* from Ritharngu into Ngandi, apparently replacing an older verbalizer **man* (found in Ngandi's close relatives Nunggubuyu and Rembarrnga) (Heath 1978: 117). The same may be true of thematizing suffix *ḏu*, discussed above, as well as several other morphemes that were borrowed to replace older native ones in the recipient languages Ngandi and Warndarang from the source languages Ritharngu and Nunggubuyu respectively. Heath does not place enough emphasis on congruence or typological similarity as a factor favoring morphological borrowing in these cases.

3.9.3 Constraints based on transparency/markedness

Perhaps the most important structural constraints on morphological borrowing are related to general principles based on markedness, and particularly on the notion of transparency. Several of Weinreich's observations on the diffusion of morphemes seem to appeal to this notion in one way or another, for instance:

- The fuller the integration of the morpheme, the less the likelihood of its transfer (Weinreich 1953: 35).
- Morphemes with complex grammatical functions seem less likely to be transferred by the bilingual than those with simpler functions (ibid.: 34).
- A relatively unbound morpheme is more likely to replace its counterpart in another language if the latter is more bound and is involved in a greater variation of alternants in fulfilling corresponding functions (ibid.: 34).
- In the interference of two grammatical patterns, it is ordinarily the one which uses relatively free and invariant morphemes in its paradigm – one might say the more explicit pattern – which serves as the model for imitation, (ibid.: 41).

As we saw above, Heath attempted a reformulation of these criteria in terms of factors reflecting the degree of transparency of a potential morphemic loan. As Thomason and Kaufman (1988:) note, all of these factors "fit well with the notion of markedness as connected with ease of learning." All fall out from a very general constraint on morphological borrowing which we might formulate as follows:

> *Morphological constraint 2 (borrowing):*
> The greater the degree of transparency of a morpheme, the greater the likelihood of its diffusion. By contrast, the more opaque (complex, bound, phonologically reduced) a morpheme is, the less likely it is to be borrowed.

Again, we find evidence of constraints based on transparency and markedness in many instances of morphological borrowing surveyed in this chapter. The clearest examples come from situations involving contact between typologically similar languages or dialects, where congruence and transparency operate simultaneously. But we find equally compelling examples in other situations. In Arnhem Land, Heath noted that most borrowed morphemes in fact satisfied all of his criteria favoring diffusability, while those resistant to borrowing did not. Among the latter were bound pronominals and verbal inflectional affixes which were typically non-syllabic (e.g., expressed by a single consonant) and, in the case of verbal inflections, multi-functional (portmanteau morphs). Interestingly, not all the morphemes that met the criteria were in fact borrowed – a fact that might be explained partly by functional factors, discussed below.

Scholars working on other contact situations have also appealed to "transparency" as an explanation for morphological borrowing. For instance, as noted in chapter 2, Dalton-Puffer (1996) used concepts such as semantic and morphotactic transparency to explain why certain French-derived derivational morphemes became productive in Middle English. She found that borrowed morphemes that were most transparent in both senses were the ones that tended to become most productive in later Middle English.

Dalton-Puffer's approach can easily be extended to cases involving the borrowing of inflectional morphology. Her concept of transparency has the advantage of appealing to both semantic and formal criteria, which are not clearly distinguished in Heath's taxonomy of factors favoring morphological borrowing. Heath's factors may be subsumed under Dalton-Puffer's two dimensions as follows:

Semantic transparency	*Morphotactic transparency*
Unifunctionality	Syllabicity
Categorical clarity	Sharp boundaries

←analogical freedom→

As noted before, constraints based on structural notions such as transparency and naturalness are related to more general cognitive principles that regulate the transfer of morphemes across linguistic systems. Weinreich himself related his structural constraints to "psychological" factors such as "economy" (1953: 24) and the preference for a more explicit pattern (ibid.: 41). Thomason and Kaufman (1988: 56) also note that structural constraints "fit well with the notion of markedness as connected with ease of learning." Approaches which treat markedness values as relative to the typological distance between the systems in contact (e.g., Mufwene 1990) would seem to be especially useful in further research on morphological borrowing (and other types). As Thomason and Kaufman (1988: 57) suggest, such an approach has the advantage of recognizing that "it is not morphology itself that is marked and unlikely to be transferred from one language to another; rather it is certain common features of morphological structure that often, but not always, make morphology hard to learn."

3.9.4 Functionally based constraints

There is some evidence that functional constraints also play a role in structural borrowing. The addition and loss of morphological categories are often dependent on such constraints. There are cases where a category present in one of the languages in contact is absent in the other(s). Depending on the direction of influence, such mismatches may lead either to the addition of a new category to the language that previously lacked it, or to its loss in the other. For cases of the former type, the constraint may be worded as follows:

> *Morphological constraint 3 (borrowing):*
> The existence of gaps in the morphemic inventory of a recipient language facilitates the importation of new morphemes and functional categories from a source language.

For cases involving loss of categories, the following constraint applies:

> *Morphological constraint 4 (borrowing):*
> The lack of a functional category in a source language may lead to loss of a similar category in a recipient language.

Evidence of functionally motivated borrowing of morphemes comes once more from Arnhem Land. For instance, the borrowing of ergative/instrumental suffix *-ṯu-* by Ngandi (from Ritharngu) and the borrowing of instrumental suffix *-miri* by Nunggubuyu (from Ritharngu) seem to have been encouraged by the lack of these categories in the recipient languages. In several other cases, however, borrowed morphemes simply replaced functionally equivalent ones in the recipient languages. In general, functional factors played a minor role, and fail to account for most cases of morphological borrowing in Arnhem Land. The Kupwar situation also provides few examples of functionally motivated borrowings, such as the introduction of an inclusive/exclusive "we" distinction into Kupwar Urdu on the model of Kannada.

Dalton-Puffer also notes that certain French derivational suffixes introduced into Middle English became productive because they filled functional gaps and conveyed distinctions not previously made in the language. These included adjective-forming suffix *-able* and feminine agentive suffix *-esse* (1996: 221).

It is clear, however, that linguistic explanations for morphological borrowing must appeal to all of the constraints discussed in this chapter, whether based on typological distance, transparency, or functional factors.

3.10 Constraints on Syntactic Diffusion

Comparatively little attention has been paid to the study of cross-linguistic influence at the level of syntax, and consequently we know little about the constraints that apply to it. Throughout this chapter, we have suggested that syntactic structure very rarely, if ever, gets borrowed. In stable bilingual situations, there are very strong constraints against such change, even in languages subjected to intense pressure from a dominant external source. As we saw in section 3.4.1, Silva-Corvalán (1998) argued that apparent syntactic changes in Spanish under English influence are relatively slight adjustments that do not affect the abstract syntactic structure of Spanish, but only its surface properties. For example, the use of *jugar* rather than *tocar* to refer to the playing of music simply introduces a surface modification of the subcategorization properties of *jugar*. This led Silva-Corvalán to propose that this kind of syntactic "borrowing" can only take place when the changes conform to the structure of the RL (1998: 226) This of course is what other scholars such as Meillet and Jakobson have argued for in the case of morphological borrowing.

When extensive syntactic diffusion does occur, as it clearly does in cases of extreme convergence, it appears to be due to mechanisms of change associated with language shift. Understanding the constraints on this kind of syntactic diffusion means, first, understanding the vehicles of such change. The chief of these is substratum influence in learner versions of a recipient language, leading to innovations that may subsequently be imitated by native RL speakers. Another closely related factor may be substitution/switching of construction types across languages in the kinds of language mixture practiced by more or less skilled bilinguals. Bilinguals who are dominant in the external language being switched to appear to play a key role in importing foreign features into an ancestral language, though these may not always be imitated by native speakers of the latter. For instance, Silva-Corvalán (1998: 233) points out that bilinguals with less proficiency in LA Spanish (that is, those who are in a more advanced stage of shift and are English-dominant) introduce more significant English-influenced changes into Spanish than more proficient speakers. Thus examples of exact calquing such as shown in (14) were produced by two speakers with extremely reduced proficiency in Spanish:

(14)	LA Span.:	Yo gusto eso
		I like-1s that
	Gen. Sp.:	A mi me gusta eso
		To me pro please-3s that
		"I like that"

Here *gustar* "to please" is reanalyzed as a transitive verb with an Experiencer subject and an accusative theme on the model of English *like*, whereas in Gen. Spanish it is a verb with a "theme" or "patient" subject and an indirect experiencer object.

In addition, bilinguals have the ability to substitute entire phrasal and clausal constituents for each other, and in many cases, to switch the "matrix" language into which they incorporate structures from the other language. As we will see in chapter 5, these strategies of language mixing are quite common in code-switching situations generally.

Hence it is not clear in what sense we can talk about constraints on syntactic diffusion in situations of convergence. We clearly need to distinguish constraints on substitution or incorporation of external features into a speaker's primary language from constraints on L1 influence on an acquired L2. Since these issues are treated in chapters 5 and 7 respectively, we can postpone our consideration of them. For the moment, we can say that, in both cases, the greater the congruence between syntactic structures in two languages in contact, the greater the likelihood that one will replace the other. For instance, Thomason and Kaufman explain the relative ease with which basic word order is borrowed or acquired by noting that patterns like SVO and SOV are functionally congruent. In other words, they "typically perform the same basic syntactic function – identification of subject and object by their position relative to each other and to the verb" (ibid.). Thomason and Kaufman cite several examples of such word order changes, including the change from SOV to SVO in Finnish under Indo-European influence, and from SVO to SOV in Austronesian languages of New Guinea under Papuan influence. However, functional congruence by itself cannot explain what factors favor or inhibit these kinds of replacement. It is not clear, for instance, whether replacement of SOV by SVO is more likely than the reverse, and if so, why.

Exercise 4
Kerswill and Williams (2000: 84) propose a number of principles that regulate processes of leveling and simplification in dialect convergence. These include the following (slightly amended):

- Majority forms found in the mix win out.
- Marked forms are disfavored.
- Phonologically and lexically simple features are more often adopted than complex ones.

How are such principles related to the structural constraints on convergence discussed in this chapter?

3.11 Summary

In this chapter we considered a continuum of contact situations ranging from those in which relatively little structural diffusion has occurred to cases involving extreme spread of both lexical and structural features. We found that there was not always a consistent relationship between degree of lexical diffusion and degree of structural diffusion. In stable bilingual situations, lexical borrowing can act as a conduit for structural innovations in the minority language, especially in derivational morphology and some aspects of (morpho-)syntax. But the affected language remains highly resistant to foreign structural interference.

In situations of unstable bilingualism, ongoing shift appears to lead to somewhat more structural innovation in an ancestral language under threat from a dominant external language. These innovations are apparently introduced by highly proficient bilinguals, especially those who use the dominant language as their primary means of communication. Some of these situations may involve high degrees of lexical diffusion, but this may not be matched by equal spread of structure.

Finally, there are situations that have led to high degrees of structural convergence across languages, to the point where they become isomorphic in structure, while still preserving lexical differences. These cases seem to involve prolonged shift, with mutual accommodation leading to a shared grammar. The selection of one of the languages in contact as a lingua franca may promote this kind of extreme convergence.

Most of these instances of structural diffusion cannot adequately be explained by the metaphor of borrowing, which implies a uni-directional process initiated by RL speakers. Rather, structural convergence seems to involve a bi-directional process of language mixing under conditions of ongoing shift. The greater the degree of shift from an ancestral language to a dominant external language, the higher the degree of structural diffusion from the latter to the former. In short, high degrees of bilingualism, ongoing shift, and mutual accommodation all appear to be factors involved in heavy structural diffusion. The mechanisms involved include those associated with both borrowing and substratum influence, each feeding the other.

It is not easy to pinpoint the particular structural and social factors that regulate the outcomes in these situations. Structural constraints differ according to whether the situation is one of stable bilingualism involving mostly borrowing, or one of shift involving substratum influence. With regard to social factors, it appears that the degree of intimacy of contact, for example, through intermarriage, frequent interaction, etc., determines the degree of structural diffusion. As usual, it is a complex interaction of linguistic, social, and attitudinal factors that determines the outcome in each case.

Notes

1 Heath's distinction is very similar to Weinreich's between "outright transfer of morphemes" from one language to another and other kinds of "interference" involving transfer of semantic content or grammatical function on their own (without the phonological forms that express them in the source language).

2 This is not to deny that the "borrowing" of some function items may have some impact on the RL grammar. Brian Joseph (p.c., July 2001) gives the example of the Persian complementizer *ki*, which was adopted by Hindi and Turkish. This resulted in a pattern of complementation quite unlike those that previously existed in the two languages.

3 According to Vinet (1984: 239), some relative clauses with preposition stranding also occur rarely in Montréal French, but the process is not as free as in PEI French.

4 As Brian Joseph (p.c., July 2001) points out, this change is not purely lexical, since it involves a structural pattern as well.

4

Code Switching: Social Contexts

4.1 Introduction

We saw in chapter 3 that bilinguals play an active role in the kinds of structural diffusion that lead to convergence of linguistic systems. In this chapter, we examine the actual performance of bilinguals who exploit the resources of the languages they command in various ways, for social and stylistic purposes. Bilinguals achieve this by alternating between their two languages, or by mixing them in different ways. These kinds of behavior are referred to as code switching.

The phenomenon known as code switching involves several types of bilingual language mixture, including the alternating use of relatively complete utterances from two different languages, alternation between sentential and/or clausal structures from the two languages, and the insertion of (usually lexical) elements from one language into the other. These kinds of language mixture have long been the norm in many communities, and have become increasingly common as a result of various sociohistorical forces that have led to increasing contact among different language groups within the same national and local communities. The sociolinguistic situations that are characterized by code switching are quite varied. First, there are stable long-term situations such as those in Switzerland, Belgium, etc., where bilingualism is the norm across wide sections of the community. Second, there are situations, particularly in Africa, South East Asia, the Caribbean, and South America, where colonization introduced European languages to serve as official vehicles of administration, education, and other public activities, alongside the pre-existing indigenous languages. Third, the increasing flow of immigrants into more industrialized nations in Europe, North America, and elsewhere has led to the establishment of linguistic minority groups who must become bilingual in the host community's language, and in some cases shift entirely to the latter in the course of a few generations. Finally, there are situations in which speakers of non-standard dialects are required to learn the standard variety of their language for purposes of educational and social advancement. The result is increasing bidialectalism, accompanied by code switching between the varieties.

Code switching is therefore a cover-term for quite varied types of bilingual and bidialectal language mixture, resulting from quite different social circumstances and motivations. Lüdi (1987) has proposed that the relevant sociolinguistic situations can be categorized in terms of two interdependent distinctions – exolingual versus endolingual interaction, and unilingual versus bilingual interaction. Exolingual interaction involves speakers of different languages, while endolingual interaction involves speakers with the same language background. Either type may involve bilingualism or unilingualism. The combination of these distinctions yields the following typology of situations:

	Bilingual	*Unilingual*
Exolingual	Interaction among speakers with different languages	Interaction between native and non-native speakers of the same language
Endolingual	Interaction among bilinguals	Interaction among monolinguals

All of these situations involve code switching of one form or another. Yet the tendency in the literature has been to focus mostly on the types of language mixture found in "endolingual bilingual" (i.e., stable bilingual) situations, and the types of code switching behavior that are typical of highly proficient bilinguals in such communities.

4.2 Defining Code Switching

Code switching has been defined as "the alternate use of two or more languages in the same utterance or conversation" (Grosjean 1982: 145). This definition is broad enough to encompass just about any kind of language alternation or mixture. Researchers, however, don't always agree on precisely what kinds of alternation should be included under the designation "code switching." Most scholars would exclude the use of different languages in different situations or activity types, of the sort found in so-called diglossic speech communities. It's questionable, however, whether such situations do in fact involve a strict complementarity of functions between the codes involved, with no language alternation within the same situation or event. Some researchers also exclude cases involving "non-contiguous stretches of talk, for example, one occurring at the beginning, the other at the end of the conversation" (Auer 1995: 116). In general, the criterion of juxtaposition of elements from the two codes is a prerequisite for code switching. For Auer, this also means that style shifting involving gradual transitions from dialect into standard cannot be included, since it works very differently from bilingual code switching (ibid.). Most researchers also exclude those types of mixture, often referred to as "interference phenomena," which occur in the speech behavior of persons acquiring a second language (i.e., in "exolingual bilingual" situations). The relationship between code switching and these interlanguage phenomena will be discussed further in section 4.2.2, below.

In general, then, code switching is taken as referring only to those cases where bilingual speakers alternate between codes within the same speech event, switch codes within a single turn, or mix elements from two codes within the same utterance. Auer (1995: 124) identifies four patterns of code switching. Pattern I involves switches from code A to code B, as in (1), or switches within a single speaker's turn, as in (2).

In (1), from Myers-Scotton (1993a: 134), a bus conductor switches from Swahili to English (in italics) in an exchange with a passenger:

(1) Conductor: Umelipa nauli ya basi?
"Have you paid the bus fare?"
Passenger: (No response)
Conductor: Unaenda wapi?
"Where are you going?"
Passenger: Nafika Jerusalem.
"I'm going to Jerusalem [housing estate]."
Conductor: *You must always say clearly and loudly where you are going to alight, OK?*

In (2), a market-vendor and a customer alternate between Swahili and English (in italics) as they negotiate prices (Myers-Scotton 1993a: 40–1):

(2) Vendor: Habari, mheshimwa. *Have some vegetables.*
"Hello, respected sir." . . .
Customer: Mboga gani? Nipe kabeji hizi. *How much is that?*
"Which vegetables? Give me these cabbages." . . .
Vendor: *Five shillings only.*
Customer: *That's too much.* Sina pesa.
"I don't have [much] money."

These types of switching often mark a shift in topic, role relationship, or activity type. Auer refers to this pattern as "discourse-related" code switching or "conversational" code switching.

Pattern II involves a negotiation of a language of interaction, with participants switching from one code to another until consensus is reached on the medium of exchange. Milroy and Li Wei (1995: 149) offer the following example of this pattern, which Auer (1995: 125) refers to as "preference-related switching." Here a mother switches between English and Cantonese in addressing her son, who finally responds in English:

(3) Mother: Finished homework?
Son: (No response) (2.0 sec.)
Mother: Steven, yiu mo wan sue?
"Steven, do you want to review your lessons?"
Son: (1.5 sec.) I've finished.

Further examples of language negotiation from Heller (1985) will be discussed later.

Pattern III involves switching between languages in a turn such that no single language can be identified as the base language. This pattern is typical of code switching as an "unmarked choice" (see below), used either to express "strategic ambiguity" (Heller 1988), or as a strategy of neutrality (Myers-Scotton 1993a: 147). In these cases, a speaker may switch from sentence to sentence or from clause to clause within the same sentence, thus leaving language choice open. Sentence (4) is an example of inter-sentential switching from Myers-Scotton (1993a: 123). A Luyia man is interviewing a Luyia woman who works as a nurse in Nairobi. She switches from English to Swahili to their shared ethnic language, Lwidakho. English elements are in italics, while those from Lwidakho are underlined.

(4) Interviewer: Unapenda kufanya kazi yako lini? Mchana au usiku?
"When do you like to do your work? Days or nights?"
Nurse: *As I told you, I like my job.* Sina ubaguzi wo wote kuhusu wakati ninapofanya kazi. *I enjoy working either during the day* au usiku yote ni sawa kwangu. Hata *family members* wangu wamezoea mtindo huu. *There is no quarrel at all.* Obubi bubulaho.
"As I told you, I like my job. I have no difficulty at all regarding when I do work. I enjoy working either during the day or at night; all is okay as far as I'm concerned. Even my family members have got used to this plan. There is no quarrel at all. There is no badness."

Example (5), from Sankoff and Poplack (1981: 11), illustrates inter-clause switching in the performance of a Spanish/English bilingual in New York city. Spanish is in italics.

(5) There was a guy, you know, *que* [that] he *se montó* [got up]. He started playing with *congas*, you know, and *se montó y empezó a brincar* [got up and started to jump] and all that shit.

Finally, pattern IV alternation refers to momentary switches which do not really change the language of the interaction. This kind of alternation is referred to as intra-sentential or, more accurately, intra-clause code switching. It produces utterances which have most of their lexicon as well as morpho-syntactic apparatus from one language, referred to as the matrix language (ML), with insertion of single words or phrases from the other language, referred to as the embedded language (EL). This type of mixture produces three kinds of constituents: mixed constituents made up of materials from both languages, EL "islands" or phrases incorporated from the EL, and ML "islands," that is, phrases entirely in the ML. Example (6) illustrates a mixed constituent consisting of an English stem (*decide*) with Swahili affixes in an otherwise Swahili utterance (Myers-Scotton 1993b: 4):

(6) Hata siku hizi ni-me-*decide* kwanza kutumia sabuni ya miti
even days these 1s-PERE-decide first to use soap of stick
"[But] even these days I've decided first to use bar soap"

Example (7) illustrates a mixed English/Swahili constituent (ni-ta-*try*) and English EL islands (*throughout the day*) as well as Swahili ML islands (Myers-Scotton 1993b: 146):

(7) Mimi ni-ta-*try* kuwa nyumbani *throughout the day*
EMPH 1s-FUT-try to be home
"As for me, I try to be at home throughout the day"

There is disagreement among researchers as to whether all types of intra-sentential alternation should be included within code switching proper. Auer, for instance, refers to this type of mixture as "transfer" or "insertion" and distinguishes it from code switching. Other researchers, such as Kachru (1978) and Singh (1985), refer to such a mixture as "code mixing," reserving the term "code switching" for patterns I , II, and III above, in which different codes are used on different occasions, or correspond to different stages in an interaction.

But it is often difficult to draw clear boundaries between the two. Poplack (1990), while accepting the distinction between inter-sentential and intra-sentential code switching, reserves the latter only for cases where entire constituents from the two languages alternate in the same utterance (i.e., cases involving EL islands). Hence Poplack and Meechan (1995: 200) define code switching as "the juxtaposition of sentences or sentence fragments, each of which is internally consistent with the morphological and syntactic (and optionally, phonological) rules of its lexifier language." This definition explicitly excludes single morpheme switches, which are treated as "nonce borrowings." This will be discussed further in section 4.3 below. Poplack also distinguishes a third type of alternation which she calls "tag-switching," that is, the insertion of a tag in language B into an utterance which is otherwise in language A, as in the following examples from Tagalog/English (Bautista 1980: 247) and English/Spanish (Poplack 1980: 596):

(8) The proceedings went smoothly, *ba* [Tagalog tag]?
"The proceedings went smoothly, didn't they?"

(9) I could understand *que* [that] you don't know how to speak Spanish, *verdad*? [right?]

Finally, Myers-Scotton (1993a, 1993b) also distinguishes between inter-sentential and intra-sentential code switching; however, *contra* Poplack, she includes single-morpheme switches within the latter category. Also, in her linguistic analysis of code switching (1993b), she focuses mainly on intra-sentential alternations, and her definition of code switching seems to present this type as prototypical: "Code switching . . . is the selection by bilinguals or multilinguals of forms from an embedded variety (or varieties) in utterances of a matrix variety during the same conversation" (1993a: 3).

These linguistically based definitions of code switching seem to imply a certain level of skilled behavior that only practiced bilinguals can manage. As we shall see, the linguistic frameworks developed for the analysis of code switching generally focus on this kind of skilled performance. The tendency to reify code switching as a unitary and clearly identifiable phenomenon has been questioned by Gardner-Chloros (1995: 70), who prefers to view code switching as a "fuzzy-edged concept." For her, the conventional view of code switching implies that speakers make binary choices, operating in one code or the other at any given time, when in fact code switching overlaps with other kinds of bilingual mixture, and the boundaries between them are difficult to establish. Moreover, it is often impossible to categorize the two codes involved in code switching as discrete and isolatable. This indeterminacy is reflected in the difficulty of distinguishing code switching from "borrowing" on the one hand, and "mixing/interference" on the other.

Exercise 1
Examine the code switching behavior of bilinguals you know, and try to determine which of the four patterns described above they tend to use. How easy is it to distinguish among the patterns?

4.2.1 Code switching versus borrowing

The single-morpheme switching which is typical of intra-clause code switching is very common across bilingual communities. Researchers have attempted to distinguish this from borrowing, but there is no consensus on the boundary between the two. The chief criteria that have been used to distinguish them include:

1 degree of use by monolingual speakers;
2 degree of morphophonemic integration.

According to the first criterion, established loans are commonly used by monolingual speakers, whereas code switches tend to be transitory phenomena. Some researchers argue, however, that frequency counts are inconclusive, and that the distinction between a switch and a borrowing is not transparent to bilinguals. The criterion of morphophonemic integration is also problematic, since both borrowings and word switches may or may not be morphologically and phonologically adapted to the ML or recipient language (Myers-Scotton 1993b: 177–91). Poplack and her associates, however, claim that borrowing involves different mechanisms than code switching, and that the latter involves more than single-morpheme insertions. Sankoff et al. (1986) argue that if an utterance has the syntax and morphology of one language, then any lexical item not native to that language must be a borrowing. This leads them to treat all single-word switches as "nonce borrowings." Poplack and Meechan (1995) support this view with evidence from noun-modification patterns on single French switches in both French–Wolof and French–Fongbe bilingual discourse. The single nouns are fully integrated into the morphosyntax of the recipient languages, and are indistinguishable from other well-established borrowings. They are quite different from multi-word French switches, which show the internal structure of French NPs, and represent true instances of code switching.

Other researchers (Myers-Scotton 1993b; Treffers-Daller 1991; Gardner-Chloros 1995) view single-word switching and borrowing as essentially similar processes which fall along a continuum, based on degree of integration or assimilation. For Myers-Scotton, code switching is in fact a major conduit for borrowing, since single switches can become borrowed forms through increased frequency of use and adoption by monolingual speakers of the ML (1993b: 182). The only clear basis for distinguishing them is frequency of occurrence – an admittedly arbitrary criterion, but one that seems to have some empirical support (ibid.). Other criteria that fail to distinguish the two phenomena include (a) the extent to which native synonyms are displaced by either, and (b) the types of grammatical category that tend to be borrowed as opposed to being switched. As Gardner-Chloros (1995: 73–4) notes, both single switches and borrowings may fill lexical gaps in the recipient language and also offer further options to native equivalents. Moreover, there is no difference in the types of lexical categories that can be switched or borrowed. Both processes display a similar hierarchy of incorporation of items, with nouns most likely to be incorporated, followed by adjectives, then verbs, prepositions, and so on, as discussed in chapter 2.

Exercise 2
Collect data on "single-word switches" from various studies and compare them with cases of lexical borrowing. What similarities and differences can you observe in the processes of integration that apply in each case? (Myers-Scotton 1993b: 177–91 and Poplack and Meechan 1995 discuss the general relationship between borrowing and code switching. Treffers-Daller 1994 and Gardner-Chloros 1991 also compare the two in the same community.)

4.2.2 Code switching versus "interference"

Most researchers also draw a distinction between code switching as practiced by competent bilinguals and the kinds of mixture found in the "interlanguage" of persons acquiring a second language (see Ludi's "exolingual bilingual" category above). Hamers and Blanc (1989: 149) refer to the former as "bilingual code switching" and the latter as "incompetence code switching." They note that the latter type is typical of certain immigrant populations who have acquired a limited functional competence in L2 but have to resort to their L1 to compensate for their lack of knowledge of L2 (ibid.). There are also cases where immigrants who have lost some of their competence in L1 resort to the L2 to fill the gaps.

Poplack (1987: 72) also distinguishes the kinds of mixture associated with fluent bilinguals from "speech errors which involve elements of both languages, and which may be properly considered 'interference.'" It may seem somewhat arbitrary to reserve the term "code switching" only for skilled bilingual behavior, and exclude phenomena associated with processes of shift and second language acquisition. However, there are clear differences, both linguistic and sociolinguistic, between the two kinds of behavior. The linguistic differences recall those between changes due to borrowing and changes due to L1 influence on L2 acquisition. Sociolinguistically too, the language mixture found in interlanguage does not follow the rules associated with bilingual code switching (Gumperz 1982).

This may explain why it is often difficult to describe interlanguage phenomena in the frameworks employed for bilingual code switching. Myers-Scotton skirts the issue, noting that "I do not pretend to detail language shift facilitated by code-switching; my only purpose here is to suggest that the mechanism exists" (1993b: 223). Attempting to treat cases of language shift (second language acquisition – SLA) in terms of gradual replacement of ML morpheme order and system morphemes, etc., by their EL counterparts (ibid.) seems to oversimplify the nature of the learning process, especially in the earlier stages of acquisition. Further discussion of language mixture in situations of SLA and language shift will be reserved for chapter 7.

Advanced learners, however, do produce code-switching phenomena similar to those of (other) competent bilinguals. In some cases, such learners may employ either the L1 or the L2 as the matrix language. For example, Nishimura (1986) describes how fluent Japanese–English bilinguals in Toronto and San Francisco produce code-switched utterances some of which have the syntactic structure of English, as in (10), while others have the structure of Japanese, as in (11). Japanese items are in italics:

(10) The ones we've seen are *bimboo na kodomo*.
poor children

(11) *Kaeri ni wa* border *de* we got stopped, eh?
return on Topic on
"On the way home, we got stopped at the border"

In some cases, Nishimura shows, it is not possible to assign code-switched utterances unambiguously to one language or the other. This will be discussed further below.

The rest of this discussion will focus on code switching as practiced by fluent bilinguals. Both inter- and intra-sentential alternation, including single morpheme switches, are included here under the umbrella of code switching. This type of performance displays properties similar to those of monolingual discourse. As Romaine (1989: 111) notes: "In code-switched discourse, the items in question form part of the same speech act. They are tied together prosodically as well as by semantic and syntactic relations equivalent to those that join passages in a single speech act."

This suggests that the code-switching performance of bilinguals is associated with an underlying competence that can be described by a system of rules and constraints analogous to those that regulate monolingual performance. The linguistic aspects of code switching will be discussed more fully in the following chapter. The rest of this chapter explores the social functions and meanings of this type of language mixture. The discussion here is also relevant to the various kinds of language behavior that are discussed throughout this book, all of which are subject to similar social forces and motivations.

4.3 Social Motivations for Code Switching

The sociocultural factors that influence code switching have been investigated primarily within three major frameworks: the sociology of language, linguistic anthropology, and the social psychology of language choice. Each of them has contributed to our understanding of the social motivations for code switching, and their insights complement one another in providing a comprehensive picture of how macro-level societal norms interact with micro-level factors to constrain the linguistic behavior of bilinguals. The sociology of language provides insight on how macro-level social institutions and group relationships influence patterns of code switching. Anthropology investigates how micro-level interpersonal relationships, participant goals, and types of interaction affect code-switching behavior in specific encounters. Within social psychology, Communication Accommodation Theory sheds light on how attitudes and group consciousness influence individuals to accommodate to one another through code switching or other linguistic compromises, or to diverge and maintain language boundaries.

4.3.1 Code switching and sociolinguistic domains

In two groundbreaking papers, Fishman (1964, 1965) introduced the concept of "sociolinguistic domains" to represent the contexts of interaction into which social life is organized, and which influence the language of interaction. Examples of domains include "family," "work," "religion," "friendship," "education," and others. Such domains are associated with specific language varieties which are seen as appropriate for a particular interaction. Fishman (1972: 441) defines domains as "institutional contexts and their congruent behavioral co-occurrences." Domains are abstract constructs, made up of a constellation of participants' statuses and role relationships, locales or settings, and subject matter (topic). As Breitborde (1983: 18) notes, "A domain is not the actual interaction (the setting), but an abstract set of relationships between status, topic and locale which gives meaning to the events that actually comprise social interaction." The relationship between "domain" and "situations" is analogous to that between a phoneme and its allophones. In other words, a domain is "a cluster of interaction situations, grouped around the same field of experience, and tied together by a shared range of goals and obligations" (Mioni 1987: 170).

Domain analysis has revealed a great deal about the situational factors that influence language alternation in different settings. While this kind of alternation is different from code switching proper, it is often the starting point for the latter, particularly since it is doubtful whether a neat separation of languages is always achieved in all the relevant domains. An often-cited example comes from studies of a New York City Puerto Rican community by Lawrence Greenfield and Fishman (1968) and Fishman and Greenfield (1970). They identified five domains of language behavior for the community: family, friendship, work, religion, and education. Table 4.1 illustrates the interrelationships among domains, their components (status/role relationship, locale and topic), and the corresponding language choices in the community. Note that the choices indicated here are majority ones; in other words, not all subjects agreed that Spanish or English was the preferred choice in the relevant domain.

As Breitborde (1983: 20) notes, the lack of unanimity in responses is significant in its own right, since it points to differences in individual interpretations of what is salient in a particular domain (e.g., topic versus status), as well as differences in the way societal norms constrain individual choice. In addition, in

Table 4.1 Selected domains of language choice among New York City Puerto Ricans

Domain	Role relationhship	Locale	Topic	Language
Family	Parent–child	Home	Family matters	Spanish
Work	Employer–employee	Workplace	Job performance	English
Education	Teacher–student	School	Homework	English

Source: adapted from L. Greenfield and Fishman (1968)

actual interactions, the components do not always correspond so neatly to the configurations shown in table 4.1. For instance, discussion of a work-related topic in the home setting may lead to conflicting language choice, as do other mismatches among the components of a domain. In such cases, the neat compartmentalization of language choice by domain often breaks down, leading to code switching proper. An example from Swiss German will be discussed in the following section.

4.3.1.1 Domains, diglossia, and code switching

The concept of sociolinguistic domains actually goes back to the work of Charles Ferguson (1964), who introduced the notion of "diglossia" (adapted from Marçais's 1930 *diglossie*) to describe situations where two related language varieties are employed in complementary distribution across different situations. In diglossic communities, one of the varieties, designated the H(igh) language, is employed in more official, public domains such as government, education, literature, etc., while the other, designated the L(ow) language, is used in more private and informal domains such as the family, friendship, neighborhood, etc. Ferguson's term was intended to describe a special type of sociolinguistic situation that differed from the usual standard-with-dialects scenario on the one hand, and from strictly bilingual situations on the other. The varieties involved in diglossia, while related, are still quite divergent in structure and lexicon, and only one of them, the L variety, is typically acquired as a first language, while the H variety has to be acquired as a second language, usually at school. A variety of other characteristics of diglossia is summed up in the following definition from Ferguson (1964: 435):

> Diglossia is a relatively stable language situation in which, in addition to the primary dialects of the language (which may include a standard or regional standards), there is a very divergent, highly codified (often grammatically more complex) superposed variety, the vehicle of a large and respected body of written literature, either of an earlier period or in another speech community, which is learned largely by formal education and is used for most written and formal spoken purposes but is not used by any sector of the community for ordinary conversation.

To illustrate his concept, Ferguson cited cases such as the alternation of vernacular and classical Arabic in Middle Eastern countries; Schwyzertüütsch and Standard German in (German-speaking) Switzerland; Dhimotiki and Katharevousa in Greece; and Kreyòl and Standard French in Haiti. Fishman adopted the concept of diglossia, but extended it to include bilingual situations characterized by a similar compartmentalization of languages across public and private domains. As Fasold (1984: 53) suggests, it is useful to distinguish "classic" diglossia in Ferguson's sense from "broad" diglossia in Fishman's sense.

An excellent example of how classic diglossia works is provided by Keller's (1982) account of language use in German-speaking Switzerland, where the diglossia is relatively stable, and everyone is aware of its existence. Keller points out that there are deliberate attempts "to cultivate diglossia by making the distinction between standard and dialect as clear as possible" (1982: 75). This is the policy of the Bund für Schwyzertüütsch, with its headquarters in Zürich (ibid.). The following example from Keller (ibid.: 79) illustrates the structural differences between the varieties (gloss and translation by Charlotte Schaengold):

(12) H: Sie konnten jenes Häuschen dort drüben nicht kaufen
they can(past) that house (dimin.) over there not buy
Es war ihnen zu teuer
it be(past) for-them too expensive
L: Si händ säb Hüüsli deet äne nid chöne chauffe
they have that house(dimin.) over there not can buy
S isch ene z tüür gsy
it is for-them too expensive be(pp)
"They couldn't buy that little house over there. It was too expensive for them"

On the whole, the complementary distribution of the functions of H and L is well maintained, with H functioning as the medium of science and technology in lectures, at conferences, in books and written instructions, as well as in other public domains such as legislation, administration, education, and so on. L, on the other hand, is obligatory for "ordinary conversation," in personal and family relationships, and so on. What is particularly interesting, however, is the fact that the pattern of separation of varieties is neither neat nor consistent in all situations. As Keller (1982: 88) notes, when there is a conflict between function and situation (e.g., if a topic involving science or technology is discussed at home), "the result tends to be a mishmash of both language forms, in other words there is a breakdown of diglossia." One manifestation of this is extensive borrowing of vocabulary from L into H, in cases where "the situation is too private for 'High', yet 'Low' is unsuited for the function. Where such a conflict occurs, the whole thought process and the mental syntax tend to be standard, the lexicon will be half 'High' and half 'Low'" (ibid.). These types of alternation have resulted in significant change in the lexicon of L, with native items continuously being replaced by "High" items, or being adapted phonologically under influence from the latter. Moreover, some structural features, such as the

Standard German future tense and present participle, are slowly being introduced into the L variety. Keller does not discuss whether L also influences H, but notes that "the German standard language has . . . a Swiss variant, the Schweizerhoch Deutsch, which is not just characterized by dialectalisms" (ibid.: 83). This variety differs from Standard German "in pronunciation, stress, orthography, lexis (semantic and lexical) and grammar (morphological and syntactical)" (ibid.: 84). Most differences appear to be due to the separate evolution of the Helvetian standard, but it seems likely that some of its features are due to "interference" from Schwyzertüütsch in the process of second language acquisition.

Keller's account makes it clear that the neat compartmentalization of functions associated with diglossia does not apply even in "classic" cases like this. The Swiss German situation offers some insight into how changing constellations of the components of domains can lead to varying degrees of code switching, resulting in contact-induced changes in both varieties.

Exercise 3

Compare situations of stable diglossia such as that in German Switzerland with unstable situations like that in Greece, where diglossia has broken down and the L language has spread into public and "high" domains. What social, political, and ideological factors favor the maintenance or loss of diglossia? (On Switzerland, see Keller 1982. On Greece, see Frangoudaki 1992 and Kazazis 1993. An extensive bibliography on diglossia can be found in Alan Hudson 1992.)

4.3.2 Micro-level analysis: code switching and conversation

Domain analysis has provided much insight into the general patterns of language choice in bilingual communities. The concept provides a link between the macro-level organization of society, with its "socio-cultural norms and expectations," and the micro-level organization of language use manifested in "individual behavior at the level of face-to-face verbal encounters" (Fishman 1972: 441). On the one hand, it is clear that the social structure constrains language choice in certain ways. On the other, individuals can and do exploit the choices available to them to manipulate situations and redefine the relationships pertinent to a particular interaction. Research in social and linguistic anthropology has greatly enhanced our understanding of these individual choices.

Hymes (1962) presented a comprehensive framework for the investigation of language choice in speech communities. His "ethnography of speaking" distinguishes a range of components that are relevant to the analysis of the speech economy of a community. Some of these, such as "situation" and "participants," have to do with the social organization of the community. Others, such as "ends," "act sequence," "key," and "norms of interpretation," have to do with the transactional nature of interactions, as negotiations aimed at achieving particular goals. In addition, they portray such interactions as ordered exchanges which rely for their success on shared understanding of sociocultural norms and the meanings assigned to specific language choices.

The major impetus for investigation of code switching as socially meaningful linguistic behavior came from Gumperz's research on Norwegian communities in the 1960s, and particularly from the highly influential study by Blom and Gumperz (1972) of the town of Hemnesberget. They found that residents of the town employed two dialects: Ranamål (the vernacular) and Bokmål (the standard variety). The scenario they present is clearly reminiscent of diglossia, with Bokmål as H and Ranamål as L language. The residents of the community fall into three socioeconomic strata. First there are locally born laborers and skilled workers with strong local network ties, including kinship. Then there is an intermediate group of wholesale/retail merchants and plant managers who have relatives within the group of artisans, and who must cultivate ties with customers of various backgrounds. Finally, there is a diversified group of service personnel, including clerks, business owners, school teachers, doctors, and the like, who are often migrants, or have stronger ties outside the town. Interestingly, Blom and Gumperz found that language choice was not directly correlated with socioeconomic divisions, but rather depended on network ties that often cut across those divisions.

Those linked primarily to local networks and values include manual workers and artisans, as well as lower-range white-collar workers. Merchants and plant managers have both local and non-local network ties, and hence divided loyalties to local versus external values. Finally, the retail owners, school teachers, doctors, and other professionals identify more with the non-local middle-class value system of the pan-Norwegian elite. It is primarily the interactions between the members of the first two networks that involve code switching. This takes two forms. First, different situations are associated with different varieties – a pattern referred to as "situational" code switching. For instance, official business between a local resident and an employee in a government office is conducted in Bokmål, but if the two engage in an informal chat, they switch to Ranamål. In general, Bokmål is used in church services, school matters, interaction with strangers, and other formal contexts. Ranamål is used among locals at home, in the workplace, and in public meeting places. This situational switching involves changes in participants' rights and obligations, that is, their status and role relationships.

But Blom and Gumperz observed that speakers often switched codes on the same occasion, particularly when there were changes of topic. For instance, locals would greet government clerks and discuss family matters in vernacular, but switch to standard for the business transaction. But even within the latter, they used the vernacular for informal comments and asides. (Compare the Swiss German situation discussed earlier.) Blom and Gumperz termed this "metaphorical" switching. The distinction between "situational" and "metaphorical" switching triggered a great deal of research on the social motivations for code switching. The distinction itself has been challenged on the grounds that it isn't based on clear criteria. As Pride (1979) pointed out, "metaphorical" switches involve the same redefinitions of status and role relationships as "situational" switches, hence the two are not distinguishable. But Breitborde (1983: 14) argues that there is "both empirical and intuitive validity in distinguishing the two." He suggests that what is involved is the difference between "two statuses operating simultaneously in one situation, and two statuses each operating in its own situation." However, Breitborde does not distinguish status from role relationship, which would add more weight to his position.

The Blom and Gumperz study was important for several reasons. It demonstrated that choice of a code is not just a mechanical product of a static domain, but that domains themselves can change as role relationships do, and interlocutors assume different stances toward the subject matter of the transaction. The study was also innovative in its use of participant-observation techniques and social network analysis to investigate the code alternation in the community. Blom and Gumperz showed that, in order to understand the social meaning of code switching, we must ask "who the speakers are, and how the codes are used. The former requires that we comprehend the social identities and social relations obtaining among speakers; the latter, that we figure out how these social identities (which are linked to linguistic varieties) are brought to bear in social interaction" (Breitborde 1983: 7).

4.3.2.1 Taxonomies of factors affecting code switching

Micro-level approaches to code switching have also attempted to construct taxonomies of the functions of code switches, to determine the various factors that trigger such switches within a conversation. Gumperz (1977) proposed three general motives for code switching:

- Choice of H to add authoritativeness to an utterance.
- Choice of H to highlight the point of a narrative in L.
- Choice of H to add seriousness to commands directed at a child.

Since then, fuller taxonomies have been developed. Auer (1995: 120) provides the following list of "conversational loci in which switching is particularly frequent":

- Reported speech.
- Change of participant constellation, particularly addressee selection.
- Parentheses or side-comments.
- Reiteration, that is, quasi-translations into the other language, for purposes of emphasis, clarification, attracting attention, etc.
- Change of activity type, also called "mode shift" or "role shift."
- Topic shift.
- Puns, language play, shift of "key."
- Topicalization, topic/comment structure.

But such taxonomies are of limited use, since, in general, they fail to provide clear explanations for specific switches within the context of an interaction. In other words, as Auer explains, such listing does not bring us closer to a theory of code alternation or tell us why code alternation may have a conversational meaning or function. What is at stake here is a theoretical framework which can explain (and ultimately predict) patterns of code switching within a conversation.

4.3.3 Toward a theory of the social meaning of conversational code switching

There have been two approaches to this problem – one focusing on the sequencing of utterances and the sequential environment of code switches (Gumperz 1982; Auer 1995), the other focusing on code choices as "indexing rights-and-obligations sets (RO sets) between participants in a given interaction type" (Myers-Scotton 1993a: 84).

The former approach builds on Gumperz's (1982) idea of code switching as a "contextualization cue" similar to monolingual choices of prosodic, paralinguistic, syntactic, and lexical features which signal a particular intent on the part of the speaker. In this approach, the meaning of a code switch depends both on its sequential position in the discourse context itself, and on the broader situational and sociocultural context which make up the background knowledge of the participants. The latter embraces the community norms for the type of interaction, and the values assigned to different language choices. The approach is therefore similar to those types of conversational analysis which attempt to explain how intended meanings are conveyed through implicatures signaled by the speaker, and inferences drawn by the listener. Hence this approach attempts to link the micro-level of conversational interaction to the macro-level societal setting in which it occurs, and without which it cannot be interpreted.

Myers-Scotton (1993a) takes a somewhat different approach to the social motivations for code switching. Her view is that speakers do not exercise linguistic choices solely because of their social identities or in response to situational factors, but rather use such choices to convey "intentional meaning of a socio-pragmatic nature" (1993a: 57). This approach stresses the role of the speaker as creative actor who uses language choice to negotiate changes in the nature of the situation and the social relationships among participants. Myers-Scotton's "markedness" model is thus a model of speakers' sociopsychological motivations for code switching (1993a: 75). It draws on concepts from a variety of disciplines, including sociology of language (domains), social anthropology (transactions, negotiations), linguistic anthropology (communicative competence), and pragmatics (implicatures and intentional meaning). Basically, the model presents code choices as "indexing" (pointing to) rights-and-obligations sets (RO sets) between the participants in a particular interaction. An RO set "is an abstraction which is based on situational factors, and represents the attitudes and expectations of participants toward each other" (1993a: 85). The model interprets code choices as negotiations of RO sets.

The idea of "markedness" relates to the community norms which apply to interaction types and which individuals may either obey or violate to achieve conversational goals. "Unmarked" choices of code are those which conform to community norms and participants' expectations. Examples would include instances of so-called "situational" switching where different RO sets are associated with different code choices. There are also instances of switching within the same conversation which signals simultaneous adherence to two positively valued social identities (e.g., the types of switching practiced among educated bilinguals in African cities like Nairobi and Dakar). The latter type of code switching is typically a strategy of neutrality that picks the middle ground between two identities and their related RO sets. "Marked" code switching, on the other hand, represents a departure from the normal, expected choice, and therefore has "shock value," signaling some ulterior intent on the speaker's part. According to Myers-Scotton, the general effect of marked code switching is "to negotiate a change in the expected social distance holding between participants, either increasing or decreasing it" (1993a: 132). Marked code switches may be used to convey anger or authority, to exclude outsiders from in-group interaction, to "flag" or emphasize messages via repitition, and so on. They may also be used to achieve more familiarity and solidarity with an addressee in a situation which normally calls for a different code choice. Though Myers-Scotton focuses on individual choices and motivations, her model requires a thorough understanding of macro-level societal norms and evaluations to interpret the transactional meaning of code switches. As she notes, such interpretation depends on "the framework of markedness which is provided by societal norms" (1993a: 109). Hence both macro- and micro-level factors are included in her model.

Most of the empirical frameworks proposed for the study of code switching attempt this kind of integration. None would claim to have achieved predictive power, though several inductive generalizations have emerged about why speakers switch on specific occasions in certain sociocultural contexts.

4.3.4 Code switching and Communication Accommodation Theory

Another important contribution to our understanding of the social meaning of code switching comes from Communication Accommodation Theory (CAT), developed by Howard Giles and his associates. A major objective of CAT is to explain the cognitive and affective factors that influence individuals to change their speech (and other forms of communication) in ways that either converge with or diverge from that of their interlocutors. Convergence (convergent accommodation) can be described as a strategy by which interlocutors accommodate to each other's speech in a variety of ways – by adjusting pronunciation and other linguistic features, or even paralinguistic features such as speech rate, pauses, and length of utterances. Divergence (divergent accommodation) refers to the ways in which speakers emphasize linguistic differences between themselves and others. The central idea behind CAT is that speakers may be motivated to adjust their speaking styles in order to evoke the listener's social approval, to increase communicative efficiency, and to maintain a positive social identity.

CAT is based on social psychological processes such as similarity attraction, social exchange, causal attribution, and inter-group distinctiveness. Speech convergence is explained primarily in terms of the first three processes, while divergence is explained in relation to inter-group processes. For instance, in convergent accommodation, speakers minimize the linguistic differences between themselves and their interlocutor with a view to increasing social attraction. The notion of social exchange refers to the speaker's assessment of the costs and rewards of accommodating. The process of causal attribution has to do with the listener's interpretation of the speaker's intention in adapting his or her style. Such accommodation is valued more positively if it is attributed to the speaker's desire to reduce social distance.

Finally, the notion of inter-group distinctiveness comes into play when speakers employ distinctive linguistic markers of their own group to emphasize their own group membership and dissociate themselves from their interlocutor. Divergent accommodation is therefore a strategy for maintaining social and psychological distance. Analysis of divergence has benefited from Tajfel and Turner's (1979) social identity theory of inter-group relations and social change. According to this, the more individuals define encounters in inter-group terms and wish to preserve a positive in-group identity, the more likely they are to diverge linguistically. The extent of the divergence depends on factors such as the individuals' perception of the social forces operating in favor of their own group, and their group's status vis-à-vis other groups (Giles et al. 1987: 29). These factors are closely linked to the concept of ethnolinguistic vitality – a construct introduced by Giles, Bourhis and Taylor (1977). The concept refers to the degree of autonomy and distinctiveness a group enjoys by virtue of factors such as demography (size, distribution, natural increase, etc.), status (economic and political power, prestige, etc.), and institutional support (degree of support in societal institutions such as the mass media, education, etc.). The assumption is that the higher the degree of ethnolinguistic vitality, the more likely it is that the group will preserve its distinctiveness and its own language. Individuals' perceptions of the ethnolinguistic vitality of their group influence the way they behave in interethnic encounters. Hence the concept offers ways of linking micro-level individual behavior to the macro-level societal structures which define interethnic group relations. This and other additions to the theory have helped CAT evolve from a strictly sociopsychological model of speech accommodation to an interdisciplinary framework for describing and explaining language choices in interethnic interpersonal interactions. The basic propositions of CAT were first summarized by Street and Giles (1982: 213–14) as follows:

(1) Speakers will attempt to converge linguistically towards the speech patterns believed to be characteristic of their interlocutors when (a) they desire their social approval and the perceived costs of so acting are lower than the rewards anticipated; and/or (b) they desire a high level of communicational efficiency and (c) social norms and/or linguistic competence are not perceived to dictate alternative speech strategies.
(2) The degree of linguistic divergence will be a function of (a) the extent of the speakers' repertoires, and (b) factors (individual differences and situation) that may increase the need for social approval and/or communicational efficiency.
(3) Speech convergence will be positively evaluated by recipients when the resultant behavior is (a) perceived as such psychologically, (b) perceived to be at an optimal sociolinguistic distance from them, and (c) attributed internally with positive intent.
(4) People will attempt to maintain their speech patterns or even diverge linguistically from those believed characteristic of their recipients when they (a) define the encounter in inter-group terms and desire a positive ingroup

identity, or (b) wish to dissociate personally from another in an interindividual encounter, or (c) wish to bring another's speech behaviors to a personally acceptable level.

(5) The magnitude of such divergence will be a function of (a) the extent of speakers' repertoires, and (b) individual differences and contextual factors increasing the salience of the cognitive or affective functions in proposition 4.

(6) Speech maintenance and divergence will be negatively evaluated by recipients when the acts are perceived as psychologically diverging, but favorably reacted to by observers of the encounter who define the interaction in intergroup terms and who share a common, positively valued group membership with the speaker.

These propositions have been revised and reformulated in more detail by Giles et al. (1987), to take account of the findings of recent research.

4.3.4.1 Code switching as accommodation

Much of the earlier work in the CAT framework consisted of experimental laboratory studies, but there has been increasing attention to observation of language behavior in natural settings (for an overview, see Giles et al. 1991). Some of the latter studies are highly relevant to understanding the social motivations for code switching. For instance, Coupland (1984) analyzed how a travel agent converged phonologically to clients of different educational and socio-economic backgrounds. Van den Berg (1985) studied code switching in Taiwan by examining over 8000 interactions in markets, shops, banks, and department stores. In most cases, it was found that interlocutors accommodated mutually to each other's code choice, which varied according to the setting. For instance, customers in banks would converge upwardly to the clerks, who converged downwardly to them. In the marketplace, however, customers converged downwardly to salespersons, who in turn converged upwardly to them. These patterns of convergence seem typical of interactions like these, where the customer's approval is sought. Other kinds of interaction are characterized by different patterns of accommodation.

Studies like these support the proposition that the greater a speaker's need to achieve social approval, social integration, or some instrumental goal, the greater the degree of convergence will be. Research of this kind can therefore shed light on patterns of code switching as a form of accommodative behavior in situations of actual or potential language shift, as well as in situations of stable bilingualism where code switching is the "unmarked" choice. As Giles et al. (1991: 20) point out, "Much of the literature on long and mid-term language and dialect acculturation can also be interpreted in convergence terms, whereby immigrants [and other linguistic minorities] seek the economic advantage and social rewards (though there are clearly also costs) that linguistic assimilation sometimes brings."

Language divergence has also been investigated from a CAT perspective in controlled experiments and in natural settings. An example of the former is Bourhis et al.'s (1979) study of how different groups of trilingual Flemish students (Flemish–French–English) reacted when recorded in "neutral" as distinct from "ethnically threatening" encounters with a French (Walloon) out-group speaker. Neutral encounters between Flemish and French speakers are often conducted in English. But when the out-group speaker posed ethnically threatening questions in English to the listeners, they initially responded in English, but half of them later switched to their in-group language, Flemish. In a follow-up study, when the Walloon speaker posed his threatening question in French, almost all listeners switched to Flemish. Studies like this demonstrate how, in such inter-group encounters, speech maintenance or divergence are (often deliberate) acts of maintaining group identity (Bourhis 1979).

Speech communities in which different ethnolinguistic groups are in conflict or wish to preserve their own distinctiveness are likely to be characterized by language divergence. This typically results in non-reciprocal patterns of code switching which disfavor the kinds of language mixture that accommodation produces in other situations. A well-documented example of this is the situation in Quebec, Canada, as described by Heller (1985, 1995). Here, interethnic interactions typically involve a process of language negotiation in which individuals attempt to choose between English and French as the language of conversation. The patterns of code switching that accompany such exchanges shed light on "how language use is bound up in the creation, maintenance or change in relations in power" (Heller 1995: 164). To understand this, one must first comprehend how power relationships between Anglophones and Francophones in Quebec have changed over the years. Until the 1960s, Anglophones were dominant in the political and economic spheres of activity, and this dominance was reflected in the imposition of English as the language of public and interethnic private communication (ibid.: 167). After World War II, however, Francophones became more and more upwardly mobile, penetrating the arenas of politics, higher education, and business enterprises. As a result, French became increasingly favored as the medium of interaction in these settings. A key factor in this development was the passing of Bill 101 by the government of Quebec in 1977. This bill declared French to be the official language of the province and required that it be used in various public domains, including government, education, and occupational spheres such as pharmacy, nursing, engineering, etc. This law in effect gave French speakers access to all areas of social and economic activity in the province, and made French the language of the work sphere. As a result, French and English came to compete directly in various domains, especially in public service encounters and in the workplace (Heller 1985: 79).

This redefinition of the power relationships between the groups and their language led inevitably to a redefinition of the norms of language use and evaluation that had characterized the older social order. Under the new dispensation, choice of one or the other language can signal a variety of meanings and intentions (presentations of self) on the speaker's part. Exclusive use of French may signal commitment to French nationalist identity, while exclusive use of English may indicate resistance to that nationalism (ibid.). Alternatively, such exclusive choices may simply be due to monolingualism. Hence interethnic interactions can proceed only when interlocutors have determined each other's ethnic affiliation, language ability and language preference, and particularly the values associated with different language choices.

Speakers react to such choices in different ways. In some cases, they may opt for deliberate divergence, emphasizing group distinctiveness in the encounter. Heller (1985: 78–9) presents the following example of a conversation at a government bureau between an Anglophone man who has come to take a French proficiency test, and a bilingual receptionist:

(13) Man: Could you tell me where the French test is?
Receptionist (in French): Pardon?
Man: Could you tell me where the French test is?
Receptionist: En français? (In French?)
Man: I have the right to be addressed in English by the government of Quebec.
Receptionist (to third person): Qu'est-ce qu'il dit? (What's he saying?)

In other cases, speakers continually switch languages until some consensus on one or the other is reached, as in the following example from Heller (1985: 81) – a telephone conversation between a patient and a clerk at a hospital:

(14) Clerk: Central Booking, may I help you?
Patient: Oui, allô?
Clerk: Bureau de rendez-vous, est-ce que je peux vous aider? ("Appointments desk? Can I help you?")
Patient: (French) (The patient begins to try to make an appointment)
Clerk: (French)

Patient: (English)
Clerk: (English)
Patient: (French)
Clerk: (French)
Patient: Êtes-vous français ou anglaise? ("Are you French or English?")
Clerk: N'importe j'suis ni l'une ni l'autre. ("It doesn't matter, I'm neither one nor the other.")
Patient: Mais . . . ("But . . .")
Clerk: Ç ne fait rien. ("It doesn't matter")
Patient: (French)
(The conversation continues in French.)

Code switching in such cases becomes a "strategy of neutrality" by which speakers avoid committing themselves to a distinct ethnic identity, choosing a middle path instead (Myers-Scotton 1993a: 147). The situation in Quebec, then, represents one way in which code alternation is linked to social processes and interactions between groups, and becomes a means of expressing relationships of power or solidarity. In other situations, the forces that promote divergence may explain why certain minority groups resist acquiring a host language with complete native proficiency (Giles et al. 1991: 31), settling instead for an ethnolect that reflects their separate status. This may also partly explain the emergence and maintenance of local or "indigenized" varieties of European languages in ex-colonial settings (see, e.g., the "New Englishes" of Africa, South East Asia, the Caribbean, etc.) It is clear that CAT offers a rich theoretical framework within which to investigate not just code switching, but other types of convergent or divergent linguistic behaviors. With respect to code switching in particular, it offers a way of explaining how and why code selection "can be the vehicle of quite opposite tendencies, from accommodation to divergence, and from language maintenance to language shift" (Gardner-Chloros 1995: 80).

4.4 Summary

This chapter examined various types of bilingual language mixture to which the label "code switching" has been applied. First we considered how best to define this term. Code switching manifests itself in various ways, from alternation between utterances in different languages to various kinds of intra-sentential and intra-clause mixture.

There is a tendency to restrict the definition of code switching only to those kinds of language mixture practiced by skilled bilinguals. Hence those kinds of mixing that characterize the interlanguage of learners acquiring a second language tend to be treated as distinct phenomena. In addition, not all researchers regard the type of intra-sentential mixture that involves momentary switches of content morphemes as "true" code switching. Some see it as a kind of lexical borrowing. It is clear that code switching is a continuum of language behaviors, and there are no sharp boundaries between it and other kinds of language mixture.

The other central focus of the chapter was on the social meanings and motivations of code switching. This kind of language performance is a reflection of the way speakers perceive their social identities and relationships to one another, in the broader context of their community's social structure. Choices of code are typically associated with different situations or sociolinguistic domains. A perhaps extreme example of this is communities characterized by diglossia, a situation in which different code choices are employed in complementary distribution in separate domains. Code switching can often be an act of identity (Le Page and Tabouret-Keller 1985) by which speakers locate themselves in social space and in relation to their interlocutors. In other cases, it may be a communicative strategy by which they attempt to achieve transactional goals. In these respects, it is similar to other kinds of stylistic variation (e.g., in monolingual communities) which are conditioned by social norms of interaction.

Choices of code are also regulated by factors such as language attitudes that reflect individuals' and groups' perception of one another. Such attitudes can lead them to accommodate to one another via code switching or other kinds of convergence, or to diverge by emphasizing linguistic differences and avoiding code switching or other accommodative behavior. Degrees and types of code switching are also constrained by other social factors, such as the extent of contact between (members of) the groups, and the degrees of bilingual competence that individuals display.

However, in the final analysis, it is the interplay between social and structural factors that determines the actual types of code switching practiced by individuals and groups. As Myers-Scotton (1993c: 476) points out, structural factors determine permissible forms of code switching, while social factors regulate the choices among the various types permitted. The role that structural factors play is the subject of the following chapter.

5

Code Switching: Linguistic Aspects

5.1 Introduction

There have been many attempts to describe the linguistic structure of code-switched utterances and identify the linguistic principles and constraints that govern their production. Studies of this type focus primarily on intra-sentential switching, rather than inter-sentential alternations, since the latter simply involve utterances that follow the grammar of one or the other language. Intra-sentential code switching, on the other hand, produces various kinds of hybrid structures that require explanation. The goal of the models proposed for this kind of code switching is to predict which utterances containing code switches are well formed or not, and to explain why certain kinds of mixture are either permitted or blocked. In short, the goal is to determine the nature of the grammar underlying bilingual mixture. As Poplack and Meechan (1995: 199) put it, "Do speakers operate with a single base grammar which is on occasion overlaid with lexical items from another language, or are different grammars activated at different times? If the latter is the case, what structural principles govern the juxtaposition?"

5.2 Structural Constraints on Code Switching

As we have seen, researchers who focus their attention specifically on the structural aspects of code switching have defined the phenomenon in different ways, depending on their own theoretical perspective. These differences in approach have implications for how the linguistic constraints on code switching are handled by different scholars.

5.2.1 Equivalence-based constraints

Poplack and her associates draw a distinction between single-word switches and those involving multi-word fragments, and claim that the distinction is crucial to the task of constructing a theory of constraints on code switching (Poplack and Meechan 1995: 224). They treat single-word switches as borrowings that are subject to different constraints from those that apply to multi-word switches. For them, the chief difference lies in the fact that "borrowing involves the grammatical structure of one language only, with the other playing a solely etymological role" (ibid.: 208). Borrowed items are structurally integrated into the morphosyntactic frame of the recipient language. Code switching, on the other hand, involves two grammars interacting with each other. The structural difference between the two phenomena is illustrated in the following examples of Wolof–French code switching from Poplack and Meechan (ibid.: 217), where the speaker first switches (1) and then borrows (2) the French noun *égalité*:

(1) sunu *idées* yu ñu am rek, xam nga ay *égalité, fraternité*, *égalité*
POSS ideas that we have ADV, know you IND
entre hommes et femmes
between men and women
"Our ideas that we have, you know, equality, fraternity, equality between men and women"

(2) ma ñəw fii, degg *affaire* u *égalité* ay *hommes* ak *femmes*
I come LOC understand thing of equality IND men and women
yooyu
DEM
"When I came here, I heard about the equality thing between men and women"

Multi-word switches are the main focus of Poplack and her associates' theory of constraints on code switching. The approach they use will be compared with that of Myers-Scotton below.

Sankoff and Poplack (1981) suggest that code switching is produced by a (context-free phrase structure) grammar which is subject to two constraints:

1 The free morpheme constraint, which predicts that a switch will not occur between a lexical stem and a bound morpheme. As Poplack (1980: 585) puts it, "Codes may be switched after any constituent provided that constituent

is not a bound morpheme." The only exceptions are when a stem has been phonologically integrated into the language of the morpheme. Thus, *flipeando* "flipping" is possible in Spanish–English code switching, but not *runeando* "running."

2 The equivalence constraint, which predicts that switches can occur only at points where the surface structures of the two languages coincide. As Pfaff (1979: 314) puts it, "Surface structures common to both languages are favored for switches."

The equivalence constraint is illustrated below (adapted from Sankoff and Poplack 1981: 6). The lines indicate permissible switch points, and the arrows indicate the surface relationships of constituents in the two languages. Switches may occur at, but not between, the lines:

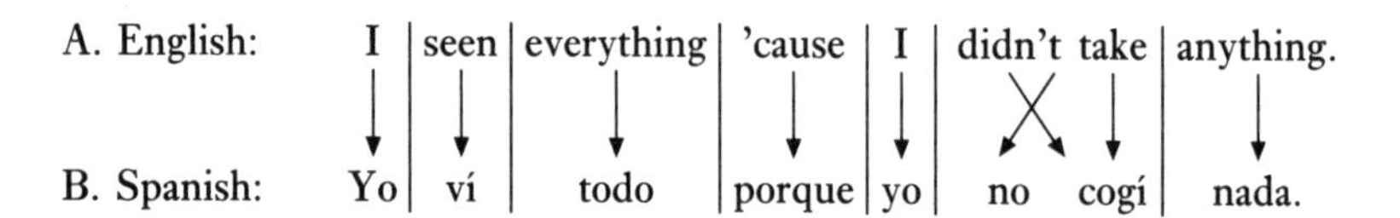

The position Poplack and her associates adopt is essentially that there is no code switching involving single morphemes, since the latter are not distinct from borrowings, and behave to all intents and purposes just like other lexical items in the recipient language. Though they acknowledge that, in theory, single-morpheme switches are possible, they discuss no examples of these. Hence the primary focus of their model of code switching is on equivalence-based switching involving multi-word fragments.

Sankoff and Poplack (1981) argue that an independent code-switching grammar, incorporating rules from the two monolingual grammars but distinct from either, produces code-switching utterances. Ability to code switch results from knowledge of the rules of both grammars, their similarities and differences (ibid.: 11). Evidence for this is that switching involves no hesitations, pauses, corrections, or other interruptions or disruptions in the rhythm of speech. This position opposes the idea that one or the other of the monolingual grammars involved in code switching acts as the "base" or "matrix" language of code-switching utterances. They argue that "no algorithm to determine 'base language' so far proposed applies consistently and convincingly to performance data containing multiply switched sentences" (ibid.: 12). This can be seen in the following examples from Spanish–English code switching (the first already cited as example (5) in chapter 4), where constituents change several times from one language to the other (Spanish items are in italics):

(3) a. There was a guy, you know, *que* [that] he *se montó* [got up]. He started playing with *congas*, you know, and *se montó y empezó a brincar* [got up and started to jump]. (Sankoff and Poplack 1981: 11)

b. Because my sister, her husband, *él es de México y asi los criaron a ellos*, you know.
"Because my sister, her husband, he's from Mexico, and they raise them like that, you know." (Pfaff 1979: 309)

Muysken (1997c: 362) refers to this type of code switching as "congruent lexicalization," a situation "where the two languages share a grammatical structure which can be filled lexically with elements from either language." Examples like these suggest that the rules used to construct code-switching utterances may be drawn at times from one language and at times from the other. Sankoff and Poplack's code-switching grammar, then, contains the combined lexicon as well as grammatical categories of the two monolingual grammars. Their model appears essentially the same as that of Woolford (1983: 523), who also investigated Spanish–English code switching. Figure 5.1 illustrates how the model generates a code-switching sentence.

For Poplack and her associates, the output of such a grammar is controlled primarily by the equivalence constraint, which ensures that switching occurs only between sentence elements that are normally ordered in the same way by the monolingual grammars. Thus, possible switch sites for Spanish–English code switching include (among others) the following boundaries:

- between subject NP and VP;
- between copula and predicate adjective;
- between verb and object NP;
- between verb and complement clause;
- between auxiliary and verb;
- between preposition and NP;
- between subordinating conjunctions and following clauses;
- between a noun and a following relative clause.

On the other hand, switching is blocked where there is a mismatch in constituency between the two languages. A simple example involves the difference in constituency between NPs in Spanish and English. The Spanish rule NP → Det N Adj has the English counterpart NP → Det Adj N. Since the ordering of nouns and adjectives differs, the equivalence constraint predicts that no switch is possible at the boundary between them. This rules out cases like *the casa white* or *the blanca house*, since these combinations are ungrammatical in one or

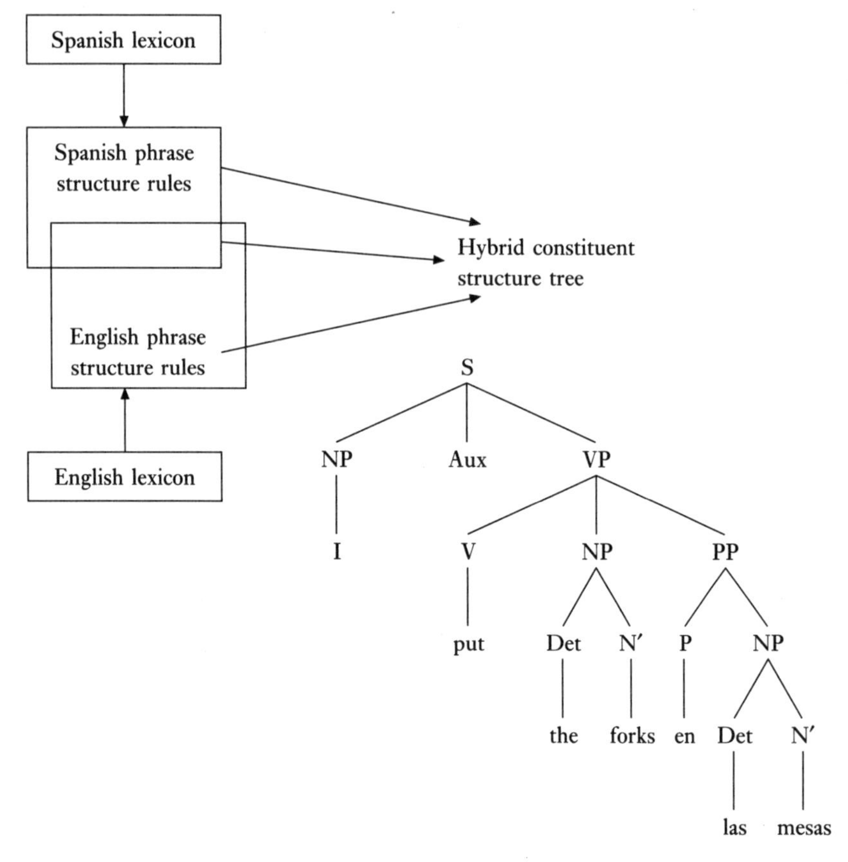

Figure 5.1 Model of a code-switching grammar
Source: adapted from Woolford (1983: 523–5)

the other language. Other prohibited switch sites in Spanish–English code switching include the following:

- Constructions involving NEG placement, which directly precedes the main verb in Spanish, but follows an auxiliary or modal in English.
- Constructions involving reflexive and object pronoun placement, which precede the verb in Spanish, and follow it in English. (Hence **She wants lo [it]*; **Lo she wants.*)

Various researchers have pointed out many exceptions to the claims of the equivalence constraint. Thus, Bentahila and Davies (1983) show that this constraint would rule out switches that occur quite commonly in Morrocan

Arabic–French code switching. For example, we would expect that switches within the NP would be possible only where the adjective follows the noun, since this is the only ordering shared by the two languages. Yet switches involving pre-nominal adjectives are found, as in the following example (Arabic in italics):

(4) j'ai vu un ancien *tilmid djali*
"I saw an old student of mine" (Bentahila and Davies 1983: 319)

Similar examples are provided by Myers-Scotton for Swahili–English code switching. Example (5) illustrates a noun-plus-adjective ordering following Swahili rules, though both noun and adjective are English (in italics):

(5) ni -ka -i- *taste* ni-ka-ona i-na *taste lousy* sana
1s-consec-obj.cl.9 1s-consec-perceive it-with taste lousy very
"And I thought it had [was with] a very lousy taste" (Scotton 1988: 74)

Sankoff and Poplack (1981) in fact acknowledged that even in the case of Spanish–English code switching, the switch site between adjective and noun represents the majority of the few attested violations of the equivalence constraint in their data.

Romaine (1989: 124) provides other counter-examples to the equivalence constraint from Panjabi–English code switching. For instance, even though Panjabi has left-branching structure and postpositions, while English has right-branching structure and prepositions, switches can occur within the PP, as in the following example (English in italics):

(6) *Parents* te *depend* hona ɛ̃
parents post depend be Aux
"It depends on the parents"

Similarly, Pandit (1990: 45) provides examples like the following from English–Hindi code switching, where an entire Hindi postpositional phrase is switched for an English prepositional phrase:

(7) John gave a book *ek larakii ko*
a girl to
"John gave a book to a girl"

Other studies which provide counter-examples to the equivalence constraint include Berk-Seligson (1986) (Spanish–Hebrew), Bokamba (1988) (Lingala–French), Forson (1979) (Akan–English), and Nartey (1982) (Adangme–

English). The wealth of counter-examples led Poplack and Sankoff (1988) to acknowledge that equivalence-based code switching (as exemplified by Spanish–English code switching in New York city) may be an extreme case. At any rate, the equivalence constraint fails to account for the common occurrence of switching under conditions of structural mismatch.

It follows that equivalence-based models also have little to say about the strategies bilinguals resort to so as to facilitate switching between typologically different languages. As Romaine (1989: 117) has pointed out, mismatches in constituent order or placement can often lead to omission or repositioning of elements. Thus, in Dutch–English code switching, subject pronouns can be omitted when they occur at points where the two languages require different word order. M. G. Clyne (1987: 752) gives the example in (8), which can be compared with the Dutch equivalent in (9):

(8) Dan make the beds and then I do the washing up.

(9) Dan maak ik de bedden (op) and dan doe ik de afwas.

The mismatch between Dutch and English placement of the pronoun is resolved here simply by omitting it in the first clause of (8). Another strategy Clyne records is to reposition a Dutch pronoun so that it conforms to the English placement rule, thus violating Dutch word order, as in (10):

(10) en dan je *realize* dat *this*, dat farmleven . . .
"And then you realize that this, that farm-life . . ."
Compare Standard Dutch: en dan besefje dat . . .

Another weakness of approaches based on surface equivalence is that they pay less attention to categorial equivalence than to equivalence in syntagmatic relations across categories. They seem to assume that the two languages involved in code switching share the same categories, when in fact categories in different languages often fail to match each other closely. Muysken (1995: 193) points to several examples of such categorial mismatch – for instance, between clitic and non-clitic pronouns, different types of determiners and demonstratives, different types of auxiliaries, and so on. These types of mismatch often result in omissions of constituents and other kinds of restructuring in code-switching discourse. For example, Berk-Seligson (1986) shows that switches from a Spanish base to Hebrew often result in omissions of articles, which Hebrew lacks. There are also omissions of prepositions and prepositional phrases, no doubt motivated by the fact that Spanish prepositions are free forms while those in Hebrew are often bound.

Amuda (1986: 411) provides an interesting example of restructuring in Yoruba–English bilingual discourse, which is due to a mismatch in copula structure between the two languages. In code-switched discourse, Yoruba copula *wa* often occurs before an English predicate adjective, as in the following example:

(11) ò wa very nice "It's very nice"

Yet Yoruba never uses *wa* in this kind of construction; predicate adjective structures lack a copula, as in the following example:

(12) ò dara pupo "It's very nice"

Of course, these kinds of innovation and restructuring in bilingual discourse pose problems for all models of code switching, not just those based on equivalence.

Among the strengths of the equivalence-based model is its recognition of congruence (typological fit) as a key factor in regulating code-switching patterns. The model has achieved some success in identifying the structural conditions under which code switching is more likely to occur, and in identifying various types of structural mismatch which inhibit code switching. For instance, its prediction that switches are rare between clitic and non-clitic pronouns, or in cases of mismatch in negative placement, etc., have generally been borne out. Unfortunately, there are still too many exceptions that the model fails to account for.

Other earlier models of code switching explain these exceptions by appealing to structural relations rather than just linear sequence. For instance, Woolford (1983) suggests that switching can occur as long as there is a match in the subcategorization frames of the relevant heads in the two languages. She explains the unacceptability of switches between object pronouns and verbs in Spanish–English code switching by noting that Spanish verbs subcategorize for a preceding object clitic, while English verbs subcategorize for a following free pronominal object. A similar view of constraints on switching is found in Azuma (1991b: 7), who says that "the subcategorization of the main verb is always preserved," and in Bentahila and Davies (1983: 329), who suggest that "switching is constrained by the requirement that there be no violation of the subcategorization rules of either language." These approaches go some way toward explaining why switches ruled out by the equivalence constraint are in fact possible. By focusing on grammatical relations rather than linear order, they provide a new perspective on how constraints on code switching operate in different language pairs.

Exercise 1

Consider the following examples of code switching from various language pairs and determine whether they comply with the equivalence constraint. Do the same for other examples of code switching that you find:

Arabic–French (Bentahila and Davies 1983)

a. il croyait *biʔana* je faisais ça exprès (p. 310)
"He thought *that* I was doing that on purpose"

b. tatbqa tat*gratter* (p. 315)
You keep DUR-scratch.
"You keep scratching"

Spanish–English (Poplack 1980)

c. But I wanted to fight her *con los puños*, you know (p. 596)
"But I wanted to fight her with my fists, you know"

d. I got a lotta *blanquito* friends (p. 600)
"I have a lot of white friends"

5.2.2 Government-based approaches to code switching

Another approach to constraints on intra-clausal code switching appeals to the notion of government as formulated within earlier X-bar theory. Government refers to the relation between the head of a construction and its complement; thus, for example, a preposition is the head of a PP and governs its complement, a noun or NP. Similarly, a verb is the head of VP, while COMP is the head of a clause, and so on. An early attempt to formulate a government-based constraint was made by DiSciullo et al. (1986), who suggested that "when a government relation holds between elements, there can be no mixing; when that relation is absent, mixing is possible" (ibid.: 4). In other words, elements related to each other by government must be drawn from the same lexicon, or, as DiSciullo et al. put it, must have the same language index.

The constraint on code switching is formulated as follows (Muysken 1995: 185):

(13) *[Xp Yq] where X governs Y, and p and q are language indices.

However, some definitions of government were extremely broad, stipulating in effect that heads governed their entire complement or maximal projection (Aoun and Sportiche 1983). As Muysken (1995: 186) points out, this broad definition was inappropriate for the government-based constraint in two ways. First, the class of governors it identified was too large, including not just lexical governors such as verbs and prepositions, but also functional categories such as inflections, complementizers, etc. A constraint based on this definition would rule out switches that are in fact frequently attested, such as between INFL and the subject, or between a complementizer and its complement clause. The following are examples of such switches in French–Italian code switching (DiSciullo et al. 1986: 14–15):

Between INFL and the subject:

(14) La plupart des canadiens *scrivono* "c"
"Most Canadians write 'c'"

Between COMP and S′:

(15) E l'altro dice come *s'appelle*?
"And the other says how is it called?"

Second, the domain of government identified in earlier approaches was too broad, including in principle the whole maximal projection. This would rule out the switches attested above, as well as others that occur, such as between verb and adverb, or between determiners or quantifiers and the nouns they modify:

Between determiner and noun:

(16) Io posso fare i *cheques*
"I can do cheques" (DiSciullo et al. 1986: 13)

For these reasons, DiSciullo et al. adopt a modified definition of government in terms of immediate c-command, as follows:

(17) X governs Y if the first node dominating X also dominates Y, where X is a major category N, V, A, P, and no maximal boundary intervenes between X and Y.

In other words, government is minimal, and switching is permitted only when "the highest element in the governed maximal projection is in the same language as the governor" (Pandit 1990: 52). Note also that DiSciullo et al. restrict the class of governors to major categories alone, excluding INFL and COMP, *contra* Chomsky (1981). Muysken (1990: 124) reformulated the constraint as follows:

(18) *[Xp Yq] where X L-marks Y, and p and q are language indices.

The revision is intended to allow for attested cases of code switching involving government by functional categories, which the broader definition of government would rule out.

The constraint makes various predictions about possible switches. For example, it predicts that, within a VP, the verb and the immediately adjacent element in its complement will be in the same language. However, the rest of the complement may be switched, as in the following made-up examples of English–Spanish code switching (italicized items are in the same language, non-italicized items are in the other language):

(19) a. I saw that *él se fué*
he left
b. I saw the *hombre* ("man")

Similarly, within a PP, the preposition and an immediately adjacent determiner must be in the same language, but the rest of the NP complement may be switched. DiSciullo et al. (1986: 12) list various other predictions of their constraint.

Researchers have presented numerous counter-examples to these predictions. Pandit (1990: 53) provides examples of switches between the verb and an adjacent complementizer in Hindi–English code switching, as in the following (Hindi in italics):

(20) a. We can't generalize *ki* [that] love marriage as such is bad.
b. *Sudhas kaa kahanna hai* that one should face life as it comes.
Sudha POSS saying is
"Sudha says that one should face life as it comes."

Other researchers have provided examples of switches between P and its complement, (21); between V and its object NP (22);[1] between indirect and direct object (23); and between a copula and its complement (24):

Hindi–English (Pandit 1990: 45)
(21) John gave a book to *ek larakii*
"John gave a book to a girl"

Arabic–French (Bentahila and Davies 1983: 313)
(22) ʔateik *une enveloppe*
"I gave you an envelope"

Morroccan Arabic–Dutch (Nortier 1990: 131)
(23) žib li-ya *een glas of water of zo*
"Get for me a glass of water or so"

(24) wellit *huisman*
"I-became 'houseman'"

The wealth of counter-examples led Muysken (1995: 188) to concede that "the government constraint, even in the revised form of Muysken (1990), cannot be maintained." He suggests that a reformulation of the constraint which takes the notion of equivalence into account may better account for code switching phenomena. The revised constraint is as follows:

> *[Xp Yq], where X L-marks Y, p and q are language indices, and there is no equivalence between the category Y in one language and the category Y in the other language involved.

In other words, an element that is lexically governed can be switched only when it is equivalent to a corresponding element in the other language. This kind of switching seems characteristic of situations involving contact between typologically similar languages. Treffers-Daller (1994: 240) finds some empirical support for this constraint in French–Dutch code switching in Brussells. However, this attempt to combine the constraints based on government and equivalence into an overarching constraint has not so far been tested against a body of code-switching data. Its virtue is that it takes account both of the principles constraining constituent structure and of the nature of the typological fit between the two languages involved. But Muysken offers no precise definition of "equivalence" that would allow one to predict what switches can or cannot occur. And at any rate, the notion of government has itself become outdated.

5.3 A Production-Based Model of Code Switching

As Treffers-Daller (1994: 227) points out, the chief problem with the equivalence and government constraints, as well as other earlier constraints, was that they attempted only to identify points at which switching was blocked, rather than explaining which constituents can be switched and why. The latter, she suggests, should be the central question in code-switching studies. Myers-Scotton (1993b) seeks to answer this question. Unlike the scholars discussed so far, she approaches code-switching phenomena from the standpoint of the language production process. In her view, code switching can be accounted for only by examining "how language is accessed and retrieved before it takes its final form" (1993b: 45). Her Matrix Language-Frame (MLF) model of code switching is a "production-based model which sees code switching constraints as set by processes which operate well before the positional level at which surface orders and structures are realized" (1993b: 6). This is diametrically opposed to earlier models of code switching, which she criticizes for "operating at a level which is too 'purely syntactic', or too close to the surface" (1993b: 45).

The MLF model is based on the assumption that one of the languages involved in code switching, referred to as the matrix language (ML), sets the grammatical frame for mixed constituents. The grammatical frame consists of morpheme order and system morphemes (system morphemes are roughly equivalent to grammatical or "function" morphemes; they are discussed more fully below). The other language involved, from which elements are incorporated into the ML frame, is the embedded language (EL). The following example from Swahili–English code switching illustrates this, with Swahili as the ML and English as the EL (Myers-Scotton 1993b: 80). Henceforth I follow Myers-Scotton's convention of marking the EL in italics in all examples involving intra-sentential code switching:

(25) Leo si- -ku- *come* na *books* z-angu
today 1s-NEG-PAST-NEG with cl-10 my
"Today I didn't come with my books"

Strictly speaking, it is the complement phrase (CP), roughly equivalent to the "clause" of traditional grammar, that is the relevant unit of analysis for this model of code switching. As Myers-Scotton (1997: 222) notes, what qualifies as a sentence in discourse may in fact contain one or more CPs. Switches from one clause to another would therefore be treated as instances of inter-sentential (or inter-clausal) switches in this framework. The MLF model is not concerned with such switches. Cases of co-ordination as in (26) and subordination as in (27) are examples of inter-clausal switches (French in italics):

Moroccan Arabic–French (Bentahila and Davies 1983: 309)
(26) *J'avais faim* w xft na:kul
"I was hungry and I was afraid to eat"

(27) *Si j'avais la maison*, maʕamri na:kul temma
"If I had the house, I would never eat there"

Intra-sentential code switching is defined as follows in the MLF framework: "A CP shows intra-sentential code switching if it contains at least one constituent with morphemes from language X and language Y" (Myers-Scotton 1997: 222). Such a mixture can result in two different kinds of mixed constituent, one involving single morpheme EL switches, as in (25) above, and the other involving EL phrases or "islands" as in (28), from Myers-Scotton (1993b: 131), citing Oloruntoba (p.c. 1990):

Yoruba–English (Oloruntoba 1990)

(28) Awon nkan ti o *come naturally to me* ni mo*like*
those things that PRO is I-like
"I like those things that come naturally to me"

Exercise 2

Examine the following examples of code switching from various language pairs and determine whether they are cases of inter-clause or intra-clause code switching. In the latter case, determine whether single morphemes or phrasal constituents are switched. Find other examples of each type of code switching on your own.

Swahili–English (Myers-Scotton 1993c: 481, 491)

a. Kweli *beer* a-na-i-*take* kwa *hours* tano
Truly beer 3sg-PROG-OBJ-take for hours five
"Truly, he was drinking beer for five hours"

b. Nikamwambia anipe ruhusa ni-end-e
and-I-told-him he-should-give me permission 1sg-go-SUBJ
ni-ka-*check for you*
1sg-CONSEC-check for you
"And I told him he should give me permission so that I go and check for you"

Japanese–English (Nishimura 1986)

c. *Mannaka ni* they're growing (p. 132)
middle in
"They're growing in the middle"

d. Camp-*seikatsu ga* made him rough (p. 136)
Camp-life NOM
"(That) camp-life made him rough"

e. He never *moratta* from anybody (p. 137)
get-PAST
"He never got (it) from anybody"

5.3.1 Hypotheses of the MLF model

The claims of the MLF model are formulated as a set of interrelated hypotheses, as follows (Myers-Scotton 1993b: 7):

I. The Matrix Language Hypothesis.
The ML sets the morphosyntactic frame for ML+EL constituents.

From this follow two related principles:

a. The morpheme order principle:
Morpheme order must not violate ML morpheme order.
b. The system morpheme principle:
All syntactically relevant system morphemes must come from the ML.

II. The blocking hypothesis.
The ML blocks the appearance of any EL content morphemes which do not meet certain congruency conditions with ML counterparts.
III. The EL island trigger hypothesis.
Whenever an EL morpheme appears which is not permitted under either the ML hypothesis or the blocking hypothesis, the constituent containing it must be completed as an obligatory EL island.
IV. The EL implicational hierarchy hypothesis.
Optional EL islands occur; generally they are only those constituents which are either formulaic or idiomatic or peripheral to the main grammatical arguments of the sentence.

To understand why these particular hypotheses and principles are proposed, it is helpful to clarify some of the theoretical underpinnings of the MLF model. It draws on psycholinguistic research which postulates three major components of speech production – the conceptualizer, which creates the pre-verbal message; the formulator, which generates a linguistic representation of the message; and the articulator, which produces actual speech. The model further assumes that sentence production by the formulator involves two stages: first, a syntactic frame is set, and second, the segmental and prosodic structure of words and their positional arrangements are established (Myers-Scotton 1993c: 487). The MLF model is primarily concerned with the first stage – how the sentential form is set and filled in.

Further motivation for the model comes from research on speech errors (Garrett 1988, 1990) and aphasic production by monolinguals (Zurif 1990), as well as psycholinguistic studies of bilingual speech (e.g., Grosjean 1988). What these studies suggest is that:

a. One language is dominant in bilingual language processing.
b. Content and system morphemes behave differently in speech errors and in aphasic language production.
c. Each language may have its own direct access to a common conceptual system in code switching production. (Myers-Scotton 1993b: 46–7)

The MLF model draws also on Levelt's view that (morpho-)syntactic processes are directed by information contained in the mental lexicon. Syntactic directions come from so-called "lemma information," or "lemmas" for short. Levelt (1989: 6) defines a lemma as the non-phonological part of an item's lexical entry, including its syntactic and semantic properties as well as certain aspects of its morphology. Lemma information regarding meaning and grammatical relations is included within the formulator, along with information concerning word order and phonological form. The MLF model follows Levelt in distinguishing three levels of representation for abstract lemmas: lexical-conceptual structure, predicate argument structure, and morphological realization patterns (Myers-Scotton and Jake 2001: 85). These distinctions are crucial to explaining congruence-related constraints on code switching (see section 5.4 below).

We can now examine how the model attempts to account for actual cases of intra-sentential code switching.

5.3.2 *Establishing the matrix language*

There is no clearly established set of criteria for identifying the ML in code-switching utterances. Some researchers (e.g., Doron 1983; Joshi 1985) define it as the language of the first word in a sentence. Others (e.g., Klavans 1983; Treffers-Daller 1991) suggest that the ML is the language of the verb or INFL. But these definitions have proven inappropriate in many cases. Nortier (1990: 159) provides the following examples from Dutch–Arabic code switching illustrating that neither the first word nor the INFL category of a code-switching utterance determines the ML (Arabic in italics):

(29) *emma* krijgen ze veel meer
there get they much more
"There they get much more"

(30) *xeṣṣ-hŭm* anders omgaan met hun
they-must differently deal with them
"They must deal with them differently"

Myers-Scotton (1993b: 68) defines the ML as "the language of more morphemes in interaction types including intra-sentential code switching." She further suggests that frequency counts must be based on a discourse sample rather than single sentences, and that cultural borrowings from the EL must not be counted as part of the latter, since they might skew the comparison.

Nortier, however, prefers to distinguish the macro-level of discourse from the micro-level of individual sentences, since "it is possible that (parts of) a conversation have language A as the base language while individual sentences in that particular conversation can have either base language A or base language B" (1990: 158). Both Myers-Scotton and Nortier acknowledge that there are individual code-switching sentences for which the ML is difficult to identify purely on the basis of a frequency count. Bentahila and Davies (1983: 309) provide the following example from Arabic–French code switching (French in italics):

(31) tajbɣiw jšufu šiħaža *qui est different*
they enjoy looking at something which is different

Nortier (1990: 159) adds the following example from her Arabic–Dutch data (Dutch in italics):

(32) ɣend-na bezzaf bezzaf *moeilijkheden* u *problemen met, eh, met*
we-have much much troubles and problems with, uh, with,
eh, nou ten eerste, de taal
uh, well, in the first place, the language

In (31), there is a switch between main and dependent clause, with each containing three words. This would probably be treated as an inter-CP switch in the MLF model. In (32), the number of Dutch morphemes exceeds that of Arabic morphemes, yet the latter language contains the main verb and begins the sentence. Here, one might argue that the syntactic core of the sentence is Arabic, and assign the ML to that language. Nortier suggests that a working definition of the ML must be based on more than one criterion, including the language of the first words of the utterance, the syntax of the sentence, and the frequency of constituents from each language. She concludes that, if the ML is still doubtful, it should be assumed there is none.

The identification of an ML can be especially problematic in cases of code switching arising from recent or ongoing language shift, where the ML can change from turn to turn even for the same speaker. Nishimura (1986) discusses such a case of code switching by Japanese–English bilinguals (whose first language is Japanese) in Toronto and San Francisco. She found that the most reliable basis for ML assignment was the syntactic pattern of the sentence, including the constituent order as well as morphological marking of syntactic functions such as subject, object, topic, etc. For instance, example (33) is assigned to Japanese as the ML, since it displays Japanese SOV (head-final) order. Note also the use of Japanese function morphemes such as topic marker *wa* and postposition *de* "on" (Japanese in italics):

(33) *Kaeri ni wa* border *de* we got stopped, eh?
return on TOP on
"On our return we got stopped at the border" (Nishimura 1986: 132)

Nishimura further argues that the English clauses in such sentences are used as equivalents of Japanese predicates, which are inflected verbs, for example, *tomerareta* "we got stopped." On the other hand, sentences like (34) would be assigned to English:

(34) I slept with her basement *de* ["in"]
"I slept with her in the basement" (Nishimura 1986: 130)

In this case there is a switch at the boundary of VP and locative PP, with the latter following Japanese constituent order. But the overall syntax of the sentence is English.

Some of Nishimura's examples recall the kinds of mixture found in second language learning, which Hamers and Blanc (1989) referred to as "incompetence switching," to distinguish them from the kinds of code switching practiced by fluent bilinguals in stable situations. Sentences (35)–(36) illustrate:

(35) Only small prizes *moratte ne*
get-past TAG
"[We] got only small prizes" (Nishimura 1986: 128)

(36) Right in the center grow-*shitara*
do-CONDIT.
"If (they) grow (it) right in the center (of it)" (ibid.: 129)

Nishimura assigns both of these sentences to Japanese on the basis of their constituent order, despite the fact that most of the words they contain are English.

Sentences similar to these are typical of the varieties of Hawai'ian Pidgin English produced by Japanese immigrants who were born in Japan and who presumably learnt the pidgin as a second language. Bickerton (1981: 9) provides examples like the following:

(37) a. mista karsan-*no tokoro* tu eika sel *shite*
Mr. Carson-POSS place two acre sell do
"I sold two acres to Mr. Carson's place"
b. *sore kara* kech *shite kara* pul ap
and then catch do then pull up
"When he had caught it, he pulled it up"

The pattern of mixture in all of these cases seems to involve the retention of abstract L1 syntactic patterns with insertion of L2 words which we find in cases of second language acquisition (see chapter 7). This once more calls into question the suggestion that the code-switching behavior of fluent bilinguals is different in kind from that of second language learners.

The opposite seems to occur in examples like the following, where a Japanese tag is added to an otherwise English sentence:

(38) The idea is bound to change *NE* ["don't you think?"] (Nishimura 1986: 134)

Similarly, we find English discourse markers attached to an otherwise Japanese sentence, as in the following (English in italics):

(39) *Anyway*, atama ga furui yo
"Anyway, they are old-fashioned" (ibid.: 134)

These cases of tag switching do not affect language assignment.

Other cases of mixture, however, prove somewhat more problematic. Among these are examples like the following, involving switches between subject and predicate (Japanese in italics):

(40) *Hakujin no heitai-san* didn't like *nihonjin* or something
white soldier Japanese
"The white soldier didn't like Japanese or something" (ibid.: 135)

(41) *Ushiro no kao wa* looks like Japanese
behind GEN face TOP
"The face of [the man in] the background looks Japanese" (ibid.)

Nishimura assigns (40) to English on the grounds that the subject NP is not marked by any Japanese case particle. On the other hand, she assigns (41) to Japanese merely because the topic marker *wa* follows the subject, despite the fact that the VP is English. This seems somewhat arbitrary, as is her argument that "for our bilingual informants, a Japanese NP without a particle is equivalent to an English subject NP" (ibid.: 136).

Another problematic example is the following:

(42) She-*wa* took her a month to come home *yo*
TOP TAG
"Talking about her, it took her a month to come home, you know" (Nishimura 1986: 136)

Nishimura apparently assigns this sentence to Japanese, claiming that its structure is identical to that of (41). She analyses *she-wa* as a Japanese topic, since it can't be the subject of the VP. But if this is so, it might be argued that *she-wa* is simply a substitute for English *as for her*, and that (allowing for the missing dummy element *it*) the rest of the sentence is English. Nishimura herself suggests the possibility that both (41) and (42) consist of a Japanese topic and an English sentence (ibid.: 137).

Finally, Nishimura offers several examples of what she calls "portmanteau sentences" (1986: 139) to which a single ML cannot be assigned. These are typically sentences in which an English clause is merged with a Japanese clause because they share an intermediate constituent, as in the following:

(43) You should see his *karada kimochi warui n da*
body appearance awful is
"You should see his body; [his body's] appearance is awful" (ibid.)

Mergers like this are possible because the final element of the English sentence (whether it is switched or not) can also function as the initial element of the Japanese clause. Such sentences may be facilitated by the mirror-image relationship between English and Japanese constituent order, for example, VO/OV; P NP/NP P, etc. These mirror-image sentences resist assignment to any one ML.

Exercise 3
Nishimura (1997: 70) provides the following example of the "mixed variety" used by a Japanese–English bilingual in Toronto. She also claims (ibid.: 32) that "no base language can be determined in such discourse." How would the MLF model characterize these switches? Japanese is in italics:

B.C. *ni iku toki, hikooki de yomou to onottekara*, I bought it, eh?
When I went to B.C., thinking that I would read it, I bought it, eh?
So, it's not finished yet. And it's hard, 'cause me-*nanka, moo*,
So, it's not finished yet. And it's hard, because a person like me, really,
Hon nanka yomu to, cover to cover *yomanakattara*, if I stop *dokka de*,
When I read a book, unless I read it cover to cover, if I stop at some point,
I forget the story. One week later *yomu deshoo*, I've got to go back.
I forget the story. When I read it one week later, I've got to go back.

All of the examples considered here raise interesting questions about the criteria for identifying the ML in a code-switched utterance. They therefore pose a challenge to models like the MLF, which treat code switching as involving a single ML grammar rather than interacting grammars.

In general, however, there appears to be strong empirical support in code-switching data cross-linguistically for the notion of a matrix language in intra-sentential code switching. According to Myers-Scotton (1993b: 69), "supporting evidence that all sentences have an ML is that code switching material in all data sets can be classified as one of the three types of code switching constituent [discussed above]." Moreover, an experimental study by Kamwangamalu and Lee (1991) showed that bilingual speakers could easily identify the ML in Mandarin Chinese–English code-switching utterances. Treffers-Daller (1994: 238) also points out that in most cases it is easy to identify the matrix language in her French–Dutch code switching data.

5.4 Constraints on Code Switching Within the MLF Model

The MLF model has devoted most of its attention to constraints on two types of single-morpheme switches, those involving "system" morphemes, and those involving content morphemes. As we will see, it has rather less to say about constraints on other kinds of code switching, such as inter-clausal switching, and switching of entire phrases or EL islands. Let us first examine the constraints it proposes for single-morpheme switches.

5.4.1 Constraints on switching of system morphemes

As we noted earlier, the MLF model appeals to the system morpheme principle to account for the fact that EL system morphemes cannot generally be inserted into the ML frame, unless they appear in EL islands. This principle simply stipulates that all syntactically relevant system morphemes in a code-switching utterance will belong to the ML. Second, the Blocking Hypothesis specifies that content morphemes can be freely switched, subject to the condition that such morphemes must be congruent in certain ways with their ML counterparts.

Note first that system morphemes form a subset of function morphemes or "closed class" items. Joshi (1985) proposed that closed class items, unlike major lexical categories, could not be switched. However, there are many counter-examples to this claim, as pointed out, for example, by Pandit (1990: 50). The MLF model refines Joshi's claim by restricting it to "system" morphemes only.

System morphemes are distinguished from content morphemes in terms of three properties (Jake and Myers-Scotton 1992):

a. [+/– Quantification]
b. [+/– Thematic-role assigner]
c. [+/– Thematic-role receiver].

First of all, morphemes involving quantification are system morphemes. These include items which express quantification over individuals, such as determiners, quantifiers, possessive adjectives, etc., or quantification over events, such as tense/aspect morphemes. On the other hand, items that are [–Quantification] are usually content morphemes. These are also either thematic-role assigners (e.g., verbs and some prepositions) or thematic-role receivers (e.g., nouns and adjectives). Any item that does not assign or receive a theta-role is a system morpheme. Table 5.1 provides examples of system morphemes.

Evidence that ML system morphemes appear freely in mixed constituents is not hard to find. A typical example is (25), repeated here as (44), from Swahili–English code switching, with Swahili as the ML:

(44) Leo si- -ku- *come* na *books* z-angu
today 1sg-NEG-PAST-NEG with cl-10-my
"Today I didn't come with my books"

Note that morphemes expressing tense and negation as well as possession all come from Swahili. The EL morphemes here are content morphemes – a verb

Table 5.1 System morphemes

System morphemes	Quantification	Theta-role assigner	Theta-role receiver
Quantifiers	+	–	–
Possessives	+	–	–
Determiners	+	–	–
Tense/aspect	+	–	–
Complementizers	–	–	–
Agr. markers	–	–	–
Copula	–	–	–
"do" verb	–	–	–
Possessive "of"	–	–	–
Dummy pronouns	–	–	–

Source: adapted from Myers-Scotton (1993b: 101)

and a noun, both integrated into the ML frame. (An exception is the plural morpheme *-s*, to be discussed below).

Myers-Scotton (1993b: 110) discusses two possible exceptions to the system morpheme principle. First, there are cases involving "double morphology," where a switched item is marked simultaneously by an EL and an ML system morpheme expressing the same meaning. For example, in Lingala–French code switching, one finds forms like *ba-jeune-s* "young people," where the French stem *jeune* is marked for plurality both by Lingala prefix *ba-* and French suffix *-s*. According to Myers-Scotton (1993b: 111), double plurals like this are very common in code switching involving European and Bantu languages, as well as in various other language pairs. She argues that these exceptions do not falsify the system morpheme principle, since the EL systems morphemes involved "have no grammatical relations external to their head constituent," such as agreement. This explanation is refined in Myers-Scotton and Jake (2001), to be discussed below.

The second exception is that, in some cases, EL content morphemes appear as "bare forms," with no morphological marking from either language. For instance, Myers-Scotton (1993b: 95) notes that many English nouns occur as switched EL items with no modifiers (adjectives, demonstratives, or possessives) or case markers in her Swahili–English corpus. She provides the following example (ibid.: 125):

(45) Hata wengine nasikia washawek-w-a *cell*
even others I hear 3-pl.-already-put-PASS-INDIC
"I even heard that some of them have already been put [in] cell[s] [i.e., jail]"

Here the noun *cell* occurs with neither an EL preposition (i.e., *in*) nor the Swahili suffix *-ni* which marks locative case.[2]

Similar bare forms have been attested in code-switching data from various language pairs, including Turkish–Dutch (Backus 1990), Moroccan Arabic–Dutch (Nortier 1990), and Louisiana French–Cajun English (Picone 1994). Picone provides the following examples (1994: 323):

(46) Il voit les *truck*
he sees the-pl
"He sees the trucks"

(47) J'ai *drive* en ville
"I drove to town"

The lack of number inflection on *truck* in (46) accords with Louisiana French morphology, where only the determiner is inflected for plurality. The lack of inflection on *drive* in (47), however, has no such motivation. This contrasts with the marking of switched verbs for imperfect aspect, as in the following example:

(48) Il *drive*-ait vingt-quatre heures
"He would drive for twenty-four hours"

Picone criticizes Myers-Scotton's approach to bare forms for assuming that all code-switching items must belong wholly either to the EL or the ML. He suggests instead that these forms be viewed as "code-intermediate" or "code-neutral" phenomena to which neither language assigns inflection. He compares them to the kinds of simplifications often found in the interlanguage of L2 learners. Myers-Scotton suggests that some bare forms surface due to a lack of congruence between the relevant ML and EL system morphemes, but she acknowledges that the motivation for other bare forms remains unclear (1993b: 97).

Another interesting example of bare forms is a strategy by which EL verbs (and other content items) are incorporated into a compound verb construction consisting of the imported item and an ML "helping" verb meaning "do/make" or "be/become." ML inflections are attached to the helping verb, thus allowing the EL item to avoid direct marking. These compound verb constructions occur in a wide variety of language pairs, including Panjabi–English (Agnihotri 1987: 120ff), Japanese–English (Azuma 1991a), Hausa–English (Bickmore 1985), Warlpiri–English (Bavin and Shopen 1985), and Turkish–Dutch (Boeschoten and Verhoeven 1985: 358). In all of these cases, the compound verb strategy has a native (ML) model. Romaine (1989) offers examples like the following from her Panjabi–English corpus:

(49) o *help* karde ne
3pl do AUX
"They help" (ibid.: 123)

(50) Baceã nũ tusĩ *force* nei kər sak-de
children ACC you NEG do can-AGR
"You can't force children" (ibid.: 129)

Romaine (ibid.: 120) notes that this structure is native to Panjabi, which has a class of compound verbs consisting of a (native) stem (a noun, verb, or adjective) plus an operator or helping verb meaning either "do" or "be." Hence the strategy of creating new compound verbs with bare EL forms conforms fully to Panjabi grammar, and is no different from other cases where EL forms are incorporated into an ML morphosyntactic frame. The key factor here and in other cases where bare forms occur in code switching seems to be the ease of integration of the EL item into an existing morphosyntactic slot. This recalls the patterns of insertion of external forms into native verb structures that Heath describes for languages in Arnhem Land, Australia (chapter 3).

Interestingly, parallel creations have been attested in other situations where no native model exists. For instance, Gardner-Chloros (1995: 78) provides examples from Cypriot Greek–English mixture consisting of an English verb form plus the Greek verb *kanno* "do/make," for example, *kamno use* "to use," *kamno develop* "to develop," etc. No model for this exists in either English or Greek, so we are dealing here with a new verbal creation. Pfaff (1976: 254–5) reports a similar construction in Californian Spanish, exemplified in the following:

(51) a. Su hija hace *teach* allá in San José
her daughter does teach there in San José
"Her daughter teaches there in San José"
b. Porqué te hicieron *beat up*?
Why you they-did beat up?
"Why did they beat you up?"

Silva-Corvalán (2000: 12) provides another example from Los Angeles Spanish:

(52) Lo hicieron *rape* a él
3obj. do-3pl past rape to him
"They raped him"

Again, there is no model for this in either of the two languages involved. Innovations like these are not easily explained by the MLF (or any other) model of code switching.

5.4.1.1 System morphemes versus other function morphemes

Another serious challenge to the system morpheme principle is how to accurately identify what counts as a system morpheme, and why other EL function morphemes are not blocked from insertion into the ML frame. The fact is that several types of function morphemes can be switched. The solution proposed by the MLF model is that the latter are in fact content morphemes and therefore subject only to the Blocking Hypothesis (see section 5.4.2).

For example, according to the criteria outlined earlier, some prepositions are system morphemes, while others are content morphemes. Thus, it is claimed that many English locative or temporal prepositions (e.g., *in, on*, etc.) are system morphemes, because they have the feature [+Quantification]. But prepositions like *of* in *I don't approve of John* and *for* in *I bought cigarettes for Mary* are content morphemes because they assign thematic roles. The same applies to prepositions like *before* and *between*. The Blocking Hypothesis therefore predicts that these latter prepositions can be switched, if they satisfy the condition of congruence. Support for this comes from Swahili–English code-switching utterances like the following (Myers-Scotton 1993b: 124):

(53) U-let-e *before* kesho jioni
2s-bring-SUBJ tomorrow evening
"You should bring [it] before tomorrow evening"

In this case, the EL preposition *before* has a close match in Swahili *kabla ya* "before," which is also a content morpheme. Hence the switch is not blocked. On the other hand, benefactive *for* cannot be substituted for its Swahili counterpart, which is a system morpheme realized as the suffix *-i-* or *-e-* (depending on vowel harmony) attached to the verb stem (Myers-Scotton 1993b: 123).

It's not always clear, however, whether the criteria for distinguishing between system and content morphemes are always valid, or whether the predictions of the MLF model hold in all cases. For instance, the model claims that "the only way for EL complementizers to appear [in code switching] is in EL islands" (Myers-Scotton 1993b: 130). But this is refuted by evidence such as the following, from Moroccan Arabic–French switching (Bentahila and Davies 1983: 310–11):

(54) il croyait *biʔana* je faisais ça exprés.
"He thought that I was doing that on purpose"

(55) matkun zjada *parce que* kul qal zjada
"There would be no increase because everybody said [there would be] an increase"

In (54) an Arabic complementizer is inserted into an otherwise French sentence, while the reverse occurs in (55). These examples suggest that the criteria for identifying system morphemes and the constraints on their ability to get switched need to be made more explicit.

5.4.1.2 Explaining double morphology

Earlier versions of the MLF model (Myers-Scotton 1993b) did not satisfactorily explain why some EL system morphemes appear in mixed constituents, as in the case of "double morphology" discussed earlier. Myers-Scotton

(1993b: 111) cites the following example from Shona–English code switching (Crawhall 1990):

(56) But ma-*day-s* a-no a-ya ha-ndi-si ku-mu-on-a
but cl6-day-pl cl6-DEM cl6-DEM NEG-1s-COP INF-3s/obj-see-fv
"But these days I don't see him much"

Here the English plural morpheme *-s* appears alongside the Shona prefix *ma-*, which also marks plurality.

To explain this, Myers-Scotton and Jake (2001: 99) suggest that plural affixes (at least in some languages) belong to a class of "early" system morphemes which are accessed simultaneously with their EL nouns during language production. By contrast, "late" system morphemes are accessed later in the production process, when the constituent structure of maximal projections is being built up. Examples of early system morphemes in English include plural markers, the definite article *the*, and particles like *at* in phrasal verbs like *look at*.

They further suggest that late system morphemes fall into two subclasses. First, there are "bridge" morphemes which integrate a content morpheme into a larger constituent, for example genitive/possessive *of* in *a friend of John* or possessive suffix *-s*. Second, there are "outsider" system morphemes which depend on grammatical information outside their own maximal projection. For example, 3rd sing. *-s* in *John eats bananas* marks agreement with the subject NP *John*, which is outside the VP. Since the revised version of the content-versus-system morpheme distinction now recognizes four categories of morphemes, Myers-Scotton and Jake (2001) refer to it as the 4-M model. They propose that the "early" versus "late" system morpheme distinction finds support in speech errors, aphasic language, and second language acquisition data which show that the two classes of morpheme behave quite differently.

It's not clear at this point how the new classification of system morphemes relates to the one presented earlier in this chapter, which was based on criteria such as quantification and thematic-role assignment. Presumably these criteria continue to apply. Further research is needed to test whether the predictions of the 4-M model are borne out by code-switching data from a variety of language pairs.

5.4.2 Constraints on switching of content morphemes

As already noted, the Blocking Hypothesis predicts that EL content morphemes will appear freely in mixed ML+EL constituents, subject to the condition that such morphemes must be congruent in certain ways with their ML counterparts. Congruence appears to be definable in terms of several kinds of similarity, viz., in semantics, categorial status, syntactic and morphological properties, subcategorization requirements where relevant, and discourse/pragmatic function (Myers-Scotton 1993b: 121). According to Myers-Scotton and Jake (2001: 105) congruence between EL and ML morphemes must be checked at three levels: lexical-conceptual structure, predicate argument structure, and morphological realization patterns.

We've already seen examples of switches involving functional content morphemes (locative prepositions, etc.) which conform to the requirement of congruence. Thus English prepositions like *before* and *between* are congruent in meaning, categorial status, and subcategorization with their respective Swahili counterparts *kabla ya* and *kati ya*. Hence the former can substitute for the latter. By contrast, English pronouns, which are closed-class content morphemes, cannot be switched for their Swahili counterparts because the latter are clitics attached to the verb stem and are system morphemes. This mismatch in categorial status, morphological realization, and positional relations blocks substitution in these cases.

For open-class items like nouns, verbs, etc., it would seem that congruence in semantics and categorial status is usually sufficient for a switch to occur.

Interestingly, there are examples of switches involving "system" morphemes, which appear to be triggered by congruence as well. For example, Bentahila and Davies (1983: 323–4) show that subordinating conjunctions introducing clauses of purpose can be switched in Moroccan Arabic–French code switching, as in the following (Arabic in italics):

(57) je peux le dire *had* le truc *hada baš* je commence à apprende
I can it say this the thing here so that I start to learn
"I can say this thing here in order that I start to learn"

(58) je vais me coucher tôt pour que *nxdem mzja:n ǰda*
"I'm going to bed early so that I may work well tomorrow."

In these sentences, Arabic complementizer *baš* and its French counterpart *pour que* both obligatorily introduce a finite clause, and thus are substitutable. Now contrast the following, where the switch is ungrammatical:

(59) *On est allé au café *baš* boire un pot
"He went to the café to have a drink" (ibid.: 323)

Here *baš* is not substitutable for French *pour*, which introduces an infinitival complement. (Compare the grammatical French equivalent *pour boire un pot.*) The mismatch in subcategorization rules out the switch. It would appear then that "system" morpheme status, by itself, is not sufficient to block switching, especially when conditions of congruence are met.

5.5 Constraints on Multi-Word Switches (EL Islands)

So far this discussion has focused on single-morpheme switches. Another type of mixed constituent consists of EL phrases or "islands" embedded in an ML clausal structure, as in the following examples from Moroccan Arabic–French code switching (Bentahila and Davies 1983: 312). French switches are italicized:

(60) *Les gens* mabqaw jxalSu:
"The people stopped paying"

(61) Kuna Yadji:n *en ville*
"We were going into town"

(62) Had l marSa *sent dégueeulasse*
"This part smells revolting"

The EL islands in these examples are maximal projections, or what Treffers-Daller (1994: 205) refers to as "full constituents." The types of constituents that can be switched include NPs, PPs, and APs. Treffers-Daller also includes clausal constituents such as S′, relative clauses, and embedded questions in her list of full constituents, but these represent inter-clausal switches rather than EL islands in the sense the term is used here, following Myers-Scotton.

We also find switches involving two constituents, as in the following example for French–Dutch code switching (Treffers-Daller 1994: 213):

(63) Aller à l'hôpital *toch niet*?
Go to the hospital really not
"You don't mean going to the hospital?"

There are as well EL islands which are part of a maximal projection, for example, a V′ or an N′. Treffers-Daller (ibid.: 214) provides the following example of a V′ switch:

(64) Ik had de *chou rave en horreur*
I had the kohlrabi in horror
"I hated kohlrabi"

Poplack and Meechan (1995: 221) give the following example of an N′ switch in their Fongbe–French code-switching corpus:

(65)

énɛ́	ɔ̀	*conséquences*	*sociales*	wɛ̀	nyí	*chômage*	mɛ̀	lɛ́	tɔ̀n
DEM	DEF	consequences	social	it's	be	unemployment	people	PLU	POSS

"These are the social consequences of unemployment"

There has been relatively little research on the constraints regulating the appearance and structure of EL islands. Researchers have taken two rather different approaches to the issue. On the one hand, Poplack and her associates suggest that multi-word switches (as they call them) are subject to the equivalence constraint. In other words, there must be surface structural congruence between the two languages for the switch to take place. Myers-Scotton argues the opposite – that EL islands are triggered precisely when there is no congruence (at a more abstract level) between the structures involved. We can consider each approach in turn, beginning with the latter.

5.5.1 The EL Island Trigger Hypothesis

Myers-Scotton's EL Island Trigger Hypothesis claims that if an EL lemma or morpheme not licensed under the ML or Blocking Hypothesis is activated or accessed, the current constituent must be completed as an EL island (1993b: 139). In particular, the lack of congruence between a blocked EL morpheme and its ML counterpart triggers a change in production, producing an EL island. For instance, in the following example from Swahili–English code switching, the speaker accesses an English possessive adjective *our*, which must occur before its head noun. Swahili has N+Adj order, so the constituent must be completed as an English island:

(66)

Tu-na-m-let-e-a	*our brother*	wa Thika
1pl-PROG-him-take-APPL-INDIC		of Thika

"We are taking [it] to our brother of Thika"

The EL island hypothesis similarly predicts that combinations like *this jioni* "this evening," *for wewe* "for you," etc. are impossible in Swahili–English code switching, because of a lack of congruence (in position and/or morphological realization) between system morphemes like *this* and *for*, and their Swahili counterparts.

However, it seems somewhat circular to explain the occurrence of EL islands as triggered by some "illicit" EL morpheme which itself forms part of the island. The goal should be to explain what kinds of constituents can in fact be switched, and under what conditions. Moreover, there are counter-examples to the MLF model's claim that any intrusion of a system morpheme into the ML must trigger an EL island. Bentahila and Davies (1983) provide several examples from their Arabic–French code-switching data in which a system morpheme in one language is followed by a constituent from the other. In the following example, an Arabic preposition is switched and followed by a French NP:

(67) il devient *bħal* un perroquet
"He becomes like a parrot" (Bentahila and Davies 1983: 315)

There are several examples of NPs containing determiners or quantifiers from one language followed by a noun from the other, for example (French in italics):

(68) ši *semaine* "some week"; *des* mraja:t "some mirrors" (ibid.: 316)

And there are cases where complementizers from one language introduce clauses from the other, as in the following:

(69) Lorsque j'ai vu que *mabqaš*
"When I saw that there was nothing left"

According to the EL Island Trigger Constraint, all the switches of system morphemes in these examples should trigger EL islands, but that is not the case.

Myers-Scotton herself acknowledges that certain kinds of multi-word switches are problematic for her hypothesis. First, there are cases like the following from Arabic–French code switching (Bentahila and Davies 1983), where an Arabic demonstrative takes a French NP as its complement:

(70) *dak* la chemise
that the shirt
"that shirt"

Myers-Scotton refers to such switches as "internal EL islands" and analyzes them as N′ categories within a ML maximal projection. This explanation makes good sense, but it constitutes a revision to the claim that EL islands are themselves maximal projections entirely in one language. Treffers-Daller (1994: 214) also provides examples of multi-word switches that are not maximal projections from her Dutch–French code-switching corpus. The following illustrate (islands in italics):

(71) Mon mari a dit que je devais venir ici *een leer halen*
my husband has said I should come here a ladder to get
"My husband said I should come here to get a ladder"

(72) Hij komt uit ne *sens unique*
he comes out a direction unique
"He comes out of a one-way street"

Treffers-Daller rightly suggests that the notion of "EL island" should be extended to partial constituents like these, though she acknowledges there is a risk that the notion might become too powerful (presumably, difficult to constrain).

There are also cases where EL islands are not fully well formed according to the rules of the EL, *contra* the prediction of the MLF model. For example, the French NP in (72) appears without an article, and similar NP islands are quite common in code switching involving other language pairs, as in the following example from Lingala–French code switching (Kamwangamalu 1989: 118):

(73) Ezali *probleme* monene te
"It's not a big problem"

Similar examples from Fongbe–French code switching (Poplack and Meechan 1995) will be discussed below.

Myers-Scotton suggests that the absence of articles in (73) may be due to the fact that Lingala has neither definite nor indefinite articles; hence there is no slot for one in the frame set by the ML. Again, this explanation makes good sense, but as Myers-Scotton admits, the EL Island Trigger Hypothesis cannot explain these cases, because it refers only to obligatory islands, not prohibited ones (1993b: 155).

Also problematic for the MLF model are cases where an EL multi-word fragment conforms to the grammar of the ML, *contra* the predictions of the EL Island Trigger Hypothesis. The following example from Swahili–English code switching (Myers-Scotton 1989: 5) illustrates:

(74) Ku-li-kuw-a na *table long* namna hii, mazee
LOC-PAST-COP-INDIC with kind this, friend
"There was a long table like this, my friend"

Myers-Scotton excludes such switches from her category of EL islands, since they fail to conform to EL rules. She explains them rather as combinations of content morphemes inserted into the ML frame in accordance with the Blocking Hypothesis (1993b: 142).

All the problematic cases discussed here suggest that the occurrence of multi-word switches cannot be predicted solely on the basis of a switch in a system morpheme that triggers an island. The explanation must be sought elsewhere.

More recent versions of the MLF hypothesis appeal once more to the notion of congruence, in order to explain the formation of EL islands. According to Myers-Scotton and Jake (1995: 995), insufficient congruence across the code-switching language pair, either in semantic/pragmatic features or in predicate argument structure, triggers EL islands. In such cases, it becomes impossible to accommodate EL material in a mixed constituent; hence the speaker resorts to an entire EL island. An example of this is the following, from Shona–English code switching (Crawhall 1990, cited in Myers-Scotton and Jake 1995: 1008). Shona items are in italics:

(75) Whenever *munhu kana-ada ku*-transfer from a certain department to
person wants INF-transfer
[another]
"Whenever a person wants to transfer from a certain department to another"

There is a mismatch here between Shona and English with respect to the subcategorization frame of "transfer." While the English verb requires a PP complement, the Shona counterpart requires an applied suffix to convey directionality. The speaker resolves the mismatch by a switch to an English EL.

5.5.2 EL islands and the notion of congruence

As we've seen, approaches based on Poplack's equivalence constraint appeal to congruence at the level of surface structure to account for the appearance of multi-word switches. Poplack and her associates refer to this type of switching as equivalence-based switching. Poplack and Meechan (1995: 213) offer the following example from Wolof–French code switching (French in italics):

(76) *Des fois* da nga y xool *un film avec des sous-titres en français*
sometimes AUX you ASP watch a film with DET subtitles in French
"Sometimes you watch a film with subtitles in French"

According to Poplack and Meechan, it is the close similarity between French and Wolof NP structure that facilitates such switches. The correspondences are illustrated in figure 5.2.

Language	Position 2	Position 1		Position 1	Position 2	Position 3
Wolof	Indef.	Adj./Numeral	NOUN	X	Def.	Rel./PP
French	Indef./Def.	Adj./Numeral	NOUN	Adj.	X	Rel./PP

Figure 5.2 Noun modifier positions in Wolof and French
Source: adapted from Poplack and Meechan (1995: 207, table 10.3)

The fact that Wolof and French share the pattern Indef. + Adj/Numeral + N facilitates switches of French NPs with that structure. In addition, mixed constituents occur which have an indefinite determiner from Wolof followed by a noun from French.

By contrast, in Fongbe–French code switching, French NP islands typically occur without determiners, because the latter occur in different slots in the two languages. Moreover, these French NPs virtually always consist of noun + adjective or numeral + noun, since these combinations are shared with Fongbe. The following example illustrates (Poplack and Meechan 1995: 222):

(77) à ḍòná ḍó *formation précise* có bó yi *aventure*
you must have training precise before and go adventure
"You must have precise training before you go on an adventure"

Poplack and Meechan refer to such switches as "constituent insertions" and explain the preference for them in Fongbe–French code switching as due to the partial structural, that is, typological mismatch between the two languages. They suggest that, in cases of such mismatch, "speakers will opt to relax one of the requirements of the equivalence constraint rather than refrain from code switching completely" (1995: 225).

Figure 5.3 illustrates the correspondences between NP structures in the two languages.

Poplack and Meechan's explanation of the lack of determiners in these French NPs recalls Myers-Scotton's explanation of the lack of determiners in French NP switches in Lingala–French code switching. Clearly congruence in constituent order plays a role in all these cases. If an entire phrasal category (maximal projection) in an EL is congruent with its counterpart in the ML, the whole constituent may be switched. If congruence is restricted to only part of the maximal projection, for example, an N′ structure, then only that part will be

Language	Position 2	Position 1		Position 1	Position 2	Position 3
Fongbe	X	Numeral	NOUN	Adj.	Indef./Def.	Rel./PP
French	Indef./Def.	Adj./Numeral	NOUN	Adj.	X	Rel./PP

Figure 5.3 Noun modifier positions in Fongbe and French
Source: adapted from Poplack and Meechan (1995: 206, table 10.3)

switched. From this perspective, the equivalence constraint is clearly relevant to predictions of code-switching patterns. However, it cannot explain why phrasal categories are switched so often in other language pairs even when they do not share the same constituent order.

Treffers-Daller (1994: 220) suggests a revision of the notion of equivalence which would help solve this problem. She argues that we should distinguish between equivalence at the constituent (phrasal) level and the level of each individual item. What she seems to be suggesting is that, if there is broad (functional) equivalence at the level of the phrasal constituent, switching is possible despite differences in word order between the two languages. This would explain switches like the following, from her Dutch–French code-switching data (1994: 220):

(78) *Le français de Brussels* spreek ik
the French of Brussels speak I
"I speak Brussels French"

Poplack's equivalence constraint rules out such switches since the word order at the switch point differs in Dutch and French (the latter has V+NP order). But in Treffers-Daller's account, the switch is possible because the French NP is functionally equivalent to its Dutch counterpart.

This notion of equivalence seems to be a more feasible basis on which to explain multi-word switches. Note that it would also explain the substitution of EL constituents for ML ones where the constituents themselves differ in word order.

This approach implies that multi-word switches are regulated by constraints similar in principle to those that govern single-word switches. In other words, both types of switches are inserted into slots made available in the syntactic frame of the ML, subject to conditions of congruence and compatibility with ML rules. This reflects the view of Bentahila and Davies (1983: 321) and Pandit

(1990: 43) that switching is always possible as long as the switched elements satisfy the subcategorization frame of the relevant ML head. Thus any EL constituent, whether it be a single word, a part of a maximal projection, or a maximal projection, can substitute for an ML counterpart with which it is functionally congruent. This explains the switches in the following examples of Dutch–French code switching from Treffers-Daller (1994: 233), which were ruled out by the equivalence constraint:

French–Dutch (Dutch in italics):

(79) Je dois je dois glisser *daan vinger hier*
I must I must slide that finger here
"I have to press here with my finger"

Dutch–French (French in italics):

(80) Ja vijf of six waren er want die *à front de rue* waren
yes five or six were there for who at front of street were
"Yes, there were five or six, who were at the street front"

In (79), the Dutch direct object *daan vinger* follows the French infinitive *glisser*, conforming to French subcategorization rules, whereas Dutch would require the direct object to immediately precede the infinitive. In (80), a French PP is positioned before the copula *waren* according to Duch syntactic rules (in French it would follow the copula).

The structure of (79) is illustrated by the tree diagram in (81), which shows how the Dutch NP is embedded within the subcategorization frame of the French verb, filling the slot of its French counterpart (**f** = French; **d** = Dutch; X = switch):

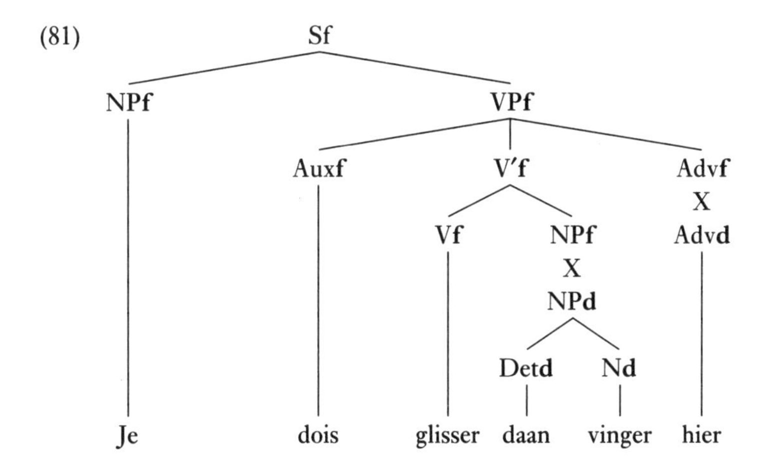

If it is true that multi-word switches are syntactically integrated into the ML just like single-word switches, this would mean, as Treffers-Daller points out, that borrowings and insertional switching are not very different in principle. An approach that stresses the unitary nature of these phenomena would seem preferable to those proposed in earlier versions of the MLF hypothesis, which offer quite different (and sometimes conflicting) explanations for the two types of insertion.

Myers-Scotton and Jake (1995) adopt a position quite similar to that proposed by Treffers-Daller (1994), Bentahila and Davies (1983), Pandit (1990), and others. Thus they note that EL islands need not be identical in composition to their ML counterparts, but their placement must follow the well-formedness conditions of the ML, not the EL (1995: 1011). This approach seems to offer a better explanation for the various kinds of EL island insertions that had proved problematic for the EL island Trigger Hypothesis.

We might note, finally that there appears to be some relationship between the frequency with which phrasal categories are switched and the degree of their centrality to the subcategorization frame of the verb. Both Myers-Scotton (1993b: 144) and Treffers-Daller (1994: 234) note that there is a hierarchy of switched EL islands, with peripheral constituents such as time and manner expressions being switched more frequently than those that are arguments of the verb (e.g., agent and object NPs). Myers-Scotton (1993b: 144) suggests the following implicational hierarchy. The implicational relationship is from bottom to top; for instance, if there are subject NPs as islands, there are also object NPs, and so on:

1 Formulaic expressions and idioms (especially as time and manner PPs but also as VP complements).
2 Other time and manner expressions (NP/PP adjuncts used adverbially).
3 Quantifier expressions (APs and NPs especially as VP complements).
4 Non-quantifier, non-time NPs as VP complements (NPs, APs, CPs).
5 Agent NPs.
6 Thematic-role and case assigners, that is, main finite verbs (with full inflections).

Treffers-Daller (1994: 226) suggests a similar hierarchy, though hers includes full clauses as well as islands. She also agrees that switches occur most frequently at "points that are loosely attached to the syntactic structure of the sentence" (ibid.: 234). As Myers-Scotton explains, since the central constituents carry the main weight of the sentence, it makes sense that they should appear either in ML islands or possibly ML+EL constituents (1993b: 144). This would explain why such constituents are switched less often. Treffers-Daller (1994: 234) also notes that bilinguals often resort to the strategy of fronting or dislocation to facilitate switching of core constituents such as Agent NPs, as in the following example from Dutch–French code switching (French in italics):

(82) *Les étrangers*, ze hebben geen geld
the strangers, they have no money
"The strangers, they don't have any money" (Treffers-Daller 1994: 207)

These strategies, as well as the hierarchy of switched constituents, suggest that switching is indeed sensitive to the subcategorization properties of ML heads, and that bilinguals have a clear sense of which constituents can be most easily switched without violating core ML rules.

Exercise 4
Discuss the extent to which (surface) congruence between structures in two languages facilitates code switching. Can Sankoff and Poplack's (1981) "equivalence constraint" be reformulated to account for switches based on such congruence? How well would such a revised constraint account for code switching in cases of typological mismatch? You can use data from studies such as Bentahila and Davies (1983), Pandit (1990), and others discussed in this chapter.

5.6 Further Issues

The study of code-switching phenomena has much to offer by way of providing more insight into all forms of bilingual language mixture and the constraints that regulate it. In particular, it has contributed much to our understanding of the notion of congruence, which is highly relevant to a wide range of contact phenomena, including borrowing, structural diffusion, and various kinds of L1 influence on an L2. However, much remains to be done before we achieve a better understanding of the relationships among these varied phenomena.

The notion of congruence and its role in determining different patterns of code switching need to be explored more fully across language pairs whose members show varying degrees of typological similarity. There is some evidence that different degrees of typological fit between the languages involved in code switching lead to different patterns of mixture. Poplack and Sankoff (1988) argue that similar typology leads to equivalence-based code switching (alternations) while conflicting typology leads to "nonce borrowings" (single-word switches) and/or "multi-word fragments" (EL islands). Muysken (1997c: 374) provides some empirical support for this. His survey of corpora from recent code-switching studies reveals that insertional code switching is more common in language pairs like Swahili–English and Tamil–English, whose members are typologically quite different. On the other hand, alternational code switching is more common in language pairs like Spanish–English, French–Dutch, and French–English, which are typologically more similar. We saw how, in the case of Spanish–English contact in New York City, the resulting code switching combines patterns of insertion and alternation to the point where it is difficult to separate the two. Here is another example from Pfaff (1979: 309):

(83) So *yo y un bunche de* guys – about twenty guys, and they were from the Ramar gang, *ellos vivían allá in Havlandale.*
"So I and a bunch of guys – about twenty guys, and they were from the Ramar gang, they lived there in Havlandale.

Recall that Muysken refers to this type of code switching as "congruent lexicalization," a type of mixture arising from code switching between languages which share a great deal of grammatical structure. Obviously, congruence in syntax is crucial in these cases. The real problem here is that one is unsure which language is being activated at a given time, since they share so much structure. But there are also cases involving typologically different languages where the mixture involves a combination of alternation and insertion, so this pattern may not be unique to typologically similar language pairs. Pandit (1990: 50–1) provides the following examples from her Hindi–English code-switching corpus:

(84) *Many* larake *interview* ke liye bulaaye gaye the *but nobody was found*
boys for called were
suitable is *job* ke liye
this for
"Many boys were called for this interview but nobody was found suitable for this job"

(85) *Life* ko *face* kiijiye *with* himmat *and faith in* apane aap
ACC do courage self
"Face life with courage and faith in self"

Both examples contain a combination of alternation and insertion, and the latter process involves both insertion of English elements into a Hindi structure (is *job* ke liye) and vice versa (*with* himmat, etc.). Clearly the problem of deciding between insertion and alternation is not restricted to pairs of typologically similar languages. The latter cases, however, do pose a greater problem for deciding language assignment.

Both the "interacting grammars" model of Sankoff and Poplack and the MLF model of Myers-Scotton and her associates would have problems generating these combinations of code-switching strategies – the former because it essentially neglects insertion, the latter because it says little about alternation. Clearly though, bilinguals' competence includes both kinds of ability, so the models of code switching should be seen as complementary rather than opposed to each other.

Finally, none of the models of code switching has so far accounted satisfactorily for certain kinds of innovation and restructuring in code-switching behavior. Phenomena such as "bare forms" and innovative compound verb constructions as well as certain types of structural convergence (discussed earlier) belong to neither of the languages in contact. Models of bilingual mixture must allow for the creative processes that generate such new structures. Furthermore, the same kinds of innovation can be found in other cases of language contact, thus raising the question whether similar processes and constraints are involved in all these situations. What unifies them is the fact that speakers in all these cases are exploiting both L1 and L2 knowledge to create innovative structures, whether these are new lexical entries or new structural patterns. Further examples of the creativity of bilinguals will be examined in the following chapter, which deals with new contact languages (so called bilingual mixed or intertwined languages) which have emerged as a result of code-switching behaviors.

5.7 Summary

The flexible and varied nature of code switching makes it difficult to characterize the phenomenon in absolute terms. It is clear that there are two broad patterns – one involving alternation of structures from two languages, the other insertion of elements from one language into the morphosyntactic frame of the other. Prototypical examples of the former are alternations between entire sentences, or entire clauses. Examples of the latter include cases in which single morphemes or phrases from language A are embedded into the structure of language B.

Different models of code switching have been proposed to account for these two broad types. Those that attempt to analyze alternational code switching propose a grammar that is a combination of the grammars of the languages involved. The code-switching grammar of Sankoff and Poplack (1981) is perhaps the best example of this approach. This model appeals to the notion of surface-level syntagmatic equivalence to constrain the kinds of alternation that occur. However, it is clear that this version of the equivalence constraint is inadequate to explain the alternations that do in fact occur across language pairs. A revised version of the constraint which appeals to congruence in categorial status and grammatical function would seem to be better suited to this task.

The dominant model of insertional code switching is the MLF model of Myers-Scotton and her associates. In this approach, code-switched utterances are seen as generated by a single grammar – that of the ML. To some extent, the grammar of the EL plays a role in determining what EL morphemes or structures can be substituted for their ML counterparts. The EL grammar appears to be more fully activated in switches involving phrases or islands. As Myers-Scotton (1993b: 36) notes, there is a "switching of procedures" from those of the ML to those of the EL in cases of EL island formation. In this model too, the notion of congruence between EL and ML elements is an essential aspect of the constraints on switching. Insertional code switching is highly sensitive to the subcategorization requirements of ML heads, whether these are verbs, prepositions, determiners, or other functional heads. As long as these ML subcategorization frames are preserved, single EL morphemes that match their ML counterparts in semantics and categorial status can be freely substituted for the latter. In fact, even functional items like prepositions, complementizers, etc. can be switched, provided their subcategorization properties match across the languages involved.

In addition, entire EL phrases, which may be maximal or partial projections of N, A, etc., can be switched, even though they may differ from equivalent ML phrases in their internal structure, provided once more that the switch does not violate the subcategorization frames of the relevant ML heads. Pandit (1990: 43) makes essentially this point when she notes that "code switching must not violate the grammar of the head of the maximal projection within which it takes place." This approach recognizes that switching of phrases is regulated by constraints similar to those that govern single-word switches.

Notes

1 Pandit (1990: 53) notes that "In fact, switching between the verb and the object NP is prolific in Hindi–English codeswitching as well as in Spanish–English codeswitching and codeswitching in general."

2 Myers-Scotton suggests that the reason "cell" is unmarked for locative case is that there is a subcategorization mismatch between Swahili *-ni* and English *in*, specifically, "*-ni*

picks out its head as a *general* locative noun, while *in* carries more specialized locative content" (1993b: 126). This argument is rather weak. It seems more likely, as she herself suggests, that the lack of marking here reflects the fact that (monolingual) Swahili does not mark locative case on certain borrowings such as *hospital*.

6
Bilingual Mixed Languages

6.1 Introduction

The previous chapter focused on bilingual mixture in situations where the two languages involved are maintained, and the mixed code itself has not achieved autonomy as a distinct language. We saw that code-switching phenomena in such situations constitute a continuum of outcomes ranging from relatively simple types of insertion to more complex types of alternation. Such patterns of mixture may persevere for generations without affecting the autonomy of the languages in contact. This seems to be the case in Brussels, Strasbourg, Nairobi, and similar communities.

Closely associated with such code switching is the emergence of "fossilized" mixed codes among bilinguals caught between two languages and their cultures. For instance, Abdulaziz and Osinde (1997) discuss two relatively stable codes, Sheng and Engsh, used by youths in Nairobi and other cities in Kenya. Sheng employs a Swahili morphosyntactic frame with lexicon from English, Swahili, and other mother tongues and is used primarily by less affluent slum dwellers. Engsh is based on English, with words from Swahili and other ethnic languages, and is used by more affluent youths. Other examples include Tsotsitaal and Isicamtho, which emerged in the Black urban townships of South Africa. Tsotsitaal is essentially non-standard Afrikaans with a significant mixture of English words, some Zulu words, and a great number of slang terms (Slabbert and Myers-Scotton 1996: 329). Among the young, especially males, Tsotsitaal has now given way to Isicamtho, which employs a Zulu (Nguni) morphsyntactic frame, with a heavy infusion of words from English and Afrikaans. Like Tsotsitaal, its lexicon includes a heavy component of slang, perhaps reflecting the origins of these vernaculars in the argot of criminals and prison inmates. Tsotsitaal translates literally as "the language of the hoodlums and thieves" (Childs 1997: 342).

All of the urban vernaculars mentioned above have the same social function of distinguishing their speakers as social groups with their own distinct identity.

They mark their speakers as "urban, hip and sophisticated" (Childs 1997: 344). Similar mixed codes also often arise among later generations of immigrants who are undergoing shift from their ancestral language to that of the host community. For instance, Agnihotri (1987: 108) describes the emergence of a mixed Panjabi–English code used among Sikh children in Leeds, England. The types of mixture range from use of a few English words in an otherwise Panjabi sentence to frequent alternations of Panjabi and English involving intricate patterns of mixture. Similarly, many persons of Hispanic descent in the United States employ mixed Spanish–English codes as an everyday vernacular and in-group language. Some of these have names of their own, such as "Tex-Mex" in Texas. Especially interesting is the argot known as Pachuco, also called Tirilí or Trilongo, used by gang members and others in cities like El Paso, Texas. Like Tex-Mex, it has a Spanish morphosyntactic base, with massive insertion of lexical items from English as well as underworld slang (Craddock 1981: 209).

Although they serve important functions as markers of group identity, these mixed codes have not generally achieved autonomy as distinct languages. Thus, Slabbert and Myers-Scotton (1996: 328) note that speakers of Tsotsitaal and Isicamtho do not think of them as unitary varieties that can be distinguished from Afrikaans, English, or Zulu.

In this chapter we will examine cases where bilingual mixture results in a new and autonomous creation – a bilingual mixed or "intertwined" language which is distinct from both of its sources, and usually not mutually intelligible with either. These new creations typically arise in situations of ongoing or completed language shift, though they do not all emerge at the same stage of the shift process, a fact which helps explain the differences in the nature and degree of mixture found in them. The styles of code switching found among immigrant groups who are acquiring the dominant language of their host community provide some interesting points of comparison with these new creations. Code-mixing patterns among these groups tend to develop in a certain order, or hierarchy, as follows (Backus 1996):

> simple insertions > more complex insertions > alternations > insertions in the other direction

This hierarchy shows some parallels with the continuum of intertwined languages that have been studied to date. On the one hand we find creations like Media Lengua which involve patterns of (massive) single-morpheme insertion from the L2 to the L1; at the other extreme we find creations like Anglo-Romani, with lexical insertions in the opposite direction, from L1 (Romani) into the L2 (English). Other creations might be placed at different points along this scale. Myers-Scotton (1999: 24) suggests a similar sequencing of bilingual code mixture in situations of shift. According to her, the first stage is characterized by classic code switching with the ancestral language as the matrix language; then a composite ML develops with the L2 contributing more and more of the grammatical apparatus; finally, there is a shift to the L2, which can in turn act as the ML for code switching. This scenario finds support in Nishimura's account of Japanese–English code switching, as discussed in the previous chapter, where fluent bilinguals use either language as the ML. The different patterns of code switching are also clearly related to cross-generational differences in the degree of proficiency achieved in the L2, as Bentahila and Davies (1992: 454) have shown. In their study, older Moroccans who are equally proficient in Arabic and French show a strong preference for inter-sentential alternation or for code switching in which French is the ML, with insertion of Arabic function words. By contrast, younger Moroccan bilinguals who are Arabic-dominant show a strong preference for intra-sentential code switching, with Arabic as the ML. If these tendencies are constant across bilingual situations, we would expect them to be reflected in the differences among the newly created mixed languages that arise at different stages of shift. As we shall see, the facts bear this out.

6.2 Definition and Classification

There is general consensus that bilingual mixed languages are composites of materials drawn from just two languages. In what are perhaps the prototypical cases, the grammar is derived primarily from one of the languages, and the lexicon primarily from the other. Examples include Anglo-Romani and Media Lengua (a blend of Spanish lexicon and Quechua grammar). However, the neat separation of grammar and vocabulary by respective source language is not found in all cases. There are cases where structural materials are derived from both sources, as in Michif, which combines French NP structure with Cree VP structure. Whatever the nature of the mixture might be, there is agreement that the resulting outcome is a new creation, distinct from either of its source languages.

It is generally easy to identify the sources of the components, particularly in cases where the source languages are typologically quite different, as in Media Lengua. But even in cases where the two languages are genetically related and hence typologically similar (e.g., Chindo, a blend of Malay and Javanese, both Austronesian, spoken by Paranakan Chinese in Indonesia), it is still possible to identify the precise sources of the components (see Dreyfuss and Oka 1979).

Thomason (1997c: 80) sums up the characteristics of bilingual mixed languages as follows:

- They evolve or are created in two-language contact situations.
- The setting involves widespread bilingualism on the part of at least one of the two speaker groups.
- In the resulting mixture the language material is easily separated according to the language of origin.
- There is little or no simplification in either component of the mixed language (reflecting the bilingualism of its creators).

There is somewhat less agreement on the classification of bilingual mixed languages and on the historical and linguistic processes involved in their creation. As we shall see, the two issues are related.

Thomason (1995) suggests a classification based simultaneously on sociohistorical and linguistic (structural) criteria. According to her, there are two broad categories of bilingual mixed languages. Category 1 is the language of a "persistent ethnic group" that has resisted total assimilation to a dominant language group, though subject to "overwhelming cultural pressure" (1995: 19). As a result, their language undergoes a long process of lexical and structural "borrowing" from the dominant language, resulting in pervasive, massive mixture in all components, and in the extreme cases, the replacement of large portions, or even all, of the inherited grammar. Examples of mixed languages with pervasive mixture though not total structural replacement include Kormakiti Arabic (an Araḅic–Greek mixture spoken in Cyprus), Asia Minor Greek (a Greek–Turkish mixture), and perhaps Wutun (a dialect of Chinese heavily influenced by Tibetan). Examples of mixed languages in which grammatical replacement has occurred include Caló (Romani lexicon with Spanish grammar), Anglo-Romani (Romani lexicon with English grammar), and Ma'a ('mixed' Cushitic–Bantu lexicon with mostly Bantu grammar).

Thomason's second category includes languages which emerge rapidly, often within a single generation, as the vernaculars of new social groups or communities that want a language of their own to symbolize their separate ethnic identity. Examples include Media Lengua, Michif, and Mednyj (Copper Island) Aleut. Structurally, these bilingual mixed languages differ from those in category 1 in that the latter show "across the board linguistic effects" while the former don't. In other words, languages in category 1 display evidence of heavy influence from the dominant group's language in all aspects of structure and grammar as well as lexicon. By contrast, languages in category 2 display a clear compartmentalization of components, or, as Thomason and Kaufman (1988: 107) put it, "categorial specificity of the structural borrowing." Thus Michif draws

Table 6.1 Thomason's (1995) classification of bilingual mixed languages

Examples	Sociohistorical characteristics	Linguistic processes
Category 1		
Kormakiti Arabic	Persistent ethnic group resisting assimilation to dominant group language	Pervasive linguistic influence from L2 on all aspects of the ethnic language
Asia Minor Greek	Overwhelming cultural pressure from dominant language	Massive replacement of L1 grammar
Ma'a and Anglo-Romani	Gradual long- term change; Language shift may or may not occur	Near-total replacement of L1 grammar
Category 2		
Media Lengua and Michif	Newly emerging social group which creates a language of its own as symbol of its identity	Clear compartmentalization of components from the two sources; structural features specific to a particular source
Mednyj Aleut	Abrupt creation, sometimes within a single generation	Structural components preserved more or less intact, with minor simplification or restructuring

its VP structure (almost) entirely from Cree, and its NP structure from French, and both components are more or less intact on all levels (phonology, lexicon, morphology, and syntax). Thomason's classification is presented in summary in table 6.1.

Bakker (1994) takes issue with Thomason and offers a quite different classification of bilingual mixed languages based, first, on the nature of the contact settings and the groups who created the mixed code and, second, on the nature of the mixtures that result. He challenges the validity of Thomason's category 1 and her view that some bilingual mixed languages arise as a result of extreme structural borrowing. In his view, a distinction should be made between languages like Kormakiti Arabic and Asia Minor Greek, which are the result of extreme structural diffusion from an external source language, and languages like Ma'a and Anglo-Romani. In Bakker's view, the latter are not the result of massive grammatical replacement in Thomason's sense, but rather arise via a process of "language intertwining," that is, the combination of the lexemes of one language with the grammatical system (phonology, morphology, syntax) of another (1994: 20). As Bakker notes, unlike "borrowing," his term does not suggest any direction of the process, but emphasizes the act of language creation. Only outcomes that arise in this way qualify as bilingual mixed languages in Bakker's classification. Hence creations like Anglo-Romani and Ma'a are essentially similar in their genesis and make-up to languages in Thomason's category 2 such as Media Lengua and Michif, though they may differ in terms of their sociohistorical background.

It seems justifiable to distinguish cases of extreme structural "replacement" from cases of language intertwining, even though both result in extreme mixture. As we saw in the previous chapter, languages like Asia Minor Greek, Wutun, etc. involve such pervasive mixture within every component of the grammar that it is well nigh impossible to separate the contributions from the source languages into neat discrete categories. Neither the lexicon nor (any component of) the grammar of these languages constitutes a homogeneous entity that derives primarily from one source. This contrasts with cases of language intertwining, where in general, the components are preserved relatively intact, and differ little from their counterparts in the source languages. This remains true even when the lexicon and/or the grammar are blends of material from different sources, as in Michif or Mednyj (Copper Island) Aleut (see section 6.7.3 below).

Henceforth, therefore, we will follow Bakker in restricting the designation "bilingual mixed" or "intertwined" languages only to those outcomes that satisfy the criteria just mentioned. We will use both of these designations to refer to these outcomes of language contact. Genetically, these mixed languages "cannot be classified as belonging solely to family A or solely to family B" (Bakker and Mous 1994: 5). Rather, they are related to both.

But even this definition has its problems. As Bakker and Mous (ibid.) suggest, the genetic classification of bilingual mixed languages "is a matter of degree, and it is not a priori clear what qualifies as a mixed language and what as a case of extreme borrowing." They suggest that the two types can be distinguished according to the extent of the lexical input from the L2 or external source language. First, in cases of extreme "borrowing", lexical borrowing never exceeds roughly 45 percent of the whole lexicon. In bilingual mixed languages, the proportion of "foreign" lexical elements is usually closer to or over 90 percent. Second, in extreme borrowing, foreign elements affect the core vocabulary only to a limited degree. In bilingual mixed languages, most of the core vocabulary tends to be from the external source language. In general, however, bilingual mixed languages are recognizable only if their history and their sources are known. Certain clues facilitate their identification. For example, the presence of sufficient bound morphology helps to establish that the source of the grammar is different from the source of the lexicon. Source languages are easier to identify when they are typologically distant, though some bilingual mixed languages arise from contact between genetically related languages (e.g., KiMwani

Table 6.2 Bakker's (1994: 24) classification of "intertwined" languages

Examples	Sociohistorical characteristics	Linguistic characteristics
Category 1		
Anglo-Romani, Caló, Callahuaya, Krekonika, etc.	Created by ex-nomadic groups who need a secret language; arise during shift from L1 to L2	L2 provides the grammar, L1 provides most of the lexicon
Category 2		
Michif, Island Carib, Chindo, Petjo, Javindo, Ilwana, etc.	Arise in mixed households with immigrant men and local women	Grammar derived from mothers' language (L1), lexicon from fathers' (L2)

(two Bantu languages) and Stedsk (two Germanic languages) (Bakker and Mous, ibid.)).

Bakker's (1994: 24) classification of bilingual mixed languages is given in table 6.2. He distinguishes two broad categories according to sociohistorical criteria, that is, the social settings and circumstances in which they arose. Category 1 includes languages created by settled ex-nomadic groups who need a secret language for communication among themselves, especially in the presence of strangers. Such languages typically have the lexicon of the original ethnic language and the grammatical system of the host language (1994: 24). Examples would include Anglo-Romani, Caló (a blend of Spanish grammar and Romani lexicon spoken in Spain), and other Romani-lexicon mixtures (see Boretzky and Igla 1994). Also included is Callahuaya, a mixture of mostly Puquina lexicon and Quechua grammar spoken by itinerant healers in Northwestern Bolivia (Muysken 1997b). A final example is Krekonika, a blend of Greek grammar and Arvanitika vocabulary, used as a secret language by masons of the Peloponnese in an area of Greece where Arvanitika used to be spoken (Konstantinopulos 1983). All of these outcomes seem to have originated in the last stages of shift from the original inherited language to the host language.

Category 2 includes languages which arise in mixed households involving men speaking language A who invade the territory of language B and marry local women (ibid.). Examples include Michif, Island Carib, Chindo, etc.

It's debatable whether Bakker's classification accounts adequately for all known cases of language intertwining. Presumably, Ma'a would fit into category 1, while Mednyj Aleut would fall into category 2, at least on sociohistorical grounds. Media Lengua might be included in category 2 on linguistic grounds, but not by the sociohistorical criteria (it didn't arise in mixed households). Note also that languages placed in different categories according to sociohistorical criteria may be quite similar in their make-up. For example, Island Carib (category 2) is a mixture of L1 lexicon and L2 grammar, similar to Anglo-Romani or Ma'a (category 1). It is clear that classifications of languages based on sociohistorical criteria do not match up exactly with those based on purely structural criteria. This reflects the fact that intertwined languages do not all conform to some ideal prototype, but rather constitute a varied assortment of outcomes, with different histories and structural characteristics. We will return later to the issues of genesis and structural change as they relate to these creations.

In the following sections, we will examine four well-known outcomes of language intertwining to provide some idea of the variety of ways in which two languages can combine to produce a new creation.

Exercise 1

Compare the classifications of bilingual mixed languages offered by Thomason (1995) and Bakker (1994). Which of their criteria do you find more satisfactory as a basis for the classification? Try to come up with your own (integrated) classification. Where would you place bilingual mixed languages like Sheng and Engsh (discussed earlier)?

6.3 Media Lengua

Media Lengua is among the best-known of the bilingual mixed languages and indeed is often taken as a prototypical exemplar of this class of contact vernaculars. The language is a blend of predominantly Quechua grammatical structure and Spanish-derived lexical forms that make up about 90 percent of the vocabulary (Muysken 1981a: 52). The language is spoken in several small towns or village communities in the central Ecuador highlands. It functions as an in-group language among Indian peasants, craftsmen, and construction workers, particularly among younger men who work in the nearby capital city Quito in industry and construction. One of the core communities where it is spoken is the town of San Miguel de Salcedo (or simply Salcedo) in the Cotopaxi province of Ecuador. Muysken (1997a: 374) notes that Media Lengua is the native language of younger adults and most children in the communities nearest to Salcedo. These villages are situated both geographically and culturally between the world of the urban centers in the valley and the Indian world of the mountain slopes (ibid.). Here Spanish is used for communication with the non-Indian world, Quechua for contact with the traditional Quechua-speaking mountain communities, and

Media Lengua for everyday interaction within the villages. Both culturally and linguistically, Media Lengua is "half-way between Quechua and Spanish" (Muysken 1981a).

The language appears to have come into being quite recently, perhaps between 1920 and 1940. Muysken explains its genesis as due to the fact that "acculturated Indians could not identify completely with either the traditional rural Quechua culture or the urban Spanish culture" (1981a: 75). Hence they created Media Lengua as a means of expressing their separate group identity. The same motivation appears to lie behind the emergence of intertwined languages in general.

6.3.1 Structural characteristics

Media Lengua (ML) emerged within the context of the long period of contact between Quechua (Q) and the colonial language, Spanish (Sp.), from the Spanish colonization of Ecuador around 1540 to the twentieth century. This contact led, as would be expected, to mutual lexical borrowing between the languages and to some degree of structural change in the second language varieties of Spanish acquired by native speakers of Quechua. It is clear, however, that Media Lengua is neither Quechua with heavy Spanish borrowing, nor Spanish subjected to substratum influence from Quechua. The language is a quite distinct creation, unintelligible to speakers of either of its source languages. The following are examples of Media Lengua sentences from Muysken (1981a: 68–9) that illustrate its unique blend of features. Spanish-derived items are italicized:

(1) a. ML: *Unu fabur*-ta *pidi*-nga-bu *bini*-xu-ni
one favor-ACC ask-NOM-BEN come-PROG-1sg
"I come to ask a favor"

b. Q: Shuk *fabur*-ta maña-nga-bu shamu-xu-ni
one favor-ACC ask-NOM-BEN come-PROG-1sg
"I come to ask a favor"

c. Sp.: Vengo para pedir un favor
I-come for ask-INF a favor

(2) a. ML: *No sabi*-ni-chu Xwan *bini*-shka-da
NEG know-1sg-NEG John come-NOM-ACC
"I don't know that John has come"

b. Q: Mana yacha-ni-chu Xwan shamu-shka-da
NEG know-1sg-NEG John come-NOM-ACC

c. Sp.: No sé que Juan ha venido
NEG I-know that John has come

As can be seen in these examples, Quechua grammar is preserved intact in Media Lengua, as reflected in the SOV word order and the rich array of verbal morphology, including affixes that mark topics, objects, person/tense, negation, subordination, and so on. On the other hand, the stems to which such suffixes are attached are Spanish-derived. However, it would be an oversimplification to say that Media Lengua consists of purely Quechua grammar with exclusively Spanish-derived stems. There are several respects in which the Quechua grammar has been modified, mostly under Spanish influence. Spanish-derived items include not just content items like nouns, verbs, adjectives, etc., but function items like prepositions and conjunctions as well as other closed-class items such as personal pronouns and question words. In addition, some stems are preserved from Quechua. On the whole, though, it is clear that Media Lengua is the result of the incorporation of Spanish phonological shapes into a Quechua morphosyntactic frame – a process that involved both adaptation of the Spanish elements to Quechua structure and some structural change in the Quechua grammar under Spanish influence.

6.3.2 Adaptation of Spanish items to Quechua structure

Muysken (1981a: 54–60) discusses several respects in which Spanish-derived items are adapted to Quechua patterns in phonology, morphology, and morphosyntax. First, Spanish sounds are replaced by their closest perceived Quechua counterparts – a process of phone substitution common in both borrowing and second language learning situations. The following are some examples of changes in vowels:

Spanish →	*Quechua*	*Examples*
e	i	*decir* > *dizi* "say"
o	u	*poder* > *pudi* "can, be able"
ie [ye]	i	*bien* > *bin* "well"; *siete* > *siti* "seven"

With regard to consonants, Spanish [v] changes to [b] as in *breve* > *brebe* "quickly." The voiced consonants [b, d, g], which are allophones of [p, t, k] respectively in Quechua, occur freely in Spanish-derived stems. Spanish intervocalic [s] becomes [z] in Media Lengua, as in *hacer* > *azi* "do, make." Spanish initial [fw] becomes [xw], as in *fuerte* > *xwerte* "strong."

The agglutinative morphology of Quechua allows suffixes to be attached to stems relatively freely, without morphophonemic alternations. Stems are easily isolatable from their suffixes, hence easily substitutable by corresponding Spanish forms. This makes for easy incorporation of both nouns and verbs, and explains why Media Lengua has been able to replace most Quechua open-class items with equivalent Spanish forms. For the most part, this process has had no impact on Quechua morphology. Spanish stems behave in all respects like Quechua stems and are fully integrated into the Quechua morphosyntactic frame.

Spanish forms are adapted in other ways. For instance, adverbs often undergo reduplication, as in the following example from Muysken (1997a: 384):

(3) *Yo*-ga *bin-bin* *tixi*-y-da *pudi*-ni
I-TOP well-well weave-INF-ACC can-1sg
"I can weave very well"

This appears to be an innovation in Media Lengua, since there is no equivalent pattern of reduplication in Quechua. Spanish forms have also undergone regularization and simplification of the sort found in informal second language learning. For instance Spanish irregular verbs are regularized, eliminating the morphological variation found in Spanish. Thus *dar* "give" is always realized as *da* in ML, whereas in Spanish it is realized in the present as *doy* (1st sing.), *das* (2nd sing.), *da* (3rd sing.), *damos* (1st pl.), *dais* (2nd pl.), and *dan* (3rd pl.), and also has different realizations in the past. Other verbs that have been simplified in this way include *ir* > *i* "go," *ver* > *vi* "see," *hacer* > *azi* "do, make," and *saber*> *sabi* "know." These stems remain invariant, with Quechua suffixes expressing differences in tense, number, person, etc. Other changes in Spanish forms include what Muysken calls "freezing," that is, the blending or fusion of separate Spanish words into a single Media Lengua word, as in the following examples:

(4)

Spanish	*Media Lengua*	*Meaning*
no hay	núway	"There is no . . ."
aún no	aúnu	"not yet"

Another instance of simplification of Spanish forms is to be found in the pronominal system. Muysken (1997a: 394) offers a comparison of personal pronouns in the three languages, shown in table 6.3.

Note how Media Lengua has eliminated all of the morphological irregularity in the Spanish pronouns, reducing each person to a single form in both singular and plural. Some of the Media Lengua pronouns are direct imports from Spanish (*yo*, *bos*, etc.) while others are combinations of Spanish forms and Quechua affixes (*bos-kuna*, *el-kuna*, etc.).

There have also been some interesting kinds of adaptation in Media Lengua derivational morphology, involving a compromise between Spanish and Quechua strategies. Quechua tends to use derivational suffixes to create new verbs from a

Table 6.3 Pronouns in Media Lengua and its source languages

Person	Quechua	Media Lengua	Spanish (nom./oblique)	
1sg.	ñuka	yo/ami + case	yo/me/mi	"I/me"
2sg.	kan	bos	tu/te/tí	"you (intimate)"
			vos/te	"you (familiar)"
			usted/le	"you (polite)"
3sg.	pay	el	él/le	"he/him"
			ella/le	"she/her"
1pl.	ñukunchi	nustru	nos(otros)	"we/us"
2pl.	kan-guna	bos-kuna	ustedes/les	"you (pl.)"
3pl.	pay-guna	el-kuna	ellos/les	"they/them (masc.)"
			ellas/les	"they/them (fem.)"

small set of roots, whereas Spanish tends to have separate verbal roots for the same concepts. The Quechua compositional forms are replaced in Media Lengua either by Spanish simplex forms, or by hybrids containing a Spanish root and the Quechua derivational suffix. Muysken (1981a: 59) offers the following illustration of the way concepts associated with the Quechua verb *riku-* "see" and its derived forms are represented in Media Lengua:

(5)	*Meaning*	*Quechua*	*Spanish*	*Media Lengua*
	"see"	riku-ø	ver	bi-
	"appear"	riku-ri	se ver	bi-ri-n
			asomar	asoma-
			aparecer	parisi-
	"show"	riku-chi	hacer ver	bi-chi
			mostrar	mustra(-chi)
	"stare"	riku-ra	espiar	bi-ra
			chapar "spy"	chapa(-ra)

Muysken (1997a: 388–93) discusses other examples of adaptation and compromise in semantics and structure in the Media Lengua lexicon.

Despite the massive incorporation of Spanish forms into Media Lengua, we find little evidence of the incorporation of Spanish morphology. The few exceptions include the gerundive suffix *-ndu* < *-ndo*, as in *trabajando* < *trabajar* "work"; the dimunitive suffix *-itu/ita*, as in *muchachito/a* < *muchacho/a* "boy/girl"; and the past participle *-do*, as in *trabajado* < *trabajar* "work." The latter two occur in Quechua as well. The dimunitive suffix is of course a derivational affix, and can be seen as a borrowing in both Quechua and Media Lengua.

Borrowing of derivational affixes is by no means rare or suprising. The past participial suffix *-do* appears only in Spanish adjectival forms (e.g., *cansado* "tired" < *cansar* "to tire") that were adopted as wholes. Hence this is not a case of borrowing of a productive inflectional morpheme. The gerundive suffix *-ndo*, on the other hand, appears to be a true structural borrowing, though its function in Media Lengua is modeled after that of the Quechua nomalizing suffixes *-sha* and *-kpi*, which are used as same subject and different subject subordinators respectively in Quechua embedded clauses. Examples of the former use in Quechua and Media Lengua are as follows (Muysken 1981a: 73–4):

(6) a. Q: Chaya-sha-mi miku-sha
arrive-NOM-AFFIRM eat-1stFUT
"I'll eat when I arrive"

b. ML: *el*-kuna-ga *asi nustru abla*-ri-k-ta-s *uye-ndu*-ga
3p-PLU-TOP thus we talk-REFL-NOM-ACC hear-NOM-TOP
aprendi-n
learn-3p
"They learn it when they hear what we speak"

There is also some incorporation of free Spanish function morphemes into ML. These include prepositions like *de* "of," *entre* "between, among," *por* "for," and others, as well as conjunctions like *pero* "but." These are exceptions to the general rule that only those lexical categories found in Quechua are to be found in Media Lengua. Quechua has only postpositions, and its conjunctions are clitics. Hence these borrowings do not follow the usual pattern of relexification, but rather introduce alternative case-marking and conjoining strategies on a limited scale. The Quechua case-marking and conjoining systems are preserved in the vast majority of cases.

Finally, Media Lengua syntax is overwhelmingly Quechua in character, with relatively little impact from Spanish. Like Quechua, Media Lengua is head-final, except for the few cases of prepositional borrowing mentioned above, and some instances of VXP order apparently due to Spanish influence. In some cases we also find Noun+Adjective order (as in Spanish) rather than the Adjective+Noun order of Quechua. Another minor change is found in comparative structures where the Quechua serial verb *yalli* "surpass" is relexified with Spanish *gana* "win," but the latter is uninflected, unlike the former. There has also been a slight change in embedded questions, where we find regular inflections on the verb instead of the Quechua strategy of nominalization. Media Lengua has also adopted a few Spanish complementizers (e.g., *ki* < *que* "that") and subordinators like *porque* "because" and *aunke* < *aun que* "even if," thus introducing a COMP-initial strategy as opposed to the COMP-final strategy found in Quechua. In general, however, Media Lengua preserves the Quechua system of nominal and adverbial marking of verbs as its subordination strategy in embedded clauses. The structural borrowings from Spanish remain marginal to the overwhelmingly Quechua character of Media Lengua syntax.

6.3.3 *Processes of change: the Relexification Hypothesis*

We might now consider what processes of contact-induced change were responsible for the creation of this language. Muysken (1981a: 61) proposed that Media Lengua arose via a process of "relexification – the process of vocabulary substitution in which the only information adopted from the target language in the lexical entry is the phonological representation." He distinguishes this process from "translexification," that is, "the process of vocabulary substitution in which, in addition to the phonological representation, all other levels of information are adopted from the target language as well" (ibid.). He notes that the boundaries between these two processes are quite fluid, and there is a continuum of possible results between the two. Lefebvre (1996: 234–5) suggests that relexification involves two steps – first, the copying of the lexical entries of an established lexicon (in this case the L1 of the creators), and second, the replacement of the original lexical entry's phonetic representation by a phonetic string drawn from another language. The process is illustrated in figure 6.1 (I have

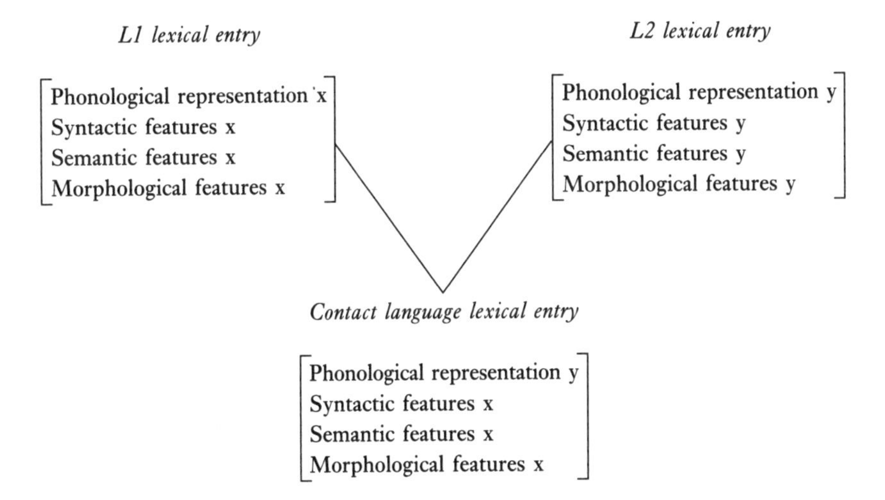

Figure 6.1 The process of relexification
Note: Syntactic features include information about category membership and, where relevant, subcategorization properties.

adapted Muysken's (1981a: 61) and LeFebvre's (1996: 235) illustrations somewhat).

The characteristic features of Media Lengua are in keeping with the view that the language was created by Quechua-dominant bilinguals. They simply relabeled the majority of Quechua content items with Spanish phonetic shapes, while retaining the Quechua morphosyntactic apparatus more or less intact. This strategy of L1 retention with incorporation of L2 lexical forms is of course common to many cases of bilingual mixture, including cases of lexical borrowing and intra-sentential code switching. More specifically, the incorporation of Spanish forms into a Quechua morphosyntactic frame in Media Lengua parallels the insertion of single morpheme switches into a matrix language frame that we find in many cases of intra-sentential code switching. What distinguishes Media Lengua is the scope of incorporation of external lexical forms, and the way they are made to conform in almost all respects to the working of Quechua grammar. The limited structural borrowing from Spanish into ML grammar is also in keeping with the view that Quechua was the matrix language.

As we will see in section 6.6 below, there are other intertwined languages with a pattern of mixture quite similar to that of Medial Lengua, except that they involve insertions from the ancestral language into the morphosyntactic frame of the newly acquired language. But first, let us consider a bilingual mixed language that displays a very different pattern of mixture.

Exercise 2

Consider the following sentences from Abdulaziz and Osinde (1997: 55, 59). Example (a) is Sheng, with a Swahili ML frame and some English words (E). (My sincere thanks to David Odden for providing me with a full gloss and translation for this sentence.) Example (b) is Engsh, with an English ML frame and some words from Swahili (S) and Kikuyu (K). Compare the patterns of mixture in these examples with that in Media Lengua. What similarities and differences do you find?

a. Woyee tichee u-si-ni-ruand-e
   Exclam. teacher (E) 2sg-NEG-me-beat-SUBJ;
   buu ndio i-li-ni-leit-isha
   bus it-is cl.9-PAST-1obj-late(E)-CAUS
   "Hey, teacher, don't beat me, it is the bus that made me late"

b. I will be gothie-ing rurayas moros.
   I will be go(K)-ing abroad (S) tomorrow (E)
   "I will be going abroad tomorrow"

6.4 Michif

Michif is another well-known and well-documented bilingual mixed language which combines, roughly speaking, Plains Cree VP structure with (Métis) French NP structure, though, as we shall see, this is somewhat of an oversimplification. The language apparently arose sometime during the early nineteenth century as a result of contact between mostly French-speaking European men and Indian women in the Red River area, near present-day Winnipeg in the province of Manitoba, Canada.

6.4.1 Sociohistorical background

The history of this contact situation goes back to the beginnings of the colonization of Canada by the British in the later seventeenth century. The British Hudson Bay Company (HBC) established trading posts on the eastern and western shores of Hudson Bay some time between 1668 and 1725. Sustained contact between the Europeans and the Indians increased during the period 1731 to 1753, when fur-trading posts managed by groups of 20–30 men were established. Most of these men apparently came from Scotland and spoke varieties of Scots English and Gaelic. There are no records of any contact vernaculars used by them for trading with the Indians. In 1784, the North West Company (NWC) was founded, and its employees were mostly speakers of French who served as guides, interpreters, canoe-men, servants, and the like, and especially as traders. The takeover of the NWC by the HBC in 1821 forced many NWC employees to settle in the Red River area. These French voyagers and traders cohabited with Cree women, producing a new population of mixed racial descent, referred to as Métis, a modern French term that means a person of mixed race, a mestizo. The term Métis itself is derived from Older French Métif/Mitif, from which Michif ([mitʃif]) – the name of the language – is derived (Bakker 1994: 14).

The Métis today number around 100,000 and live in various rural and urban communities in Manitoba and other Canadian provinces west of it, as well as in North Dakota, Montana, and Oregon in the United States. Most Métis speak only English, though some also speak Indian languages like Plains Cree and Ojibwe, and many in Canada speak French. According to Bakker (1994: 14), speakers of Michif today number perhaps 1000, though the Métis themselves put the number as high as 5000. Bakker (1997: 3) suggests that the number of speakers was probably several thousands around the year 1900, though never much higher than this. The language is spoken in scattered communities in

Manitoba and Saskatchewan (Canada) as well as North Dakota and Montana (USA), with pockets of speakers elsewhere. Most Michif speakers are over 60 years of age, and the language is no longer being acquired as a first language.

Bakker (1997: 13) argues that Michif arose as an expression of the separate identity of the Métis, who viewed themselves as a new people of mixed ancestry. Other cases involving cohabitation between groups of men and women speaking different languages have produced similar bilingual mixtures that serve as the language of the descendants of such unions. Examples include the Island Caribs (Arawak mothers and Carib fathers), the Krojos (Javanese mothers, Dutch fathers), and the Griekwas and Basters of South Africa (Khoekhoes mothers and Afrikaans fathers). (See Bakker 1997: 206–8 for discussion.) The creation of Michif seems to have been brought about especially by the coming together of Métis who traveled west from Manitoba to engage in bison hunting after 1821. The Métis apparently started to regard themselves as a distinct people in the 1820s, and according to Métis oral tradition, the Michif language was already in use between 1820 and 1840 (Bakker 1997: 26). Some of the communities in which Michif is spoken today may well have been first established as winter camps for buffalo hunting. Bakker (1997: 190) suggests that Michif may have originated between 1812 (the emergence of a separate ethnic identity of the Métis) and 1820 (the beginning of the large bison hunts).

6.4.2 Sources of Michif structure

As noted earlier, the source languages of Michif are Métis French and Plains Cree. The former contributed most (roughly 90 percent) of the nouns as well as the NP structure, while the latter contributed practically all of the verbs and their inflections, along with grammatical categories such as question words, personal pronouns, postpositions, and so on. The following piece of a narrative recorded by Bakker (1997: 78) in Brandon, Manitoba, illustrates the nature of the mixture. French items are italicized:

(7) e:gwanıgi *li: sava:z* ki:pa:ʃamwak *la vyâd*
they the Indians dried the meat
la vjâd ɔrıja:l, la vjâdi ʃovrø, tut ki:pa:ʃamwak
the meat moose, the meat-of deer, all they-dried it
da: dibčca:k ki:a:ʃta:wak mana
in little-bags they-put-it usually
"These Indians dried the meat. Moose meat, deer meat, they dried it all. They used to put it in little bags."

Table 6.4 Sources of grammatical categories of Michif

Category	Source languages
NP elements	
Nouns	94% French; rest from Cree, Ojibwe, and English
Adjectives	All from French, but Cree noun-modifying strategies often used
Articles	French
Numerals	Almost all French
Demonstratives	Almost all Cree
Personal pronouns	Almost all Cree
VP elements	
Verbs	88–99% Cree; a few French verbs; some mixed Cree and French verbs
Copulas	Some French, but Cree copula constructions predominate
Negation	Roughly 70% French, 30% Cree
Function Items	
Question words	Almost all Cree
Postpositions	Almost all Cree
Prepositions	70–100% French; 5% English
Co-ordinating conjunctions	55% Cree; 40% French; 5% English
Adverbial particles	70% Cree; 30% French
Discourse particles	Mostly Cree

Table 6.4, adapted from Bakker (1997: 117) provides a summary of the sources of Michif grammatical categories. (I have amended his table somewhat by including categories like articles, adjectives, and copulas that were omitted in the original.)

6.4.3 *Phonology*

The rough division between French NP and Cree VP structure in Michif is reflected in quite separate phonological systems associated with each component. The pronunciation of French NP elements is typically that of Michif French. On the other hand, Southern Plains Cree phonological units and rules are faithfully preserved in the Cree component. There are minor differences such as the presence of nasal vowels in Michif but not in Plains Cree, and the use of /č/ and /ʃ/ in Michif where Plains Cree has /c/ and /s/. Fuller details can be found in Bakker (1997: 80–6) and Bakker and Papen (1997: 307–12). On the whole, the French and Cree phonological systems are independent of each other, though there is evidence of some Cree influence on the French system, involving mid-vowel raising, assimilation of sibilants, and vowel length (Bakker and Papen 1997: 311). The co-existence of two separate phonological systems parallels the co-existence of two distinct subsystems of grammar in Michif, making this language unique among contact vernaculars.

6.4.4 NP structure

As table 6.4 shows, Michif nouns, articles, and quantifiers are mostly derived from French, though Cree has provided some quantifiers, while some nouns are from English, Ojibwe, or Cree. Demonstratives all come from Cree (except for a few French demonstratives in frozen expressions). This is related to the fact that Cree demonstratives play a key role in the syntax, since they express distinctions between animate and inanimate gender. All French nouns in Michif are assigned to one or the other of these genders, and the demonstratives agree in gender and number with them, as in Cree. Interestingly, the French gender system is also preserved in the Michif NP, hence Cree demonstratives are accompanied by either a French possessive or article which must agree in French gender (masculine/feminine) and number with the noun. The following examples from Bakker and Papen (1997: 328) illustrate (French items in italics):

(8) a. awa *lɨ* *garsũ*
DEM the-masc. boy
"this boy"
b. awa *la* *fij*
DEM the-fem. girl
"this girl"
c. u:ma *la* *bwet*
DEM the-fem. box
"this box"

In addition, the verb is marked for agreement in animacy/inanimacy with its subject and/or object. Further details of Michif NP structure can be found in Bakker (1997).

Exercise 3
Compare the structure of the Michif noun phrases in (8) with that of noun phrases containing demonstratives in Arabic–French code switching (Bentahila and Davies 1983), as discussed in chapter 5. What similarities and differences do you find?

6.4.5 VP structure

The VP of Michif is essentially that of Plains Cree, with only minor incursions from French. For instance, some French and a few English verbal stems are integrated into the Cree verbal morphology, while a few French verbs occur with French inflections. An example of the former is the following, from Bakker and Pappen (1997: 318):

(9) *Lɨ pɛ:r* ki:-*lɨ*-*bɨn*-w *lɨ mûd*
ART priest PAST-ART-bless-INF-TA.3→3 ART people
"The priest blessed the people"

In general, though, Cree verbal paradigms are well preserved in Michif. There are four stem classes divided according to animacy and transitivity (animate transitive and intransitive; inanimate transitive and intransitive), each with different inflections for subject/object, and often different stem forms too. The morpheme order of the Cree verb is also faithfully preserved in Michif. For instance, tense/aspect distinctions are expressed by prefixes, while "preverbs" express notions like "start" and "try" as well as adverbial notions like "strongly." Suffixes express distinctions of voice/valency and person/number agreement, among others. Here are some more examples from Bakker (1997: 87, 93):

(10) Ki:wanɪst-a:w *li žwal su liku*
PAST-lose.it-3→4 the horse his halter
"The horse lost his halter"

(11) *Li nasjũ æ̃ træti* aja:-w-ak nu SI-nutɪn-ɪto-čik
DEF nation INDEF treaty have-3sobj-PL NEG COMP-fight-RECIP-3pl
"Nations have treaties not to fight each other"

Michif also preserves the Cree distinction between two main orders in the verb complex (that is, different verb forms) – the independent order, used in main clauses, and the conjunct order, used in embedded clauses and in *wh*-questions. The marking of negation and person agreement differs in these two orders.

Copular-type constructions in Michif are also predominantly Cree in character, lacking copula verbs. Ascriptive constructions (the equivalent of predicate adjective structures) employ stative verbs, as in (12) below, or a verbalized French noun to which the suffix -ɪwɪ is attached, as in example (13) below (Bakker and Papen 1997: 338). Equative constructions consist of a nominal predicate followed by a Cree demonstrative, as in (14) below (ibid.: 379). However, some copula constructions are more French in character, employing a French copula derived from inflected forms of *être* "to be," with cliticized pronouns, as in (15) below (ibid.: 339):

(12) *La bwɛt* mɪša:-w
ART box be.big-INAN.INTR-3p.
"The box is big"

(13) *La-pusjɛr*-iw-an *lɨ pɔrtmãtũ*
ART-dust-be-INTR ART suitcase
"The suitcase is dusty"

(14) *Ma tãt* ana
my aunt DEM.ANIM.sg.
"That's my aunt"

(15) e:waku *la rɔb ilɨ kwarɛk*
that ART dress COP correct
"That dress is appropriate"

This brief overview fails to convey the full complexities of Michif/Cree VP structure, fuller details of which can be found in Bakker (1997: 97–100) and the references he provides.

6.4.6 *Syntax of Michif*

Word order in Michif is based on Cree, and is rather free, though it tends to conform more to French SVO order when more French elements are used. Grammatical relations in the sentence are marked by affixes on the verb. Complex sentences generally follow Cree patterns of subordination, for example in relative clauses, embedded questions, and complement clauses. However, adverbial clauses are often introduced by French subordinating conjunctions (e.g., *akuz* "because," *apre* "after," etc.) which control a Cree conjunct clause, as in the following example (Bakker and Papen 1997: 342):

(16) *Nu* pe:ht-am *akuz* e:-pa:kɪ-paym-ɪyɪ-k *su zaraj*
NEG hear-TI.3→4 because COMP-thick-become-PS-II.4 his ear
"S/he doesn't hear it because of an ear infection"

As we saw earlier, Michif has adopted other function morphemes from both Cree and French. Thus prepositions are from French while postpositions are from Cree. Interrogative pronouns and adjectives are generally Cree. Adverbs, negators, and co-ordinators tend to be drawn from both source languages.

6.4.7 *Convergence and innovation in Michif*

It should be clear from the above sketch that Michif is not simply a blend of pure French NP structure with pure Cree VP structure. Both components have been subject to varying degrees of modification, as we would expect in a language contact situation. First, some aspects of the Cree VP have been changed under French influence. For instance, some French (and a few English) verb stems have been incorporated and adapted to Cree verb morphology, while a few French verbs are conjugated as in French (Bakker and Papen 1997: 317). Michif also employs French nouns or adjectives to create property-denoting stative verbs (by attaching the suffix *-ɪwɪ*) or transitive verbs (by attaching the suffix *-ɪhke*: "to make"). French copulas have also been incorporated into Michif, as have a variety of function morphemes, as mentioned above. Finally, French has exerted considerable influence on the system of modality and on impersonal constructions in Michif.

In the second place, the French-derived NP structure of Michif has undergone some modification under Cree influence. While French is the source of most nouns as well as articles and possessives, demonstratives are all Cree and agree in animacy with their nouns according to Cree rules. Quantifiers are derived from both French and Cree. Although many adjectives have been incorporated from French, Michif still favors the Cree strategy of using relative clauses to express property concepts (Cree lacks adjectives). Possessive and genitive constructions follow Cree word order, even when French possessives are used, as in the following example (Bakker and Papen 1997: 347):

(17) *Joe* u-ma:ma:-wa ki:-apɪ-w *dã la šãbr*
Joe his-mother-OBV PAST-sit-3p in ART room
"Joe's mother was sitting in the parlor"

Michif also distinguishes between alienable and inalienable possession, like Cree and unlike French. Finally, the French NP component of Michif has lost several semantic distinctions made in French, including the count versus mass noun distinction and that between definite and indefinite plurals. Gender distinctions, while retained for nouns, have been lost in pronouns and verb clitics as well as in post-nominal (though curiously not pre-nominal) adjectives. These changes explain why Michif NP structure, while basically French in syntax, is essentially Cree in its semantics (Bakker 1997: 239).

To sum up, then, the overall pattern of mixture in Michif is one in which "the grammatical and bound elements are Cree, and the lexical and free elements are French" (Bakker 1997: 233). A variety of processes of contact-induced change were involved in this language intertwining. In the first place, we have the overall blending of French NP structure with Cree VP structure. Any attempt to explain Michif origins must account for how this particular combination of components occurred. Furthermore, the modifications that each of these components underwent must also be explained. Unfortunately, there is still some disagreement over the mechanisms of change responsible for this outcome.

Exercise 4
Compare the kinds of language mixture found in Media Lengua and Michif with those found in the code mixing of Japanese–English bilinguals as described by Nishimura (1986, or 1997: 95–114). What similarities and differences do you find? See the discussion of Nishimura's data in chapter 5.

6.4.8 *Mechanisms and processes in the genesis of Michif*

Scholars have debated whether Michif is the product of code switching, structural borrowing, relexification, or some other process such as "language intertwining." None of these terms seems to account adequately for the genesis of the language. The problem seems to reside in a failure to distinguish the actual mechanisms of change involved from their manifestations as different kinds of bilingual mixture.

For instance, the fact that Michif is reminiscent of some kinds of code switching simply implies that its creation involved processes similar to those that produce code-switching behavior. As we saw in the previous chapter, code switching itself is not a "mechanism" but rather a form of behavior in which certain strategies of mixture come into play. There is a similar problem with the concept of "language intertwining," mentioned earlier, which Bakker (1994: 24) defines as a distinct process in its own right. But this label just describes the outcome, not the processes involved, and does not account for the very different patterns of structural and lexical mixture that are found in different intertwined languages.

The notion of "relexification" also seems ill-suited to explain the mechanisms of Michif formation. The term is more appropriate for the process of single morpheme insertion into a maintained ML frame that we saw in Media Lengua. However, there are parallels between Michif and other patterns found in code switching. The incorporation of French NPs and PPs into the Cree morphosyntactic frame of Michif is similar to constituent or EL island insertion. The main difference is that Michif restricts this process to French NPs (and some prepositional phrases), and of course applies it consistently, at least for NPs. But even this account is somewhat simplistic, since French NP structure is not imported intact, but modified so as to conform to Cree morphosyntax and semantics.

There is also the question why this particular pattern of insertion, so different from that in Media Lengua, is found in Michif. What motivates the incorporation of French elements into Cree NP structure, rather than its VP structure? Bakker (1997: 224ff) suggests that the typological relationship between French and Cree can explain this. Whereas French is inflectional, Cree is a polysynthetic language with simple noun derivation and highly complex verbal structure. Since neither Cree nor French noun morphology is very complex, and since noun stems can be easily isolated in both, this facilitates the substitution of Cree noun stems by their French counterparts. The latter can therefore take Cree nominal affixes.

As we saw in chapter 5, the primary constraints on this kind of constituent substitution are, first, there must be congruence of function between the relevant constituents and, second, the subcategorization requirements of the relevant ML heads must be met. So, while Michif may not appear identical to the products of intra-sentential code switching, the mechanisms and constraints involved in both kinds of mixture appear to be the same.

By contrast, Cree verbs are highly complex in structure, consisting only of bound grammatical elements. This applies even to verb roots, which cannot be isolated easily. The following example from Bakker (1997: 228) illustrates (AN = animate; REC = reciprocal):

(18) nôhtê-wâp-am-ito-w-ak
want-look-AN-REC-3-PL
"They want to see each other"

It is difficult to separate stems from affixes here. Even apparent roots like *-wâp-* never occur in isolation. Hence it is difficult to identify a specific stem that might be substituted with a French verb (Bakker 1997: 229).

Here is another example from Bakker (ibid.: 230), illustrating a complex verbal form with initial, medial, and final elements (3→3 = 3rd p. subject, 3rd p. object):

(19) mihkw-âpisk-isw-êw
INIT-MED-FINAL-INFL
red-stone-by.heat-3→3
"He makes the stone red hot"

Here again, even the stems themselves are combinations of bound forms that are not easily substitutable by French forms. The very different typological structure of the Cree VP would therefore constitute a strong barrier to the incorporation of French elements. This explanation is supported by the fact that similar constraints seem to operate in other cases of contact between Algonquian languages similar to Cree and European languages like English and French. Bakker (1997: 181f) discusses instances of Cree–English and Naskapi–English code mixing from Saskatchewan and Montréal (Quebec) respectively. He notes that they all display a similar pattern of insertion of English nouns, noun phrases, and prepositional phrases into the Algonquian frame, with the VP left intact. This is also true of the pattern of Montagnais–French code mixing found in the community of Betsiamites, Quebec. In this case, however, French verbs are also incorporated, along with French nouns, prepositions, etc. The verbs are inserted as infinitival forms that combine with a helping verb *-tut-* "do," which bears all necessary inflections. This strategy is quite common in borrowing and code-switching behavior, as we saw in chapter 5. Its occurrence in Montagnais–French code mixing suggests that the strong structural constraints on the incorporation of verbs that we mentioned earlier can be overridden.

In general, all these examples suggest that contact involving different pairs of languages with similar typological distance will lead to similar patterns of mixture (Bakker 1997: 186). Presumably this is because the same constraints apply in all cases.

Finally, there is a need to account for the modifications in French NP structure as well as the intrusion of some French structural apparatus into the Cree syntactic frame of Michif. The processes involved in the first case seem quite similar to those that characterize the integration of elements introduced into a recipient language from a foreign source. Similarly, the incorporation of French function morphemes such as prepositions, copulas, modals, etc. has parallels in both "borrowing" and code-switching behavior. All of these French elements are free forms that could easily be accommodated within the Cree grammar. This is in keeping with the view that Michif was created by Cree–French bilinguals who inserted French elements into a maintained Cree grammatical frame.

6.5 Creations Associated with Language Shift

The cases we have examined so far all involve maintenance of basic L1 structure, with incorporation of features from an external source. But several bilingual mixed languages appear to have arisen after a process of shift in which an original ethnic language is replaced by a host language. The newly acquired host language is then used as the grammar-source or matrix language into which (mostly) lexical material is incorporated from the original ethnic language, thus creating a new intertwined language. Many of the languages that arose in this way were created by nomadic groups who used them either as secret in-group languages or as symbols of their separate ethnic status. As noted earlier, they include Anglo-Romani and other mixed Romani varieties such as Caló and Armenian Romani, as spoken by various Roma or Gypsy groups; Ma'a or Mbugu; Krekonika and Callahuaya. Other intertwined languages have been documented for nomadic groups in Afghanistan, Ireland, and Scotland (Hancock 1984), India, the Middle East (Kenrick 1976–7), and elsewhere.

The genesis of these shift-induced mixed languages has also been the subject of some disagreement. Some researchers (e.g., Thomason 1995) attribute their formation to massive grammatical borrowing or replacement. Others (e.g., Boretzky 1985) argue that they arose when the ethnic group shifted to the language of the host community but retained most of the vocabulary of their original language. Before we decide on the merits of either position, let us examine one such outcome, the language known as "Ma'a" or "'inner' Mbugu."

6.6 The Case of Ma'a

Ma'a is spoken in several communities in the Usambara mountains of Northeastern Tanzania by groups who migrated to the region several hundred years ago. Almost all of its grammar is Bantu, and closely similar to that of Pare, a neighboring language spoken by immigrants from the Pare mountains. Roughly half of its lexicon comes from (mostly) Southern Cushitic, while the rest is drawn from Bantu languages. The group refers to itself as the Ma'a – a term which is also used for the mixed language they speak. Outsiders refer to them as the Mbugu, which is also the name of the Bantu language they speak. Ma'a, or in-group (inner) Mbugu, is identical to Mbugu except for the lexicon and some minor structural differences.

6.6.1 Historical background

Oral tradition has it that the Mbugu were originally from Lukipya (present-day Lackipya in Kenya). To escape harassment by the Masai, they apparently migrated to the northern Pare mountains, then to the south Pare mountains, from where many later moved to the Usambara mountains. It is generally agreed that the Mbugu originally spoke some variety of (Southern?) Cushitic, and preserved it for a long time before shifting to Pare (or in some cases to Shambaa, the dominant language of the Usambara region). Those who call themselves Ma'a apparently resisted assimilation longest, and created a mixed language as a sign of their resistance and their autonomy as a distinct ethnic group. The language is considered incomprehensible by their neighbors.

6.6.2 Structural features

6.6.2.1 Lexicon

Roughly half of Ma'a's lexicon is Cushitic, according to Ehret (p.c.) cited in Thomason (1997b: 475). The basic vocabulary is primarily Cushitic, and much of its cultural vocabulary also comes from that source. The rest of the vocabulary is drawn from different Bantu languages such as Pare, Shambaa, and Swahili, as well as from Maasai of the Eastern Nilotic family, and includes many verbs, some body parts, and cultural words. In certain semantic fields such as color, the lexical semantics of Bantu-derived words is Cushitic. This particular pattern of intertwining of basic and cultural vocabulary from two primary sources is probably unique among bilingual mixed languages.

6.6.2.2 Grammar

The combination of Bantu grammar and Cushitic vocabulary typical of Ma'a is illustrated in the following example from Mous (1994: 176). Non-Bantu items are in italics (APL = applicative; IT = "Itive"; F = final vowel):

(20) hé-*ló* i-*ʔazé* i-wé áa-*sé* va-*maʔa* na va-sitá na
16-have 5-day 5-one 1:PAST-call 2-Mbugu with 2-Shambaa with
va-*ʔariyé* vá-*so* vá-zé-m-hand-í-ya ma-*gerú* *kuʔu*
2-Pare 2:SUBJ-go 2:SUBJ-IT-01-plant-APL-F 6-bananas his
"On a certain day, he called the Mbugu, Shambaa and Pare people to go and plant his banana trees."

It seems clear from this example that Ma'a is for the most part structurally identical to Mbugu, which in turn is practically identical to Pare. The exceptions are minor, and generally marginal to the grammar. In most cases, these non-Bantu structural elements derive from Cushitic. For instance, the phonemic inventories of Ma'a and Mbugu are identical except for a few non-Bantu phonemes in the former. These include voiceless lateral fricative /hl/, the glottal stop /ʔ/, the voiceless velar fricative /x/, and the complex sound /n̥x/ (voiceless nasal + voiceless velar fricative). As might be expected, these are found only in Ma'a words of non-Bantu origin (Mous 1994: 197).

Ma'a nouns and verbs have all of the inflectional and derivational morphology of Pare, again with minor differences. For example, many Cushitic-derived nouns lack a noun-class prefix, while both Ma'a and Mbugu have a noun class (14: 2) which Pare lacks. Some Ma'a verbs ending in *-a* fail to inflect the final vowel, unlike Mbugu and Pare.

Some of the closed classes of Ma'a show more significant non-Bantu influence. There are three non-Bantu demonstratives that show no agreement with their nouns, unlike those in Mbugu. The precise source of these forms is unclear. Ma'a also has different personal and possessive pronouns than Mbugu. Moreover, possessives fail to show agreement in Ma'a as they do in Mbugu. One or two pronominal forms show some slight resemblance to forms in Cushitic languages, but in most cases a specific source language cannot be established. Note, however, that despite the formal differences, both demonstratives and personal pronouns in Ma'a show the same semantic distinctions as those in Mbugu, differing somewhat in that respect from Cushitic languages.

Ma'a syntax generally follows Bantu patterns, with SVO and noun–adjective order, as well as prepositions, where Cushitic has dominant SOV and adjective–noun order and postpositions. Interestingly, some Ma'a prepositions (e.g., *he* "to" and *na* "from") derive from Cushitic lexical items. In cases where Bantu and Cushitic are typologically similar, Ma'a may employ constructions from both. This is true of genitive and copula constructions, for example. The copula is obligatory in Ma'a, following Cushitic and unlike Bantu, which frequently omits this marker. Other Ma'a features due to Cushitic influence include its large class of adjectives (Bantu has few of these) and the use of a verb *-lo* "have" to express possession. For the latter, Bantu uses a pronoun-connective combination (e.g., *a-na* "he-with") in present contexts, and a form "to be with" for other tenses/aspects (Thomason 1983a: 214–16).

Finally, several derivational suffixes in Ma'a are of Cushitic origin. Some of these are apparently still productive, such as causative *-ti* (attached to verbs) and "amplicative" *-ʃa* (attached to both nouns and verbs) (Thomason 1983a: 214). Others have ceased to be productive, while a few survive as fossilized forms. At the same time, however, many Bantu affixes have become part of the Ma'a derivational system (ibid.).

Exercise 5

Thomason (1983a: 218) offers a more detailed account of the similarities and differences between Ma'a, Bantu' and Cushitic. Make your own list of these and decide to what extent the features peculiar to Ma'a might be attributed to L1 influence under shift as opposed to borrowing. How far do they provide evidence for Thomason's claim that Ma'a arose through a process of "massive grammatical replacement"?

6.6.3 The genesis of Ma'a

The various non-Bantu structural elements described here have been the focus of a continuing debate over Ma'a origins. As noted earlier, some scholars (e.g., Thomason 1997a, 1997b) explain its genesis as the result of gradual but massive structural "borrowing" or replacement (similar to Asia Minor Greek), with maintenance only of core Cushitic vocabulary. I suggest below (section 6.7.3) that Copper Island Aleut is a better point of comparison with Asia Minor Greek. Others (e.g., Bakker 1994: 24) argue that Ma'a arose as a result of the intertwining of a Bantu grammatical system and Cushitic vocabulary. This suggests that the language originated in a way similar to languages like Media Lengua, except that the matrix language in this case was a newly acquired L2, rather than the group's ancestral language.

Thomason (1997b: 481–3) uses the evidence of Cushitic structural features and core vocabulary as well as what appear to be chronologically ordered changes in Ma'a to support her view that the language arose via gradual Bantuization of a previously Cushitic grammar. She finds further support for this scenario in Whiteley's (1960: 96) observation that the Bantu affix system is better established among the younger people than the older generation. But neither piece of evidence seems sufficient. The Cushitic structural features could just as well be explained as L1 retentions which accompanied the shift to Bantu. In other words, the shift may have produced an imperfectly learnt second language variety of Bantu with some degree of substratum influence from Cushitic. If we assume that it was this variety of Bantu (Pare) that served as the grammar-source language for the initial creation of Ma'a, the Cushitic retentions can be explained (as well as perhaps the inter-generational differences in the use of the Bantu affix system). Younger people's greater use of these affixes would then be due to continuing contact with Bantu and more successful learning of its structure.

In short, all of the non-Bantu structural features in Ma'a are consistent with what might be expected in a case of language shift. Some (like the loss of agreement in demonstratives and possessives) are simplifications, while others (like the actual forms of demonstratives and pronouns as well as the non-Bantu phonemes) appear to be retentions from Cushitic. The interweaving of Cushitic vocabulary with Bantu grammar, on the other hand, seems to have been the result of a process of content morpheme insertion ("relexification") similar to that found in other bilingual mixtures like Media Lengua and Anglo-Romani. This appears to offer the most feasible explanation for the genesis of Ma'a. In other words, the language was created at the point where the shift to a Bantu language (Pare) was (almost) complete. The second language variety of Pare, with substratum influence from Cushitic, provided the morphosyntactic frame for Ma'a. This is similar to the position taken by scholars such as Brenzinger (1987), Sasse (1992a), and Bakker (1997).

The shift scenario has two advantages over alternative explanations. First, it allows us to group together a number of contact languages that arose under similar historical circumstances. These would include, apart from Ma'a, various Romani-lexicon contact languages such as Anglo-Romani, Armenian Romani, and Caló. Thomason (1995: 19) in fact accepts the shift scenario in the case of Anglo-Romani and Armenian Romani, but rejects it for Ma'a and Caló, as noted earlier.

Consigning these intertwined languages to distinct categories seems to be somewhat unmotivated, given their basic similarity in history as well as linguistic make-up. The shift scenario at least provides a unified treatment of the processes involved, while allowing for the retention of structural and lexical features that distinguish Ma'a and Caló from other intertwined languages in the group. Perhaps the difference between Asia Minor Greek on the one hand, and Ma'a and Caló on the other, is merely a matter of the degree to which the shift took place. But the creation of the latter seems to have followed the shift, rather than being products of shift-induced changes. As Bakker (1997: 205) has pointed out, we need to distinguish the historical process of shift from the actual linguistic processes that created these languages.

The second advantage of the shift scenario is that it allows us to identify similarities in such processes across bilingual mixed languages with different histories. It seems likely that the intertwined languages that originated after language shift were created by processes quite similar to those that produced languages like Media Lengua and Michif. In both cases, the dominant language of bilinguals provided the matrix language (ML) frame into which elements from the other language were incorporated. The only difference would be that, in the case of Ma'a, Anglo-Romani, etc., the ML was the newly acquired language, while for Media Lengua, Michif, etc., it was the ancestral language. In either case, as Bakker (1994: 24) notes, "it is the language that is best known that provides the grammatical system." In short then, while their sociohistorical scenarios may differ, languages like Anglo-Romani and Ma'a appear to have arisen through the same linguistic processes that led to the genesis of Media Lengua and Michif.

Exercise 6

Bentahila and Davies (1992) describe differences in code-switching patterns between older and younger Arabic–French bilinguals. The former typically use French as the ML, while the latter use Arabic. To what extent are these differences analogous to those between Anglo-Romani and Media Lengua?

6.7 The Strange Case of Copper Island Aleut

The last of the intertwined languages we examine closely in this chapter is Mednyj (Copper) Island Aleut (CIA), once widely spoken on Copper Island, one of the two Russian-owned Commander Islands in the Aleutian Islands chain. The language is spoken by only a few older persons today, most of whom reside on Bering Island. Like Aleut, it has all but given way to Russian on these islands. This contact language is characterized by a blending of Russian and Aleut (primarily Attu) elements in most components of the grammar, but most profoundly in the verbal morphology. Golovko and Vakhtin (1990: 111) summarize the mixture thus: "[The Aleut component] comprises the majority of the vocabulary, all the derivational morphology, part of the simple sentence syntax, nominal inflexion and certain other grammatical means. The [Russian component] comprises verbal inflexion, negation, infinitive forms, part of the simple sentence syntax, and all of the compound sentence syntax." This summary should not be interpreted to mean that the Russian and Aleut contributions to Copper Island Aleut are equal. As we shall see, this is not entirely accurate. At any rate, the pattern of mixture is quite unlike any that have been recorded for other intertwined languages, though it bears some resemblance to the latter. Before we examine the structural details more closely, let us consider the sociohistorical context in which the language arose.

6.7.1 Sociohistorical background

Trading between Russia and the Aleutian Islands began in 1741 and continued through the nineteenth century. But closer contact between the groups began in 1826 when the Russian-American company established permanent settlements on the two previously uninhabited Commander Islands, Copper Island and Bering Island (Golovko and Vakhtin 1990: 98). Dozens of Aleut and creole families were brought in from the Aleutian, Kurch, and Pribylof Islands, and from Kamchatka. They supplied the labor for processing of skins and other activities associated with the trade in seal furs. There was also a minority of Russian employees of the company, mostly men, who settled on the islands.

By 1860, there were 90 people on Copper Island, including Russian traders, Aleuts from various islands, creoles, and a few persons of other ethnic background (ibid.: 114). By 1879, the Copper Island population is said to have comprised an equal number of Aleuts and creoles and by 1897 the creoles outnumbered the Aleuts (ibid.: 116). It was this creole population that played the major role in creating Copper Island Aleut, which eventually became a badge of their distinct social identity. Thomason (1997b: 461) suggests that the language arose sometime between 1826 and 1900. Let us now examine its structural characteristics in some detail.

6.7.2 Structural characteristis of Copper Island Aleut

6.7.2.1 The lexicon and phonology

The vocabulary of CIA is overwhelmingly Aleut. According to Sekerina (1994: 29), 94 percent of the verbs and 61.5 percent of the nouns in her corpus were Aleut. A significant percentage of the nouns are Russian, though these loanwords are not more numerous than those found in some Aleut varieties, such as that on Bering Island (Golovko 1996: 64). Russian loans include some verbs denoting activities new to Aleut speakers, for example, *kraasil* (< *krasit'*) "paint" and *muučil* (< *mučit'*) "torture" (ibid.). Several adverbs and function words (conjunctions and prepositions) as well as most pronouns also come from Russian (Golovko and Vakhtin 1990: 104, 110).

Given the nature of the vocabulary, it is not surprising that CIA phonology is very similar to that of Aleut. In fact, their phonological inventories are identical except for a few changes introduced into CIA under Russian influence. These include sounds like /p, b, f, g/, mostly restricted to Russian loanwords, and not found in Aleut (Thomason 1997b: 455). According to Golovko (1996: 65), Aleut /v/ has been split into /p/ and /b/ in CIA. Three Aleut phonemes (/ð, hŋ, hw/) are absent from CIA, while the velar versus uvular distinction in the stop and fricative series has also been lost. The latter may be a recent change (Thomason 1997b: 456).

6.7.2.2 Syntax

Only a brief overview of key aspects of CIA syntax and morphology is possible here. With regard to the former, the rigid SOV order of Aleut has been abandoned in favor of variable word order, with Russian-like patterns predominating. In complex sentence constructions, Aleut structures are often replaced by more Russian-like ones in which Russian complementizers or subordinating conjunctions appear. Some examples will illustrate some of the complex patterns of intertwining that characterize the syntax of the language. The following two CIA sentences are synonymous and equally acceptable to CIA speakers (Golovko 1996: 72–3). Russian elements are in italics (I have replaced some of Golovko's symbols with corresponding IPA symbols):

(21) a. *ja segodnja* čχuuʁi-n inka-ča-*l* qaka-ča-anga
I today linen-PL hang-CAUS-3sgPAST dry-CAUS-INT
b. ja *segodnja* čχuuʁi-n inka-ča-*l* *čtoby ego* quaka-ča-*t'*
I today linen-PL hang-CAUS-3sgPAST in order it dry-CAUS-INF
"Today I hung linen in order to dry it"

These sentences may be compared with their Aleut (Bering Island) (BIA) and Russian (RUS) equivalents;

(22) a. RUS: ja segodnja bel'e povesi-l-a (čtoby ego) vyusuši-t'
I today linen hang-PAST-FEM (in order it) dry-INF
b. BIA: wan angaliχ čχuuʁis qaka-t-iingan inka-t-na-χ
this day linen dry-CAUS-INTR hang-CAUS-PAST-3sg
"Today I hung linen in order to dry it"

We note first that the CIA word order is more Russian-like. There is also alternation between the Aleut intentional form *qaka-ča-anga* and the Russian-like purpose construction. The latter contains a Russian complementizer and an infinitival form of the verb, marked by Russian suffix *-t'*. Another interesting instance of Russian influence is the use of the Russian subject pronoun *ja*. CIA uses the full range of Russian subject pronouns (*ti* "you-sg.," *on* "he," *mi* "we," *vi* "you-pl.," *oni* "they"). Aleut has no subject pronouns. The Russian pronouns are used to convey differences in person particularly in the past tense, for reasons we shall see below. CIA also employs Russian object pronouns (e.g., *ego* in example (1b). Aleut object pronouns survive in the language (e.g., *ti* "me," *tin* "you," *txin* "(s)he") but they are used only as objects of reflexive verbs (Golovko and Vakhtin 1990: 104).

A few other (morpho-)syntactic features in CIA also derive from Russian. These include the negative prefix *ni-*, rather than the two Aleut negative suffixes *-lakaʁ* (negation of actual action) and *(-ʁ)ula-(x)* (negation of non-actual event) (Golovko 1996: 72). The difference between CIA and Bering Island Aleut is shown in the following examples:

(23) a. CIA: iglu-ŋ *n'i* tuta-qaʁi-*it*
grandson-1sgPOSS NEG hear-DETRAN-3sgPRES
b. BIA: iglu-ŋ tutu-qaʁi-laka-χ
grandson-1sgPOSS listen-DETRAN-NEG-3sgPRES
"My grandson doesn't listen [obey]"

In addition, CIA, like Russian and unlike Aleut, lacks a copula in the present tense (Thomason 1997b: 460). The language has also adopted some Russian modal verbs like *nado* "ought to," *dolžen* "must," etc., which have replaced Aleut suffixes. Finally, CIA has introduced several Russian conjunctions in compound sentences, replacing the conjunctive suffixes of Aleut. The general pattern in CIA morphosyntax is to replace the bound suffixal morphology of Aleut with analytic strategies derived from Russian.

Despite these changes, CIA has preserved certain aspects of Aleut syntax. Among them is the rather unusual pattern of topic–number agreement illustrated in the following example (Golovko 1996: 69):

(24) kaju-ŋi huzu-ŋi nana-*it*
muscle-3plPOSS each-3plPOSS ache-3sgPRES
"All his muscles ache"

Notice how the verb inflection *-it* agrees not with the subject "muscles" but with the singular possessor (the "topic"). But Golovko and Vakhtin (1990: 107) note that Russian-type agreement also occurs in these types of CIA structure.

6.7.2.3 Morphology

CIA has preserved practically all of the nominal and most of the verbal morphology of Aleut. For instance, the whole system of derivational suffixes, both nominal and verbal, remains intact. The most striking change has occurred in the verb forms, where Russian tense suffixes have entirely replaced their Aleut counterparts. The paradigm for the verb "to stand" in (25) illustrates this (Golovko 1996: 70):

(25)		*CIA*	*Russian*
	Verb stem	anqaχta-	sto-
	1sg.	anqaχta-ju	sto-ju
	2sg.	anqaχta-iš	sto-iš
	3sg.	anqaχta-it	sto-it
	1pl.	anqaχta-im	sto-im
	2pl.	anqaχta-iti	sto-ite
	3pl.	anqaχta-jut (-jat)	sto-jat

Examples (21), (23a), and (24) above illustrate the unusual blend of bound morphology from the two sources. They show that CIA preserves the Aleut verbal suffixes that change the valency (argument structure) of the verb. These include the marker of factitive causation *-ča-* (21), detransitivizer *-qaʁi-* (23a), and several others (Golovko 1996: 66–8). In addition, CIA has retained those Aleut suffixes that convey aspectual and similar notions, such as "want, begin, stop," etc.

In general, then, the basic verbal morphology is Aleut, but Russian has made a significant contribution to it as well. Table 6.5 summarizes (most of) the

Table 6.5 Aleut and Russian features in CIA verbal and nominal morphology

Features	Aleut	Russian
Nominal morphology	All	None
Verbal morphology	Valency-changing suffixes	Tense suffixes
	Aspectual suffixes	Analytic future
	Some dependent forms	Negative prefix
	Topic–number agreement	Infinitival suffix
		Person agreement (pronouns)
Function words	Reflexive object pronouns	Subject and object pronouns
	Postpositions	Modal verbs and words
	Demonstratives	Several complementizers

Source: Golovko and Vakhtin (1990); Golovko (1996)

contributions from Aleut and Russian to the nominal and verbal morphology of Copper Island Aleut.

The somewhat detailed overview of CIA presented above helps us place the Russian contribution to its grammar in perspective. Though striking, this influence was by no means overwhelming, and the basically Aleut character of CIA remains predominant. How then did this unusual mixture come about?

6.7.3 Processes and constraints in Copper Island Aleut origins

The pattern of mixture in CIA is obviously different from those we found in Media Lengua and Michif. Yet there are several respects in which CIA resembles these other intertwined languages. In the first place, it consists of a basically Aleut matrix language (ML) frame into which Russian elements have been incorporated. Furthermore, the adoption of Russian lexical items as well as pronouns, complementizers, etc. is not unlike what we find in other intertwined languages. So for that matter is the substitution of Russian constructions such as purpose clauses for their Aleut counterparts – which seems somewhat similar to EL island insertion. But clearly the intrusion of Russian morphosyntactic apparatus into the Aleut ML frame of CIA is much more pervasive than in other intertwined languages.

This kind of convergence could have been accomplished only by bilinguals who were highly proficient in both Aleut and Russian. Children in particular may have played a key role in this creation. The pattern of mixture itself conforms to certain principles that we have seen operating in other cases of convergence.

To take the most striking feature first, the intrusion of Russian tense suffixes into CIA must have been facilitated by a certain typological similarity between Aleut and Russian tense inflections. Both occupy a slot at the end of the inflected verb, as illustrated in the following examples from Golovko (1996: 71):

(26)	a.	RUS:	ty menja spraŝiva-*eš*
			you me ask-2sgPRES
	b.	BIA:	tiŋ ahmayaaχta-ku-*χt*
			me ask-REAL-2sgPRES
	c.	CIA:	ty menja hamayaaχta-ku-*iš*
			you me ask-2sgPRES
			"You are asking me"

The substitution here is similar to the morphological adoptions from Ritharngu into Ngandi in Arnhem Land, Australia, which we discussed in chapter 3, section 3.6.1.

Exercise 7
Compare the morphological influence from Russian on Copper Island Aleut with that from Ritharngu on Ngandi. To what extent are the patterns similar? To what extent does typological similarity between the languages involved in each case account for the patterns?

In other cases, as Golovko (1996: 116) observes, the typological differences between Aleut and Russian block certain kinds of influence from the latter. For example, the absence of prefixes in Aleut may explain why practically no Russian prefixes were incorporated into CIA.

In several cases, the typological differences between the two source languages are resolved in favor of selections that achieve greater transparency. Examples include the substitution of much Aleut suffixal morphology by Russian-derived analytic strategies such as pronouns, negation, and future marking. Such changes seem to result from processes of convergence similar to those we found in the contact between Urdu and other languages in Kupwar (chapter 3, section 3.7.3). In all these cases, bilinguals create compromises by replacing certain syntactic strategies with others that are simpler or more transparent.

The pervasive mixture of elements from two sources in every component of CIA grammar led to a new creation that appears to have few parallels elsewhere. Apart from the cases of convergence we just mentioned, similar patterns of mixture can be found in languages like Asia Minor Greek and Wutun. In both these cases, elements and structures from the respective sources have combined to produce composite systems of phonology, morphology, and syntax. All of these contact languages are clearly the work of skilled bilinguals who recombine structures from their two languages to create a new composite language. The chief difference between intertwined languages like CIA and composites like Asia Minor Greek is that the former outcomes seem to arise relatively quickly, and achieve stability and autonomy as new norms. By contrast, as we saw in chapter 3, section 3.7.2, Asia Minor Greek was the result of gradual intrusion of Turkish elements over a long period, duing which it was in a state of continual flux. Moreover, intertwined languages display neater patterns of mixture than languages like Asia Minor Greek, perhaps because they involve more deliberate acts of creation. There are also some differences in the types of diffusion characteristic of each case. For instance, EL elements incorporated into intertwined languages are usually overt and identifiable surface forms. In addition to such forms, however, languages like Asia Minor Greek display evidence of "pattern transfer," that is, diffusion of abstract structural patterns from the source language. These kinds of diffusion do not seem to be typical of intertwined languages. On the whole, however, there is no reason to suppose that the actual processes of mixture involved in the creation of intertwined languages were unique to these languages.

Exercise 8
Compare some of the changes in Kupwar Urdu (chapter 3, section 3.7.3) with those resulting from Russian influence in the creation of CIA. To what extent are they similar?
Advanced: Do the same for the changes in Asia Minor Greek under Turkish influence. See Thomason and Kaufman 1988: 215–22.

6.8 Summary

In this chapter, we examined a variety of bilingual mixed codes that are used as in-group languages, and were created by more or less skilled bilinguals. Some of these are transient and not likely to survive, for instance the mixed Panjabi–English code used by younger generations of Sikhs in England. Others are restricted in scope of use, like Tsotsitaal, the blend of Zulu, English, and Afrikaans used by younger people in South African townships. Though the creation of such mixed codes appears to be quite common, few have achieved autonomy as distinct languages. The few that have done so constitute the class of bilingual mixed or intertwined languages.

We examined four well-known exemplars of this type of contact language – Media Lengua, Michif, Ma'a, and Copper Island Aleut. They display noticeable differences in their patterns of mixture and provide some sense of the diversity of these outcomes of contact. In general, intertwined languages differ from other contact varieties in that their components, whether lexical or structural, are preserved relatively intact, and can be easily traced back to the respective source languages. There is still some disagreement over the precise origins and classification of these languages. Much of it is due to the fact that distinctions made according to purely structural criteria do not always match those that are made according to sociohistorical criteria.

6.8.1 Sociohistorical background and social motivations

Bilingual mixed languages have arisen under a variety of sociohistorical circumstances; hence it is not easy to generalize about the social motivations for their creation. However, two broad scenarios can be identified. On the one hand, there are languages like Michif, Copper Island Aleut, Chindo, and others that were created by newly emerged social groups who wanted a language of their own. For the most part, these groups are "creoles" of mixed race who see themselves as distinct from either of the cultural groups from which they descended. But in certain cases, such as Media Lengua, the group involved is not of mixed race, but is caught between competing cultures. The same motivation to express a separate social identity lies behind mixed codes like Tsotsitaal and others that have not achieved autonomy.

On the other hand, there are languages like Ma'a, Anglo-Romani, Caló, and others which arise when a group's ancestral language has almost been replaced by a dominant host language. Among such groups are ex-nomads like the Roma and the Callahuaya healers, who need a secret, in-group language. Like the Ma'a, these groups wish to preserve some of their old traditions and culture by retaining parts of their ancestral language in their new language. This reflects their attempt to resist total assimilation to the dominant culture.

6.8.2 Processes and origins

Most of the intertwined languages known to us display characteristics found in the code-switching behavior of skilled bilinguals. For instance, the pattern of mixture in Media Lengua involves an extreme form of the single content morpheme insertion found in some types of code switching. On the other hand, the mixture in Michif is reminiscent of the type of code switching known as EL island insertion, the main difference being that Michif does this across the board, replacing Cree nouns consistently with French ones. In both cases, it is possible to identify a matrix language – Quechua in the case of Media Lengua, and Plains Cree in the case of Michif – into which EL elements (from Spanish and French respectively) are incorporated. Similar processes lie behind the creation of most other bilingual mixed languages, though the ML is the ancestral language in some cases (like the two above), while it is a newly acquired language in others (like Ma'a and Anglo-Romani). The constraints on the mixture found in these cases are quite similar to those that operate in code switching generally.

The case of Copper Island Aleut is quite different. The blend of Russian and Aleut structure represents a very unusual pattern of mixture. The processes involved in this case seem similar to those found in cases of convergence, particularly those involving extreme structural diffusion, as for instance in some varieties of Asia Minor Greek. The product in each case is pervasive mixture in every component of the grammar. In CIA, however, the pattern of intertwining is much more regular, displaying the neat compartmentalization of components typical of intertwined languages.

Despite the intricate pattern of mixture, the processes of intertwining in Copper Island Aleut appear to conform to the usual contraints on structural diffusion or convergence. Typological differences between Russian and Aleut block certain kinds of substitution, while others, for example, the wholesale incorporation of Russian tense suffixes, are facilitated by (partial) congruence between verbal structures in both languages.

On the whole, therefore, while intertwined languages are relatively rare creations, the processes and constraints that were involved in their genesis are not different from those that operate in other kinds of bilingual mixture.

7

Second Language Acquisition and Language Shift

I AN OVERVIEW OF INDIVIDUAL SECOND LANGUAGE ACQUISITION

7.1 Introduction

The types of cross-linguistic influence we have considered in previous chapters have all, by and large, involved changes in a maintained language under the agency of its own speakers. In a majority of these cases, recipient language (RL) speakers "borrow" or incorporate foreign (SL) features into their L1. This process of borrowing, as we have seen, is subject to quite strict constraints. In some cases, for example, those involving structural convergence, both RL and SL agentivity seem to be involved, with active bilinguals playing a crucial role. In the next few chapters, we will be concerned with situations involving various kinds of second language acquisition, in which the target language (TL) is changed to varying degrees under the agency of learners.

Speakers attempting to communicate in a language they are acquiring may resort to various strategies to achieve success. In doing so, they create versions of the TL that differ in many ways from the varieties used by its native speakers. The strategies and changes involved in this procedure of trial and error offer fascinating insight into the creativity that is part of second language acquisition (henceforth SLA). Attempts to describe and explain this creative activity and the principles that regulate it have led to some degree of understanding, though there is also much disagreement on several issues.

Researchers traditionally make a distinction between second language acquisition and foreign language acquisition (see Ellis 1994: 11–12). The former involves the learning of a language in "natural" settings, for instance by immigrants who have to acquire the dominant language of a host community. The latter refers usually to the learning of a foreign language through formal instruction, for example in the classroom. Henceforth I will refer to both types as SLA, except where it may become necessary to distinguish the two. Research has shown that both types of learning are similar in many ways, and each can provide a great deal of insight into the other. Our concern, however, is primarily with so-called "natural" SLA. This takes place in community settings where learners attempt to acquire the TL through more or less direct interaction with its speakers (or with others who have learnt it), usually without benefit of instruction. In such reallife situations, as van Coetsem (1988: 19) notes, "the primary aim is communication, not the acquisition of an optimal knowledge of the TL." Hence learners may freely adapt the TL in ways that best facilitate their need to communicate.

Our ultimate concern will be with language shift or second language acquisition by groups or communities of speakers. But since individual SLA feeds group SLA, we need to understand the former in order to fully explain the latter. It won't be possible to consider all aspects of individual SLA here; we will focus only on those that seem most relevant to our present interest. Both individual and group SLA provide a rich laboratory for investigating the changes that arise from learners' creativity, as well as the principles and constraints that guide them. In general, such changes fall into three categories: (a) L1 or substratum influence on the learner version of the TL or "interlanguage"; (b) various kinds of simplification of TL structures (see section 7.3 below); and (c) changes that are internal to the interlanguage system. These changes arise from strategies that learners employ to simplify the task of learning, and to compensate for lack of acquisition (mastery) of TL features (see van Coetsem 1988: chapter 3). These strategies will be discussed further below.

7.2 L1 Influence in SLA

It has long been recognized that learners' versions of a TL are subject to varying degrees of influence from their native or primary (dominant) language. The latter may not be the same as the former; however, I will henceforth refer to either of these as the L1. Weinreich (1953) was among the first to attempt a comprehensive account of these types of influence, which he referred to as "interference" phenomena. Though Weinreich himself did not always distinguish interference due to borrowing from that due to L1 influence, most of his illustrations in fact deal with the latter. Hence some scholars use the term "interference" only in the sense of L1 influence on a TL. Most scholars of

SLA, however, prefer to use the term "transfer" instead. This term has been used in different senses. Lado (1957) interpreted it as the use of overt L1 elements or structures in the L2. This narrow interpretation failed to take account of all the ways in which the L1 might influence the L2. Moreover, Lado's idea of the transfer of linguistic habits seemed somewhat too closely tied to behaviorist theories of language acquisition which later scholars challenged. Odlin (1989: 27) offered a much broader interpretation of transfer as "the influence resulting from similarities and differences between the target language and any other language that has been previously (and perhaps imperfectly) acquired." While this allows for a greater range of influence than Lado's definition, it raises the question whether all of the possible types of L1 influence can be properly subsumed under the concept of "transfer."

Part of the problem lies in the varied uses to which this term is currently put. It may refer both to the manifestations of L1 influence and to the psycholinguistic processes that bring them about. In the former sense, it refers to the final manifestations or products of certain kinds of L1 influence on an outcome of SLA. In other words, it is possible to claim, in retrospect, that certain L1 properties have been "transferred" into learner versions of a TL, changing it in some way. Such an approach views learners' innovations purely from the perspective of the original TL, rather than from the perspective of the interlanguage grammar itself. We shall adopt the latter perspective, and use the term in the sense of a strategy or process. We will continue to use the more neutral term "L1 influence" to refer to the results of this process. L1 influence manifests itself in the form of L1 features that learners introduce into their developing version of the L2, or interlanguage (henceforth IL). Such features might be referred to as "L1 retentions," which constitute a significant input to the restructuring of the early IL system.

As Jarvis and Odlin (2000: 537) suggest: "Much of what is called cross-linguistic influence [in SLA] can be viewed in terms of retentions: Whenever challenges of using or understanding a second language arise, learners may retain something from their L1 or some other language to aid in coping with the new challenges." Such retentions, as we shall see, can be overt or direct, as in the use of L1 sounds, words, and sometimes morphemes in the IL, or it may be covert, involving more abstract L1 categories or patterns. In cases where L1 and L2 match each other closely, L1 retentions may result in relatively close approximations to the target element or structure, leading to what is called "positive transfer." In cases of mismatch, such retentions often lead to "imperfect learning," and represent forms of "negative transfer." Or, as Weinreich (1953: 1) puts it: "The greater the difference between the systems . . . the greater is the learning problem and the potential area of interference."

7.2.1 L1 influence on the TL lexicon

In the simplest cases, learners may retain features of their L1 to compensate for their unfamiliarity with equivalent features of the TL. For instance, they may retain overt lexical items from the L1. Nemser (1991: 352–3) provides several examples of such L1 lexical retentions in the spoken and written L2 English of German-speaking Austrian students. Beginning and intermediate students use lexical items like *brills* "eyeglasses" and function words like *außer* "except." More advanced learners employ words like *grammatik* for "grammar" and *dement* for "deny." L1 influence on the L2 lexicon may be more covert, leading learners to reinterpret TL words in terms of the semantics of similar L1 forms, thus creating new meanings for the former. For instance, Nemser's students used *meager* to mean "thin" (cf. German *mager* "thin"), and *guilty* to mean "valid" (cf. German *gültig* "valid") (1991: 348). Appel (1996: 392) refers to this as "negative transfer of word form." Such L1–L2 word pairs are often called *faux amis* or "false friends." Similar examples of such pairs in English–French include *demand* versus *demander* "ask," *ignore* versus *ignorer* "not to know," etc. Negative transfer can occur in both directions, that is, when either language is the TL.

Just as insidious from the learner's viewpoint are cases where an L2 form only partly matches an L1 form in meaning, but the learner assumes complete overlap between the two. For instance, German learners of English may extend the meaning of *carry* to include both "transport" and "wear (clothes)" on the model of German *tragen*. Note the similarity to cases of semantic extension in borrowing. Finally, learners often create loan translations employing L2 forms combined according to an L1 pattern. Nemser (1991: 358) cites examples such as *ill-car* "ambulance" (cf. German *Krankenwagen* lit. "sick-car") and *alp-dream* "nightmare" (cf. German *Alptraum* lit. "alp(?)-dream"). These coinages were created by learners at an intermediate stage of acquisition of L2 English.

All of these types of lexical contact phenomena recall those found in borrowing, except that the direction of influence is reversed. As we will see in chapter 9, similar kinds of reinterpretation of superstrate lexical forms on the model of substrate semantic patterns are also common in creole formation.

It seems clear that learners rely heavily on their L1 lexical structure in creating their L2 lexicon. This assumption lies behind the Semantic Equivalence Hypothesis, which claims that "conceptual patterns and linguistic/semantic coding practices in the L1 provide the essential criteria for those in the L2" (Ijaz 1986: 437). Other studies have provided support for this view, for example, Graham and Belnap (1986), Hoeks (1985), etc. But L1 influence cannot explain all that is involved in L2 lexical acquisition. For that we still need a broader lexical theory that will explain the stages of the acquisition process and the ways in which learners solve the problems they encounter.

Exercise 1

L2 learners' uses of L1 lexical knowledge in interpreting L2 lexical items appear quite similar to certain kinds of adaptation characteristic of lexical borrowing from an L2 into an L1 (see discussion in chapter 2). What similarities and differences do you find?

7.2.2 L1 influence on L2 phonology

As Weinreich (1953: 14) noted, L1 influence on L2 phonology occurs when "a speaker perceives and reproduces the sounds of one language, which might be designated secondary, in terms of another, to be called primary." In other words, speakers make "interlingual identifications" between L1 and L2 sounds, and simply replace the latter with the former. Similar kinds of reinterpretation may affect the phonotactics as well as the prosodic features of the TL (that is, the version of it that is acquired by the learners).

Phone substitution may involve the simple replacement of a target sound by a close counterpart in the L1, without further consequences for the phonemic system as a whole. Weinreich refers to this as "actual phone substitution," where two sounds are identified as equivalent in the two languages in contact, though their actual phonetic realizations may differ somewhat. For instance, English learners of L2 French substitute their native /u/ for French /u/ without realizing that the two sounds differ acoustically, and hence do not accurately produce the former (Flege 1987).

When there is a significant mismatch between the L1 and L2 phonological categories, phone substitution can have various consequences for the learner version of the TL. In some cases, it results in loss of phonemic distinctions. For example, Spanish learners of English may substitute their native /i/ for both /iy/ and /ɪ/ of English, so that both *ship* and *sheep* are pronounced as /ʃip/.

Exercise 2

Weinreich (1953) suggests that what he calls "phonic interference" can be categorized into the following subtypes: (a) actual phone substitution; (b) underdifferentiation of phonemes; (c) overdifferentiation of phonemes; and (d) reinterpretation of distinctions. Explain what each of these refers to, and find suitable examples to illustrate each. How satisfactory do you think Weinreich's classification is?

Similarly, Japanese learners of English often fail to distinguish between /l/ and approximant /ɹ/, substituting their only native liquid sound for both. Weinreich (1953: 18) refers to this as "underdifferentiation of phonemes," and identifies several other kinds of phonological reinterpretation that result from the substitution of L1 sounds or sound patterns for those in the TL.

Learners may also introduce changes in the phonotactics of their version of the TL under the influence of their L1. For instance, German learners of Swedish transfer their L1 rule that requires devoicing of final obstruents to their L2 Swedish (Hammarberg 1997: 170). German learners of English tend to do the same, pronouncing words like *job* as [jɔp]. Various studies have shown that "transfer" of L1 syllabification rules is the primary influence on the syllable structures produced by learners of L2 English from a variety of language backgrounds (Leather and James 1991: 327). Finally, there have been similar findings on the effects of L1 influence on prosodic features of an L2 such as word stress, rhythm, and intonation patterns (ibid.: 326).

On the whole, it seems clear that the beginning learner, in attempting to make sense of L2 speech, relies heavily on the phonetic categories of the L1. However, it would be simplistic to assume that learners simply substitute L1 sounds for L2 "equivalents" as the classic theory of transfer predicted (Lado 1957). The process by which learners imitate and approximate L2 sounds involves a complex interplay of perception and production that can only be fully understood through detailed phonetic and phonological analysis.

7.2.3 L1 influence on L2 Morphology

Unlike lexical and phonological elements, L1 morphemes tend not to be transferred directly into learner approximations of the TL as substitutions for equivalents in the latter. Bound morphology, in particular, is difficult for beginning learners to recognize, far less replace with native morphology, particularly when there is substantial typological distance between the L1 and the TL. The preferred strategy is to reduce or eliminate TL inflectional apparatus and to use periphrastic means of expression instead. Hence early learner L2 varieties commonly lack grammatical categories that convey notions such as agreement, gender, number, and case, as well as tense, aspect, and so on. In some cases, however, close typological similarity between L1 and L2 may facilitate substitution of certain L1 morphemes for their TL counterparts. For example, Nemser (1991: 353) reports that some German-speaking learners of English created plurals like *dog-e* "dogs" and *girl-en* "girls," employing German plural suffixes. Similarly, Dusková (1984) notes that Czech learners of Russian tend to substitute L1 bound morphemes for Russian ones in their L2 Russian, producing words like *rabotnice* "workwomen" with the Czech suffix *-nice* instead of Russian *-nicy*.

On the other hand, more indirect L1 influence on L2 morphology or morphosyntax is often in evidence. It can lead to the reinterpretation of L2 categories, as when French or German learners of L2 English use the perfect *have+V-ed* construction as a preterite (*I have written the letter yesterday*) on the model of their native category, which is used to convey preterite meaning (cf. *Ich habe den Brief gestern geschrieben*).

L1 influence can also lead to the emergence of "new" grammatical categories in the interlanguage variety. This is typically accomplished via reinterpretation or reanalysis of TL lexemes in terms of L1 functional categories. These kinds of morphosyntactic change are fairly common in cases of group SLA, including situations of language shift. A well-known example is the so-called "hot news" perfect construction in Hiberno-English, consisting of *be* + *after* + *V-ing* (e.g., *She's after painting the house* "She's just painted the house"). This is apparently modeled on an Irish (Gaelic) construction (see section 7.9.1 below). We will see in chapter 9 that these kinds of L1 influence are also quite common in creole formation.

7.2.4 L1 influence on TL syntax

A learner's L1 can exert varying degrees of influence on the syntax of the approximative (interlanguage) systems she or he constructs at different stages of acquisition. In the earlier stages, the use of L1 word order in attempting to produce TL utterances is quite common, though certainly not absolute. For example, English-speaking learners of L2 French often generalize the SVO order of simple declaratives to sentences containing pronominal objects, which must precede the verb in native French. Thus we find sentences like the following:

(1) il n'est [*sic*] pas prend le
"He doesn't take it" (Gundel and Tarone 1983: 292)

In these cases, mismatches in syntactic structure between L1 and L2 can impede successful acquisition, and prompt the use of L1 strategies, or "negative transfer."

Similarly, French-speaking learners of English may employ yes/no questions like the following:

(2) Is the breakfast is good?

Structures like these appear to be modeled on French yes/no questions containing nominal objects, like the following:

(3) Est-ce que Mari est une touriste?
Is-it that Mari is a tourist
"Is Marie a tourist?" (Zobl 1980)

By contrast, the same learners produce acceptable English yes/no questions with pronominal subjects, like the following:

(4) Is he a tourist?

The reason appears to be that such questions have a more or less identical structure in French, as in (5):

(5) Est-il un tourist?

This shows that L1 influence can also have a positive effect on the acquisition of L2 structures, a phenomenon that SLA researchers refer to as "positive transfer." Another example of this is the relative ease with which English-speaking learners acquire German copular structures and vice versa. Since the structures are quite similar in the two languages, they are easier to learn, and tend to be mastered quite early. Felix (1977: 151) provides the following examples of L2 German copula sentences produced by English-speaking child learners:

(6) a. das ist ein Wind
"That is a wind"
b. das ist grün
"That is green"

However, there are also cases where L1 influence can delay successful acquisition of a TL structure because of a similarity between the L1 and an early developmental stage of acquisition of the structure in question. For instance, most learners of English employ early negative structures consisting of *no* + Verb, which they eventually abandon in favor of more TL-like structures. However, Spanish and Italian learners of English remain in the *no* + Verb stage much longer than, say, Japanese learners, because the former languages employ *no* + Verb structures and therefore promote retention of such structures in the learner versions of English.

It is difficult to generalize about the ways an L1 might influence the learner's acquisition of TL syntax, since that depends not only on the degree of typological similarity between the languages, but also on the stage of acquisition the learner has reached, and other constraints to be discussed below. As learners pass through various stages of acquisition, L1 influence interacts with their growing proficiency in different ways.

For instance, Meisel et al. (1981) propose four stages of acquisition of German word order by English, Italian, and other learners. In the first stage, learners use canonical SVO order, which conflicts for the most part with acceptable German word order. In stage 2, learners acquire a rule that requires particles and non-inflected verbs to appear in sentence-final position:[1]

(7) Ich habe den Wagen verkauft
I have the car buy-PP
"I sold the car"

In stage 3, learners master the so-called inversion rule, which inverts the subject with the inflected verb in *wh*-questions as well as in sentences with preposed adverbs:

(8) Wann gehst du Heim?
When go you home
"When are you going home?"

Finally, in stage 4, learners acquire the rule that moves an inflected verb to clause-final position in an embedded clause:

(9) Ich ruf(e) dich an wenn ich nach Hause gehe
I call-1sg you at? when I to home go
"I'll call you when I go home"

A similar pattern of acquisition is reported by Pienemann (1984) for children learning German as a second language. Given this order of acquisition, it follows that early learners may employ L1 word order in, say, subordinate clauses, even after they have abandoned it in *wh*-questions and other structures.

L1 grammar can also influence the acquisition of other TL syntactic features such as the argument structure of TL verbs. Nemser (1991: 360) reports that his German-speaking learners produced L2 English sentences like (10), which seems to be modeled on the German equivalent in (11):

(10) Explain me something.

(11) Erklär mir was.

In this case, the subcategorization properties of German *erklären* have been "transferred" to *explain*. The reanalysis may also be motivated by analogy with English verbs like *tell*, *show*, etc. The same learners also produce L2 English (E.) utterances like the following (German (G.) equivalents are provided):

(12) L2 E.: I would suggest him to go
G.: Ich empfehle ihm zu gehen

(13) L2 E.: You just finished to eat
G.: Du hast gerade aufgehört zu essen

Again, these may be reinforced by analogy with other English verbs that take infinitival complements, for instance, *like*, *expect*, etc. in the case of *suggest*, and *start*, *agree*, etc. in the case of *finish*. Here again, it is interaction between L1 influence and advanced learning that seems to produce such reanalysis.

Exercise 3
Find as many examples as you can of L1 influence on a learner's version of L2 English, focusing on syntax. Try to explain the reasons for such influence.

7.3 Simplification in SLA

Another major strategy employed by learners as compensation for partial or incomplete acquisition is simplification. This term is somewhat controversial since it can refer to a variety of different processes of change, as well as the final product or consequences of such changes. I will use it here as a cover-term for processes that include reduction of TL structures, rule regularization, and other strategies aimed at achieving ease of perception and production. These processes interact both with L1 influence and with changes that are internal to the developing L2 grammar.

Learner versions of the TL are typically reduced in lexicon and structure, and consequently in communicative power, especially in the early stages of acquisition. Meisel (1977) refers to this as "restrictive simplification." Such reduction is, in the first instance, a direct consequence of the learner's limited knowledge of the TL. To compensate for this deficiency, the learner may resort to avoidance, or rely on the L1, or on other strategies of grammar building internal to the developing L2 system. All of these may result in simplification of some kind. Bound morphology is usually among the first victims of reduction, since it tends to be difficult to learn, even in cases where it is similar to L1 morphology. The avoidance or elimination of TL morphology therefore represents a common means by which early learners simplify their version of the TL.

Some cases of reduction may be partly due to L1 influence. For instance, learners may eliminate phonemic or morphemic oppositions in their version of the TL because their own native language lacks them. For example, the three-way phonemic distinction between /i/, /ü/, and /u/ in Dutch is usually reduced to a two-way distinction (/i/ versus /u/) by English speakers. Similar kinds of reduction can be found in morphology and morphosyntax. Jarvis and Odlin (2000) discuss how Swedish and Finnish learners of English employ prepositions to convey locative, directional, and other meanings in the TL. While both groups often produced the right preposition (e.g., *in* in *sit in the grass*), the Finnish learners frequently used zero prepositions in all the spatial contexts examined, whereas the Swedish learners never did. Also, both groups often used the "wrong" preposition. For example, Finnish speakers produced phrases like *sit to the grass* while both groups used *in* rather than *to* in sentences like *take Chaplin in the car*.

The researchers attribute the Finns' use of zero prepositions both to simplification (that is, reduction due to avoidance) and to the effects of "transfer" due to the fact that Finnish employs bound case morphology rather than prepositions to express spatial relationships. This, they suggest, leads Finnish learners to "disregard pre-posed function words as relevant spatial markers" (Jarvis and Oddlin 2000: 550). By contrast, the Swedish learners, whose L1 employs prepositions which often match their English equivalents in meaning, never resorted to omitting prepositions in any context. The differences in the choice of "wrong" prepositions also seem to be due to L1 influence. For example, Finnish has case inflections corresponding to English preposition *to* which might explain their use of *sit to the grass*, while there is no model for this in Swedish.

There are other kinds of simplification that are due to internal forces at work in learners' attempts to systematize the L2 grammar. Meisel (1977) refers to this as "elaborative simplification." For instance, learners may compensate for loss of morphology by employing periphrastic means instead. Thus, they may use adverbs to convey time reference, or fixed word order to distinguish subjects from objects, etc. Other strategies include analogical leveling and (over-) generalization, for instance the extension of past tense suffix *-ed* to irregular verbs like *run* or *see* in L2 English. These kinds of strategy are found in L1 acquisition as well, suggesting that both first and second language acquisition share certain "universal" developmental tendencies. Some of these will be discussed in the following sections. Elaborative simplification seems to be guided by the need for more transparency in the developing grammar. This motivation lies behind various changes or innovations that are internal to the developing interlanguage system.

Exercise 4

J. H. Schumann (1986) found significant differences in the use of zero and overt prepositions in the L2 English of Cantonese and Japanese learners on the one hand, and Spanish learners on the other. Examine Schumann's data, and suggest possible reasons for the difference, with special reference to the role of simplification and L1 influence.

7.4 Internal Developments in L2 Systems

Learners do not merely adopt elements from their L1 and the TL in their attempt to achieve communication in the latter. They also creatively adapt the resources they use, formulating and testing hypotheses to expand their developing L2 grammar (see Schachter 1992). The strategies they use include various kinds of regularization of grammatical structure, or other types of "elaborative simplification" that compensate for their limited knowledge of TL grammar.

Among the most common strategies of regularization is (over-)generalization of rules. Nemser (1991) provides several examples of these in the L2 English of his German-speaking students. For instance, early learners produce forms such as *leaved* for *left*, *buyed* for *bought*, *thinked* for *thought*, etc., overgeneralizing the "regular" past tense suffix *-ed* to irregular verbs (Nemser 1991: 348). They similarly overgeneralize the rule for plural formation, producing *sheeps* for *sheep* (pl.), *informations*, etc. Similar examples are found in derivational morphology, as when advanced learners produce *sparsity* for *sparseness* (apparenty by analogy with *scarcity*) or *unsmell* for "air out." Advanced learners also produce several other types of (incorrect) innovations, some based on analogical extension (e.g., *cruelism, cowardish*, etc.); others on back formation (e.g., *a jean* < *jeans*, *nocent* "guilty" < *[in]nocent*); and others on false (folk) etymology (e.g., *dumbfolded* for *dumbfounded*, *matter language* for *metalanguage*, and so on (ibid.: 349).

Innovative word coinage, especially through compounding, is also common in interlanguage. Extra and van Hout (1996: 105) cite examples like *yongen familie* "young family" for "nephew" and *boermensen* lit. "farmer-men" for *boeren* "farmers" in the L2 Dutch of a Moroccan learner.

In some cases, L1 morphological patterns reinforce the tendency to overgeneralize. Thus, German-speaking learners of L2 English produce innovations like *nervosity* (cf. German *Nervosität*) and *unguilty* (cf. German *unschuldig*) (Nemser 1991: 360). Similarly, English learners of Dutch tend to overgeneralize use of Dutch plural *-s* (which matches English *-s*) to cases where Dutch requires *-en*. All of these creative innovations testify simultaneously to learners' command of new L2 structural patterns and to their incomplete mastery of the rules. Such "errors" disappear as learners achieve greater familiarity with the TL.

All of the processes described here are also found in first language acquisition (L1A) as well as in internally motivated language change. These tendencies seem to be regulated by universal principles, constrained to some extent by the structure of the language itself. The main motivation seems to be the need to achieve maximum regularity and transparency in the grammar. One means of doing so is to assign an invariant meaning to an invariant form – a learning strategy attributed to the so-called one-form–one-meaning principle, also referred to as isomorphism. (See further discussion below.)

The same principle may lie behind the communicative strategies that learners adopt to compensate for loss (avoidance) of morphological distinctions. One example is the use of periphrastic (analytic) means to convey notions like time reference, discussed earlier. In rebuilding TL structure as they progress toward better acquisition, learners continue to seek optimality in structure as far as possible. Eventually, however, many of the generalizations they create must yield to irregularities in certain aspects of the TL grammar.

7.5 Developmental Stages in SLA

We have seen so far that the course of SLA follows a complicated path that involves gradual acquisition of TL elements and structures, interacting with L1 input, processes of reduction and other kinds of simplification, and processes internal to the developing interlanguage. These contributory factors remain active throughout the acquisition process, though with different effects at each stage. As Brown (1980: 163) notes: "By a gradual process of trial and error and by hypothesis testing, the learner slowly and tediously succeeds in establishing closer and closer approximations to the system used by native speakers of the language."

Studies of SLA have revealed a number of clear stages in the acquisition of specific areas of TL grammar such as negation, question formation, and so on. Most of these are based on classroom learning. Some studies (J. H. Schumann 1978; Huebner 1983; Perdue 1993a, 1993b) have focused on "natural" acquisition and attempted a more comprehensive picture of how learner's approximations to the TL develop over time. It is important to investigate these stages if we are to fully understand the role of TL input, reduction, L1 "transfer" or retention, and internal change in the learning process, as well as the principles that constrain it. These developmental stages, as well as the processes and constraints that guide them, are (also) very relevant to the emergence of contact vernaculars such as pidgins, creoles, and the "indigenized" varieties of a TL that result from group SLA or language shift.

We've already seen that, in the early stages of SLA, learners have only a highly reduced version of the TL, and rely to varying extents on their L1 and their creative ingenuity to build this first approximation. For instance, English-speaking children learning German begin with some sentence imitation and two-word utterances before producing multi-word phrases. The pattern of development is from two-word utterances, to copular sentences, to sentences containing auxiliaries, to sentences with main verbs (Felix 1977). A similar pattern has been reported for Italian-speaking children learning German (Pienemann 1980), a Chinese child acquiring English (Huang and Hatch 1978), and a Spanish-speaking adolescent acquiring English (Butterworth and Hatch 1978). It's not clear whether this order of acquisition of sentence types is the same for every L2, or specific to certain languages.

The L2 acquisition of particular syntactic structures also follows relatively clear stages. For instance, Spanish-speaking learners of L2 English acquire rules of negation in the following order (Cancino et al. 1978: 229; J. H. Schumann 1978; Stauble 1978; examples are from J. H. Schumann 1978: 13):

(14) a. *no* + V — *I no see; I no understand.*
b. *don't* + V — *I don't understand.*
c. aux-neg — *You can't tell her.*
d. Analyzed *do* + *not* — *He doesn't/didn't know.*

A similar pattern has been reported for German-speaking children learning English (Wode 1981), with slight differences, some apparently due to the influence of the respective L1 negation structures.

Stages of SLA have also been investigated for question formation, word order, relative clause formation, and other aspects of syntax. The studies reveal a certain order of acquisition in which a single invariant rule is applied across the board in the first stage, followed by gradual acquisition of more specific rules in later stages (see Braidi 1999: 19–47 for further details).

The questions that interest us at this point are as follows: What are the general characteristics of the interlanguage systems that learners construct in the earlier stages of learning? What strategies and processes are involved at each stage? What principles and constraints regulate the process of grammar building?

7.5.1 General characteristics of early interlanguage

In many cases, especially in "natural" SLA, learners' progress halts at a certain stage of development, resulting in "fossilization" or "acquisition failure" (van Coetsem 1988: 56). This phenomenon is particularly relevant to our concern with the possible outcomes of arrested SLA. Of special interest is the fact that many learners, especially adults, develop only a basic variety of the TL. In other words, they seem to get stuck at a relatively early stage of the acquisition process.

Perdue, Klein, and their associates studied the acquisition of second languages by 40 adult immigrants in Europe over the period 1981 to 1988, recording their L2 production for thirty months in each case (Perdue 1993a, 1993b). The subjects were of various language backgrounds, including Arabic, Finnish, Italian, Panjabi, Spanish, and Turkish. The TLs were various European languages, including Dutch, English, French, German, and Swedish. The study was designed to allow for comparison of acquisition of the same TL by different immigrant groups, as well as different TLs by the same group. Interestingly, the investigation revealed that all learners developed a basic variety of each TL that was surprisingly uniform in its general structure. About a third of the learners got stuck at this stage of acquisition, though some continued to add more vocabulary items to their system.

The basic variety was characterized by a small but expanding lexicon, drawn mostly from the TL, but with some L1 items. It consisted mostly of nouns and verbs and a smaller inventory of adjectives and adverbs. It also contained a small number of function words such as quantifiers, a few determiners, a single negative marker and a few prepositions. The pronominal system distinguished only between the speaker, the hearer, and a third person. This basic variety completely lacked inflectional morphology and, by extension, grammatical categories such as tense and aspect, case, gender and number, agreement, etc. In syntax, it lacked complementizers and subordination in general. Sentence structures were limited to three simple patterns with slight variations, as follows:

(15) a. NP – V – (NP) (NP)
b. NP – Cop – XP (Adj, NP or PP)
c. V – NP

In general, this order reflected that of the TL. Klein and Perdue (1997) note, however, that the position of an NP does not always determine its role as subject or object. Instead, argument position is determined by a pragmatic principle ("focus last") which places the focused element last in an utterance, and a semantic principle ("controller first") which places first an NP whose referent controls the event. Whether these constraints hold universally for these and other early learner versions of a TL is a matter of some disagreement. However, the essentials of the basic variety's syntactic structure seem to match those found in other early adult interlanguages. In fact, this is true of the overall structural characteristics of the basic varieties.

Also worth noting is the fact that some degree of L1 influence is evident in the basic variety as well. Such influence appears in phonology, in noun-compounding strategies, and in the expression of spatial relations (Klein and Perdue 1997: 312). Some variation in word order is also ascribable to L1 influence. In general, however, the basic variety is essentially independent of both the L1 and the TL in its structural organization.

The findings of Perdue and his associates are interesting because they suggest that all (adult) L2 learners go through a similar early stage of SLA in which they create a stable but rudimentary version of the TL which is shaped by similar principles of organization and structure. Whether these organizational principles are universal is still unclear. But it has been argued that they apply also to early L1 acquisition, as well as to the process of pidgin formation. We return to the latter in the next chapter.

As noted earlier, learners progress beyond the basic variety by adding more vocabulary, morphological apparatus, and syntactic rules drawn primarily from the TL. With increasing acquisition comes decreasing reliance on reduction, L1 input (transfer), and changes internal to the IL. At this point, it may be useful to ask how these IL phenomena relate to the actual strategies that learners employ to achieve communication in the TL.

7.6 Strategies and Processes in SLA

Before we proceed any further, some clarification of terminology is in order. Terms like "strategy" and "process" are often applied to the same phenomena, though conceptually they are quite distinct. For instance, Kellerman (1978) refers to transfer as a learning and/or communication strategy, while Gass (1983) refers to it as a process in which L1 structure is imposed on L2 structure. Both interpretations may be appropriate, depending on the perspective one takes. Thus Hammarberg (1997: 162) suggests that transfer can be considered at different levels of analysis as follows:

> (a) at the level of *strategy*, with regard to the learner's plan of action to solve a particular problem; (b) at the level of *execution*, with regard to the event or process

of carrying out the strategy; and (c) at the level of *solution*, with regard to the product (as manifested in the learner's L2 performance) of the applied strategy.

So each strategy a learner uses can be associated with a certain (linguistic) process, and a certain result. We will try to keep these different aspects of transfer apart as far as possible in the following discussion.

The learner is faced with two tasks – learning as well as producing TL structures. To accomplish them, he or she resorts to various learning and communication strategies, each subject to certain constraints. Learning strategies include, for instance, memorizing, guessing, using deductive reasoning through comparison of L1 and L2 elements, translating, and testing various hypotheses. Learners may also actively seek out more opportunities to access L2 input, for example, through interaction with L2 speakers, reading, watching television, and so on. These have been referred to as "social/affective" strategies. All of these strategies directly feed the process of grammar building.

In attempting to communicate via the L2, learners will obviously employ the elements they have acquired, but, to compensate for those they lack, they resort to various communication strategies. These may be divided into avoidance strategies (e.g., avoidance of certain elements or topics) and compensatory strategies. The latter include use of L1 elements and rules, IL-internal strategies such as generalization or paraphrase, and, often, non-linguistic strategies such as mime, gesture, etc. (Poulisse 1996).

Learning and communication strategies complement one another in the task of grammar restructuring, though the former are more difficult to observe than the latter. The relationship between them may be somewhat analogous to that between competence and performance. Hence it is generally agreed that a full picture of learner's IL grammar must come from investigation of not just their production, but also their comprehension and intuitive judgments. At any rate, the communicative strategies themselves, as represented in learners' attempted production of the TL, provide much insight into the developing IL grammar. Indeed, it is precisely these strategies that lie behind the three major processes of IL creation – simplification, L1 retention (transfer), and IL-internal innovation, as discussed earlier. Recall that these processes compensate for incomplete acquisition of the TL. Our task at this point is to describe how acquisition of TL features, learning strategies, and communication strategies interact to help build up the learner's IL system.

Studies conducted in the 1970s and 1980s revealed that communication strategies, including resort to the L1, were more common among less proficient (early) than advanced learners (see Poulisse 1996: 149 for an overview). This is in keeping with what we saw of the structural characteristics of the basic interlanguage system that early learners create. Strategies of avoidance would account in part for the reduction of morphology, the absence of syntactic operations like embedding, and so on. Of course, absence of these in learners' early IL may be also due to simple ignorance or lack of awareness, that is, failure to notice and process (especially bound) morphology (Ellis 1994: 361–2). Other compensatory strategies would explain, for instance, the use of L1 elements and rules, as well as IL-internal processes like word coinage, overgeneralization, paraphrase, etc.

As noted earlier, the elaboration of IL grammar goes through several stages. Learners acquire, for instance, more specific rules of negation, word order, and so on. They gradually master TL morphology, introducing into their system grammatical categories like tense and aspect, number and agreement, and so on. What cognitive and linguistic principles guide learners in this attempt to reconstruct TL grammar? What constraints regulate that process? Let us consider these issues briefly.

7.7 Principles and Constraints on SLA

The progress of L2 acquisition is determined by various factors, both linguistic and non-linguistic. The latter include motivation, degree of access to and interaction with TL speakers, opportunities to use the TL, attitudes to the culture, and so on. The linguistic factors include the nature of the TL input, the degree of structural similarity between the TL and the learner's L1, and various principles and constraints that regulate the learner's attempt at grammar construction. For the moment, let us focus on the last of these.

SLA researchers have suggested that certain cognitive and linguistic principles are at work at every stage of L2 acquisition, interacting with various constraints that either facilitate or impede successful acquisition. It's of course impossible to provide here a complete picture of all the (psycho-)linguistic factors that influence the course of L2A. But a brief overview will suffice.

7.7.1 The early stages of SLA: processing and learning principles

In the early stages of L2A, the main task of the learner is to make sense of the L2 input and discover the structure underlying it. In this task, one is guided by general cognitive principles of language processing and learning. Researchers suggest that learners of both first and second languages rely on certain "operating" principles to help them analyze input. These include, for instance, maxims like the following:

- Pay attention to the ends of words.
- Store any perceptually salient stretch of speech.
- Pay attention to the order of words.
- Avoid exceptions, etc. (Slobin 1973, 1985; Andersen 1984, 1990)

Other processing principles determine which aspects of the input learners tend to process earlier. For instance, Van Patten (1996: 14–15) suggests the following, among others:

- Learners process input for meaning before they process it for form.
- Learners process content words first.
- Learners tend to process lexical items before grammatical items for semantic information.

Principles like these might explain why early interlanguage tends to include mostly lexical rather than function morphemes, and no bound morphology. Such principles also constrain the actual amount of input that makes its way into the learner's developing IL system. This modified input, or intake, constitutes the primary material for the construction of the early IL grammar.

The process of grammar building, in turn, is regulated by certain general learning principles, as well as by constraints of a specifically linguistic nature. The learner comes equipped with certain expectations about grammatical structure which help impose order on the intake data. The principles that have been suggested in this connection include:

> A. The uniqueness principle (one form expresses one meaning);
> B. The principle of continuity (constituents that belong together are placed together);
> C. The principle of canonical word order (main clause word order constitutes the basic word order. (Jordens 1996: 32)

We might conceive of such principles as guides that regulate the other kinds of constraint, particularly those that apply to L1 influence and other kinds of creative restructuring in the building of IL grammar. For example, we saw earlier that L1 influence plays some role in learners' decisions as to what constitutes basic word order in the TL. They then generalize this word order across the board, in keeping with the principle of canonical word order, which is closely related to the "One to One Principle" (see below). Jordens (1996: 417) discusses this with regard to the acquisition of L2 Dutch by speakers of Moroccan Arabic and Turkish. Since Dutch allows the lexical verb to occur in first, second, or sentence-final position, the input to learners includes both OV and

VO patterns. Turkish speakers select OV as the basic word order in their L2 Dutch, since that is the pattern in their L1. On the other hand, Moroccan Arabic speakers assume that the basic order is VO, for the same reason. A similar explanation may lie behind the overgeneralization of SVO order in the early L2 German and L2 French of English learners, as discussed in section 7.2.4.

Other researchers have proposed additional principles that guide learners' interpretation of sentence structure. For instance, Van Patten (1996: 32) suggests that learners adopt a default assumption that the first noun in a sentence is the agent. This is part of a more general principle that learners rely on word order as their primary cue to interpreting sentences or utterances. However, they may adopt different hypotheses based on semantic or pragmatic principles (see Klein and Purdue's argument earlier) or on L1 knowledge (see below).

General processing and learning principles such as these allow learners to maximize ease of perception and production. They explain many of the typical structural characteristics of the basic L2 variety that emerges in the early stages of SLA, as discussed earlier. Andersen (1984, 1990) ascribes many of these structural characteristics to the workings of his "One to One Principle," which seems to subsume the uniqueness principle and the principle of canonical word order mentioned above. Andersen's principle states that "an interlanguage system should be constructed in such a way that an intended underlying meaning is expressed with one clear invariant surface form [or construction]" (1989: 79). He cites examples such as canonical SVO order in early L2 German, and the use of an invariant negative marker *no* in early L2 English, among others. The One to One Principle seems to apply both to processing and to grammar building. Principles more or less identical to this have been proposed for pidgin and creole formation. We will explore the links between these contact vernaculars and SLA in later chapters.

7.7.2 Constraints in the elaboration of L2 grammar

In elaborating their earliest version of the TL, learners gradually acquire more complex rules of word order, movement, etc., as well as a variety of morphological operations like number and person marking, tense and aspect, and so on. The sequence and path of this restructuring are also subject to general linguistic principles and constraints that regulate the design of grammars. Some of these may be universal in nature, applying to both L1A and L2A, or they may be specific to the L2. Others have to do with the interaction between L1 and L2 grammar, and the influence the former has on the latter.

As we would expect, learners continue to formulate and test various generalizations about the way L2 grammar is organized. For instance, learners of L2

English have to figure out the range of application of rules such as *wh*-question and relative clause formation. With regard to the former, they must acquire rules of inversion as well as various restrictions on *wh*-extraction. Cancino et al. (1978: 230) show that early learners of L2 English employ the same word order in all *wh*-questions, as in the following:

(16) a. Who is coming?
b. What John is doing?

Later, they learn rules of inversion which they sometimes overgeneralize to embedded questions as well:

(17) a. What is John doing?
b. I know what is John doing.

Eventually they learn that inversion applies only to direct rather than embedded *wh*-questions. In addition to this, learners have to acquire rules of *wh*-extraction from different levels of embedding, as in the following;

(18) a. $What_i$ did Mary do t_i?
b. $What_i$ did Mary write about t_i?
c. $What_i$ did Mary tell a story about t_i?

Research by Wolfe Quintero (1992) suggests that learners first acquire *wh*-extraction in sentences like (18a), then in sentences like (18b), and finally in those like (18c). Part of the explanations for this seems to lie in the different levels of embeddedness involved in the three structures (extraction from VP in (18a); from a PP within a VP in (18b); and from a PP within an NP within a VP in (18c)).

Finally, learners must master various restrictions on *wh*-questions. For instance, they must discover that *wh*-extraction is possible from some embedded clauses, but not others, as in the following (see Bley-Vroman et al. 1988):

(19) a. Who_i did Mary try to find t_i?
b. *Who_i did Mary say that t_i left?

In short, learners have to discover the "domains of generalization" for rules of *wh*-question formation (Jordens 1996: 411). A similar developmental pattern seems to apply to the acquisition of other kinds of structure, such as relative clauses, to which we will return later. The principles and constraints that govern the generalization of such rules are not clearly understood. But part of the explanation may be that different levels of wh-extraction reflect a hierarchy of markedness, and that learners acquire wh-questions in order of less to more marked (see below). Processing constraints may also be involved in determining both what is more marked, and what restrictions apply. In some cases too, learners may be aided by similarities between their L1 and the TL.

It has also been proposed that learners may acquire a number of L2 rules or properties simultaneously because such properties form a closely related cluster. A great deal of attention has been devoted to such clustering by scholars working within the framework of Universal Grammar (UG). UG is made up of a set of principles and parameters. The former determine or restrict the form of grammars. The latter represent those areas of grammar that vary from language to language. One of the assumptions of the theory is that the setting of a particular parameter results in a cluster of related properties. For instance, earlier approaches hypothesized that pro-drop in languages like Spanish implied a set of characteristics including null subject pronouns, subject–verb inversion in declarative sentences, and extraction of subjects (leaving a trace) out of embedded clauses with overt complementizers (as in (19b) above). On the other hand, languages without pro-drop, like English, would have none of these characteristics. On this basis, it was assumed that learners who mastered one characteristic (e.g., [lack of] pro-drop) would simultaneously master all the associated properties. However, studies of the acquisition of English by speakers of Spanish, French, and other languages show no evidence that learners acquire the relevant cluster of English properties as a whole, or even recognize any relationship among all of them (see discussion in Gass 1997: 33–5). Part of the reason seems to be that there is no underlying rationale – for example, some type of structural relationship – for the cluster proposed. Nor is there any clear structural principle that might explain the relationship. There may well be a tendency in such approaches to confuse UG principles with specific structural properties of a language. Future research in SLA will no doubt attempt to provide a clearer rationale to explain how learners acquire related structures in an L2.

This is not meant to deny the importance of certain general linguistic principles of UG in L2 acquisition. Structural principles such as subjacency do seem to constrain the sequence and extent of acquisition of certain related structures, such as the various kinds of *wh*-extraction discussed above, or different kinds of relative clause formation, to be discussed below. Other UG principles such as the empty category principle and the Binding principles seem to impose constraints on IL grammar construction as well (see Felix 1997 for some discussion). We will suggest below that such UG principles may be related to processing constraints as well.

7.7.3 Typological universals and SLA

Scholars working in the area of language typology take a somewhat different approach to the question of how universal linguistic principles constrain SLA. Based on cross-linguistic comparison of a broad sample of languages, Greenberg (1966) first proposed 45 universals of grammatical structure. These typological universals are statements about structural characteristics and relationships that apply across languages. Some of these are absolute or unrestricted, such as "all languages have vowels," while others are tendencies, such as "SOV languages tend to have postpositions." Typological universals may be either implicational or non-implicational. A well-known example of the former is the Noun Phrase Accessibility Hierarchy (NPAH), which ranks the grammatical functions of noun phrases that are accessible to relativization in relative clauses (Keenan and Comrie 1977). It states that nouns with different functions (subject, object, etc.) in such clauses lend themselves to relativization in the following order:

> subject > direct object > indirect object > object of preposilion > genitive > object of comparison

The symbol ">" here means "more accessible than." Thus, if a language allows relativization of grammatical functions lower down the hierarchy (those to the right) then it will also allow relativization with those to the left. But the reverse does not hold.[2]

Integral to the study of typological universals is the notion of markedness – a rather complex concept that has been interpreted in different ways by typologists and generative linguists. Markedness has to do with the relationship between two poles of an opposition, for example between categories like singular versus plural, or between rules or constructions. Typologists define markedness in several ways, using various criteria, some based on structure, some on distribution and frequency, both within a single language and cross-linguistically. In general, the unmarked value of an opposition has less complex structure, is found in more environments, and has a wider cross-linguistic distribution and frequency than the marked value (Croft 1990: 92). Generative linguistic approaches define markedness somewhat differently, in very theory-specific terms, which need not concern us here (see Battistella 1990, 1996 for further discussion). Of particular interest to SLA researchers is the fact that, in recent approaches, the concept has been linked closely to theories of learnability. Some researchers suggest that "via markedness, UG provides an inherent learning hierarchy, which is reflected in the process of second language acquisition" (Battistella 1996: 118).

In general, we might say that forms or structures that are more basic, simpler, easier to learn, and more frequent are unmarked, while marked forms are more complex, infrequent, and harder to learn. There is still much disagreement about what constitutes a marked feature, and the precise linguistic grounds for identifying markedness are not clear. Nevertheless, there are some generally accepted claims about markedness at various linguistic levels, like the following:

- Complex consonantal codas are highly marked while vowel codas are unmarked.
- Polysynthetic morphology is more marked than agglutinative morphology.
- *Wh*-extraction from deeply embedded constituents is more marked than *wh*-extraction from less deeply embedded constituents.

The notion of (typological) markedness has figured prominently in discussions of SLA, as well as other kinds of language contact such as pidgin and creole formation. The assumption in the former case is that the degree of markedness of TL structures is directly related to the ease and order of their acquisition. This hypothesis has found support in studies of the acquisition of relative clauses and question formation in L2 English, Swedish, and other languages. For example, Gass (1979, 1980) investigated the acquisition of L2 English relative clauses by speakers of nine different languages, including Arabic, Chinese, French, and others. She found that relative clauses attached to nouns in more accessible positions on the NPAH were produced more frequently and accurately than for the less accessible (more marked) positions. A similar conclusion was reached by Hylstenstam (1981), who examined the acquisition of relative clauses in L2 Swedish by speakers of Finnish, Greek, Persian, and Spanish.

It would appear then that typological universals do play a role in SLA, though the full extent of that role remains unclear. This may well be in keeping with both processing constraints and linguistic principles that restrict the scope of certain syntactic operations, especially those involving embedding, as discussed earlier. The three types of constraint, processing, structural and typological, appear to be related in some way.

7.7.4 *Markedness constraints and L1 influence in SLA*

So far, we have been treating markedness as though it was an absolute property that could be defined in universal terms. However, as we saw in chapter 3, markedness may also be viewed in relative terms, as a function of the degree of typological distance between the systems in contact. This is what lies behind approaches that attempt to integrate markedness into a theory of L1 influence on SLA.

Earlier SLA researchers attempted to account for the role of the L1 in SLA in terms of the approach proposed by Lado (1957) which came to be known as the Contrastive Analysis Hypothesis (CAH). This hypothesis claimed to predict potential areas of difficulty for learners of an L2 purely on the basis of differences between the learner's L1 and the TL. Though many of its predictions were borne out by research, many others failed. There were cases where learning was successful despite differences between the L1 and L2, and others where it proved difficult in the absence of any differences between the two. It became clear that there was a need to identify specific principles that regulate L1 influence on L2 acquisition.

One such attempt was Eckman's (1977) Markedness Differential Hypothesis (MDH). This was intended to remedy the shortcomings of the CAH by linking the notion of congruence between L1 and L2 to the concept of (typological) markedness. The MDH included the following stipulations (Eckman 1985: 291):

> *The Markedness Differential Hypothesis*
> The areas of difficulty that an L2 learner will have can be predicted on the basis of a comparison of the NL [native language] and the TL such that:
>
> (a) those areas of the TL that are different from the NL and are relatively more marked than in the NL will be difficult;
> (b) the degree of difficulty associated with those aspects of the TL that are different and more marked than in the NL corresponds to the relative degree of markedness associated with those aspects;
> (c) those areas of the TL that are different than the NL but are not relatively more marked than in the NL will not be difficult.

For instance, the MDH predicts that native speakers of languages like Japanese which have no word-final consonant clusters will have greater difficulty learning stop + stop clusters than fricative + stop clusters in final position. This is premised on the typological evidence that final stop + stop clusters are more marked than final fricative + stop clusters (Eckman 1985: 291).

Exercise 5
Revisit the discussion of phonemic differences between English and Hindi in chapter 2. What difficulties would the MDH predict that L1 Hindi learners would face in acquiring L2 English phonology, and vice versa?

Some predictions of the MDH have been borne out in various studies (see Eckman 1985: 299 for a brief summary). For instance, it has been claimed that the MDH explains the order of acquisition of relative clauses in L2 English and Swedish by learners of various language backgrounds. The MDH predicts that the order of acquisition of relative clauses should follow the order of accessibility in the NPAH. Also, it predicts that acquisition would be facilitated in cases where the L1 relativization matches that of the L2. Support for this comes from Hyltenstam's study of L2 Swedish relative clauses by Finnish, Greek, Persian, and Spanish learners, referred to earlier. Eckman (1977) also claimed that the data from Schachter (1974) supported the MDH with respect to acquisition of L2 English relative clauses by Arabic, Chinese, Japanese, and Persian learners. However, some questions have been raised about discrepancies in various analyses of relative clause formation in the four languages, which cast doubt on Eckman's conclusion. Further research may clarify the part that L1 influence plays in these cases. Note, however, that the explanations of acquisitional development offered by the MDH are quite compatible with those that depend on structural principles such as subjacency, as discussed earlier.

Exercise 6

What stages would you predict for the acquisition of question formation (both yes/no and *wh*-questions) in L2 English? (See Braidi 1999: 28–32 for some help.) Do you see any similarity with the case of relative clause acquisition? Find out whether there are typological universals that relate to question formation. What order of difficulty would be predicted by the MDH? (See Braidi 1999: 85–6 and Eckman et al. 1989 for some discussion.)

7.7.5 Constraints on transfer

The MDH simply notes that some TL structures will be easier to acquire than others based on the degree of typological similarity between L1 and L2. But it offers no explanation for the kinds of L1 influence that may come into play, or the principles that constrain it. For instance, it's not clear how the MDH would explain why acquisition is not always accurate in cases of closer typological fit or congruence between L1 and TL. A tacit assumption of this hypothesis seems to be that the learner can simply substitute certain L1 properties or structures for matching counterparts in the TL. But this may lead to either positive or negative transfer.

This kind of L1 influence, based on some perceived congruence between L1 and L2 features (cf. Weinreich's "interlingual identifications"), is the focus of Andersen's (1983) Transfer to Somewhere Principle. This states that:

> A grammatical form or structure will occur consistently and to a significant extent in the interlanguage *if and only if* (1) natural acquisitional principles are consistent with the L1 structure or (2) there already exists within the L2 input the potential for (mis)generalization from the input to produce the same form or structure. (1983: 182)

A frequently quoted example of this is the fact that English learners of L2 French tend to place object pronouns after the verb in their French IL, on the model of their native syntax. Thus they produce structures like **je vois le*, lit. "I see him," instead of the correct French structure *je le vois* "I him see." The Transfer to Somewhere Principle explains this as follows. Post-verbal placement of full NP objects is required in both English and French, and this provides a model for the post-verbal placement of pronouns by English learners of French. By contrast, French learners find no English model for pre-verbal placement of pronominal objects, hence they do not produce structures like **I him see*.

To take another example, it's often the case that TL sounds that are perceived as quite similar to L1 sounds prove quite difficult for learners to produce accurately. There is much evidence that learners typically fail to accurately reproduce the acoustic properties of TL sounds that have close counterparts in the L1. Flege (1987) showed that advanced English learners of L2 French were in fact more successful in producing French /y/, which has no English equivalent, than French /u/, which differs acoustically from English /u/. In fact, it seems that in general, learners find it harder to master a sound that is closely similar to one in the L1 than a sound that they have to learn from scratch (Leather and James 1991: 313). In other words, interlingual identifications based on learner's perceptions often lead to inaccurate production. These kinds of misidentification are the phonological equivalent of the "false friends" we mentioned earlier with respect to L1 influence on the acquisition of L2 vocabulary (section 7.2.1). Similar phenomena can be found in morphosyntax, as we saw in section 7.2.3. In all these cases, learners seem to be projecting L1 categories onto TL forms.

This kind of transfer, then, is triggered by some type of congruence, whether semantic, functional, or structural, between L1 and L2 elements. We will discuss constraints on transfer further, in section 7.12.2 below. It seems clear from all the above that L1 influence is constrained in various ways by general structural principles.

7.7.6 Cognitive principles and IL development

The structural constraints on IL development that we have considered so far, whether based on general linguistic principles or on typological markedness, are often linked to cognitive principles and constraints of a more abstract psycholinguistic nature. Just as we suggested for the early stages of L2A, these cognitive principles also guide the process of hypothesis testing and rule formulation that brings learners closer to the TL system. The principles are reflected in various processing constraints on the emergence of more complex IL structures. Clahsen (1984: 221) suggested that structures requiring more processing would be acquired later than those requiring less. This idea was taken up by Pienemann (1997), whose Processability Theory states that "the learner cannot access . . . hypotheses which he/she cannot process" (1997: 3). This approach attempts to link a processing model of speech production to a model of grammar construction so as to account for developmental stages in SLA (see discussion in Braidi 1999: 123–7). Research on the links between processing and structural constraints in L2 grammar construction is still very much in its infancy. But it promises to shed light on the central issue of how universal cognitive and linguistic principles interact with TL input and L1 influence to regulate the path of SLA. This is the ultimate goal of a comprehensive theory of SLA.

This brief sketch of L1 influence on L2 acquisition falls far short of revealing the full complexity of the strategies and operations learners employ in producing some approximation to the TL. The learner's success depends on a number of factors, cognitive, linguistic, and sociolinguistic. We have focused our attention on those cognitive and linguistic principles that regulate the learning process and help learners to maximize ease of perception and production. We will see in the next section how such principles are relevant to cases of group SLA, that is, language shift by an entire community.

Though the sociolinguistic factors that influence individual SLA are also quite important, we will not consider them in any detail here. Such factors include, for instance, the learner's age and maturation, motivation to learn, degree of social integration and acceptance among TL speakers, and her or his attitudes toward the TL community and its culture. Factors such as these are also relevant to group SLA, to which we now turn our attention.

II GROUP SECOND LANGUAGE ACQUISITION OR LANGUAGE SHIFT

7.8 Introduction

As our brief survey of SLA has shown, we have a fairly good idea of how individuals go about learning a second or foreign language. But what happens when an entire community or group acquires a TL as their second language, or shifts entirely to it? Very often, the outcome of such shift is a contact language significantly different from the original TL. Among the examples we will consider here are Irish English (also referred to as Hiberno-English) and Colloquial Singapore English. Like other outcomes of group SLA, both show striking linguistic peculiarities due in part to influence from ancestral languages, or processes of simplification in the course of shift. How do such contact vernaculars originate? What factors, structural and non-structural, influence the form they take? Questions like these can be difficult to answer clearly, since all we have to go on are the outcomes themselves, and we seldom have the opportunity to observe the actual process of their formation. We therefore have to rely on what we can find out about the linguistic inputs to the contact situation, and the social context of the contact itself, in order to try to reconstruct this process of language creation. The insights gained from the detailed examination of individual SLA are obviously of great value in this undertaking.

For a start, we can assume that the same structural principles and processes that operate in individual SLA are at work in group SLA as well. Hence we would expect that the various kinds of innovation and creative restructuring found in individual SLA would have their counterparts in the outcomes of group shift as well. But of course the two situations are not identical. The differences between them might be characterized in terms of Weinreich's well-known distinction between "interference in speech" and "interference in language." The former he compares to sand carried by a stream, while the latter is "the sedimented sand deposited on the bottom of the lake" (1953: 11). In other words, contact-induced changes in individual production are variable and ephemeral, while such changes in language are fixed and permanent. One of our tasks is to explain why some features are selected or conventionalized as part of the communal grammar, while others are discarded.

The creation of new contact vernaculars involves a stage of continuing interaction and competition among individual interlanguage grammars that is eventually resolved into a shared communal system. The actual resolution depends on a variety of sociolinguistic factors, including the demographics of the groups in contact, the extent of inter-group versus intra-group interaction, the length of contact, the power relationship between the groups, their attitudes toward each other, and so on. In order to explore the origins of contact vernaculars, we must have the clearest possible picture of all these factors, as well as of the linguistic structures of the languages involved at the time of the contact (Thomason 1993). Before we explore these issues further, it may be useful to examine particular outcomes of shift and their settings.

In chapter 1, we outlined two broad types of situation in which group language shift can occur. The first of these involves settings in which minority groups form part of a larger host community speaking a different language.

Members of such groups usually become bilingual in the host language, or shift entirely to it, often by the third generation. In most of these cases, children born in the third generation acquire native proficiency in the host language. When demographic and other sociocultural conditions are right, some immigrant groups may develop their own distinctive version of the TL, which they preserve as an in-group vernacular and a badge of separate identity. The variety of American English known variously as African American Vernacular English or Ebonics is such an example. So too are some varieties of English spoken by Chicano and other Latino groups in the US.

The second type of situation can be found in (former) colonies where conquerors have introduced their own language, but have remained a minority. In such cases, the indigenous community acquires its own version of the foreign language, either replacing their ancestral language with it, or employing both in different domains. In the following discussion, I will focus my attention on situations of the second type, though it should be kept in mind that the processes involved in both types of shift are the same. Let us first examine the well-known case of Irish English.

7.9 Irish English

English was first introduced to Ireland in the twelfth century by settlers who spoke various regional dialects of English. The major input seems to have come from southern and southwest Midlands English (Kallen 1997: 140). The contact between English and Irish resulted in a distinctive form of medieval Irish English with substantial influence from Irish. This early contact variety no doubt had some influence on the emergence of modern Irish English. For the next several centuries, English remained very much a minority language in Ireland, with most of the population maintaining Irish as their only language. The English-speaking population grew steadily over the period 1500 to 1700, due to migration of settlers from other parts of Britain, as well as to education and informal second language learning among the Irish (Odlin 1992: 182).

British colonial settlements were established in Ulster (Northern Ireland) and eastern Ireland. Large numbers of settlers were introduced to Ulster from Scotland and northern England, while eastern Ireland attracted settlers from various regions of England, especially the south and southwest Midlands. Another important factor in the spread of English was the seasonal migration of Irish workers to other parts of Ireland as well as Scotland and England (Odlin 1997a: 11). Over the next two centuries, English gradually spread at the expense of Irish, establishing itself first in the towns and eventually throughout most of Ireland. Odlin (1997a) provides a fuller account of the sociohistorical background.

The differences in the settlement patterns as well as the patterns of contact in general resulted in the emergence of two broad varieties of Irish English, northern and southern. The former includes the variety known as Ulster Scots, originally introduced by Scottish settlers, as well as two other varieties, mid-Ulster and south Ulster English (Kingsmore 1995: 20). The latter two, though they share many features with Ulster Scots, seem to have been more influenced by regional varieties of southern English. Despite their differences, northern and southern Irish English have a great deal in common due to shared superstratal input and substratum influence from Irish (Odlin 1997a: 29). In keeping with practice in contact linguistics, I will henceforth use the term "substratum influence" as a synonym for L1 influence.

The varieties of Irish English that most interest us are those spoken as everyday informal vernaculars, particularly by persons of rural and/or working-class background. These non-standard varieties share various characteristics that include continuities from early Modern English dialects as well as features due to Irish substratum influence and other processes of contact-induced change. The effects of such change are most noticeable in parts of Ireland once having a high degree of bilingualism, and in conservative rural speech (Harris 1984: 305).

Examples of early Modern English dialectal continuities in Irish English include the variable absence of subject pronouns in relative clauses, as in (20), and the use of *for to* as a complementizer where Standard English uses *to*, as in (21):

(20) I know a girl works in that shop.

(21) It's not easy for to do that.

Structures like these are still found in some contemporary regional dialects of England and Scotland, and Irish English presumably adopted them from the ancestors of these dialects.

Many other distinctive lexical and structural characteristics of Irish English are also direct continuities of features found in earlier English dialects, including literary varieties. They include demonstratives like *them* "those"; *yon/thon* "that/those further away"; use of concord *-s* with both singular and plural third person subjects (*the women knows; the men is/was*); reduction of "strong" verb paradigms from a three-way to a two-way distinction (*go/went/went* versus Standard English *go/went/gone*); multiple negation (*I never said nothing to nobody*); positive *anymore* used in the sense of "nowadays" as well as "from now on" (*Wool is expensive anymore; We can do our homework on this [desk] anymore, can't* *we?*). Example sentences are from Kallen (1997: 153). For a more detailed account of these and other continuities from earlier English, see Harris (1993).

Many lexical items that are now rare or obsolete in British English can still be found in contemporary Irish English. Some of these came from Scotland and northern England, for example *palatic* "drunk," *skite* "drinking session, party," etc. Others came from southern England, for example *ledge* "a row of mown hay," *pill* "river tributary," etc. (Kallen 1997: 146–7).

7.9.1 Substratum influence on Irish English

There seems to be general agreement that, while Irish English is based on mid-seventeenth-century English dialects, many of its features are due to influence from Irish, the first language of its learners. As Bliss (1972: 63) puts it: "This seventeenth century English was acquired gradually and with difficulty, by speakers of Irish; and in the process of their acquisition of it they modified it, both in pronunciation and syntax, toward conformity with their own linguistic habits."

This L1 or substratum influence is apparent at all levels of Irish English structure. In phonology, the following are among the characteristics that can be found, especially in more conservative rural speech:

- Interdental fricatives /θ/ and /ð/ are realized as affricates, that is, they are co-articulated with alveolar or dental stops as /tθ/ and /dð/ respectively.
- Velar stops tend to undergo palatalization more frequently than they do in other varieties of British English.
- Alveolar fricative /s/ is produced with fortis articulation.
- The labio-dental fricative /f/ and /v/ have the allophones /ɸ/ and /β/ respectively.

All of these have counterparts in Irish (Odlin 1997a: 30).

The morphosyntactic features ascribed to Irish influence include tense/aspect categories like "hot news" perfect and habitual *be*; the imperative expressed by *let*, and peculiar uses of prepositions, as in *Hugh is buried with years* (= has been buried for years) (Harris 1993: 171–3). These features are not exact replicas of those in Irish, but represent compromises between English and Irish structure. For instance, the overall organization of the tense/aspect system of Irish English is a blend of continuities from both source languages. Irish English preserves earlier English perfect constructions like the following:

(22) She's nearly her course finished
"She's nearly finished her course" (Harris 1984: 307)

It also preserves other categories such as present, past, and future tense, progressive and past habitual aspect, etc. But, as noted above, the "hot news" perfect and the present habitual are clearly due to Irish influence.[3] The former is expressed by a construction consisting of *be* + *after* + *V-ing*, as in the following:

(23) She's after selling the boat
"She's just sold the boat"

Irish has a very similar construction, exemplified in the following:

(24) Tá sí tréis an bád a dhíol
Be+nonpast she after the boat selling (Harris 1984: 319)

As can be seen, the Irish English construction conforms to English rather than Irish word order, but the Irish influence is clear. Similarly, Irish English makes a distinction between the simple present copula and habitual *be*, as in the following:

(25) a. She's here now
b. She be's here often
"She's often here"

The same distinction is found in Irish, as in:

(26) a. Tá sí anseo anois
Be+nonpast she here now
b. Bíonn sí anseo go minic
be+nonpast+hab. she here often

Irish English also employs *do* as a present habitual auxiliary with *be* and non-copular verbs, as in the following examples from Harris (1986: 176):

(27) a. They do be fighting among other
"They're usually fighting among themselves"
b. He does help us. He does plough the field for us
"He helps us. He ploughs the field for us"

Present habitual *do* appears to derive from simple periphrastic *do* in seventeenth-century English dialects, especially those of the southwest, which were a major input to Irish English. The reanalysis of *do* as a habitual auxiliary seems to have been motivated both by the fact that it often conveyed habitual meaning, and the fact that Irish had a distinct habitual category that provided a model for its reinterpretation (Harris 1986: 180). A similar reinterpretation of *do* occurred in Bajan (Barbadian English) for much the same reasons (see chapter 9, section 9.4).

Several other distinctive features of Irish English syntax can also be attributed to compromise between English and Irish structure, and to congruence between the inputs from the two sources. For instance, Irish English (IE) has a distinctive use of *and* as a subordinating conjunction, which appears to have counterparts in British English dialects (Filppula 1991; Odlin 1992). However, Odlin (1992) argues that these constructions are modeled primarily on similar constructions in Irish which are introduced by *agus*, the Irish equivalent of *and*. The following examples from Odlin (1992: 186–7) illustrate:

(28) a. Irish: Agus é san IRA, phós sé Albanach buí
And him in-the IRA married he Scot yellow
"He married an orange [Protestant] girl while in the IRA"
b. IE: The sergeant ran for his life. And he going out over the wall, he hit against a tomb

Irish substratum influence is also apparent in other areas of Irish English grammar, including cleft constructions (e.g., *It was painting I was*) and use of reflexive pronouns where Standard English doesn't permit the (e.g., *I don't remember himself*) (Odlin 1997b: 40–1) Also of interest are various idiomatic expressions (Odlin 1991), and the use of *sorrow* and *devil* as negators, as in the following examples (Odlin 1995, 1996):

(29) a. Divil a one ever I seen
"I never saw one"
b. Sorra one o' them was equal to Charlie
"Not one of them was equal to Charlie"

Odlin (1997a: 14) suggests that these forms of negation are the result of combined Scots superstrate and Irish superstratum influence.

7.10 "Indigenized" Englishes and Similar Contact Varieties

We have used Irish English as an illustration of the kinds of changes that characterize contact vernaculars that arise in scenarios of group shift involving influence from the group's native language(s) and other processes of change. Similar kinds of restructuring can be observed in all of the "new" or "indigenized" Englishes that emerged in other colonial settings. We include here other situations in the British Isles that involved contact between (speakers of) English and indigenous languages like Welsh and Scottish Gaelic, out of which emerged contact varieties such as Welsh English and (especially Highland) Scots. Interestingly, these varieties are seldom highlighted in discussions of the "new" colonial Englishes, though they clearly form part of this category (Kachru 1992: 231). English remained confined to the British Isles until the end of the sixteenth century. As a result of colonial expansion from the early seventeenth century on, English came into contact with Niger Congo languages in Africa, Indic and Dravidian languages in India, and Sinitic and Austronesian languages in South East Asia and the Pacific. Contact varieties of English emerged in all these settings, serving as lingua francas to ethnically and linguistically diverse populations.

We will not be concerned here with those colonial settings that are associated with the emergence of pidgin and creole languages. These will be dealt with in subsequent chapters. Our concern is with situations where the spread of English was linked to the spread of English-medium education, for instance in Ireland, India, South East Asia, parts of Africa, and areas of the Pacific such as Fiji and Papua New Guinea. This occurred during the course of the late eighteenth to nineteenth centuries, in the later phases of British colonial expansion, when the British acquired trading and political control of these areas. In addition to India, countries like Singapore, Malaysia, and African nations like Kenya and Nigeria are good examples of such situations. It was socially and economically rewarding to learn English, and local varieties of the language became prestigious second languages for the more educated and elite sections of the community. In the course of time, the New Englishes were increasingly adopted as everyday vernaculars for use in inter-group, and later in-group, communication.

Of course, English was not the only language to be subjected to these forces of change in colonial settings. Similar contact varieties of French, Spanish, Portuguese, and other languages emerged in their respective colonies. Non-European languages have also undergone similar processes of change under conditions of shift. Taiwanese Mandarin, heavily influenced by Taiwanese, a southern Min dialect of Chinese, is one such example (see discussion below). All these situations share the fact that the shifting group has a strong sense of its autonomy and separate identify vis-à-vis the TL group. This motivated the emergence of a distinctive local variety of the TL that serves as an in-group vernacular, and symbolizes the group's ethnic or national identity.

Exercise 7
Compare the sociohistorical background to the emergence of Irish English with that of Singapore English (discussed below) or any of the "New Englishes." To what extent did the historical and social contexts of the contact influence the types and extent of change that took place in each case? (On Irish English, see Odlin 1997a; on Singapore English, see Ho and Platt 1993 and Gupta 1992; on the New Englishes, see Kachru 1997 and references therein; also the journal *World Englishes*.)

7.11 Issues in the Study of Language Shift

Cases of group language shift raise many issues for scholars in various fields of enquiry, including sociologists interested in language maintenance and shift, psychologists interested in convergent and divergent accommodation in group behaviors, language planners concerned with issues of education, and so on. We cannot investigate all of these issues here. We will be concerned primarily with the issues that the outcomes of group shift raise for linguistic theories of contact-induced change. These fall into three broad categories: those issues relating to the linguistic processes through which these outcomes emerged; those relating to the role played by sociocultural and other non-linguistic factors in their formation; and those relating to their place in a classification of contact vernaculars.

7.11.1 Processes of formation

The origins of contact vernaculars like the New Englishes and other "indigenized" varieties clearly require explanation in terms of a theoretical framework for SLA in general. The processes of grammar construction that resulted in these outcomes of shift are the same as those that we discussed earlier, in relation to individual SLA. Thus we can ascribe different aspects of their grammar to TL input, L1 influence, processes of simplification, and internally driven changes.

Scholars within the field known as "English as a world language" (EWL) have long recognized the similarities in the processes of restructuring that characterize both individual and group SLA. They often use the terminology of SLA studies, including such concepts as transfer, interference, etc., to describe the emergence of the New Englishes. Much of the EWL literature has focused on two central processes of language change – "nativization" and "acculturation."

According to Kachru (1992: 235), "Nativization involves the approximation of a language to the linguistic and discoursal characteristics of the native (or dominant) language of the area into which it has been transplanted." On the other hand, "acculturation focuses on the people learning the transplanted language; it refers to the reflection of their sociocultural identities in a nativized language." This emphasis on both linguistic and sociocultural aspects of language shift reflects our own concern with both structural and non-structural factors in contact linguistics.

The term "nativization" is somewhat problematic, since creolists use it in a quite different sense, that is, to refer to the adoption of an erstwhile second language as the first or native language of a community. That is the sense in which we will use it here. In Kachru's use, the term clearly refers to what we have called L1 or substratum influence. We have already seen ample evidence of this process at work in the formation of Irish English.

Similar kinds of reanalysis (or transfer, if you prefer) can be found in other outcomes of group SLA. For instance, the colloquial variety of Mandarin spoken in Taiwan shows evidence of significant influence from Taiwanese (southern Min), the ancestral language of most of the population. For example, certain grammatical morphemes appear to have resulted from the reanalysis of standard (Beijing) Mandarin forms in terms of Taiwanese functional categories. A well-known example of this is the use of Mandarin *you* "have" as an auxiliary marking perfective aspect, where standard Mandarin has verb-final particle *-le*. This use of *you* is modeled on a similar use of Taiwanese *u* "have," which functions both as a main verb and as an auxiliary marking perfective aspect. The following examples from Lin (1997) illustrate (Tw = Taiwanese; BM = Beijing Mandarin; TM = Taiwanese Mandarin).[4] Tones are omitted:

(30)	a.	Tw:	wa	kinali	u	chia	dyongdao
			I	today	have	eat	lunch
	b.	TM:	wo	jintian	you	chi	zhongfan
			I	today	have	eat	lunch
	c.	BM:	wo	jintian	chi-le		zhongfan
			I	today	eat-PFTV		lunch
			"I have eaten lunch today"				

Various other examples of Taiwanese influence on TM have been documented for morphosyntax (Cheng 1985; Kubler 1985).

Taiwanese has also influenced the phonology of TM. For example, the retroflex initials, /tʂ'/, /tʂ/ and /ʂ/ of standard Mandarin have been replaced in TM by their non-retroflex Taiwanese equivalents, /ts'/, /ts/ and /s/ respectively. Taiwanese lacks the retroflex sounds, so its speakers simply substitute the most similar L1 sounds for them. Several other phonological features of TM can also be attributed to Taiwanese influence (Kubler 1979).

7.11.2 Degrees of "fossilization" or approximation in group SLA

The notion of so-called "fossilization" is also relevant to group learning, since different outcomes of shift seem to reflect different developmental stages in the acquisition of the TL. The term itself may not be appropriate when applied to group SLA, since it assumes that the community involved is aiming at a faithful reproduction of the TL. As Escure (1997: 275) notes, the term also "fails to capture the dynamic, innovative, and – at least subconsiously – intentional use of old features" to preserve a group identity distinct from that of the TL group.

Some outcomes, for example African American Vernacular English and Irish English, approximate their TL sources more closely. Others, such as Singapore English, display stronger effects of L1 influence and simplification that are characteristic of earlier stages of IL development. Different stages of fossilization may also be observed in different regional or social varieties of the same contact vernacular. As we saw earlier, Irish English really consists of a regional continuum, with western varieties more heavily influenced by Irish than those in the east (Odlin 1997a: 31; Filppula 1991). Moreover, there is some evidence that certain substratal features such as "sorrow negation" found in earlier Irish English have apparently been lost in the contemporary language (Odlin 1997a: 14).

In general, however, it is difficult to identify the precise developmental stages involved in cases of shift in the way we can do for individual SLA. The main reason is that we cannot always observe the changes that take place in the former. Moreover, there is often no single variety that we can identify as the TL. Witness the diversity of the English dialectal input to the formation of Irish English, or African American Vernacular English (AAVE) (Winford 1997d, 1998). Often too, the shift can take place over several generations, and involve successive stages of bilingualism among different sections of the shifting group. As a result, over time, the target for new learners would have been second language varieties of the TL spoken by bilinguals (Odlin 1997a: 27). Situations like these, where learners interact primarily among themselves rather than with native speakers of the TL, promote the preservation of contact-induced changes or innovations.

7.11.3 Colloquial Singapore English: a case of early IL "fossilization"?

The differences in stages of "fossilization" among outcomes of shift can be illustrated by comparing Irish English with another indigenized variety, Colloquial

Singapore English (Sing. E.). In general, despite the changes it has undergone, Irish English is quite English in character, showing a great deal of continuity from its British dialectal sources. The same cannot be said of vernacular or colloquial Sing. E., which diverges significantly from its English sources.

Sing. E. emerged in the period 1930–60 in a complex contact situation involving English (taught as a second language in schools) and various substrate languages, including southern varieties of Chinese (especially Hokkien and Cantonese), Mandarin, and varieties of Malay (Gupta 1992: 327). It became a lingua franca for the ethnically diverse population, and is now increasingly being used as a first or primary language by younger generations of Singaporeans.

Ho and Platt (1993) document various aspects of Sing. E. structure that are due to the familiar effects of L1 influence, simplification, and internal developments. For instance, Sing. E. has serial verb constructions like the following, which reflect the syntax of similar constructions in Hokkien and Cantonese, two of the principal substrates:

(31) Sing. E.: You sit car come here, ah?
Hokkien: lí che chhia lâi chit-tau ah
you sit car come here QP
"Did you come here by car?"

Other features that are clearly due to Chinese influence (sometimes reinforced by Malay) include the use of *one* as a relative marker, or as a marker of emphasis in sentence-final position (Ho and Platt 1993: 10); the use of "emphatic" *got* (ibid.: 77); yes/no questions (Gupta 1992: 338); and several discourse particles, for example, *ma, ah, lah*, etc., adopted directly from Chinese.

Sing. E. also displays the effects of simplificatory processes of reduction and regularization. Thus we find variable omission of copula/auxiliary *be*, omission of subject pronouns, and omission of plural and past tense marking. There are several innovations in Sing. E. due to internal developments. For instance, *used to* is generalized to express both present and past habituality. The auxiliaries *is* and *was* are used as markers of present and past time reference respectively, as in the following examples from Ho and Platt (1993: 35):

(32) a. My father is stay here what
"My father lives here"
b. I was study in primary school
"I studied in a primary school"

The extent of substrate influence in colloquial Sing. E. has led some scholars (e.g., Ritchie 1986) to suggest that this contact vernacular is typologically closer to Chinese than to English. Later in this chapter, we will consider some possible reasons for the greater prevalence of substrate and other features in Sing. E. than in Irish English, and what this implies for their place in a classification of contact vernaculars. For the moment, let us return to the processes of change and the constraints that regulate them.

7.12 Linguistic Constraints in Language Shift

The situations we have considered here should suffice to illustrate the similarities in the processes of change found in both individual and group SLA. Presumably also, the changes that occur in both cases are subject to similar linguistic constraints, at least in relation to the role of individual learners in the acquisition process. We can conceive of group shift as involving two broad stages, one in which individual learners create their own IL grammars, and another in which the competition among features of those is resolved in favor of a set of community norms. Each stage is associated with its own processes of change and their attendant constraints.

At the level of individual acquisition, the same cognitive and linguistic principles come into play in all situations. As we have seen, different principles regulate different aspects of IL construction such as processes of simplification, L1 influence, and internally motivated change. Each of these can be observed in cases of group shift.

The general reduction of bound morphology, copulas, etc. in Sing. E. appears to be due to input processing principles similar to those we discussed earlier in relation to simplification as a learning strategy (see section 7.7.1). Similarly, the overgeneralization of SVO to questions, as well as the choice of *used to* as a general marker of habituality, conform to the One to One Principle, which favors canonical word order and isomorphism of form and meaning. L1 influence from Chinese no doubt played some role here as well. Similar principles might explain such developments as the use of *is* and *was* as markers of present and past respectively. The motivation in all these cases is apparently to maximize transparency in the form–function relationship.

7.12.1 Constraints on L1 influence

This brings us to the role played by learners' L1s in cases of language shift. What principles or constraints regulate such influence? To understand this better, we need first of all to come to grips with what L1 influence involves.

7.12.2 The concept of "transfer" in group SLA

We saw earlier that SLA researchers conceive of L1 influence primarily in terms of "transfer." We also noted that the term is used by some in a very broad sense, to refer to all forms of L1 influence (Odlin 1989: 27). But most studies of transfer focus on only one type of L1 influence, that resulting from learners' perception, whether conscious or not, of some similarity between L1 and L2 elements or structures.

As we saw earlier, Andersen (1983) refers to this kind of influence as "transfer to somewhere," noting crucially that it can result in both successful and unsuccessful imitation of the TL (positive and negative transfer respectively). But L1 influence also occurs frequently where no similarity appears to exist between L1 and L2, on the basis of which learners can make "interlingual identifications." Some have referred to these kinds of L1 influence as "transfer to nowhere" (Kellerman 1995) or "blind transfer" (Kean 1986). Kellerman cites examples from Slobin (1993) such as the preference for use of progressives rather than preterites in the L2 English narratives of Panjabi learners. He suggests that this is due to transfer of the Panjabi use of imperfectives in narratives, and to the fact that Panjabi is aspect-dominant. But it is arguable that this and the other examples Kellerman provides are actually cases of transfer to somewhere, based on misidentification. In this case, the English progressive is assigned functions associated with the Panjabi imperfective. This then is not a true case of transfer to nowhere. But the notion itself is worth pursuing further.

The main idea behind the notion of "transfer to nowhere" is that learners find certain aspects of the TL more difficult to acquire if they have no counterparts in the L1. Of course, not all such features pose difficulty. Some of them are transparent and hence easy to acquire, such as the singular/plural distinction in English, which is learnt by speakers of languages like Chinese, which do not mark the distinction morphologically. However, those differences that do constitute a barrier can have consequences for both learning and use of the TL. In attempting to use the TL, learners may resort to strategies based on their L1. It is such strategies that are apparently being associated with "transfer to nowhere." A possible example of this might be the strategy Andersen (1990: 62) refers to as "relexification," though Andersen doesn't make this connection himself. The strategy is subject to the following "relexification principle":

> When you cannot perceive the structural pattern used by the language you are trying to acquire, use your native language structure with lexical items from the second language.

In other words, this suggests that learners may use abstract L1 syntactic patterns as a template into which they insert L2 words. Andersen points out that this strategy may be more common in "natural" SLA settings, especially where access to L2 input is restricted. This appears to be quite true. For instance, Mesthrie and Dunne (1990: 35–7) discuss cases of "transfer of relativization strategies from [Indic and Dravidian] substrates" in South African Indian English (SAIE). Indic languages employ a correlative construction with a pre-nominal relative clause, as illustrated by example (33) from Gujarati:

(33) Je vepārī marī sathe avyo, te vepārī Harilal ka
CORRELAT. businessman me with came that businessman Harilal of
bhaī che
brother is
"The businessman who came with me is Harilal's brother"
[Lit: Which businessman came with me, that businessman is Harilal's brother]

The same strategy is found in the L2 English employed by older speakers whose L1 is an Indic language. This is illustrated in (34):

(34) Which-one I put in the jar, that-one is good
"The ones [i.e. pickles] I put in the jar are the best"

Dravidian languages, on the other hand, employ a pre-nominal external relative clause without a relative pronoun, as illustrated in example (35) from Tamil:

(35) Vaṇṇeñe aṭicca taccān cenneki
washerman.ACC beat.past.rel. part carpenter.NOM Madras.DAT
pōnān
go.past.3sgmasc
"The carpenter who beat the washerman went to Madras"
[Lit. The washerman-beat(ing) carpenter went to Madras]

Again, a similar strategy is found in the L2 English of Dravidian speakers, as in the following example:

(36) People who got [working for them] sons, like, for them nice they can stay
"It is nice for people who have sons [who are] working for [the company], since they are allowed to stay on [in the barracks]"

The SAIE relative structures, of course, are quite different from relatives in other varieties of English, though it might be argued that they are similar to structures that English would allow.

Interestingly, similar cases of syntactic retention can be found in the code-mixing behavior of bilinguals who are not very proficient in the L2, such as the Japanese–English bilinguals studied by Nishimura (1986), whom we discussed in chapter 5. Compare also the retention of Japanese verb-final order and other features in the versions of Hawai'i Pidgin English used by Japanese immigrants in Hawaii, as in the following examples from Bickerton (1981). Japanese items are in italics:

(37) a. mista karsan-*no* *tokoro* tu eika sel *shite*
Mr. Carson-POSS place two acre sell do
"I sold two acres to Mr. Carson's place"
b. da pua pipl awl poteito iit
"The poor people ate only potatoes"

Strategies like these are not quite the same as the cases of word-order change we discussed earlier, in the IL of German learners of L2 English, such as the following example, repeated here for convenience:

(38) I would suggest him to go.

Cases like this do seem to involve transfer to somewhere, in that the English verb has been assigned the subcategorization properties of its German counterpart *empfehlen* "suggest." It is possible that this explanation also applies to the cases of so-called "transfer to nowhere" that we just discussed. In other words, these may involve the same kinds of "projection" of syntactic properties of L1 categories onto L2 elements as occurs in (38), and may simply be a more complex case of "transfer to somewhere." (See chapter 9, section 9.9.2, for discussion of similar kinds of "transfer" in creole formation.)

Another strategy that might be viewed as an instance of "transfer to nowhere" is the use of L1 content or function morphemes to convey meanings for which the L2 means of expression has not (yet) been acquired. We saw examples of this in the early interlanguage of German-speaking learners of L2 English, who use words like *brills* for "eyeglasses," and German plural inflection, as in *doge* "dogs." In all these cases, learners seem to follow the maxim, "When in doubt, fall back on L1 knowledge."

It is clear then that L1 influence can manifest itself in various ways, and typically involves transfer to somewhere, though there may be a role for transfer to nowhere. This notion, however, remains tenuous and has not gained wide acceptance among SLA researchers.

7.12.3 Transfer as psycholinguistic process

We noted earlier that the concept of transfer refers essentially to a psycholinguistic process by which learners manipulate L1 and L2 inputs to restructure their IL grammar. In cases involving transfer to somewhere, learners project the categories of their L1 onto L2-derived forms that have become part of their ILs. In other cases, learners try to compensate for unfamiliarity with certain TL structures by employing L1-based strategies that have no models in the TL.

This restructuring involves specific strategies and processes through which learners exploit L1 knowledge in creating the IL grammar. The strategies include:

1 Retention of overt L1 elements in the IL, when L2 counterparts are unknown or non-existent.
2 Retention of L1 structural patterns with insertion of L2 vocabulary (so-called "relexification").
3 Retention of L1 elements as substitutes for L2 counterparts perceived as similar (e.g., substitution of English /u/ for French /u/).
4 Covert retention of L1 semantic categories via reanalysis/reinterpretation of L2 forms that learners identify with L1 forms (e.g., reanalysis of *after* as a marker of perfect aspect in Irish English).

The first type of retention, (1), involves "transfer to nowhere" and by definition results in a departure from the TL (negative transfer). Type (2) can involve transfer either to somewhere or to nowhere, while types (3–4) involve transfer to somewhere. These three types (2–4) may have either positive or negative results in terms of accurate imitation of the TL.

Transfer, then, can be seen as the process by which certain L1 categories and structures are retained and projected onto L2-derived forms. It should also be borne in mind that L1 categories and structures may not be replicated exactly in the IL grammar. Learners may create compromises between L1 and L2 grammar, or other innovations that have no exact counterparts in either of the source languages.

Understanding these processes is a prerequisite to understanding the linguistic constraints on these types of L1 influence. The constraints have to do with the interlingual identifications learners make between L1 and L2 elements, based on the degree of congruence between these elements. Principles such as the Transfer to Somewhere Principle and the Relexification Principle can in fact be rephrased in terms of congruence-based constraints like the following:

- L2 structures that are highly congruent with those in the L1 will be acquired more easily (and successfully) than those that are not.
- L2 forms that are partially congruent with or partly similar in semantics or function to L1 forms will tend to be reanalyzed on the model of the latter.
- Certain L2 structures or elements that have no counterparts in the L1 may be difficult to learn. Learners may simply ignore such structures or employ L1 strategies by way of compensation.

Whether one interprets these as constraints on L1 influence or constraints on acquisition of L2 features is really a matter of perspective. Congruence-based constraints can also be interpreted in terms of markedness relations between L1 and L2 elements, as noted earlier.

We've suggested some ways in which L1 properties and elements may end up in the IL of individual learners. But under what conditions are such elements selected as part of a new contact vernacular? The answer to this lies primarily in social factors, which we can consider now.

7.13 Non-Structural Factors in Language Shift

Contact vernaculars like the New Englishes, Taiwanese Mandarin, etc. all seem to have arisen in settings characterized by limited interaction between native speakers of the TL and the groups learning it as an L2. In general, the TL is taught in schools, and earlier learners' versions of it then become targets of acquisition for later learners. Since native speakers of the original TL are typically in a small minority and have higher social status, only the more educated and elite sections of the community have access to native TL models. Hence they tend to learn closer approximations to the TL, which may become the basis of a new local standard variety. The fact that most members of the community interact primarily among themselves rather than with native speakers of the TL means that the contact variety of the TL itself becomes the primary target of learning. Indeed, even teachers of the TL in the schools may speak a "local" version of it. These are perhaps the most important factors in the eventual preservation of features due to simplification, L1 influence, etc. in the new vernacular.

Siegel (1997) proposed certain "reinforcement principles" that guide the selection process in these cases. In the first place, the greater the linguistic homogeneity of the population, the more likely it is that similar strategies of L1 retention etc. will be found across the shifting group. Irish English, of course, meets this criterion well, since only one substrate language was involved. In the case of Singapore English, the numerical dominance of speakers of Chinese dialects ensured that the ILs of these groups exerted most influence on the outcome. This said, it is of course impossible to predict exactly which features will be adopted, and which discarded. Siegel (ibid.) suggests that the key factor in this case is the salience of competing variants, as determined for instance by their frequency and/or transparency. However, we still know relatively little about the role of these or other factors. Some light may be shed on this by a comparison with processes of dialect leveling or koiné formation (Siegel 1985; Kerswill and Williams 2000). The factors that favor selection of certain variants over others in those situations are relevant here as well (see discussion in chapter 3, section 3.10).

Certain differences in the patterns of contact between indigenous and L2 groups also seem to promote differences in the outcomes of shift. For example, in addition to schooling, migratory labor seems to have played an important role in the emergence of Irish English (Odlin 1997a). Many speakers of Irish traveled either to parts of Britain or to English-speaking towns in Ireland to obtain work. This pattern of migration dated back to the fifteenth century, and reached a peak in the late eighteenth century when massive migrations to Britain occurred. On the one hand, most workers from Ulster tended to go to Scotland, thus reinforcing the establishment of Ulster Scots in that area. On the other hand, southern Irish tended to migrate to southern parts of England or to the English settlements in eastern Ireland, thus reinforcing the southern English influence on southern Irish English. There was also a great deal of trade between southern Ireland and England in this period (Kallen 1997: 146). The greater degree of contact with native English speakers in the Irish case seems to have resulted in Irish English being closer to its superstrate sources than Singapore English.

The persistence of bilingualism within the shifting group is another important factor in language shift. In both eighteenth- to nineteenth-century Ireland and twentieth-century Singapore, the majority of those who acquired the TL maintained their ancestral language(s) as well. Odlin (1997a: 4–5) suggests that there were large numbers of illiterate bilinguals in nineteenth-century Ireland, judging from the figures in the 1851 census. It is reasonable to assume also that childhood bilingualism was quite common, and that bilingual children played a role in the regularization of Irish English grammar. These factors would also have favored the retention of Irish features in the English of such speakers. Support for this comes from the fact, noted earlier, that Irish features are most pronounced in those varieties of contemporary Irish English spoken in areas that recently had or still have significant numbers of bilinguals. The Singapore situation is also characterized by high degrees of bilingualism, which may explain the pervasive substratal retentions in that variety.

No doubt there are many other factors relating to the community settings, demographics, patterns of interaction, etc. that played a role in these outcomes of shift. Gal's (1979) pioneering investigation of the shift from Hungarian to German in Oberwart, Austria, explores some of these factors. She attributes the shift to several causes, including economic change, social mobility and opportunity, changing social network structures, and speakers' choices of social identity. All of these sociocultural factors offer fruitful grounds for research on the causes and outcomes of shift.

Gal's point about choices of social identity is particularly germane to the case of indigenized varieties. The preservation of distinctive characteristics in these languages has much to do with their value as symbols of national or ethnic identity for their speakers. They are often acquired as first languages, and serve as the primary means of everyday interaction, or in some cases as "link" languages across ethnic groups, as in Singapore. Hence they have become associated with shared community membership and belonging. This has resulted in a range of problems concerning the status of these vernaculars, especially in cases where they co-exist with a lexically related standard variety. Whether we focus on African American English, Singapore English, or Taiwanese Mandarin, the sociolinguistic reality remains the same. The vernacular varieties exist in a diglossic relationship with the standard dialects, leading to ambivalence both in attitudes and in public policy toward them. Studies of Irish English in Belfast (Milroy 1987; Milroy and Milroy 1992) reveal a tug-of-war between the status-oriented ideologies that confer prestige on the standard variety, and the identity-oriented values that confer legitimacy on the non-standard vernacular as a symbol of group cohesion. The pattern extends to all cases of unequal status between standard and non-standard varieties.

Our focus has shifted here from diachrony to synchrony, which links the study of shift situations to the broader sociolinguistic investigation of contact situations in general. The synchronic sociolinguistic study of indigenized varieties is still somewhat new, but it can contribute much to our understanding of the sociocultural contexts of language contact. From a more practical perspective, such research can also address the problems associated with diglossia and its consequences for education, social opportunity, and public planning.

7.14 Questions of Classification

Where exactly do cases of shift fit into a typology of contact vernaculars? The answer to this is far from straightforward, since there is little consensus on what such a typology should look like in the first place. Even generally accepted categories such as "pidgin," "creole," and "bilingual mixed language" are subject to great controversy. The category of "outcomes of shift" is similarly vague and malleable. These outcomes range from fairly close approximations to a TL to highly divergent versions of it. The degree of change in some of these cases has led researchers to treat them as close to creoles, which share similar processes of grammar restructuring.

For instance, Gupta (1992: 342) refers to the formation of Singapore English as a case of "creolization." Similarly, Ho and Platt (1993: 1) refer to Sing. E. as "creoloid." They argue that it "shares many of the features of a creole, e.g., serial verb constructions, variable marking of past tense, variable occurrence of articles and replacement of articles by other items, variable copula and auxiliary *be*." Given all these characteristics, it is perhaps not surprising that Sing. E. should be categorized as creole-like. But this approach assumes that there is a set of structural characteristics that is definitive of creole status, when in fact there isn't. It is quite true that creoles share the characteristics that Ho and Platt list. But these are not unique to creoles. Rather, they result from processes of change and restructuring that creole formation shares with other cases of language contact, especially those involving natural SLA. If vernacular Sing. E. has serial verb constructions, for instance, it is because the L1s of the learners of English in this contact situation (particularly Chinese dialects) have serial verb structures which were incorporated into Sing. E. via L1 retention, just as West African serial verb constructions were incorporated into Caribbean and other creoles (see chapter 9). On the other hand, the fact that the outcomes are not identical in all cases suggests that differences in the linguistic inputs and in the social settings play a significant role in determining the nature and extent of the change that takes place.

One way to classify the outcomes of shift might be to place them on a continuum ranging from cases of relatively successful SLA at one extreme to cases of radical creole formation at the other end. The chief criterion for placement would be the degree of L1 influence and perhaps simplification in the contact variety. Indigenized varieties would occupy the mid-range of this continuum, though they are by no means a homogeneous group.

Contact varieties like AAVE and Irish English might be placed closer to one end (say the left) on the scale than varieties like Sing. E. Creoles also pose a problem for placement, since they too fail to constitute a homogeneous group. I will suggest in chapter 9 that we make a broad distinction between "radical" creoles like Sranan Tongo and "intermediate" creoles such as Bajan (vernacular Barbadian English). The former would be placed on the extreme right of our continuum, while the latter would fall somewhere to the left of these, along with Singapore English. Figure 7.1 is a rough sketch of the proposed continuum.

Less L1 retention etc. ⟵⟶ *More L1 retention, simplification, etc.*

Advanced SLA	Somewhat indigenized	Highly indigenized	Intermediate creoles	Radical creoles
Native-like L2	AAVE, Irish English	Sing. E.	Bajan	Sranan

Figure 7.1 A continuum of outcomes of language shift

This is not meant to be an exhaustive or definitive classification of outcomes of shift. As already noted, there is no clear set of criteria that could be used to establish such a typology for contact outcomes in general. We will return to this issue in subsequent chapters, when we discuss pidgins and creoles.

III FIRST LANGUAGE ATTRITION AND DEATH

7.15 Introduction

Our discussion of language shift so far has focused on the changes that occur in a TL during a process of group learning. But it is of equal interest and theoretical import to consider the changes that a speaker's or group's ancestral language (AL) can undergo as a result of shift to a new language. In many cases, the acquisition of a new language promotes the gradual abandonment of the AL, leading to increasing attrition and eventually the obsolescence and death of the latter. The processes of language decay and loss have traditionally been studied within the subdiscipline known as language death studies, which has evolved in recent decades into a somewhat autonomous field of enquiry. However, as we will see, the phenomena involved in language attrition and death are similar to those found in many other cases of contact discussed throughout this book. Moreover, the social forces and changes that motivate language death are the same as those that promote contact-induced changes in language structure and behavior in general.

As Brenzinger and Dimmendaal (1992: 3) points out, "a language is considered to be extinct when there is no longer a speech community using [it]." Gradual language shift is the primary but not the only cause of language death. Sometimes languages become extinct because all their speakers die or are killed quickly, as in the case of Tasmania. In other cases, a group may suddenly abandon its language as a strategy of self-defense in the face of extreme repression, as happened with Lenca and Cacopera in El Salvador (Campbell and Muntzel

1989: 182). But the vast majority of cases of language death are due to gradual abandonment of an AL.

Roughly half of the world's known languages have disappeared within the last 500 years (Sasse 1992a: 7). Hundreds more are in danger of dying. Most of these will probably not be remembered in the way in which long-extinct languages like Gothic, Hittite, Sumerian, etc. are. Great effort is being made to at least preserve records of these endangered languages, and in some cases even revitalize them. But the sad truth is that many if not most of them will be lost to us in the near future. The social and other external forces promoting such loss are often too powerful to counteract. Discussions of current attempts at language revitalization in various situations can be found in Fishman (1991, 2001).

7.16 External (Social) Factors in Language Death

As Sasse (1992a: 10) has pointed out, there are three general aspects of the study of language death. The first two focus on the macro- and micro-level social factors that lead to language obsolescence. The third focuses on the linguistic consequences for the dying language. Let us briefly examine the first two. Fortunately, there are several detailed studies of dying languages by scholars like Dorian (1981) on East Sutherland Gaelic, Sasse (1991) on Arvanítika in Greece, Gal (1979) on Hungarian in Austria, and others. These have given us a great deal of insight into the social ecology of language death.

7.16.1 Macro-level social factors

Communities undergoing first language attrition tend to be minority or at least subordinate groups who have come under the control of larger or more powerful ones. Some of the factors leading to this kind of situation were discussed in chapter 1 (sections 1.4.2 and 1.6.2) and chapter 3 (section 3.8). They include the colonization of smaller ethnic groups by larger ones, and the formation of larger national polities that relegate some groups to subordinate status. Some of these factors were also discussed in section 7.13 with respect to the shift from Irish to English in nineteenth-century Ireland.

Within such conglomerates, a variety of social forces come into play to compel the minority groups to assimilate to the dominant language and culture. The cultural, political, and socioeconomic superiority of the dominant group is one such factor. This is usually reflected in the lower status ascribed to the minority language, often by language policies that stigmatize it and deny it a place in education, politics, and other important spheres of life. In addition, increasing modernization, urbanization, and economic changes have made it difficult for minority groups to retain their autonomy. Finally, the increasing availability of modern transportation and the reach of supra-regional communication media have made it difficult for previously isolated groups to avoid the pressure of the dominant language.

In the face of such pressure, some groups may deliberately decide to give up their AL in favor of a more prestigious or socially advantageous language. Brenzinger (1992b: 213) mentions the case of the Yaaku of Kenya, who apparently held a public meeting in the early 1930s and decided to abandon Yaaku and teach their children Maasai from then on. Most cases of shift, however, seem to involve an unconscious agreement that is slowly forced on the community by social forces within the community itself. Before we consider these internal social factors, let us consider the stages involved in the attrition and eventual death of an AL.

7.16.2 Stages of language attrition and death

As Batibo (1992: 90–2) informs us, language attrition occurs in several stages, which overlap to varying degrees. There is first a stage of monolingualism in the AL, followed by a period of growing bilingualism with the AL dominant. At this point, the AL is used in most kinds of in-group interaction, in domains like the family, neighborhood, etc. The L2 is used for wider inter-group communication. Stage 3 is a period of continuing bilingualism during which more and more speakers adopt the L2 as their primary language. Both stages 2 and 3 involve varying degrees of diglossia, allowing for code-switching behavior. The gradual breakdown of diglossia, wherein the L2 intrudes more and more on the domains of the AL, signals the beginning of complete shift. In the fourth stage, the members of the community display more limited knowledge and production of the AL. The final stage is the complete replacement of the AL by the L2. Traces of the AL often survive in the newly acquired L2 as substratum features, as we saw earlier in the case of Irish English and other indigenized varieties. The five stages are not discrete, since different speakers shift toward the L2 to different extents at different times.

To summarize, the chief symptoms of first language attrition include a rapid decrease in the number of speakers, reduction in domains of use, and gradual loss of competence on the part of a growing number of speakers. The first two symptoms are more sociolinguistic in nature, and might be referred to as "quantitative attrition." The third symptom has to do with the linguistic consequences of reduced competence, and might be referred to as "qualitative attrition." This distinction is similar to that made by Rickford (1987: 34) between "quantitative" and "qualitative" decreolization, which involves the gradual incursion of a standard language into the structure of a lexically related creole language.

7.16.3 Sociolinguistic factors within the shifting community

Sociolinguistic approaches to language death are particularly concerned with the factors that come into play in quantitative L1 attrition. These factors are not different from those that regulate language choice in bilingual communities in general, which we discussed in chapter 4. It is their specific configuration that promotes shift in some cases and inhibits it in others. The overall sociolinguistic structure of the community, its patterns of language usage, its size, and its ideology toward language all determine the extent to which its ancestral language is prone to decay. One overriding factor that promotes language maintenance is a high degree of vitality in an ethnolinguistic group. Giles et al. (1977: 308) defined group vitality as "that which makes a group likely to behave as a distinctive and collective entity within the inter-group setting." The higher the degree of vitality, the greater the degree of loyalty to the AL is likely to be. (See also the discussion in chapter 4, section 4.3.4.) On the other hand, the pursuit of socioeconomic opportunity and social advancement, in concert with sociopsychological pressure from the dominant group, may lead to negative evaluation of the AL, thus providing strong motivation for shift.

Exercise 8

Examine any situation in which a minority group's language is under threat from a dominant language, for instance, Spanish in the US, French in eastern Canada. Try to determine what social factors either promote or inhibit shift in the community of your choice. (Suggested reading: Dressler and Wodak-Leodolter 1977, Seliger and Vago 1991a, Dorian 1989, and Fishman 2001 contain many interesting case studies of endangered languages.)

7.17 The Linguistic Consequences of L1 Attrition

Studies of the linguistic consequences of first language attrition are particularly interested in the final three stages of the process of language death. Sasse (1992a: 20) labels these stages as follows:

- Primary language shift, in which shifting speakers become more proficient in the L2 and use it more often than the AL (Batibo's stage 3, above).
- Language decay, characterized by significant structural change in the AL (Batibo's stage 4).
- Language death and replacement, that is, monolingual competence in the L2 and total loss of competence in the AL (Batibo's stage 5).

Each of these stages is characterized by particular linguistic changes in the dying language.

During the period of primary language shift, L2 elements increasingly intrude into the AL, encouraged by frequent code switching and code mixing. L2-dominant bilinguals are the chief agents of the diffusion of L2 lexicon and structure into the AL. Early manifestations of this process can be seen in the various situations of incipient shift that we discussed in chapter 3. For instance, languages like Prince Edward Island French, LA Spanish, and Pennsylvania German all show evidence of lexical and structural interference from English. This is particularly true of those varieties of the ALs that are spoken by English-dominant bilinguals.

Change in a threatened language under influence from a dominant L2 involves the same mechanisms and processes as those we saw earlier in these cases of convergence. They include direct transfer of L2 lexical and structural elements as well as the diffusion of L2 structural patterns into the L1. Seliger and Vago (1991b: 7–10) discuss many examples of such diffusion in the attriting L1 German and Hungarian of speakers for whom L2 English had become the primary language. L2 rules of word order, preposition stranding, patterns of subordination, etc. are adopted into the L1. Loan translations, semantic extensions, etc. on the pattern of the L2 become common in the L1, whose lexicon as a whole is increasingly forgotten and replaced by L2 items. As Haugen (1978: 37) puts it: "As the learner builds new systems in the language he acquires, he dismantles and reorders the systems of the language he already knows."

Some languages involved in a long period of gradual shift manage to retain something of their autonomy despite a great deal of influence from an encroaching language. But they usually pay the price of losing a great deal of their former character, evolving into linguistic hybrids that are substantially different from earlier forms of the language. Examples include Ngandi, now becoming extinct as its speakers shift to Ritharngu or to pidgin and creole varieties of English in Arnhem Land, Australia (chapter 3, section 3.6). An extreme case of survival at the expense of massive change is Cappadocian Greek, which suffered pervasive interference from Turkish at every level of its structure (chapter 3, section 3.7.2). The same might be said of the Kupwar situation, where local varieties of Urdu, Marathi, and Kannada have all undergone significant structural change due to convergence (chapter 3, section 3.7.3). In all these cases, with the exception of Cappadocian Greek, the languages concerned have not become extinct, and continue to meet their speakers' communicative needs. Those aspects of their structure that were lost are simply replaced by others from the L2, so there is no loss of communicative power. However, a different picture emerges in cases where the AL is undergoing not just interference, but also decay.

7.17.1 Language decay

The decision to give up an AL and cease transmitting it to one's descendants signals the start of serious attrition in the language. This is the period of decay both in individual idiolects and in the communal language. This stage is associated with the emergence of speakers with limited competence in the AL. The degree of proficiency they have depends on how they acquired the AL, and what opportunities they have to use it. Sasse (1992b: 77, fn. 2) cites Dorian's (p.c.) classification of limited proficiency speakers into two broad categories: formerly fluent speakers (sometimes called "rusty" speakers) and semi-speakers. The latter can be further divided into those who acquired the AL as children but abandoned it at school and those who experienced "abnormal acquisition" due to inadequate exposure to the language. The latter are "prototypical" semi-speakers. Semi-speakers are also referred to as "terminal" speakers (Tsitsipis 1989).

Formerly fluent speakers often preserve or can recover much of their original knowledge, so that their language "dies with its morphological boots on" (Dorian 1978: 608). Others (the "forgetters") have significantly reduced competence, like the remnant speakers of Menomini described by Bloomfield (1927). In fact, such speakers really belong to the category of "semi-speakers." An example of a semi-speaker who abandoned his AL early is Michal, a child who gradually lost command of Hebrew as he shifted to English between the ages of 2:7 and 4:6 (D. Kaufman and Aronoff 1991). His dying Hebrew passed through all the stages of attrition typical of decaying languages, as discussed earlier. Semi-speakers of different kinds are the primary producers of decayed language. Their performance in the AL ranges from reasonably fluent speech to distorted output somewhat similar to those kinds of aphasic speech characterized by agrammatism (Menn 1989). The extent of attrition correlates closely with age differences, with younger speakers displaying less competence than older ones. In the final stages of death, such speakers make up the vast majority of the speech community.

Manifestations of language decay include increasing replacement of L1 elements by L2 counterparts, and various kinds of reduction and simplification in the L1 itself. The more speakers come to rely on the L2 for communication, the more their AL disintegrates. This manifests itself especially in loss of morphological and morphophonemic apparatus, such as verbal and nominal inflection and derivation. Reduction in allomorphic variation and overgeneralization of forms result in greater paradigmatic regularity. For example, Dimmendaal (1992) reports the loss of nominal affixes marking number and gender in semi-speaker varieties of Kore, a language spoken on Lamu Island off the Kenyan coast. The verbs used by these semi-speakers are also invariable, having lost inflectional markers of tense, aspect, and negation, as well as number and person agreement. Sasse (1992b: 70–1) reports similar kinds of morphological simplification in a semi-speaker variety of Arvanítika.

Loss of inflection must sometimes be compensated for by fixed word order to express grammatical relations. This is why semi-speaker varieties of immigrant Finnish in northern Minnesota have fixed word order whereas Finnish word order is variable. Larmouth (1974: 359) gives the following examples of differences in the language of first- versus fourth-generation speakers:

(39)	G1:	a.	Mieheltä kuoli äiti
			man-ABLAT died (the) mother
	OR	b.	Miehan äiti kuoli
			man-GEN mother died
	G4:		Miehen äiti kuoli
			[Only the genitive construction is used.]

Other changes at the syntactic level include the loss of synthetic constructions in favor of periphrastic ones, as well as the loss of subordination mechanisms. For instance, the "conjugating" prepositions of Gaelic are replaced by analytic prepositional phrases in semi-speaker varieties. Dorian (1981) provides examples like the following:

(40)	*Proficient speaker*	*Semi-speaker*	*Gloss*
	rium	ri mis'	"to me"
	dhomh	orn mis'	"for me"

Maher (1991) provides a comprehensive overview of all these types of simplification and regularization in semi-speaker varieties found in various immigrant enclave communities. Sasse (1992b: 71) gives further examples from Arvanítika, while Annette Schmidt (1985) provides others from Dyirbal.

In phonology too, we find various kinds of leveling in decaying languages. For example, semi-speaker varieties of Kore have lost the opposition between voiceless plosives and voiced implosives, as well as distinctions of length and tongue root position for vowels. Interestingly, though, they preserve tone distinctions, possibly because these may be less marked than segmental distinctions (Dimmendaal 1992: 129–30). In general, many of the changes at all levels of structure appear to involve the loss of more marked features or structures and the preservation of less marked ones.

Exercise 9
Examine any two case studies of language attrition and compare the kinds of changes that occur in each. Which ones are due to L2 influence on the AL? Which are due to "internal" processes of simplification? If there are differences, how can we explain them? (Case studies of L1 attrition can be found in Brenzinger 1992a, Seliger and Vago 1991a, and Dorian 1989, among others.)

7.18 Language Attrition in Relation to Other Contact Phenomena

There has been some disagreement concerning the extent to which the structural changes that occur in a dying language are unique to such situations or similar to other kinds of contact-induced change. For instance, Sasse (1992b: 60) questions the view of Dorian (1981: 151) and others that the same kinds of change occur in both dying and healthy languages subjected to contact. Sasse argues that, in principle, borrowing and interference in what he calls "normal language contact situations" are quite different from the process of reduction and loss in a decaying language. On the other hand, researchers like Dimmendaal (1992: 130) compare language decay to pidginization. Can these different positions be reconciled?

Part of the problem here is that researchers are not always comparing the right phenomena. Sasse's comparison of borrowing and interference with later stages of language decay is a case in point. It would be more appropriate to compare the former phenomena with those found in earlier stages of shift, especially that of primary language shift where the AL begins to converge toward the L2. As argued earlier, the types of externally influenced changes that occur in the AL at this stage are in fact quite similar to the convergence phenomena found in many other situations of bilingualism.

On the other hand, as Sasse (1992b: 63) in fact suggests, the proper point of comparison for the decaying language of semi-speakers is cases of imperfect acquisition, including pidgin formation. This applies especially to those terminal speakers who experienced "random" acquisition due to inadequate input and/or limited opportunity to use the AL. The systematic reduction and simplification of structural apparatus found in their version of the AL are quite comparable to those found in pidgins (see chapter 8), or indeed, in very early interlanguage. Maher (1991: 81) also suggests that the common element linking semi-speaker varieties and pidgins is "inadequate exposure to the target language." It also seems reasonable to compare the types of simplification found in the less decayed output of formerly fluent speakers to those found in "simplified" languages (chapter 8).

While there are no doubt some differences between pidgins and decaying language, these vary depending on the degree to which the decay has progressed. The semi-speaker varieties of Kore described by Dimmendaal retain features such as morphological verb classes, compounds, and tone distinctions – features not usually found in "prototypical" pidgins. But some of these can be found in simplified languages and expanded pidgins (chapter 8). This suggests that both language decay and pidginization vary along a continuum, and attempts to compare them must focus on similar points along each continuum. In general, however, all of these contact phenomena are "manifestations of a universal tendency . . . from the marked to the unmarked" (Dimmendaal 1992: 130).

Exercise 10
Based on the case studies you examined for the previous exercise, compare phenomena of reduction and simplification in obsolescent languages with those found in pidgins and simplified languages. What similarities and differences do you find? (See chapter 8, section 8.4, for discussion of structural characteristics of pidgins.)

7.19 Summary

In this chapter, we examined the processes of individual and group second language acquisition, focusing primarily on the strategies learners employ in their attempt to acquire a TL. These strategies include appealing to L1 knowledge, simplifying and avoiding TL structures that are difficult to learn, and creatively adapting those L2 elements that have been acquired.

In section I, we saw that L1 influence can manifest itself in the individual learner's interlanguage at every level of structure, from the lexicon to the syntax. Such influence is particularly strong at earlier stages of SLA, though it remains active at all stages. Also in the early stages, processes of simplification, including reduction of bound morphology and more complex syntactic structures, yield a fairly simple IL system. Learners also employ strategies of rule generalization, innovative word formation, etc. to expand the capacity of their developing IL. The learner is guided by general cognitive principles that regulate the processing of the L2 input. For instance, learners tend to process content words before grammatical items and pay attention only to salient features of the input. This explains in part why early IL systems are highly reduced, though regular. The outcome of this early stage is usually a "basic variety" of the TL which learners continue to expand if they have motivation and opportunity to do so. Some learners in "natural" settings fail to advance beyond this stage.

The elaboration of the IL grammar involves acquisition of increasingly complex morphological and syntactic operations, as well as expansion of the vocabulary. The restructuring process follows a certain sequence and path of development that are subject once more to general linguistic principles and constraints. For instance, research has shown that learners acquire rules of negation, question formation, relativization, etc. in a relatively fixed order in each case. This order seems to follow a hierarchy of complexity, with simpler structures acquired first. This has been taken as evidence that the ease and order of acquisition are directly related to the degree of markedness of the relevant TL structures.

Markedness-based constraints also appear to regulate the role of the L1 in SLA. TL structures that are more marked in relation to equivalent L1 structures are harder to learn. By the same token, acquisition is facilitated in cases where the TL structure is either universally unmarked or typologically similar (and hence relatively unmarked in relation) to the corresponding one in the L1. In general, the degree of congruence between L1 and TL elements is a crucial factor in determining the kinds of L1 transfer that occur in the elaboration of the IL. Perceived congruence or "interlingual indentifications" may cause learners to project or impose L1 categories or functions onto TL-derived forms.

Each stage of IL development involves a particular set of learning and communication strategies, all of which are subject to general cognitive principles, as well as constraints based on markedness and typological distance. There appears to be a hierarchical relationship among these three. Typologically based constraints can be viewed as a subset of markedness-based constraints, which in turn are subject to cognitively driven constraints based on processing principles.

In section II, we examined cases of group SLA or language shift that produce new contact varieties of a TL. Like the ILs of individual learners, these contact varieties display the effects of L1 influence as well as simplification and internal innovation. The cases discussed in this section included Irish English, Singapore English, and Taiwanese Mandarin. All of these "indigenized" varieties show evidence of significant substratum influence from the first languages of their creators. Irish English has various phonological and (morpho-)syntactic features that can be traced to Irish influence. Likewise, much of the grammar of Singapore English and Taiwanese Mandarin is modeled on Cantonese and Taiwanese respectively.

Both transfer to somewhere and transfer to nowhere play a role in the creation of these vernaculars. In the former case, learners project the properties of L1 elements onto TL-derived forms that they perceive as equivalent in some sense to the former. In the latter case, they compensate for unfamiliarity with TL structures by resorting to L1 structures that have no model in the TL. These strategies of transfer are subject to the same principles and constraints that operate in individual SLA. The main difference is that, in the case of group SLA, a new contact language emerges via leveling of competing features across individual I(nternal)-languages. Various social factors determine the nature of this leveling, and the types of innovations that will become conventionalized as part of the community E(xternal)-language. These factors include the demographics of the groups in contact, their patterns of interaction, the persistence of bilingualism within the shifting group, and so on. Factors such as speakers' network structures, social mobility, and choice of social identity also play a role.

Cases of group SLA pose interesting questions for a classification of contact vernaculars. In some respects, they have much in common with extended pidgins (chapter 8) and creoles (chapter 9). All of these outcomes can be placed on a continuum, at one extreme of which are cases of relatively successful approximation to a TL, while "radical" creoles occupy the other extreme. Indigenized varieties and "intermediate" creoles occupy the mid-points of the continuum.

Finally, in section III, we considered the consequences of shift for the L1 or ancestral language of the shifting group, particularly in cases where the shift leads to the attrition and even extinction of the AL. The same external pressures and social forces that initiate language shift can often lead individuals or groups to abandon their AL altogether. The changing sociolinguistic structure of the speech community and its degree of ethnolinguistic vitality are the main determinants of how far the process of abandonment will go.

Language attrition begins with a period of bilingualism and (broad) diglossia during which the L2 assumes dominance. This is followed by a period of disintegration and decay when speakers no longer learn the AL in the normal way or have limited opportunity to use it. Such "semi-speakers" are the chief producers of decayed versions of the AL.

The contact-induced changes that occur in the AL under influence from the L2 during the period of bilingualism are quite similar to those found in other cases of convergence. By contrast, the changes that occur during the period of decay involve processes of reduction and simplification typical of pidgin formation or early IL construction, though there are differences. In short, both the social motivations and the linguistic processes involved in language attrition and death can be found in other situations of language contact.

Notes

1 My thanks to Bettina Migge (p.c. August 2001) for providing some of the German example sentences.
2 A few examples of the grammatical functions of nouns that can be relativized are as follows: (a) subject: *The girl that loves John*; (b) object: *The girl that John loves*; (c) indirect object: *The girl that John wrote a letter to*; (d) object of preposition: *The girl that John talked about*; etc.
3 Irish English also expresses the sense of a "continuative" or "extended" perfect with present tense forms rather than *have*, for example, *She's here since last week*. This has been attributed primarily to superstrate influence, though it is possible that substrate influence also played some role (Odlin 1997a: 32).
4 My thanks to Hannah Lin, Jinyi Wang, and Janice Fon for help with the Taiwanese data. They inform me that a TM sentence like (30b) can be used only in certain pragmatic contexts, for instance, in reply to a question like "Did you have lunch?"

8

Pidgins and Pidginization

8.1 Introduction: Definitions

Like other labels used to describe the outcomes of contact, the term "pidgin" is fairly recent. The types of contact vernaculars it refers to existed long before linguists attempted to attach any label to them. To take one of the best-known examples, the Mediterranean Lingua Franca is believed to have been in existence since the Middle Ages, and texts of this contact variety survive from the sixteenth century. There is also evidence of the existence of numerous pidgins in pre-colonial Africa, Asia, and North America. No doubt many others emerged even earlier, whenever the need arose. Such languages arose to facilitate communication between groups of different linguistic backgrounds in restricted contexts such as trade, forced labor, and other kinds of marginal contact. Because of such restrictions in the scope of their use, these contact varieties were highly reduced and simplified, fashioned solely for the limited purposes they served. By definition, then, pidgins are adult creations, involving processes of learning and selective adaptation of linguistic resources that are reminiscent of those found in adult SLA.

It is now generally accepted that the term *pidgin* derives from the English word *business*, reflecting the most commonplace function of these languages as vehicles for trading transactions. The label seems to have been first applied to Chinese Pidgin English, which served as a lingua franca between speakers of Chinese and English (as well as others) on the southern China coast from roughly 1715 on. The first texts in this pidgin appeared in 1743 (Baker and Mühlhäusler 1990). The label was popularized in a Chinese Pidgin English phrase book used in the early 1900s. Eventually the term became a generic label for all contact varieties of this type. Before that, terms like "jargon" and "lingua franca" were used to refer to pidgins. This is why we find, for instance, names like "Chinook Jargon" and "Mobilian Jargon" being applied to two well-known pidgins that emerged in early colonial or perhaps even pre-colonial America.

All of the labels mentioned so far were first used by lay people or non-specialists before they were adapted as technical labels by linguists. Non-specialists, of course, tend to use such terms in rather loose and derogatory senses, to refer to forms of speech that they perceive as defective or corrupt in some way. One thing that all specialists agree on, however, is that pidgins and other contact vernaculars are not corruptions or ungrammatical versions of their source language(s), but rather legitimate languages with a grammar of their own, which can be learnt like other languages.

Notwithstanding this, there still remains a great deal of indeterminacy and confusion in the use of the term "pidgin," even among linguists. It is necessary for us to sort things out before we proceed any further. In the first place, there is the problem of distinguishing "pidgins" from "jargons," cases of "imperfect" L2 learning, and "foreigner talk," the simplified version of a language that its own native speakers sometimes use in communicating with outsiders. The differences among these kinds of simplified language are by no means absolute, since similar processes of change apply to all.

Terms like "jargon" and its French counterpart "baragouin" (also spelt "barogoin") date back to the colonial period, when they were used by Europeans to refer in derogatory terms to second language varieties of their languages used by indigenous peoples trying to communicate with them (Chaudenson 1992: 12). Since we can refer to such varieties more appropriately as unconventionalized or idiosyncratic forms of interlanguage, the term "jargon" serves no useful purpose here. By the same token, its use in reference to pidgins is redundant as well as inappropriate, given its associations of "corrupt" or "debased" language in its original lay usage. For that reason we will henceforth break with established practice and refer to so-called Chinook Jargon, Mobilian Jargon, etc. as Chinook Pidgin, Mobilian Pidgin, and so on.

We can further distinguish pidgins from early interlanguage varieties ("imperfect learning") and foreigner talk by noting that pidgins, unlike the other two, are conventionalized systems of communication that serve as targets of learning in their own right. (See further discussion in section 8.5, below.) Weinreich's analogy of sand in the stream versus sand deposited on the lake-bed (see p. 236) is relevant here as in other cases of contact. Idiosyncratic interlanguage varieties and forms of foreigner talk (as input to the former) provide the materials (sand) which are shaped (deposited) into a stable pidgin grammar. Foreigner talk is further distinguished from early interlanguage and pidgins by not being subject to substratal influence or admixture.

The second problem that faces us is how to delimit the scope of reference of the term "pidgin" in a realistic way. The reason is that the label now encompasses a wide variety of contact vernaculars with varying degrees of complexity in structure and use. It can refer to "rudimentary" languages like Russenorsk or

Delaware Pidgin, as well as to "full-fledged" languages like Hiri Motu, which serves as a lingua franca in Papua, the southern half of Papua New Guinea. The problem, as usual, revolves around the criteria of definition one applies. If one emphasizes criteria such as lack of native speakers, or restricted use as a lingua franca, then any language that fits this profile could be regarded as a "pidgin." If on the other hand we try to use structural criteria in our definition, we are faced with the problem that the relevant outcomes of contact lie on a continuum, with considerable overlap among them. Precisely where do we draw the boundaries between "true" pidgins and other contact varieties, particularly "extended pidgins" and "creoles"?

One solution is to distinguish prototypical pidgins from other contact varieties that depart in varying degrees from the prototype (Thomason 1997c: 76). The concept of "prototypical pidgin" is in fact quite close to the traditional wisdom on what constitutes a pidgin. It is a concept based on both structural and sociocultural criteria, captured well by Hymes (1971b: 84): "Pidginization is that complex process of sociolinguistic change comprising reduction in inner form, with convergence, in the context of restriction in use. A pidgin is the result of such a process that has achieved autonomy as a norm." Other definitions have appealed variously either to structural characteristics or to second language status or to restriction in use as criteria for pidgin status. But it is a combination of all these properties that best characterizes true pidgins.

Henceforth, then, our use of the term "pidgin" as a classificatory label will refer only to those contact vernaculars characterized by highly reduced vocabulary and structure, which are native to no one, and serve as lingua francas for certain restricted communicative functions such as trade. Other contact varieties that have been referred to as "pidgins" but fail to meet the criteria just outlined will be classified in different ways. As we shall see, they include "extended pidgins" (e.g., varieties of Melanesian Pidgin) which bear striking similarities to "creoles," as well as "simplified languages" (e.g., Hiri Motu and Kituba) which closely resemble cases of group SLA. The reasons for these classifications will be discussed later in the chapter.

8.2 Social Contexts of Pidgin Formation

Pidgins have arisen in a variety of social situations involving limited contact between groups, where neither group has the opportunity or the real need to learn the other's language. Some have emerged in domestic settings for use in employer–servant interactions, for instance Indian Butler English (Hosali

1992). Others have been formed in situations involving military invasion or occupation, for instance American, French, and British military activity in various parts of Asia and the Pacific in the twentieth century. Varieties such as Japanese Pidgin English (Goodman 1967) and Vietnamese Pidgin French or Tây Bôi (Reinecke 1971) arose in this way. It is claimed that some pidgins have emerged as vehicles for interaction with tourists, for example the Turkish-derived pidgin described by Hinnenkamp (1982). However, it's not clear how stable or conventionalized such varieties are.

The two most common as well as most important types of pidgin are those that have arisen either in contexts of mass migrant labor, or in trading situations. Well-known examples of the former include Pidgin Hawaiian and (earlier) Hawai'i Pidgin English, both employed on the plantations of Hawaii in the nineteenth century. Varieties of early Pacific Pidgin English which arose for purposes of trade were later adopted for use on plantations in Queensland (Australia) and Samoa. Plantation and other labor pidgins may not always conform strictly to the criteria associated with "prototypical" pidgins. They tend to be somewhat more elaborate than the latter because labor settings permit of more continuous contact between groups. In such cases, extension of the functions of these pidgins beyond the restricted context of labor led to the emergence of more complex contact vernaculars. Examples include the "extended pidgins" of the Pacific and (later) Hawai'i Pidgin English, which eventually became Hawai'i Creole English, (though its speakers still call it "pidgin"). For this reason, plantation pidgins pose more problems both in terms of the degree to which they diverge from the prototype, and with regard to determining the boundaries between their stages of development and expansion. We return to this below.

The most commonly found pidgins are those that have arisen in contexts of trade. Such contact varieties have been documented in a great many areas throughout the world and throughout recorded history. Most of them no longer survive, and the only record we have of many is brief mention in historical documents – for instance, Pidgin Macassarese in northern Australia, Arabic–Chinese pidgin of Canton, Pidgin Siassi of New Guinea, etc. (Mühlhäusler 1986: 77). There were, no doubt, many others in prehistory about whose existence we will never know.

Fortunately, records in the form of texts and commentaries survive for many others that are no longer in use, and for some that are. Among these are indigenous American pidgins such as Chinook Pidgin (also known as Cinúk Wawa, or simply Wawa "speech"), Mobilian Pidgin, Delaware Pidgin, and varieties of Eskimo Pidgin. The first three of these may well have arisen in pre-colonial times as lingua francas for use among different Native American groups, but were eventually also adopted for use between Indians and Europeans. Varieties of Eskimo Pidgin, on the other hand, seem to have emerged from about the seventeenth century specifically for trade between the Inuit (used here to refer to Eskimo-speaking people in general) and Europeans, whom the Inuit referred to as "Qallunaat."

The circumstances in which these pidgins arose and were used are representative of those typical of trade pidgins in general. The best-known of them, Chinook Pidgin, probably originated in pre-European times for use in slave trading and shell-money commerce in the Northwest Pacific area. The earliest records of this pidgin date back to 1778, the year when Captain James Cook first explored Nootka sound. Use of the pidgin extended from Southern Alaska to Northern California and from the Pacific coast to Western Montana (Johnson 1978; cited in Drechsel 1981: 101). It was used by speakers of perhaps a hundred or more mutually unintelligible Native American languages belonging to different language families (Athapascan, Penutian, Salishan, Wakashan) as well as between American Indians and non-American Indians (English, French, Russian, Hawaiian, and others). This pidgin was highly mixed in lexicon, but seems to have drawn materials primarily from Lower Chinook or some other closely related language. Chinook Pidgin was unique among indigenous American pidgins in being adopted as a primary language by children of intertribal and interethnic families in the late nineteenth to early twentieth centuries. It has been suggested that the pidgin was in fact "creolized" by such children at the Grande Ronde reservation in Northwestern Oregon (Zenk 1988).

Further details of the origins and use of Chinook Pidgin and other indigenous pidgins of the US can be found in Drechsel (1981, 1996) and the references there. According to Drechsel (1996: 1226) they all shared a number of sociolinguistic characteristics. All (except perhaps Eskimo Pidgin) were used in a variety of communicative functions, both among American Indians of diverse linguistic backgrounds, and later between American Indians and non-American Indians. Their primary contexts of use included trading, hunting, and similar activities, as well as political associations and alliances. They were also used in gatherings between kin, and across communities linked by intermarriage. All existed in situations of great linguistic diversity involving much bi- and multilingualism. In post-Columbian times, they functioned as lingua francas not only in trade with Europeans, but also in European exploration and missionary work among the American Indians, and in European employment (or enslavement) of Native Americans. At least two of them, Chinook Pidgin and Mobilian Pidgin, were also used in narration, song, and other kinds of entertainment. These pidgins were also characterized by heavy use of gesture and other kinds of body language, to a much greater extent than in their source languages. Many of these sociolinguistic characteristics can also be found in other indigenous pidgins, such as those of Papua New Guinea.

Other trade pidgins, such as Russenorsk, Chinese Pidgin, and Eskimo Pidgin, arose primarily in contact between indigenous and foreign groups, and were more restricted to trading activity, though some, for example, Chinese Pidgin English, later developed more general uses and hence more elaborate structure. In the following section, we take a brief look at Russenorsk by way of illustrating what a typical pidgin looks like. The choice of Russenorsk is deliberate, since questions have been raised about its status as a genuine or prototypical pidgin. It will help us clarify precisely what criteria are relevant to this designation.

8.3 Russenorsk: A Brief Sketch

Russenorsk (henceforth RN) was first used in trading between Russian fishermen and Norwegian merchants in northern Norway from about the end of the eighteenth century to the 1920s. The contact between the two groups was restricted to a few months in summer, during which time the Norwegians traded their fish for Russian grain and other commodities. The Russian Revolution in 1917 effectively ended the trade, as a result of which RN died.

Because of the equal status between the two groups, the pidgin they developed drew almost equally from both Russian and Norwegian for its vocabulary. Though more words appear to have come from Norwegian, this may be due to the fact that almost all of the texts that survive were collected from Norwegian speakers of the language (Jahr 1996: 120, fn. 10). RN seems to have employed a core vocabulary of just 150–200 words, and in many cases there are both Russian- and Norwegian-derived words for the same concept. Some 10 percent of the vocabulary (about 20 words) comes from other languages, including English. To compensate for the small size of the core vocabulary, new words were sometimes formed through compounding, for example, *kuasjorta* lit. "cow-shirt" = "cow-hide," and *kuasalt* lit. "cow salt" = "salted meat" (I. Broch and Jahr 1984: 37). The lexicon consisted mainly of nouns, verbs, adjectives, and a few adverbs. Only two pronouns were frequently used: *moja* first person and *tvoja* second person (sometimes *ju*), with no inflections for case. Hence RN was sometimes referred to as *moja på tvoja* "me on (?) you." It was also sometimes called *kaksprek* "how-speak" (Fox 1983: 101).

Given the almost equal contribution from Russian and Norwegian to the vocabulary, it is not surprising that RN phonology is a kind of compromise between the phonologies of the two source languages. Sounds shared by them are retained in the pidgin, while those that occur only in one are for the most part eliminated. For example, Russian /x/ becomes RN /k/, thus, Russian *orech* "nut" > RN *oreka* (I. Broch and Jahr 1984: 31).

Like all pidgins, RN entirely lacks inflectional morphology as well as any complex (especially bound) derivational morphology of the sort found in its source languages. It also lacks categories such as tense, aspect, person, number, etc. Notions like time reference are expressed through use of adverbials, as in the following example:

(1) stari gammel, snart på kjæka slipom
old old soon on church sleep
"I'm old, I shall die soon" (H. Stanges, in Jahr 1996: 119)

Modal verbs like *ville* "want" and *skulle* "should" can convey futurity, but they are not tense auxiliaries:

(2) Moja vil spraek på principal
"I want to speak with the captain" (I. Broch and Jahr 1984: 45)

As in the case of pidgins generally, functional categories are either missing or very rare in RN. The pidgin lacks copulas (see example (3)), and employs almost exclusively only one preposition *på/po* (from Norwegian and Russian respectively) and one apparently subordinating conjunction *kak* (< Russian *kak*), which seems to be essentially a question word (see example (4)):

(3) Russman bra mann.
Russian-man good man
"The Russian is a good man"

(4) Moja smotrom kak ju pisat
I see that(how?) you write (I. Broch and Jahr 1984: 37)

Finally, RN has a very basic syntax, lacking any kinds of embedding or subordination (with the possible exception of *kak* clauses above). Clauses are combined only by paratactic means, either through juxtaposition or via co-ordinating conjunctions (*i, ja, jes*). The basic word order of the pidgin is SVO, though it has a tendency to use SOV order in sentences with adverbials. Compare (5) and (6):

(5) Moja kopom fiska
"I buy fish"

(6) Moja tvoja på vater kasstom
I you on water throw
"I'll throw you into the water" (Jahr 1996: 115–16)

In short, in its overall structural design, RN is very much like any other prototypical pidgin. This raises some interesting questions concerning the claims that have been made about the defining features of "true" pidgins.

8.4 Structural Characteristics of Pidgins

It is interesting to note that there have been challenges to Russenorsk's status as a "true" pidgin. For example, Fox (1983) argues that it does not conform to Whinnom's (1971) stipulation that pidgins are due to a process of "tertiary hybridization," which comes about when the pidgin is used among different "substrate" groups whose members are not native speakers of the "superstrate" or lexifier language. By this criterion, only contact varieties like Chinook Pidgin or Hawai'i Pidgin English would qualify as true pidgins. Note that this would deny pidgin status not only to Russenorsk, but also to Ndjuka-Trio Pidgin (Huttar and Velantie 1997), Chinese Pidgin English (Baker and Mühlhäusler 1990), and others that most linguists would regard as pidgins. (Ndjuka-Trio pidgin developed in a two-language contact situation for use in trade between Ndjukas and Trio Indians in the interior of Suriname from about the nineteenth century on.)

Disagreements like this are not uncommon, and tend to be based on scholars' different definitions and assumptions. Some argue that pidgins have a grammar drawn from one source, and a vocabulary from another; others claim that pidgins are compromises between grammars in contact. Still others insist that excessive lexical variation rules out pidgin status. None of these stipulations offers a definitive basis on which to identify pidgins. The simple way to resolve this would be to recognize that there is in fact a great deal of diversity among pidgins in the way they put their source materials together, and that they do not all fit into a single mold. What unites them as a distinct typological class of contact vernaculars is a set of shared structural and non-structural characteristics.

8.4.1 Pidgin morphology and syntax

Perhaps the most definitive structural characteristics of pidgins are to be found in morphology and syntax. Among these are the following, as suggested in Bickerton (1981) and Drechsel (1996: 1225):

Morphology:

- Absence of morphological apparatus such as affixation and inflection; hence no morphological expression of categories like number, person, agreement, etc.
- Absence of other functional categories such as tense and aspect, with limited expression of deontic modality (e.g., desire).
- Minimal inventory of function morphemes such as articles, quantifiers, prepositions, conjunctions, complementizers, etc.
- Restricted number of question words and pronouns. Most pidgins have only three pronouns: first, second and third person, undifferentiated for gender or number.
- Use of one universal negative marker.

Syntax:

- Analytic structures, with word order as the primary means of determining grammatical functions such as "subject," "object," etc.
- A reduced number of sentence patterns, due to lack of rules for changing word order to create derived structures, for example, "movement" rules for topicalization, passivization, inversion in questions, etc.
- A lack of derivational depth, due to absence of any mechanisms for subordination or embedding (e.g., of relative or complement clauses).

Pidgins also share certain core characteristics in their lexicon and phonology, though both of these components allow for some variation both across and within pidgins.

8.4.2 Pidgin lexicon

All pidgins have very restricted lexical inventories. Estimates range from 150–200 words in the case of Russenorsk (Jahr 1996: 109) to about 500 in the case of Chinook Pidgin (Grant 1996: 1186). These numbers refer to words most commonly used. The count may be higher if we include words whose use was restricted, or confined to specific places. According to Grant (ibid.) this would bring the count for Chinook Pidgin up to about 1500 words. The general character of pidgin lexicons is well summed up by Drechsel's (1996: 1225) remarks about the three best-documented Native American Pidgins (Chinook, Delaware, and Mobilian pidgins). He notes that all three had "parsimonious vocabularies consisting of generic lexical entries that were often semantically and grammatically ambiguous, as well as polysemous. The lexicon could be expanded via compounding, metaphorical extension or simple borrowing of words from the speaker's L1 or a foreign language." These properties are shared across all pidgins, despite differences in the degree of diversity in the sources of their vocabulary.

Most pidgins in fact draw their vocabulary primarily from one source language. For example, Delaware Pidgin has its lexical (and grammatical) base mostly in Unami, a dialect of Delaware (Goddard 1997: 43). But as with pidgins generally, other languages in the contact situation contributed to the lexicon as well. In some cases this resulted in a high degree of mixture and variation, as we saw in the case of Russenorsk. Ndjuka-Trio pidgin also draws its vocabulary from both of its source languages, Ndjuka and Trio, though Trio contributed the smaller share, consisting mostly of nouns.

There is even greater mixture in the lexicon of Chinook and Mobilian Pidgins, reflecting the greater linguistic diversity of the groups who used them. Thus, while words from Lower and Upper Chinook constitute the majority of the core lexicon of Chinook Pidgin, there were also significant contributions from other American Indian languages as well as from French and English. For instance, Nootka provided about two dozen words and several others came from Salishan, Sahaptuan, and other language families (Grant 1996: 1189). English and French provided a substantial portion of words, expressing various objects or concepts associated with European trade, religion, etc. Even the basic lexicon of Chinook Pidgin is quite mixed, with several words from French and English, though Chinook words are most frequent (Grant 1996: 1190). The diversity in the vocabulary is directly related to the gradual spread of the pidgin from its original locale in the coastal areas, where Chinook was spoken, to various parts of the Pacific Northwest. Despite the diversity, it can still be claimed that Chinook Pidgin is based on Chinook (Grant 1996: 1188).

8.4.3 Pidgin phonology

The shared characteristics of pidgin phonology include a reduced inventory of phonemes as well as phonological contrasts and processes, by comparison to those of the major lexifier language. This reduction is primarily due to the elimination of sounds that are not shared across the languages in contact, particularly those of the major lexifier language that are marked in relation to those of the learners' L1s. For example, Ndjuka-Trio Pidgin preserves only the five vowels Ndjuka shares with Trio, which has seven. Also, it lacks contrasts of nasalization, vowel length, tone, and voicing of stops, which are characteristic of Ndjuka but not of Trio (Huttar and Velantie 1997: 104). Note that a pidgin may retain marked sounds in cases where they are shared across the languages in contact. For instance, the varieties of Chinook Pidgin spoken by Native Americans retained lateral obstruents and affricates, including the complex sound /tɬ'/ (Thomason and Kaufman 1988: 260). Native American speakers also kept such features as glottalization and a distinction between velar and uvular obstruents. European speakers of Chinook Pidgin could not reproduce such features, but tended to replace the difficult sounds with the closest equivalents from their own languages. But some loss of marked features occurred even in the speech of American Indians. In general, "highly marked sounds converged with less marked counterparts across language boundaries," forming "systems of phonological common denominators" (Drechsel 1981: 95–6).

Apart from this common core, however, some pidgins display substantial variation in phonology, due to influence from speakers' L1s. This is especially true of pidgins like Chinook and Mobilian pidgins which were used by a wide variety of linguistic groups. This diversity and variation in pidgin lexicon and phonology contrast sharply with the uniformity of their reduced morphological and syntactic components. Let us now examine how these components arose.

8.5 Pidgin Formation in Relation to Early SLA

We have seen that most pidgins have their lexical base primarily in one source language and that some aspects of their structure (e.g., phonology) might be viewed as attempted approximations to the lexifier language. This invites the conclusion that pidgins are learner varieties of the lexifier language, a kind of early-fossilized stage of L2 acquisition. Many pidgins seem to fit this profile. Thus Goddard (1997: 43) refers to Delaware Pidgin as "a pidginized form of Unami." On the other hand, however, there are pidgins that do not seem to fit this profile. For instance, Ndjuka-Trio Pidgin cannot be regarded as a "reduced" version of Ndjuka, its main lexifier. Most of its grammar derives from Trio, its "substrate" (Huttar and Velantie 1997: 105). But the difference here may be one of degree rather than kind, since all pidgins as well as early IL manifest some degree of influence from learners' L1s.

Still, it seems oversimplistic to claim that pidgins can be equated fully with early learner approximations to a TL. Even for pidgins like Delaware Pidgin which have both their lexical and grammatical base in one primary source language, it may be misleading to think of that source as a TL in the strict sense. The aim of the original creators of the pidgin was not to learn the other group's language, but to forge some limited practical means of communication.

Once it was established, this compromise system, and not the lexifier language, became the target of learning for later arrivals on the scene.

It could be argued that another difference between pidgin formation and early IL construction lies in the nature of the input to each. As we have seen, it is widely claimed that the primary input to pidgins came from foreigner talk versions of the major source or lexifier language. Thus it might be argued that this deliberately reduced and simplified model was the source of many characteristic pidgin features such as absence of morphology and syntactic complexity. On the other hand, it seems to be assumed that the TL input to early SLA is richer and more complex. If so, the processes of reduction and simplification found in early IL would be due primarily to the agentivity of L2 learners rather than TL speakers. It's not clear, however, that such a sharp distinction can be made. It would seem, in fact, that much of the input to early SLA, especially in "natural" settings, consists of foreigner talk versions of the TL that its native speakers use in communicating with outsiders. Hinnenkamp (1982) and Harding (1984) discuss the kinds of foreigner talk used by German and English native speakers respectively in talking to foreign immigrants. As Hinnenkamp (1984: 157) shows, such varieties display many of the kinds of reduction and simplification associated with pidgins. This would mean that pidgin formation and the early stages of "natural" SLA have similar TL inputs, and this may account for certain similarities in their outcomes.

Finally, one might argue that treating pidgin formation as a form of early SLA also assumes that all of the structural properties of pidgins can be traced to one source. Yet it turns out that much of pidgin grammar is quite independent of the source language grammars. Again, however, this is true to some extent of early IL too. As we saw in chapter 7 (section 7.5.1), early IL grammar is also quite independent of both the L1 and the TL in its organization. Perhaps the most important distinction between pidgin formation and early IL construction is that the former involves eventual conventionalization of a set of distinctive norms shared by the groups in contact. Hence, unlike individual SLA, it is subject to social forces that promote leveling and compromise across individual grammars, just as in the case of group SLA or language shift.

Keeping all of the above caveats in mind, we will compare processes of pidgin formation with those involved in early IL construction. In fact, such a comparison can lead to better understanding of how pidgins arise. The two forms of language creation share similar strategies, properties, and processes of restructuring. Like "basic" L2 varieties, pidgins are born out of communicative strategies involving massive reduction and simplification, in a context of limited access (in the case of early IL, limited knowledge of the TL). In many ways also, pidgin formation is subject to principles and constraints similar to those that regulate the early stages of SLA.

8.5.1 Processes of pidgin formation

Traditionally, the processes involved in pidgin formation have been referred to collectively as "pidginization," a term which is not unproblematic, but which we will use for convenience. Hymes (1971b: 70) suggests that pidginization is "a complex process, comprising the concurrence of several component processes." For Hymes, these include three linguistic processes: simplification, reduction of "inner form," and admixture. Also involved are social processes such as restriction in scope of use, and use between groups with different languages. We focus here on the linguistic processes.

Trudgill (1996: 5) echoes Hymes, providing explanations of each process. Reduction involves impoverishment, as reflected in a small vocabulary, limited syntactic structures, a narrower range of styles, etc. Simplification is defined as involving "regularization of irregularities, loss of redundancy . . . and. . . . an increase in analytic structures and transparent forms" (ibid.: 6). Admixture is equated with "interference – the transfer of [structural] features from the native language to the new language, an obvious feature of adult SLA" (ibid.: 5).

Both of these accounts leave out a crucial component of pidgin formation, that is, the internally motivated processes of restructuring that lead to innovations not found in the source languages. Taking this into account, we find that pidgin formation shares the following linguistic processes with early SLA:

- Simplification: Used here to include both "reduction" and "regularization" of structures.
- L1 influence: Retentions from the native languages of those creating, and later learning, the pidgin.
- Internal developments: Innovations due to creative restructuring using internal resources.

As in the case of early IL creation, these processes are manifestations of communication strategies (avoidance, compensation) that all learners employ in their first attempts to communicate in a foreign language.

8.5.1.1 Reduction and simplification in pidgin formation

We have already illustrated the processes of reduction and simplification in pidgin formation in our sketch of Russenorsk, above. The phenomena we observed there – reduced vocabulary, absence of bound morphology, a limited range of syntactic structures, etc. – parallel those found in early stages of SLA. Indeed, the structural characteristics of pidgins are strikingly similar to those that Klein and Perdue (1997) describe for the "basic variety" of a TL created by immigrant learners in various European host countries. (See chapter 7, section 7.12.1). In both cases, we find a highly reduced vocabulary consisting mainly of content words and only a few function words. Both pidgins and basic L2 varieties lack inflectional morphology, grammatical categories like tense, aspect, case, number, etc., and syntactic phenomena such as movement, embedding, and similar devices.

In both cases, too, learners employ both avoidance and compensatory strategies of communication to make up for their lack of competence in the language being learnt. Pidgin formation provides some especially interesting examples of how learners systematize their rudimentary grammar and compensate for the limited resources they have at their disposal.

For example, in attempting to communicate with Eskimo-speaking peoples in the latters' language, European and other traders reduced the complex polysynthetic morphology in ways that yielded a more transparent form-to-meaning relationship in both lexicon and grammar. Thus, where Eskimo uses verbal affixes to express categories of person, Eskimo pidgin employs free pronominal forms, derived from emphatic pronouns whose use is pragmatically restricted in Eskimo. Example sentence (7) is the modern West Greenlandic (WG) Eskimo rendition of "I told you." Its highly synthetic structure may be contrasted with the analytic structure of its pidgin equivalent, (8), from Hudson Bay Pidgin Eskimo (Hanbury 1904, quoted in van der Voort 1997: 378):

(7) Modern WG: Oqaluttuup-pakkit
tell-I.you

(8) Hudson Bay: Awonga igbik ukak-tūk
I you talk-he
"I told you"

Also interesting is the fact that the pidgin sentence consists of word forms with fossilized inflections that have completely lost their original meanings. A word-for-word translation of (8) into modern WG would yield the completely ungrammatical and incoherent sentence in (9):

(9) *uanga illit oqar-poq
I you talk-he
"I, you, he talked" (van der Voort 1997: 378)

There are many other similar examples of how pidgin speakers reanalyzed complex Eskimo words to express a single invariant meaning. Here are some West Greenlandic examples from van der Voort (1997: 380–1):

(10)

Pidgin	*Meaning*	*Eskimo*
bos.amia	"sealskin"	WG: puisi-p ami-a
seal-skin		seal-ERG skin-his
uvanga nulia	"my wife"	nulia-ra
I wife(.his)		wife-my

(Note that *nulia* here may be either a reduced form of *nuliaq* "wife" or the third person singular form of the word *nulia* "his wife": van der Voort 1997: 390, fn. 7.)

With regard to syntax, many of the innovations in pidgin grammar can be explained as simplifications of more complex constructions found in one or another source language. For instance, most negative constructions in Chinook Pidgin consist of NEG S V, as in the following example from Thomason (1983b: 853):

(11) wik aɬqi msayka atá nayka
NEG FUT 2pl wait-for 1sg
"You won't have to wait for me"

Thomason shows that this pattern is a simplification of much more complex structures in the American Indian languages, in which sentence-initial negatives occur.

8.5.1.2 L1 influence in pidgin formation

Falling back on the resources of an L1 is another compensatory strategy common to both early SLA and pidgin formation. While it is generally agreed that L1 influence plays some role in pidgin formation, the degree and importance of such influence relative to others, for example, universals, remains under dispute. This is not surprising, since one can reach quite different conclusions about L1 influence depending on which pidgin one chooses to examine. As we saw earlier (section 8.4), different pidgins manifest different degrees of lexical and structural input from learners' L1s, as opposed to the lexifier language. L1 influence seems to manifest itself most in pidgin phonology. Thus Drechsel (1981: 95) points out that speakers of both Eskimo Pidgins and Chinook Pidgin "essentially followed the rules of pronunciation characteristic of their own native tongues." Baker and Mühlhäusler (1990: 112) make the same point about Chinese Pidgin English.

In the case of Eskimo pidgins, this meant a significant reduction both in phonemic inventory and in phonological contrasts in the pidgin by comparison with Eskimo proper. This was because the L1s of the mostly European learners of the pidgin lacked many of the Eskimo features. On the other hand, in the case of Chinook Pidgin, as we saw earlier, several marked sounds shared by Chinook and the other Native American languages in contact were preserved in the varieties of pidgin used by these groups. European speakers of the pidgin, however, did not employ sounds which their L1s lacked.

As far as syntax is concerned, we also noted earlier that some pidgins (e.g., Delaware Pidgin) draw primarily on the lexifier (superstrate) language, while others draw primarily on the learners' L1(s). Ndjuka-Trio Pidgin exemplifies perhaps an extreme case of the latter type, since practically all of its syntax is based on that of its substrate, Trio. Its syntax resembles that of the lexifier, Ndjuka, only where the latter matches Trio. Like Trio, the pidgin has basic SOV order which becomes OSV when the subject is a pronoun, whereas Ndjuka consistently has SVO (Huttar and Velantie 1997: 105). Also, like Trio, the pidgin marks negation with a post-verbal morpheme and has postpositions; by contrast, Ndjuka has a pre-verbal negative morpheme and prepositions (ibid.: 110–11). Various other syntactic characteristics of the pidgin can also be traced to Trio. In general, it may be the case that two-language contact situations favor greater structural influence from the substrate on the pidgin.

Most other pidgins show far less evidence of influence from learners' L1s on their syntax. When such influence appears, it tends to affect word order in particular. For example, Delaware Pidgin had variable SOV and SVO order, the former reflecting that of the American Indian languages, the latter that of European languages. Similarly, Eskimo Pidgin, which has dominant SOV order (like Eskimo), also allows some SVO, again reflecting European influence.

In general, however, pidgins have grammars that are substantially different from those of their primary source languages. To a large extent, this is due to those processes of simplification, regularization, and innovative restructuring that characterize pidgin formation. Pidgin grammar is therefore best seen as the result of interaction among various factors, of which L1 influence is just one.

Exercise 1

Thomason (1983b: 821) notes that "all C[hinook] J[argon] speakers produced CJ utterances containing systematic features not present in their native languages." Identify some of these features and try to explain their origins in terms of the various processes of pidgin formation discussed here.

8.5.1.3 Internal innovation in pidgin formation

One defining characteristic of pidgins that is generally agreed on is the innovative character of their grammar. Pidgins, in other words, have grammatical features that do not derive (directly) from their source languages. Like L2 learners, pidgin speakers creatively exploit their limited resources to achieve their communicative ends. They expand the lexicon through polysemy, compounding, and paraphrase, assign new functions to available morphemes, and create new syntactic rules.

The most common strategy for creating new pidgin words is compounding. We mentioned examples of this earlier, for Russenorsk (section 8.3). Godard (1997: 72) provides examples of similar coinages in Delaware pidgin, such as *hââs táckquin* "skin clothing," lit. "skin wear" (cf. Southern Unami *xé.s* "skin" + *nták.wi.n* "I wear it"), and *Hockung Tappin* "God," lit. "above sit" (cf. N. Unami *hokunk* "above" + S Unami *ntáp.i.n* "I sit/am (there)"). The pidgin also creates new expressions using *hátte* "have" and *maranijto* "do, make." Thus we find *hwisásse hátte* "be afraid," lit. "fear have," and *maranijto manúnckus* "abuse, do wrong to," lit. "make bad" (ibid.). The latter strategy is widespread in bilingual mixture in general, including code switching, as we saw in chapter 5. Finally, Baker and Mühlhäusler (1990: 100–3) provide many examples of innovative lexical expansion in Chinese Pidgin English, yielding compounds with *man* (*doctor man, josh man* "priest") and *side* (*topside* "upstairs, on top," *shoreside* "by/at the shore," etc.) and interrogative words with *what* (*what for* "why," *what side* "where," etc.).

Russenorsk also provides good examples of innovations in pidgin morphology. These include the use of suffix *-om* as an apparent marker of verbal status, for example, *kopom* "buy," *drinkom* "drink." This trait may have been borrowed from an English–Russian pidgin used in Archangel (Jahr 1996: 114). Nouns in RN also tend to end in *-a* (e.g., *groppa* "grain," *fiska* "fish," etc.), though there are exceptions such as nouns ending in *-i* from Russian (*kruski* "cup" < *kružki* "cups") or single-syllable nouns from Norwegian (e.g., *skip* "ship").

We also find innovations in pidgin syntax that have no counterparts in the source languages. Again, Russenorsk provides examples. The preference for SOV order in sentences with adverbials is one such innovation. This word order is not found in Norwegian, and is somewhat unusual in Russian. There is too a rule that requires the negator (Russian *nyet* or Norwegian *ikke*) to appear in second position, with a few exceptions. Neither Russian nor Norwegian has such a rule.

Innovations in pidgin grammar often reflect (incipient) patterns of grammaticalization that are quite common in language change and SLA. One such example is the use of verbs meaning "stay," "stop," etc. in a function similar to that of a locative copula. Kotsinas (1996: 133–4) compares the following examples from Russenorsk and Immigrant Swedish (IS), viz., the L2 variety of Swedish used by a Greek immigrant in Sweden (Swedish, of course, is quite similar to Norwegian, to the point of mutual intelligibility):

(12) a. RN: kor yu tannom på gammel ras
where you stay on old time
"Where were you last time?"
b. IS: den tjugo år stanna Joannina
it twenty year stay Joaninna.
"She lived in Joannina [a town] for twenty years"[1]

Another common innovation in pidgins which has parallels to early IL development is the use of a single preposition in a variety of functions. For example, Kotsinas (1996: 139) informs us that both Russenorsk and Immigrant Swedish employ the preposition *på* to mark various spatial meanings such as location, direction, and origin. *På* is also used as a case marker in both contact varieties, to mark indirect objects and possession, as in the following examples from Kotsinas (1996: 141–2):

(13) a. RN: moja på ju presentom baanbaan
I P you give candy
"I will give you candy"
b. IS: Köpa på barn
buy P child
"[I] bought [clothes] for [my] child"

(14) a. RN: mangeli klokka på ju?
how-much clock P you
"What time is it?"
[Lit. how much is your clock?]
b. IS: Stan på din mamma
town P your mother
"Your mother's village"

In other uses, *på* seems to have the potential to function either as a preverbal marker of some kind of desiderative mood (example (15)), or as a complementizer (example (16)) in both RN and IS (examples from Kotsinas 1996: 144–5):

(15) a. RN: Moja på-slagom på tvoja
I P hit P you
"I will hit you"
b. IS: den barn sex månar kommer på skriva på kyrka.
it child six month come P write P church
"The child became six months old and we had to register him at church"

(16) a. RN: gå på slipom
go P sleep
"Go to sleep"
b. IS: och gå vi på simma och åta
and go we P swim and eat
"And we went to swim and eat"

Example (16b) is from the L2 Swedish of a Spanish immigrant, and it is possible that this use of *på* is influenced by the similar use of Spanish *para* (Kotsinas 1996: 150).

Though *på* has not been grammaticalized as either an auxiliary or a purpose complementizer in Russenorsk, its similarity to other all-purpose prepositions such as *long* (< *along(a)*) in Tok Pisin and *fu* (< *for*) in Atlantic creoles is striking. These examples demonstrate that even the limited resources of pidgins and early IL offer much potential for (internal) expansion of the grammar. As Ingvild Broch and Jahr (1984: 21) note, Russenorsk could have developed functionally and grammatically if contact between Norwegians and Russians had been intensified and further extended. In later sections of this chapter, we take a look at cases where circumstances were ripe for such expansion.

8.5.2 Principles and constraints in pidgin formation

The brief overviews of Russenorsk and Eskimo Pidgin provide ample evidence of how pidgin creators shape basic grammars in conformity with the same universal principles and constraints as regulate early SLA. The resemblance between pidgins and early IL was noted by earlier scholars such as J. H. Schumann (1978), Andersen (1981), Huebner (1983), and others. It was argued that, like pidgins, early IL represents a variety of natural language stripped of all marked characteristics. Moreover, different scholars proposed very similar principles to explain how early IL and pidgins were created.

In both cases, similar operating and processing principles regulate the ways in which the input materials are selected as part of the simplified variety (see chapter 7, section 7.7.1). Such principles help to explain why both pidgins and early IL have mostly lexical rather than functional morphemes, no bound morphology, and a highly reduced syntax. These principles apply regardless of whether the agents simplifying the input were native speakers of the putative TL or primary source language, or learners attempting to communicate with them in it. As we saw earlier, foreigner talk (Hinnenkamp 1984) displays the same kinds of simplification and isomorphism of form and function found in pidgins and early IL. It seems reasonable to assume that they are all subject to the same universal principles.

The claim that universal principles regulate pidgin formation has sometimes been (mis)interpreted to mean that such principles actually dictate and prescribe specific structural characteristics of pidgin grammar such as word order. Thus, Goddard (1997) rejects a "universalist" explanation for certain word order patterns in Delaware Pidgin, such as optional placement of object before the verb, the optional (but preferred) placement of the negative particle in sentence-initial position, and the possibility of given information following new. He argues that "these features are characteristic of Unami [the principal source of Delaware Pidgin], absent or rare in Germanic [the European languages involved in the contact], and unmotivated by putative universal patterns of unmarked word order" (1997: 83). However, Goddard's assumption that universal principles permit only certain patterns is erroneous. Rather, as we saw in the case of early IL (chapter 7, section 7.7.1), their role is simply to constrain selection among (possibly competing) choices. Recall, for example, the choice of invariant VO order in L2 German by Moroccan Arabic learners, as opposed to the choice of OV by Turkish learners. In the case of Delaware Pidgin, universal principles selected the word order patterns that were most common or preferred in the input.

Universal cognitive principles also regulate the process of grammar building in both pidgins and early IL. Corresponding to Andersen's One to One Principle of early IL construction is Naro's (1978) "Factorization Principle" for pidgin formation. The latter states: "Express each invariant, separately intuited meaning by at least one phonologically separate, invariant stress bearing form . . . and . . . avoid excessive accumulation of separately intuited elements of meaning" (1978: 340–1). As Bever and Langendoen (1972) note, general cognitive principles like these play a role in all cases of language learning as well as language change. In their attempts to communicate across language boundaries, learners aim to achieve maximum ease of perception and production through isomorphism of form and grammatical function, the elimination of opacity and redundancy, and the regularization of structure.

The view that pidgin formation is regulated by universal principles in fact goes back as far as Coelho (1880–6), and was further developed by Kay and Sankoff (1974) and Bickerton (1981). More recently, it was recast by Macedo

(1986) in terms of the core versus periphery theory advanced within the Principles and Parameters framework. According to this view, pidgins have a core grammar consisting of structures that are "maximally general and unmarked," reflecting the unmarked parameter settings of Universal Grammar (Macedo 1986: 73). Elaboration of pidgin grammar, from this perspective, involves the development of more "peripheral" rules and structures that are marked. The idea is an interesting one, which merits further development within a theoretical model. (For such an attempt, see Bresnan's 2000 discussion of pidgin pronominal systems from the perspective of Optimality Theory.)

8.6 Elaborated or Extended Pidgins

Most pidgins disappear quite quickly once the reasons for their use no longer exist. But many have developed into more elaborate systems of communication when social conditions have promoted extension of their use. Among the well-known cases are Chinook Pidgin, which developed into a more elaborate vernacular on the Grande Ronde reservation of Northwest Oregon, and varieties of early to mid-nineteenth-century Pacific Pidgin English, which developed into the languages known collectively as Melanesian Pidgin. Although these contact vernaculars are usually referred to as "extended pidgins," there is a very thin line separating them from those traditionally known as "creoles." For the sake of convenience, however, we will continue to refer to them as extended or elaborated pidgins.

There is another group of contact languages that are usually referred to as "pidgins," but which have much more elaborate grammars than prototypical pidgins. They include languages like Sango and Kituba in Central Africa, Hiri Motu in Papua New Guinea, and so on. The historical records are insufficient for us to claim with any certainty that these languages were the result of elaboration of an earlier prototypical pidgin. But the linguistic evidence, as we will see, indicates that they are really somewhat simplified versions of one source language – a fact which distinguishes them from elaborated pidgins like Melanesian Pidgin and makes them perhaps more akin to cases of group SLA. At any rate, we will henceforth refer to these contact varieties as "simplified languages." For instance, Hiri Motu is essentially a simplified form of Motu.

Both extended pidgins and simplified languages pose problems for a classification of contact vernaculars, as well as for the distinction between processes of "pidginization" and "creolization" and their relation to processes of contact-induced change in general. It is important to realize, first, that the labels we use to reify the outcomes of contact – "pidgin," "creole," "simplified language," etc. – imply a discreteness of status and characteristic structure that does not exist in reality. This is because all these outcomes have much in common in so far as their origins and processes of formation and development are concerned. Hence terms like "pidginization" and "creolization," which also imply distinct developmental paths of origin for each outcome, can in fact be misleading. If we are to achieve more accuracy in our understanding of both the outcomes and their origins, we need to examine in detail the inputs and processes – both social and linguistic – that brought them into being.

8.6.1 The origins and development of extended pidgins

We will focus here on the origins of Melanesian Pidgin, which emerged in the Loyalty Islands, New Caledonia, Vanuatu (formerly the New Hebrides), the Solomon Islands, and Papua New Guinea in the course of the nineteenth century. Its best-known modern descendants include Bislama of Vanuatu, Solomon Islands Pijin, and Tok Pisin ("talk pidgin") of Papua New Guinea. Melanesian Pidgin (henceforth MP) is in a direct line of descent from earlier varieties of Pidgin English that were used for trade between (mostly) English speakers and indigenous Pacific peoples from the early nineteenth century on. Baker and Mühlhäusler (1996) show that the path of MP's development involved differing inputs from various English-lexicon pidgins that emerged throughout the Pacific from roughly the 1790s on, from the China coast to Melanesia and Australia. The essentials of the sociohistorical background to the emergence of MP are outlined in the following sections.

8.6.2 Social contexts of early Pacific Pidgin English

European exploration of the Pacific began in 1488, when the Portuguese Magellan rounded the Cape of Good Hope. But contact between Europeans and Pacific peoples was generally rare or limited during the sixteenth to seventeenth centuries. Thereafter, the Portuguese established closer ties with various parts of South and South East Asia, including India, Ceylon, Macao, and parts of the East Indies. A number of Portuguese-lexicon contact vernaculars emerged in these areas, several of which survive today. Our concern, however, is with contact involving English and Pacific languages.

A trade in sea-otter furs from North America to China via Hawaii began in 1786. From then on, English-speaking (American and British) traders and others established continuing contact with Chinese ports like Macao, Whampoa, Canton, and (later) Shanghai, etc. This soon led to the emergence of Chinese

Pidgin English (CPE), which was the earliest of the Pacific English-lexicon pidgins to become stabilized and established.

In the 1790s, large-scale whaling operations began in the Pacific, and soon became a dominant factor in European–Oceanic contact. This lasted until the 1860s (Clark 1983: 12). By the 1830s, a (variable) form of pidgin English had become well established throughout the South Pacific, in Micronesia, Polynesia, Australia, and New Zealand. Clark (1983: 13) refers to this trade pidgin as "South Pacific Jargon," but I shall refer to it henceforth as South Pacific Pidgin (SPP). Clark notes that it was based mostly on foreigner talk English (FTE) that sailors, traders, and others employed in talking to South Pacific islanders – a view that Baker (1993a: 60) concurs with. This FTE apparently included lexical and grammatical features derived from other pidgin traditions in Atlantic and Asian ports. These were incorporated into SPP along with innovations introduced by Pacific islanders. SPP was also one of the inputs to the pidgins that developed in Australia, particularly in the Sydney area of New South Wales (NSW) from about 1800 on, and in Queensland, in the 1840s.

Early texts, like the following from NSW and the Marquesas respectively, show that these early contact varieties displayed many characteristics associated with prototypical pidgins (though the presence of features like past marker *been* and conjunction *cos* (< because) suggests they were somewhat more developed):

(17) *A pidgin text from New South Wales 1826*:
I been see Cope crammer plenty belonging to store; dat put it under arm like it dis, den dat run all along creek; dent me see it no more, cos I been run along Micky, and piola William. Den when look out along William dat gone.

"I saw Cope steal lots of things from the store. He put them under his arm like this. Then he ran down to the creek. Then I didn't watch any longer because I ran with Micky to inform William. When we searched with William, Cope had gone." (R. Dawson 1830: 297, quoted in Baker and Mühlhäusler 1996: 557)

(18) *A pidgin text from the Marquesas, South Pacific*:
Why you no like to stay? Plenty moee-moee (sleep) – plenty ki-ki (eat) – plenty whi-henee (young girls) – Oh, very good place Typee! Suppose you no like this bay, why you come? (Melville 1846: ch. 33, quoted in Clark 1983: 14)

SPP never became established in Micronesia and Polynesia, and its use declined along with whaling activities by the 1860s.

8.6.3 The emergence of early Melanesian Pidgin

From the 1840s on, SPP became the lingua franca used in various Southern Melanesian islands involved in the lucrative sandalwood and bêche-de-mer (< Portuguese *bicho do mar* "trepang") trade. These islands included the New Hebrides (modern Vanuatu), New Caledonia, and the Loyalty Islands (now politically part of New Caledonia). The trade required the establishment of more or less fixed settlements, thus leading to regular contact between English speakers and a multilingual native population. Conditions were therefore ripe for the emergence of relatively stable and more conventionalized pidgins. The distinct status of these pidgins is reflected in the fact that they obtained names of their own – Sandalwool English and Beach-la-Mar. The latter name, apparently an Anglicized version of bêche-de-mer, survives as Bislama, the name of the contemporary language spoken in Vanuatu. Henceforth we will refer to the mid-nineteenth-century varieties of MP as Early MP.

The English pidgin which had become well established by 1820 in the Sydney area of New South Wales (henceforth NSW Pidgin) seems to have exerted significant influence on early forms of MP, especially during the period 1840 to 1860 (Clark 1979; Baker 1993a: 13). This was because Sydney was the most frequent port of call in the Pacific for ships engaged in trading and related activities. Hence pidgin features were diffused by sailors, islanders, and other travelers from NSW to Melanesia and other parts of the Pacific. This is reflected in the fact that Early MP shares many lexical and grammatical features with Australian pidgin English and several with CPE. Some of these appear to be features of FTE, such as preposed negator *no*, zero copula, and *me* "I." Others seem to have been derived from pidgins that developed earlier in the Atlantic and parts of Asia, especially the China Coast. These "worldwide" features include "past" marker *been*, *suppose* "if," *allsame* "as, like," future adverbial *by and by*, and other grammatical items. Lexical items include, for example, *got* "have," pre-verbal intensifier *too much*, *plenty* "a lot of," *savi* "know," and *piccaninny* "young child." The latter two came from earlier Portuguese pidgin (Baker and Mühlhäusler 1996: 554).

The following sample of Early MP, from the New Hebrides in 1859, displays several of these features:

(19) *An Early MP text (1859) from Tanna, New Hebrides*:
You see . . . no good missionary stop Tanna. Suppose missionary stop here, by and by he speak, "Very good, all Tanna man make a work." You see that no good: Tanna man he no too much like work. By-and-by missionary speak, "No good woman make a work; very good,

> all man he only get one woman." You see Tanna man no like that: he speak, "Very good plenty woman; very good woman make all work." Tanna man no savé work . . . he too much lazy; he too much gentleman! (Clark 1983: 19)

NSW Pidgin was also diffused to other parts of Australia, including Queensland (1840s), where it formed the basis of Queensland Pidgin English (QPE), used initially for interaction between Whites and Aborigines.

QPE was used on plantations established in Queensland between 1863 and the turn of the century, the period of the labor trade. Laborers were recruited from different Pacific islands to work on these plantations for a few years, after which they returned home. The relatively stable plantation pidgin that emerged in this period became the basis for modern MP. The inputs to this developing contact variety came both from QPE and from early forms of MP introduced by New Hebrideans and Solomon Islanders.

Baker and Mühlhäusler (1996: 555–9) demonstrate that many features found in post-1863 MP have their earliest attestations (and presumably their source) in Australian Pidgin English. Among these are grammatical features first attested in NSW, such as transitive marker *-Vm*, *make-Vm (NP) VP*, pre-verbal intensifier *plenty*, and possessive marker *belong*. Lexical features of MP first attested in Australia include some *fellow* compounds (*blackfellow*, *whitefellow*), *walkabout* "wander," *mary* "woman," etc. Several of these grammatical and lexical features appear to be due to influence from Aboriginal languages, whose role in the formation of Australian Pidgin English is still somewhat underresearched (but see Koch 2000).

Further significant input to the development of plantation QPE came from the forms of early MP spoken by labor recruits and innovations they created as they elaborated this medium of interethnic communication. During the first 20 years of the labor trade, the vast majority of the recruits came from the New Hebrides, with smaller numbers from the Southeast Solomons and Micronesia. Siegel (1999: 11) shows that between 1863 and 1882, out of a total of 25,532 recruits in Queensland, 21,717 came from the New Hebrides, 2599 from the Southeast Solomons, and 1123 from the Loyalty Islands. The rest came from various other islands. It should not be surprising, then, that Southern Melanesians had a great impact on the pidgin used on Queensland plantations. Many features of MP first attested during the labor trade can be attributed to their influence. These include grammatical features such as *what name* (relative), *finish* (postposed completive), and three new pronouns: *me fellow*, *he fellow*, and *all he* "they." New lexical features include *beach la mar* "Bislama," *belly* "seat of the emotions," *liklik* "little," etc. (Baker and Mühlhäusler 1996: 560).

The following text, from Tanna (New Hebrides) in 1877, illustrates the further grammatical development of MP during the labor trade:

(20) *A text from the New Hebrides, 1877*:
Me been work long-a Marboro. Misse White my massa . . . You savvee Misse White, my word me plenty work long that fellow massa long-a-soogar . . . Misse White no good he plenty fight, too much kill-em me; he been give me small fellow box, no good, me fine fellow man, very good you give me tambacco, me too much like-em smoke.
What name you want-em man he do? (Giles 1968: 37, 40, quoted in Clark 1983: 22)

Texts like the above provide evidence that the early forms of MP underwent significant elaboration after 1865. This was due, as noted earlier, to their adoption for wider communication between heterogeneous groups not only on the plantations, but also in the home territories of the recruits after they returned there. The same scenario was repeated for other varieties of MP. Thus, Tok Pisin had its origins in the plantation pidgin that emerged on the German copra plantations of Samoa from 1878 on (Clark 1979: 39–40). Workers from New Britain and New Ireland started being recruited for work on these plantations in 1879. They learned pidgin from the New Hebrideans and Solomon Islanders who greatly outnumbered them at the start. As in other cases, returning workers took the pidgin back with them to Papua New Guinea, where it continued to develop as a medium of interethnic communication. The development of the different varieties of MP is discussed in Siegel (1998).

8.6.4 Further elaboration of MP grammar

Once established in their respective home territories, all varieties of MP continued to expand their resources through direct lexical borrowing from native languages, internal developments, and structural innovations due to substrate (L1) influence. Tok Pisin shows the highest degree of lexical borrowing from indigenous languages, with roughly 20 percent of its vocabulary from these sources, and about 80 percent derived from English, with a smattering of German words (Wurm 1971: 1010). This and other characteristics peculiar to this language reflect its relative isolation from 1890 to 1920, when New Guinea and Samoa fell under German administration. Southern varieties of MP, viz., Bislama and Solomon Islands pidgin, derive 90–5 percent of their lexicon from English (ibid.). Of special interest here are the structural innovations in MP that are due either to internal developments or to substrate influence. As a result of such changes, all MP dialects have developed quite elaborate grammars, including complex pronominal and tense/aspect systems, strategies of relativization, complementation and other types of embedding, and so on. Let us examine some of these.

8.6.4.1 L1 influence in MP development

The elaboration of Early MP from 1863 on involved a great deal of creative adaptation on the part of its speakers, who drew both on their limited lexical resources and on their L1 knowledge in building up the grammar. The role of substrate influence in this process has been well documented by Keesing (1988), Siegel (1999), and others. As Siegel (1999: 12) points out, the native languages of the creators of modern MP belonged to the Central Eastern Oceanic (CEO) subgroup of the Austronesian family. They included Southern Oceanic (Vanuatu, Loyalty Islands, New Caledonia), Southeast Solomons, and Central Pacific languages. The first two of these subgroups figured prominently in the development of MP. All of these languages are very similar typologically – a fact which no doubt promoted very similar kinds of innovation in the varieties of pidgin used by Islanders with different L1s.

Keesing (1988) identifies many aspects of MP (morpho-)syntax which he attributes at least partly to the role of substrate influence from CEO languages. First of all, in general MP syntax is highly paratactic in structure, reflecting that of the substrates. There are also many aspects of its morphosyntax that have more or less close parallels in CEO. A few examples will suffice. For a more comprehensive overview, see Keesing (1988: 105–32).

MP, like CEO, employs a subject-referencing pronoun (SRP) in the verb phrase. The function of this marker is to "reiterate an explicit subject NP and reference a subject indexically or anaphorically in subsequent clauses" (Keesing 1988: 98). The following examples from Siegel (1999: 13) illustrate the parallels between MP and its substrates:

(21) a. Arosi (SE Solomons): E noni a ome-si-a i ruma
ART man 3sg. see-TR-3sg ART house
"The man saw the house"

b. Bislama: Man ya i stil-im mane
"The man stole the money"

These sentences also illustrate another feature MP shares with its substrates, viz., the productive use of a transitivising suffix *-Vm* in a variety of functions that parallel those of transitivizing suffixes in CEO languages. Compare Arosi

-si in (21a) with Bislama *-im* in (21b). The transitivizing suffix converts intransitive verbs into transitive ones, as in (22), and is used to form causative verbs from statives, as in (23) (Keesing 1988: 120–1):

(22)	a.	Kwaio (SE Solomons):	*(aga)aga* "look" *fana* "shoot"	*aga-si* "see" *fana-si* "shoot" (tr.)
	b.	Solomons Pidgin:	*(luk)luk* "look" *sut* "shoot"	*luk-im* "see" *sut-im* "shoot" (tr.)
(23)	a.	Kwaio:	*mou* "be broken"	*mou-si* "break it"
	b.	Solomons Pidgin:	*birek* "break" (intr.)	*birek-em* "break it"

This feature already existed in New South Wales Pidgin, but CEO substrate influence reinforced its use and productivity in MP.

The features described here represent only a small sample of the many parallels in grammar between MP and CEO languages. The pervasiveness of the latters' influence led Keesing (1988: 96) to observe that the grammar of MP "incorporates in a simplified way the core grammatical system more or less common to . . . mainly (Eastern) Oceanic languages."

8.6.4.2 Internal innovation in the elaboration of MP

The case of MP illustrates the kinds of interplay between internally driven development and substrate influence that are typical of the elaboration of pidgin grammar. The transitivizing suffix *-Vm* apparently had its source in the English pronoun *(h)im* (and perhaps *(th)em*) which was often attached to verbs in the FTE that Europeans used with Pacific Islanders in the early nineteenth century. CEO speakers reanalyzed the form as a transitivizing suffix equivalent to those in their L1s. The functions of *-Vm* then expanded to match those of its equivalents in the substrates.

A similar collaboration between internal forces and L1 influence is seen in the development of MP's pronominal system. The inventory of English-derived pronouns in early Pacific pidgin consisted only of a few forms: *mi* "I," *yu*, and *i* (< *he*). Later, *ol(geta)* "they" (< *altogether*) emerged, first attested in Queensland between 1842 and 1858 (Baker and Mühlhäusler 1996: 558). This limited system was first expanded through internal processes of compounding, yielding new forms such as *yumi* (< *you and me*) as well as various compounds with *-fela* (<*fellow*), which was becoming increasingly productive as a derivational morpheme. Thus we find new pronouns like *mi-fela*, and *yu-fela* coined by analogy with established compounds like *dis-fela* (< *this fellow*), *dat-fela* (< *that* *fellow*), etc. These innovations are first attested in Queensland during the period of the labor trade, and were very probably created by CEO speakers. Eventually, this process of expansion and restructuring, employing the pidgin's own lexical resources, resulted in an MP pronominal system that was very similar to that of CEO languages. The modern MP system distinguishes singular, dual, trial, and plural numbers, and has an inclusive/exclusive opposition in the first person non-singular paradigm, just like CEO languages.

Siegel (1999: 16–17) provides the following comparison of the pronominal systems of Tangoa (Vanuatu) and Bislama. Note that in Tangoa, *rua* and *tolu* are free forms meaning "two" and "three" respectively:

(24) *The pronominal system of Tangoa (Camden 1979)*:

	Singular	*Dual*	*Trial*	*Plural*
1st person inclusive	–	eñrarua	eñratolu	eñra
1st person exclusive	enau	kamamrua	kamamtolu	kamam
2nd person	egko	kamimrua	kamimtolu	kamim
3rd person	enia	enrarua	enratolu	enra/enira

(25) *The pronominal system of Bislama (Siegel 1999: 17)*:

	Singular	*Dual*	*Trial*	*Plural*
1st person inclusive	–	yumitu(fala)	yumitrifala	yumi
1st person exclusive	mi	mitufala	mitrifala	mifala
2nd person	yu	yutufala	yutrifala	yufala
3rd person	(h)em	tufala	trifala	olgeta

Several other features of MP syntax can be attributed more or less directly to internal grammaticalization processes, sometimes triggered or reinforced by substrate influence. These include strategies of embedding such as the use of *sapos* (< *suppose*) "if" to introduce conditional clauses, a *se* (< *say*) complementizer to introduce complements of verbs of assertion, etc., an all-purpose locative preposition *long*, also used to introduce clauses of purpose, and so on. Also of interest is the grammaticalization of tense/aspect markers such as future *bai* (< *by and by*), past *been*, completive *finis/pinis* (< *finish*), etc. More will be said about the interplay between internal processes and substrate influence in the elaboration of pidgin TMA systems in the following chapter.

The brief overview provided in this chapter so far suggests that the origins and development of pidgin grammar involve the same basic processes of simplification, L1 retention, and internal innovation found in IL development in SLA. The difference is that the role and contribution of these three processes become increasingly attenuated in the course of SLA, as learners achieve more mastery of TL lexicon and grammar. In pidgin elaboration, by contrast, the full lexical and grammatical resources of the lexifier language are not available to learners. Hence they draw increasingly on their own L1 knowledge and on creative internal restructuring to expand the resources of the pidgin.

As Baker and Mühlhäusler (1996: 578) note, this pattern of elaboration is true of many other contact situations in which contact varieties have been acquired as additional languages to serve as media of interethnic communication. This includes situations in which so-called "creoles" arose. In the following chapter, we will see that "extended pidgins" and (prototypical) creoles have much in common with regard to the circumstances and processes of their creation.

8.7 Simplified Languages

Our overview of pidgin formation would not be complete without a brief look at a class of contact languages which have traditionally been classified as pidgins, but which seem to be different from either prototypical or extended pidgins. These include Sango, Kituba, and others in Africa, Yimas Pidgin and Hiri Motu in Papua New Guinea, and so on. On the one hand, these languages differ from prototypical pidgins in having more elaborate lexical and grammatical apparatus than the latter. On the other hand, they differ from extended pidgins in drawing far more of their grammatical resources from the lexifier language than the latter do.

The reasons for such languages being labeled "pidgins" have to do with the fact that they are typically used as lingua francas for inter-group communication, and are structurally simpler than their source language. For example, according to Dutton (1997), Hiri ("Trade") Motu (formerly Police Motu) originated as a simplified form of Motu which native speakers of that language employed with other groups who came to visit or trade with them. It became the lingua franca of the Port Moresby area after about 1880, when groups of various ethnolinguistic backgrounds settled the area. It was also adopted for use by the first police force, established in 1890 (hence the name "Police Motu"). Later, it became the principal, though unofficial, language of administration in surrounding areas.

The fact that this language came to be employed in a broad range of functions explains why it displays a richer and more complex structure than prototypical pidgins. However, Hiri Motu is still quite simplified by comparison with Motu proper. It lacks most of the inflectional and derivational morphology of Motu, its distinction between alienable and inalienable possession, its irregular verbs, etc. In phonology, many of Motu's phonemic oppositions have been lost, for example, /g/ and /ɣ/ merge to /g/, /r/ and /l/ to /l/, etc. The vocabulary of Hiri Motu comes mostly from Motu, but some of it comes from other Papuan languages, or from pidgin English. There are also a number of non-Motu features in Hiri Motu, apparently due to substrate influence from the languages of its learners, but their sources are difficult to trace (Dutton 1997: 32).

Languages like Hiri Motu are difficult to categorize because their structural characteristics, histories, and use overlap with those of different types of contact vernaculars. The difficulty is compounded by the fact that we know so little about their developmental histories. Did they originate as prototypical pidgins that later became elaborated, like MP? Were they the result of "imperfect" second language acquisition, which would account for the fact that their grammar and lexicon come from one primary source? Or were they the result of deliberate simplification of their L1s by speakers of the source language who wanted either to facilitate outsiders' efforts to communicate with them, or to prevent them from fully learning their language? If so, how much input came from the foreigner talk version of the language, and what contribution did learners' L1s make to the grammar? All of the above explanations have been offered for one or the other of these contact languages. It may well be the case that different explanations apply to different outcomes, or that a combination of causes explains a particular outcome.

At any rate, some distinction must be made between these cases and those we have classified (on the basis of clearer sociohistorical and linguistic evidence) as either prototypical or extended pidgins. Henceforth, we will refer to languages like Hiri Motu, Yimas Pidgin, etc. as "simplified languages," that is, simplified forms of their respective source languages. Some simplified languages have names of their own. Thus Kituba (spoken in West-central Africa) is a simplified form of "ethnic Kikongo" – a label representing a cluster of Kikongo varieties such as Kiyómbe, Kimanyánga, etc. (Mufwene 1997: 203, fn. 3). Similarly, Sango (spoken in the Central African Republic) appears to be based primarily on Yakoma, an Ngbandi variety already established as a lingua franca of the area. There were also inputs from other Bantu languages including Kituba and Lingala (themselves "simplified languages") as well as some West African languages, not to mention French.

All of these contact varieties differ from extended pidgins primarily in having far less substratal input to their grammars than the latter do. This seems to be due in part to the continuing access that learners had to (close approximations of) the TL. Higher TL input reduces the need for reliance on L1 knowledge and other kinds of creative restructuring. (See discussion in chapters 7 and 9.) This makes simplified languages somewhat more akin to cases of group SLA such as "indigenized" varieties than to extended pidgins such as Melanesian Pidgin. Indeed, Pasch (1997: 260) argues that "Sango is the result of a series of significant changes, losses and innovations which occurred due to imperfect acquisition of Yakoma by second-language speakers." Later in the same paper, however, she claims that "Sango is a creole language which has emerged out of a pidgin." These two descriptions may not be as inconsistent as they appear to be at first glance. There are certainly no clear lines separating languages like Sango from creoles, or either of them from "imperfectly learned" second languages. As we shall see in chapter 9, some so-called creoles like Bajan and urban Guyanese are much closer approximations to their superstrate sources than more "radical" ones such as the Surinnamese creoles. The difference here also has much to do with degree of continuing access to varieties of the TL models as used by native speakers or more proficient learners. Simplified languages seem to occupy a position somewhere between intermediate creoles and second language varieties that closely approximate the TL. All of these contact vernaculars share many similar processes of development (see also the discussion in chapter 7, section 7.14). However, that does not necessarily mean that attempts to classify them differently on both sociohistorical and structural criteria are futile.

Exercise 2

Morrill (1997: 352) argues that a pidgin "is a new linguistic creation that may not be placed onto any existing family tree." He therefore denies pidgin status to Sango on the grounds that it is simply a "distinct variety of Ngbandi" to which it is genetically related in the normal sense of the term. Read Pasch's (1997) and Samarin's (2000) descriptions of Sango and use the facts presented there to argue for or against Morrill's position.

8.8 Issues of Classification Revisited

The lack of consensus on the classification of the various types of contact vernaculars surveyed in this chapter is reflected in the fact that different scholars (and sometimes the same scholar) apply different labels to the same or similar languages. Thus Samarin (2000) insists that Sango is a pidgin, based on a variety of (mostly structural) criteria. Among these are:

- the drastic simplificatory changes which distinguish it from its primary source (Ngbandi),

- the rapidity of these changes (ibid.: 308), and
- its highly reduced vocabulary of roughly 1000 words (ibid.: 321).

For Samarin, Sango is a pidgin because it is a "new" language, and "remarkably reduced by comparions with its source language" (2000: 320). At the same time, he concedes that it does not meet "all the definitions of pidgins," and "it certainly fails to have what are claimed to be typical features of pidgins in general" (ibid.). Presumably by this he means absence of features such as bound morphology, a TMA system, embedding strategies, etc., all of which Sango possesses.

This contrasts with Pasch's view, mentioned above, that Sango, though once a pidgin, is now a "creole." Her primary reasons for this include its elaboration and extension of use as a primary vernacular. She equates this process of "vernacularization" with "creolization." Mufwene (1997) uses the same argument to claim that Kituba is a creole. Finally, Morrill (1997) argues that Sango is just a variety of Ngbandi that arose through somewhat imperfect SLA. How do we reconcile such different positions? The only solution, it seems, is to recognize that there are no absolute structural or non-structural criteria by which so-called "extended pidgins," "creoles," "simplified languages," and "imperfectly learned" second language varieties can be distinguished. They all share certain processes of change and restructuring. They differ primarily in the extent to which one or the other process applies in their creation and development.

For these reasons, students of contact linguistics must be wary of terms like "pidginization," "creolization," and the like, which imply some unitary process of change and development leading to the emergence of pidgins, creoles, etc. We have tried to establish that pidginization is a cover-term for a complex of interrelated processes. Hence there is no single dimension along which pidgins, extended pidgins, and simplified languages can be compared for the purpose of placing them on a continuum reflecting degrees of "pidginization." It may be possible to compare these outcomes in terms of particular processes – degrees of reduction and simplification (to the extent that we can define these), or degrees of substratal influence, internally motivated change, etc. Intuitively, it seems possible to establish a cline of outcomes involving, for example, degrees of simplification. Prototypical pidgins might occupy the end of the scale furthest from their lexifier language, with more successfully learnt second language varieties at the other extreme, and simplified languages like Sango somewhere in the middle. But this would depend on consensus about the processes involved and the structural criteria for defining each type.

Even so, such a scale could not easily accommodate extended pidgins and similar outcomes (e.g., creoles and some indigenized varieties) characterized by heavy substratal influence. In the following chapter, we will consider the process of creole formation in the light of what we have discovered in this chapter. We will also question the concept of a uniform process of "creolization" in much the same way as we did for "pidginization." We will postpone until then discussion of the principles and constraints relevant to the formation of extended pidgins, since these are similar to those involved in the formation of (prototypical) creoles.

8.9 Summary

This chapter has tried to address issues concerning the classification, origins, and development of various kinds of contact languages to which the term "pidgin" has been applied. Our approach has been essentially a conservative one, which identifies a class of "prototypical" pidgins distinguished from other contact languages by a well-defined set of structural and sociolinguistic attributes. The former include a highly reduced vocabulary and grammar, while the latter include severe restrictions in range of functions and use as a marginal second language between groups of different language background.

This characterization still allows for some degree of diversity among "prototypical" pidgins. There may be differences in degree of input from one or another source language to the pidgin's lexicon or grammar. Some pidgins may draw on one primary source language for both components, while others may draw their lexicon from one primary source and model their grammar on another. Many prototypical pidgins have arisen in multilanguage contact situations through a process of "tertiary hybridization," that is, through use as a medium of interethnic communication among groups speaking different "substrate" languages. But others (Russenorsk, Chinese Pidgin English, etc.) have arisen in two-language contact situations, and display the characteristics associated with any prototypical pidgin. In short, there is no single formula for pidgin formation, and no fixed or invariant blueprint for pidgin structure. Rather than attempting to fit pidgins into a single mold, our concern should be to explain how particular configurations of social and linguistic factors promote differences in lexical and grammatical input, and in the eventual outcomes of pidgin formation.

We also cautioned against unqualified use of the term "pidginization" to describe the changes that create pidgins out of their inputs. For one thing, the term implies that there is always a single source language that is "pidginized." But we saw that not all cases of pidgin formation involve a single source. Even more problematic is the fact that the term implies a unidimensional and unidirectional process of change. But we noted that so-called pidginization is really a complex combination of different processes of change, including reduction and simplification of input materials, internal innovation, and regularization of structure, with L1 influence also playing a role. Also problematic is the notion of "degrees of pidginization," which suggests that languages can be "pidginized" to varying extents. We saw, in fact, that the processes involved in pidgin formation are also found in other cases of language change and restructuring. But not all such situations lead to the emergence of a pidgin. Of special interest are "simplified" languages such as Yimas Pidgin and Hiri Motu. Are these cases of "pidginization," or do they just happen to share certain processes of change with prototypical pidgins? If we are to speak of "degrees of pidginization" we must clarify which of these processes is being referred to. We then face the problem of how to measure degrees of simplification, reduction, etc.

We highlighted in particular the structural and developmental similarities between prototypical pidgins and early IL systems. While acknowledging the differences between the two types of language creation, we cannot but recognize the similarities in the component processes that characterize them. Both involve input from an external source language, interacting with input and influence from learners' L1s, processes of simplification, and internally motivated innovations. The strategies and processes of grammar construction in both cases are regulated by the same principles and constraints. These guide learners in their attempts to maximize ease of processing and production, to achieve economy, and to establish common ground.

Finally, we distinguished prototypical pidgins from two other (somewhat less clearly defined) types of contact language – "extended pidgins" and "simplified languages." Seen as final products, the latter two are in some sense mirror-images of each other. Extended pidgins begin as prototypical pidgins and are elaborated in both lexicon and grammar when called upon to fulfill the functions of a primary vernacular. This process of elaboration draws heavily on input from the L1s of the groups that adopt the erstwhile pidgin as a language of wider everyday communication. Hence the grammars of extended pidgins are much closer to those of their substrates than to that of their lexifier language. By contrast, simplified languages have the appearance of outcomes to which certain processes of "pidginization" have applied in much smaller measure than in the case of prototypical pidgins. Hence they represent closer approximations to their lexifier language in both vocabulary and grammar.

It remains unclear, however, whether simplified languages and extended pidgins can be so clearly differentiated in their earlier stages of development. Do simplified languages also begin as prototypical pidgins that learners create, and which they subsequently elaborate by drawing more lexical and structural input from the TL? Or are they created in the round by speakers of the TL who simplify it for the benefit of the learners? Intuitively, it would seem that both explanations apply. Only detailed examination of the sociohistorical contexts and earlier stages of development, as represented in actual samples of the relevant languages, can answer these questions with certainty.

What we do know of the history of extended pidgins and simplified languages reveals that changes in the social ecology of a language can result in quite significant change in the language itself. As Baker and Mühlhäusler (1990: 112) note, longitudinal studies of such contact vernaculars as Chinese Pidgin English, Melanesian Pidgin, and others reveal that they go through phases of stability interspersed with periods of fluctuation and sometimes drastic breaks. Thus CPE expanded significantly from aboout 1830 on, when its use first spread beyond trading to interactions between Europeans and Chinese in more fixed domestic master–servant contexts. Changes in the social circumstances of their use also led to drastic elaborative change in all varieties of Melanesian Pidgin, when they became the primary media of interethnic communication in their home territories. Today, languages like Bislama and Tok Pisin are recognized as official languages in Vanuatu and Papua New Guinea respectively. They continue to expand their resources in response to the growing demands placed on them. They demonstrate, in all stages of their history, the ways in which social factors can shape the very character of a language.

Note

1 Panos Pappas (p.c., Feb. 2002) informs me that the verb *meno* in Greek is used to mean "live," but its literal sense is "stay." Hence the use of *stannom* in example (12b) may also be due to L1 transfer.

9

Creole Formation

> The human mind is the same in every clime; and accordingly we find nearly the same process adopted in the formation of language in every country. The Negroes have been proved to be in no degree inferior to other nations in solidity of judgement, or fertility of imagination.
>
> W. Greenfield 1830: 51, cited in Holm 1988: 22

9.1 Introduction

No other contact languages have generated as much debate, disagreement, and controversy as those traditionally referred to as "creoles." They emerged in colonial settings in the New World, the Indian Ocean, and West Africa, where European powers subjected African, Asian, and other populations to their rule in the course of the fifteenth through nineteenth centuries. They were created by slaves and other subordinated groups who fashioned materials from the colonial languages and their own mother tongues into new media of communication. Eventually these languages came to function as community vernaculars acquired by children as first languages.

Their birth among the oppressed and enslaved, and their continued association with such disadvantaged groups, explain the low esteem in which most laypeople hold them. From the earliest periods of their emergence, they provoked the scorn and derision of Europeans who encountered them on their travels to the colonies. For example, Mrs Carmichael had this to say about the creole language spoken in St Vincent in the nineteenth century (Carmichael 1833: vol. 1, 5): "I could comprehend little or nothing of what they said; for though it was English, it was so uncouth a jargon that to one unaccustomed to hear it, it was almost unintelligent as if they had spoken in any of their native tongues." Even today, most laypeople continue to condemn these languages as vulgar and uncouth corruptions of standard languages. Their use has been subject to disapproval and even punishment from parents and other authority figures, especially in the schools. Even some scholars of language once held the view that creoles were unworthy of serious scientific study, and until recently, these languages remained "the unwanted stepchildren of linguistic science" (Lounsbury 1968: 205).

But linguists have come to view creoles as exciting creations that challenge the conventional wisdom about language change and mixture, and offer fascinating insights into the workings of the human language faculty. Scientific study of these languages dates back to the nineteenth century, in particular the work of Van Name (1871), Coelho (1880–6), Schuchardt (1882, 1883, etc.), Hesseling (1897), and others. These early studies explored many of the issues still being hotly debated today, such as the role of substrate influence versus universals in creole formation, the relationship between creoles and first or second language acquisition, and the implications of these languages for theories of language change.

But before we examine these issues in more detail, we must first clarify what we mean by "creoles," and whether there are clear criteria for identifying them as a distinct class of languages.

9.2 Defining Creoles

The speakers of the languages that linguists call creoles do not all use this term to refer to their form of speech. Many of these languages have names of their own, for instance Patwa (English-lexicon) in Jamaica, Papiamentu (Iberian-lexicon) in the Dutch Antilles, Sranan Tongo ("Suriname Tongue," English-lexicon) in Suriname, Papia Kristang (Portuguese-lexicon) in Malacca, and Tayo (French-lexicon) in New Caledonia. Sometimes the popular names match those used by linguists, for instance "Kweyòl" (French) in St Lucia, "Kreyòl" (French) in Haiti, "Creolese" (English) in Guyana, "Krio" (English) in Sierra Leone, and "Creole" (English) in Belize.

How then did the term "creole" become a cover-label for such different outcomes of contact? The story behind this is quite similar to what happened in the case of "pidgins." The term "creole" was used long before linguists adopted it as a technical label. In fact, it was first applied not to languages but to people who were born in the colonies, first Europeans, then persons of mixed descent, and eventually all locally born people. The earliest known attestation of the term is the Spanish word *criollo*, which appeared in a book published in 1590, and translated into English in 1604 (Corominas 1967: 171, cited in Holm 1988: 15). The English citation reads: "Some Crollos [sic], for so they call the Spaniards borne at the Indies." The term was adopted into French as *créole*, and then into English.

Not surprisingly, the term "creole" and its cognates came to refer to the languages spoken by persons born in the colonies – "the creole(s') language(s)." Used in this sense, it referred to a fairly diverse set of contact vernaculars. Some of these were quite similar in structure to the dialects introduced by European settlers. Others were more divergent from these source languages, drawing significantly more of their resources from substrate languages. It is partly for this reason that there is no current consensus on how best to define creoles. As DeCamp (1977: 3) noted, labels like "creole" and "pidgin" are not comparable to those that classify other groups of languages on the basis of genetic relationship (e.g., "Romance" languages), geographical location (e.g., the Balkan languages), or shared typology (e.g., tone or serializing languages). Of course, all of these classifications are problematic in one way or another. But the problem is especially vexing in the case of creoles.

As with pidgins, the identification of these contact vernaculars is based on a variety of often conflicting criteria, including their putative origins, their communicative functions, and their structural characteristics. According to the first two criteria, creoles have traditionally been defined as pidgins that were adopted as native languages ("nativized") by newly emergent creole societies. To serve this function, the erstwhile pidgin had to be elaborated in lexicon and grammar. This process of structural expansion, it is argued, involved the "restructuring" or reconstitution of a viable grammar more complex and efficient than that of the pidgin ancestor. The nature of this restructuring will be discussed further below.

There is continuing disagreement concerning the true impetus for this process of elaboration. The "nativization" scenario implies that pidgins are elaborated into creoles by children who adopt the former as a first language. However, there are various situations in West Africa (Nigerian and Ghanaian Pidgin English), Central Africa (Sango), and Papua New Guinea (Tok Pisin) where erstwhile "pidgins" have been nativized without significant structural change. The "nativization" account also implies that the process of creole formation is rather quick or "abrupt." Yet recent research on the early stages of creole formation in Suriname and elsewhere suggests that creole grammar emerged over several decades, and that adults as well as children played crucial roles in its development.

These considerations would imply that there is little distinction between creoles and "expanded pidgins" in terms of the nature and speed of their development (see chapter 8). Both involve similar processes of restructuring over time, and there are no structural criteria that can distinguish one from the other. This is particularly true in cases where the same contact vernacular is used as both a first and a second language by different groups within the same community. (See cases like Tok Pisin and Sango, for example.) Hence some have attempted to distinguish creoles from pidgins on purely functional grounds. For instance, Gilman (1979: 274) argues that creoles, unlike pidgins, are languages of reference for an ethnic group. While this may be true, it would once more assign different statuses to varieties that are structurally and developmentally quite similar, for example Krio and varieties of West African Pidgin English. Similar objections can be made to those definitions that equate "creolization" with "vernacularization" of a pidgin (Mufwene 1997; Pasch 1997).

Much of the confusion over how best to define creoles is due to indeterminacy in the definition of the "pidgins" from which they are claimed to have arisen. Some have tried to clear up this confusion by specifying that creoles are elaborations of "prototypical" pidgins that have become nativized. But such a definition can apply only to a certain subset of creoles – the so-called "radical" creoles like those of Suriname which display extreme divergence from their lexifier languages. And to complicate things further, we have no clear evidence that many creoles (including some "radical" ones) emerged directly from earlier pidgins. The reality is that creoles constitute a motley assortment of contact vernaculars with different histories and lines of development, though of course they still have much in common.

This diversity in the origins and evolution of creoles explains why they have resisted classification on structural or typological grounds as well. In the first place, there are no structural characteristics that all creoles share. And second, there are no structural criteria that can distinguish creoles from other types of language. Attempts to identify a list of such structural diagnostics of creole status have generally failed. This is true even of efforts that focus only on "radical" creoles.

For instance, Bickerton (1981) identified a set of 12 features which he claimed were diagnostic of "prototypical" creoles. These included the use of "adjectives" as verbs; a tripartite opposition in the TMA system between Anterior tense, Nonpunctual aspect, and Irrealis mood; a distinct locative copula; and so on. Most of these are discussed in section 9.6 below. Bickerton cited Hawai'i Creole English, Sranan Tongo, Jamaican Creole, (rural) Guyanese creole, and Haitian Kreyòl as paradigm examples of the creole prototype. But it turns out that none of these creoles has all the definitive characteristics, and all of them exhibit particular structural features not found in the others. Moreover, even a casual overview of other creoles reveals significant differences among them.

A more recent attempt to "vindicate" creoles as a typological class (McWhorter 1998) claimed that there were three structural features that "prototypical" creoles share. But, as Mufwene (2000: 67) points out, the criteria in question reduce the set of prototypical creoles to a mere handful. More importantly, each of these "prototypical" creoles lacks one or another of the putative typological features.

This is not to deny that there are also striking similarities across creoles, particularly in the areas mentioned by Bickerton and McWhorter. Some of them can be explained as the result of similar kinds of superstrate and/or substrate influence, or similar processes of simplification and grammaticalization (see section 9.8 below). Others can be explained as the result of diffusion, as creole speakers migrated from one area to another. The similarities among Western Caribbean creoles like those in Jamaica, Belize, and Providence Island are clearly due to such migration. The same is true of the similarities between Bajan, Trinidadian, and urban Guyanese, the latter two being largely modeled on the first (Winford 1997a). The diffusion of English-lexicon and French-lexicon creoles throughout the Atlantic area has also been discussed in Huber and Parkvall (1999) and Corne (1999) respectively.

Despite the problems of definition we have pointed to so far, there is still justification for treating creoles as a separate and identifiable class of languages. The grounds for doing so are primarily sociohistorical in nature, as Thomason (1997c), Mufwene (2000), and others have argued. From this perspective, creoles are simply contact languages that emerged primarily in plantation settings in various European colonies throughout the world. Such settings shared a number of sociopolitical and demographic characteristics, including the use of large numbers of slaves who were transplanted from their homelands and placed under the control of a small minority of Europeans. The details of the settlement history and social organization of these plantation societies will be discussed below. Suffice it to say for now that differences in the social settings of each colony led to diversification in the outcomes of the contact between Europeans and the oppressed groups.

In some cases, for instance in most of the Spanish colonies as well as in Brazil and the southern United States, social conditions promoted the acquisition of the language of the dominant group. These colonial dialects of Spanish, Portuguese, English, and other languages are not usually referred to as creoles. However, some scholars (e.g., Mufwene 1997) have advocated their inclusion in that category, on the basis that they shared a similar sociohistorical development. In other colonies, the combination of social factors and linguistic inputs favored the emergence of contact vernaculars that were highly divergent from their respective European lexifier languages. The most divergent of these constitute the class of "radical" creoles. Other creoles occupy various mid points in the continuum between colonial dialect and radical creole.

To explain the diversity in the outcomes of creole formation, we must explore the sociohistorical background to their emergence, and the social contexts in which they arose.

9.3 The Sociohistorical Background to Creole Formation

9.3.1 Portuguese colonization

European colonial expansion from the fifteenth through nineteenth centuries brought (speakers of) European languages into contact with a multitude of indigenous languages in the colonized territories. Portugal was the first European power to engage in the quest for a colonial empire, providing in many ways a model to be imitated by other European powers in succeeding centuries.

Portuguese exploration of the North African coast began in the early 1400s, at first motivated primarily by pursuit of military action against the Muslims they had succeeded in driving from the Iberian Peninsula. In the course of the fifteenth century, the Portuguese traveled south along the West African coast, from Morocco (1415) to Cape Verde (1444) and eventually down to Angola and the Cape of Good Hope (1488). They soon realized that there were lucrative opportunities for trade with the various nations they encountered, in commodities like ivory, gold, spices, and later slaves. They established settlements on islands like Madeira and the Azores in the early fifteenth century and later in the Cape Verde islands and the Gulf of Guinea islands, Sao Tomé, Principe, and Annobón (1470s). At first, they engaged in small farming and most of the labor was done by Portuguese peasants. Soon, however, they began importing slaves in ever increasing numbers to cultivate crops and raise livestock in the Cape Verde islands, and to meet the demand for labor on the sugar plantations they established in the Gulf of Guinea islands.

This kind of plantation economy was eventually carried over the Atlantic to Brazil, "discovered" by Cabral in 1500. It became the model for the plantation colonies established by other European powers in the New World and elsewhere.

The trading contacts between the Portuguese and West Africans led to the emergence of a Portuguese-lexicon pidgin that was used extensively along the West African coast from the fifteenth through eighteenth centuries. This pidgin may have provided a partial model for pidginized forms of versions of other European languages that emerged later on the West African coast. The sociolinguistic situation in the islands where plantations had been established created the right conditions for the earliest known creoles to arise. Such languages – Cape Verdian, Principense, and Annobonese – survive today as the primary vernaculars of these communities. By contrast, the contact situations on the West African mainland did not produce Portuguese-lexicon creoles. The one exception is the creole spoken in Guinea-Bissau, which may have been transported there from the Cape Verde islands (Holm 1989: 254).

Portuguese colonial expansion continued beyond Africa to South and South East Asia after Vasco da Gama rounded the Cape of Good Hope in 1488, and reached India in 1498. The Portuguese established a vast trading empire from India to Japan, but eventually withdrew from most of Asia. By this time, creole varieties of Portuguese had arisen in several of these Southern Asian settlements. Among those still spoken today, though endangered, are Papia Kristang of Malacca (Baxter 1985), Korlai Portugese of Korlai in the state of Maharashtra, India (Clements 1996), and Daman Creole of Northwest India (Holm 1989: 286).

Some scholars have claimed that a Portuguese pidgin was the ancestor of Ternateño, a Spanish-lexicon creole that emerged on the Phillipine island of Ternate in the sixteenth century. This creole was later transported to three other locations in the Phillipines: Zamboanga in the southern island of Mindanao, and the towns of Cavite and Ternate on the northern island of Luzon. Scholars remain divided on whether these creoles emerged directly from contact with Spanish, or from an earlier Portuguese pidgin whose lexicon was replaced by Spanish items.

From the seventeenth century on, other European powers, Dutch, French, and English, followed in the wake of the Portuguese, establishing trading contacts with West Africa, particularly in slaves. These supplied labor for the large-scale plantation economies that all these powers (as well as Spain) introduced to their colonies in the Caribbean, North and South America, the Indian Ocean, and parts of the Pacific. Like the Portuguese plantation islands off the West African coast, these New World settings were favorable to the emergence of creoles. To explore the details of these settings, let us turn our attention to the Caribbean colonies.

9.3.2 The social contexts of creole formation

The plantation economies established in the Caribbean and elsewhere in the New World and Indian Ocean were based on the forced labor of large numbers of slaves transplanted from Africa and controlled by a small number of Europeans. In general, colonization in these areas involved the repeopling of lands made empty by the extermination of indigenous Caribbean peoples. Hence the newcomers, both European and African, came together in a social, cultural, and linguistic vacuum, into which each group introduced some part of its cultural traditions (Mintz 1971: 484).

Mintz (1971: 481) identifies three general social conditions that influenced the emergence and character of creole languages in the New World:

- The demographics of each colony, that is, the relative numbers of Europeans, Africans, and other groups present in each colony over time.

- The nature of the contact among these groups, and in particular, "the codes of social interaction governing the relative statuses and the relationships of these differing groups in particular societies."
- The types of community settings within which the groups mixed and interacted.

There has been a tendency among some scholars to focus primarily on demographics (population ratios) in attempts to explain creole origins. For instance, Bickerton (1981: 4) suggested that creoles typically arose in settings where the dominant group made up no more than 20 percent of the population. Expanding on this, Baker (1982, 1993b) proposed that a major factor was the timing of three crucial developments in the population make-up, which he termed events 1, 2, and 3. Event 1 was the time when the number of slaves exceeded that of the slave-owners. Event 2 occurred when the number of locally born slaves exceeded that of non-slaves, both locally and foreign born. Event 3 was when the importation of slaves ceased. In this scenario, the period between events 2 and 3 is most favorable to the emergence of a creole, provided all other circumstances are right (Baker 1993b: 138). Bickerton (1984), drawing on Baker's account, proposed a "pidginization index" which could measure the degree to which a creole diverged from its lexifier language. However, Singler (1990a, 1993, 1995) has demonstrated that this approach makes the wrong predictions about creole development.

It is clear that the analysis of population ratios must be complemented by in-depth investigation of the changing contexts and patterns of interaction among the groups concerned. For instance, there were different ratios between Europeans and slaves in different contact settings within the same colony. In the American South, for example, the high ratios of Africans to English settlers on the Carolina coast contrasted with the higher proportions of Europeans elsewhere in the southern colony. The disproportion in the former setting was a key factor in the formation of Gullah, the only English-lexicon creole of North America. The latter kind of contact led to the emergence of varieties of African American English that were much closer to their English dialectal sources.

Also relevant was the role played by indentured servants brought from Europe to work alongside the slaves. In Barbados, for instance, the high ratios of such workers and settlers from South West England in the first 40 years of settlement led to a contact variety, Bajan, that was closely modeled on those settler dialects. Another crucial demographic factor was the degree of natural increase versus mortality in the plantation colonies. Most of these were characterized by low rates of natural increase and high rates of (especially infant) mortality. This resulted in not only a small number of locally born children but also a continuing importation of new slaves. Suriname represents perhaps the extreme case of this scenario. Contrasting with it were colonies like those in

Barbados and the Southern United States, where natural increase was more common. Singler (1992) has argued that the more locally born children there were (especially in the earlier period of settlement), the more the likelihood that the emerging contact language would approximate its lexifier. The contrasting cases of Barbados and Suriname seem to bear this out.

9.3.3 Community settings and codes of interaction

The nature of the community settings differed in the same colony over time, as well as from colony to colony. As Singler (1993) has noted, the type of economic activity – crop selection in particular – made for significant differences in patterns of contact. In most cases, the earlier periods of settlement were characterized by small farm or homestead economies, devoted to the cultivation of crops like tobacco. In such settings, there were more equal if not higher proportions of Europeans to Africans, and closer interaction between the two groups. The longer such settings survived, the more likely they were to produce creole varieties closer to the settler dialects. This occurred in colonies like (French) Reunion, and, not surprisingly, Barbados. In both cases, there was a fairly long period of close contact between Europeans and non-Europeans in homestead settings. The second language varieties of the superstrate which emerged in that period prevailed, even when slave importation increased dramatically in later years. By then, they had already become community vernaculars.[1]

By contrast, the early introduction of large-scale plantation economies to other colonies made conditions more favorable to the emergence of more radical creoles. The shift to sugar cultivation and increasing slave importation meant less opportunity for the latter to acquire closer approximations to European languages. In addition, the linguistic heterogeneity of the slave groups and their numerical dominance and limited contact with superstrate speakers contributed to the creation of a contact variety that diverged significantly from its lexifier source. This is why Mauritius, colonized by the French in 1721, presents such a sharp contrast to Reunion, settled some 58 years earlier. The contact language that developed in the former colony was and is far more divergent from French, reflecting greater influence from Malagasy and other substrate languages, as well as from internal restructuring.

Various other factors played a role in determining patterns of interaction between Europeans and others. Among these were the codes of social relations regulating such interaction. In general, as Mintz (1971: 487) notes, the colonies differed in three respects. First, different European powers exercised different degrees of control over the affairs of their colonies. In general, Spain kept stricter watch than either France or England.

Second, there were differences in the slave codes in each colony. These regulated whether slaves could participate in institutions like the church, the speed with which they attained freedom, and so on. In the Spanish colonies, for example, the rate of manumission was in general rapid and continuous, compared with that in the French and English colonies. The class of freed slaves had closer contact with Europeans, and thus acquired the latters' language. The codes also determined the sexual and mating practices between the groups. In colonies like Reunion, European male settlers often had non-European spouses. Hence there was a significant number of locally born, free persons of mixed race in the earlier stages of settlement. The emergence of second language varieties of the superstrate in such colonies seemed to be directly related to the linking function of the mixed-race and free groups in such colonies (Hoetink 1967: 178). By contrast, in colonies like Mauritius, the strict separation of groups prevented such cohabitation. This helps in part to explain the more divergent linguistic outcomes in these cases (Baker 2000: 53; Corne 1982).

Third, there were differences in the ideologies of the dominant classes regarding each colony's relationship to the pertinent European power. Hence the emergence of a distinct "creole" identity varied from colony to colony. For instance, Mintz (1971: 487) suggests that Spanish colonists identified more fully with their new homes in the Caribbean than either the French or the English. The different political and social climate in the Spanish colonies may explain the paucity of Spanish-lexicon creoles in the New World (but see McWhorter 1995 for a different explanation). All of the factors discussed here can help us to understand why different creole cultures emerged in different colonies, with varying degrees of acculturation toward or divergence from European cultural and linguistic practice.

Finally, in each colony, there were differences in privilege and status among different categories of slaves. Domestic slaves had more contact with Europeans and presumably learnt second language varieties of the latters' languages. Skilled slaves had more freedom of movement than those who labored in the field. In many cases, such differences led to linguistic continua ranging from second language varieties of the superstrate to highly divergent creoles.

Similarly, the creoles that arose in different colonies form a kind of continuum, with more "radical" creoles such as those in Suriname furthest removed from their lexifiers, and "intermediate" creoles like Bajan much closer. Most of the English-lexicon creoles of the Caribbean – the so-called "basilectal" varieties of Guyanese Creole, Jamaican Creole, etc. – fall somewhere in the middle of this continuum.

To sum up, each mix of ecological factors constituted a recipe for different linguistic consequences of contact (Mufwene 2001). As Hymes (1971b: 83) put it: "What would be constant would be the fundamental terms, or variables, and variables they would be, such that differences in their values would result in different outcomes."

Exercise 1
Using Mintz's (1971) framework for describing the sociohistorical background to creole formation, compare the roles of demographic and other social factors in the emergence of any "intermediate" creole such as Bajan, and any more "radical" creole such as Jamaican or Sranan. How far do Mintz's criteria help to explain the different outcomes? (On Bajan see Winford 1997a, 2000a; on Jamaican Creole, see Lalla and D'Costa 1990; on Sranan, see Arends 1995b.)

9.4 The Emergence of "Intermediate" Creoles: Bajan

9.4.1 The social context

"Intermediate" creoles like Bajan and Reunionnaise must be seen as creations in their own right, independent of the more radical creoles. Their formation is the result of a peculiar mix of social factors and linguistic inputs that favored the emergence of a contact variety closer to its superstrate sources. It was once commonly assumed that these creoles arose from more radical ones via a process of "decreolization," that is, contact-induced change in a more radical creole due to continuing contact with its lexifier (e.g., Rickford 1992). But that view has been challenged by various researchers (Winford 1997a). Let us focus on Bajan.

For roughly 25 years after its colonization in 1627, Barbados relied on a small farm economy in which English and Irish settlers and servants were in close contact with Africans. Moreover, Whites outnumbered Blacks by margins of at least 6 to 1 up to 1642, when the ratio became more even. Based on these facts, among others, we can assume that by 1650, there was a sizeable group of Africans speaking second language varieties of settler dialects, especially those used by the indentured servants with whom Blacks had closest contact. These were the basis of modern Bajan. Several other factors favored the spread and survival of this variety. Even after large-scale plantations were introduced to Barbados from about 1650 on, White indentured servants continued to work alongside African slaves (Beckles 1989: 121). Moreover, the growth of the slave population during the plantation period was due mostly to natural increase, rather than continuous resupply from Africa. Hence, by the mid-1700s the majority of Barbadian slaves were locally born (Rickford and Handler 1994: 237). In addition, there soon emerged a significant number of children of mixed European and African parentage who were free. All of these factors, and others, encouraged the spread and consolidation of the intermediate variety modeled closely on the settler/servant dialects. The parallels with Reunion, mentioned earlier, are clear.

There is also evidence that a more radical creole emerged in Barbados, probably among field slaves, but also spreading to some poor Whites, during the peak plantation period in the eighteenth century, when Blacks vastly outnumbered Whites. This more divergent creole survives in isolated rural villages today (Roy 1986; Rickford 1992). But the intermediate variety remains the primary and majority vernacular of Barbados.

9.4.2 Linguistic inputs and outcomes in Barbados

Bajan grammar reflects heavy influence from southern English dialects, especially those of the South West of England. The vast majority of settlers and indentured servants came from the latter region. However, Bajan grammar is not an exact replica of these sources. It shows evidence of both simplification in morphology and morphosyntax, and substratum influence from West African languages, although the latter influence is much slighter than that found in more radical creoles. By way of brief illustration, table 9.1 (from Winford 2000a: 229) compares the inventory of tense/aspect categories in Bajan with those of earlier

Table 9.1 Correspondences between Bajan and SW English dialects in tense/aspect marking

Time/aspect marking	Bajan	Seventeenth-century SW English dialects
Time reference		
Simple present	ø (statives)	*do/does* + V or V + pres. infl.
Simple past	ø (non-statives)	*did* + V OR V + past infl.
Relative past	*did* + V	–
Future	*go(n)* + V	*shall/will* + V
Prospective	*goin to* + V	*be going to* + V
Aspectual reference		
Present Habitual	*does* + V	*do/does* + V or V + pres. infl. (+ adverbs)
Past Habitual	*useto* + V	*used to* + V
Progressive	V-*in*	*(do) be* + *(a)* V-*ing*
Perfect	*done* + V	*be/have (done)* + V-*ed*?

SW English dialects as described by Barnes (1886), Elworthy (1877, 1886), and Klemola (1996).

As can be seen, most of the Bajan markers are derived directly from the SW English dialects, and several of them preserve meanings similar to those they had in the latter. However, the Bajan system also departs in several respects from its sources. The differences seem to be due to a combination of simplification and substrate influence. For instance, the loss of auxiliary *be* in Progressive structures and of inflection in verbs is typical of simplificatory processes in second language acquisition. On the other hand, the discourse uses of unmarked verbs and the Habitual expressed by *does* seem to reflect substrate influence, though the latter auxiliary shows similarity to present periphrastic "do" in the English dialects as well.

In addition, Bajan lacks the serial verb constructions, common in more radical creoles, that have their source in West African languages (see section 9.6.5.2 below). Its systems of copular predication, complementation, and other aspects of its syntax have stronger parallels in its English sources than its substrates (Winford 2000a).

All of these characteristics are in keeping with the view that Bajan was the result of relatively successful shift toward a fairly accessible target language. This is true of other intermediate Caribbean English creoles like urban Guyanese and Trinidadian creole, which are closely related historically to Bajan. In these respects, the intermediate creoles resemble "indigenized" varieties much more than they resemble "radical" creoles.

9.5 The Emergence of Radical Creoles: Suriname

The creoles that arose in Suriname are often cited, with justification, as prime examples of "radical" creoles. They include Sranan Tongo, various dialects of the Eastern Maroon Creole (Aluku-Boni, Ndjuka or Okanisi, and Paamaka), Saamaka, and its mutually intelligible offshoot Matawai. Sranan is spoken both as a first language and as a lingua franca for inter-group communication throughout the coastal areas, including the capital city, Paramaribo. The Eastern Maroon (EMC) and Saamaka dialects are spoken in the interior in maroon communities founded by escaped slaves in the early to mid-eighteenth century. Sranan and the EMC varieties are usually classified as English-lexicon creoles because most of their vocabulary is drawn from this source. Saamaka and Matawai, on the other hand, draw roughly 30 percent of their vocabulary from Portuguese, and the rest mostly from English. These creoles also preserve a certain number of African words, with higher numbers in the maroon varieties.

All of the contemporary Surinamese creoles have their origins in the early Plantation Creole that emerged on the coastal plantations in the late seventeenth to early eighteenth centuries. Since modern Sranan Tongo is a more direct continuation of this early contact language, we will refer to the latter as "early Sranan."

9.5.1 The sociohistorical background

Suriname was colonized by the English in 1651, but ceded to the Dutch in 1667. Most of the English settlers and their slaves came from Barbados, with others coming from England and the Leeward Islands (especially St Kitts). The first 30 years of settlement were characterized by small-scale farming, with relatively equal or small (2:1) ratios of Blacks to Whites, and close interaction between the two groups. It is therefore likely that most slaves spoke second language varieties of the lexifier, which they had either acquired in previous places or learnt in Suriname.

A radical change in the demographics of the colony came between 1668 and 1680, when most of the English settlers and the slaves they had brought with them left the colony. As a result, the English population declined from about 2000 in 1666 to about 38 in 1680 (Voorhoeve and Lichtveld 1975: 2–3). In the early 1680s the Dutch established a successful plantation system, importing increasing numbers of slaves over the next couple of centuries. In 1668, there had been a total population of roughly 2920, of whom 1850 were Black and 1070 White. In 1684, by contrast, out of a total of about 3984, 3332 were Africans and only 652 were European, mostly Dutch, with smaller numbers of English, Portuguese, and German settlers (Mulert 1917, quoted by Migge 1998: 223). Over the next 40 years, the proportion of Africans to Europeans increased dramatically, from 5:1 in 1684 to 15:1 by 1720 (Migge 1998: 221).

The almost total withdrawal of the English settlers and their slaves by 1680 meant that the English-lexicon contact varieties that had emerged by that time became the primary source of European input to the continuing development of early Sranan. This, added to the constant replenishment of the slave supply due to high mortality and low fertility rates among the Africans, undoubtedly contributed to the "radicalization" of the emerging creole. The continuing importation of slaves meant that new arrivals were continually acquiring the contact varieties that had already been established. This would be in keeping with the view that creole formation in Suriname was largely a process of second language acquisition by several new waves of African-born adults (Arends 1995b: 235). It would also explain the significant role played by West African languages in shaping the grammar of the plantation creole. We will return to this below.

Exercise 2
The following is a dialogue between speakers A and B from modern Sranan Tongo. Try to identify those aspects of phonology, morphology, and syntax that distinguish it from its lexifier, English. For instance, what kinds of phonological changes have occurred in English words? How are time and aspectual reference conveyed? (Dutch loanwords are in italics.)

A: Ma fa a pikin fu Oom N ø du dede dan?
But how the child of uncle N do die then
"But how did Uncle N's child actually die, then?"

B: Ayi, a wan moi *vraag*, noh. Wel, mi ben de a Novar.
Yes, COP one nice question, TAG. Well, I PAST be LOC Novar
Mi ø de a Novar, mi ø de nanga wan man, ben (e) taki tori nanga wan man.
I be LOC Nover, I be with one man, PAST IMP talk story with one man
"Yes, it's a good question, no? Well, I was at Novar. I was at Novar, I was with a guy, I was talking to a guy."
Dan wan man ø *ry* kon nanga wan *bromfiets*, ma a man di ø kon teki mi,
Then one man ride come with one bike, but the man REL come take me
en nanga den suma dati no ø de bun. Dan a man ø tan a strati,
he and the-pl people DEM NEG COP good. Then the man stay LOC street
dan a e bari kari mi "D, D, Oom N, Oom N, Oom N"
then he IMP shout call me "D, D uncle N. uncle N uncle N"
"Then a guy came on a moped, but the guy who came to pick me up, he and those people (I was talking to) were not on speaking terms. So the guy stayed in the street, then he called me 'D, D, Uncle N, Uncle N, Uncle N'")
Dan mi e taki taki a man ø abi mi fanowdu, san a man no e kon.
Then I IMP talk COMP the man have me need why the man NEG IMP come
Mi no e go. Okay, dan a man, a man di mi nanga en e taki,
I NEG IMP go. Okay, then the man, the man REL I and he IMP talk,
a man ø taki, yu kan go want a man no e kon. A no o kon dya.
the man say, you can go because the man NEG IMP come. He NEG FUT come here

"So I was saying that the guy needed me, why wasn't the guy coming to me? I'm not going. Okay, then the guy, the guy I was talking to, the guy said, you can go for he's not going to come. He won't come here"
Di mi ø go a man ø taigi mi taki taki "Oom N, sidon a baka a fiets.
When I go the man tell me say say "Uncle N, sit LOC back the bike
Oto ø naki a boi fu yu." Mi ø taki "san! oto ø naki en."
Car hit the boy of you." I say "what, car hit him."
Mi ø taki efu oto naki en a o dede. *Merkwaardig* . . .
I say if car hit him he FUT die. *Oddly* . . .
"When I went, the guy told me 'Uncle N, sit on the back of the bike. A car has knocked down your son.' I said 'what! a car knocked him down?' I said if a car has knocked him down he'll die. Oddly enough . . ."

9.6 Some Aspects of Creole Grammar

Given the wide differences across creoles, it is difficult to generalize about their structural characteristics. This is true even if we limit our attention to the more radical creoles. However, certain general features can be identified.

9.6.1 Creole phonology

In general, creole phonology appears to be the result of varying degrees of reinterpretation of superstrate phonology in terms of substrate phonetic categories and phonological rules. Relatively little research has been done so far on this aspect of creole structure, far less its sources. Hence we have only a vague picture of the substrate contribution.

It would appear that creoles generally preserve sounds that are similar in the input languages. Among the consonants, these include a variety of stops such as /p, t, k, b, d, g/, and nasals like /m, n/. Where there is a mismatch between superstrate and substrate sounds, the former are generally substituted by their closest equivalents in the latter. This kind of L1 influence is of course characteristic of second language acquisition in general. It helps explain, for instance, the substitution of /b/ for /v/, /t/ for /θ/, d for /ð/, /l/ for /r/, and so on. Some radical creoles such as the Surinamese creoles and Krio (Sierra Leone) preserve West African words containing coarticulated and prenasalized stops (e.g., /gb, kp, mb/, etc.) which are fairly common in their substrates (Holm 1988: 127–30).

However, it is also clear that creoles owe certain aspects of their phonology to their superstrate sources too. For instance, several distinctive features of Caribbean English-lexicon creoles can be traced back to regional English dialects. These include loss of initial /h/ in words like *'ospital*, the palatization of /k, g/ in words like /kyari/ "carry," /gyal/ "girl," etc., insertion of the glide /w/ in words like *bwai* "boy," *gwine* "going," etc. Even features such as the substitution of /b/ for /v/ in words like *bery* "very," /t/ for /θ/, and /d/ for /ð/ were also typical of some regional dialects of English, and of nautical English too (Lalla and D'Costa 1990: 51–60, 100). Using contemporary Standard English phonology as a point of comparison with English-lexicon creole phonology would therefore be quite misleading with regard to the superstrate sources of the latter.

Creole vowels similarly tend to be those common to their source languages, though some vowel systems are more complex than others are. Practically all creoles have at least the five vowels /i, e, a, o, u/, though some have /ɛ/ and /ɔ/ in addition. Holm (1988: 114) suggests that "the seven vowel system found throughout much of West Africa is also the basic system of the Atlantic creoles." Again, however, some aspects of creole vowel systems appear to derive from superstrate sources. With reference to English-lexicon creoles, Lalla and D'Costa (1990: 60–4, 107) mention such features as the use of /a/ for /ɔ/ in words like *drop*, /ie/ for /e/ in words like *game*, /ai/ for /ɔi/ in words like *boil*, etc.

There is evidence of substrate influence on creole phonotactics too. A general feature is the simplification of both initial and final consonant clusters. In some English-lexicon creoles, initial /s/ is lost in clusters like /sp/, /st/, and /sk/, yielding, for instance, *puun* "spoon," *tan* "stand," and *kin* "skin." Interestingly, French-lexicon creoles generally preserve such initial clusters (Parkvall 2000: 32) – something we might not expect, given the strong tendency for such clusters to be simplified in creoles and early L2 varieties. Similarly, /t, d, k/ are lost in final clusters like /st, sk/, and /ld/, yielding *laas* "last," *ool* "old," *des* "desk," etc. This phenomenon is also common in French creoles. The simplification of final consonant clusters also has models in English regional dialects (Lalla and D'Costa 1990: 100, 107).

Also typical of many Atlantic creoles is the use of paragoge (the addition of a vowel, especially to European stems that end in a consonant). This yields words in Sranan like *luku* "look," *kiri* "kill," etc., containing a CVCV syllable pattern typical of many West African languages. Lalla and D'Costa (1990: 65) suggest that "syllabic structure in early JC [Jamaican Creole] was West African," citing now obsolete words like *wharra* "why," *killee*, *preachy*, etc. found in earlier JC texts. Here again, they suggest that this pattern might have been reinforced by a similar syllabic structure found in southwest dialectal English words such as *hearee* "to hear," *caree* "to care," etc.

Finally, certain suprasegmental features found in some Atlantic creoles seem to have their source in substrate influence. It has been claimed that some Caribbean English-lexicon creoles preserve vestiges of West African tone systems, though they are not tone languages in the strict sense (Carter 1979: 3, 1987; Devonish 1989). Also of interest is the apparent retention in some Atlantic creoles of tone- or pitch-based distinctions between "intensive" and "distributive" reduplications. Thus in Jamaican we find *smaal smaal* (even pitch) "very small" versus *smaal smaal* (falling pitch) "smallish" (Carter 1987; Gooden 2001).

In general, much more research needs to be done before we have an adequate understanding of creole phonology and its origins.

9.6.2 Creole lexicon

There are three major sources of creole lexicon: input from the superstrate, which supplies the bulk of the vocabulary, retentions from substrate languages, and internal innovations.

Many superstrate items have their phonological shapes and meanings fairly well preserved in creoles. Most of these come from the regional dialects introduced by settlers and servants in the early period of colonization. But a significant number of items also came from so-called "nautical" language, as used by sailors and other seafarers. In Jamaican creole, for instance, we find such survivals as *jerk* "barbecued" (originally "to salt and smoke dry meat"), *cow* "any horned cattle," *kotlash* "machete," and *tsokop* "chock full" (Lalla and D'Costa 1990: 101). Other items from English dialects include *buss* "kiss," *maaga* "thin" (< *meagre*), and *eerie* "smart, excellent," the possible source of the popular Rastafarian term *irie* [airi] "excellent, very fine" (ibid.: 226). Many JC compounds also derive from English dialectal sources, including *morning-time*, *self-same* "identical," *was-mout* "liquor," and others. Several such items are found in Suriname too, suggesting a similar nautical or dialectal English source. They include *no so* "otherwise," *too much* "very," *before time* "long ago," etc.

Superstrate-derived lexical items often undergo semantic and even categorial change, sometimes under substrate influence. For instance, in JC, *wind* (vb) has come to mean "twist and turn [the hips] provocatively," while *sweet* is a verb meaning "please greatly." In the Surinamese creoles, English prepositions like *round* and *up* are reanalyzed as the verbs *lontu* "go around" and *opo* "lift" respectively. The Atlantic creole cognates of *foot* and *hand* refer to the entire limb, including "arm" and "leg" respectively, not just to the extremity. These kinds of semantic reanalysis are also found in extended pidgins. Thus Tok Pisin *as* (< Engl. *arse*) means not just "buttocks," but also "cause, foundation." Similarly, *bel* means not just "belly," but also "seat of the emotions." These parallel the range of meaning expressed by equivalent words in the substrate.

Creoles also derive a significant number of words from their substrates, and to a lesser extent from other languages, usually via pidgin varieties of the latter. These tend to be lost over time, so earlier creole texts provide a clearer picture of the contribution from these sources. Lalla and D'Costa (1990: 77) identify approximately 250 words in earlier (seventeenth- to nineteenth-century) JC texts, which required etymological commentary. Of these, 180 or three-fourths were from English dialects, 36 were West African, 14 "Hispanic," and 25 of unknown or multiple origin. Modern JC preserves a fair number of the West African items, including *backra* "white person, boss" (< Ibo, Efik *mbakara* "white man"), *kongkongsa* "deceit, deceitful" (< Twi *ŋkongkongsá* "falsehood, deceit"), *nyam* "eat, food" (multiple West African sources), *tata* "father, elder" (multiple West African sources), and so on.

Another interesting aspect of creole lexicon is the formation of compounds modeled on both superstrate and substrate patterns. In JC, compounds derived from Early Modern English dialects provided not just a source, but also a model for lexical expansion. Thus we find innovations like *man-crab* "male crab," *good-belly* "good-natured," *hard-ears* "stubborn," *pick-mouth* "troublesome," etc. Some compounds are clearly calques on West African equivalents, and are widely distributed across Atlantic English lexicon creoles. They include CEC forms like *bad-mouth* "to speak ill of" (cf. Mandingo *da-jugu*, Hausa *mugum-baki* "bad-mouth"), *eye-water* "tears," *suck-teeth* "a disapproving sound" (multiple West African sources), and *cut-eye* "a scornful look" (Rickford and Rickford 2000: 95). A final word formation strategy that has its sources partly in the substrates and partly in internal motivation is reduplication, discussed in the previous section. The richness of creole derivational patterns belies the myth that creoles lack bound morphology, an idea that no doubt arose because creoles generally lack inflectional morphology. (See DeGraff 2001 for a discussion of the richness of Haitian Creole morphology.)

9.6.3 *Creole morphology and morphosyntax*

The general lack of inflectional morphology in creoles is the result of processes of simplification that emergent creoles share with pidgins, or (early) second language varieties. Hence categories such as case, agreement, etc. are lacking in these languages. Simplification also has consequences for various aspects of

Table 9.2 The pronominal system of Jamaican Creole

Number/person	Subject	Object	Possessive
Singular			
1st person	mi	mi	mi/fi mi
2nd person	yu	yu	yu/fi yu
3rd person	im	im	im/fi im
Plural			
1st person	wi	wi	wi/fi wi
2nd person	unu	unu	unu/fi unu
3rd person	dem	dem	dem/fi dem

creole morphosyntax. For instance, case and gender distinctions are reduced or eliminated in the pronominal system, though number distinctions are preserved. Table 9.2 illustrates the pronominal system of JC, which is generally representative of Caribbean English creoles outside of Suriname.

Some creoles have more complex systems than this. For instance, in their singular pronoun paradigm Principense and other Gulf of Guinea creoles make distinctions between emphatic and non-emphatic forms, as well as between stressed and unstressed forms (Holm 1988: 202). This appears to be due to substrate influence, as we saw in the case of Melanesian Pidgin in the previous chapter.

Creole systems of copular predication are also organized quite differently from those of their lexifiers. Most creoles employ overt (and distinct) copulas only in predicate nominal and locative constructions. These are invariant forms, with no distinctions of number and agreement. The following examples from JC illustrate:

(1) Jan a di liida
John COP the leader
"John is the leader"

(2) Mieri de a skuul
Mary COP LOC school
"Mary's at school"

Moreover, creoles generally lack copulas in ascriptive-type predication, that is, those corresponding to predicate adjective constructions in their lexifiers. Example (3) illustrates:

(3) Di mango raip
"The mango is ripe"

The property items (corresponding to adjectives) in these constructions tend to behave more like verbs. They can be preceded by TMA markers, undergo predicate cleft, occur in comparative constructions with serial *paas* or *moro* "exceed" and display other verbal properties. The following sentences from Sranan illustrate:

(4) A pikin e bigi
The child IMP big
"The child is getting big"

(5) A breiti a man breiti
FOC happy the man happy
"The man is HAPPY"

(6) Kofi langa moro yu
Kofi tall surpass you
"Kofi is taller than you"

The degree of verbal behavior varies according to the semantic class of the property item, and from creole to creole (Winford 1997b: 256).

9.6.4 Creole TMA systems

Perhaps the best-known and most debated area of creole morphosyntax is their TMA systems. With very few exceptions, creoles express temporal, modal, and aspectual meanings via pre-verbal markers. There are striking similarities in the sources, functions, and distribution of these functional heads across creoles, regardless of what their lexifiers were.

Practically all of the Atlantic English-lexicon creoles, for instance, employ a Past tense derived from *been*, a Future derived from *go*, and a Terminative Perfect expressed by *done* (or, in the Surinamese creoles, *kaba* < Portuguese *acabar* "finish"). In addition, the unmarked verb has very similar interpretations and functions (dictated by the context) in all these creoles. Table 9.3 gives a brief overview of some basic temporal and aspectual categories in three of these creoles.

This is not meant to imply that the TMA systems of Atlantic English creoles are identical in all respects. There are significant differences, especially in some

Table 9.3 Some tense/aspect categories in three Atlantic English-lexicon creoles

Categories	Jamaican	Guyanese	Sranan
Tense			
Relative Past	(b)en	bin	ben
Future	wi	go	(g)o
Prospective	a go	a go	e go
Aspectual			
Perfective	unmarked	unmarked	unmarked
Progressive	a/de	–	–
Imperfective	–	a	(d)e
Perfect	don	don	VP final kaba

areas of aspectual marking, as well as in modality and auxiliary combinations (see Winford 1993, 2001).

French-lexicon creoles have a similar set of pre-verbal markers, including a Past derived from *etait* "was" or *eté* "been" and a Future derived from forms of *aller* "go". In Haiti, for example, Future *(a)va* derives from *va(s)*, the present singular forms of *aller*. Eastern Caribbean French creoles, on the other hand, have a future marker *ke* (with variants *kay, kale* in Guyanais) derived from Progressive *ka* + *aller*. There are also differences among French creoles in the Progressive marker, which in some cases is *ap*, derived from *après* (e.g., Haitian Creole) and in the eastern Caribbean *ka*, a form of uncertain etymology (see Goodman 1964: 82ff for discussion of possible sources).[2] Some French creoles also have a quasi-perfect marker derived from *finir* "finish." The following examples from Haitian (Spears 1990: 121) illustrate. I have amended Spears's labels for the categories somewhat:

(7) Mwen te pale avè l
1sg PAST talk with 3sg
"I talked with him"

(8) L (a)va vin dokté
3sg FUT become doctor
"S/he'll become a doctor"

(9) M ap pale ak Mari
1sg PROG talk with Marie
"I'm talking to Marie"

(10) Nou fin(i) sakle
we finish weed
"We've finished weeding" (Degraff to appear: 41)

Spanish and Portuguese lexicon creoles also display certain parallels in TMA marking with their English and French counterparts, However, the organization of these systems is far from identical across these creoles.

Still, the striking similarities led earlier scholars such as Thompson (1961), Taylor (1963, 1971), and others to propose that a certain inventory as well as a fixed (T–M–A) ordering of pre-verbal markers were definitive of creoles. For such scholars, this was evidence that all creoles were in fact descended from a common ancestor, perhaps a Portuguese pidgin. This "monogenetic" theory of creole origins found little support in either the sociohistorical or linguistic evidence from studies of various creoles (see Arends et al. 1995: 87–8 for an overview).

Bickerton (1981, 1984) used the similarities in creole TMA and other areas of grammar as evidence to support his "Language Bioprogram Hypothesis" (LBH). This explained many aspects of creole grammar as due to the creativity of young children who resorted to the bioprogram (a genetically determined set of principles for the organization of language) when acquiring a deficient pidgin as their first language. However, evidence from recent studies shows that there is in fact a great deal of diversity among creole TMA systems (Singler 1990b), and indeed other areas of the grammar, despite a certain degree of similarity.

Exercise 3

Find out which features of creole grammar Bickerton (1981: ch. 2) attributed to a putative language bioprogram. Focusing on TMA or any other of these features, discuss alternative explanations for the similarities found across creoles. (On TMA similarities, see Winford 2001 for Caribbean English-lexicon creoles and DeGraff to appear for French-lexicon creoles).

9.6.5 Creole Syntax

Unlike prototypical pidgins, creoles have elaborate syntactic systems, including movement rules, relativization strategies, various types of complementation, and other forms of subordination, for example temporal and conditional clauses. Once more, however, creoles differ considerably in the extent to which these syntactic resources diverge from those found in their lexifiers. In the more radical creoles, as we would expect, such divergence is partly a reflection of substrate influence and partly due to internal developments.

A brief look at the more radical Atlantic creoles should suffice to illustrate some of the more definitive aspects of their syntax. Those that show clear evidence of substrate influence include identificational (contrastive) focus constructions and a variety of serial verb constructions.

9.6.5.1 Contrastive focus constructions

Contrastive focus involves the fronting of a constituent introduced by a focus marker identical to the equative copula. Consider the following sentence from Jamaican Creole, for example:

(11) Jan tiff di mango yesidee
"John stole the mango yesterday"

Any one of the constituents of this sentence can be fronted, yielding the following:

(12) a. a jan tiif di mango yesidee
FOC John steal the mango yesterday
"It was John who stole the mango yesterday"
b. a di mango jan tiif yesidee
"It was the mango that John stole yesterday"
c. A yesidee jan tiif di mango
"It was yesterday that John stole the mango"

Interestingly also, even the verb can be fronted, though a copy must appear in its original position. This construction, sometimes referred to as "predicate clefting," is illustrated in (13):

(13) a tiif jan tiif di mango
"John STOLE the mango"

There is some evidence that these focus constructions have models in the substrate languages of the Atlantic creoles (see section 9.8.2.2 below).

9.6.5.2 Serial verb constructions

Among the best-known aspects of Atlantic creole syntax are serial verb constructions (SVCs) in which the serial verb (usually appearing after a main verb) performs functions associated with categories like prepositions and complementizers in the lexifier languages. Examples of the former type include "directional" as well as "dative/benefactive" SVCs.

In directional SVCs, a main verb of motion requires a serial verb such as "go," "come," etc. to indicate the direction of motion. The following sentences from Jamaican Creole illustrate (Winford 1993: 231–2):

(14) a. dem bring di pikni kom a tong
They bring DET child come LOC town
"They brought the child (hither) to town"
b. Dem a waak go a maakit
They PROG walk go LOC market
"They're walking (thither) to the market"

In dative/benefactive SVCs, the serial verb "give" marks either the recipient or the beneficiary of the action of the main verb. The following examples from the Paamaka variety of the Eastern Maroon Creole illustrate (Migge 1998: 236–8):

(15) a. A langa a buku gi mi (Recipient)
3sg hand DET book give me
"S/he handed the book to me"
b. A bai wan moi doo gi Saafika (Benefactive)
3sg buy a nice door give Saafika
"S/he bought a nice door for Saafika"

Other types of SVC shared across the Atlantic English creoles include comparative constructions in which a serial verb meaning "surpass" conveys the comparison, and "instrumental" SVCs in which a verb "take" governs the instrument of the action expressed by a following verb. Examples (16) and (17) illustrate the two respective types:

(16) Amba tranga pasa/moro Kofi (Sranan, Sebba 1987: 52)
Amba strong pass/surpass Kofi
"Amba is stronger than Kofi"

(17) Mi tek naif kot di bred (JC, Winford 1993: 263)
I take knife cut DET bread
"I cut the bread with a knife"

Again, not all Caribbean English creoles display the same range of SVCs. Moreover, even for a particular type of SVC there are differences in the productivity of the construction. For instance, the Surinamese creoles use serial verb "give" in a wider range of functions than the most divergent varieties of Guyanese Creole (GC), JC, etc. (Migge 1998). The Surinamese creoles also have a richer inventory of serial verbs expressing directionality (Winford 1993: 233–4).

There are many other areas of creole grammar that cannot be explored fully here. They include strategies of question formation, relativization, factive and purposive complementation, passivization, and so on. All of these show significant divergence from superstrate syntax in the more radical creoles.

Let us now turn our attention to current theories or hypotheses about how creoles came into being.

9.7 Theories of Creole Formation

Contemporary scholars remain divided over the relative contribution of superstrate and substrate languages as well as the role of language universals in creole formation. Some still adhere to Bickerton's LBH or some version of it that ascribes the primary role in creole creation to innate universal principles (Bickerton 1999). Others maintain that, *contra* the LBH, creoles did not develop from pidgins but began as second language varieties of the lexifier or "superstrate" languages and gradually diverged more and more from the latter via a process of "basilectalization" (Mufwene 1996a, 1996b). Some scholars who hold this view maintain that most of creole grammar can be traced to the lexifier language (Chaudenson 1992, 2001). Others allow for significant influence from substrate languages (Mufwene 1990). Then there are those who claim that the major influence on the grammar of "radical" creoles in fact came from the substrate languages (Lefebvre and Lumsden 1994; Lefebvre 1996; Lumsden 1999; etc.).

Recently, however, there has been a trend toward a compromise which acknowledges that creole formation involved varying degrees of "input" from both superstrate and substrate sources, and was guided by principles that regulate all cases of language contact (Mufwene 1990; DeGraff 1999b). More specifically, there is now wide agreement that creole formation was akin in many respects to a gradual process of group second language acquisition.

Exploring the precise nature of the similarities and differences between creole formation and (other) cases of group SLA promises to enrich our understanding of both. The main question that arises is what differences in the social contexts and linguistic inputs set creole formation apart from cases of shift (group SLA) such as we examined in chapter 7. Before attempting to answer this question, we must again take into account the differences among the creoles themselves. As noted already, intermediate creoles like Bajan and Reunionnaise are essentially similar to "indigenized" varieties such as Hiberno-English, Indian English, and Singapore English. Indeed, it is arguable that Singapore English is more divergent from its superstrate source than either Bajan or Reunionnaise. It seems reasonable to treat these creoles as cases of shift in which access to the TL was not severely limited. Radical creoles, however, pose a more difficult problem. But before we attempt to reconstruct their history, some caveats are in order.

9.7.1 Reconstructing creole formation: a caveat

Several problems arise in the attempt to faithfully reconstruct the ways creoles came into being. One, already mentioned, is the unavailability of data from the earliest stages of the process. This makes it difficult to determine not only the nature of early creole grammar, but also the nature of the linguistic inputs to it. We are still not sure of the exact superstrate input, though we know something about the settler dialects that were involved. As far as the substrates are concerned, we can assume that their structure was essentially the same then as it is now. As Thomason (1993) reminds us, 300 years is not a very long time in the history of a language. With regard to the creoles, however, such an assumption may be dangerous. Many creoles (e.g., Jamaican, Guyanese, etc.) have been subject to continuing influence from their European lexifiers, and have changed in their direction. There is evidence, for instance, that earlier JC phonology and morphosyntax may have diverged more from English than contemporary JC does (Lalla and D'Costa 1990: 37–46). Moreover, because earlier creoles were dynamic and developing systems, they have continued to change both under internal motivation and external contact, sometimes with languages other than their lexifiers. For example, Haitian Creole (Baker 1993b) and Sranan (Arends 1989) show evidence of several recent internal developments. In addition, Sranan has borrowed a great deal of vocabulary and some grammatical formatives and patterns from Dutch.

Finally, as Arends (1989, 1993) and Baker (1995, 1997) have argued, we cannot assume that all of the features of earlier creole grammar were established in a single generation, as Bickerton claimed. The evidence from available historical texts of Sranan, for instance, suggests that many features, including some TMA markers and combinations, relativization strategies, etc., emerged over time. In short, the process of creole formation was a gradual one (Arends 1993). All of these caveats must be kept in mind in any attempt to reconstruct early creole formation.

Exercise 4
Alleyne (2000) argues that Old Haitian Creole was closer to Français Populaire than modern Haitian. What kinds of evidence does he adduce for this claim, and how convincing is it? (See also Baker 1993b: 136; DeGraff to appear; Detgers 2000.)

9.8 Radical Creole Formation as SLA

The parallels between creole formation and SLA were noted as early as the nineteenth century by scholars like Hesseling (1897), and later by Jespersen (1922). Most creolists now espouse the view that creoles are products of a special form of SLA. In both cases, we find an early stage of grammar construction that yields a "basic" or pidginized variety of the L2 with a reduced lexicon and grammatical apparatus. Both also involve processes of elaboration in which three major sources of input are involved. These include input (intake) from the target language, L1 influence, and internally driven changes which regularize and expand the grammar. Still, the parallels between the two cases of acquisition are not identical. For instance, questions arise about the nature of the language that was the target of acquisition.

9.8.1 The target of acquisition

It is questionable whether radical creoles like Sranan are instances of targeted SLA in the usual sense of that term. For one thing, the designation would imply that the creators of such creoles were not only targeting (dialects of) English, French, Portuguese, etc., but had adequate access to them. Both of these assumptions are questionable, as Arends (1995b), Baker (1990), Singler (1993), and others have argued. Rather, it would seem that most slaves brought to these colonies, particularly at the height of the plantation system, were attempting to learn an already established contact variety quite distinct from the superstrates.

Baker (1990) suggests that this contact variety, or "medium of interethnic communication" (MIC), was itself the target. While this clearly applies to later arrivals, it still leaves open the question of how the MIC originated, and what the inputs to its earliest formative stage were. We can only speculate about this for most colonies, because we lack historical and textual records of the earliest period of settlement. However, in some cases, such records are quite revealing about the process by which the MIC first emerged.

For instance, evidence from Hawaii makes it clear that the formation of Hawaii Creole English (HCE) involved elaboration of an earlier English-lexicon pidgin that became a target of learning for adult immigrants and their locally born children in the late nineteenth century (S. J. Roberts 2000; Siegel 2000). Both adults and children had a major role in elaborating this pidgin into HCE. Siegel (2000) argues in particular that children of Portuguese and Chinese immigrants, bilingual in their ancestral languages and the pidgin, contributed much to the elaboration of the latter's grammar. This explains why many aspects of HCE grammar can be traced to substrate influence from Cantonese and Portuguese. Siegel demonstrates that several key features of HCE grammar (including TMA categories) that had been ascribed to the putative language bioprogram could in fact be explained as the result of such substrate influence. Indeed he concludes that "in the use of the copula, non-verbal adjectives, combinations of tense markers, functions of the [+ Non punctual] marker [the Progressive] and *for* complementation, HCE is more similar to Portuguese than to other creoles" (2000: 230).

In short, *contra* the LBH, the evidence suggests that HCE was the result of a typical three-generation process of language shift. It started being acquired as a first language only after its grammar had been extensively restructured by the previous generation(s). Children acquiring it (later) as a first language may have helped regularize the grammar and perhaps introduced more innovations such as auxiliary combinations. However, HCE was essentially a creation by persons (including children) who already had a first language.

This scenario closely resembles that outlined in chapter 8 for the creation of "extended" pidgins such as Melanesian. Based on this, it might seem reasonable to assume that the first stage of radical creole formation involved a similar process, in which the grammar of a pidgin or simplified variety of the superstrate was elaborated by learners appealing to L1 knowledge and guided by universal principles of SLA. This new creation in turn became a target of learning for later arrivals. In places like Suriname, social and demographic conditions (see above) promoted the continuous relearning of the contact variety by successive waves of new slaves.

However, not all scholars accept that this "pidgin to creole" scenario applies to all cases of creole formation. Chaudenson (1992, 2001), Mufwene (1996a, 1996b), and others suggest that the initial stages of contact produced second language varieties of the superstrate that were restructured and "basilectalized" via a process of repeated SLA. In this approach, there is no need to assume that everyone spoke or targeted a stable superstrate-derived pidgin spoken as the lingua franca for some period before its elaboration into a creole began. Such an alternative may well be plausible for some cases of creole formation, for example, Haiti (Alleyne 2000). But it is not inconsistent with the view that radical creole formation began with the restructuring of simplified, even pidginized forms of the superstrate, regardless of what input was previously available. Given the severe lack of access to full superstrate input that we find in all cases of radical creole formation, we can assume two things. First, individual learners, particularly new arrivals, began with a basic variety of the superstrate, based on whatever intake they could process from the available input. Second, lacking continued input from the full superstrate sources, learners/creators elaborated this basic variety by drawing more on their L1 knowledge and other compensatory strategies. Whichever scenario one chooses, it seems that creole formation was essentially a process of SLA with highly restricted TL input under unusual social circumstances.

9.8.2 Restructuring in creole grammar

The elaborative stages of creole formation have traditionally been referred to as "creolization," which Hymes (1971b: 84) defined as "that complex process of sociolinguistic change comprising expansion in inner form, with convergence, in the context of extension in use." However, the term has been used in so many (sometimes conflicting) senses, that its usefulness has been seriously compromised (Winford 1997c: 136). We will therefore avoid it here.[3] Instead we will describe the elaboration of creole grammar as "restructuring," in the sense in which this term is used in the literature on first and second language acquisition. With regard to L1 acquisition, van Buren (1996: 190) defines restructuring as "discarding old grammars for new ones." He adds, "As soon as new relevant data are encountered, the current grammar is restructured to accommodate the new input" (ibid.). SLA researchers define the concept in similar ways. For instance, Hulstijn (1990: 32) describes it as "the establishment of new procedures which reorganize a body of facts and rules previously acquired." Similarly, Lalleman (1996: 31) defines it as "the process of imposing organization and structure upon the information that has been acquired" as new input is encountered. Note that this is very different from the sense in which creolists sometimes use the term, viz., to refer to restructuring of the lexifier language. This implies that creole creators began with the lexifier, modifying it over time.

The major issue facing creolists today is the nature of this process of restructuring and the relative contributions of the three major inputs referred to earlier. In addition, there is the question of the role of "universals" in the elaboration of creole grammar.

Before we proceed further, it is important to emphasize that the process of creole formation is both an individual and a community phenomenon. The restructuring process goes on primarily in individual learners' attempts to construct and expand their IL system. The innovations introduced by these learners then become available for selection as part of the community's language. Consequently, creole formation must be seen as a product both of individual grammar construction (I-language) and of the spread of features across individual grammars, yielding a shared community vernacular (E-language). We will return to the latter process later.

9.8.2.1 Restructuring and superstrate input to creole formation

The frequently stated view that the superstrate contributes lexicon while the substrate languages contribute most of the grammar to creole formation is quite simplistic, even when applied to the most radical creoles. The reality is rather more complex. In the first place, some aspects of superstrate grammar do find their way into creoles, though they are generally transformed in various ways. For example, features such as infinitival and complementizer *fo(r)*, found throughout Atlantic English creoles, have models in English regional dialects (Lalla and D'Costa 1990: 107). Similarly, the Progressive/Imperfective marker *(d)a* found in most Caribbean English creoles appears to derive from present periphrastic *do* (often pronounced /də/) of southwest English dialects, probably reinforced by the prefix *a-* found in English dialectal progressive constructions such as *He's a-hunting*.

In the second place, the lexical features that creoles derive from their superstrate sources are often modified in various ways in the emerging grammar. For instance, we saw earlier how many superstrate-derived lexical items undergo changes in semantics and function, so that their lexical entries no longer match those of their counterparts in the European source language. On the other hand, it is clear that creoles draw on both lexical and structural resources of the substrates, though, as we will see, they do not replicate the latter exactly. Moreover, aspects of creole grammar often result from the interaction of both superstrate and substrate inputs. A case in point is the emergence of the complementizer *se* "that" in JC, which resembles both English *say* and Twi complementizer *se* "that," used after *verba dicendi* and verbs of knowing, etc. (Lalla and D'Costa 1990: 77).

In the more radical creoles, these phenomena reflect learners' limited access to the native varieties of the superstrate, and their heavy reliance on L1 knowledge in processing whatever input those sources provide. As we have already noted, the higher this input is, the closer the creole grammar is to that of its lexifier.

9.8.2.2 Restructuring and substrate influence

One of the major differences between creole formation and (other types of) SLA lies in the perseverance of L1-based strategies in the former. As it progresses, SLA typically involves replacement of such strategies (and other compensatory ones) by those adopted from the TL. By contrast, radical creoles, and to a lesser extent the intermediate ones, continue to draw on the substrate languages and their own internal resources as the grammar develops.

The role of substrate influence in creole formation has been convincingly demonstrated in many recent studies. In the case of the Surinamese creoles, studies by Arends (1986), McWhorter (1992), Sebba (1987), and Smith (1996) have argued for Kwa substrate influence on serial verb constructions. Research by Bruyn (1994) points to influence from Gbe (and to some extent Kikongo) on complex prepositional phrases in Sranan. Finally, Migge has argued for Gbe influence on various Paamaka constructions, including "give"-type SVCs (1998), attributive (property) predication (2000), and the copula system (to appear).

By way of brief illustration, consider the case of "give"-type SVCs in Paamaka. There are strong parallels between such structures and those in the principal Kwa substrates – Gbe and Akan. The "give" serial verb in all cases performs a variety of functions, assigning recipient, benefactive, and substitutive roles, among others, to its complement NP. The following are examples of the first type, from Migge (1998: 236):

(18)	Paamaka:	a.	Mi seli a osu gi en
			I sell DET house give 3s
			"I sold the house to him/her"
	Ewegbe:	b.	Ye dʒra maʃin-a ne Amba
			3pl sell machine-the give Amba
			"They sold the computer to Amba"
	Twi:	c.	Me tɔɔn me dan ma-a no nnera
			I sell-PAST my house give-PAST him yesterday
			"I sold my house to him yesterday"

Migge provides many examples of similar correspondences in other types of "give" SVC. Correspondences between the Surinamese creoles and their Kwa substrates can be found in other types of SVC mentioned earlier, including comparative and instrumental-type constructions.

Smith (1996) also demonstrates strong parallels between contrastive (identificational) focus constructions in Saamaka (SM) and Fongbe (Fon). In fact, Saamaka uses exactly the same focus marker (*wɛ̀*), in the same position (following the focused element), as Fon does. The following examples illustrate:

(19) SM: a. di mujee wɛ̀ mi bi bel, naa di womi
DET woman FOC 1sg PAST phone NEG DET man
"It was the WOMAN I telephoned, not the man"
b. kaí wɛ̀ mi kaí kó a di baáka dendu
fall FOC 1sg fall come LOC DET hole inside
"I FELL into the hole"

(20) Fon: a. mɔ́tò ɔ̀ wɛ̀ súnù ɖé gbà
car DET FOC man DET destroy
"It was the CAR a man destroyed"
b. gbà wɛ̀ súnù ɖé gbà mɔ́tò ɔ́
destroy FOC man DET destroy car DET
"The man DESTROYED the car (he didn't fix it)"

Migge (to appear) shows that there are strong correspondences between Paamaka and Gbe with regard to presentational and contrastive (idenficational) focus constructions. However, the Paamaka constructions are not direct replicas of those in Gbe. (See further discussion below in section 9.8.2.4.)

The correspondences between these radical creoles and their substrates suggest that creole formation involved, in part, the retention of abstract substrate syntactic patterns, into which superstrate-derived lexical forms were incorporated. For instance, the abstract pattern underlying recipient "give" SVCs is as follows:

Semantic elements:	Agent	Transfer	Theme	Dative	Recipient
Syntactic elements:	NP	Vtrans	NP	"give"	NP

Similar shared patterns underlie other SVCs. How such patterns become part of creole grammar will be discussed below, in sections 9.9.3–9.9.5.

Strong syntactic parallels like these led Sylvain (1936) to assert that Haitian Creole was a language with Ewe grammar and French words. Similarly, Wilson (1962: ix) described Guinea Bissau creole as a West African language. Berbice Dutch even preserves overt grammatical morphemes from its primary substrate, Eastern Ijo (Kalabari) (Smith et al. 1987). In the last case, the homogeneity of the substrate was no doubt a factor in allowing such retentions. In the case of Guinea Bissau creole, the strong substrate influence was partly due to its continued co-existence with its substrates. But, these exceptions aside, radical creoles do seem to preserve much of substrate grammar, though they hardly replicate it exactly.

9.8.2.3 The Relexification Hypothesis

The most comprehensive attempt to identify substrate influence on a creole is the research done on Haitian Creole (HC) origins by LeFebvre, Lumsden, and their associates (Lefebvre and Lumsden 1994; Lumsden 1999). They developed a particularly strong version of the substratist theory of creole formation, known as the Relexification Hypothesis (RH). The process of relexification will be discussed more fully below, in section 9.9.2.1. According to this theory, most of HC grammar is derived more or less directly from that of Fongbe, its principal substrate language.

However, this account of HC origins has been strongly challenged by several scholars, including Chaudenson (1996), DeGraff (1999b), and Singler (1996). In the first place, the RH rests on a somewhat limited account of the sociohistorical background to HC formation, neglecting the role of substrate languages other than Fongbe. Second, the RH has little to say about the precise sources of the superstrate input to HC formation. As Chaudenson (1992) and others have shown, it was provincial French dialects of the seventeenth and eighteenth centuries that provided this input. Moreover, many aspects of HC grammar can be traced to these sources.

Finally, the RH seems to present only a partial picture of the mechanisms and constraints involved in creole formation. Its critics have questioned whether relexification constitutes the only mechanism of substratal influence or indeed the only mechanism of change involved in creole formation. Singler (1996: 218) points out that substrate influence (and by extension the RH) cannot account for certain features of creoles which are due to universals of acquisition or internal motivation. Lumsden (1999: 230, fn. 7) acknowledges this, pointing out that "the RH is NOT a claim that relexification is the one and only process involved in creole genesis, nor is it argued that relexification can account for all the properties of creole languages." Such an account must address both superstrate and substrate inputs, as well as the principles that determined the selection of particular source language features and not others. In addition, it must account for innovations in creole grammar that arose independently of such input. We will discuss the various mechanisms and principles involved in all of these aspects of creole formation below, in sections 9.9 and 9.10.

9.8.2.4 Restructuring and internal developments

The elaboration of early creole grammar, like that of developing interlanguage and expanding pidgins, involves innovations driven by tendencies already present in the developing system. Kouwenberg (1996), while acknowledging Kalabari (Eastern Ijo) as the source of several aspects of Berbice Dutch grammar, also points to several others that cannot be explained in this way. Some of the latter can be attributed to Dutch influence, for instance features like adjectives, prepositions, and postnominal relatives. However, this still leaves several features that can be explained in terms of neither superstrate nor substrate influence. They include invariant SVO order, pre-verbal auxiliaries and negative marker, predicate cleft, and a serial verb construction in which a verb "say" introduces complement clauses.

Features like these appear to be due to processes of internal restructuring similar to those found in developing IL and in the elaboration of pidgins. In all cases, speakers exploit intake from both L1 and L2 sources to create a maximally simple grammar, and this can lead to innovations peculiar to the developing language. In the case of Berbice Dutch, this creativity may explain the features listed above, though this explanation doesn't necessarily hold for similar features in other creoles. For instance, in English-lexicon Atlantic creoles, features such as SVO and pre-verbal TMA and negation have parallels in the substrate languages.

More generally, internally driven innovations in creole grammar seem to arise from the restructuring of superstrate and substrate input, regulated by universal principles of acquisition (the need for economy and simplicity). A case in point is the development of the copula systems of Sranan and Ndjuka. In these creoles, the form *na/da* is employed as the focus marker in presentative and contrastive focus constructions and in equative (identificational) constructions lacking TMA marking. The following Paamaka examples from Migge (to appear: 19, 22) illustrate:

(21) a. Mi na Sa D
1sg COP Ms D
"I am Ms D"

b. na a udu ya, a fu mi
COP DEM wood here, 3sg for me
"It's THIS WOOD that's mine (not that one)"

On the other hand, the copula *de* is employed in locative constructions and in equative constructions containing negation or TMA marking, as in the following Paamaka examples (ibid.: 33):

(22) a. A o de wan laulau sani
it FUT COP one badbad thing
"It'll be an unimportant thing"

b. Mi an de a fesiman
1sg NEG COP ART leader
"I'm not the leader"

This distribution of copulas has no exact parallel in the substrates, or indeed in other Atlantic creoles. First, unlike the creoles in question, the substrates employ contrastive focus markers distinct from their equative/presentative copula (Migge to appear: 23). In addition, the focus markers follow the focused constituent in the substrates, but precede it in the creoles (recall that Saamaka follows the Gbe pattern in this respect). Moreover, the generalization of copula *de* beyond locative environments to equative environments that are specified for TMA and negation is not found in the substrates.[4] The latter employ an equative copula distinct from the locative copula in all these cases. The creoles therefore have restructured their copula domain to create a simplified and more transparent system distinct from those of the substrates. How do we explain these developments?

Arends (1986, 1989) argues convincingly that the equative copula *da/na* derives from the demonstrative *da* (< that) found in early Sranan equative constructions like the following:

(23) a. Da mi, Filida
That ø me, Filida
"It's me, Filida" (van Dyck, n.d.: 73, cited in Arends 1986: 108)

b. "adjossi," da Bakkratongo
"adjossi," that ø bakra tongue
"'Adjossi' is Europeans' Sranan" (C. Schumann 1783: 46, cited in Arends 1986: 113)

Sentences like these appear to represent the kind of simplified English that formed the early input to the Surinamese plantation creole. This would explain the initial position of *da/na* as focus markers, as well as the fact that in earlier Sranan, the negative marker followed the equative copula (a pattern still found today in competition with structures containing *no* followed by *de*):

(24) Hertoch a no yu mati
Hertoch COP NEG your friend

Copula *de*, on the other hand, appears to have arisen via reinterpretation of adverbial *de* (< *there*) in early Sranan structures like the following:

(25) a. Mastra soopie de
master drink there
"Master, there is the drink" (van Dyck n.d., cited in Arends and Perl 1995: 170)

b. Mastra, wini no de na battra
master wine NEG there? LOC bottle
"Master, there's no more wine in the bottle" (Arends and Perl 1995: 180)

Migge (to appear: 53) argues that the resemblance of such strings to existential and locative structures in Gbe and Kikongo triggered an interlingual identification between *de* and the substrate copulas. Compare the following sentences from Xwelagbe (Migge to appear: 53, 34):

(26) a. makikʔkwe ɖé
bananas COP
"There are bananas"

b. ixhe mɔ ɖé dɔ mɛ kliya
fish PAST COP net in IDEO
"Fish were in the net in great quantity"

Substrate influence, then, can partly explain the emergence of *de* as an existential/locative copula in the creoles. But it can't explain the generalization of *de* to other copula constructions. The latter must be due to internal developments in Sranan and Ndjuka. The fact that the locative copula *de* found in other Atlantic creoles has not been generalized in this way would lend support to this suggestion.

The conclusion to be drawn from this overview of creole formation is that this process was a complex one, involving a variety of linguistic inputs and strategies of restructuring. The theories of creole origins that have been proposed ("superstratist," "substratist," and "universalist") tend to focus only on one or another aspect of this complex process.[5] The challenge to contemporary scholarship is how to integrate these sometimes conflicting accounts into a unified explanation of creole creation.

9.9 Mechanisms, Constraints, and Principles in Creole Formation

Creolists generally agree that, in the emergence of creole grammar, superstrate-derived lexical items (or their phonetic shapes) are selected to express the morphological and syntactic categories of the creole. The processes by which these forms are integrated into creole grammar, and the principles and constraints governing their selection, remain subjects of debate. This is compounded by disagreement over the degree to which superstrate lexicon and grammar, as opposed to substratal input and universal principles, contribute to the formation of creoles.

Several questions arise here. First, what constrains the degree of superstratal as opposed to substratal input? Second, what principles regulate the selection of specific elements, lexical as well as structural, from each of the inputs? Third, what mechanisms and constraints are involved in the interaction between superstratal and substratal input? Finally, what role do universal principles play in this and other aspects of creole development?

9.9.1 Constraints on the linguistic inputs

Siegel (1997: 137) has proposed a number of "availability" constraints – that is, external and internal factors that determine the input to the earlier stages of creole development. Essentially, the input consists of the data available to learners as a target or model for acquisition. A crucial factor here is whether learners have relatively full as opposed to simplified input from the relevant L2. The external factors that influence this include those discussed earlier, in section 9.3, for example, the demographics of the groups in contact and the social contexts of the contact. Both external and internal (linguistic) factors influence the nature of learners' intake from the superstrate, that is, the actual L2 materials they acquire and employ in the construction of their interlanguage. The internal factors are constraints on learners' ability to process the L2 input, which lead to strategies of reduction and simplification of that input. Such strategies are common to all early attempts to achieve communication across language boundaries, including pidgin formation and early IL, as we have seen in earlier chapters. On the other hand, we can assume that the full resources of their L1s were available to creole creators when they needed to compensate for limited mastery of the L2 (whatever variety of it they were exposed to). This raises the question of what types of L1 features creole creators actually use, and what constraints there are on this compensatory strategy.

9.9.2 Substrate influence: mechanisms and constraints

As we saw earlier, in addition to overt retention of L1 forms, L1 influence in creole formation takes two general forms: use of abstract syntactic patterns into which superstrate phonetic shapes are incorporated, and reinterpretation of these superstrate forms in terms of substrate morphosyntactic and lexicosemantic categories. The same is true of extended pidgins, as discussed in the previous chapter. Hence the discussion of mechanisms and constraints here applies equally to them.

Two rather different explanations have been offered for these kinds of L1 influence. First, there are approaches such as Lefebvre's and Lumsden's (mentioned earlier) which appeal to notions like "relexification" and "reanalysis." Then there are approaches like Siegel's (1999, 2000) which appeal to "transfer," a central concept in SLA (see chapter 7). Let us examine each of these approaches in turn.

9.9.2.1 Relexification and substrate influence

Lumsden (1999: 225) defines relexification as "a mental process that allows a language learner to create a new vocabulary of lexical categories (i.e., nouns, verbs, adjectives, prepositions and adverbs) by linking new phonological forms with syntactic and semantic information that is already established in the lexicon of his native language." The classic example of this process is of course Media Lengua, which we discussed in chapter 6. For example, the Media Lengua verbal root *bi-* "see" derives its phonological shape from Spanish *ver* "to see," but it displays the semantics and derivational properties of Quechua *riku-* "see" (chapter 6, section 6.3.2). Relexification in this case explains the reinterpretation of L2 forms in terms of L1 lexicosemantic categories.

The RH also explains the similarity between abstract syntactic patterns in creoles and their substrates by arguing that the phonetic shapes of superstrate verbs assume the syntactic and semantic representations of substrate counterparts. For example, Lumsden (1999: 241) argues that, in Haitian Creole, French-derived forms like *voye* "send," *vann* "sell," etc. assume the argument structure of Fongbe verbs like *sɛ́* "send," *sà* "sell," etc. Thus we find syntactic similarities like the following (Lumsden 1999: 239):

(27) Haitian: M voye rad la pou Mari
I send clothing DET for Mari
"I sent the clothing for the benefit of Mari"

(28) Fongbe: Báyí sɛ́ àwù i dó Ajwá
Bayi send clothing DET for Ajwa
"Bayi sent the clothing for the benefit of Ajwa"

Lefebvre (1996) also appealed to the RH to explain the emergence of creole morphosyntactic categories such as TMA. Again, superstrate lexical forms are reinterpreted as labels of substrate categories. Lumsden (1999) revises this somewhat, suggesting that relexification accounts only for the entry of the superstrate lexical shapes into the early creole. These forms were subsequently reanalyzed as the signals of substrate grammatical categories through a process Lumsden (ibid.: 250) refers to as "grammaticalization" (see further discussion below).

Exercise 5
Lumsden's (1999) account of the role of relexification in creole formation seems to imply that certain aspects of creole grammar (e.g., syntactic structures) emerged earlier than others (e.g., grammatical categories). What evidence is there that this was true? Does this also apply in the case of extended pidgins?

9.9.2.2 Substrate influence as "transfer"

All of the types of substrate influence described in the preceding section have also been explained in terms of the "transfer" of L1 features onto L2-derived forms (Siegel 1999; Wekker 1996). This approach has paid more attention to morphosyntactic than to lexicosemantic or syntactic structures. Siegel (1999), for instance, examines seven core morphosyntactic features of Melanesian Pidgin (MP) and argues that they derive directly from Central Eastern Oceanic (CEO) languages, the relevant substrates. One of his examples is the organization of the MP pronominal system, discussed in chapter 8. Here distinctions such as exclusiveness and a four-way number opposition, and even the morphemic composition of the pronominal forms, directly parallel those in CEO languages. Other examples include the use of a subject-referencing marker in the VP and the use of property items as verbs. Both of these features are illustrated in the following examples, which compare Bislama with Tangoa, a language of Vanuatu (Siegel 1999: 14–15):

(29) a. Bislama: Haos ya i big-fala
house DET 3sg. big-adj
"This house is big"

b. Tangoa: Tamioci sei mo para mo malokoloko
man DET 3sg fat 3sg tired-tired
"This man is fat and lazy" (Camden 1979: 107)

These features are explained in terms of the strategy of transfer, according to which L2 forms that are congruent in meaning and/or position with L1 forms acquire the properties of the latter. Siegel (2000) offers a similar explanation for the emergence of various morphosyntactic features of Hawai'i Creole English. For example, the selection of *stay* as copula and progressive marker was due in part to L1 Portuguese learners who identified it with *estar*, the copula used in such functions in Portuguese. In this case, reinforcing influence may have come from Cantonese, another principal substrate, which uses the verb *háidouh* "to be (t)here" as a progressive marker (Jeff Siegel, p.c., Feb. 2002). Siegel refers to this as "substrate reinforcement," where features from different substrate languages reinforce the retention of reanalyzed L2 forms.

Exercise 6
Lefebvre (1996) argues that the TMA categories of Haitian Creole derive their semantics and functions directly from Fongbe via relexification and reanalysis. How similar is this explanation to that offered by Siegel for the emergence of TMA categories in Hawai'i Creole English? How convincing are the respective arguments for substrate influence?

9.9.2.3 Transfer and creole syntax

In cases where there is some degree of congruence between L1 and L2 structures, creole syntax reflects the common ground. Thus, SVO ordering in Atlantic English-lexicon creoles has parallels in both English and the relevant substrates. Again, such cases can be explained as "transfer to somewhere" (recall, for example, English learners' placement of object pronouns after the verb in their L2 French). On the other hand, those substrate-derived aspects of creole syntax that have no counterparts in the superstrate (input) would presumably be treated as cases of "transfer to nowhere" and explained in terms of Andersen's "relexification principle" (see chapter 7, section 7.12.2). Recall that, according to this, learners will use their L1 structure when they cannot perceive certain L2 structural patterns. That would explain the emergence of structures such as SVCs in the Atlantic creoles. Andersen does not make it clear whether his conception of relexification is similar to that of Lumsden. Are abstract syntactic patterns "transferred" *in toto*, so to speak? Or do they result from the transfer or projection of substrate semantic and lexical representations onto superstrate-derived lexical forms? The latter approach would be closer to that of Lefebvre and Lumsden, though they view the process the other way around, that is, as calquing of superstrate-derived forms onto substrate categories.

9.9.2.4 Relexification or transfer?

Differences in the terminology used for describing L1 or substrate influence on learner versions of an L2 merely reflect differences in perspective. The terms themselves, "relexification" or "transfer," refer to the same objective psycholinguistic process of restructuring. Transfer views the effects of L1 influence from the perspective of (learner versions of) the TL, focusing on the ways in which input (intake) is changed under that influence. The relexification scenario views the process more from the perspective of the L1 (input), focusing on how L2 items are incorporated into the learner system as labels for L1-derived semantic/functional categories. The dichotomy between the two approaches is only an illusion.

Both "transfer" and "relexification" are consistent with the notion that creole creators (or L2 learners) retain certain abstract categories or structures in terms of which they reanalyze or reinterpret substrate- or L2-derived forms. Such abstract continuities are in principle no different from the retention of overt L1 lexical (and sometimes grammatical) forms, which occurs in both LSA (see chapter 7, section 7.2) and creole formation.

Whether learners "project" L1 categories onto L2 forms or "calque" the latter onto the former, the resulting reanalysis is the same. Moreover, the principles and constraints regulating this process are the same, whichever perspective we take.

Both relexification and transfer scenarios identify the same constraints on the reanalysis of L2-derived forms. Both appeal, for instance, to the notion of congruence leading to interlingual identifications between L1 and L2 forms, as we saw earlier. Siegel (1999) also argues that the selection of superstrate forms is determined by factors such as perceptual salience, transparency, and frequency. As we noted in chapter 7 (section 7.7.3), all of these notions can be subsumed under the concept of markedness. We return to this below.

9.9.3 Leveling in creole formation

So far, we have been considering processes of creole formation primarily from the perspective of individual learners. As DeGraff (1999b: 485) has noted, these individuals create I-languages (IL systems) on the basis of the linguistic data available to them. These I-languages provide the lexical and grammatical features that are adopted into the community language. Hence a theory of creole formation must also explain how a stable grammar emerges via a process of leveling, from among the competing variants introduced by different individuals or groups of speakers. Siegel (1997: 126) describes the process of leveling as involving the reduction or attrition of variants in ways similar to koinéization.

In this connection, the "reinforcement principles" proposed by Siegel (1999), which we discussed in chapter 7 (section 7.13), are highly relevant. Recall that these principles determine which features will be retained and which discarded. A key principle seems to be that features shared across the individual ILs will be retained. In case where (the majority of) the substrate languages are typologically similar, such features occur frequently as a result of similar kinds of L1 influence. They constitute part of the common ground that learners seek in communicating across language boundaries. In cases where competing variants arise, the more transparent or salient ones survive. In both instances, then, features that are less marked by virtue of similarity, frequency, and transparency are most likely to be retained in the emerging community language. This would explain, for instance, why Melanesian Pidgin grammar retains a common core of features shared across its CEO substrates (Keesing 1988: 123).

There is also reason to believe that children acquiring emergent creoles play a role in ironing out the variation due to influences from different source languages. Children themselves may introduce certain innovations into creoles, such as TMA markers and auxiliary combinations. We saw earlier that children bilingual in their ancestral language and Hawai'i Pidgin English introduced several such innovations into Hawai'i Creole English. It is very likely that children bilingual in West African languages and early forms of creole made a similar contribution to the latter.

It also seems reasonable to assume that children acquiring an established creole as a first language would have contributed toward systematizing and expanding the grammar. Studies by Newport (1999) and Kegl, Senghas, and Coppola (1999) demonstrate that children acquiring American Sign Language and Nicaraguan Sign Language respectively as their first language imposed regularity and order on the disparate and variable input they received from adult signers.

As DeGraff (1999b: 494) suggests: "Via L2A [SLA], ... adults introduce innovative patterns into the linguistic ecology of language learners, whereas children, via L1A [first language acquisition], play a key role in restructuring adults' (and their own) innovations into stable grammars." In this, children (and adults) are guided by "UG [Universal Grammar] acting as a sieve and guiding grammatical invention" (ibid.: 497).

9.10 Universal Principles and Creole Formation

The view that "universal principles" have priority over substrate influence in creole formation goes back, as we have noted, to scholars of the late nineteenth century such as Coelho (1880–6). It was later given fuller expression by Bickerton (1981, 1984), who claimed that the bulk of creole grammar was due to UG, the innate language faculty. This approach treated creole formation as essentially a case of first language acquisition, in which adults had little role to play, except as suppliers of degenerate pidgin input. Some scholars still hold this view. For example, Veenstra (1996) argued that serial verb constructions in Saamaka were due to the workings of UG principles. In his view, absence of verbal morphology and consequently of verb movement to INFL triggered children's creation of SVCs in this creole (ibid.: 176). He does not, however, rule out the possibility that adults (and hence substrate influence) also played a role, but at later stages of creole development (ibid.: 194).

This strong position on the role of UG has given way lately to a more eclectic view. There is now broad consensus that the role of UG is to constrain the processes of restructuring by which superstrate and substrate inputs (intakes) are shaped into a viable grammar – one that conforms to universal principles of language design. Such principles play a role in all phases of creole formation – the early pidginization stage, the elaborating stages, and the later developmental stages.

Absence of bound morphology, fixed word order, invariant pre-verbal negation, and other instances of "reductive" simplification are presumably introduced into creoles via input from their pidginized antecedents. Such cases of simplification reflect the same processing and learning principles that apply to the early stages of SLA (chapter 7, section 7.71) and pidgin formation (chapter 8, section 8.5.2). There is therefore no need to repeat them here. We are concerned only with the elaborative and later developmental stages of creole formation.

9.10.1 Universals and L1 influence

The same principles that regulate the role of the L1 in the elaboration of early IL in SLA operate to constrain the interaction between substrate and superstrate input to creole formation. As we suggested in chapter 7 (section 7.7.5), cognitive constraints based on processing principles conspire with structural constraints based on typological distance to regulate restructuring in IL development. As in SLA research, some theories of creole formation attempt to explain these constraints in terms of markedness principles. For instance, scholars like DeGraff (1999: 509) and Muysken (1981b) see creole grammar as reflecting the least marked parameter settings triggered by the input. Other (not incompatible) approaches appeal to notions such as ease of perception and ease of learning – two notions central to markedness theory. Thus, Seuren and Wekker (1986: 65–6) argue that the need for semantic transparency was a major factor in creole formation. This would explain general properties of creole grammar such as "uniformity" (isomorphism of form and function), "universality" (maximal use of rules that are least language specific), and "simplicity" (minimal processing required to get from semantic to surface structures and vice versa).

As Keesing (1988: 110), following Kay and Sankoff (1974), notes: "the more speakers simplify and the deeper they dig, the more closely languages converge on basic minimally marked and maximally natural patterns." To cast this in different terms, creole grammar might be seen as representing the unmarked core of language as distinct from the periphery of marked elements and constructions (DeGraff 1999b: 510; Macedo 1986). As we noted earlier, children may have played a role in creating these properties of creole grammar.

9.10.2 Universals and internal developments

Those features of creole grammar that arise via internal processes and have no counterparts in either substrate or superstrate sources are of particular interest to universalist theories of creole origins. Such innovations may be due either to creativity in the process of creole formation itself, or to subsequent internally motivated change. In both cases, children may have played a vital role.

Some developments in the TMA system of Sranan will serve to illustrate these types of innovation. For example, the emergence of *go* as Future marker and *been* as Past marker seem to have been driven more by internal motivation than by either superstrate or substrate influence. This may explain why these forms were reinterpreted in similar ways in various Atlantic English creoles, as well as in Hawai'i Creole English. In the pidgin from which the latter developed, both forms already displayed the potential to develop into TMA markers (Siegel 2000). We can assume the same to be true in early Sranan and Caribbean English creoles generally. In both Hawai'i Creole English and Atlantic English creoles, the grammaticization of Future *go* was further encouraged by the existence of substrate and superstrate models in which a form derived from "go" indicated futurity. But in addition to this, the fact that *go* and other verbs of motion tend to develop into Future markers cross-linguistically (Bybee et al. 1994) suggests that universals were also at work. In the case of Past *been* in Sranan, however, no substrate model appears to have existed. Hence this is a likely candidate for an explanation in terms of universal principles of grammaticization (see Detgers 2000).

The emergence of auxiliary combinations in creoles is another internal development that seems to owe its origin partly to universal principles. Again, however, substrate influence played some role in the Atlantic creoles. For instance, the classic TMA ordering found in the Surinamese creoles has models in Gbe. Jondoh (1980: 52) informs us that this is the order of auxiliary elements in Gengbe. The following examples illustrate (ibid.:)

(30) Sranan: En dan a man ben musu e breiti
And then the man PAST MUST IMPFV happy
"So the man should have been happy"

(31) Gengbe: é lá téɰ no du glí
he FUT can PROG eat gali
"He will be able to eat gali"

Similarly, Siegel (2000: 221) suggests that auxiliary order in Hawai'i Creole English has a model in Portuguese.

In addition, however, the Surinamese and other Atlantic English creoles have far more complicated patterns of auxiliary ordering, all of which seem to have developed internally. The following examples from Sranan and Belize creole illustrate:

(32) Sranan, elicited: a. A ben e musu e taki nanga unu
T A M A
"S/he usually had to be talking with us"

Sranan, elicited: b. A ben sa e musu e wani go na foto
T M A M A
"S/he would have had to be wanting to go to Paramaribo"

(33) Belize Creole: a. Jan don mi wã di iit if i mi kom in taim
A T T A
"John would have already been eating if he had come in time"

Belize Creole: b. Jan mos mi wa kom ya laas nait if i mi de da
M T T
Belize
"John would certainly have come here last night if he was in Belize"

Again, without models in either the substrates or the superstrates, these complex tenses must be the result primarily of internal developments.

9.10.3 Grammaticalization in creoles

The emergence of grammatical categories in earlier creoles has sometimes been attributed to a process of "grammaticalization." This term has been defined in various ways (Joseph 2001: 165), but in general it refers to the language-internal process(es) by which grammatical morphemes develop gradually out of lexical morphemes (Bybee et al. 1994: 4–5). As Joseph (2001: 166) points out, the term "grammaticalization" is really a cover-term that describes the results of "other recognized mechanisms of change, especially sound change, analogy, or reanalysis." One example is the gradual reanalysis of the Old English verb *willan* "to want" as the Future tense auxiliary *will*. A similar example is the emergence of the modern Greek Future prefix *θa* from Medieval Greek structures like the following (Joseph 2001: 181):

(34) thélo: hina grápho:
want-1sg that write-1sg
"I want to write"
[lit.: "I-want that I-write"]

Later, through processes of phonological reduction, *thélo*: and *hina* became /θe/ and /na/ respectively. Thus we find future constructions like the following (ibid.):

(35) thé na grápho:
FUT write-1sg
"I will write"

Eventually, *θé* + *na* were further condensed to the modern Future form *θa*.

In short, grammaticalization involves gradual change that is internally motivated. Bruyn (1996: 30) has pointed out that the term, in its usual sense, should not be applied without qualification to the reanalysis of superstrate-derived items as creole grammatical categories. In the first place, this reanalysis is not gradual, but the result of a relatively rapid change. Second, it is promoted by external (usually substrate) influence, as opposed to purely language-internal motivation. This means that the creation of creole grammatical categories is due to direct calquing, unlike the processes of analogy, metaphorical transfer, and phonological reduction found in "ordinary" grammaticalization. The former type of innovation might instead be referred to as "grammaticization," to distinguish it from the more gradual historical process. Note, however, that some scholars use "grammaticization" as a synonym for "grammaticalization."

Note also that grammatical elements in some creoles appear to derive from superstrate grammatical morphemes that are simplified and reanalyzed. For example, Detgers (2000: 150ff) argues convincingly that the Past marker *te* of French-lexicon creoles derives from the French auxiliary *était*, used in constructions of the type *il était à écrire* "He was writing." This is somewhat different from the change of lexemes into grammatical formatives referred to above.

Some creole grammatical categories seem to emerge via calquing followed by internally driven processes of change. One such case is the development of the earlier Sranan Progressive marker *de* into an Imperfective. The progressive function of copula *de* was apparently due to substrate influence. Gbe, like other West African languages, uses the same form as both a locative copula and a progressive marker. The following Gengbe examples from Jondoh (1980: 46) illustrate:

(36) é lè ekplɔ̃-a ʤi
it be table-the on
"It's on the table"

(37) é lè nú ḍùḍǔ kɔ̀
he be thing eating at
"He's eating"

The progressive function seems to have been transferred to copula *de* in earlier Sranan, as in other Caribbean English creoles such as Belizean and some varieties of JC. In contemporary Sranan, however, *(d)e* functions as a true Imperfective marker, conveying notions such as "progressive" and "habitual" and used with predicates of all types, stative and non-stative. This development has no models in Gbe or other substrate languages, which employ distinct Habitual and Progressive categories. Nor did it take place in Belize or Jamaica. Hence the broadening of *de*'s functions seems to be an internally motivated development in Suriname. The change of Progressives into Imperfectives is of course common cross-linguistically (Bybee et al. 1994: 82) and seems to be promoted by similar principles of semantic extension.

We also find innovations in creole morphosyntax that are due to grammaticalization in the traditional sense. These represent another instance where universal principles of change shape the grammar of creoles. A case in point is the development of the modal auxiliary *man* in Sranan (van den Berg 2000; van den Berg and Arends 2001). In the contemporary language, *man* conveys the sense of ability constrained by physical law or other forces beyond the agent's control (Winford 2000c: 77). In the following example, a woman complains that poverty prevents her from being able to afford a peanut butter sandwich:

(38) A diri k'falek, yu no man bai en. Mi no man
It expensive terrible, you NEG can buy it. I NEG can
"It's terribly expensive. You can't buy it. I can't"

In early Sranan, however, *man* was clearly a noun, meaning "male human being." It was used in structures like the following:

(39) a. Mingo, yu no man
Mingo you NEG man
"Mingo, you're not man [enough] (You don't dare)" (Sranan text 1707; van den Berg 2000: 14)
b. Mi no man va hoppo dati
I NEG man for lift that
"I'm not man [strong] enough to lift that" (C. Schumann 1783)

Over time, its meaning must have extended from "being man enough" to "being strong enough" to "being physically able to" to the more general sense of ability it now conveys. The fact that a woman utters the example in (38) underscores the change.

Similar paths of internal change have occurred in all creoles, sometimes leading to drastic differences between the earlier and later stages of these languages. DeGraff (1999b: 497) points to various cases of "grammatical invention" in Haitian Creole that are due to such internal processes. These have caused contemporary Haitian to diverge significantly from earlier HC (see also Alleyne 2000).

9.11 Externally Motivated Change in Later Creole Development

In addition to the kinds of internally motivated changes discussed so far, creoles continue to change under external influence. Sranan, for example, borrowed the modal auxiliary *mag* from Dutch, the official language of Suriname. The modal expresses only permissibility, as in the following example:

(40) Yu mag go prei baka te yu kaba wasi den doti sani
you may go play after when you finish wash the-pl dirty thing
"You may go and play after you finish washing the dirty dishes"

There is also evidence of Dutch influence on certain areas of Sranan syntax, such as attributive (property) predication and comparative structures. With regard to the former, conservative varieties of Sranan employ structures in which the predicative property item is verbal, as in the following (Winford 1997b: 257f):

(41) a. A liba sa bradi
The river POT broad
"The river may be wide"
b. A pikin musu weri
"The child must be weary"
c. A watra faya tumsi
The water hot too-much
"The water is too hot"

However, in some (second language) varieties of contemporary Sranan, such structures are giving way to alternatives in which the copula *de* is used, suggesting that the property items are adjectives. The following illustrate:

(42) a. A liba sa de bradi
the river POT COP broad
"The river may be wide"
b. A pikin musu de weri
"The child must be weary"
c. A watra de tumsi faya
"The water is too hot"

This tendency is reinforced by the continuing borrowing of Dutch adjectives that require copula support, as in the following examples (Winford 1997b: 283):

(43) a. A man de ernstig
"The man is serious"
b. Mi de enthoesiast
"I'm enthusiastic"

With regard to comparatives, conservative Sranan also preserves structures like the following, in which a verb *moro* (< *more*) "surpass" conveys the comparison:

(44) Hertoch bigi moro Ronald
Hertoch big surpass Ronald
"Hertoch's bigger than Ronald"

Under Dutch influence, alternative comparative structures like the following have emerged:

(45) Hertoch de moro bigi leki Ronald
Hertoch COP more big than Ronald
"Hertoch is bigger than Ronald"

Here *moro* is an adverbial modifier qualifying the adjective *bigi*, and the comparative structure on the whole is closely modeled on that of Dutch. Many native speakers of conservative Sranan are aware of these changes, and comment openly on them (Winford 1997b: 278).

Varieties of Sranan spoken by native speakers of Dutch or Dutch-dominant have long been subject to these kinds of external influence (Eersel 1971). However, there is an increasing tendency for these changes to spread into native Sranan as well, especially among the young (Arends 1989: 51). This is not surprising, given that Sranan speakers are generally bilingual in Dutch.

We could adduce many further examples of more recent contact-induced changes in creoles. The most widely discussed cases of this are the Atlantic English-lexicon creoles outside of Suriname. These have been subject to continuing influence from English, and have converged toward the latter in a process known as "decreolization." Such creoles have always been part of a continuum ranging from more acrolectal (English-like) to mesolectal (intermediate) to basilectal (most divergent). Hence it is not always easy to identify the line separating the creole varieties from each other, and from the acrolect. This makes it difficult to determine which features of the more basilectal varieties are innovations due to external influence, as opposed to variation long inherent in the grammar. For example, basilectal Guyanese Creole employs modal auxiliaries like *wuda* "would" (< *would have*), *kuda* "could" (< *could have*), *shuda* "should" (< *should have*), etc., which compete with auxiliary combinations like *bin go/sa*, *bin kan*, *bin mos*, etc. respectively. The following are examples:

(46) a. Jan bin kyan kom yesidee
John PAST can come yesterday
"John could have come yesterday"

b. Jan bin go du am
John PAST FUT do it
"John would have done it"

(47) a. Jan kuda (bin) kom yesidee
"John could have come yesterday"

b. Jan wuda (bin) du am
"John would have done it"

Are the auxiliary combinations giving way to the single forms, or have they always been in competition? A comparison with the Surinamese creoles, which have only the auxiliary combinations, would suggest the former. If this is the case, did this process of change also occur in creoles like Jamaican, which disallows the combination Past + Future (*ben* + *wi*) but allows Past + Prospective (*ben a go*)? Did the contemporary JC Future auxiliary *wi* (< *will*) replace an earlier *go* future similar to that found in the eastern Caribbean English creoles?

Questions like this are almost impossible to answer, given the dearth of early textual evidence from these creoles. Yet some researchers (e.g., Alleyne 1980) believe that creoles like JC and GC were once much closer to the Surinamese creoles in many areas of their grammar. Further research will no doubt clarify whether this is true.

9.12 Summary

We've seen in this chapter that the languages called "creoles" include a diverse set of contact vernaculars that arose in European colonies in the fifteenth through nineteenth centuries. There are no absolute criteria, either sociolinguistic or structural, that define creoles as a type. In general, however, we can distinguish among them in terms of their degree of divergence from the European (superstrate) languages from which they derived most of (the phonological shapes of) their lexical and grammatical items. Creoles range from second language varieties that are close approximations to the superstrates, to "radical" outcomes that depart significantly from the latter. Between these two extremes there is a continuum of outcomes, with "intermediate" creoles like Bajan closer to the superstrate and "basilectal" creoles like rural Guyanese and Jamaican closer to the radical end. To a large extent, these differences are due to varying degrees of substratal influence from the L1s of their creators, as well as to internal developments within the creoles themselves.

These differences among creoles are due primarily to differences in the social contexts in which they were created. The relevant factors include the demographic make-up of the groups in contact, the types of community settings in which they interacted, and the social codes regulating that interaction. In general, creoles arose in plantation colonies where transplanted slaves or subjugated indigenes were subjected to control by smaller numbers of Europeans.

Intermediate creoles like Bajan and Reunionnais arose in small farm or homestead settings where there were higher or at least equal ratios of Europeans to slaves. These settings allowed for closer interaction between the groups over several decades, promoting the consolidation of second language varieties of the

European languages. The intermediate varieties display characteristics due to simplification and substrate influence, but these are far less pronounced than the continuities from their superstrate sources. In effect, then, these creoles are akin to colonial dialects of the European languages. Similar second language varieties arose even in classic plantation societies, within those sectors of the slave and free non-European population that had more privilege and hence greater access to the superstrate models.

In other colonies to which the plantation system was introduced early, the *société d'habitation* (homestead) phase of contact was neither long nor intense enough to override the effects of the massive demographic and sociopolitical changes that accompanied the rise of large plantations. In these cases, more radical creoles emerged among the majority of the slave population, particularly the field slaves. These outcomes displayed significant influence from substrate languages and from internally motivated innovations, resulting in greater divergence from their superstrates.

The effects of substratum influence on creoles can be found in many aspects of their phonology, lexicon, and (morpho-)syntax. At the same time, there are continuities from their superstrate sources, though that input was subjected to varying degrees of simplification and reanalysis. This accounts for characteristic features of creoles such as the loss of bound morphology and the reduction of case, gender, and other distinctions.

More radical creole formation involves a variety of complex interrelated processes by which learners restructure input (intake) from the source languages into new grammars. The various theories that attempt to account for this kind of language creation tend to focus on one or the other aspect of the process. Some argue for the primacy of the superstratal contribution, while others assign more significance to substrate influence. Still others maintain that universal principles of language acquisition account for much of creole grammar. These disagreements are compounded by a lack of consensus on the precise nature of the superstrate input to creole formation, particularly whether it consisted of a previous pidgin or second language varieties acquired by earlier slaves.

Despite these differences of opinion, creolists generally accept that creole formation was primarily a process of second language acquisition in rather unusual circumstances. Moreover, children may have played a role in regularizing the developing grammar. The processes of restructuring that created creoles are in principle the same as those found in SLA and to a lesser extent first language acquisition, modulo differences in the inputs and the social constraints on access to the target. In general, like SLA, creole formation involves the selective adaptation of both superstrate and substrate input, and is guided by universal principles of language acquisition and design. There is also agreement that radical creoles result from the continuing relearning of previously acquired contact varieties by successive waves of newly arrived slaves over several decades.

The restructuring of available materials into a creole grammar also involves processes familiar in SLA. First, processes of simplification operate on the available input to produce a maximally transparent grammar. Second, processes of elaboration come into play, reshaping previously acquired grammars by drawing more on L1 sources as well as internally driven change. This interaction between L1 knowledge and learners' intake from superstrate-derived input operates within the developing IL system itself – or more accurately, within the minds of individual learners creating IL systems or I-languages.

Various mechanisms and principles similar to those that operate in SLA guide this process of restructuring. Simplificatory processes are regulated by principles of economy and transparency. L1 influence, whether described as "relexification" or "transfer," leads to reanalysis of superstrate-derived lexical (and sometimes grammatical) forms in terms of substrate semantic and functional categories. Factors such as congruence and markedness determine which forms are selected and which features from the input will be retained. Processes of internally driven elaboration result in innovations peculiar to the creole. Such developments appear to be motivated by universal principles of acquisition and change.

Competition among features and innovations introduced into individual ILs is resolved in a process of leveling, via which a common core of features is retained and conventionalized in the new community language. Over time, other changes take place in creole grammar under both internal and external motivation. Processes of grammaticalization lead to the former, while continuing co-existence with an official language (usually but not always the lexifier) leads to contact-induced change.

The course of creole development and its relation to language evolution in general are neatly summed up by Ian Roberts (1999: 317): "Creoles are particularly interesting because they represent an extreme of language change, but it is the mechanisms of language change, which are ubiquitous in the history of every language and every language family, that have made creoles what they are."

Notes

1 In Barbados, a more divergent creole variety of English emerged among slaves in the later plantation settings, and apparently co-existed with the "intermediate" variety (Bajan) that had emerged earlier. This more "basilectal" variety still survives in isolated rural and coastal villages today (Rickford 1992; Roy 1986).

2 My thanks to Michel DeGraff for pointing this out.

3 For similar reasons, it seems preferable to use the term "nativization" rather than "creolization" to refer to the adoption of an erstwhile second language variety or lingua franca as a first language.

4 Migge (to appear: 5), apparently following Arends (1986), claims that Sranan Tongo has gone further than Ndjuka in extending the functions of *de*, using it also in equative constructions expressing class membership (that is, attributive predicate nominal structures), as in *Lina de wan datra* "Lina is a doctor." However, an analysis of my own Sranan data by Dawson (2002) shows that *(n)a* is the usual choice in these cases, though *de* is also sometimes used.

5 For a detailed discussion of these various theories, see Arends et al. (1995: chs 8–11).

References

Abdulaziz, Mohamed H. and Ken Osinde. 1997. Sheng and Engsh: development of mixed codes among the urban youth in Kenya. *International Journal of the Sociology of Language* 125, 43–63.

Agnihotri, Rama Kant. 1987. *Crisis of Identity: Sikhs in England.* New Delhi: Bahri Publications Private.

Alleyne, Mervyn. 1980. *Comparative Afro-American.* Ann Arbor: Karoma.

Alleyne, Mervyn. 2000. Opposite processes in "creolization." In Newmann-Holzschuh and Schneider 2000: 125–33.

Amuda, A. A. 1986. Yoruba/English code switching in Nigeria: Aspects of its functions and form. PhD dissertation, University of Reading.

Andersen, Roger. 1981. Two perspectives on pidginization as second language acquisition. In Roger Andersen (ed.) *New Dimensions in Second Language Acquisition Research*, 165–95. Rowley, Mass.: Newbury House.

Andersen, Roger W. 1983. Transfer to somewhere. In S. M. Gass and L. Selinker (eds) *Language Transfer in Language Learning*, 177–201. Rowley, Mass.: Newbury House.

Andersen, Roger W. 1984. The One to One Principle of interlanguage construction. *Language Learning* 34, 77–95.

Andersen, Roger W. 1990. Models, processes, principles and strategies: second language acquisition inside and outside the classroom. In Bill VanPatten and James F. Lee (eds) *Second Language Acquisition/Foreign Language Learning*, 45–66. Philadelphia: Multilingual Matters.

Aoun, Y. and D. Sportiche. 1983. On the formal theory of government. *Linguistic Review* 2.3, 211–36.

Appel, René. 1996. The lexicon in second language acquisition. In Peter Jordens and Josine Lalleman (eds) *Investigating Second Language Acquisition*, 381–403. Berlin: Mouton de Gruyter.

Appel, René and Pieter Muysken. 1987. *Language Contact and Bilingualism.* London: Edward Arnold.

Arends, Jacques. 1986. Genesis and development of the equative copula in Sranan. In Pieter Muysken and Norval Smith (eds) *Substrata versus Universals in Creole Genesis*, 103–27. Amsterdam: Benjamins.

Arends, Jacques. 1989. Syntactic developments in Sranan. PhD dissertation, University of Nijmegen.

Arends, Jacques. 1993. Towards a gradualist model of creolization. In Francis Byrne and John Holm (eds) *Atlantic Meets Pacific*, 371–80. Amsterdam: Benjamins.

Arends, Jacques (ed.). 1995a. *The Early Stages of Creolization*. Amsterdam: Benjamins.

Arends, Jacques. 1995b. Demographic factors in the formation of Sranan. In Arends 1995a: 233–85.

Arends, Jacques and Matthias Perl. 1995. *Early Suriname Creole texts: A Collection of 18th Century Sranan and Saramaccan Documents*. Frankfurt: Vervuert.

Arends, Jacques, Pieter Muysken, and Norval Smith (eds). 1995. *Pidgins and Creoles: An Introduction*. Amsterdam: Benjamins.

Auer, Peter. 1995. The pragmatics of code-switching: a sequential approach. In Lesley Milroy and Pieter Muysken (eds) *One Speaker, Two Languages: Cross-Disciplinary Perspectives on Code-Switching*, 115–35. Cambridge: Cambridge University Press.

Azuma, S. 1991a. Processing and intrasentential code switching. PhD dissertation, University of Texas at Austin.

Azuma, S. 1991b. Two level processing hypothesis in speech production: evidence from intrasentential code switching. Paper presented at the 27th meeting of the Chicago Linguistics Society.

Backus, A. 1990. Turkish–Dutch code switching and the frame process model. Paper presented at the International Workshop on Ethnic Minority Languages in Europe. Tilburg, Netherlands.

Backus, A. 1996. Two in one: bilingual speech of Turkish immigrants in the Netherlands. Doctoral dissertation, Katholieke Universiteit Brabant, Tilburg.

Bailey, Charles-James and K. Maroldt. 1977. The French lineage of English. In Jürgen M. Meisel (ed.) *Langues en contact – pidgins – créoles – Languages in Contact*, 21–53. Tübingen: TBL Verlag, G. Narr.

Baker, Philip. 1982. On the origins of the first Mauritians and of the creole language of their descendants: a refutation of Chaudenson's "Bourbonnais" theory. In Philip Baker and Chris Corne, *Isle de France Creole. Affinities and Origins*, 131–259. Ann Arbor: Karoma.

Baker, Philip. 1990. Off target. *Journal of Pidgin and Creole Languages* 5, 107–19.

Baker, Philip. 1993a. Australian influence on Melanesian Pidgin English. *Te Reo* 36, 3–67.

Baker, Philip. 1993b. Assessing the African contribution to French-based creoles. In Mufwene 1993: 123–55.

Baker, Philip. 1995. Some developmental inferences from the historical studies of pidgins and creoles. In Arends 1995a: 1–24.

Baker, Philip. 1996. The origins and diffusion of Pidgin English in the Pacific. In Stephen A. Wurm, Peter Mühlhäusler, and Darrell T. Tryon (eds) *Atlas of Intercultural Communication in the Pacific, Asia and the Americas*, vol. II.I, 551–94. Berlin: Mouton de Gruyter.

Baker, Philip. 1997. Directionality in pidginization and creolization. In Spears and Winford 1997: 91–109.

Baker, Philip. 2000. Theories of creolization and the degree and nature of restructuring. In Newmann-Holzschuh and Schneider 2000: 41–63.

Baker, Philip and Peter Mühlhäusler. 1990. From business to pidgin. *Journal of Asian Pacific Communication* 1, 87–115.

Bakker, Peter. 1994. Michif, the Cree–French mixed language of the Métis buffalo hunters in Canada. In Bakker and Mous 1994: 13–33.

Bakker, Peter. 1997. *A Language of Our Own. The Genesis of Michif, the Mixed Cree–French Language of the Canadian Métis*. Oxford: Oxford University Press.

Bakker, Peter and Maarten Mous (eds). 1994. *Mixed Languages: 15 Case Studies in Language Intertwining*. Amsterdam: Institute for Functional Research into Language and Language Use (IFOTT).

Bakker, Peter and Robert A. Papen. 1997. Michif: a mixed language based on Cree and French. In Thomason 1997a: 295–363.

Barnes, William. 1886. *A Glossary of the Dorset Dialect with a Grammar of its Word Shapening and Wording*. London: Trübner. (Reprinted 1970, Guernsey: Steven Cox, Toucan Press.)

Batibo, Herman. 1992. The fate of ethnic languages in Tanzania. In Brenzinger 1992a: 85–98.

Battistella, Edwin L. 1990. *Markedness: The Evaluative Superstructure of Language*. Albany: State University of New York Press.

Battistella, Edwin L. 1996. *The Logic of Markedness*. Oxford: Oxford University Press.

Bautista, M. L. S. 1980. *The Filipino Bilingual's Competence: A Model Based on an Analysis of Tagalog–English Code-Switching*. Pacific Linguistics Series C-59. Canberra: Australian National University.

Bavin, E. and T. Shopen. 1985. Warlpiri and English: languages in contact. In M. Clyne (ed.) *Australia: Meeting Place of Languages*. Pacific Linguistics Series C-92. Canberra: Australian National University.

Baxter, Allan N. 1985. A description of Papia Kristang (Malacca Creole Portuguese). PhD dissertation, Australian National University, Canberra.

Beckles, Hilary. 1989. *White Servitude and Black Slavery in Barbados, 1627–1715*. Knoxville: University of Tennessee Press.

Bentahila, Abdelâli and Eirlys Davies. 1983. The syntax of Arabic–French code switching. *Lingua* 59, 301–30.

Bentahila, Abdelâli and Eirlys E. Davies. 1992. Code-switching and language dominance. In R. J. Harris (ed.) *Cognitive Processing in Bilinguals*, 443–58. Amsterdam and New York: North-Holland, Elsevier Science.

Berk-Seligson, Susan. 1986. Linguistic constraints on intrasentential code switching: a study of Spanish/Hebrew bilingualism. *Language in Society* 15, 313–48.

Betz, Werner. 1949. *Deutsch und Lateinisch: die Lehnbildungen der altochdeutschen Benediktinerregel*. Bonn: H. Bouvier.

Bever, Thomas and D. Terence Langendoen. 1972. The interaction of speech perception and grammatical structure in the evolution of language. In R. Stockwell and R. Macaulay (eds) *Linguistic Change and Generative Theory*, 32–95. Bloomington: Indiana University Press.

Bickerton, Derek. 1981. *Roots of Language*. Ann Arbor: Karoma.

Bickerton, Derek. 1984. The language bioprogram hypothesis. *Behavioral and Brain Sciences* 7, 173–88.

Bickerton, Derek. 1999. How to acquire language without positive evidence: what acquisitionists can learn from creoles. In DeGraff 1999a: 49–74.

Bickmore, L. S. 1985. Hausa–English code switching. MA thesis, University of California at Los Angeles.

Bley-Vroman, R. W., S. W. Felix, and G. L. Ioup. 1988. The accessibility of universal grammar in adult language. *Second Language Research* 4, 1–32.

Bliss, A. J. 1972. Languages in contact: some problems of Hiberno-English. *Proceedings of the Royal Irish Academy* 72, 63–82.

Blom, J. P. and John J. Gumperz. 1972. Social meaning in linguistic structures: code-switching in Norway. In J. J. Gumperz and Dell Hymes (eds) *Directions in Sociolinguistics*, 407–34. New York: Holt, Rinehart and Winston.

Bloomfield, Leonard. 1927. Literate and illiterate speech. *American Speech* 2, 432–9.

Bloomfield, Leonard. 1933. *Language*. New York: Holt, Rinehart and Winston.

Boeschoten, H. and L. Verhoeven. 1985. Integration niederländischer lexicalischer Elemente ins Turkische: Sprachmischung bei Immigranten der ersten and zweiten Generation. *Linguistische Berichte* 98, 347–64.

Bokamba, E. 1988. Code-mixing, language variation, and linguistic theory: evidence from Bantu languages. *Lingua* 76, 21–62.

Boretzky, Norbert. 1985. Sind Zigeunersprachen kreols? In Norbert Boretzky, Werner Enninger, and Thomas Stolz (eds) *Akten des 1. Essener Kolloquiums uber "Kreolsprachen und Sprachkontakte*," 43–70. Bochum: Studienverlag Dr. N. Brockmeyer.

Boretzky, Norbert and Birgit Igla. 1994. Romani mixed dialects. In Bakker and Mous 1994: 35–68.

Bourhis, R. Y. 1979. Language in ethnic interaction: a social psychological approach. In Howard Giles and B. Saint-Jacques (eds) *Language and Ethnic Relations*, 117–41. Oxford: Pergamon.

Bourhis, R. Y., H. Giles, J. P. Leyens, and H. Tajfel. 1979. Psycholinguistic distinctiveness: language divergence in Belgium. In Howard Giles and R. St. Clair (eds) *Language and Social Psychology*, 158–85. Oxford: Blackwell.

Braidi, Susan M. 1999. *The Acquisition of Second Language syntax*. London: Arnold.

Braun, Maximilian. 1937. Beobachtungen zur Frage der Mehrsprachigkeit. *Göttingsche Gelehrte Anzeigen* 199, 116–30.

Breitborde, L. B. 1983. Levels of analysis in sociolinguistic explanation. *International Journal of the Sociology of Language* 39, 5–34.

Brenzinger, Matthias. 1987. Die sprachliche und kulturelle Stellung der Mbugu (Ma'a). MA thesis, University of Cologne.

Brenzinger, Matthias (ed.). 1992a. *Language Death: Factual and Theoretical Explorations with Special Reference to East Africa*. Berlin: Mouton de Gruyter.

Brenzinger, Matthias. 1992b. Lexical retention in language shift: Yaaku/Mukogodo-Maasai and Elmolo/Elmolo-Samburu. In Brenzinger 1992a: 213–54.

Brenzinger, Matthias and Gerrit J. Dimmendaal. 1992. Social contexts of language death. In Brenzinger 1992a: 3–5.

Bresnan, Joan. 2000. Pidgin genesis and optimality theory. In Jeff Siegel (ed.) *Processes of Language Contact: Studies from Australia and the South Pacific*, 145–73. Montréal: Fides.

Broch, Ingvild and Ernst Håkon Jahr. 1984. Russenorsk: a new look at the Russo-Norwegian pidgin in northern Norway. In P. Sture Ureland and Iain Clarkson (eds) *Scandinavian Language Contacts*, 21–65. Cambridge: Cambridge University Press.

Broch, Olaf. 1927. Russenorsk. *Archiv für slavische Philologie* 41, 209–67.

Brown, H. D. 1980. *Principles of Language Learning and Teaching*. Englewood Cliffs, N.J.: Prentice Hall.

Bruyn, Adrienne. 1994. Some remarkable facts in Sranan: a discussion of possible accounts. Paper presented at the joint meeting of the SCL and SPCL. Georgetown, Guyana.

Bruyn, Adrienne. 1996. On identifying instances of grammaticalization in Creole languages. In Philip Baker and Anand Syea (eds) *Changing Meanings, Changing Functions: Papers Relating to Grammaticalization in Contact Languages*, 29–46. London: University of Westminster Press.

Butterworth, G. and E. Hatch. 1978. A Spanish-speaking adolescent's acquisition of English syntax. In E. Hatch (ed.) *Second Language Acquisition: A Book of Readings*, 231–45. Rowley, Mass.: Newbury House.

Bybee, Joan and Oesten Dahl. 1989. The creation of tense and aspect systems in the languages of the world. *Studies in Language* 13.1, 51–103.

Bybee, Joan, W. Pagliuca, and R. Perkins. 1994. *The Evolution of Grammar: Tense, Aspect and Modality in the Languages of the World*. Chicago: University of Chicago Press.

Camden, Pastor B. 1979. Parallels in structure of lexicon and syntax between New Hebrides Bislama and the South Santo language as spoken at Tangoa. In Peter Mühlhäusler et al. (eds) *Papers in Pidgin and Creole Linguistics, No. 2*, 51–117. Pacific Linguistics Series A-57. Canberra: Australian National University.

Campbell, Lyle. 1976. Language contact and sound change. In W. Christie (ed.) *Current Progress in Historical Linguistics*, 181–94. Amsterdam: North-Holland.

Campbell, Lyle and Martha C. Muntzel. 1989. The structural consequences of language death. In Dorian 1989: 181–96.

Campbell, Lyle, Terrence Kaufman, and Thomas Smith-Stark. 1986. Meso-America as a linguistic area. *Language* 62.3, 530–70.

Cancino, H., E. J. Rosansky, and J. Schumann. 1978. The acquisition of English negatives and interrogatives by native Spanish speakers. In E. Hatch (ed.) *Second Language Acquisition: A Book of Readings*, 207–30. Rowley, Mass.: Newbury House.

Carmichael, A. C. 1833. *Domestic Manners and Social Conditions of the White, Coloured and Negro Population of the West Indies*, vols 1 and 2. London: Whittaker, Treacher.

Carter, Hazel. 1979. Evidence for the survival of African prosodies in West Indian creoles. *Society for Caribbean Linguistics, Occasional Paper* 13.

Carter, Hazel. 1987. Suprasegmentals in Jamaican: some African comparisons. In Glenn Gilbert (ed.) *Pidgin and Creole Languages: Essays in Memory of John E. Reinecke*, 213–63. Honolulu: University of Hawaii Press.

Chaudenson, Robert. 1992. *Des îsles, des hommes, des langues*. Paris: L'Harmattan.

Chaudenson, Robert. 1996. Démystification de la relexification. *Études Créoles* XIX. 1, 93–109.

Chaudenson, Robert. 2001. *Creolization of Language and Culture*. London and New York: Routledge. (Revised version of Chaudenson 1992, in collaboration with Salikoko Mufwene.)

Cheng, Robert L. 1985. A comparison of Taiwanese, Taiwan Mandarin, and Peking Mandarin. *Language* 61.2, 352–77.

Childs, G. Tucker. 1997. The status of Isicamtho, an Nguni-based urban variety of Soweto. In Spears and Winford 1997: 341–70.

Chomsky, Noam. 1981. *Lectures on Government and Binding*. Dordrecht: Foris.

Clahsen, H. 1984. The acquisition of German word order: a test case for cognitive approaches to L2 development. In R. W. Andersen (ed.) *Second Languages: A Cross-Linguistic Perspective*, 219–42. Rowley, Mass.: Newbury House.

Clark, Ross. 1979. In search of Beach-la-Mar. Towards a history of Pacific Pidgin English. *Te Reo* 22, 3–64.

Clark, Ross. 1983. Social contexts of early South Pacific pidgins. In Ellen Woolford and William Washabaugh (eds) *The Social Contexts of Creolization*, 10–27. Ann Arbor: Karoma.

Clements, J. Clancy. 1996. *The Genesis of a Language: The Formation and Development of Korlai Portuguese*. Amsterdam: Benjamins.

Clyne, Michael G. 1987a. Constraints on code switching: how universal are they? *Linguistics* 25, 739–64.

Clyne, Michael G. 1987b. History of research on language contact. In H. von Ulrich Ammon, Norbert Dittmar, and Klaus J. Mattheier (eds) *Sociolinguistics – Soziolinguistik*, vol. 1, 452–9. Berlin: Walter de Gruyter.

Coelho, F. A. 1880–6. Os dialectos românicos ou neolatinos na África, Asia, e América. *Bolletim da Sociedade de Geografica de Lisboa*. (Republished in J. Morais-Barbosa (ed.) 1967, *Crioulos: estudos linguísticos. Introducas e notous de Jorge Morais-Barbosa*, 1–234. Lisbon: Academia Internacional de Cultura Portuguesa.)

Corne, Chris. 1982. A contrastive analysis of Reunion and Isle de France Creole French: two typologically diverse languages. In Philip Baker and Chris Corne *Isle de France Creole: Affinities and Origins*, 8–129. Ann Arbor: Karoma.

Corne, Chris (ed.). 1999. *From French to Creole: The Development of New Vernaculars in the French Colonial World*. Westminster Creolistics Series 5. London: University of Westminster Press.

Coromines, J. 1967. *Breve diccionario etimológico de la lengua castelleana*. Madrid: Biblioteca románica hispánica.

Coupland, N. 1984. Accommodation at work: some phonological data and their implications. *International Journal of the Sociology of Language* 46, 49–70.

Craddock, Jerry R. 1981. New World Spanish. In Charles A. Ferguson and Shirley Brice Heath (eds) *Language in the USA*, 196–217. Cambridge: Cambridge University Press.

Crawhall, Nigel. 1990. Unpublished Shona/English data.

Croft, William. 1990. *Typology and Universals*. Cambridge: Cambridge University Press.

Dalton-Puffer, Christiane. 1996. *The French Influence on Middle English Morphology*. Berlin and New York: Mouton de Gruyter.

Dawkins, R. M. 1916. *Modern Greek in Asia Minor: A Study of the Dialects of Sílli, Cappadocia and Phárasa with Grammars, Texts, Translations and Glossary*. Cambridge: Cambridge University Press.

Dawson, Hope. 2001. The linguistic effects of the Norse invasion of England. Unpublished ms, Dept of Linguistics, Ohio State University.

Dawson, Hope. 2002. The copulas in Sranan Tongo. Unpublished research paper. Dept of Linguistics, Ohio State University.

Dawson, R. 1830. *The Present State of Australia: [. . .]*. London: Smith, Elder.

DeCamp, David. 1977. The development of Pidgin and Creole studies. In Albert Valdman (ed.) *Pidgin and Creole Linguistics*, 3–20. Bloomington: Indiana University Press.

DeGraff, Michel (ed.). 1999a. *Language Creation and Language Change: Creolization, Diachrony and Development*. Cambridge, Mass.: MIT Press.

DeGraff, Michel. 1999b. Creolization, language change, and language acquisition: an epilogue. In DeGraff 1999a: 473–543.

DeGraff, Michel. 2001. Morphology in creole genesis: linguistics and ideology. In Michael Kenstowicz (ed.) *Ken Hale: A Life in Language*, 53–121. Cambridge, Mass.: MIT Press.

DeGraff, Michel. To appear. Morphology and word order in "creolization" and beyond. In Guglielmo Cinque and Richard Kayne (eds) *Handbook of Comparative Syntax*. New York: Oxford University Press.

Detgers, Ulrich. 2000. Two types of restructuring in French creoles: a cognitive approach to the genesis of tense markers. In Newmann-Holzschuh and Schneider 2000: 135–62.

Devonish, Hubert. 1989. *Talking in Tones*. London: Karia Press.

Dimmendaal, Gerrit. 1992. Reduction in Kore reconsidered. In Brenzinger 1992a: 117–35.

DiSciullo, A. M., P. Muysken, and R. Singh. 1986. Government and code-mixing. *Journal of Linguistics* 22, 1–24.

Dorian, Nancy. 1978. The fate of morphological complexity in language death: evidence from East Sutherland Gaelic. *Language* 54, 590–609.

Dorian, Nancy. 1981. *Language Death: The Life Cycle of a Scottish Gaelic Dialect*. Philadelphia: University of Pennsylvania Press.

Dorian, Nancy (ed.). 1989. *Investigating Obsolescence: Studies in Language Contraction and Death*. Cambride: Cambridge University Press.

Doron, E. 1983. On formal models of code switching. *Texas Linguistics Forum* 22, 35–59.

Drechsel, Emanuel J. 1981. A preliminary sociolinguistic comparison of four indigenous pidgin languages of North America (with notes towards a sociolinguistic typology in American Indian Linguistics). *Anthropological Linguistics* 23.3, 93–112.

Drechsel, Emanuel J. 1996. Native American contact languages of the contiguous United States. In Stephen A. Wurm, Peter Mühlhäusler, and Darrell T. Tryon (eds) *Atlas of Intercultural Communication in the Pacific, Asia and the Americas*, vol. II.2, 1213–39. Berlin: Mouton de Gruyter.

Dressler, Wolfgang U. 1985. On the predictiveness of natural morphology. *Journal of Linguistics* 21, 321–37.
Dressler, Wolfgang and Ruth Wodak-Leodolter. 1977. Language preservation and death in Brittany. *International Journal of the Sociology of Language* 12, 33–44.
Dreyfuss, Gail Raimi and Djoehana Oka. 1979. Chinese Indonesian: a new kind of language hybrid? *Papers in Pidgin and Creole Linguistics* 2, 247–74. Pacific linguistics series, no. 57. Canberra: Research School for Pacific Studies.
Dusková, Libuse. 1984. Similarity – an aid or hindrance in foreign language learning? *Folia Linguistica* 18, 103–15.
Dutton, Tom. 1997. Hiri Motu. In Thomason 1997a: 9–41.
Eckman, Fred R. 1977. Markedness and the contrastive analysis hypothesis. *Language Learning* 27, 315–30.
Eckman, Fred R. 1985. Some theoretical and pedagogical implications of the markedness differential hypothesis. *Studies in Second Language Acquisition* 7, 289–307.
Eckman, Fred R., E. A. Moravcsik, and J. R. Wirth. 1989. Implicational universals and interrogative structures in the interlanguage of ESL learners. *Language Learning* 39, 173–205.
Eersel, Christian. 1971. Prestige in choice of language and linguistic form. In Hymes 1971a: 317–22.
Ellis, R. 1994. *The Study of Second Language Acquisition.* Oxford: Oxford University Press.
Elworthy, Frederick Thomas. 1877. *An Outline of the Grammar of the Dialect of West Somerset. Illustrated by Examples of the Common Phrases and Modes of Speech Now in Use Among the People.* London: Trübner.
Elworthy, Frederick Thomas. 1886. *The West Somerset Word Book: A Glossary of Dialectal and Archaic Words and Phrases used in the West of Somerset and East Devon.* London: Trübner.
Emeneau, Murray B. 1962. *Brahui and Dravidian Comparative Grammar.* University of California Publications in Linguistics 27. Berkeley and Los Angeles: University of California Press.
Emeneau, Murray B. 1980. *Language and Linguistic Area.* Stanford: Stanford University Press.
Escure, Genevieve. 1997. *Creole and Dialect Continua: Standard Acquisition Processes in Belize and China.* Amsterdam: Benjamins.
Extra, Guus and Roeland van Hout. 1996. Second language acquisition by adult immigrants: a multiple case study of Turkish and Moroccan learners of Dutch. In Peter Jordens and Josine Lalleman (eds) *Investigating Second Language Acquisition*, 87–113. Berlin: Mouton de Gruyter.
Fasold, Ralph. 1984. *The Sociolinguistics of Society.* Oxford: Blackwell.
Felix, Sascha W. 1977. Early syntactic development in first and second language acquisition. In C. A. Henning (ed.) *Proceedings of the Los Angeles Second Language Research Forum*, 147–59. Los Angeles: University of California at Los Angeles.
Felix, Sascha W. 1997. Universal Grammar in L2 acquisition: some thoughts on Schachter's Incompleteness Hypothesis. In Lynn Eubank, Larry Selinker, and Michael

Sharwood Smith (eds) *The Current State of Interlanguage*, 139–51. Amsterdam: Benjamins.

Ferguson, Charles A. 1964. Diglossia. In Dell Hymes (ed.) *Language in Culture and Society*, 429–39. New York: Harper and Row. (Reprinted from *Word* 15 (1959), 325–40.)

Filppula, M. 1991. Subordinating *and* in Hiberno-English: Irish or English origin? In P. Ureland and G. Broderick (eds) *Language Contact in the British Isles*, 617–31. Tübingen: Max Niemeyer.

Fishman, Joshua A. 1964. Language maintenance and language shift as a field of inquiry. *Linguistics* 9, 32–70.

Fishman, Joshua A. 1965. Who speaks what language to whom and when? *La Linguistique* 2, 67–8.

Fishman, Joshua A. 1972. Domains and the relationship between micro- and macro-sociolinguistics. In J. J. Gumperz and Dell Hymes (eds) *Directions in Sociolinguistics*, 435–53. New York: Holt, Rinehart and Winston.

Fishman, Joshua. 1991. *Reversing Language Shift: Theoretical and Empirical Foundations of Assistance to Threatened Languages*. Clevedon: Multilingual Matters.

Fishman, Joshua (ed.). 2001. *Can Threatened Languages Be Saved? Reversing Language Shift, Revisited: A 21st Century Perspective*. Clevedon: Multilingual Matters.

Fishman, Joshua and Lawrence Greenfield. 1970. Situational measures of normative language views in relation to person, place and topic among Puerto Rican bilinguals. *Anthropos* 65, 602–18.

Fishman, Joshua, V. Nihitny, J. Hoffman, and R. Hayden. 1966. *Language Loyalty in the United States*. The Hague: Mouton.

Flege, J. E. 1987. Effects of equivalence classification on the production of foreign language speech sounds. In A. James and J. Leather (eds) *Sound Patterns in Second Language Acquisition*, 9–39. Dordrecht: Foris.

Forson, B. 1979. Code switching in Akan–English bilingualism. PhD dissertation, University of California at Los Angeles.

Fox, James A. 1983. Simplified input and negotiation in Russenorsk. In Roger W. Andersen (ed.) *Pidginization and Creolization as Language Acquisition*, 94–108. Rowley, Mass.: Newbury House.

Frangoudaki, Anna. 1992. Diglossia and the present language situation in Greece: a sociological approach to the interpretation of diglossia and some hypotheses on today's linguistic reality. *Language in Society* 21, 365–81.

Fuller, Janet M. 1996. When cultural maintenance means linguistic convergence: Pennsylvania German evidence for the Matrix Language Turnover Hypothesis. *Language in Society* 25, 493–514.

Gal, Susan. 1979. *Language Shift: Social Determinants of Linguistic Change in Bilingual Austria*. New York: Academic Press.

Gardner-Chloros, Penelope. 1985. Choix et alternance des langues à Strasbourg. Thèse pour l'obtention du doctorat en psychologie, Université Louis Pasteur, Strasbourg.

Gardner-Chloros, Penelope. 1991. *Language Selection and Switching in Strasbourg*. Oxford: Clarendon Press.

Gardner-Chloros, Penelope. 1995. Code-switching in community, regional and national repertoires: the myth of the discreteness of linguistic systems. In Lesley Milroy and Pieter Muysken (eds) *One Speaker, Two Languages: Cross-Disciplinary Perspectives on Code Switching*, 68–89. Cambridge: Cambridge University Press.

Garrett, M. F. 1988. Process in sentence production. In F. Newmeyer (ed.) *Linguistics: The Cambridge Survey*, vol. III, 69–96. Cambridge: Cambridge University Press.

Garrett, M. F. 1990. Sentence processing. In D. Osherson and H. Lasnick (eds) *An Invitation to Cognitive Science*, 133–75. Cambridge, Mass.: MIT Press.

Gass, Susan M. 1979. Language transfer and universal grammatical relations. *Language Learning* 29, 327–44.

Gass, Susan M. 1980. An investigation of syntactic transfer in adult second language learners. In R. C. Scarcella and S. D. Krashen (eds) *Research in Second Language Acquisition*, 132–41. Rowley, Mass.: Newbury House.

Gass, Susan M. 1983. Language transfer and universal grammatical relations. In S. M. Gass and L. Selinker (eds) *Language Transfer in Language Learning*, 69–82. Rowley, Mass.: Newbury House.

Gass, Susan M. 1997. Universals, SLA, and language pedagogy: 1984 revisited. In Lynn Eubank, Larry Selinker, and Michael Sharwood Smith (eds) *The Current State of Interlanguage*, 31–42. Amsterdam: Benjamins.

Giles, Howard, R. Y. Bourhis, and D. M. Taylor. 1977. Towards a theory of language in ethnic group relations. In Howard Giles (ed.) *Language, Ethnicity and Inter-group Relations*, 307–48. London: Academic Press.

Giles, Howard, Nikolas Coupland, and Justine Coupland. 1991. Accommodation theory: communication, context and consequence. In Howard Giles, Justine Coupland, and Nikolas Coupland (eds) *Contexts of Accommodation: Developments in Applied Sociolinguistics*, 1–68. Cambridge: Cambridge University Press.

Giles, Howard, A. Mulac, J. J. Bradac, and P. Johnson. 1987. Speech accommodation theory: the next decade and beyond. In M. Mclaughlin (ed.) *Communication Yearbook 10*, 13–48. Newbury Park, Calif.: Sage.

Giles, W. E. 1968. *A Cruise in a Queensland Labour Vessel to the South Seas*. Canberra: Australian National University Press.

Gilman, C. 1979. Cameroonian Pidgin English: a neo-African language. In Ian Hancock, E. Polomé, M. Goodman, and B. Heine (eds) *Readings in Creole Studies*, 269–80. Ghent: E. Story-Scientia.

Goddard, Ives. 1997. Pidgin Delaware. In Thomason 1997a: 43–98.

Golovko, Evgenij V. 1996. A case of nongenetic development in the Arctic area: the contribution of Aleut and Russian to the formation of Copper Island Aleut. In Ernst Håkon Jahr and Ingvild Broch (eds) *Language Contact in the Arctic: Northern Pidgins and Contact Languages*, 63–77. Berlin: Mouton de Gruyter.

Golovko, Evgenij V. and Nikolai B. Vakhtin. 1990. Aleut in contact: the CIA enigma. *Acta Linguistica Hafniensia* 22, 97–125.

Gonzales, Ambrose. 1922. *The Black Border: Gullah Stories of the Carolina Coast*. Columbia, S.C.: State Company.

Gooden, Shelome. 2001. A case for distributive reduplication in Jamaican Creole. Unpublished ms submitted as a pre-candidacy paper, Dept of Linguistics, Ohio State University.

Goodman, J. S. 1967. The development of a dialect of English–Japanese pidgin. *Anthropological Linguistics* 9.6, 43–55.

Goodman, Morris. 1964. *A Comparative Study of French Creole Dialects*. The Hague: Mouton.

Graham, C. Ray and R. Kirk Belnap. 1986. The acquisition of lexical boundaries in English by native speakers of Spanish. *International Review of Applied Linguistics* 24, 275–86.

Grant, Anthony P. 1996. Chinook Jargon and its distribution in the Pacific Northwest and beyond. In Stephen A. Wurm, Peter Mühlhäusler, and Darrell T. Tryon (eds) *Atlas of Intercultural Communication in the Pacific, Asia and the Americas*, vol. II.2, 1185–1208. Berlin: Mouton de Gruyter.

Greenberg, Joseph H. 1966. *Language Universals, with Special Reference to Feature Hierarchies*. Janua Linguarum, Series Minor, 59. The Hague: Mouton.

Greenfield, Lawrence and Joshua A. Fishman. 1968. Situational measures of language use in relation to person, place and topic among Puerto Rican bilinguals. In Joshua A. Fishman, Robert L. Cooper, Roxana Ma, et al. (eds) *Bilingualism in the Barrio*, 430–58. New York: Yeshiva University Press.

Greenfield, W. 1830. *A Defense of the Surinam Negro-English version of the New Testament. . . .* London: Bagster. (Reprinted in the *Journal of Pidgin and Creole Languages* (1986) 1.2, 259–66ff.)

Grosjean, F. 1982. *Life with Two Languages: An Introduction to Bilingualism*. Cambridge, Mass.: Harvard University Press.

Grosjean, F. 1988. Exploring the recognition of guest words in bilingual speech. *Language and Cognitive Processes* 3, 233–74.

Gumperz, John J. 1977. The social significance of conversational code switching. *Regional English Language Center Journal* 8.2, 1–34.

Gumperz, John J. 1982. *Discourse Strategies*. Cambridge: Cambridge University Press.

Gumperz, John J. and Robert Wilson. 1971. Convergence and creolization: a case from the Indo-Aryan/Dravidian border in India. In Hymes 1971a: 151–67.

Gundel, J. K. and E. E. Tarone. 1983. Language transfer and the acquisition of pronominal anaphora. In S. M. Gass and L. Selinker (eds) *Language Transfer in Language Learning*, 281–96. Rowley, Mass.: Newbury House.

Gupta, Anthea Fraser. 1992. Contact features of Singapore Colloquial English. In Kingsley Bolton and Helen Kwok (eds) *Sociolinguistics Today: International Perspectives*, 323–45. London: Routledge.

Guthrie, Malcolm. 1967–71. *Comparative Bantu: An Introduction to the Comparative Linguistics and Prehistory of the Bantu Languages*. 4 vols. Farnborough: Gregg.

Hamers, Josiane F. and Michel H. A. Blanc. 1989. *Bilinguality and Bilingualism*. Cambridge: Cambridge University Press.

Hammarberg, Björn. 1997. Conditions on transfer in phonology. In Allan James and Jonathan Leather (eds) *Second-Language Speech: Structure and Process*, 161–80. Berlin: Mouton de Gruyter.

Hanbury, David T. 1904 [1902]. *Sport and Travel in the Northland of Canada*. New York: Macmillan.

Hancock, Ian. 1984. Shelta and Polari. In Peter Trudgill (ed.) *Language in the British Isles*, 384–403. Cambridge: Cambridge University Press.

Harding, E. 1984. Foreigner talk: a conversational-analysis approach. In Mark Sebba and Loreto Todd (eds) *Papers from the York Creole Conference, September 24–27 1983*, 141–52. York Papers in Linguistics 11. Heslington: University of York.

Harris, John. 1984. Syntactic variation and dialect divergence. *Journal of Linguistics* 20, 303–27.

Harris, John. 1986. Expanding the superstrate: habitual aspect markers in Atlantic Englishes. *English World-Wide* 7, 2, 171–99.

Harris, John. 1993. The grammar of Irish English. In James Milroy and Lesley Milroy (eds) *Real English: The Grammar of English Dialects in the British Isles*, 139–86. London: Longman.

Haugen, Einar. 1950a. Problems of bilingualism. *Lingua* 2, 271–90.

Haugen, Einar. 1950b. The analysis of linguistic borrowing. *Language* 26, 210–31.

Haugen, Einar. 1953. *The Norwegian Language in America: A Study in Bilingual Behavior. Vol. 1: The Bilingual Community; Vol. II: The American Dialects of Norwegian.* Bloomington: Indiana University Press. (Reprinted 1969.)

Haugen, Einar. 1978. Bilingualism, language contact, and immigrant languages in the United States: a research report 1956–1970. In Joshua Fishman (ed.) *Advances in the Study of Societal Multilingualism*, 1–112, The Hague: Mouton.

Heath, Jeffrey. 1978. *Linguistic Diffusion in Arnhem Land*. Australian Aboriginal Studies: Research and Regional Studies 13. Canberra: Australian Institute of Aboriginal Studies.

Heath, Jeffrey. 1981. A case of intensive lexical diffusion. *Language* 57, 335–67.

Heath, Jeffrey. 1984. Language contact and language change. *Annual Review of Anthropology* 13, 367–84.

Heller, Monica. 1982. Negotiations of language choice in Montréal. In John J. Gumperz, (ed.) *Language and Social Identity*, 108–18. Cambridge: Cambridge University Press.

Heller, Monica. 1985. Ethnic relations and language use in Montréal. In Nessa Wolfson and Joan Manes (eds) *Language of Inequality*, 75–90. Berlin: Mouton.

Heller, Monica. 1988. Strategic ambiguity: code-switching in the management of conflict. In Monica Heller (ed.) *Code Switching: Anthropological and Sociolinguistic Perspectives*, 77–96. Berlin: Mouton de Gruyter.

Heller, Monica. 1995. Code switching and the politics of language. In Lesley Milroy and Pieter Muysken (eds) *One Speaker, Two Languages: Cross-Disciplinary Perspectives on Code Switching*, 158–74. Cambridge: Cambridge University Press.

Henderson, Eugenia J. A. 1965. The topography of certain phonetic and morphological characteristics of South East Asian languages. *Lingua* 15, 400–34.

Herbert, Robert K. 1995. The sociohistory of clicks in Southern Bantu. In Rajend Mesthrie (ed.) *Language and Social History: Studies in South African Sociolinguistics*, 51–67. Cape Town: David Philip.

Herzog, George. 1941. Culture change and language: shifts in the Pima vocabulary. In Leslie Spier, A. Irving Hallowell, and Stanley S. Newman (eds) *Language, Culture and Personality. Essays in Memory of Edward Sapir*, 66–74. Menasha, Wis.: Sapir Memorial Publication Fund.

Hesseling, Dirk Christiaan. 1897. Het Hollandsch in Zuid-Afrika. *De Gids* 60.1, 138–62. (Reprinted in English in Dirk Hesseling (1979) *On the Origin and Formation of Creoles: A Miscellany of Articles*, 1–22. Ann Arbor: Karoma.)

Hesseling, Dirk Christiaan. 1899. *Het Afrikaansch: Bijdrage tot de geschiedenis der Nederlandsche taal in Zuid-Afrika*. Leiden: Brill.

Hesseling, Dirk Christiaan. 1905. *Het Negerhollands der Deense Antillen: Bijdrage tot de geschiedenis der Nederlandsche taal in Amerika*. Leiden: Sijthoff.

Hilts, Craig. 2001. A featural presentation of Atepec Zapotec–Spanish linguistic contact. Qualifying paper, linguistics, Ohio State University, spring.

Hinnenkamp, V. 1982. *Foreigner Talk and Tarzanisch*. Hamburg: Helmut Buske Verlag.

Hinnenkamp, V. 1984. Eye-witnessing Pidginization? Structural and sociolinguistic aspects of German and Turkish foreigner talk. In Mark Sebba and Loreto Todd (eds) *Papers from the York Creole Conference, September 24–27 1983*, 153–66. York Papers in Linguistics 11. Heslington: University of York.

Hinskens, Frans. 1998. Dialect leveling: a two dimensional process. In P. Auer (ed.) *Dialect Levelling and the Standard Varieties in Europe*, special issue of *Folia Linguistica* 32.1–2, 35–51.

Hinskens, Frans and K. Mattheier (eds). 1996. *Convergence and Divergence of Dialects in Europe*. Special issue of *Sociolinguistica* 10.

Ho, Mian-Lian and John T. Platt. 1993. *Dynamics of a Contact Continuum: Singapore English*. Oxford: Clarendon Press.

Hock, Hans. 1991. *Principles of Historical Linguistics*. 2nd edition. Berlin: Mouton de Gruyter.

Hoeks, Jimmy A. 1985. Transfer of homonymy and polysemy with special reference to Dutch and English. *Toegepaste Taalwetenschap in Artikelen* 23, 45–54.

Hoetink, Harmannus. 1967. *The Two Variants in Caribbean Race Relations*. Oxford: Oxford University Press.

Holm, John. 1988. *Pidgins and Creoles*. Vol. 1. Cambridge: Cambridge University Press.

Holm, John. 1989. *Pidgins and Creoles*. Vol. 2. Cambridge: Cambridge University Press.

Hosali, Priya. 1992. Syntactic peculiarities of Butler English. *South Asian Language Review* 2.2, 58–74.

Huang, J. and E. Hatch. 1978. A Chinese child's acquisition of English. In E. Hatch (ed.) *Second Language Acquisition: A Book of Readings*, 118–31. Rowley, Mass.: Newbury House.

Huber, Magnus and Mikael Parkvall. 1999. *Spreading the Word: The Issue of Diffusion among the Atlantic Creoles*. Westminster Creolistics Series 6. London: University of Westminster Press.

Hudson, Alan. 1992. Diglossia: a bibliographic review. *Language in Society* 21, 611–74.

Huebner, Thom. 1983. *A Longitudinal Analysis of the Acquisition of English*. Ann Arbor: Karoma.

Hulstijn, J. H. 1990. A comparison between the information-processing and the analysis/control approaches to language learning. *Applied Linguistics* 11, 30–45.

Huttar, George and Frank J. Velantie. 1997. Ndjuka–Trio Pidgin. In Thomason 1997a: 99–124.

Hylstenstam, K. 1981. The use of typological markedness conditions as predictors in second language acquisition. Paper presented at the European–North American Workshop on Cross-Linguistic Second Language Acquisition Research. Los Angeles.

Hymes, Dell. 1962. The ethnography of speaking. In T. Gladwin and W. C. Sturtevant (eds) *Anthropology and Human Behavior*, 15–53. Washington, D.C.: Anthropological Society of Washington.

Hymes, Dell (ed.). 1971a. *Pidginization and Creolization of Languages*. Cambridge: Cambridge University Press.

Hymes, Dell. 1971b. Section III. General conceptions of process: introduction. In Hymes 1971a: 65–90.

Ijaz, I. Helene. 1986. Linguistic and cognitive determinants of lexical acquisition in a second language. *Language Learning* 36, 401–51.

Ishiwata, Toshio. 1986. English borrowings in Japanese. In Wolfgang Viereck and Wolf-Dietrich Bald (eds) *English in Contact with Other Languages: Studies in Honor of Broder Carstensen on the Occasion of his 60th Birthday*, 457–71. Budapest: Akadémia Kiado.

Jahr, Ernst Håkon. 1996. On the pidgin status of Russenorsk. In Ernst Håkon Jahr and Ingvild Broch (eds) *Language Contact in the Arctic: Northern Pidgins and Contact Languages*, 107–22. Berlin: Mouton de Gruyter.

Jake, Janice and Carol Myers-Scotton. 1992. Testing the fit: syntactic theory and intrasentential codeswitching. Paper presented at the Annual Meeting of the Linguistic Society of America.

Jakobson, Roman. 1938. Sur la théorie des affinités phonologiques entre des langues. *Actes du Quatrième Congrès Internationale de Linguistes*, 48–59. (Reprinted in Jakobson (1962) *Selected Writings*, vol. 1, 234–46. The Hague: Mouton.)

Jarvis, Scott and Terence Odlin. 2000. Morphological type, spatial reference and language transfer. *Studies in Second Language Acquisition* 22, 535–56.

Jespersen, Otto. 1922. *Language: Its Nature, Development, and Origin*. London: Allen and Unwin.

Johnson, Samuel V. 1978. Chinook Jargon: A computer analysis of variation in American Indian Pidgin. PhD dissertation, Dept of Anthropology, University of Kansas.

Jondoh, Edina Elemawusi Ayaba. 1980. Some aspects of the predicate phrase in Gengbe. PhD dissertation, Indiana University.

Jordens, Peter. 1996. Input and instruction in second language acquisition. In Peter Jordens and Josine Lalleman (eds) *Investigating Second Language Acquisition*, 407–49. Berlin: Mouton de Gruyter.

Joseph, Brian. 1983. *The Synchrony and Diachrony of the Balkan Infinitive: A Study in Areal, General and Historical Linguistics*. Cambridge: Cambridge University Press.

Joseph, Brian. 1986. A fresh look at the Balkan *Sprachbund*: Some observations on H. W. Schaller's Die Balkansprachen. In Alexander Borg and Paul Wexler (eds) *Mediterranean Language Review*, vol. 3, 105–14. Wiesbaden: Otto Harrassowitz.

Joseph, Brian. 2000. Processes of spread for syntactic constructions in the Balkans. In C. Tzitzilis and C. Symeonidis (eds) *BalkanLinguistik: Synchronie und Diachronie*, 139–50. University of Thessaloniki, Greece.

Joseph, Brian D. 2001. Is there such a thing as "grammaticalization"? *Language Sciences* 23, 163–86.

Joshi, A. 1985. Processing of sentences with intrasentential codeswitching. In D. Dowty, L. Karttunen, and A. Zwicky (eds) *Natural Language Parsing*, 190–205. Cambridge: Cambridge University Press.

Kachru, Braj. 1978. Toward structuring code mixing: an Indian perspective. *International Journal of the Sociology of Language* 16, 27–47.

Kachru, Braj B. 1992. The second diaspora of English. In Tim W. Machan and Charles T. Scott (eds) *English in its Social Contexts: Essays in Historical Sociolinguistics*, 230–52. Oxford: Oxford University Press.

Kachru, Braj. B. 1997. World Englishes 2000: resources for research and teaching. In Larry E. Smith and Michael Forman (eds) *World Englishes 2000*, 209–51. University of Hawai'i: College of Languages, Linguistics and Literature, and the East–West Center.

Kallen, Jeffrey L. 1997. Irish English and world English: lexical perspectives. In Edgar W. Schneider (ed.) *Englishes Around the World. Vol. 1: General Studies, British Isles, North America*, 139–57. Amsterdam: Benjamins.

Kamwangamalu, Nkonko Mudipanu 1989. Some morphosyntactic aspects of French/English-Bantu code-mixing: evidence for universal constraints. In Bradley Music, Randolph Graczyk, and Caroline Wiltshire (eds) *CLS 25. Part Two: Papers from the Parasession on Language in Context*, 157–70. Chicago: Chicago Linguistic Society.

Kamwangamalu, N. M. and C. L. Lee. 1991. "Mixers" and "mixing": English across cultures. *World Englishes* 10, 247–61.

Kaufman, Dorit and Mark Aronoff. 1991. Morphological disintegration and reconstruction in first language acquisition. In Seliger and Vago 1991a: 175–88.

Kaufman, Eugen. 1939. Der Fragenkreis ums Fremdwort. *Journal of English and Germanic Philology* 38, 42–63.

Kay, Paul and Gillian Sankoff. 1974. A language-universals approach to pidgins and creoles. In David DeCamp and Ian F. Hancock (eds) *Pidgins and Creoles: Current Trends and Prospects*, 61–72. Washington, D.C.: Georgetown University Press.

Kazazis, K. 1993. Dismantling Greek diglossia. In Eran Fraenkel and Christina Kramer (eds) *Language Contact – Language Conflict*, 7–25. New York: Peter Lang.

Kean, M. 1986. Core issues in transfer. In E. Kellerman and M. Sharwood Smith (eds) *Crosslinguistic Influence in Second Language Acquisition*, 80–90. Oxford: Pergamon.

Keenan, E. L. and B. Comrie. 1977. Noun phrase accessibility and universal grammar. *Linguistic Inquiry* 8, 63–99.

Keesing, Roger. 1988. *Melanesian Pidgin and the Oceanic Substrate*. Stanford: Stanford University Press.

Kegl, Judy, Ann Senghas, and Marie Coppola. 1999. Creation through contact: sign language emergence and sign language change in Nicaragua. In DeGraff 1999a: 179–237.

Keller, R. E. 1982. Diglossia in German-speaking Switzerland. In W. Haas (ed.) *Standard Languages, Spoken and Written*, 70–93. Manchester: Manchester University Press.

Kellerman, Eric. 1978. Giving learners a break: native language intuitions as a source of predictions about transferability. *Working Papers on Bilingualism* 15, 59–92.

Kellerman, Eric. 1995. Crosslinguistic influence: transfer to nowhere? *Annual Review of Applied Linguistics* 15, 125–50.

Kenrick, Donald. 1976–7. Romanies in the Middle East. *Roma* 1.4, 5–8; 2.1, 30–6; 2.2, 3–39.

Kerswill, Paul and Ann Williams. 2000. Creating a new town koiné: children and language change in Milton Keynes. *Language in Society* 29.1, 65–115.

King, Ruth. 2000. *The Lexical Basis of Grammatical Borrowing: A Prince Edward Island Case Study*. Amsterdam: Benjamins.

Kingsmore, Rona K. 1995. *Ulster Scots Speech: A Sociolinguistic Study*. Tuscaloosa: University of Alabama Press.

Klavans, Judith L. 1983. The syntax of code switching: Spanish and English. In L. D. King and C. A. Matey (eds) *Selected Papers from the 13th Linguistic Symposium on Romance Languages*, 213–32. Amsterdam: Benjamins.

Klein, Wolfgang and Clive Perdue. 1997. The basic variety (or: couldn't natural languages be much simpler?). *Second Language Research* 13.4, 301–47.

Klemola, Juhani. 1996. Non-standard periphrastic DO: a study in variation and change. PhD dissertation, University of Essex.

Kloss, Heinz. 1927. Spracherhaltung. *Archiv für Politik und Geschichte* 5.4, 456–62.

Kloss, Heinz. 1929. Sprachtabellen als Grundlage für Sprachstatistik, Sprachenkarten und für eine allgemeine Sozologie der Sprachgemeinschaften. *Vierteljahresschrift für Politik und Geschichte* H.2.1, 3–17.

Koch, H. 2000. The role of Australian Aboriginal languages in the formation of Australian Pidgin grammar: transitive verbs and adjectives. In Jeff Siegel (ed.) *Processes of Language Contact: Studies from Australia and the South Pacific*, 13–46. Montréal: Fides.

Konstantinopulos, Christos G. 1983. *Oi paradosiakoi chtistes tes Poloponnesou*. Athens: Melissa.

Kopitar, Jernej. 1829. Albanische, walachische und bulgarische Sprache. *Jahbücher der Literatur* 46, 59–106.

Kotsinas, Ulla-Britt. 1996. Aspect marking and grammaticalization in Russenorsk compared with immigrant Swedish. In Ernst Håkon Jahr and Ingvild Broch (eds) *Language Contact in the Arctic: Northern Pidgins and Contact Languages*, 123–54. Berlin: Mouton de Gruyter.

Kouwenberg, Silvia. 1996. Short note: substrate or superstrate: what's in a name? *Journal of Pidgin and Creole Languages* 11.2, 343–7.

Kubler, Cornelius C. 1979. Some differences between Taiwan Mandarin and "textbook Mandarin." *Journal of the Chinese Language Teachers Association* 14.3, 27–39.

Kubler, Cornelius C. 1985. The influence of Southern Min on the Mandarin of Taiwan. *Anthropological Linguistics* 27.2, 156–76.

Kurath, Hans. 1956. The loss of long consonants and the rise of voiced fricatives in Middle English. *Language* 32, 435–45.

Lado, R. 1957. *Linguistics Across Cultures*. Ann Arbor: University of Michigan Press.

Lalla, Barbara and Jean D'Costa. 1990. *Language in Exile: Three Hundred Years of Jamaican Creole*. Tuscaloosa: University of Alabama Press.

Lalleman, Josine. 1996. The state of the art in second language acquisition research. In Peter Jordens and Josine Lalleman (eds) *Investigating Second Language Acquisition*, 3–69. Berlin: Mouton de Gruyter.

Larmouth, Donald W. 1974. Differential interference in American Finnish cases. *Language* 50, 356–66.

Leather, Jonathan and Allan James. 1991. The acquisition of second language speech. *Studies in Second Language Acquisition* 13, 305–41.

Lefebvre, Claire. 1996. The tense, mood, and aspect system of Haitian Creole and the problem of transmission of grammar in creole genesis. *Journal and Pidgin and Creole Languages* 11.2, 231–311.

Lefebvre, Claire and John S. Lumsden. 1994. Relexification in creole genesis. Paper read at the MIT Symposium on the Role of Relexification in Creole Genesis: The case of Haitian Creole.

Leland, Charles G. 1874. *The Gypsies and their Language*. London: Trübner.

LePage, Robert B. and A. Tabouret-Keller. 1985. *Acts of Identity*. Cambridge: Cambridge University Press.

Levelt, Willem. 1989. *Speaking, from Intention to Articulation*. Cambridge, Mass.: MIT Press.

Lewis, Glyn E. 1978. Types of bilingual communities. In James E. Alatis (ed.) *International Dimensions of Bilingual Education*, 19–34. Washington D.C.: Georgetown University Press.

Lin, Hannah H. 1997. Taiwan Mandarin – a case of substratum interference. Unpublished research paper, Dept of Linguistics, Ohio State University.

Louden, Mark L. 1997. Linguistic structure and sociolinguistic identity in Pennsylvania German society. In James R. Dow and Michèle Wolff (eds) *Languages and Lives: Essays in Honor of Werner Enninger*, 79–91. New York: Peter Lang.

Lounsbury, Floyd G. 1968. One hundred years of anthropological linguistics. In J. O. Brew (ed.), *One Hundred Years of Anthropology*, 153–225. Cambridge, Mass.: Harvard University Press.

Loveday, Leo J. 1996. *Language Contact in Japan: A Socio-linguistic History*. Oxford: Clarendon Press.

Lüdi, G. 1987. Les marques transcodiques: regards nouveaux sur le bilinguisme. In G. Lüdi (ed.) *Devenir bilingue – parler bilingue. Actes du 2e colloque sur le bilinguisme, Université de Neuchâtel, 20–22 Septembre, 1984*, 1–21. Tübingen: Max Niemeyer.

Lumsden, John S. 1999. Language acquisition and creolization. In DeGraff 1999a: 129–57.

Macedo, Donaldo P. 1986. The role of core grammar in pidgin development. *Language Learning* 36.1, 65–75.

Maher, Julianne. 1991. A crosslinguistic study of language contact and language attrition. In Seliger and Vago 1991a: 67–84.

Marçais, W. 1930. La diglossie arabe. *L'Enseignement Public* 97.12, 401–9.

Masica, Colin P. 1976. *Defining a Linguistic Area: South Asia*. Chicago: University of Chicago Press.

McWhorter, John H. 1992. Substratal influence on Saramaccan serial verb constructions. *Journal of Pidgin and Creole Languages* 7, 1–53.

McWhorter, John H. 1995. The scarcity of Spanish-based creoles explained. *Language in Society* 24.2, 213–44.

McWhorter, John H. 1998. Identifying the creole prototype: vindicating a typological class. *Language* 74, 788–818.

McWhorter, John H. (ed.). 2000. *Language Change and Language Contact in Pidgins and Creoles*. Amsterdam: Benjamins.

Meillet, Antoine. 1921. *Linguistique historique et linguistique générale*. Paris: Champion.

Meisel, Jürgen M. 1977. Linguistic simplification: a study of immigrant workers' speech and foreigner talk. In S. P. Corder and E. Roulet (eds) *The Notions of Simplification, Interlanguages and Pidgins in their Relation to Second Language Pedagogy*, 88–113. Geneva: Droz.

Meisel, Jürgen M., H. Clahsen, and M. Pienemann. 1981. On determining developmental stages in natural second language acquisition. *Studies in Second Language Acquisition* 3, 109–35.

Melville, Herman. 1846. *Narrative of Four Months' Residence among the Natives of a Valley of the Marquesas Islands* (*Typee*). London: John Murray.

Menn, Lise. 1989. Some people who don't talk right: universal and particular in child language, aphasia, and language obsolescence. In Dorian 1989: 335–45.

Mesthrie, Rajend and Timothy T. Dunne. 1990. Syntactic variation in language shift: the relative clause in South African Indian English. *Language Variation and Change* 2.1, 31–56.

Migge, Bettina. 1998. Substrate influence in creole formation: the origin of *give*-type serial verb constructions in the Surinamese Plantation Creole. *Journal of Pidgin and Creole Languages* 13.2, 215–65.

Migge, Bettina. 2000. The origin of the syntax and semantics of property items in the Surinamese plantation creole. In McWhorter 2000: 201–34.

Migge, Bettina. To appear. The origin of the copulas *(d/n)a* and *de* in the Eastern Maroon Creole. *Diachronica*.

Milroy, Lesley. 1987. *Language and Social Networks*. 2nd edition. Oxford: Blackwell.

Milroy, Lesley and J. Milroy. 1992. Social network and social class: toward an integrated sociolinguistic model. *Language in Society* 21, 1–26.

Milroy, Lesley and Li Wei. 1995. A social network approach to code-switching: the example of a bilingual community in Britain. In Lesley Milroy and Pieter Muysken (eds) *One Speaker, Two Languages: Cross-Disciplinary Perspectives on Code-Switching*, 136–57. Cambridge: Cambridge University Press.

Mintz, Sidney W. 1971. The socio-historical background to pidginization and creolization. In Hymes 1971a: 481–96.

Mioni, Alberto M. 1987. Domain. In H. von Ulrich Ammon, Norbert Dittmar, and Klaus J. Mattheier (eds) *Sociolinguistics–Soziolinguistik*, vol. 1, 170–8. Berlin: Walter de Gruyter.

Mkude, Daniel J. 1986. English in contact with Swahili. In Wolfgang Viereck and Wolf-Dietrich Bald (eds) *English in Contact with Other Languages*, 513–32. Budapest: Akadémiai Kiadó.

Moeliono, Anton M. 1994. Contact-induced language change in present-day Indonesian. In Tom Dutton and Darrell T. Tryon (eds) *Language Contact and Change in the Austronesian World*, 377–88. Berlin and New York: Mouton de Gruyter.

Mordinov, A. and G. Sanžejev. 1951. Nekotoryje voprosy razvitija mladopismennyx jazykov S.S.S.R. *Bol'ševik* 8, 38–48.

Morrill, C. H. 1997. Language, culture and society in the Central African Republic: the emergence and development of Sango. PhD dissertation, Indiana University.

Mougeon, Raymond and Edouard Beniak. 1991. *Linguistic Consequences of Language Contact and Restriction: The Case of French in Ontario, Canada*. Oxford: Oxford Universiy Press.

Mous, Maarten. 1994. Ma'a or Mbugu. In Bakker and Mous 1994: 175–200.

Mufwene, Salikoko. 1990. Transfer and the substrate hypothesis in creolistics. *Studies in Second Language Acquisition* 12, 1–23.

Mufwene, Salikoko (ed.). 1993. *Africanisms in Afro-American Language Varieties*. Athens, Ga.: University of Georgia Press.

Mufwene, Salikoko. 1996a. The development of American Englishes: some questions from a creole genesis perspective. In Edgar W. Schneider (ed.) *Focus on the USA*, 231–64. Varieties of English Around the World G16. Amsterdam: Benjamins.

Mufwene, Salikoko. 1996b. The Founder Principle in creole genesis. *Diachronica* 13, 83–134.

Mufwene, Salikoko. 1997. Kituba. In Thomason 1997a: 173–208.

Mufwene, Salikoko. 1998. What research on creole genesis can contribute to historical linguistics. In Monika S. Schmid, Jennifer R. Austin, and Dieter Stein (eds) *Historical Linguistics 1997*, 315–38 Amsterdam: Benjamins.

Mufwene, Salikoko. 2000. Creolization is a social, not a structural, process. In Newmann-Holzschuh and Schneider 2000: 65–83.

Mufwene, Salikoko. 2001. *The Ecology of Language Evolution*. Cambridge: Cambridge University Press.

Mühlhäusler, Peter. 1986. *Pidgin and Creole Linguistics*. Oxford: Blackwell.

Mulert, F. E. 1917. De bewoners van Suriname in 1675. *De Navorscher* 26, 401–6.

Müller, Friedrich Max. 1875. *Lectures on the Science of Language*, vol. 1. New York: Scribner, Armstrong.

Muysken, Pieter. 1981a. Halfway between Quechua and Spanish: the case for relexification. In Arnold Highfield and Albert Valdman (eds) *Historicity and Variation in Creole Studies*, 52–78. Ann Arbor: Karoma.

Muysken, Pieter. 1981b. Creole tense/mood/aspect systems: the unmarked case? In Pieter Muysken (ed.) *Generative Studies on Creole Languages*, 181–99. Dordrecht: Foris.

Muysken, Pieter. 1990. A unified theory of local coherence in grammar contact. In H. Nelde (ed.) *Confli(c)t*, 123–8. ABLA Papers 14. Brussels: ABLA.

Muysken, Pieter. 1995. Code switching and grammatical theory. In Lesley Milroy and Pieter Muysken (eds) *One Speaker, Two Languages: Cross-Disciplinary Perspectives on Code Switching*, 177–98. Cambridge: Cambridge University Press.

Muysken, Pieter. 1997a. Media Lengua. In Thomason 1997a: 365–426.

Muysken, Pieter. 1997b. Callahuaya. In Thomason 1997a: 427–47.

Muysken, Pieter. 1997c. Alternation, insertion, congruent lexicalization. In Martin Pütz (ed.) *Language Choices: Conditions, Constraints and Consequences*, 361–80. Amsterdam: Benjamins.

Myers-Scotton, Carol. 1989. Code switching with English: types of switching, types of communities. *World Englishes* 8, 333–46.

Myers-Scotton, Carol. 1993a. *Social Motivations for Code-Switching: Evidence from Africa*. Oxford: Clarendon Press.

Myers-Scotton, Carol. 1993b. *Dueling Languages: Grammatical Structure in Code-Switching*. Oxford: Clarendon Press.

Myers-Scotton, Carol. 1993c. Common and uncommon ground: social and structural factors in code switching. *Language in Society* 22, 475–503.

Myers-Scotton, Carol. 1997. Code switching. In Florian Coulmas (ed.) *The Handbook of Sociolinguistics*, 217–37. Oxford: Blackwell.

Myers-Scotton, Carol. 1999. Putting it all together: the matrix language and more. In Bernt Brendemoen, Elizabeth Lanza, and Else Ryen (eds) *Language Encounters across Time and Space*, 13–28. Oslo: Novus Press.

Myers-Scotton, Carol and Janice Jake. 1995. Matching lemmas in a bilingual competence and production model: evidence from intrasentential code switching. *Linguistics* 33, 981–1024.

Myers-Scotton, Carol and Janice Jake. 2001. Explaining aspects of codeswitching and their implications. In Janet Nicol (ed.) *One Mind, Two Languages: Bilingual Language Processing*, 84–116. Oxford: Blackwell.

Naro, Anthony J. 1978. A study on the origins of pidginization. *Language* 54, 314–47.

Nartey, J. 1982. Code switching, interference or faddism? Language use among educated Ghanaians. *Anthropological Linguistics* 24.2, 183–92.

Nelde, Peter Hans. 1997. Language conflict. In Florian Coulmas (ed.) *The Handbook of Sociolinguistics*, 285–300. Oxford: Blackwell.

Nemser, William. 1991. Language contact and foreign language acquisition. In Vladimir Ivir and Damir Kalagjera (eds) *Languages in Contact and Contrast: Essays in Contact Linguistics*, 345–64. Berlin: Mouton de Gruyter.

Newmann-Holzschuch, Ingrid and Edgar W. Schneider (eds) 2000. *Degrees of Restructuring in Creole Languages*. Amsterdam: Benjamins.

Newport, Elissa L. 1999. Reduced input in the acquisition of signed languages: contributions to the study of creolization. In DeGraff 1999a: 161–78.

Nishimura, Miwa. 1986. Intrasentential code switching: the case of language assignment. In J. Vaid (ed.) *Bilinguals: Psycholinguistic and Neuropsychological Perspectives*, 123–43. Hillsdale, N.J.: Erlbaum.

Nishimura, Miwa. 1997. *Japanese/English Code Switching: Syntax and Pragmatics*. New York: Peter Lang.

Nortier, Jacomine. 1990. *Dutch–Moroccan Arabic Code Switching among Moroccans in the Netherlands*. Dordrecht: Foris.

Odlin, Terence. 1989. *Language Transfer*. Cambridge: Cambridge University Press.

Odlin, Terence. 1991. Irish English idioms and language transfer. *English World-Wide* 12, 175–93.

Odlin, Terence. 1992. Transferability and linguistic substrates. *Second Language Research* 8, 171–202.

Odlin, Terence. 1995. *Causation in Language Contact: A Devilish Problem.* CLCS Occasional Paper No. 41. Dublin: Trinity College, Centre for Language and Communication Studies.
Odlin, Terence. 1996. *Sorrow Penny Yee Payed for My Drink: Taboo, Euphemism, and a Phantom Substrate.* CLCS Occasional Paper No. 43. Dublin: Trinity College, Centre for Language and Communication Studies.
Odlin, Terence. 1997a. *Hiberno-English: Pidgin, Creole or Neither?.* CLCS Occasional Paper No. 49. Dublin: Trinity College, Centre for Language and Communication Studies.
Odlin, Terence. 1997b. Bilingualism and substrate influence: a look at clefts and reflexives. In Jeffrey Kallen (ed.) *Focus on Ireland*, 35–50. Varieties of English Around the World G21. Amsterdam: Benjamins.
Oksaar, Els. 1972. Bilingualism. In Thomas A. Sebeok (ed.) *Current Trends in Linguistics. Vol. 9: Linguistics in Western Europe*, 476–511. The Hague: Mouton.
Ortoz, Carmelia. 1949. English influence on the Spanish of Tampa [Florida]. *Hispania* 32, 300–4.
Otheguy, Ricardo. 1995. When contact speakers talk, linguistic theory listens. In E. Contini-Morava and B. Sussman (eds) *Meaning as Explanation: Advances in Linguistic Sign Theory*, 213–42. Berlin: Mouton de Gruyter.
Pandit, Ira. 1990. Grammaticality in code switching. In Rodolfo Jacobson (ed.) *Codeswitching as a Worldwide Phenomenon*, 33–69. New York: Peter Lang.
Pap, Leo. 1949. *Portuguese-American speech: An Outline of Speech Conditions among Portuguese Immigrants in New England and Elsewhere in the United States.* New York: King's Crown Press.
Parkvall, Mikael. 2000. Reassessing the role of demographics in language restructuring. In Newmann-Holzschuch and Schneider 2000: 185–213.
Pasch, Helma. 1997. Sango. In Thomason 1997a: 209–70. Amsterdam: Benjamins.
Paul, Hermann. 1886. Prinzipien der Sprachgeschichte. Halle: Max Neimeyer.
Perdue, Clive (ed.). 1993a. *Adult Language Acquisition: Cross-Linguistic Perspectives. Vol. 1: Field Methods.* Cambridge: Cambridge University Press.
Perdue, Clive (ed.). 1993b. *Adult Language Acquisition: Cross-Linguistic Perspectives. Vol. 2: The Results.* Cambridge: Cambridge University Press.
Pfaff, Carol. 1976. Functional and structural constraints on syntactic variation in code switching. *Papers from the Parasession on Diachronic Syntax*, 248–59. Chicago: CLS.
Pfaff, Carol. 1979. Constraints on language mixing: intrasentential code switching and borrowing in Spanish/English. *Language* 55, 291–318.
Picone, Michael D. 1994. Code-intermediate phenomena in Louisiana French. In Katharine Beals, Jeannette Denton, Robert Knippen, Lynette Melnar, Hisam Suzuki, and Erica Zeinfeld (eds) *CLS 30-I: Papers from the Thirtieth Regional Meeting of the Chicago Linguistic Society. Vol. 1: The Main Session*, 320–34. Chicago: CLS.
Pienemann, Manfred. 1980. The second language acquisition of immigrant children. In S. W. Felix (ed.) *Second Language Development: Trends and Issues*, 41–56. Tübingen: Gunter Narr.
Pienemann, Manfred. 1984. Psychological constraints on the teachability of languages. *Studies in Second Language Acquisition* 6, 186–214.

Pienemann, Manfred. 1997. A unified framework for the study of dynamics in language development – applied to L1, L2, 2L1 and SLI. Unpublished ms.

Platt, John Talbot. 1977. A model for polyglossia and multilingualism (with special reference to Singapore and Malaysia). *Language in Society* 6.3, 361–78.

Platt, John T., Heidi Weber, and Mian Lian Ho. 1983. *Singapore and Malaysia. Varieties of English Around the World*, vol. 4. Amsterdam: Benjamins.

Poplack, Shana. 1980. Sometimes I'll start a sentence in English Y TERMINO EN ESPAÑOL: toward a typology of code switching. *Linguistics* 18, 581–618. (Also in J. Amastae and L. Elias-Olivares (eds) 1982, *Spanish in the United States: Sociolinguistic Aspects*, 230–63. Cambridge: Cambridge University Press.)

Poplack, Shana. 1981. Syntactic structure and social function of codeswitching. In R. Duran (ed.) *Latino Language and Communicative Behavior*, 169–84. Norwood, N.J.: Ablex.

Poplack, Shana. 1987. Contrasting patterns of code switching in two communities. In E. Wande, J. Anward, B. Nordberg, L. Steensland, and M. Thelander (eds) *Aspects of Multilingualism: Proceedings from the Fourth Nordic Symposium on Bilingualism 1984*, 51–77. Sweden: University of Uppsala.

Poplack, Shana. 1990. Variation theory and language contact: concept, methods and data. In *Papers for the Workshop on Concepts, Methodology and Data, Basel, January 12–13, 1990*, 33–66. Strasbourg: European Science Foundation. (Also in D. Preston (ed.) 1993, *American Dialect Research: An Anthology Celebrating the 100th Anniversary of the American Dialect Society*, 251–86. Amsterdam: Benjamins.)

Poplack, Shana. 1996. The sociolinguistic dynamics of apparent convergence. In Gregory Guy et al. (eds) *Towards a Social Science of Language: Papers in Honor of William Labov*, vol. 1, 285–308. Amsterdam: Benjamins.

Poplack, Shana and Marjorie Meechan. 1995. Patterns of language mixture: nominal structure in Wolof-French and Fongbe-French bilingual discourse. In Lesley Milroy and Pieter Muysken (eds) *One Speaker, Two Languages: Cross-Disciplinary Perspectives on Code Switching*, 199–232. Cambridge: Cambridge University Press.

Poplack, Shana and David Sankoff. 1988. Code switching. In H. von Ulrick Ammon, Norbert Dittmar, and Klaus J. Mattheier (eds) *Sociolinguistics – Soziolinguistik*, vol. 2, 1174–80. Berlin: Walter de Gruyter.

Poplack, Shana, David Sankoff, and Christopher Miller. 1988. The social correlates and linguistic processes of lexical borrowing and assimilation. *Linguistics* 26, 47–104.

Poulisse, Nanda. 1996. Strategies. In Peter Jordens and Josine Lalleman (eds) *Investigating Second Language Acquisition*, 135–63. Berlin: Mouton de Gruyter.

Pride, J. B. 1979. A transactional view of speech functions and code switching. In W. McCormack and S. Wurm (eds) *Language and Society*, 27–53. The Hague: Mouton.

Rayfield, J. R. 1970. *The Languages of a Bilingual Community*. The Hague: Mouton.

Reed, Carol E. 1948. The adaptation of English to Pennsylvania German morphology. *American Speech* 23, 239–44.

Reinecke, John E. 1971. Tây Bôi: notes on the Pidgin French of Vietnam. In Hymes 1971a: 47–56.

Rickford, John Russell. 1987. *Dimensions of a Creole Continuum: History, Texts and Linguistic Analysis of Guyanese Creole*. Stanford: Stanford University Press.

Rickford, John Russell. 1992. The creole residue in Barbados. In N. Doane, J. Hall, and D. Ringler (eds) *Old English and New: Essays in Language and Linguistics in Honor of Frederick G. Cassidy*, 183–201. New York: Garland.

Rickford, John Russell and Jerome Handler. 1994. Textual evidence on the nature of early Barbadian speech, 1675–1835. *Journal of Pidgin and Creole Languages* 9, 221–55.

Rickford, John Russell and Russell Rickford. 2000. *Spoken Soul: The Story of Black English*. New York: John Wily.

Ritchie, W. C. 1986. Second language acquisition and the study of non-native varieties of English: some issues in common. *World Englishes* 5, 15–30.

Roberts, Ian. 1999. Verb movement and markedness. In DeGraff 1999a: 287–327.

Roberts, Sarah Julianne. 2000. Nativization and the genesis of Hawaiian Creole. In McWhorter 2000: 257–300.

Romaine, Suzanne. 1989. *Bilingualism*. Oxford: Blackwell.

Rosensweig, Jay B. 1973. *Caló. Gutter Spanish*. New York: E. P. Dutton.

Roy, John D. 1986. The structure of tense and aspect in Barbadian Creole English. In Manfred Görlach and John Holm (eds) *Focus on the Caribbean. Varieties of English Around the World. G8*, 141–56. Amsterdam: Benjamins.

Samarin, William J. 2000. The status of Sango in fact and fiction: on the one-hundredth anniversary of its conception. In McWhorter 2000: 301–33. Amsterdam: Benjamins.

Sandfeld, Kristian. 1930. *Linguistique balkanique: problèmes et résultats*. Paris: Klincksieck. (Reprinted 1968.)

Sankoff, David and Shana Poplack. 1981. A formal grammar for code switching. *Papers in Linguistics* 14, 3–46.

Sankoff, David, Shana Poplack, and S. Vanniarajan. 1986. *The Case of the Nonce Loan in Tamil*. Technical Report 1348. Centre du récherches mathematiques, University of Montréal.

Sapir, Edward. 1921. *Language*. New York: Harcourt, Brace and World.

Sasse, Hans-Jürgen. 1991. *Arvanítika: Die albanischen Sprachreste in Griechenland*. Part 1. Wiesbaden: Harrassowitz.

Sasse, Hans-Jürgen. 1992a. Theory of language death. In Brenzinger 1992a: 7–30.

Sasse, Hans-Jürgen. 1992b. Language decay and contact-induced change: similarities and differences. In Brenzinger 1992a: 59–80.

Schachter, Jacqueline. 1974. An error in error analysis. *Language Learning* 24, 205–14.

Schachter, Jacqueline. 1992. A new account of language transfer. In S. M. Gass and L. Selinker (eds) *Language Transfer in Language Learning*, 32–46. Amsterdam: Benjamins.

Schaller, Helmut W. 1975. *Die Balkansprachen: Ein Einführung in die Balkanphilologie*. Heidelberg: Carl Winter Universitätsverlag.

Schmidt, Annette. 1985. *Young People's Dyirbal: An Example of Language Death from Australia*. Cambridge: Cambridge University Press.

Schmidt, Johannes. 1872. *Die Verwantschaftsverhältnisse der indogermanischen Sprachen*. Weimar: H. Bohlau.

Schuchardt, Hugo. 1882. Kreolische Studien I. Ueber das Negerportugiesische von S. Thomé (Westafrika). *Sitzungsberichte der kaiserlichen Akademie der Wissenschaften zu Wien* 101.2, 889–917.

Schuchardt, Hugo. 1883. Kreolische Studien V. Ueber das Melaneso-englische. *Sitzungsberichte der kaiserlichen Akademie der Wissenschaften zu Wien* 105.1, 151–161. (Reprinted in English in Hugo Schuchardt (1979), *The Ethnography of Variation: Selected Writings on Pidgins and Creoles*, ed. and trans. Thomas L. Markey, 18–25. Ann Arbor: Karoma.)

Schuchardt, Hugo. 1884. *Slawo-deutsches und Slawo-italienisches.* Graz: Leuschner and Lubensky.

Schumann, Christian. 1783. Neger–Englisches Wörterbuch. Ms. (Published in André Kramp (1983), Early creole lexicography: a study of C.L. Schumann's Manuscript dictionary of Sranan, 44–305. PhD dissertation, University of Leiden.)

Schumann, John H. 1978. *The Pidginization Process: A Model for Second Language Acquisition.* Rowley, Mass.: Newbury House.

Schumann, John H. 1986. Locative and directional expressions in basilang speech. *Language Learning* 36, 277–94.

Scotton, Carol M. 1988. Code switching and types of multilingual communities. In P. Lowenberg (ed.) *Language Spread and Language Policy*, 61–82. Washington, D.C.: Georgetown University Press.

Sebba, Mark. 1987. *The Syntax of Serial Verbs.* Amsterdam: Benjamins.

Seiler, Freidrich. 1907–13. *Die Entwicklung der deutschen Kulture im Spiegel des Lehnwortes.* 4 vols. Halle: Buchhandlung des Waisenhauses.

Sekerina, Irina A. 1994. Copper Island (Mednyj) Aleut (CIA): a mixed language. *Languages of the World* 8, 14–31.

Seliger, Herbert W. and Robert M. Vago (eds) 1991a. *First Language Attrition.* Cambridge: Cambridge University Press.

Seliger, Herbert W. and Robert M. Vago. 1991b. The study of first language attrition: an overview. In Seliger and Vago 1991a: 3–15.

Seuren, Pieter and H. C. Wekker. 1986. Semantic transparency as a factor in creole genesis. In Pieter Muysken and Norval Smith (eds), *Substrata versus Universals in Creole Genesis*, 57–70. Amsterdam: Benjamins.

Sherzer, Joel. 1976. *An Areal-Typological Study of American Indian Languages North of Mexico.* Amsterdam: North-Holland.

Siegel, Jeff. 1985. Koinés and koinéization. *Language in Society* 14.3, 357–78.

Siegel, Jeff. 1987. *Language Contact in a Plantation Environment.* Cambridge: Cambridge University Press.

Siegel, Jeff. 1997. Mixing, leveling, and pidgin/creole development. In Spears and Winford 1997: 111–49.

Siegel, Jeff. 1998. Substrate reinforcement and dialectal differences in Melanesian Pidgin. *Journal of Sociolinguistics* 2, 347–73.

Siegel, Jeff. 1999. Transfer constraints and substrate influence in Melanesian Pidgin. *Journal of Pidgin and Creole Languages* 14.1, 1–44.

Siegel, Jeff. 2000. Substrate influence in Hawai'I Creole English. *Language in Society* 29, 197–236.

Silva-Corvalán, Carmen. 1994. *Language Contact and Change: Spanish in Los Angeles.* Oxford: Clarendon.

Silva-Corvalán, Carmen. 1998. On borrowing as a mechanism of syntactic change. In Armin Schwegler, Bernard Tranel, and Myriam Uribe-Etxebarria (eds) *Romance Linguistics: Theoretical Perspectives*, 225–46. Amsterdam: Benjamins.

Silva-Corvalán, Carmen. 2000. El contacto Español–Inglés en Los Angeles: aspectos demográficos y sociolinguísticos. Paper presented at UC Davis, April.

Singh, R. 1985. Grammatical constraints on code switching: evidence from Hindi–English. *Canadian Journal of Linguistics* 30, 33–45.

Singler, John. 1990a. On the use of sociohistorical criteria in the comparison of creoles. *Linguistics* 28, 645–69.

Singler, John (ed.). 1990b. *Pidgin and Creole Tense-Mood-Aspect Systems.* Amsterdam: Benjamins.

Singler, John. 1992. Nativization and pidgin/creole genesis: a reply to Bickerton. *Journal of Pidgin and Creole Languages* 7, 319–33.

Singler, John. 1993. African influence upon Afro-American language varieties: a consideration of sociohistorical factors. In Mufwene 1993: 235–53.

Singler, John. 1995. The demographics of creole genesis in the Caribbean: a comparison of Martinique and Haiti. In Arends 1995a: 203–32.

Singler, John. 1996. Theories of creole genesis, sociohistorical considerations, and the evaluation of evidence: the case of Haitian Creole and the relexification hypothesis. *Journal of Pidgin and Creole Languages* 11.2, 185–230.

Slabbert, Sarah and Carol Myers-Scotton. 1996. The structure of Tsotsitaal and Iscamtho: code switching and in-group identity in South African townships. *Linguistics* 34, 317–42.

Slobin, Dan I. 1973. Cognitive prerequisites for the development of grammar. In C. I. Ferguson and D. I. Slobin (eds) *Studies of Child Language Development*, 175–276. New York: Holt, Rinehart and Winston.

Slobin, Dan I. 1985. *The Cross-Linguistic Study of Language Acquisition.* Hillsdale, N.J.: Erlbaum.

Slobin, Dan I. 1993. Adult language acquisition: a view from child language study. In C. Perdue (ed.) *Adult Language Acquisition: Cross-Linguistic Perspectives*, vol. II, 239–52. Cambridge: Cambridge University Press.

Smith, Norval. 1996. Wɛ-focus in Saramaccan: substrate feature or grammaticalization? In Philip Baker and Anand Syea (eds) *Changing Meanings, Changing Functions: Papers Relating to Grammaticalization in Contact Languages*, 113–28. London: University of Westminster Press.

Smith, Norval, Ian Robertson, and K. Williamson. 1987. The Ijo element in Berbice Dutch. *Language in Society* 16, 49–90.

Spears, Arthur. 1990. Tense, mood and aspect in the Haitian Creole preverbal marker system. In Singler 1990b: 119–42.

Spears, Arthur and Donald Winford (eds). 1997. *The Structure and Status of Pidgins and Creoles.* Amsterdam: Benjamins.

Stauble, A.-M. 1978. The process of decreolization: a model for second language development. *Language Learning* 28, 29–54.

Street, Richard L. and Howard Giles. 1982. Speech accommodation theory: a social cognitive approach to language and speech behavior. In Michael E. Roloff and Charles R. Berger (eds) *Social Cognition and Communication*, 193–226. Beverley Hills: Sage.

Sylvain, S. 1936. *Le créole haïtien. Morphologie at syntaxe*. Wetteren: De Meester.

Tajfel, H. and J. C. Turner. 1979. An integrative theory of inter-group conflict. In W. G. Austin and S. Worchel (eds) *The Social Psychology of Inter-Group Relations*, 33–47. Monterey, Calif.: Brooks/Cole.

Taylor, Douglas. 1963. The origin of West Indian Creole languages: evidence from grammatical categories. *American Anthropologist* 64.4, 800–14.

Taylor, Douglas. 1971. Grammatical and lexical affinities of creoles. In Hymes 1971a: 293–6.

Thomason, Sarah Grey. 1983a. Genetic relationship and the case of Ma'a (Mbugu). *Studies in African Linguistics* 14.2, 195–231.

Thomason, Sarah G. 1983b. Chinook Jargon in areal and historical context. *Language* 59.4, 820–70.

Thomason, Sarah G. 1993. On identifying the sources of creole structures: a discussion of Singler's and Lefebvre's papers. In Mufwene 1993: 280–95.

Thomason, Sarah Grey. 1995. Language mixture: ordinary processes, extraordinary results. In Carmen Silva-Corvalán (ed.) *Spanish in Four Continents: Studies in Language Contact and Bilingualism*, 15–33. Washington, D.C.: Georgetown University Press.

Thomason, Sarah Grey (ed.). 1997a. *Contact Languages: A Wider Perspective*. Amsterdam: Benjamins.

Thomason, Sarah Grey. 1997b. Ma'a (Mbugu). In Thomason (1997a: 469–87).

Thomason, Sarah Grey. 1997c. A typology of contact languages. In Spears and Winford 1997: 71–88.

Thomason, Sarah G. and Terrence Kaufman. 1988. *Language Contact, Creolization and Genetic Linguistics*. Berkeley: University of California Press.

Thompson, R. W. 1961. A note on some possible affinities between the creole dialects of the Old World and those of the New. In Robert B. LePage (ed.), *Creole Language Studies 2: Proceedings of the 1959 Conference on Creole Language Studies*, 107–13. London: Macmillan.

Thurston, William R. 1987. *Processes of Change in the Languages of Northwest New Britain*. Pacific Linguistics Series B, No. 99. Dept of Linguistics, Australian National University, Canberra.

Thurston, William R. 1994. Renovation and innovation in the languages of Northwestern New Britain. In Tom Dutton and Darrell Tryon (eds) *Language Contact and Change in the Austronesian World*, 573–609. Berlin and New York: Mouton de Gruyter.

Treffers-Daller, Jeanine. 1991. Towards a uniform approach to code switching and borrowing. *Papers for the Workshop on Constraints, Conditions and Models*, 259–79. Strasbourg: European Science Foundation.

Treffers-Daller, Jeanine. 1994. *Mixing Two Languages: French–Dutch Contact in a Comparative Perspective*. Berlin: Mouton de Gruyter.

Treffers-Daller, Jeanine. 1999. Borrowing and shift-induced interference: contrasting patterns in French-Germanic contact in Brussels and Strasbourg. *Bilingualism: Language and Cognition* 2.1, 1–22.

Troubetzkoy, Nikolai S. 1928. [Proposal 16]. First International Congress of Linguists, Actes, 17f. Leiden.

Trudgill, Peter. 1986. *Dialects in Contact.* Oxford: Blackwell.

Trudgill, Peter. 1996. Dual-source pidgins and reverse creoloids: northern perspectives on language contact. In Ernst Håkon Jahr and Ingvild Broch (eds) *Language Contact in the Arctic: Northern Pidgins and Contact Languages*, 5–14. Berlin: Mouton de Gruyter.

Tsitsipis, Lukas D. 1989. Skewed performance and full performance in language obsolescence: the case of an Albanian variety. In Dorian 1989: 117–37.

van Buren, Paul. 1996. Are there principles of universal grammar that do not apply to second language acquisition? In Peter Jordens and Josine Lalleman (eds) *Investigating Second Language Acquisition*, 187–207. Berlin: Mouton de Gruyter.

van Coetsem, Frans. 1988. *Loan Phonology and the Two Transfer Types in Language Contact.* Dordrecht: Foris.

van den Berg, M. E. 1985. *Language Planning and Language Use in Taiwan.* Dordrecht: ICG Printing.

van den Berg, Margot. 2000. "Mi no sal tron tongo": Early Sranan in court records 1667–1767. MA thesis, Katholieke Universiteit Nijmegen.

van den Berg, Margot and Jacques Arends. 2001. Court records as a source of authentic early Sranan. Paper presented at the SPCL meeting, Washington, D.C., January 2001.

van der Voort, Hein. 1997. New light on Eskimo Pidgins. In Spears and Winford 1997: 373–93.

van Dyck. n.d.[*c.*1765]. *Nieuwe en nooit bevoorens geziene onderwyzinge in het Bastert Engels, of Neeger Engels, zoo als het zelve in de Hollandsze Colonien gebruikt word.* Amsterdam: Jacobus van Egmont.

Van Name, A. 1871. Contributions to creole grammar. *Transactions of the American Philological Association 1869–70* I, 123–67.

Van Patten, B. 1996. *Input Processing and Grammar Instruction in Second Language Acquisition.* Norwood, N.J.: Ablex.

Veenstra, Tonjes. 1996. *Serial Verbs in Saramaccan: Predication and Creole Genesis.* Dordrecht: ICG.

Vinet, Marie-Thérèse. 1984. La syntaxe du québécois et les emprunts à l'anglais. *Revue de l'Association québécoise de linguistique* 3, 221–42.

Voorhoeve, Jan and U. M. Lichtveld. 1975. *Creole Drum: An Anthology of Creole Literature in Suriname.* New Haven: Yale University Press.

Wackernagel, J. 1904. Sprachtausch und Sprachmischung. *Nachrichten der königlichen Gesellschaft der Wissenschaften.* Göttingen.

Weinreich, Uriel. 1953. *Languages in Contact: Findings and Problems.* New York: Linguistic Circle of New York. (Reprinted 1968, The Hague: Mouton.)

Wekker, Herman. 1996. Creolization and the acquisition of English as a second language. In Herman Wekker (ed.) *Creole Languages and Language Acquisition*, 139–49. Berlin: Mouton de Gruyter.

Whinnom, Keith. 1971. Linguistic hybridization and the "special case" of pidgins and creoles. In Hymes 1971a: 91–115.

Whiteley, Wilfred Howell. 1960. Linguistic hybrids. *African Studies* 19.2, 95–7.

Whiteley, Wilfred Howell. 1967. Swahili nominal classes and English loan words: a preliminary survey. In *La classification nominale dans les langues négro-africaines*. Paris: Centre Nationale de la Récherche Scientifique.

Whitney, W. D. 1881. On mixture in language. *Transactions of the American Philosophical Association* 12, 5–26.

Wilson, W. A. A. 1962. *The Crioulo of Guiné*. Johannesburg: Witwatersrand University Press.

Winford, Donald. 1993. *Predication in Caribbean English Creoles*. Amsterdam: Benjamins.

Winford, Donald. 1997a. Re-examining Caribbean English Creole continua. In Salikoko Mufwene (ed.) *Symposium on English-to-Pidgin Continua*, 233–79. Special issue of *World Englishes* 16.2.

Winford, Donald. 1997b. Property items and predication in Sranan. *Journal of Pidgin and Creole Languages* 12, 237–301.

Winford, Donald. 1997c. Guest column. Creole formation in the context of contact linguistics. *Journal of Pidgin and Creole Languages* 12.1, 131–51.

Winford, Donald. 1997d. On the origins of African-American Vernacular English – a creolist perspective. Part I: the sociohistorical background. *Diachronica* 14, 304–44.

Winford, Donald. 1998. On the origins of African-American Vernacular English – a creolist perspective. Part II: linguistic features. *Diachronica* 15, 99–154.

Winford, Donald, 2000a. "Intermediate" creoles and degrees of change in creole formation: the case of Bajan. In Newmann-Holzschuh and Schneider 2000: 215–46.

Winford, Donald. 2000b. Tense and aspect in Sranan and the creole prototype. In McWhorter 2000: 383–442.

Winford, Donald. 2000c. Irrealis in Sranan: mood and modality in a radical creole. *Journal of Pidgin and Creole Languages* 15.1, 63–125.

Winford, Donald. 2001. A comparison of tense/aspect systems in Caribbean English Creoles. In Pauline Christie (ed.) *Due Respect: Papers on English and English-Related Creoles in the Caribbean in Honour of Professor Robert LePage*, 155–83. Kingston, Jamaica: University of the West Indies Press.

Wode, H. 1981. *Learning a Second Language*. Tübingen: Gunter Narr.

Wolfe Quintero, Kate. 1992. Learnability and the acquisition of extraction in relative clauses and *wh*-questions. *Studies in Second Language Acquisition* 14, 39–70.

Woolford, Ellen. 1983. Bilingual code switching and syntactic theory. *Linguistic Inquiry* 14, 520–36.

Wurm, Stephen A. 1971. Pidgins, creoles and lingua francas. *Current Trends in Linguistics* 8, 999–1021.

Zenk, Henry Benjamin. 1988. Chinook jargon in the speech economy of Grande Ronde Reservation. *International Journal of the Sociology of Language* 71, 107–24.

Zentella, Ana Celia. 1997. *Growing Up Bilingual: Puerto Rican Children in New York*. Oxford: Blackwell.

Zobl, H. 1980. The formal and developmental selectivity of L1 influence on L2 acquisition. *Language Learning* 30, 43–57.

Zurif, E. B. 1990. Language and the brain. In D. Osherson and H. Lasnick (eds) *An Invitation to Cognitive Science*, 177–98. Cambridge, Mass.: MIT Press.

Index

AAVE *see* African American Vernacular English
Abdulaziz, Mohamed H. 168
Aboriginal languages 27, 31, 74–9, 292
Acadian French 68–70
accommodation 5, 39, 40, 41, 100
code switching as 121–4, 125
convergent *see* convergence
divergent *see* divergence
see also Communication Accommodation Theory (CAT)
acculturation
in language change 243–4
language and dialect 121–2
acquisition
abnormal 261
failure *see* fossilization
random 263–4
Adangme, and English 131–2
admixture 280
adstratum 16
affinité linguistique see Sprachbünde
Africa
New Englishes in 27, 242
see also West Africa
African American Vernacular English 237, 245, 254, 255
Afrikaans
and Khoekhoes 184
and Zulu and English 168, 205
agentivity 12, 16, 25, 62, 64
see also recipient language (RL) agentivity; source language (SL) agentivity
Agnihotri, Rama Kant 149, 169
agrammatism, in aphasia 261
Akan 335
and English 131
AL *see* ancestral language
Alawa 74
Albanian 13, 71, 72, 73
foreign vocabulary in 59
Aleut, and Russian 19, 198–205
Algonquian languages 31, 192
Alleyne, Mervyn 332, 352, 355
Alsatian, and French in Strasbourg 37, 41, 66
Aluku-Boni 316
Amara 13, 14, 87–9
American English 15
influence on Japanese 38
lexical borrowing from immigrant groups 34
lexical borrowing from indigenous languages 31
American Portuguese 44
American Sign Language 346
Amerindian languages
of Central and South America 31
Spanish loanwords in 63
Amuda, A. A. 133
ancestral language
attrition and death 256–67
and group SLA 236–7
linguistic consequences of shift 259–63, 266
as matrix language in code switching 170, 198
structural change in 69, 84, 97–8, 99, 206

Anderlecht 40
Andersen, Roger 233–4, 248–9, 286, 344
  One-to-One Principle 226, 227, 287
Anêm 13, 86–9
Anglo-Romani 4–5, 19, 169, 170, 171, 172, 174, 175, 193, 197, 206
Annobonese 309
anthropology, linguistic 110, 114–15, 118
Aoun, Y. 134
aphasia 140, 152
  agrammatism in 261
Appel, René 9, 51, 211
approximation, degrees in group SLA 245–7
Arabic 29, 222, 231
  and Dutch 136–7, 141, 142, 148, 226
  and English 48–9
  and French in Morocco 130–1, 136, 138, 142, 151, 153, 154, 156, 170
  and German 287
  and Greek, in Cyprus 171
  and Persian 52
  vernacular and classical 112
Arabic–Chinese pidgin of Canton 271
Arawak, and Carib 184
Arends, Jacques 317, 326, 330, 331, 335, 339, 340, 351, 354
argots 168–9
Aria 87–9
Armenian Romani 193, 197
Arnhem Land, Australia 27, 74–9, 150, 260
  convergence in 52, 75, 78–9, 90–1, 92, 93–4, 96, 203
Aronoff, Mark 261
Arosi 294
Aruba 21
Arvanítika 257, 262
  and Greek 174
Aukan *see* Okanisi
Asia Minor Greek 171, 172, 173, 196, 197, 204, 206
  and Turkish 56, 83–4, 204
Athapascan language family 272
Atlantic creoles 321–2, 324–5, 327–9
  English-lexicon 325 table 9.3, 334, 338–9, 344, 348, 349, 354
attrition
  qualitative 258
  quantitative 258
Attu 198
Auer, Peter 102–5, 117
Australian English, lexical borrowing from indigenous languages 31
Australian pidgin English 291, 292
  see also New South Wales Pidgin; Queensland Pidgin English
Austria 27, 254
  German and English 211
  Hungarian 257
Austronesian languages 13, 86, 242, 294
  shared characteristics 88–9
  word order 98
Azuma, S. 133, 149

back formation 49
Backus, A. 148, 169
Bailey, Charles-James 34
Bajan (Barbadian English) 22, 241, 255, 299, 308, 313, 330, 355
  emergence of 311, 314–16
  linguistic inputs and outputs in Barbados 315–16
  social context of 314–15
  and SW English dialects 315 table 9.1
Baker, Philip 268, 275, 282, 284, 289–92, 295–7, 303, 311, 313, 330, 331
Bakker, Peter 183–93, 196, 197–8
  classification of "intertwined languages" 172–4 table 6.2
Balkan languages 71
Balkans 7, 8, 11, 13, 64
  Sprachbund 70, 71–4
Balochi, and Brahui 64
Bantu languages 53, 298
  borrowings from Khoesan into Southern 41
  and Cushitic languages 171, 193–8
  diffusion of click consonants into 70
  and European languages 148
baragouin (barogoin) 269
Barbadian English *see* Bajan
Barbados, linguistic inputs and outputs in 315–16

Bariai language family 13, 87–9
Barnes, William 316
basilectal creoles 313, 355
basilectalization 329, 332–3
Basque 27, 33
Basters 184
Batibo, Herman 258, 260
Battistella, Edwin L. 230
Bautista, M. L. S. 106
Bavin, E. 149
Baxter, Allan N. 310
Beach-la-Mar 291
bêche-de-mer trade 291
Beckles, Hilary 314
Belfast, Irish English in 254
Belgium 101
Belize Creole 305, 308, 349, 351
Belnap, R. Kirk 211
Beniak, Edouard 69
Bentahila, Abdelâli 130–1, 133, 136, 138, 142, 151, 153, 154, 156, 160, 162, 170
Berbice Dutch 21, 336, 338
Bering Island Aleut 198, 199, 200, 201
Berk-Seligson, Susan 131, 132
Betsiamites, Quebec 192
Betz, Werner 42
Bever, Thomas 287
Bibling language family 13, 87–9
Bickerton, Derek 3, 20, 143, 250, 275, 287, 307, 308, 311, 326, 347
  Language Bioprogram Hypothesis (LBH) 326, 329
Bickmore, L. S. 149
bidialectalism, and code switching 102
bilingual language processing, one dominant language in 140
bilingual mixed languages 7, 19, 168–207
  Bakker's classification 172–3
  characteristics 171–2
  definition and classification 170–5 table 6.1
  genetic classification 173–4
  processes and origins 206–7
  social motivations 205–6
  sociohistorical background 205–6
  Thomason's classification 171–2
  see also "intertwined languages"
bilingual speech, psycholinguistic studies 140
bilingualism 9
  in ancestral language and colonial official language 27
  bounded or subordinate 33
  contact in settings of unequal 33–7
  degree of 25, 26
  degrees of in structural convergence 64–5, 100
  different kinds of competence 14, 125
  individual 27
  lexical borrowing in settings of equal 37
  one-way 64
  persistence in language shift 253, 266
  see also stable bilingualism; unstable bilingualism
bilinguals
  cohabitation, different language 184
  initiators of structural change 62, 69, 83–4, 99, 203, 204
  skilled and code switching 101, 102, 106–7, 109–10, 124–5
  unskilled substitution/switching of construction types 97–8
binding principles 229
bioprogram 326, 332
Bislama 21, 289, 291, 293, 295, 296, 303
  and Tangoa 343
Blanc, Michel H. A. 108, 143
blending *see* hybridization
blends 42
  compound 43, 45
  derivational 44, 45
Bley-Vroman, R. W. 228
Bliss, A. J. 239
Blom, J. P. 115–16
Bloomfield, Leonard 6, 39, 261
Boeschoten, H. 149
Bokamba, E. 131
Bonaire 21
Boretzky, Norbert 174, 193
borrowability, hierarchy of 51
borrowing
  compared with insertional switching 162–3
  constraints on L2 into L1 208

borrowing (*cont'd*)
defined 12
degree and kind 12
direct, of structural features 63, 63–4
distinguished from shift 17
gender assignation in 49–50
implicational constraint 54
morphological constraints 91–7
phonological constraints 55–6
and substratum influence 50
or substratum influence in structural diffusion 63–4, 79–89, 100
syntactical constraints 97–9
versus code switching 107–8
see also lexical borrowing
borrowing interference, use of term 12
borrowing scale, Thomason and Kaufman's 29–30 table 2.1, 80, 83–4
borrowing situations 11–12, 23 table 1.2
bound morphology, reduction in SLA 218
Bourhis, R. Y. 120, 122
Brahui, and Balochi 64
Braidi, Susan M. 221, 235
Braun, Maximilian 8
Breitborde, L. B. 111, 116
Brenzinger, Matthias 197, 256, 258
Bresnan, Joan 288
Broch, Ingvild 273, 274, 286
Broch, Olaf 8
Brown, H. D. 220
Brussels, Flemish/Dutch and French 27, 37, 39, 40, 41, 49–50, 51–2, 53, 137, 168
Bruyn, Adrienne 335, 350
Buddhism, Chinese in Japan 36
Bulgarian 13, 71, 72, 73
and Meglenite Rumanian 63, 93
Bund für Schwyzertüütsch 113
Bush-Hottentot languages 70
Butterworth, G. 221
Bybee, Joan 348, 350, 351

Cabral, Pedro Alvarez 309
Cacopera 256
CAH *see* Contrastive Analysis Hypothesis
Cajun English, and Louisiana French 148–9
Californian Spanish, and English 150
Callahuaya 174, 193, 206
Caló 1, 171, 174, 193, 197, 206
and Armenian Romani 193
calques 44, 45, 62
calquing 53, 64, 68, 98, 345, 350–1
Camden, Pastor B. 296
Campbell, Lyle 56, 70, 256
Canadian French 68–9
Cancino, H. 221, 228
canonical word order principle 226, 227
Cantonese 4, 246, 332, 344
and English 104
and Taiwanese 266
Cape Verde Crioulo 22, 309
Cappadocian Greek 83, 260, 261
and Turkish 260
Carib, and Arawak 184
Caribbean creoles 22, 255, 310–14, 320
English-lexicon 316, 317, 321, 323, 328–9, 348, 351, 355
Carmichael, A. C. 304
Carter, Hazel 321
CAT *see* Communication Accommodation Theory
Central Eastern Oceanic languages 294–6, 343, 346
Central Pacific languages 294
Central and South America, Amerindian languages 31
Chaudenson, Robert 269, 329, 332, 337
Cheng, Robert L. 244
Chicano English in US 237
children, and creoles 346–7
Childs, G.Tucker 168–9
China, Opium Wars (1839–42 and 1850–60) 31–2
Chindo 170, 174, 206
Chinese 3, 70, 231
and English 221, 248
influence on Japanese lexicon 32, 36–7
southern Min dialect 242, 244
and Tibetan 52–3, 171
Chinese Pidgin 273
Chinese Pidgin English 20, 268, 273, 275, 282, 284, 289–90, 291
longitudinal studies 303

Chinook
Lower 272, 277
Upper 277
Chinook Jargon *see* Chinook Pidgin
Chinook Pidgin 268, 271, 275, 278, 282, 283, 288
lexicon 276, 277
origins 272
Chomsky, Noam 135
Cinúk Wawa *see* Chinook Pidgin
Clahsen, H. 235
Clark, Ross 290, 291, 293
classification, of contact vernaculars 254–6, 266, 288–9, 299–301, 306–8
classroom SLA 16, 209, 220
Clements, J. Clancy 310
clipping, of loanwords 44, 50
cluster simplification 47
Clyne, Michael G. 6, 8, 9, 132
code mixing 105
pattern hierarchy 169
code switching
as accommodation 121–4, 125
alternational 164–5
bilingual 8, 108
common conceptual system postulated for production 140
and Communication Accommodation Theory (CAT) 110, 119–24
and congruence 163–5
as a contextualization cue 117–18
as a continuum of language behaviors 125
and conversation 103, 114–17
conversational loci for 117
defining 102–10, 124–5
domains and diglossia 112–14, 125
equivalence-based constraints 127–34
fronting or dislocation to switch core constituents 163
government-based approaches 134–7
incompetence 108–10, 143
as indexing rights-and-obligations sets 117, 118–19
insertional 164–5, 166
see also Matrix Language-Frame (MLF) model
inter-sentential 14, 104–6, 107, 125, 170
intra-sentential 105, 107, 125, 126–67, 138, 170
linguistic aspects 126–67
and markedness 118–19
Matrix Language-Frame (MLF) model 137–46
metaphorical 116
overlap with convergence 65, 98
patterns of 103–5
preference-related 104
production-based model 137–46
situational 115–16, 118
situations 14–15
social contexts 101–25
social motivations for 110–24
and sociolinguistic domains 101–2, 110–14, 125
as a strategy of neutrality 104, 123–4
structural constraints on 126–37
structural factors 126–67
taxonomies of factors affecting 116–17
theory of the social meaning of conversational 117–19
versus borrowing 107–8
versus interference 108–10
code switching grammar
MLF model 137–54, 166
model 129–30 fig. 5.1
Sankoff and Poplack's 158–65, 166
codes of interaction, community settings 312–14
Coelho, F. A. 287, 305, 347
cognitive principles
and IL development 234–5, 265, 347
and pidgin formation 287
coinages, involving compounds 44, 219
Colloquial Singapore English 4, 236, 253, 254
early IL fossilization in 245–7, 265
colonization 15, 21, 22, 31, 34, 101, 176, 183, 242, 257, 304
and creole formation 308–12
Portuguese 308, 309–10
Spanish 308, 312–13
common conceptual system, postulated for code switching production 140

Communication Accommodation Theory (CAT) 8
basic propositions 120–1
and code switching 110, 119–24
communicative strategies 224–5, 280–1
avoidance 224–5, 281
compensatory 224–5, 251, 281, 282
periphrastic 218, 220
community E(xternal)-language 247, 266, 334
community settings
and codes of interaction 312–14
norms of behavior 40, 118–19
types 25, 26–8
comparative linguistics 7, 9
competence, and performance 224
compounding
in creoles 322
innovative 33, 44–6, 219
in pidgins 284
truncated 33
compounds, coinages with 44, 46
compromise language 83
computerese, spread of 58
Comrie, B. 230
congruence
code switching and 133, 163–5
defined 152–3
EL islands and 158–63
and the MLF hypothesis 158
perceived *see* interlingual identifications
in transfer strategies 251–2, 357
congruent lexicalization 129, 164
conquest 70, 271
constituent insertion *see* EL islands
constraints, "availability" in creole formation 341
contact
"casual," and lexical borrowing 30–3
history and length of 25
intensity of 29, 38
intimate 74–9, 84–6
in settings of "unequal" bilingualism 33–7
contact linguistics
field of 9–11
objective 5, 10–11
subject matter 1–6
contact situations
archetypal 26–8
continuum of 99
outcomes 22–4
overview 22–4
taxonomy 22–4 table 1.2
types of 10, 11–22
typologies of 90
contact vernaculars
classification of 254–6, 266, 288–9, 299–301, 306–8
status of 254
content morphemes
as bare forms 148–9
constraints on switching 152–4
prepositions as 150–1
in speech errors and aphasia 140
use of L1 in L2 250
continuity principle 226
Contrastive Analysis Hypothesis (CAH) 232
contrastive focus construction
Jamaican Creole 327
Saamaka and Fongbe 335–6, 339
convergence
in ancestral language during bilingual period 266–7
in Balkan Sprachbund 71–4
code switching and 119–24
in Kupwar 84–6
in Northwest New Britain 86–9
situations 13–14, 23 table 1.2
types of transfer involved in 63
see also structural convergence
convergence areas *see* Sprachbünde
conversation
and code switching 103, 114–19
non-contiguous stretches of talk 102
conversational analysis 117–19
Cook, Captain James 272
Copper Island Aleut 19, 171, 172, 173, 174, 196, 198–205
convergence in 206–7
lexicon and phonology 199–200
morphology 202–3 table 6.5
processes and constraints in origins 203–5
and Russian 198–205

sociohistorical background 199
structural characteristics 199–203
syntax 200–1
Coppola, Marie 346
core versus periphery theory 288, 348
Corne, Chris 308, 313
Coromines, J. 305
Costa Rican Spanish 42
Coupland, Nikolas 121
Craddock, Jerry R. 169
Crawhall, Nigel 152, 158
creations
associated with language shift 169, 193
hybrid 45, 46
and lexical borrowing 43
native 44, 45
using only foreign morphemes 44, 45
creativity 1–2, 44–6, 50, 59–60, 165, 209, 219, 338, 348
Cree
and English 192
and French 19, 170, 172, 183–93
creole continuum 22, 266, 308, 354, 355
creole development, and language change 305, 357
creole formation 8, 211, 227, 304–58
internal innovation 337–40
L1 influence in 347–8, 357
leveling in 345–6, 357
and markedness 347–8
mechanisms, constraints and principles in 340–6
pidgin-to-creole scenario 332
radical as SLA 331–40
reconstructing 330
Relexification Hypothesis 337
relexification or transfer 342–3, 344, 345, 357
restructuring and substrate influence 335–6
restructuring and superstrate input 334
social contexts of 310–12
sociohistorical background to 309–14
substratum influence 322, 329, 330, 335–6, 341–5, 356
superstrate input 319, 321, 329, 330, 334, 356
theories of 329–31, 340
universal principles and 333, 338–9, 346–52, 356
créole (French) 306
creole grammar 319–29, 350–2
core and periphery 348
isomorphism 348
restructuring in 306, 333–40
creole lexicon 321–2
creole morphology and morphosyntax 322–4
creole phonology 319–21
creole syntax 326–9
and transfer 344
creoles 7, 21–2, 304–5, 355
child innovations into 346–7
defining 21, 305–8
diffusion of English-lexicon and French-lexicon 308
or extended pidgins 288, 306–7
externally motivated change in later development 352–5
grammaticalization in 350–2, 357
and group SLA 266
of mixed race 183–4, 206
"monogenetic" theory of origins 326
as nativized pidgins 306
TMA systems 324–6, 338–9, 348
terms used for 305
as a typological class 307–8
use of label 18–19, 305–6
see also intermediate creoles; prototypical creoles; radical creoles
creolists, use of term "nativization" 244
creolization
Chinook Pidgin 272
defined 333
Singapore English 255
use of term 289, 300, 301
vernacularization and 300, 307
creoloid 255
criollo (Spanish) 305–6
Croatian 6
Croft, William 230
cross-disciplinary approach 6, 9
cross-generational differences, in L2 proficiency 170, 196

cultural pressure 29, 38–9, 65–70, 90, 206
Curaçao 21
Cushitic languages 53, 84
  and Bantu languages 171, 193–8
Cypriot Greek, and English 150
Czech
  and German 54
  and Russian 213–14

Dalmatian 6
Dalton-Puffer, Christiane 35, 57, 58, 95, 97
Daman Creole Portuguese 21, 310
Danelaw 34, 80
Danes 34, 80
Davies, Eirlys 130–1, 133, 136, 138, 142, 151, 153, 154, 156, 160, 162, 170
Dawkins, R. M. 56, 83
Dawson, Hope 82
Dawson, R. 290
D'Costa, Jean 320, 322, 330, 334
DeCamp, David 306
decreolization 314, 354
  quantitative and qualitative 259
DeGraff, Michel 7, 322, 326, 329, 337, 346, 347, 348, 352
Delaware Pidgin 270, 271, 276, 283, 284, 287
  source language Unami 277, 278, 287
demographic factors 25, 311, 341
derivational morphology, constraints on borrowing 62, 91, 95
Detgers, Ulrich 348, 351
Devonish, Hubert 321
Dhayʔyi 74
Dhimotiki, and Katharevousa 112
Dhuwal 78
dialects
  contact between 81–2
  leveling 253
  speakers of non-standard 101–2
diffusion areas *see* Sprachbünde
diglossia 14, 27, 35, 36, 112, 254
  classic and broad 112–13
  definition 112
  domains and code switching 112–14, 125
  as stage in language attrition 258
diglossic speech communities 102
Dimmendaal, Gerrit J. 256, 262, 263, 264
direct transfer, compared with structural convergence 62
directionality 18, 25
DiSciullo, A. M. 134, 135, 136
divergence 5
  code switching and 119–20
  and Communication Accommodation Theory (CAT) 122–4
domain analysis 114
domains
  defined 111
  diglossia and code switching 112–14, 125
  examples 111
  or situations 111
Dorian, Nancy 257, 261, 262, 263
Doron, E. 141
double morphology 148, 151–2
Dravidian languages 64, 84, 242, 249
Drechsel, Emanuel J. 272, 275, 276, 278, 282
Dressler, Wolfgang U. 58
Dreyfuss, Gail Raimi 170
Dunne, Timothy T. 249
Dusková, Libuse 213–14
Dutch 21, 222, 330, 338
  and Arabic 136–7, 141, 142, 148, 219, 226
  and English 43, 132, 218
  and French 49–50, 146, 154, 156–7, 160, 161–2, 163, 164
  gender assignation of borrowings 49
  and Javanese 184
  and Sranan 352–4
  Standard (Belgian) 40, 49–50
  and Turkish 148, 149
Dutton, Tom 297–8
Dyirbal 262

Early Modern English 37–8
  borrowing from Latin and Greek 57
  dialect influence on Irish English 237–8
  influence of French writing on 36, 55
  in Jamaican creole 322
East Sutherland, Scottish Gaelic 257
Eastern Caribbean French creoles 325
Eastern Ijo (Kalabari) 336, 338

Eastern Maroon Creole 22, 316
Paamaka variety, SVCs 328
see also Okanisi; Paamaka (Paramaccan)
Eastern Nilotic language family 194
Ebonics *see* African American Vernacular English
Eckman, Fred R. 232–3
Ecuador 19
education, English-medium 237, 242
Eersel, Christian 354
Ehret, Christopher 194
EL islands 159, 191, 206
constraints on multi-word switches 138, 154–63, 166
implicational hierarchy of switched 162
internal 156–7
and the notion of congruence 158–63, 164
Trigger Hypothesis 140, 155–8
El Salvador 256
elaborated pidgins *see* extended pidgins
Ellis, R. 208, 225
Elworthy, Frederick Thomas 316
embedded language (EL) 105, 138
see also EL islands
Emeneau, Murray B. 64, 70
empty category principle 229
endangered languages 257
endolingual bilingualism 102
English 222, 229, 233
and Adangme 131–2
and Akan 131
and Arabic 48–9
borrowing into American Norwegian 39
and Cantonese 104
and Chinese 221, 248
and Cree 192
and Cypriot Greek 150
and Dutch 43, 132, 218
East Midlands 81
examples of contact-induced changes 3
and Finnish 218
and Florida Spanish 43
and French 43, 54, 164, 212, 214, 214–15, 234
and French in Ottawa/Hull 40, 66
and French in Prince Edward Island 68–70
and French in Quebec 40, 122–4
and German 44, 211, 213, 214, 215, 219–20, 221, 250
as a Germanic language 35, 59
and Gujarati 249
and Hausa 149
and Hebrew 261
and Hindi 47, 47–8, 131, 136, 164
influence on Japanese lexicon 31–3 table 2.2, 39, 42, 52
and Italian 215
and Japanese 149, 170, 250
and Japanese in San Francisco 109, 142–3
and Japanese in Toronto 109, 142–3
and Latin 56
lexical borrowings in 29
and Malay 15
and Mandarin Chinese 146
and Naskapi 192
Norse influence on Standard 81–2
Northern dialect, as a koiné 81, 82–3
northern in Ireland 237, 239
and Panjabi 131, 149, 169, 205, 248
and Pennsylvania German (PG) 65
question formation 228–9, 231
"Romance" phonological rules 55
and Romani 4–5, 171
and Shona 152, 158
southern and southwest Midlands in Ireland 237–8, 239
southwestern dialects, and Bajan 315 table 9.1, 334
and Spanish 14, 42, 43, 44, 97, 106, 128–9, 131, 133, 136, 164, 169, 212, 215, 221
and Spanish in New York City 105, 132, 164
spread of 38
and Swahili 103, 104, 105, 131, 138, 147–9, 151, 155, 157, 164, 168
and Swedish 218
and Tagalog 106
and Tamil 164, 249
and Warlpiri 149
and Yiddish 17–18 table 1.1, 44

English (*cont'd*)
  and Yoruba 133, 139
  Zulu and Afrikaans 168, 205
  see also American English; Early Modern English; foreigner talk English; "indigenized" varieties of English; Middle English (ME); nautical English; New Englishes; Old English (OE)
English as a world language (EWL) 243–5
English-lexicon creoles 21, 22, 316–17, 320, 324–5, 332, 334, 338–9
Engsh 168
epenthesis 47
equivalence 160
equivalence constraint 128–33, 166
  in equivalence-based switching 158–60, 163–4
  on multi-word switches 155
  revised 137
equivalence-based constraints on code switching 127–34, 137
Escure, Genevieve 245
Eskimo Pidgin 273, 281–2, 283
  varieties 271–2
Eskimo Trade Pidgin 20
Ethiopic Semitic 84
ethnic group, "persistent" 171, 172, 194
ethnic minorities *see* minorities
ethnography of speaking 114–15
ethnolect 124
ethnolinguistic vitality 12, 259, 266
European languages
  and Bantu languages 148
  colonization and 308–10
  indigenized varieties of 124
Ewe, and French 336
Ewegbe 335
EWL *see* English as a world language (EWL)
exogamy 70, 74
exolingual bilingualism 102, 108
expanded pidgins *see* extended pidgins
extended pidgins 20–1, 264, 270, 271, 288–97, 302–3
  or creoles 288, 306–7, 332
  and group SLA 266
  origins and development of 289
extensions, semantic 33, 43, 45
external (social and psychological) factors 2, 8, 9, 24, 341
  in language death 257–9
E(xternal)-language, community 247, 266, 334
externally motivated change, in later creole development 352–5
Extra, Guus 219
extralinguistic factors 25

Factorization Principle (Naro), for pidgin formation 287
"false friends" (*faux amis*) 211, 234
"family tree" model *see* Stammbaum model
fashion 38
Fasold, Ralph 113
Felix, Sascha W. 215, 221, 229
Ferguson, Charles A. 112
Fiji 242
Filppula, M. 241, 245
Finnish 98, 222, 231
  and English 218
  in northern Minnesota 262
first language acquisition 220
  children and creole formation 346
first language attrition
  and death 256–67
  linguistic consequences of 259–63
Fishman, Joshua A. 8, 110–11, 112–13, 114, 257
Flege, J. E. 212, 234
Flemish
  and French in Brussels 27, 37, 39
  French and English 122
Florida Spanish, and English 43
Fongbe 335–6, 337
  and French 107, 155, 157, 159, 160 fig. 5.3, 342
foreign language *see* second language
foreign language acquisition 208–9
  see also second language acquisition (SLA)
foreigner talk 269, 279, 287
foreigner talk English 279, 290, 291, 295
Forson, B. 131

fossilization 222
  degrees of in group SLA 245–7
  inflection in pidgins 281
Fox, James A. 273, 275
free morpheme constraint 127–8
freezing of forms 178
French 29, 222, 229, 231
  and Alsatian in Strasbourg 37, 41, 66
  and Arabic in Morocco 130–1, 136, 138, 142, 151, 153, 154, 156, 170
  contact varieties of 242
  and Cree 19, 170, 172, 183–93
  and Dutch 49–50, 146, 154, 156–7, 160, 161–2, 163, 164
  efforts to rid it of borrowings 41
  and English 43, 54, 164, 212, 214, 214–15, 234
  and English in Montréal 27
  and English in Ottawa/Hull 40, 66
  and English in Prince Edward Island 68–70
  and English in Quebec 40, 122–4
  and Ewe 336
  and Flemish/Dutch in Brussels 27, 37, 39, 137
  and Fongbe 107, 155, 157, 159, 160 fig. 5.3, 337, 342
  gender assignation of borrowings 49
  German borrowings from 52
  influence on derivational morphology of Middle English (ME) 62, 95, 97
  influence on lexicon of Middle English (ME) 34–6, 37, 39, 54–5, 56–7 table 2.5
  influence of writing on Early Modern English 36, 55
  and Italian 135
  and Kreyòl in Haiti 112
  and Lingala 131, 148, 157, 159
  and Montagnais 192
  as official language of Quebec 122–3
  Old Central 35
  Old Northern 35
  in Reunion 312
  and Wolof 107, 127, 158–9 fig. 5.2
  see also Acadian French; Canadian French; Norman French
French-lexicon creoles 21, 320, 325–6, 351
Fuller, Janet M. 65
function morphemes 150–1, 153
  see also system morphemes
function words, direct borrowing of 63

Gaelic *see* Irish (Gaelic); Scottish Gaelic
Gal, Susan 27, 254, 257
Gama, Vasco da 310
Gardner-Chloros, Penelope 37, 41, 106, 108, 124, 150
Garrett, M. F. 140
Gass, Susan M. 223, 229, 231
Gbe 22, 335, 336, 339, 340, 349, 351
Geg 71
gender assignation of borrowings 49–50
generations, shift over 237, 245, 332
generative linguistics 230–1
"genetic affiliation" 6, 7
  effects of borrowing on 59
Gengbe 348, 351
German 34, 222
  and Arabic 287
  borrowings from French and Russian 52
  and Czech 54
  and English 44, 211, 213, 214, 215, 219–20, 221, 250
  foreigner talk to immigrants 279
  gender assignation of borrowings 49
  of "guestworkers" 15
  and Italian 221
  and Russian 8
  shift from Hungarian to 27, 254
  and Slavic 7
  stages of acquisition of word order by learners 216–17
  Standard and Schwyzertüütsch in Switzerland 27, 112, 113–14
  and Swedish 213
  in Tok Pisin 293
  see also Pennsylvania German; Swiss German
Germanic languages 287
  English 35, 59
gesture, use in pidgins 272–3
Ghanaian Pidgin English 306
Giles, Howard 8, 39, 119–24, 259

Gilman, C. 307
Goddard, Ives 277, 278, 284, 287
Golovko, Evgenij V. 198–204
Gonzales, Ambrose 1
Gooden, Shelome 321
Goodman, J. S. 271
Goodman, Morris 325
Gothic 257
government, approaches to code switching 134–7
Graham, C. Ray 211
grammar
  constraints in the elaboration of L2 grammar 227–9
  IL 224–5
  and lexicon fusion 19
  model of a code switching 129–30 fig. 5.1
  underlying code switching 126–66
  see also creole grammar
grammaticalization
  in creoles 343, 348, 350–2, 357
  defined 350
  in pidgins 284–5, 295–6
grammaticization 348, 350
Grant, Anthony P. 276, 277
Greek 13, 37, 71, 72, 73, 231, 350
  in Albanian 59
  and Arabic in Cyprus 171
  and Arvanítika 174
  Asia Minor 13
  and English 57
  as a High language 71
  Medieval 73
  Middle 64
  see also Cappadocian Greek; Cypriot Greek
Greenberg, Joseph H. 230
Greenfield, Lawrence 111
Greenfield, W. 304
Griekwas 184
Grosjean, F. 102, 140
Guarani 14, 27
Guinea Kriyol (Portuguese lexicon) 22
Guinea-Bissau creole 22, 309, 336
Gujarati, and English 249
Gulf of Guinea creoles 22, 323
Gullah 1, 311
Gumperz, John J. 27, 84–6, 109, 115–16, 117
Gundel, J. K. 214
Gupta, Anthea Fraser 246, 255
Guthrie, Malcolm 70
Guyana
  Berbice Dutch in 21
  Creolese 305
Guyanais 325
Guyanese 21, 313, 329, 330, 354
  rural 307, 355
  urban 22, 299, 308, 316
Gypsies *see* Roma

Haiti, Standard French and Kreyòl 112
Haitian creole (French lexicon) 21, 322, 325, 330, 336, 337, 342, 352
Haitian Kreyòl 305, 307
Hamers, Josiane F. 108, 143
Hammarberg, Björn 213, 223–4
Hanbury, David T. 281
Hancock, Ian 193
Handler, Jerome 315
Harding, E. 279
Harris, John 238, 239, 241
Hatch, E. 221
Haugen, Einar 8, 9, 34, 39, 43, 44, 47, 51, 260
Hausa 322
  and English 149
Hawai'i Creole English (HCE) 271, 307, 332, 344, 346, 348, 349
Hawai'i Pidgin English 3, 20, 271, 275, 346
  of Japanese immigrants 143–5, 250
HCE *see* Hawai'i Creole English (HCE)
Heath, Jeffrey 27, 53, 62, 74, 74–8, 92, 94, 95, 150
Hebrew 34
  and English 261
  and Spanish 131, 132
  and Yiddish 57
Heller, Monica 104, 122–3
Hemnesberget, Norway 115–16
Henderson, Eugenia J. A. 70
Herbert, Robert K. 41
Herzog, George 8, 42
Hesseling, Dirk Christiaan 8, 305, 331

Hiberno-English 22, 330
  "hot news" construction 214, 240
  see also Irish English
High (H) language variety 27, 112–14
Hindi, and English 47, 131, 136, 164
Hindi-Urdu 13, 85
Hinnenkamp, V. 271, 279, 287
Hinskens, Frans 83
Hiri Motu 270, 288, 297, 302
  origins of 297–8
Hispanics, in US 27, 33, 66, 169
historical linguistics 7, 9, 91
Hittite 257
hlonipha 41
Ho, Mian-Lian 246, 255
Hock, Hans 47–8
Hoeks, Jimmy A. 211
Hoetink, Harmannus 313
Hokkien 246
Holm, John 304, 305, 309, 310, 320, 323
Hosali, Priya 270
Huang, J. 221
Huber, Magnus 308
Hudson Bay Pidgin Eskimo 281
Huebner, Thom 220, 286
Hulstijn, J. H. 333
human language faculty 304–5, 347
Hungarian
  in Austria 257
  shift to German 27, 254
Huttar, George 275, 277, 278, 283
hybrid languages 19, 260
hybridization 33
  tertiary 275, 301
hybrids 43
Hylstenstam, K. 231, 233
Hymes, Dell 114–15, 270, 280, 313–14, 333
hypothesis testing 235

Icelandic 59
identifications, interlingual 37, 48
identity
  code switching and 116, 118, 122–5
  differences in perception of 41
  divergence and group 122–4
  in-group vernaculars 242
  mixed codes as markers of group 168–9, 176
  and urban vernaculars 168–9, 206
ideologies and attitudes 25, 313
Igla, Birgit 174
Ijaz, I. Helene 211
IL *see* interlanguage (IL)
imitations of foreign words 42
immigrant groups
  and dominant language 33–7, 101
  own version of TL 237
Immigrant Swedish, and Russenorsk 285–6
imperfect learning *see* transfer, negative
importation
  versus imposition 80
  versus substitution 43, 47
imposition
  importation versus 80
  use of term 16
incorporation, hierarchy of 108
indentured servants 311, 314
India
  creoles in 21, 22
  New Englishes in 27, 242
Indian Butler English 20, 270
Indian English 15, 330
Indic languages 47, 242, 249
"indigenized" varieties
  colonization and 15, 237
  continuum of 255–6 fig. 7.1
  intermediate creoles and 316, 330
  as link languages 254
"indigenized" varieties of English
  origins and formation 243–5
  and second language learning 4
  and similar contact varieties 241–3
  substratum influence 239–41, 265–6
indigenous American pidgins 271–2
  sociolinguistic characteristics 272–3
indigenous peoples, lexical borrowing from European languages 31
I(nternal)-languages 247, 266, 333–4, 345, 357
Indo-European family 59, 84, 98
Indonesia, Paranakan Chinese in 170
Indonesian 38, 39

inflectional morphology
constraints on borrowing 62, 91–2, 95
direct borrowing of 63–4
innovations
borrowing as 42
in language shift 265
inter-community contact, example 74–9
interference 62, 109, 280
code switching versus 108–10
defined 12
degrees in bilinguals' languages 17–18 table 1.1
L1 influence on TL 209–10
phenomena or code switching 103
phonological 55–6
in speech or in language (Weinreich) 236
studies 9–10
through shift 16, 80
use of term 10, 12
see also transfer
interlanguage (IL) 16, 108, 209
code switching and 103, 108–9, 125
cognitive principles and development of 234–5, 265, 347
early as basic variety of TL 265, 267
early fossilization in 245–7
elaboration of grammar 227–9, 265
general characteristics of early 222–3, 264–5, 279, 296
grammar characteristics 224–5
internal innovation 224
one-to-one principle 227
prototypical pidgins and early 269, 279, 286, 302
simplifications 149
stages of development 220–3, 265
interlingual identifications 233–4, 248–9, 265, 345
intermediate creoles 22, 255–6, 266, 313, 330, 355
emergence of 314–16
internal innovation
in creole formation 337–40
in pidgin formation 284–6, 295–7
internal (linguistic) factors 2, 9, 24, 341
I(nternal)-language 247, 266, 333–4, 345, 357
internet, and lexical borrowing 31
"intertwined languages" 172–3, 190–1, 205, 206–7
Bakker's classification 172–4 table 6.2
continuum of 169
creations 193
Inuit, and Europeans 272
invasions, contact through 34–6
Irish English 15, 17, 237–41, 245, 252, 255, 265
in Belfast 254
emergence of 253
northern and southern varieties 238
substratum influence on 239–41, 246, 265–6
see also Hiberno-English
Irish (Gaelic), and Irish English 237–41, 257, 265
Ishiwata, Toshio 32
Isicamtho 168, 169
Island Carib 174, 175, 184
Isle de France creole 21
isomorphism 220, 247
in creole grammar 348
structural 13, 90, 99–100
Italian 222
and English 215
and French 135
and German 221
and Slavic 7

Jahr, Ernst Håkon 273, 274, 275, 276, 286
Jake, Janice 147, 148, 152, 153, 158, 162
Jakobson, Roman 24, 97
Jamaican Creole 21, 307, 308, 313, 320, 321, 322, 334, 351, 355
continuing influence from European languages 330
contrastive focus construction 327
pronominal system 323 table 9.2
SVCs 328
James, Allan 213, 234
Japanese 3, 26, 34, 44, 232
Chinese influence on lexicon 36–7
Chinese writing system 36
and English 149, 170, 250

English influence on lexicon 31–3 table 2.2, 39, 42, 52
and English in San Francisco 109, 142–3
and English in Toronto 109, 142–3
influence of American English on 38
pronunciation of loanwords 47
treatment of English loans 50
Japanese immigrants, Hawai'i Pidgin English 143–5, 250
Japanese Pidgin English 271
jargon 268, 269
Jarvis, Scott 210, 218
Javanese
and Dutch 184
and Malay 170
Jespersen, Otto 331
Johnson, Samuel V. 272
Jondoh, Edina Elemawusi Ayaba 351
Jordens, Peter 226–7, 228
Joseph, Brian 55, 71–4, 350
Joshi, A. 141, 146
Judeo-Espagnol 71
Judezmo 71

Kabana 87–9
Kachru, Braj B. 105, 242, 244
Kalabari (Eastern Ijo) 336, 338
Kallen, Jeffrey L. 237, 239, 253
Kamwangamalu, Nkonko Mudipanu 146, 157
Kannada 13, 260
Marathi and Urdu 84–6, 93, 97
Katharevousa, and Dhimotiki 112
Kaufman, D. 261
Kaufman, Eugen 42
Kaufman, Terrence 6, 7, 9, 12, 17, 22, 52, 53, 54, 55–6, 57, 61, 64, 79–84, 89, 90, 93, 94–5, 98–9, 171–2
borrowing scale 29–30 table 2.1, 34, 80, 83–4
on pidgins 278
Kay, Paul 287, 348
Kean, M. 248
Keenan, E. L. 230
Keesing, Roger 294, 295, 346, 348
Kegl, Judy 346
Keller, R. E. 113–14
Kellerman, Eric 223, 248
Kenrick, Donald 193
Kenya 242, 258
Kerswill, Paul 83, 253
Khoekhoes, and Afrikaans 184
Khoesan 41
Kikongo 298, 335, 340
Kiminyánga 298
KiMwani 173
King, Ruth 68–9
Kingsmore, Rona K. 238
Kituba 270, 288, 297, 298, 300
Kiyómbe 298
Klavans, Judith L. 141
Klein, Wolfgang 222–3, 227, 281
Klemola, Juhani 316
Kloss, Heinz 8
Koch, H. 292
koiné
formation 253
Northern English as a 81, 82–3
koinéization 345
Konstantinopulos, Christos G. 174
Kopitar, Jernej 8
Kore 262, 264
Korlai Portuguese 310
Kormakiti Arabic 171, 172
Kotsinas, Ulla-Britt 285–6
Kouwenberg, Silvia 338
Kove 87–9
Krekonika 174, 193
Kreyòl 305
and Standard French in Haiti 112
Krio (English lexicon) 22, 307
Krojos 184
Kubler, Cornelius C. 244–5
Kupwar, India 13, 27, 260
convergence in 84–6, 87, 90, 93, 97, 204
Kannada, Marathi and Urdu 84–6
Kurath, Hans 54
Kwa 335
Kweyòl 305

L1 *see* ancestral language; first language; native language

L1 influence 62, 209
constraints on language shift 247
in pidgin formation 282–3, 294
in SLA 209–17, 231–3, 264–5
and universals in creole formation 347–8, 357
see also substratum influence
L1 retentions 210, 211, 224
L1A *see* first language acquisition
L2 *see* second language
Ladino 71
Lado, R. 210, 213, 232
Lalla, Barbara 320, 322, 330, 334
Lalleman, Josine 333
Lamogai 13, 87–9
Lamu Island 262
Langendoen, D. Terence 287
language attitudes, code switching and 125
language attrition 79, 266
age differences 261
first language 256–67
quantitative and qualitative 258–9
in relation to other contact phenomena 263–4
stages of 258–9, 266
structural influence in 69
Language Bioprogram Hypothesis (LBH), Bickerton's 326, 329
language change 6
and creole development 305, 357
directionality of 18, 25, 64–5
mechanisms of 65–100
nativization and acculturation in 243–4
sources of 64–5
theories of 18, 243
"wave" model 7
language contact
history of research on language 6–9
in its social setting 25–8
major outcomes 23–4 table 1.2
social contexts of 24–8
and speech communities 26–9
Language Contact and Conflict, First World Congress on (1979) 9
language creation, new contact languages 18–22, 24 table 1.2
language death 16, 79
external (social) factors in 257–9
final three stages 259–60
first language 256–67
sociolinguistic factors in 259
language decay 260, 261–3, 266–7
compared with pidginization 263–4
language ideology 40–1
language maintenance 8, 11–15, 23
with bilingualism 68
defined 11
and lexical borrowing 29–60
resistance to extreme structural changes 74, 89
structural diffusion in 61–100
language mixture 1–2, 6
language obsolescence, due to ongoing shift 84
language policies 41, 243, 257–8
language production, and code switching 137–46
language shift 8, 15–18, 23–4 table 1.2
collapse of stable bilingualism 27
continuum of outcomes 255–6 fig. 7.1
creations associated with 169, 193
distinguished from borrowing 17
extreme convergence and 97, 99–100
and creation of "indigenized" varieties 243–5
individual and group distinguished 17
issues in the study of 243–7
linguistic constraints in 247–52
non-structural factors in 252–4
over generations 237, 245, 332
persistence of bilingualism 253, 266
primary 260, 263
radical creoles as cases of 22
reinforcement principles in 252–3
and second language acquisition 208–67
sequencing of bilingual code mixture 170
structural change in 84
"untutored" or targeted 16
see also second language acquisition (SLA), group
language teaching 26

languages
single-parent 6, 7
typological similarity 2
Larmouth, Donald W. 262
Latin 29, 35, 37, 55
in Albanian 59
and English 56, 57
Latino, in US 237
LBH *see* Language Bioprogram Hypothesis (LBH)
learnability theories 230–1
Leather, Jonathan 213, 234
Lee, C. L. 146
Leeds, England, Panjabi and English 169, 205
Lefebvre, Claire 182, 329, 337, 342–3, 344
Lehnprägung (loancoinage) 42
Lehnwort (loanword) 42
Leland, Charles G. 5
lemmas 141
levels of representation for 141
Lenca 256
LePage, Robert B. 125
leveling
in creole formation 345–6, 357
dialect 253
see also simplification
Levelt, Willem 141
Lewis, Glyn E. 33
lexical borrowing 1, 8, 26, 59–60, 61
"casual" contact and 30–3
code switching as 125
defining and classifying 42–6
impact on lexicon 58–9
impact on morphology 56–8
impact on phonology 54–6
and innovations in minority language 99
and language maintenance 29–60
linguistic constraints on 51–3
mediates structural transfer 62
processes and products of 42–6
in settings of equal bilingualism 37
social motivations for 37–42
structural consequences of 53–9
see also loanshifts; loanwords
lexical contact phenomena, classification 44–5 table 2.3
lexical diffusion, and structural diffusion 99
lexicalization, congruent 129, 164
lexicon
creole 321–2
and grammar fusion 19
impact of lexical borrowing on 58–9
of pidgins 276–7, 293–4
lexifer language *see* superstrate language
Lichtveld, U. M. 317
Lin, Hannah H. 244
Lingala 298
and French 131, 148, 157, 159
lingua franca
contact varieties of English as 242
as instance of extreme convergence 100
pidgin English as 3, 21
use of term 268
linguistic areas *see* Sprachbünde
linguistic constraints 25, 61–2, 91–7
loan creations 44
loan renditions 44
loan translations 44, 45, 211, 260
loanblends 43, 44, 45
loans
established 40
semantic 43–4
loanshifts 43, 45, 64
subtypes 43–4, 45
loanwords 17, 43, 45
clipping of 44, 50
integration of 46–51
morphological integration 48–51
phonological integration 46–8
pure 43, 45
London English 81
Los Angeles Spanish 65, 66–8, 98, 150, 260
Louden, Mark L. 65
Louisiana French, and Cajun English 148–9
Lounsbury, Floyd G. 305
Loveday, Leo J. 26, 31, 33, 36, 39, 44, 50
Low (L) language variety 27, 112–14
loyalty, language 40–1
Lucio, G. 6
Lüdi, G. 102, 108
Lumsden, John S. 329, 337, 342–3, 344
Lusi 13, 87–9

Luyia 104
Lwidakho 104

Ma'a 53, 171, 172, 174, 175, 193
  case of 193–8
  genesis of 196–8, 206
  grammar 194–6
  historical background 194
  lexicon 194
  structural features 194–6
Maasai 194, 258
Macedo, Donaldo P. 287–8, 348
Macedonian 13, 71
McWhorter, John H. 307, 308, 313, 335
Magellan, Ferdinand 289
Maher, Julianne 262, 264
maintained language, linguistic constraints on structural diffusion 61–2, 91–7
Malagasy 312
Malay 246
  English and 15
  and Javanese 170
Malaysia 15, 21, 242
Mandarin Chinese 15, 246
  Beijing 244–5
  and English 146
Mandingo 322
Marathi 13, 90, 260
  and Urdu 84–6, 93
markedness
  code switching 118–19
  and creole formation 347–8
  and ease of learning 96
  hierarchy in rule generalization 229
  structural constraints based on 92, 94–6, 345
  and typological universals 230–1
markedness constraints, and LI influence in SLA 231–3, 265
Markedness Differential Hypothesis (MDH) 232–3
markers, foreignness 43
Maroldt, K. 34
maroon communities 316–17
Marquesas, South Pacific, pidgin text 290
Masica, Colin P. 70
mass media
  and lexical borrowing 31
  and pressure of dominant language 258
Matawai 316
matrix language (ML) 105, 138
  ancestral language as 198, 206
  defined 141
  dominant language as 198
  establishing the 141–6, 206
  host language as 193
Matrix Language-Frame (MLF) model
  blocking hypothesis 140, 146, 150–1, 152
  of code switching 137–46, 166
  constraints on code switching 146–54
  EL implicational hierarchy hypothesis 140, 162
  EL island trigger hypothesis 140, 155–8
  hypotheses 139–41
  matrix language hypothesis 140
Mauritius 21, 312, 313
Mayan 56
  and Spanish 52
Mbugu 193, 195
  see also Ma'a
MDH *see* Markedness Differential Hypothesis
Media Lengua 19, 169, 170, 171, 172, 174, 175–82, 197, 342
  adaptation of Spanish items to Quechua structure 177–81, 206
  processes of change 181–2
  pronouns in 178–9 table 6.3
  structural characteristics 176–7, 191, 206
Mediterranean Lingua Franca 268
"medium of interethnic communication" (MIC) 331
Mednyj Aleut *see* Copper Island Aleut
Meechan, Marjorie 106, 107, 126, 127, 155, 157, 158–60
Meglenite Rumanian, and Bulgarian 63, 93
Meillet, Antoine 6, 91, 97
Meisel, Jürgen M. 216, 217, 218
Melanesian Pidgin 288, 289, 298, 323, 332, 343, 346
  emergence of early 291–3
  grammar 293–7
  internal innovation in 295–7

L1 influence in development 294–5
longitudinal studies 303
varieties of 270
Menn, Lise 261
Menomini 261
mental lexicon 141
Meso-America Sprachbund 70
Mesthrie, Rajend 249
mestizo 183–4, 206
Métis (mixed race) 183–4
MIC *see* "medium of interethnic communication" (MIC)
Michif 19, 170, 171–2, 174, 183–93, 206
convergence and innovation in 189–90
mechanisms and processes in the genesis of 190–3, 206
NP structure 186–7
phonology 185–6
sociohistorical background 183–4
sources of grammatical categories 173, 185 table 6.4
sources of structure 184–5
syntax 188–9
VP structure 187–8
micro-level analysis, code switching 114–17
Middle English (ME)
derivational morphemes borrowed from French 62, 95, 97
French influence on lexicon 34–6, 39, 54–5, 56–7, 58
Norman French shift to English 15
Northern dialect
compared with Old English and Viking Norse 81 table 3.1
Norse impact on 80–2
phonemicization of voiced fricatives and affricates 54, 55
Romance suffixes via French loanwords 57 table 2.5
Migge, Bettina 317, 328, 329, 335, 338–9, 340
migration, to and from Ireland 253
military occupation 20, 271
Milroy, J. 254
Milroy, Lesley 104, 254
minorities, and majority national language 8, 26–7, 33–7, 101, 236–7
minority languages
cultural pressure from dominant host language 65–70, 257–8
resistance to host language 123–4
Mintz, Sidney W. 310, 312, 313
Mioni, Alberto M. 111
mismatch, categorial, code switching and 132
mixed codes, "fossilized" 168
mixed race 183–4, 206
Mkude, Daniel J. 48–9
ML *see* matrix language
MLF *see* Matrix Language-Frame (MLF) model
Mobilian Jargon *see* Mobilian Pidgin
Mobilian Pidgin 268, 271, 272, 276, 277, 278
modernization 37
Moeliono, Anton M. 38, 39
monolingualism 26
Montagnais, and French 192
Montréal French 49
and English 27
Mordinov, A. 43
Moroccan Arabic
and Dutch 136–7, 141, 142, 148, 219
and German 287
Arabic–French code switching 130–1, 138, 151, 153, 154, 170
morphemes
categories of (4-M model) 152
diffusability of 92, 95
see also content morphemes; function morphemes; system morphemes
morphology
borrowing of 64
constraints based on congruence 93–4
constraints based on transparency/ markedness 94–6
constraints on borrowing 91–7
creole 322–4
functionally based constraints 96–7
impact of lexical borrowing on 56–8
LI influence on L2 213–14
natural 58
of pidgins 275–6
see also derivational morphology; double morphology; inflectional morphology

morphosyntax, creole 322–4
Morrill, C. H. 300
Motu 21, 288, 297–8
Mougeon, Raymond 69
Mouk 13, 87–9
Mous, Maarten 173–4, 194–5
MTT (morphotactic and semantic transparency) *see* transparency, semantic and morphotactic
Mufwene, Salikoko 7, 17, 96, 298, 300, 307, 308, 313, 329, 332
Mühlhäusler, Peter 268, 271, 275, 282, 284, 289–92, 295–7, 303
Mulert, F. E. 317
Müller, Friedrich Max 6, 24
multi-word switches, constraints on 154–63
multilingualism
  community 65, 71–4
  degree of 26, 64–5
  individual 27
  stable 90–1
Muntzel, Martha C. 256
Muysken, Pieter 9, 19, 51, 129, 132, 134–5, 137, 164, 174, 347
  on Media Lengua 175–82
Myers-Scotton, Carol 103–6, 107, 108, 109, 117–19, 125, 131, 147, 148, 151–2, 153, 158, 162, 165, 166, 168, 169, 170
  EL Island Trigger Hypothesis 155–8
  Matrix Language-Frame (MLF) model 137–46

Nairobi 168
Naro, Anthony J. 287
Nartey, J. 131
Naskapi, and English 192
Native American languages 272, 278
  see also indigenous American pidgins
native language
  influence on language shift 15–16, 17
  influence in SLA 209–17
nativization
  creolists' use of term 244
  in language change 243–4, 306
nautical English 320, 321
Navajo 31
Ndjuka 277, 278, 283, 316, 338, 340
Ndjuka-Trio Pidgin 275, 277, 278, 283
need 36, 37, 39, 268
negation, order of acquisition of rules 221
neighborhood 40
Nelde, Peter Hans 9
Nemser, William 211, 213, 216, 219–20
new contact languages, creation 11, 18–22, 89, 204, 265–6
New Englishes 4, 27, 124, 242, 252
  see also "indigenized" varieties of English
New South Wales Pidgin 291, 292, 295
  pidgin text 290
New York City
  Puerto Ricans in 14, 111–12 table 4.1
  Spanish and English 105, 132, 164
Newport, Elissa L. 346
Ngandi 74, 79, 94, 260
  and Ritharngu 75, 76–8, 79, 93–4, 96, 203, 260
Ngbandi 298, 299–300
Nguni 41, 168
Nicaraguan Sign Language 346
Niger Congo languages 242
Nigeria, New English in 242
Nigerian Pidgin English 20, 21, 306
Nishimura, Miwa 109, 142–3, 144–5, 170, 250
nomadic groups, and bilingual mixed languages 193, 206
non-Austronesian languages 13
non-structural factors, in language shift 252–4
nonce borrowings 40, 41, 106, 107, 164
Nootka 277
Norman French 15, 34
Norse, Viking
  compared with Old English and Northern Middle English 81 table 3.1, 93
  influence on Old English (OE) 34
North America
  English colonialization 31
  immigrant languages in 8
Northwest New Britain 11, 13, 27
  convergence in 86–9, 90
  languages in contact 86–9 table 3.2

Nortier, Jacomine 136, 141, 142, 148
Norwegian,
  Ranamal and Bokmal 115–16
  and Russian 20, 21, 273–5, 284
Norwegian immigrants, United States 34, 39
Noun Phrase Accessibility Hierarchy (NPAH) 230–1
NPAH *see* Noun Phrase Accessibility Hierarchy
Nunggubuyu 74, 94, 96
  and Warndarang 75, 78

Oberwart, Austria 27, 254
Odlin, Terence 210, 218, 237–8, 239, 241, 245, 248, 253
official and national language, vernaculars as 38
Ojibwe 183, 186
Oka, Djoehana 170
Okanisi (Aukan) 316
Oksaar, Els 6
Old English (OE) 350
  compared with Viking Norse and Northern Middle English 81 table 3.1
  influence of Old Norse on 34, 80–3
  phonemicization of allophonic pairs 54
Old Norse, influence on Old English 80–3
Oloruntoba, Y. 138–9
one-to-one principle 226, 227, 247, 287
  see also isomorphism
Optimality Theory 288
Ortoz, Carmelia 43
Osinde, Ken 168
Otheguy, Ricardo 67
Ottawa/Hull, French and English 40, 51, 66
overgeneralization 247, 262

Paamaka (Paramaccan) 316, 336, 338
  SVCs 328, 335
Pachuco 169
Pacific Islands 20, 22, 242
Pacific Northwest Sprachbund 70
Pacific Pidgin English 271, 288
  social contexts of early 289–90
Pacific Trade Pidgin 21
Papiamentu in Dutch Antilles 305
Pandit, Ira 131, 135, 136, 146, 160, 162, 164, 166
Panjabi 222
  and English 131, 149, 169, 205, 248
Pap, Leo 8
Papen, Robert A. 187, 188, 189
Papia Kristang 21, 305, 310
Papiamentu 21
Papua New Guinea 13, 21, 242
  see also Northwest New Britain
Papuan languages 86
paragoge 320–1
Paraguay 14
Paramaccan *see* Paamaka
Paranakan Chinese, in Indonesia 170
Pare 193, 194, 195, 197
Parkvall, Mikael 308, 320
participant observation 116
Pasch, Helma 298, 300, 307
pattern transfer 53, 62, 77, 204
Patwa in Jamaica 305
Paul, Hermann 6, 42
Pennsylvania Dutch 27, 33
Pennsylvania German (PG) 43, 44, 260
  and English 65
Penutian language family 272
Perdue, Clive 220, 222–3, 227, 281
performance, and competence 224
Perl, Matthias 340
Persian 231
  and Arabic 52
Pfaff, Carol 128, 129, 150, 164
phone substitution, by learners 78, 212–13
phonic interference 212
phonology
  constraints on borrowing 55–6, 62
  creole 319–21
  impact of lexical borrowing on 54–6
  LI influence on L2 212–13
  pidgins 277–8
  types of borrowing 54–5 table 2.4
Picone, Michael D. 148–9
pidgin English
  in Japan 20
  as lingua franca 3, 20
  trade varieties 289

pidgin formation 8, 223, 227, 263
  Factorization Principle (Naro) 287
  internal innovation in 284–6
  L1 influence in 282–3, 294–5
  principles and constraints in 286–8
  processes 280–6
  reduction and simplification in 280–2
  in relation to early SLA 278–88
  social contexts of 270–3, 289–90
  universal principles 287–8
Pidgin Hawaiian 271
Pidgin Macassarese 271
Pidgin Siassi of New Guinea 271
pidginization
  definition 270
  language decay compared with 263–4
  and pidgins 268–303
  use of term 280, 289, 300, 301–2
  see also pidgin formation
"pidginization index" 311
pidgins 7, 20–1
  core grammar 288
  definition 268–70, 307
  lexicon 276–7, 293–4
  morphology and syntax 275–6
  phonology 277–8
  and pidginization 268–303
  structural characteristics of 275–8
  use of label 18–19, 20, 268
  see also extended pidgins; prototypical pidgins
Pienemann, Manfred 216, 221, 235
Pima 42, 44
Plains Cree 183
plantations 20, 21, 22, 271
  creoles 308, 309, 312, 314, 317, 355–6
  pidgins 271, 292
Platt, John T. 15, 246, 255
polyglossia 14
Poplack, Shana 40, 49–50, 51, 52, 66, 105, 106, 107, 109, 126, 131, 132, 155, 157, 165, 166
  equivalence constraint 127–9, 158–60, 163–4
portmanteau sentences 145
Portuguese 3, 21, 316, 324, 332, 344, 349
  colonization 309–10
  contact varieties of 242, 289, 291
  see also American Portuguese
Portuguese-lexicon creoles 22, 326
Portuguese-lexicon pidgin, West Africa 309
Poulisse, Nanda 224
power relations 25
  and code switching 122–4
pragmatics 118
predicate clefting *see* contrastive focus construction
prediction, goal of 9–10
preposition stranding 68–9
prepositions, as system or content morphemes 150–1
prestige 34–5, 36, 37, 38, 39, 254, 257–8
Pride, J. B. 116
Prince Edward Island French 260
  and English 68–70
Principense 22, 309, 323
Principles and Parameters
  core versus periphery theory 288
  UG 229
pro-drop languages 229
Processability Theory (Pienemann) 235
pronouns, subject-referencing, in Melanesian Pidgin 294–6
prosody, L1 influence on L2 213
prototypical creoles, features of 307
prototypical pidgins 20, 264, 270, 301
  concept of 270
  and creoles 307
Providence Island creole 308
psycholinguistics 140, 243
  factors in SLA 225–35
  process of transfer 210, 251–2
Puerto Ricans, in New York City 14, 111–12 table 4.1
Puquina, and Quechua 174

Qallunaat 272
Quebec
  Betsiamites 192
  French and English 40
  language negotiation 122–4

Quechua
and Puquina 174
and Spanish 19, 51, 170, 175–82, 342
Queensland Pidgin English 292
question formation, English 228–9, 231

radical creoles 22, 255–6, 266, 307, 308, 355
emergence of 313, 316–19, 356
formation as SLA 329, 331–40, 356–7
target language 331–3
Rayfield, J. R. 17
recipient language (RL) 12, 44, 208
agentivity 80, 82
borrowing and rules of 50
source language features imposed on 62, 63
reduction 217
in early IL formation 267
of "inner form" in pidgins 280
in language decay 261–2
in pidgin formation 280–2
Reed, Carol E. 8
Reinecke, John E. 271
reinforcement principles, in language shift 252–3, 346
relativization 229, 230, 231
transfer in South African Indian English 249–50
relexification 191, 251
in creole formation 342, 342–3
defined 342
principle 248, 251–2, 344
process 181–2 fig. 6.1
or transfer in creole formation 345, 357
Relexification Hypothesis 181–2, 337, 342–3
Rembarrnga 94
restructuring
creole grammar 306, 333–40
defined 333
psycholinguistic process 345
and substrate influence in creole formation 335–6
and superstrate input to creole formation 334
Reunionnais 312, 313, 314, 315, 330, 355
Rickford, John Russell 259, 314, 315, 322
Rickford, Russell 322
Ritchie, W. C. 246
Ritharngu 74
and Ngandi 75, 76–8, 79, 93–4, 96, 203, 260
RL *see* recipient language (RL)
Roberts, Ian 357
Roberts, Sarah Julianne 332
Roma (Gypsies) 1, 4–5, 193, 206
Romaine, Suzanne 110, 131, 132, 149
Romance languages 6, 55, 71
Romani 174, 193
and English 4–5, 171
and Spanish 1, 171
Romanian 71, 72, 73
Romany 71
Rosenzweig, Jay B. 1
Roy, John D. 315
rule formulation 235
rule generalization 219–20, 227–9, 265
rule regularization 217, 219–20
Rumanian 64, 73
see also Meglenite Rumanian
rural speech, Irish English 238, 239
Russenorsk 20, 21, 269, 273–5, 280–1, 284
and Immigrant Swedish 285–6
lexicon 276
status as a true pidgin 275
Russian 26, 43
and Aleut 19
and Copper Island Aleut 198–205
and Czech 213–14
and German 8
German borrowings from 52
and Norwegian 20, 21, 273–5, 284

Saamaka (Saramaccan) 22, 316, 335–6, 339, 347
Sahaptuan language family 277
SAIE *see* South African Indian English (SAIE)
St Vincent creole 304
Salishan language family 272, 277
Samarin, William J. 299–300
San Francisco, Japanese–English bilinguals 109, 142–3
Sandalwood English 291

Sandfeld, Kristian 73
Sango 288, 297, 298–9, 299–300, 306
Sankoff, David 105, 107, 127–8, 131, 132, 163–4, 165, 166
Sankoff, Gillian 287, 348
Sanskrit, and Tibetan 52–3
Sanzejev G. 43
Sâo Tomé 22
Sapir, Edward 6, 91
Saramaccan *see* Saamaka
Sasse, Hans-Jürgen 83, 197, 257, 259–60, 261, 262, 263
Schachter, Jacqueline 219, 233
Schaengold, Charlotte 113
Schaller, Helmut W. 71
Schmidt, Annette 262
Schmidt, Johannes 6, 7
Schuchardt, Hugo 6, 7, 8, 305
Schumann, Christian 339, 352
Schumann, John H. 220, 221, 286
Schweizerhoch Deutsch 114
Schwyzertüütsch, and Standard German in Switzerland 27, 112, 113–14
Scots English 183
  Highland 242
  and Irish English 241
  in Ulster 237, 238
Scottish Gaelic 27, 33, 183, 242, 262
  in East Sutherland 257
Sebba, Mark 328, 335
second language
  constraints in the elaboration of grammar 227–9
  internal developments in 219–20
second language acquisition (SLA) 208–9
  adult compared with pidgins 268
  classroom setting 16, 209, 220
  developmental stages in 220–3
  formation of radical creoles as 329, 331–40
  individual 208–35
  interference phenomena 103, 108–10, 114
  and language shift 208–67
  LI influence 209–17, 231–3, 264–5
  markedness constraints 231–3
  operating principles 225–6
  pidgin formation in relation to early 278–88, 280, 296–7
  principles and constraints on 225–35
  processing and learning principles in early stages 225–7
  psycholinguistic factors 225–35
  simplification in 217–19
  strategies and processes in 208, 223–5, 264–5
  typological universals and 230–1
  untutored 89
second language acquisition (SLA), group 235–56
  compared with simplified languages 270, 298–9
  concept of transfer in 248–50
  degrees of fossilization or approximation in 245–7
  see also language shift
second language learning
  imperfect 269, 298
  incompetence switching 143
  and "indigenized" varieties of English 4
  source language agentivity 12
secret languages 174, 193, 206
Seiler, Friedrich 42
Sekerina, Irina A. 199
Seliger, Herbert W. 260
Semantic Equivalence Hypothesis 211
semantic extensions/loans 33, 43, 45, 211, 260
semantic restriction 33
semi-speakers 261, 266
Semitic *see* Ethiopic Semitic
Senghas, Ann 346
sentence types, order of acquisition 221
Serbian 72
Serbo-Croatian 71, 72, 73
  and Chakavian dialects 93
serial verb constructions (SVCs), in Atlantic creoles 327–9, 344
servants and employers 20, 270
Seuren, Pieter 347–8
Seychelles 21
Shambaa 194
Sheng 168
Sherzer, Joel 70

Shona, and English 152, 158
Shopen, T. 149
Siegel, Jeff 82, 83, 252–3, 292, 293, 294, 296, 332, 341, 342, 343–4, 345, 346, 348, 349
Sierra Leone Krio 22, 305, 319
Silva-Corvalán, Carmen 66–8, 97, 98, 150
simplification 10, 16, 52, 63, 82, 209
  in creoles 322–3, 347
  in early IL construction 149, 224, 236, 247, 267
  elaborative 218–19
  in language decay 261–2
  in language shift 197–8
  in pidgin formation 280–2
  in pidgins 280
  restrictive 217–18
  in SLA 217–19, 264–5
  use of term 217
  see also reduction; rule regularization
simplified languages 20, 21, 264, 270, 288, 297–9, 302–3
Singapore 15, 21
  New Englishes in 27, 242, 253, 254
Singapore English 22, 245, 330
  as creolization 255
  see also Colloquial Singapore English
Singh, R. 105
Singler, John 311–12, 326, 331, 337
Sinitic languages 242
situations, or domains 111
SL *see* source language (SL)
SLA *see* second language acquisition (SLA)
Slabbert, Sarah 168, 169
slang 168–9
slaves 3, 21, 309–11, 313, 331
Slavic
  in Albanian 59
  and German 7
  and Italian 7
Slavic languages 71
Slobin, Dan I. 226, 248
Smith, Norval 335–6
social anthropology 118
social class 40
social contexts
  code switching 101–25
  of creole formation 310–12, 314–15, 355
  of language contact 8, 10, 24–8
  of pidgin formation 270–3, 289–90
  of structural convergence 64–5, 90–1
social distance, and code switching 118–19, 119–20
social ecology 25, 257, 303, 313
social factors 1, 25, 28, 303
  in code switching 101–25
  group relationships and loyalty 5
  in language death 257–9
  in language shift 252–4, 266
  in lexical borrowing 37–42
  macro-level 257–8
  in structural diffusion 74–9, 84–6, 100
social motivations, bilingual mixed languages 205–6
social network analysis 40, 116
social psychology of language choice 8, 110, 119–24
social settings, for language contact 25–8
social solidarity 39
social values 39
société d'habitation (homestead) phase of contact 356
sociocultural factors 25–8, 243
  in code switching 110–24
sociohistorical background
  bilingual mixed languages 205–6
  to creole formation 309–14, 317–19
sociolinguistic domains, and code switching 101–2, 110–14, 125
sociolinguistic factors
  in group SLA 236–7
  macro- and micro- 38–42, 257
sociolinguistics 8, 9
sociology of language 8, 110, 118, 243
sociopolitical factors 1
Solomon Islands Pidgin 289, 293
source language (SL) 12, 16
  agentivity 80, 91
  features imposed on recipient language 62, 63
South Africa, black urban townships 168, 205

South African Indian English (SAIE), relativization transfer 249–50
South Asia Sprachbund 70
South East Asian languages 21, 70, 242
South Pacific Jargon *see* South Pacific Pidgin
South Pacific Pidgin 290–1
Southeast Solomons language 294
Southern Cushitic 193–4
Southern Oceanic 294
Southern Plains Cree 185–6
Spanish 31, 34, 222, 229, 231
  in Amerindian languages 63
  contact varieties of 242
  and English 14, 42, 43, 44, 97, 106, 128–9, 131, 133, 136, 164, 169, 212, 215, 221
  and English in New York City 105, 132, 164
  and Guaraní 14, 27
  and Hebrew 131, 132
  in Los Angeles 65, 66–8, 98, 260
  and Mayan 52
  and Portuguese 21
  and Quechua 19, 51, 170, 175–82, 342
  and Romani 1, 171
  in US 27, 33, 66
Spanish-lexicon creoles 310, 313, 326
Spears, Arthur 325
Speech Accommodation Theory *see* Communication Accommodation Theory (CAT)
speech communities
  contiguous *see* Sprachbünde
  defined 26
  and language contact 26–9
speech errors, research on 140, 152
speech production
  major components of 140
  processing model and grammar model 235
Sportiche, D. 134
Sprachbünde 8, 11, 13
  structural diffusion 70–4
  term coined 70
Sranan Tongo 3, 21, 22, 255, 305, 307, 316, 330, 331, 338, 349, 351–4
  early Sranan 317, 320, 328, 339–40
  SVCs 328
  TMA system developments 348
stable bilingualism 101, 102
  code switching as unmarked choice 121
  collapse of 27
  structural convergence in 65–70, 99
Stammbaum ("family tree") model 6, 7
Stanges, H. 274
Stauble, A.-M. 221
Stedsk 174
Strasbourg, French and Alsatian 37, 41, 168
Street, Richard L. 8, 120–1
structural borrowing 79–80
  categorial specificity 171–2
  distinguished from language intertwining 173
  and lexical borrowing 54, 61
structural convergence
  compared with direct transfer 62
  degrees of 99–100
  factors affecting 64–5
  situations 11, 13–14, 23 table 1.2
  social contexts of 64–5, 90–1
  in stable bilingual situations 65–70
structural diffusion
  borrowing or substratum influence 62–3, 79–89
  continuum of 99
  in language maintenance 61–100
  and lexical diffusion 99
  linguistic constraints on 91–7
structural factors
  code switching 126–67
  and non-structural 10
structural features, directness of borrowing 63–4
structuralism 6
style shifting 103
stylistics, in borrowing 39, 58–9
subcategorization frames, code switching if match in 133, 161–3, 166, 191
subjacency 229
substitution
  or importation 43, 47
  morphemic 43
  system-based pattern 47–8

substrate languages 21, 301
substrate reinforcement 344
substratum influence 62, 209, 244
  and borrowing 50, 63
  or borrowing in structural diffusion 63–4, 79–89, 91, 100
  in creole formation 322, 329, 330, 335–6, 341–5, 356
  defining 17
  and grammar 334
  intermediate stages of 84
  on Irish English 239–41
  in learner versions of recipient language 97
  phone substitution 78
  role of 8
  on sounds, syntactic patterns and morphology 17
  use of term 16
  see also L1 influence
Sumerian 257
superstrate language 16, 21, 22
  input to creole formation 319, 321, 329, 330, 334, 345
  and lexicon 334
superstratum 16
Suriname Tongue *see* Sranan Tongo
Surinamese creoles 299, 307, 313, 319, 324, 335, 349, 355
  emergence of 311–12, 316–19
  SVCs 329
  sociohistorical background 317–19
SVCs *see* serial verb constructions (SVCs)
Swahili 194
  and English 103, 104, 105, 131, 138, 147–9, 151, 155, 157, 164, 168
  noun classes 48–9
Swedish 222, 231, 233
  and English 218
  and German 213
  Immigrant 285–6
  Low German vocabulary 59
Swiss German 112
Switzerland 101, 112, 113–14
syllabification of glides 47
syllabification rules, transfer of 213
Sylvain, S. 336
symbolic value 10
syntax
  constraints on diffusion 62, 97–9
  creole 326–9
  LI influence on L2 214–17
  of pidgins 276, 283
system morphemes 138
  bridge morphemes 152
  congruence and 153–4
  constraints on switching of 146–52
  early and late 152
  outsider 152
  properties 147 table 5.1
  in speech errors and aphasia 140
  versus other function morphemes 150–1

Tabouret-Keller, A. 125
tag-switching 106
Tagalog, and English 106
Taiwan, code switching in 121
Taiwanese 242, 244–5
  and Cantonese 266
Taiwanese Mandarin 22, 242, 244–5, 252, 254, 265, 266
Tajfel, H. 120
Tamil, and English 164, 249
Tampa Spanish 43
Tangoa 296
  and Bislama 343
Tanna, New Hebrides, early Melanesian Pidgin texts 291–2, 293
target language (TL) 15, 16
  changed by learners 208
  early IL as basic variety of 265, 281
  inadequate exposure to 264
  learner version *see* interlanguage (IL)
  LI influence on lexicon 211–12
  of radical creoles 331–3
  simplified languages and 298–9
  unsuccessful acquisition hypothesis of creoles 22
Tarone, E. E. 214
Tasmania 256
Tây Bôi 271
Taylor, D. M. 120, 326
Tayo 305

tense, mood, and aspect (TMA) systems 324–6, 338–9, 348
terminal speakers *see* semi-speakers
Ternateño 310
"Tex-Mex" 169
Thai 70
Thomason, Sarah Grey 6, 7, 9, 12, 17, 19, 22, 52, 53, 54, 55–6, 57, 61, 64, 79–84, 89, 90, 93, 94–5, 98–9, 193, 236, 308, 330
  borrowing scale 29–30 table 2.1, 34
    Level 5 situations 80, 83–4
  classification of bilingual mixed languages 171–2 table 6.1
  on Copper Island Aleut 199, 200, 201
  on Ma'a 194–7
  on pidgins 270, 278, 282
Thompson, R. W. 326
Thurston, William R. 7, 13–14, 27, 87–8
Tibetan 13, 83
  and Chinese 52–3, 171
  and Sanskrit 52–3
time reference, periphrastic communicative strategies 218, 220
Tirilí 169
TL *see* target language (TL)
TMA *see* tense, mood, and aspect (TMA) systems
Tok Pisin 20, 21, 97–9, 286, 289, 303, 306, 322
  German words in 293
  origins 293
tokens, and types 51
Torlak dialects of Serbo-Croatian 71
Toronto, Japanese–English bilinguals 109, 142–3
Tosk 71
Tourai 87–9
tourism 26, 271
trade 20–1, 70, 199, 253, 268, 271–3, 289–90
Trade Motu 21
  see also Hiri Motu
transfer
  at different levels of analysis 223–4
  blind (or to nowhere) 248, 250, 251, 344
  constraints on 233–4
  and creole syntax 344
  defined 16
  distinguished from code switching 105
  in group SLA 248, 248–50, 266
  negative 210, 211, 214, 248, 251
  positive 210, 215, 248
  as psycholinguistic process 210, 251–2
  or relexification in creole formation 341, 345, 357
  substrate influence in creole formation as 343–4
  use of term 210
  see also direct transfer; interference; pattern transfer
Transfer to Somewhere Principle 233–4, 248, 250, 251–2, 344
translexification 181
transmission, "normal" and "abnormal" 7
transparency
  in convergence 204
  semantic and morphotactic 58, 95–6, 347–8
  in SLA and L1A 220, 247
  structural constraints based on 94–6
travel 26
Treffers-Daller, Jeanine 37, 39, 40, 41, 49–50, 51–2, 53, 108, 137, 141, 154, 156–7, 160, 161–3
Trilongo 169
Trinidadian creole 22, 308, 316
Trio 277, 278, 283
Troubetzkoy, Nikolai S. 8, 70
Trudgill, Peter 82, 280
Tsitsipis, Lukas D. 261
Tsotsitaal 168, 169, 205, 206
Turkish 13, 71, 73, 222, 287
  and Asia Minor Greek 56, 83, 204
  and Cappadocian Greek 260
  and Dutch 148, 149, 226
  pidgin for tourists 271
Turner, J. C. 120
Twi 334, 335
types, and tokens 51
typological distance 92, 192, 204, 207, 232, 265

typological similarity
in code switching 163–4
in structural borrowing 81, 83, 133, 191–2, 195, 203
typological universals, and SLA 2 30–1, 265

UG *see* Universal Grammar (UG)
Ulster, mid-Ulster and south Ulster English 238
Ulster Scots 237, 238, 253
Unami 277, 278, 284, 287
uniqueness principle 226, 227
United States
Hispanics in 27, 33, 66, 169
immigrant groups 15, 27
Norwegian immigrants 34, 39
Universal Grammar (UG) 5, 347
children and 346
learning hierarchy in 230–1
Principles and Parameters 229, 288
role in creole formation 346–7
universal principles, and creole formation 304, 329, 338, 346–52, 356, 357
universals
and internal developments in creole formation 348–9
and L1 influence in creole formation 329, 333, 347–8
typological in SLA 230–1
unstable bilingualism, structural consequences of contact 68–70, 99
urban vernaculars, identity and 168–9
Urdu 260
and Kannada 84–6, 93, 97, 204
and Marathi 84–6
see also Hindi-Urdu

Vago, Robert M. 260
Vakhtin, Nikolai B. 198, 199, 201, 202
van Buren, Paul 333
van Coetsem, Frans 12, 16, 209, 222
van den Berg, Margot 121, 351, 352
van der Voort, Hein 281
van Dyck, P. 339, 340
van Hout, Roeland 219
Van Name, A. 305
Van Patten, B. 226, 227
Vanuatu 21
Veenstra, Tonjes 347
Velantie, Frank J. 275, 277, 278, 283
Verhoeven, L. 149
vernacularization, and creolization 300, 307
vernaculars
creoles as community 304
as official and national language 38
Vietnamese 70
Vietnamese Pidgin French 271
vocabulary borrowing 17
basic or core, constraints on 53
Voorhoeve, Jan 317
vowels, creole 320

Wackernagel, J. 10
Wakashan language family 272
Walloon 39, 122
and Flemish 39
Warlpiri, and English 149
Warndarang 74, 79, 94
and Nunggubuyu 75, 78
Wawa *see* Chinook Pidgin
Wei, Li 104
Weinreich, Uriel 8, 9–10, 12, 25, 37, 43–4, 48, 52–3, 54, 55, 63–4, 78, 92, 93, 94, 96, 269
interlingual identifications 233–4, 265
on SLA 209, 210, 212–13, 236
Wekker, Herman 343, 347–8
Welsh 242
Welsh English 242
West Africa, Portuguese-lexicon pidgin 309
West African languages 21, 298, 315, 316, 320, 321, 351
creoles 22, 255, 317, 336, 346
West African Pidgin English 21, 307
West Greenlandic 281, 282
Western Caribbean creoles 308
whaling 290
Whinnom, Keith 275
Whiteley, Wilfred Howell 48–9, 196
Whiteman family 87
Whitney, W. D. 7, 8, 51
Williams, Ann 83, 253
Wilson, Robert 27, 84–6
Wilson, W. A. A. 336

Winford, Donald 245, 308, 314, 315, 316, 324, 325, 328, 329, 333, 351, 353–4
Wode, H. 221
Wolfe Quintero, Kate 228
Wolof, and French 107, 127, 158–9 fig. 5.2
Woolford, Ellen 129–30, 133
word formation, creative 44–6, 265
word order
  borrowing and acquisition of 98–9
  canonical principle 226, 227
  L1 influence on L2 214–15
word structure, typological differences and borrowing strategies 52–3
Wurm, Stephen A. 293
Wutun 13, 83, 84, 171, 173, 204

X-bar theory, government in 134
Xwelagbe 340

Yaaku 258
Yakoma 298, 299
Yakut 43
Yaqui 42, 46
Yiddish 34
  American 63–4
  and English 17–18 table 1.1, 44
  and Hebrew 57
Yimas Pidgin 21, 297, 302
Yoruba, and English 133, 139
Yuulgnu languages 74–9

Zapotec 42
Zenk, Henry Benjamin 272
Zobl, H. 215
Zulu, English and Afrikaans 168, 205
Zurif, E. B. 140